The Princeton Review®

Cracking the
GMAT®

PREMIUM
2019 Edition

The Staff of The Princeton Review

PrincetonReview.com

Penguin
Random
House

The Princeton Review
110 East 42nd Street, 7th Floor
New York, NY 10017
Email: editorialsupport@review.com

Published in the United States by Penguin Random House LLC,
New York, and in Canada by Random House of Canada, a division
of Penguin Random House Ltd., Toronto.

Some of the content in the "GMAT Insider" has previously
appeared in *The Best 296 Business Schools* and *Business
School Essays That Made a Difference*, both published as trade
paperbacks by Random House in 2012; and *Do I Need an MBA?
Figuring Out if Business School Really Fits Your Future Needs*,
published as an eBook by Random House in 2012.

ISBN: 978-1-5247-5788-5
eBook ISBN: 978-1-5247-5823-3
ISSN: 1936-4040

GMAT is a registered trademark and owned by the Graduate
Management Admission Council (GMAC).

The Princeton Review is not affiliated with Princeton University.

Editor: Meave Shelton
Production Artist: Deborah Weber
Production Editors: Liz Rutzel and Jim Melloan

Printed in the United States on partially recycled paper.

10 9 8 7 6 5 4 3 2 1

2019 Edition

Editorial
Rob Franek, Editor-in-Chief
Casey Cornelius, Chief Product Officer
Mary Beth Garrick, Executive Director of Production
Craig Patches, Production Design Manager
Selena Coppock, Managing Editor
Meave Shelton, Senior Editor
Colleen Day, Editor
Sarah Litt, Editor
Aaron Riccio, Editor
Orion McBean, Associate Editor

Penguin Random House Publishing Team
Tom Russell, VP, Publisher
Alison Stoltzfus, Publishing Director
Amanda Yee, Associate Managing Editor
Ellen Reed, Production Manager
Suzanne Lee, Designer

Acknowledgments

Our GMAT course is much more than clever techniques and powerful computer score reports; the reason our results are great is that our teachers care so much about their students. Thanks to all the teachers who have made the GMAT course so successful, but in particular the core group of teachers and development people who helped get it off the ground: Alicia Ernst, Tom Meltzer, Paul Foglino, John Sheehan, Mark Sawula, Nell Goddin, Teresa Connelly, Phillip Yee, Kimberly Beth Hollingsworth, Bobby Hood, Chris Chimera, Chris Hinkle, Peter Hanink, and Cathy Evins.

Special thanks to John Fulmer, Kyle Fox, Jim Havens, Ted Klein, and Keith Hehr for their valuable contributions to the 2019 edition of this book.

Special thanks to Adam Robinson, who conceived of and perfected the Joe Bloggs approach to standardized tests and many of the other successful techniques used by The Princeton Review.

We are also, as always, very appreciative of the time and attention given to each page by Liz Rutzel, Jim Melloan, and Deborah Weber.

Contents

Get More (Free) Content

1 Go to **PrincetonReview.com/cracking.**

2 Enter the following ISBN for your book: 9781524757885.

3 Answer a few simple questions to set up an exclusive Princeton Review account. (If you already have one, you can just log in.)

4 Click the "Student Tools" button, also found under "My Account" from the top toolbar. You're all set to access your bonus content!

Need to report a potential **content** issue?

Contact **EditorialSupport@review.com.**
Include:
- full title of the book
- ISBN number
- page number

Need to report a **technical** issue?

Contact **TPRStudentTech@review.com** and provide:
- your full name
- email address used to register the book
- full book title and ISBN
- computer OS (Mac/PC) and browser (Firefox, Safari, etc.)

The Princeton Review®

Once you've registered, you can...

- Take 6 full-length practice GMAT exams

- Download additional practice material excerpted from 3 other Princeton Review GMAT titles

- Plan your review sessions with study guides based on your schedule—4 weeks, 8 weeks, 12 weeks

- Watch short video tutorials in which top-notch Princeton Review teachers discuss GMAT question types and strategies, working through problems step by step

- Research admissions rates and average test scores for dozens of popular business schools

- Read successful b-school application essays, interviews with administrators, and articles containing a wealth of advice about admissions and financial aid

- Check to see if there have been any corrections or updates to this edition

- Get our take on any recent or pending updates to the GMAT

Look For These Icons Throughout The Book

PREMIUM STUDENT TOOLS

 ONLINE VIDEO TUTORIALS

ONLINE ARTICLES

ONLINE PRACTICE DRILLS

ONLINE PRACTICE TESTS

 PROVEN TECHNIQUES

 APPLIED STRATEGIES

 TIME-SAVING TIP

 MORE GREAT BOOKS

 WATCH OUT

Part I
Orientation

Chapter 1
Introduction

Congratulations on your decision to attend business school, and welcome to *Cracking the GMAT,* 2019 Edition! Preparing for the GMAT is an important part of the process, so let's get started. This chapter will provide you with a strategic plan for acing the GMAT, as well as an overview of the test itself, including question formats and information on how the test is scored.

HOW TO USE THIS BOOK: A STRATEGIC PLAN FOR ACING THE GMAT

1. Learn the Famed Princeton Review Test-Taking Strategies

In the next few chapters, you'll find the strategies that have given our GMAT students the edge for the past 20 years.

2. Learn the Specific Math and Verbal Skills You'll Need

Our courses include an extremely thorough review of the math and verbal skills our students need to ace the GMAT, and this book will give you that same review.

3. Practice Each Type of Question—at the Difficulty Level You Need to Master

Two of the GMAT's sections, the Quantitative and Verbal sections, are computer adaptive. These sections quickly hone in on your ability level and then mostly give you questions at or just above that level. It makes sense for you to practice on the level of problem you will actually see during the test. *Cracking the GMAT* is the only book out there with practice questions grouped by difficulty. Page after page of practice questions are arranged at the back of this book in difficulty "bins"—just like the questions on the real GMAT—so that you can concentrate on the question level you will have to answer on the actual test in order to get the score you need.

The Integrated Reasoning section of the GMAT is *not* computer adaptive. We've provided two complete Integrated Reasoning sections at the back of this book to help you prepare for this section of the test.

4. Periodically Take Simulated GMATs to Measure Your Progress

As you work through the book, you'll want to take our online practice tests to see how you're doing. These tests closely mimic the GMAT so you can become familiar with the test's content and structure. Our tests include adaptive sections for the Quantitative and Verbal sections and a non-adaptive section for the Integrated Reasoning section. Our practice tests can be found at **PrincetonReview.com**. In addition, we actively encourage students to use *The Official Guide for GMAT Review*, which is published by the Graduate Management Admission Council (GMAC). It contains actual test questions from previous administrations of the GMAT. You should also take at least one of the real practice tests available through the GMAT website, **www.mba.com**.

Make sure that you register your book to access your tests. Please refer to the "Get More (Free) Content" spread a few pages back to learn how to do just that.

5. Hone Your Skills

Using the detailed score reports from your practice exams, you'll be able to zero in on problem areas and quickly achieve mastery through additional practice. And as your score rises on the adaptive sections, this book is ready with more difficult question bins to keep you on track for the score you need. You can use the two practice Integrated Reasoning sections in this book to help you prepare for your practice tests and your real GMAT.

Important Websites
To register for the GMAT:
www.mba.com

6. Keep Track of the Application Process

Throughout the book, you will find informative sidebars explaining how and when to register for the test, how and when to apply to business school, the advantages and disadvantages of applying early, and much more. Plus, at **PrincetonReview.com**, you'll be able to take advantage of our powerful web-based tools to match yourself with schools that meet your needs and preferences.

WHAT IS THE GRADUATE MANAGEMENT ADMISSION TEST?

The Graduate Management Admission Test (GMAT) is a standardized test used by business schools as a tool to decide whom they are going to let into their MBA programs.

Where Does the GMAT Come From?

The GMAT is published and administered by the Graduate Management Admission Council (GMAC). GMAC is a private company. We'll tell you more about them later on in this book.

More Great Books!
Check out our survey-driven guide, *The Best 294 Business Schools*, for profiles of the nation's top b-schools.

What Does the Test Look Like?

The GMAT is offered only on computer. The 3.5 hour test is administered at a secure computer terminal at an approved testing center. You enter your multiple-choice answers on the screen with a mouse; you must compose your essay for the Writing Assessment section on the computer as well.

1. One 30 minute essay to be written on the computer using a generic word processing program
2. One 30 minute, 12 question, multiple-choice Integrated Reasoning section. Some Integrated Reasoning questions can have multiple parts. (optional break)
3. A 75 minute, 37 question multiple-choice Math section (optional break)
4. A 75 minute, 41 question multiple-choice Verbal section

On average, this would give you two minutes for each math question and a little less than two minutes for each verbal question—but you will find that our Princeton Review strategies will slightly revise these times. You must answer a question in order to get to the next question—which means that you can't skip a question and come back to it. And while you are not required to finish any of the sections, your score will be adjusted downward to reflect questions you did not complete.

On each of the Math and Verbal sections, approximately one-quarter of the questions you encounter will be experimental and will not count toward your score. These questions, which will be mixed in among the regular questions, are there so the test company can try out new questions for future tests. We'll have much more to say about the experimental questions later.

But Wait, There's More

One of the first options you'll encounter when taking the GMAT is the option to choose from one of three possible orders for the exam sections. You pick your preferred section order on the day of the test.

Here are the possible section orders:

Order #1 (Classic Order)	Order #2 (Verbal First)	Order #3 (Math First)
Analytic Writing Assessment	Verbal	Quantitative
Integrated Reasoning		
Optional 8 minute break		
Quantitative	Quantitative	Verbal
Optional 8 minute break		
Verbal	Integrated Reasoning	Integrated Reasoning
	Analytical Writing Assessment	Analytical Writing Assessment

How Do You Know What Order to Pick?

The answer to that depends on your goals for the test and your level of comfort with the different sections. Are you looking to get a high Math score, but you don't care so much about the Verbal? Has your school told you they never consider the essay and Integrated Reasoning section? Are you good at Verbal but not so good at Math?

The answer to these questions and other questions like them help to inform your section order choice.

How Does This Impact Your Studying?

We recommend that you take your first two tests using the classic order. A major goal of your first practice test is to simply get acquainted with the sections, question types, content, and timing of the GMAT. A major goal of your second practice test is to start putting into use some of the basic approaches for important question types.

Taking your first two tests using the classic section order provides a baseline score. Having established a baseline score, you can then try out different sections orders for the remaining tests. Compare the results of the tests with different section orders to the results of the tests with the classic section order and see if there are any improvements.

In addition to looking for score improvements, you should also pay attention to a handful of other factors about your preferences in test taking.

For instance, do you like to ease into a test or hit the ground running? If you like to ease into a test, you may want to stick with the classic section order. While all parts of your GMAT score are important, most schools do attach less importance to your AWA and Integrated Reasoning scores than your Quantitative and Verbal scores. Remember, as well, that only the Quantitative and Verbal scores are used in calculating the overall score. So, if you like to ease into a test, the AWA and Integrated Reasoning can provide that way to ease in.

Do you like to do the section you're most worried about first? Some test takers like to get the section that they are most worried about out of the way. If that's you, you'll probably want to pick either the Verbal First or Math First orders, depending on which section you are most worried about!

Are you worried about fatigue? Most test takers find the GMAT both fast-paced and tiring. Fatigue can be a very real issue. If you are worried about fatigue, you probably want to do either the Verbal First or Math First orders as they place the two least consequential sections at the end of the test.

What Information Is Tested on the GMAT?

You will find several different types of multiple-choice questions on the GMAT.

Math (37 questions total)
- Problem Solving—approximately 19 questions
- Data Sufficiency (a strange type of problem that exists on no other test in the world)—approximately 18 questions

Verbal (41 questions total)
- Reading Comprehension (tests your ability to answer questions about a passage)—approximately 13 questions
- Sentence Correction (a grammar-related question type)—approximately 17 questions
- Critical Reasoning (a logic-based question type recycled from the LSAT)— approximately 11 questions

Integrated Reasoning (12 questions total)
- Table Analysis—data is presented in a sortable table (like an Excel spreadsheet); each question usually has three parts.
- Graphics Interpretation—a chart or graph is used to display data; each question usually has two parts; answers are selected from drop-down boxes.
- Multi-Source Reasoning—information (a combination of charts, text, and tables) is presented on two or three tabs; each set of tabbed information is usually accompanied by three questions.
- Two-Part Analysis—each question usually has five or six options of which you need to pick two.

How Is the GMAT Scored?

As soon as you've finished taking the GMAT, your computer will calculate and display your unofficial results, not including your Writing Assessment score. You can print out a copy of your unofficial results to take with you. Within 20 days, you will receive your score report online; a written report will be available only by request.

Most people think of the GMAT score as a single number, but in fact there are five separate numbers:

1. Math score (reported on a scale that runs from 0 to 60)
2. Verbal score (reported on a scale that runs from 0 to 60)
3. Total score (reported on a scale that runs from 200 to 800 and based only on the results of Math and Verbal sections)
4. Analytic Writing Assessment score (reported on a scale of 0 to 6, in half point increments; 6 is the highest score)
5. Integrated Reasoning score (reported on a scale from 1 to 8 in one point increments)

The report will look something like this:

Math	%	Verbal	%	Total	%	AWA	%	Integrated Reasoning	%
36	42	30	56	550	48	4.5	38	6	75

Many business schools tend to focus on the total score, which means that you may make up for weakness in one area by being strong in another. For example, if your quantitative skills are better than your verbal skills, they'll help pull up your total score—although some of the more selective schools say they prefer to see math and verbal sub-scores that are balanced. Total scores go up or down in ten-point increments. In other words, you might receive 490 or 500 on the GMAT, but never 494 or 495.

The Integrated Reasoning section is scored from 1 to 8 in one-point increments. Questions have multiple parts, and you must answer each part correctly to get credit for the question. The Integrated Reasoning score is not included in the Overall score.

You will also see a percentile ranking next to each score. For example, if you see a percentile of 72 next to your Verbal score, it means that 72 percent of the people who took this test scored lower than you did on the Verbal section.

Where Will Your Scores Take You?
Get The Princeton Review's definitive list of admissions rates and average test scores for dozens of top business schools. Visit your Student Tools for more info.

WHAT IS THE PRINCETON REVIEW?

The Princeton Review is a test-preparation company founded in New York City. It has branches in more than 50 cities across the country, as well as abroad. The Princeton Review's techniques are unique and powerful, and they were developed after a study of thousands of real GMAT questions. They work because they are based on the same principles that are used in writing the actual test. The Princeton Review's techniques for beating the GMAT will help you improve your scores by teaching you to:

- think like the test writers
- take full advantage of the computer-adaptive algorithms upon which the GMAT is based
- find the answers to questions you don't understand by using Process of Elimination
- avoid the traps that test writers have set for you (and use those traps to your advantage)

A Warning

Many of our techniques for beating the GMAT may be very different from the way that you would naturally approach problems. Some methods may even seem counterintuitive. Rest assured, however, that many test takers have used our methods to get great GMAT scores. To get the full benefit of our techniques, you must trust them. The only way to develop this trust is to practice the techniques and persuade yourself that they work.

Practice with Real Questions

One reason coaching books do not use real GMAT questions is that GMAC won't let them. So far, the council has refused to let anyone (including us) license actual questions from old tests. As we mentioned above, the council has its own review book called *The Official Guide for GMAT Review*, which we heartily recommend that you purchase. GMAC also puts out preparation software called *GMATPrep*, which can be downloaded for free from **www.mba.com**. This software includes two computer-adaptive tests plus additional practice sets, all of which feature real GMAT questions. By practicing our techniques on real GMAT items, you will be able to prove to yourself that the techniques work and increase your confidence when you actually take the test.

And, remember, by using The Princeton Review's practice questions grouped by level of difficulty at the back of this book, you'll be able to concentrate on types of questions you are actually likely to see.

Additional Resources

In addition to the material in this book, we offer a number of other resources to aid you during your GMAT preparation.

Register your book at **PrincetonReview.com** to gain access to your Student Tools, the companion website to this book. There you will find 6 full-length GMAT exams, assorted videos that demonstrate step-by-step approaches to GMAT question types and strategy, extra drills and practice, and tons of useful articles, essays, and information.

Premium Student Tools
To gain access, follow the instructions on page vi.

Summary

○ By using a combination of The Princeton Review's Integrated Reasoning introduction, math and verbal reviews, the practice questions contained in this book, and periodic simulated tests, you will be able to improve your score on the GMAT.

○ The test itself is taken on computer. It consists of the following:

Analytical Writing Assessment			
• Analysis of an argument	1 essay on business or a topic of general interest.	30 minutes	Scoring: 0–6 in half point-increments

Quantitative Section			
• Problem Solving • Data Sufficiency	37 questions total. Roughly 50% Problem Solving.	75 minutes	Scoring: 0–60

Verbal Section			
• Sentence Correction • Critical Reasoning • Reading Comprehension	41 questions total. Roughly 40% Sentence Correction and 30% each for Reading and Critical Reasoning.	75 minutes	Scoring: 0–60

Overall score: 200–800 (based only on the Quantitative and Verbal sections)

Integrated Reasoning Section			
• Table Analysis • Graphics Interpretation • Multi-Source Reasoning • Two-Part Analysis	12 questions total. But most questions require multiple responses.	30 minutes	Scored on a scale from 1 to 8 in one-point increments.

Chapter 2
How to Think
About the GMAT

If you think the GMAT tests your business knowledge or shows how smart you are, you're in for a surprise. This chapter will give you a new way to look at the GMAT to guide your studies in the right direction.

How Do You Think About Standardized Tests?

If you're like most people, you think standardized tests measure how smart you are. If you score 800 on the GMAT, you may think of yourself as a genius (and the future manager of a corporate empire). If you score 200, you may think of yourself as an idiot (and the future manager of…well…nothing). You may think that the GMAT measures your verbal and math abilities. At the very least, you probably believe the GMAT is an accurate predictor of how you'll do in business school.

What Does the GMAT Measure?

The GMAT is not a test of how smart you are. Nor is it a test of your business acumen or even a predictor of your grades in business school. It's simply a test of how good you are at taking the GMAT. In fact, you will learn that by studying the very specific knowledge outlined in this book, you can substantially improve your score.

The GMAT as a Job Interview

The first axiom of any how-to book on job interviewing is that you must always tell your interviewer what he or she wants to hear. No matter whether this is good job-hunting advice, it happens to be a very useful strategy on the GMAT. The test writers think in predictable ways. You can improve your score by learning to think the way they do and anticipating the kinds of answers that they think are correct.

How Closely Does The Princeton Review Monitor the GMAT?

Very closely. Each year, we publish a new edition of this book to reflect the subtle shifts that happen over time, or, in the case of the introduction of the Integrated Reasoning section, the major changes to the GMAT. For the latest information on the GMAT, please visit our website **PrincetonReview.com**.

Is This Book Just Like The Princeton Review Course?

No. You won't have the benefit of taking ten computer-adaptive GMATs that are scored and analyzed by our computers. You won't get to sit in small classes with only three other highly motivated students who will spur you on. You won't get to work with our expert instructors who can assess your strengths and pinpoint your weaknesses. There is no way to put these things in a book.

What you *will* find in this book are some of the techniques and methods that have enabled our students to crack the system—plus a review of the essentials that you cannot afford not to know.

If at all possible, you should take our course. If that is not possible, then there is this book.

How to Crack the System

In the following chapters, we're going to teach you our method for cracking the GMAT. Read each chapter carefully. Some of our ideas may seem strange at first. For example, when we tell you that it is sometimes easier to answer GMAT questions without actually working out the entire problem, you may think, "This isn't the way I conduct business."

Remember: The GMAT Isn't About Business

We're not going to teach you business skills. We're not going to teach you math and English. We're going to teach you the GMAT.

Chapter 3
Cracking the Adaptive Sections: Basic Principles

This chapter will show you how the computer-adaptive sections of the GMAT really work. You will learn to pace yourself and to take advantage of the test's limitations.

HOW THE COMPUTER-ADAPTIVE GMAT SECTIONS WORK

To understand how to beat the computer-adaptive sections (Math and Verbal) of the GMAT, you have to understand how they work.

Unlike paper-and-pencil standardized tests that begin with an easy question and then get progressively tougher, the computer-adaptive sections always begin by giving you a medium question. If you get it correct, the computer gives you a slightly harder question. If you get it wrong, the computer gives you a slightly easier question, and so on. The idea is that the computer will zero in on your exact level of ability very quickly, which allows you to answer fewer questions overall and allows the computer to make a more finely honed assessment of your abilities.

To check out which b-schools are the "Toughest to Get Into," take a look at the Business School Ranking lists at PrincetonReview. com.

What You Will See on Your Screen

During the test itself, your screen will display the question you're currently working on, with little circles next to the five answer choices. To answer the question, you use your mouse to click on the circle next to the answer choice you think is correct. Then you press a button at the bottom of the screen to verify that this is the answer you want to pick.

What You Will Never See on Your Screen

What you will *never* see is the process by which the computer keeps track of your progress. When you start each adaptive section, the computer assumes that your score is average. So, your starting score for each section is around a 30. As you go through the test, the computer will keep revising its assessment of your score based on your responses.

Let's watch the process in action. In the left-hand column on the next page, you'll see what a hypothetical test taker—let's call her Jane—sees on her screen as she takes the test. In the right-hand column, we'll show you how GMAC keeps track of how she's doing. (We've simplified this example a bit in the interest of clarity.)

Note: The answer choices on the actual GMAT don't have letters assigned to them. Instead, you select your response by clicking on an adjacent oval. For the sake of clarity and brevity, we'll refer to the five answer choices as (A), (B), (C), (D), and (E).

WHAT JANE SEES:

To regard the overwhelming beauty of the Mojave Desert is <u>understanding the great forces of</u> nature that shape our planet.

- ○ understanding the great forces of
- ○ to understand the great forces to
- ⊗ to understand the great forces of
- ○ understanding the greatest forces in
- ○ understanding the greater forces on

WHAT JANE *DOESN'T* SEE:

When you start each adaptive section, the computer assumes that your score is average. So, your starting score for each section is around a 30. Jane gets the first question correct, (C), so her score goes up to a 35, and the computer selects a harder problem for her second question.

WHAT JANE SEES:

Hawks in a certain region depend heavily for their diet on a particular variety of field mouse. The killing of field mice by farmers will seriously endanger the survival of hawks in this region.

Which of the following, if true, casts the most doubt on the conclusion drawn above?

- ○ The number of mice killed by farmers has increased in recent years.
- ○ Farmers kill many other types of pests besides field mice without any adverse effect on hawks.
- ○ Hawks have been found in other areas besides this region.
- ○ Killing field mice leaves more food for the remaining mice, who have larger broods the following season.
- ○ Hawks are also endangered because of pollution and deforestation.

WHAT JANE *DOESN'T* SEE:

The computer happens to select a Critical Reasoning problem.

Oops. Jane gets the second question wrong (the correct answer is (D)), so her score goes down to a 32, and the computer gives her a slightly easier problem.

current score: 32

WHAT JANE SEES:

Nuclear weapons being invented, there was wide expectation in the scientific community that all war would end.

- ○ Nuclear weapons being invented, there was wide expectation in the scientific community that
- ○ When nuclear weapons were invented, expectation was that
- ○ As nuclear weapons were invented, there was wide expectation that
- ○ Insofar as nuclear weapons were invented, it was widely expected
- ✓ With the invention of nuclear weapons, there was wide expectation that

WHAT JANE *DOESN'T* SEE:

Jane has no idea what the correct answer is on this third question, but she guesses (E) and gets it correct. Her score goes up to a 33.

You get the idea. At the very beginning of the section, your score moves up or down in larger increments than it does at the end, when GMAC believes it is merely refining whether you deserve, say, a 42 or a 43. The questions you will see on your test come from a huge pool of questions held in the computer in what the test writers call "difficulty bins"—each bin with a different level of difficulty.

The Experimental Questions

Unfortunately, approximately one-fourth of the questions in each adaptive section (Math and Verbal) won't actually count toward your score; they are experimental questions being tested out on you. The difficulty of an experimental question does not depend on your answer to the previous question. You could get a question correct and then immediately see a fairly easy experimental question.

So, if you are answering mostly upper-medium questions and suddenly see a question that seems too easy, there are two possibilities: a) you are about to fall for a trap, or b) it's an experimental question and really is easy. That means it can be very difficult for you to judge how you are doing on the section. Your best strategy is to simply try your best on every question.

Remembering that experimental questions are included throughout the adaptive sections can also help you use your time wisely. When you get stuck on a question—even one of the first ten questions—remember that it might be experimental. Spending an inordinate amount of time on one question could cause you to rush and make silly mistakes later. Would you really want to do that if the question turned out to be experimental?

In those situations, eliminate as many answer choices as you can, guess, and move on to the next question.

What the Computer-Adaptive GMAT Uses to Calculate Your Score

The GMAT keeps a running tally of your score as it goes, based on the number of questions you get correct and their levels of difficulty—but there are two other important factors that can affect your score:

- Early questions count more than later questions.

- Questions you leave unanswered will lower your score.

How much can leaving questions at the end unanswered damage your score? GMAC says that somebody who was on track to score in the 91st percentile will drop to the 77th percentile by leaving just five questions unanswered. Answer every question!

Why Early Questions Count More Than Later Questions

At the beginning of the test, your score moves up or down in larger increments as the computer hones in on what will turn out to be your ultimate score. If you make a mistake early on, the computer will choose a much easier question, and it will take you a while to work back to where you started from. Similarly, if you get an early problem correct, the computer will then give you a much harder question.

However, later in the test, a mistake is less costly—because the computer has decided your general place in the scoring ranks and is merely refining your exact score.

While it is not impossible to come back from behind, you can see that it is particularly important that you do well at the beginning of the test. Answering just a few questions correctly at the beginning will propel your interim score quite high.

Pace Yourself

Make sure that you get these early questions correct by starting slowly, checking your work on early problems, and then gradually picking up the pace so that you finish all the problems in the section.

Still, if you are running out of time at the end, it makes sense to spend a few moments guessing intelligently on the remaining questions using Process of Elimination (POE) rather than random guesses or (let's hope it never comes to this) not answering at all. You will be pleased to know that it is possible to guess on several questions at the end and still end up with a 700.

On the next page, you'll find our pacing advice for Math and Verbal. The charts will tell you how much time you should spend for each block of ten questions based on a practice test score.

MATH

Score	1–10	11–20	21–30	31–37

	Question numbers			
Score	1–10	11–20	21–30	31–37
Under 35	30 min.	25 min.	15 min.	5 min.
35–42	30 min.	20 min.	15 min.	10 min.
Above 42	25 min.	20 min.	20 min.	10 min.

VERBAL

	Question numbers			
Score	1–10	11–20	21–30	31–41
Under 28	30 min.	25 min.	10 min.	10 min.
28–34	27 min.	20 min.	18 min.	10 min.
Above 34	25 min.	20 min.	15 min.	15 min.

The Princeton Review Approach to the GMAT

To help you ace the computer-adaptive sections of the GMAT, this book is going to provide you with

General Test Strategies
Go to your Student Tools to watch a video on effective ways to approach and tackle the GMAT exam, no matter which section you're in.

- test-taking techniques that have made The Princeton Review famous and that will enable you to turn the inherent weaknesses of the computer-adaptive sections of the GMAT to your advantage
- a thorough review of all the major topics covered on the GMAT
- a short practice test to help you predict your current scoring level
- practice questions to help you raise your scoring level

Know Your Bin

According to classic theory, the average test taker spends most of his or her time answering questions at his level of competency (which he gets correct) and questions that are just above his level of competency (which he gets wrong). In other words, most test takers will see questions from only a few difficulty "bins."

This means that to raise your score, you must learn to answer questions from the bins immediately *above* your current scoring level. At the back of this book, you will find a short diagnostic test to determine your current scoring level and then bins filled with questions at various scoring levels. When combined with a thorough review of the topics covered on the GMAT, this should put you well on your way to the score you're looking for.

But first, let's learn with some test-taking strategies.

Summary

- The computer-adaptive sections of the GMAT always start you off with a medium question. If you get it correct, you get a harder question; if you get it wrong, you get an easier question. The test assigns you a score after each answer and quickly (in theory) hones in on your level of ability.

- Mixed in with the questions that count toward your score will be experimental questions that do not count toward your score. The testing company is using you as an unpaid guinea pig to try out new questions. Approximately one-fourth of the questions in each of the adaptive sections are experimental.

- Because the test is taken on a computer, you must answer each question to get to the next question—you can't skip a question or come back to it later.

- Because of the scoring algorithms, early questions count more than later questions—so check your work carefully at the beginning of the test.

- The GMAT computer-adaptive sections select questions for you from "bins" of questions at different levels of ability. The Princeton Review method consists of finding your current bin level through diagnostic tests and then practicing questions from that bin, ~~gradually moving to higher bins~~ as you become more proficient.

Chapter 4
Cracking the Adaptive Sections: Intermediate Principles

This chapter provides an introduction to one of the key Princeton Review techniques: Process of Elimination.

Imagine for a moment that you are a contestant on *Jeopardy*. You are hoping to stumble upon a coveted Daily Double, but first you've got to answer every question that gets thrown your way.

As you answer assorted questions about myriad topics (including "Potent Potables," no doubt), you wish that there were some way that you could know where the Daily Doubles are placed on the board and jump to those. But you can't—you can't opt to skip any of the questions and continue to dominate that game.

Let's Make a GMAT

Normally when you don't know the correct answer on a test, you skip the question and come back to it later. But on the computer-adaptive sections of the GMAT, as in *Jeopardy*, you can never skip the question.

To Get to the Next Question, You Have to Answer This One

Because of the way the computer-adaptive sections of the GMAT's scoring algorithm works, the question you see on your computer screen at any particular moment depends on your response to the previous question. This creates an odd situation for the test designers: If they allowed you to skip a question, they wouldn't know which question to give you next.

It's clear from articles that GMAT test designers have published that they know test takers are at a real disadvantage when they can't skip a problem and come back to it later. Still, the idea of using a computer to administer tests was too tempting to give up. In the end, GMAC decided that you should generously be willing to make the sacrifice in the name of progress.

So whether you know the answer to a problem or not, you have to answer it in order to move on.

This means that, like it or not, you may have to do some guessing on the GMAT. Ah, but there's guessing, and then there's *guessing*.

If You Don't Know the Correct Answer, Don't You Dare Just Pick an Answer at Random

This may sound a little loony, but it turns out that you don't always have to know the correct answer to get a question correct.

Try answering the following question:

What is the unit of currency in Sweden?

What? You don't know?

Unless you work for an international bank or have traveled in Scandinavia, there is no reason why you should know what the unit of currency in Sweden is. (By the way, the GMAT doesn't ask such factual questions. We're using this one to make a point.) As it stands now, because you don't know the answer, you would have to answer this question at random, right?

Not necessarily. GMAT questions are written in multiple-choice format. One of the five choices has to be the answer. You just have to find it.

Look for Wrong Answers Instead of Correct Ones

Let's put this question into multiple-choice format—the only format you'll find on the GMAT—and see if you still want to answer at random.

> What is the unit of currency in Sweden?
>
> ◯ the dollar
> ◯ the franc
> ◯ the pound sterling
> ◯ the yen
> ◯ the krona

PROCESS OF ELIMINATION

Suddenly this question isn't difficult anymore. You may not have known the correct answer, but you certainly knew enough to eliminate the wrong answers. Wrong answers are often easier to spot than correct answers. Sometimes they just sound weird. Other times they're logically impossible. While it is rare to be able to eliminate all four of the incorrect answer choices on the GMAT, you will almost always be able to eliminate at least one of them—and frequently two or more—by using Process of Elimination. Process of Elimination (POE for short) will enable you to answer questions that you don't have the time to figure out exactly. We will refer to POE in every single chapter of this book. It is one of the most important and fundamental tools you will use to increase your score.

Try another example:

> Which of the following countries uses the peso as its unit of currency?
>
> ◯ Russia
> ◯ Canada
> ◯ Venezuela
> ◯ England
> ◯ Chile

Process of Elimination is a key strategy and can play a huge role in helping you to find the correct answer choice!

This time you can probably get rid of only three of the five answer choices using POE. The answer is clearly *not* Russia, Canada, or England, but most people probably don't know for sure whether the answer is Venezuela or Chile.

You've got the question down to two possibilities. What should you do?

Heads or Tails

A Chilean might flip a peso. You have a fifty-fifty chance of getting this question correct, which is much better than if you had guessed at random. And because the GMAT forces you to guess anyway, it makes sense to guess intelligently.

In the chapters that follow, we'll show you specific ways to make use of POE to increase your score. You may feel uncomfortable about using these techniques at first, but the sooner you make them your own, the sooner you'll start to improve your score.

Is It Fair to Get a Question Correct When You Don't Know the Answer?

If you took any math courses in college, you probably remember that the correct answer to a problem, while important, wasn't the only thing you were graded on. Your professor was probably more interested in *how* you got the answer, whether you wrote an elegant equation, or if you used the right formula.

If your equation was correct but you messed up your addition at the end, did you get the entire question wrong? Most college professors give partial credit for an answer like that. After all, what's most important is the mental process that goes into getting the answer, not the answer alone.

On the GMAT, if you don't click the correct circle with your mouse, you're wrong. It doesn't matter that you knew how to do the problem or that you clicked the wrong answer by mistake. GMAC doesn't care: You're just wrong. And a wrong answer means that the running score GMAC is keeping on you will go down by 10 or 20 points, and you'll be forced to answer several easier questions correctly before you get back to the level at which you were.

This really isn't fair. It seems only fitting that you should also be able to benefit from the flip side of this situation: If you click on the correct circle, GMAC doesn't care how you got that answer either.

Scratch Work

Process of Elimination is a powerful tool, but it's powerful only if you keep track of the answer choices you've eliminated. On a computer-adaptive test, you obviously can't cross off choices on the screen—but you can cross them off on your scratch paper. Don't be afraid to use it!

You only have so many tools at your disposal, and the scratch paper the testing center provides is one of them. Many test-takers often ignore the scratch paper—especially on the Verbal side of the test. Don't be one of them! Use the scratch paper to keep track of eliminated answer choices, jot down notes about questions and passages, and keep yourself organized.

The bottom line about scratch paper:

Make the test easier on your brain by writing things down instead of keeping them in your head.

So, What Are the Appropriate Uses of Your GMAT Score?

1. Selection of applicants for graduate study in management
2. Selection of applicants for financial aid on the basis of academic potential
3. Counseling and guidance

Source: *Graduate Management Admission Council*

Summary

○ Because of the way the GMAT is designed, you will be forced to answer questions whether or not you know the correct answer.

○ However, not knowing the exact answer to a question does not mean that you have to get it wrong.

○ When you don't know the correct answer to a question, look for wrong answers instead. This is called POE, or Process of Elimination.

Chapter 5
Cracking the
Adaptive Sections:
Advanced Principles

In this chapter, you will learn how the GMAT is constructed with obvious answers. You will also learn how to use this information to radically increase your score.

The people who write the computer-adaptive section of the GMAT think that this part of the test is wonderful—and not just because they wrote it, or because it makes them a lot of money. They like it because it ensures that the only problems a test taker gets to see are problems at, and slightly above and below, her level of ability. One of the things they always hated about the paper-and-pencil test was that a student scoring 300 could guess the correct answer to a 700-level question.

But They Have This Little Problem

The questions on the GMAT are still multiple-choice.

That may not seem like a problem to you, but consider the following situation. Suppose a student takes the GMAT. She's answered 36 of the 37 problems on the Math section. There's one left, and as she looks at this last question, she realizes she has absolutely no idea how to answer it. However, one of the answer choices just "seems" correct. So she picks it.

And she gets it correct.

The test writers get nightmares just thinking about this situation. Say that student was supposed to get 500. She "deserved" 500. But by guessing the correct answer to one last problem, she may have gotten 510.

Ten points more than she "deserved."

GMAC's Solution

GMAC's tests wouldn't be worth much if students could routinely guess the correct answer to difficult questions by picking answers that seemed correct.

So the test writers came up with a wonderful solution:

On some difficult questions, answer choices that seem correct are wrong.

Choosing Answers That Seem Correct

Almost everybody gets stuck on at least a few questions when they take the computer-adaptive sections of the GMAT. After all, the questions keep getting harder as you get questions right. Sooner or later, you may run into a question that you just don't know how to do. If you're like most people, you'll get as far as you can, and then choose the answer that seems correct. In other words, you play a hunch. For some questions, you may pick an answer because it "just looks right" or something about it seems to go naturally with the question.

What Happens When a Person Takes the GMAT?

Many people pick the answer that seems correct on every problem. Sometimes these hunches are correct; sometimes they are not.

- On easy questions, the obvious answer tends to be the correct answer.
- On medium questions, the obvious answer is correct only some of the time.
- On difficult questions, the obvious answer is almost always wrong.

What Do Most People Think about the GMAT?

Most people have a few preconceived notions about the GMAT.

- The GMAT is constructed to be fair.
- Knowing the content is enough to get most questions right.
- GMAC wants you to get the questions right if you have the knowledge needed.

Unfortunately, none of these is true.

The Truth about the GMAT

- The GMAT is constructed to make you miss questions you *should* get right.
- You can completely understand the content behind the question and still get it wrong. In fact, almost all GMAT test takers miss some questions this way.
- GMAC wants to trick you into getting the question wrong, even if you understand the concepts.

Don't Be Predictable

Because most people trust the test, they feel confident reading a problem, solving it in a way that seems correct, and picking the answer that appears in the answer choices.

To ace the GMAT, it is not enough to know how to read and to understand math and grammar topics. You have to be able to dodge GMAC's traps. In this section, we'll discuss how to use the traps to your advantage and make yourself more likely to pick the right answer, since understanding the content is not a guarantee that you will get the question right. First, let's understand how GMAC constructs these traps.

Put Yourself in GMAC's Shoes

Imagine you are writing a multiple-choice test. Here is a problem you've written:

During a sale, a store sells $\frac{1}{5}$ of its books. The following day, the sale continues and the store sells $\frac{1}{5}$ of the remaining books. What fraction of the original books remain in the store?

Because you enjoy making people miserable, you decided to write a question that was very tricky. To solve this problem correctly, a student needs to understand that the second $\frac{1}{5}$ is coming out of the books that are remaining after the first day. That is, there are $\frac{4}{5}$ of the books left after the first day, and the store sells $\frac{1}{5}$ of those books, not another $\frac{1}{5}$ of the total.

$\frac{1}{5}$ of $\frac{4}{5}$ is $\frac{4}{25}$ (solve by replacing "of" with multiplication). So the store sold $\frac{1}{5}$ of the total and then another $\frac{4}{25}$ of the total, for a final total of $\frac{9}{25}$ of the original books sold. Then the student has to subtract that from 1 because the question asks what fraction *remain* in the store: the answer is $\frac{16}{25}$.

So that is already a pretty tough question. By itself, it would be rated a high medium. You have to make one of the answer choices $\frac{16}{25}$, since that's the answer, but how should you come up with the other answer choices? You could make up random fractions, but if a student did the problem wrong, his or her answer probably wouldn't be on there and the student would realize that he or she did it wrong. Then the student might figure out the correct way to solve the problem or even decide to take a random guess and get the answer right. You can't allow that.

Making the Problem Extra Tricky Just Because You Can

You want to make sure that this student doesn't get the answer right. You only want a student who understood the question the first time to get it right and to weed out students who could get it right if they realized they'd made a mistake.

To do that, you create answer choices based on what a student might do wrong. So let's figure out what that is.

A student might think the second $\frac{1}{5}$ was coming from the total and add $\frac{1}{5} + \frac{1}{5}$, and get $\frac{2}{5}$. That would be a good answer choice to use.

Another student might get that same part wrong but understand that the question was asking about how many are left: $\frac{3}{5}$ would be another good answer to use.

A student who really doesn't understand the problem might just multiply the two fractions. $\frac{1}{5} \times \frac{1}{5} = \frac{1}{25}$. Make another answer choice $\frac{1}{25}$.

How about a student who did everything correct but misread the question? The student gets that the store sold $\frac{9}{25}$ of the books over the two days and is so excited that he or she didn't fall in a trap in the first couple steps that the student sees $\frac{9}{25}$ in the answer choices and goes ahead and picks it without rereading the question.

So now you've made sure that most students who don't know how to solve the problem don't get it right. Either they do it wrong but don't realize it because their answer is on there, or they look at the answer choices and find one that seems like it could be correct based on the numbers in the problem. But your correct answer is disguised—it isn't obvious how to get to it because it's the result of several steps. This bumps up the difficulty level to medium-hard because you've ensured that it would be almost impossible for a student to get the problem right without knowing exactly how to do it and carefully avoiding your traps.

Here's your finished question:

During a sale, a store sells $\frac{1}{5}$ of its books. The following day, the sale continues and the store sells $\frac{1}{5}$ of the remaining books. What fraction of the original books remain in the store?

- ○ $\frac{1}{25}$
- ○ $\frac{9}{25}$
- ○ $\frac{2}{5}$
- ○ $\frac{3}{5}$
- ○ $\frac{16}{25}$

Use GMAC's Tricks Against Them

Knowing how these questions are constructed makes you GMAC's worst nightmare. Now, rather than a great trap question, this just became much easier than it was without the trap choices. Why? Because you might not be able to solve the problem yourself, but you know how **not** to solve it!

You see the phrase *of the remaining books* and you realize that something tricky is happening. You add the fractions, get (C), subtract them from 1, get (D), and eliminate both of them, because you *know* there's a trick that you're not seeing, so *those answers can't be right*. A little quick estimating can eliminate (A) too—there's no way those numbers are going to get **that** low.

Now this medium-hard question just became a 50/50 shot, and you had no idea how to solve it.

Nice job.

No Relief on the Verbal Portion

Let's pretend again: you still work for GMAC, and you write a reading passage. Let's use a short one, to keep it simple.

> For most of this century, big companies dominated an American business scene that seemed to thrive on its own grandness of scale. The expansion westward, the growth of the railroad and steel industries, an almost limitless supply of cheap raw materials, plus a population boom that provided an ever-increasing demand for new products (although not a cheap source of labor) all coincided to encourage the growth of large companies.

Then you write a question:

> To what does the passage credit as bolstering the growth of large companies?

And you write the correct answer:

> The combination of a variety of conditions favorable to big businesses

B-School Lingo

back of the envelope: a quick analysis of numbers, as if scribbled on the back of an envelope

benchmarking: comparing a company to others in the industry

burn rate: the amount of cash a money-losing company consumes during a period of time

Source: *The Best 294 Business Schools*

Why did you write an answer choice like that instead of something that is explicitly stated in the passage? Well, because you're thinking like GMAC. You only want students who have a good understanding of the passage as a whole and read the answer choices carefully to get the question correct.

Read Carefully...Or Else

Next you make some trap answers to direct students away from the correct answer. Would you write a trap answer like, *The lack of government intervention prior to the Sherman Anti-Trust Act?* No, because nothing in there was mentioned in the passage and a student isn't likely to pick it.

You want to write trap answers that a student will find tempting. How about:

> The high cost of labor for expanding businesses

The passage says this more or less, but it doesn't answer this particular question because high labor costs don't help businesses grow. It's a trap because students might pick it if they forget what the question is actually asking, or if they misunderstand the meaning of the word *bolster*.

You might also write:

> Large companies' ability to transport steel via railroads

> Greater demand for new products in the West than in the East

> Cheap labor as a result of a population boom

Notice that all of these are not supported by the passage but have some elements that are found within the passage. In fact, they are, respectively, examples of the common GMAT trap answer types: Recycled Language, No Such Comparison, and Reversal. We'll go into much greater detail on these later on. Your correct answer, however, is 100% supported by what is in the passage but doesn't have a lot of memory traps that make you want to pick it immediately after reading the passage.

How to Use this to Your Advantage

Now that you know how GMAC constructs wrong answers, you can use that to your advantage to avoid picking them.

Here are two examples of how you might do that.

1. You read a problem and immediately know what to do. You do one step on paper or solve quickly in your head and see that answer in the answer choices. You're super excited to click on the answer and you're sure you got such an obvious problem correct.

    Stop! Don't pick that answer. You aren't likely to see many, if any, questions that are so easy you barely have to do any work. If you think you know the answer right away, go back and reread the problem carefully. Reread the question and the answer choices as well. You have probably made a mistake.

    If you have been doing well on the last few questions, the questions are going to get harder, and that means less obvious answers!

2. You can't figure out why your "obvious" answer is wrong OR you have no idea how to actually solve the problem.

Look at the answer choices and eliminate anything that is obvious. Ask yourself what answer choice you could get by doing one or two simple steps. Or maybe you know the first step of the problem and see that answer on there but you know there's more to do. Eliminate any answer choices that you can tell are not correct and take a guess among whatever is left.

This applies to the Verbal as well. You should never just pick out an answer choice that immediately seems correct. It is probably a trap. Use POE and think carefully about what the passage actually means.

What This Means for your Bin

Higher-level questions tend to have more trap answers. In fact, that's often what makes a higher-level question rated as so difficult. It's not that the math is hard or the passage is complex, but that many students are fooled and miss the question.

Harvard and the GMAT

For 12 years, Harvard University's Business School would not even look at the GMAT scores of its applicants. The class of 1997 was the first in more than a decade that was required to submit GMAT scores.

If you know most of your questions are coming from the medium-hard and hard bins, look out for those trap answers. If you've noticed a trap and avoided it, you can feel more confident that your answer is correct.

If your questions are drawing mostly from the easy and medium bins, there will still be trap answers. The most important thing to keep in mind is that while GMAC considers those questions easier, they're not easy for you since the test is designed to give you questions at or above your appropriate level. Even if the questions are more straightforward, answer choices are always constructed based on common errors and misreadings.

Be honest with yourself! Practice, evaluate your performance, and develop a solid understanding of what bins you can reasonably handle. The techniques you will learn and practice will increase what you can handle, but don't try to jump ahead of yourself. What kind of practice is more likely to improve your score? What kind of practice is more likely to just be frustrating?

- Correctly answering 90% of the problems in a challenging bin
- Incorrectly answering 90% of the problems in a *really* challenging bin

Even if you want your score to go up significantly, take it one step at a time.

Summary

o   Almost everyone approaches the GMAT by choosing the answer that seems correct, all things considered.

o   The GMAT is constructed with incorrect answer choices that the test writers think you might like. If it's a mistake a person might easily make on a problem, it's probably an answer choice.

o   If a question seems easy to you, STOP, and re-read the question. Make sure you haven't fallen into a trap. If you caught a twist or trick along the way, you can feel more confident.

o   Knowing why an answer choice is a trap can help you eliminate and improve your chances—even on problems you don't know how to solve.

Chapter 6
Taking the GMAT

How do you register and practice for the GMAT? What is taking the actual test really like? What do you do if something goes wrong? This chapter will answer these and other practical questions.

REGISTERING TO TAKE THE GMAT

The easiest way to register for the exam is by telephone or online. You will be given a list of dates, times, and testing centers that are located near you. One of the actual advantages of the GMAT is that you get to schedule the time of the exam. If you are not a morning person, ask for an afternoon time slot. If you can't think after midday, ask for a morning time slot.

Keep in mind that certain slots get filled quickly, so be sure to call ahead of time. The registration fee is $250 (worldwide). Those who schedule an exam in certain countries will incur taxes. Tax rate information is available at **www.mba.com** in the GMAT registration section. Note that checks or money orders payable in U.S. dollars must be drawn from banks located in the United States or Canada.

> To register for the GMAT, call 1-800-717-GMAT or visit the website at **www.mba.com**.

PRACTICING TO TAKE THE GMAT

As you prepare for the GMAT, it's important to know—in advance—what the experience of taking the test is like so that you can mimic those conditions during practice tests. When you are taking a practice test, turn off your telephone, and try to strictly observe the time limits of the test sections, and even the time limits of the breaks in between sections. To mimic the experience of working with a scratch booklet, buy a spiral notebook filled with grid paper. If you know when you will be taking the real GMAT, try to schedule your practice tests around the same time of day.

If you are the sort of person who likes to have a mental picture of what a new experience will be like, you might even consider visiting the test center ahead of time. This serves two purposes: first, you'll know how to get there on the day of the test, and second, you'll be familiar with the ambiance in advance.

The Days Before the Test

Try to keep to your regular routine. Staying up late to study the last few nights before the test is counterproductive. It's important to get regular amounts of exercise and sleep. Continue the study plan you've been on from the beginning, but taper off toward the end. You'll want to take your last practice exam no later than several days before the real test, so you'll have time to go over the results carefully. The last day or so should be devoted to any topics that still give you trouble.

The Night Before the Test

Get together the things you will need to take with you for the test: a government-issued ID card; directions to the test center (if you haven't already been there); a mental list of the five schools you wish to receive your test scores (if you can't identify these when you take the test, you will have to pay $28 extra per school to get scores sent out later); and a snack and some water. Snacks and water are not allowed in the testing room, but they can be placed in your locker and consumed during a break. Don't bother to take a calculator—no calculators are permitted for the adaptive sections (Quantitative and Verbal) of the GMAT. An on-screen calculator is provided for the Integrated Reasoning section.

(give 5 schools)

What to Take to the Test Center
1. A government-issued ID
2. A snack
3. A bottle of water

Once you have gathered everything you need, take the night off. Go to a movie. Relax. There is no point in last-minute cramming. You are as ready as you are going to be.

The Day of the Test

If you are taking the test in the morning, get up early enough that you have time to eat break-fast, if that is your usual routine, and do a couple of GMAT questions you've already seen in order to get your mind working. If you are taking the test in the afternoon, make sure you get some lunch, and, again, do a few GMAT problems. You don't want to have to warm up on the test itself.

Take a snack to the test center. Use your breaks to eat the food you've brought or to run to the bathroom.

At the Testing Center

Unlike testing sessions you may have attended in the past, where hundreds of people were lined up to take the same test, you may well be the only person at your testing center taking the GMAT. You'll be asked to present your government-issued ID, and an employee will take your photograph and scan your palm using a palm vein scanner. Finally, you'll be led to the computer station where you will take the test. The station consists of a desk with a computer monitor, a key-board, a mouse, a scratch booklet, and a black, fine-tipped marker. The marker they will give you to write in your scratch booklet has tendency to dry up when left uncapped—so during breaks, remember to cap it. If you need another marker or another scratch booklet during the test, simply raise your hand, and a proctor will bring it. However, the timer won't stop while the proctor brings you another scratch booklet or marker. Use your practice tests to learn to fit your scratch work into one scratch booklet. Before the test starts, make sure you're comfortable. Is there enough light? Is your desk sturdy? Don't be afraid to speak up; you're going to be spending four hours at that desk.

There will almost certainly be other people in the same room at other computer stations taking other computer-adaptive tests. You might be seated next to someone taking the licensing exam for architects, or a test for school nurses, or even a test for golf pros.

None of the people in the room will have necessarily started at the same time. The testing center employee will show you how to begin the test, but the computer itself will be your proctor from then on. It will tell you how much time you have left in a section, when your time is up, and when to go on to the next section.

The test center employees will be available if you have a question. They will also monitor the room for security purposes. Just in case their eagle eyes aren't enough, video and audio systems will record everything that happens in the room.

The process sounds less human than it really is. Our students have generally found the test center employees to be quite nice.

What Your Screen Will Look Like

During most of the test, your screen will look a lot like this:

The problem you're working on at any particular moment will be near the top of the screen (by the way, the answer to this one is the third choice). At the top right will be a readout of the time remaining in the section, the number of the question you're working on, and how many total questions there are in the section. Here are the main interface items you will see on the screen:

End Exam—By clicking on this button, you can end the test at any moment. We don't recommend that you do this unless you actually become ill. Even if you decide not to have your test scored (an option they will give you at the end of the exam), you might as well finish—it's great practice, and besides, GMAC has no intention of giving you a refund.

Time—The time you have left to complete the section is displayed in the upper right of the screen. You can hide the time by clicking on it, and you can make it reappear by clicking on the icon in its place. During the last few minutes of the test, the time is automatically displayed and you cannot hide it.

Question Number—The question number that you are on is also displayed in the upper right, and it works just like the time display: You can hide it by clicking on it or make it reappear by clicking on the icon. During the last few minutes of the test, the question number is automatically displayed and cannot be hidden.

Help—During the test, this button provides test and section directions and information about using the software.

Next—When you've answered a question by clicking on the small bubble in front of the answer you think is correct, you press this button.

Confirm—After you press "Next," a pop-up window will open and ask you to confirm your answer. Select "yes" to continue to the next question.

What Happens If You Get Stuck on a Question?

Everyone knows that sinking feeling of not knowing how to do a test problem, but before you start panicking, there are a few things to bear in mind about the GMAT.

First of all, as any Princeton Review graduate will tell you, seeing hard questions on the adaptive (Math and Verbal) sections of the GMAT is a good sign. Because these sections are adaptive, you don't get a hard question until you've answered a bunch of increasingly difficult medium questions correctly—which means you are probably already on track for a good score.

Second, if you have gone through this book and taken the practice tests, then chances are good that if you reread the question and think about it for a few seconds, you may get an idea of how to start it (and starting is half the battle).

Third, you should remember that approximately one-fourth of the questions on the adaptive sections of this test don't even count. They are "experimental questions" being tried out for future versions of the GMAT, so there's no point in getting too upset over a question that might not even get scored.

And fourth, if you are really stuck, then you can pull out The Princeton Review's arsenal of POE (Process of Elimination) techniques to do some very shrewd guessing.

Admissions Insight No. 2: Research
All business schools are NOT alike. To begin your admissions research, go to **PrincetonReview. com**, and take advantage of our Advanced Business School Search tool. Our school profiles present detailed facts and figures on admissions, academics, student body, and career outlook.

What Happens If You Don't Get to Every Question in a Section?

If you run out of time without having answered all the questions in one of the adaptive sections, the computer just moves you on to the next section. As we said earlier, for adaptive sections, the computer keeps an updated estimate of your score as you move through the section. If you don't get to answer some questions, the computer deducts points (based on an algorithm) and gives you a score based on the questions you *have* answered. So, you could get a score on the adaptive sections by answering only one math and one verbal question. Of course, that score would be pretty low!

For the Integrated Reasoning section, you also cannot skip a question and move on to the next question. For questions that have multiple parts, you also need to answer every part of the question before you move onto the next question. Like the adaptive sections, you can run out of time, however, and leave questions unanswered. Doing so, however, can have a drastic impact on your Integrated Reasoning score. With scores that range from only 1 to 8, and only 12 questions that are scored all or nothing, answering every question is important on this section.

It Is Actually in Your Interest to Answer *All* the Questions—Even If You Have to Guess

You might think it would be better to skip any questions you don't have time to answer at the end of an adaptive section—but in fact, the reverse is true: If time is running out, you will almost certainly get a higher score by clicking through and answering any remaining questions at random. This is because the penalty for getting a question wrong diminishes sharply toward the end of each adaptive section (when the computer has already largely decided your score). The penalty for each question skipped at the end of an adaptive section is actually greater than the penalty for getting one of those last questions wrong.

But You Can Do Much Better Than Guessing at Random

In the following chapters, we will give you all the specific math and verbal skills you need to ace the Math, Verbal, and Integrated Reasoning sections. We will also raise the Process of Elimination to a fine art—in case you have to guess.

Zen and the Art of Test Taking

As you begin each new question, put the previous question behind you. Don't get rattled if you think you got the previous question wrong. Even if your current question seems easier, it could be experimental. Just do your best to answer the current question correctly.

At the End of the Test

When you finish, the computer will ask you if you want the test to count. If you say no, or you just walk away, the computer will not record your score, and no schools will ever see it. Of course, neither will you. GMAC will let you look at your score with their Score Preview feature so you can decide whether you want to keep it or cancel before sending off to your prospective schools. You are given 2 minutes to decide whether to accept your scores, but if you do not decide within this time, your score will be canceled. Also note that if you do cancel your scores, your future score reports will not show this.

If you tell the computer that you want the test to count, then it will give you your unofficial score right then and there on the screen. This will include your Integrated Reasoning score but not your essay score. (Test center employees can print out the unofficial score report for you.) Within 20 days, you'll receive your official results online. If you choose to cancel at the test site, you have up to four years and 11 months after your exam date to change your mind, for a $50 fee.

If Something Weird Happens at the Test Center...

We have found that almost nothing ever goes wrong at the test centers. They are professionally run. But in the unlikely event that there is a technical glitch with your assigned computer, or if you want to complain about test center conditions or some other anomaly, it is best to start the process before you leave the test center by filing a complaint immediately after the test is over. If possible, get the test center staff to corroborate your complaint. Then, as soon as possible after the test is over, contact either Pearson VUE or GMAT Customer Service by one of the following methods:

> **Email:** pvtestsecurity@pearson.com
> **Web:** www.pearsonvue.com/contact/gmat/security
> **Phone:** 800-717-GMAT or 952-681-3680

> **Admissions Insight No. 3: When to Apply**
> Although many schools have a filing range that stretches from six to eight months, early applications often have a better chance. This is because there are more spots available in the beginning of the process.

One Final Thought Before You Begin

No matter how high or low you score on the test and no matter how much you improve your performance with this book, you should *never* accept the score GMAC assigns you as an accurate assessment of your abilities. The temptation to see a high score as evidence that you're a genius, or a low score as evidence that you're an idiot, can be very powerful.

When you've read this book and practiced our techniques on real GMAT questions, you'll be able to judge for yourself whether the GMAT actually measures much besides how well you do on the GMAT.

Think of this as a kind of game—a game you can win.

Summary

o Register for the GMAT either online or by telephone. Schedule the test for a time that is convenient for you, but that meets your schools' deadlines.

o In the days leading up to the test, follow the study plan you set up in the beginning. Be sure to get plenty of rest, particularly the night before the test.

o Get together all the things you'll need on the day of the test: directions to the test center, a list of five schools to which you want to submit scores, a snack, water, and photo ID.

o At the testing center, make sure you are comfortable at the computer they assign to you. Tune out everyone else. Start working through the test. It should look exactly like the practice tests you have taken online. If you get stuck on a question, use POE to make an educated guess and move on. Remember, some of the questions are experimental and may not count toward your score.

o Because there is a penalty for unanswered questions at the end of the test, it makes sense to use POE to guess on any remaining questions rather than to leave them blank.

Part II
How to
Crack the
Math GMAT

Chapter 7
GMAT Math:
Basic Principles

If *absolute value* sounds familiar, but you can't quite remember it, this chapter can help. It provides a comprehensive review of the math terms and rules you haven't had to think about since high school.

Math and the Integrated Reasoning Section

Before we get started talking about the Quantitative section of the GMAT, let's take a moment to talk about the Integrated Reasoning section. The Integrated Reasoning section tests a blend of math and critical reasoning (verbal) skills. However, some questions test math skills. The good news is that those math skills are the same math skills that the GMAT has been testing for years. So, while we'll be mostly discussing the Quantitative section in this and the following chapters, you'll want to remember that you'll also use the math reviewed in these chapters to answer some of the Integrated Reasoning questions.

What's Covered in the Math Section

The 37 math questions on the GMAT come in two different formats. About half of the questions are regular Problem Solving questions of the type you're familiar with from countless other standardized tests, such as the SAT. The other half of the questions, mixed in among the regular Problem Solving questions, are of a type unique to the GMAT: They're called Data Sufficiency questions, and they ask you to determine whether you can answer a math question based on two pieces of information. We've devoted two entire chapters to Data Sufficiency.

But whether the question falls into the category of Problem Solving or Data Sufficiency, GMAT questions test your general knowledge of three subjects:

> 1. Arithmetic
> 2. Basic algebra
> 3. Basic geometry

What Isn't Covered in the Math Section

The good news is that you won't need to know calculus, trigonometry, or any complicated geometry. The bad news is that the specialized, business-type math you're probably good at isn't tested, either. There will be no questions on computing the profit on three ticks of a particular bond sale, no questions about amortizing a loan, no need to calculate the bottom line of a small business.

Ancient History

For the most part, what you'll find on the GMAT is a kind of math that you haven't had to think about in years: junior high school and high school math. Because most people who apply to business school have been out of college for several years, high school math may seem a bit like ancient history. In the next few chapters, we'll give you a fast review of the important concepts, and we'll show you some powerful techniques for cracking the system.

Order of Difficulty

The first problem on the computer-adaptive Math test is of medium difficulty. Based on your response to that first question, you will next be presented with an easier or a more difficult problem.

The Princeton Review Approach

Because it's probably been a long time since you've needed to reduce fractions or remember how many degrees there are in a quadrilateral, the first thing to do is review the information tested on the GMAT by going through our math review. Along the way, you'll learn some valuable test-taking skills that will allow you to take advantage of some of the inherent weaknesses of standardized testing.

When you've finished the math review, you should read our chapter on Data Sufficiency and then take our diagnostic math test. Based on your approximate score on our diagnostic, you can then practice working through problems at, or just above, your scoring range. By becoming familiar with the general level of difficulty of these problems and the number of steps required to solve them, you can increase your score on the real GMAT.

Stay Focused!
Always keep in mind that if your purpose is to raise your GMAT score, it's a waste of time to learn math that won't be tested. Don't get us wrong, we think the derivation of ϖ is fascinating, but…

Extra Help

Although we can show you which mathematical principles are most important for the GMAT, this book cannot take the place of a basic foundation in math. We find that most people, even if they don't remember much of high school math, pick it up again quickly. Our drills and examples will refresh your memory if you've gotten rusty, but if you have serious difficulties with the following chapters, you should consider a more thorough review, like *Math Workout for the GMAT*, from The Princeton Review. This book will enable you to see where you need the most work. Always keep in mind, though, that if your purpose is to raise your GMAT score, it's a waste of time to learn math that won't be tested.

No Calculators on Quant!
One form of extra help you won't be allowed during the Quantitative section of the GMAT is a calculator. (For the Integrated Reasoning section, there's an onscreen calculator.) All calculations for the Quant section must be done the old fashioned way—by hand. To get used to this, you should retire your calculator (especially during practice tests) until after you have finished with your real GMAT.

BASIC INFORMATION

Try the following problem:

How many even integers are between 17 and 27 ?

○ 9
○ 7
○ 5
○ 4
○ 3

Extra Practice
Visit your Student Tools to download a free excerpt from *Math Workout for the GMAT*.

This is an easy GMAT question. Even so, if you don't know what an integer is, the question is impossible to answer. Before moving on to arithmetic, you should make sure you're familiar with some basic terms and concepts. This material isn't difficult, but you must know it cold. (The answer, by the way, is (C).)

Integers

Integers are the numbers we think of when we think of numbers. Integers are sometimes called whole or natural numbers. They can be negative or positive. They do not include fractions. The positive integers are:

1, 2, 3, 4, 5, etc.

The negative integers are:

–1, –2, –3, –4, –5, etc.

Zero (0) is also an integer. It is the only number that is neither positive nor negative. Sometimes the GMAT will reference a number that is not positive, or non-negative. That is another way to refer to zero as a potential part of a question.

Ancient History 101
The GMAT will test your (probably rusty) knowledge of high school math.

Positive integers get greater as they move away from 0; negative integers get lesser. Look at this number line:

2 is greater than 1, but –2 is less than –1.

Positive and Negative

Positive numbers lie to the right of zero on the number line. Negative numbers lie to the left of zero on the number line.

There are three rules regarding the multiplication of positive and negative numbers:

Having Trouble Memorizing?
If you're having trouble memorizing GMAT math terminology, consider making flash cards to help you review.

positive × positive = positive

positive × negative = negative

negative × negative = positive

If you add a positive number and a negative number, subtract the number with the negative sign in front of it from the positive number.

$$4 + (-3) = 1$$

If you add two negative numbers, you add them as if they were positive, then put a negative sign in front of the sum.

$$-3 + -5 = -8$$

Digits

There are ten digits:

0, 1, 2, 3, 4, 5, 6, 7, 8, 9

All integers are made up of digits. In the integer 246, there are three digits: 2, 4, and 6. Each of the digits has a different name:

6 is called the units (or ones) digit.
4 is called the tens digit.
2 is called the hundreds digit.

A number with decimal places is also composed of digits, although it is not an integer. In the decimal 27.63, there are four digits:

2 is the tens digit.
7 is the units digit.
6 is the tenths digit.
3 is the hundredths digit.

Remainders

If an integer cannot be divided evenly by another integer, the integer that is left over at the end of division is called the **remainder**. Thus, remainders *must* be integers.

$$2\overline{)7} \\ \underline{-6} \\ 1 \leftarrow \text{remainder}$$

with quotient 3 above.

Odd or Even

Even numbers are integers that can be divided evenly by 2, leaving no remainder. Here are some examples:

$$-6, -4, -2, 0, 2, 4, 6, \text{etc.}$$

Any integer, no matter how large, is even if its last digit is divisible by 2. Thus 777,772 is even.

Odd numbers are integers that cannot be divided evenly by 2. Put another way, odd integers have a remainder of 1 when they are divided by 2. Here are some examples:

$$-5, -3, -1, 1, 3, 5, \text{etc.}$$

Any integer, no matter how large, is odd if its last digit is not divisible by 2. Thus 222,227 is odd.

There are several rules that always hold true for even and odd numbers:

even × even = even

odd × odd = odd

even × odd = even

even + even = even

odd + odd = even

even + odd = odd

It isn't necessary to memorize these, but you must know that the relationships always hold true. The individual rules can be derived in a second. If you need to know *even × even*, just try 2 × 2. The answer in this case is even, as *even × even* always will be.

?

Q: 20,179.01792
In the number above, which of the following two digits are identical?

(A) The tens digit and the hundredths digit
(B) The ones digit and the thousandths digit
(C) The hundreds digit and the tenths digit
(D) The thousands digit and the tenths digit
(E) The thousands digit and the hundredths digit

Turn to page 60 for the answer.

Consecutive Integers

Consecutive integers are integers listed in order of increasing value without any integers missing in between. For example, –3, –2, –1, 0, 1, 2, 3 are consecutive integers. Only integers can be consecutive.

Some consecutive even integers: –2, 0, 2, 4, 6, 8, etc.

Some consecutive odd integers: –3, –1, 1, 3, 5, etc.

Distinct Numbers

If two numbers are **distinct**, they cannot be equal. For example, if x and y are distinct, then they must have different values.

Prime Numbers

A **prime number** is a positive integer that is divisible only by two numbers: itself and 1. Thus 2, 3, 5, 7, 11, 13 are all prime numbers. The number 2 is both the least and the only even prime number. Neither 0 nor 1 is a prime number. All prime numbers are positive.

Divisibility Rules

If there is no remainder when integer x is divided by integer y, then x is said to be **divisible** by y. Put another way, divisible means you can evenly divide the greater number by the lesser number with no remainder. For example, 10 is divisible by 5.

Some Useful Divisibility Shortcuts:

- An integer is divisible by 2 if its units digit is divisible by 2. Thus, 772 is divisible by 2.
- An integer is divisible by 3 if the sum of its digits is divisible by 3. We can instantly tell that 216 is divisible by 3, because the sum of the digits (2 + 1 + 6) is divisible by 3.
- An integer is divisible by 4 if the number formed by its last two digits is divisible by 4. 3,028 is divisible by 4, because 28 is divisible by 4.
- An integer is divisible by 5 if its final digit is either 0 or 5. Thus, 60, 85, and 15 are all divisible by 5.
- An integer is divisible by 6 if it is divisible by both 2 and 3, the factors of 6. Thus, 318 is divisible by 6 because it is even, and the sum of 3 + 1 + 8 is divisible by 3.
- Division by zero is undefined. The test writers won't ever put a zero in the denominator. If you're working out a problem and you find yourself with a zero in the denominator of a fraction, you've done something wrong. By the way, a 0 in the numerator is fine. Any fraction with a 0 on the top is 0.

$$\frac{0}{1} = 0$$

$$\frac{0}{4} = 0$$

$$\frac{4}{0} = \text{undefined}$$

Factors and Multiples

An integer, x, is a factor of another integer, y, if y is divisible by x. So, in other words, $y = nx$, where y, n, and x are all integers. For example, 3 is a factor of 15 because 15 = (3)(5). All the factors of 15 are 1, 3, 5, and 15.

The **multiples** of an integer, y, are all numbers 0, $\pm1y$, $\pm2y$, $\pm3y\ldots$, etc. For example, 15 is a multiple of 3 (3×5); 12 is also a multiple of 3 (3×4). When you think about it, most numbers have only a few factors, but an infinite number of multiples. The memory device you may have learned in school is "factors are few; multiples are many."

Every integer greater than 1 is both its own greatest factor and least positive multiple.

Q: Which of the following numbers is prime?

0, 1, 15, 23, 33

Turn to page 62 for the answer.

Least Common Multiples

If an integer, x, is divisible by two integers, n and m, then x is a common multiple of n and m. For example, 30 is a common multiple of 5 and 6. The least common multiple of two integers is called the **least common multiple**. For our example, 30 is also the least common multiple of 5 and 6.

The most straightforward way to find a least common multiple is to simply start listing the positive multiples of both integers. When you find a number that is on both lists, that number is the least common multiple.

For example, here's how you find the least common multiple of 4 and 6.

>   **Multiples of 4:** 4, 8, 12, 16, 20,…

>   **Multiples of 6:** 6, 12,…

Since 12 is on both lists, 12 is the least common multiple of 4 and 6.

Greatest Common Factor

If two integers, n and m, are both divisible by an integer, x, then x is a common factor of n and m. For example, 6 is a common factor of both 12 and 18. The greatest factor that two numbers have in common is referred to as the **greatest common factor**. For our example, 6 is also the greatest common factor of 12 and 18.

The most straightforward way to find a greatest common factor is to simply list the factors of both numbers. Then you just need to find the greatest number that is on both lists.

For example, here's how you find the greatest common factor of 12 and 18.

>   **Factors of 12:** 1, 2, 3, 4, 6, 12

>   **Factors of 18:** 1, 2, 3, 6, 9, 18

Since 6 is the greatest number on both lists, 6 is the greatest common factor of 12 and 18.

Prime Factors

If an integer, x, that is a factor of an integer, y, is also prime, then x is called a **prime factor** of y. For example, 3 and 5 are prime factors of 15.

To find the prime factors of an integer, use a factor tree:

All positive integers greater than 1 have unique prime factorizations, a fact that the GMAT frequently tests. So, it doesn't matter which pair of factors you start with when you use the factor tree.

Here are some symbols you should know for the GMAT:

Symbol	Meaning
=	is equal to
≠	is not equal to
<	is less than
>	is greater than
≤	is less than or equal to
≥	is greater than or equal to

The prime factorization of 12 is 2 × 2 × 3.

Absolute Value

The **absolute value** of a number is the distance between that number and 0 on the number line. The absolute value of 6 is expressed as $|6|$.

$$|6| = 6$$

$$|-5| = 5$$

Challenge Question #1

x and y are integers less than 60 such that x is equal to the sum of the squares of two distinct prime numbers, and y is a multiple of 17. Which of the following could be the value of $x - y$?

- ○ −19
- ○ −7
- ○ 0
- ○ 4
- ○ 9

NOW LET'S LOOK AT THE INSTRUCTIONS

During the test, you'll be able to see test instructions by clicking on the "Help" button at the bottom of the screen. However, to avoid wasting time reading these during the test, read our version of the instructions for Problem Solving questions now:

Problem Solving Directions: Solve each problem and choose the best of the answer choices provided.

Numbers: This test uses only real numbers; no imaginary numbers are used or implied.

Diagrams: All problem solving diagrams are drawn as accurately as possible UNLESS it is specifically noted that a diagram is "not drawn to scale." All diagrams are in a plane unless stated otherwise.

Summary

o   Without a review of the basic terms and rules of math tested on the GMAT, you won't be able to begin to do the problems.

o   Study the vocabulary and rules in the preceding chapter to get this stuff back into your head. If you find that you need an even more comprehensive review, consider getting *Math Workout for the GMAT* or *Math Smart*, both published by The Princeton Review.

Chapter 8
POE and
GMAT Math

This chapter delves deeper into Process of Elimination
for GMAT Math problems, focusing on what to look
for when eliminating incorrect answer choices.

In Chapter 4, we introduced you to Process of Elimination—a way to increase your chances of picking a correct answer by eliminating incorrect answers. In Chapter 5, we delved into POE a little more deeply by exploring the mind of the test writer and showing you ways to use GMAC's tricks against them by not being predictable.

In this chapter, we are going to focus on what to look for when using POE on GMAT math problems.

But, first things first.

Break Glass In Case Of Emergency

The strategies we're going to outline for you in this chapter are often misunderstood by students. It's not that the concepts are overly difficult or foreign. In fact, they rely mostly on straightforward logical reasoning and simply paying close attention to the problem.

However, many students believe that these strategies are a one-stop shop for GMAT success. This is emphatically not the case.

When you are confronted with a GMAT math problem, your goal should be to solve the problem using the math concepts and strategies covered in this book. Solving the question should be your goal every time a new math question appears on your screen. You should take an internal inventory of the question—determine the kind of math being tested, the possible steps for completing the problem, the information provided by the problem—and then you should reach into your math toolkit to pull out the appropriate tools to solve the problem.

So, these POE strategies are not a silver bullet to solving math problems. They should not be your first resort.

These strategies should be considered an emergency valve. They are a rip cord for you to pull when you need it the most. That usually means that you are either stuck—the solution isn't working out—or that you are running out of time.

Hard Questions

Unless you are a truly masterful mathematician, or for some reason the adaptive portion of the GMAT testing algorithm is broken that day (hint: it won't be), you will eventually run into a math problem that you don't know how to solve. What do you do? Spending a lot of time hammering away at a problem is not necessarily the best idea, as you have other problems that you need to work on that may be easier to solve. So, you decide to guess and move on. That's a good idea!

But wait! Before you make a blind guess, take a second and apply the POE strategies outlined in this chapter to see whether you can eliminate any answer choices. You may still need to guess but your odds of guessing correctly will be greater if you've already eliminated some answer choices. This way, you have the best possible chance at answering an additional hard question correctly, which will improve your score.

Running Out Of Time

Let's say you're nearing the end of the allotted time for the math section and you look up only to realize that you have more questions left than you have time to work on. You know it's in your best interest to click on an answer for all the questions on the test, so you decide to guess on the remaining questions.

But wait! Don't guess blindly. Try some of these POE strategies for these remaining questions. If you can eliminate some answers before you guess, great!

Let's Get To Work

Now that we've established when you should use these POE strategies, it's time to discuss the actual strategies. For the remainder of this chapter, we are going to assume that you have already tried to answer the question using math concepts and that you were unsuccessful. Or, that you are running out of time and need to make quick, educated guesses about the answers. You are ready to break the glass and use your emergency tools. But, what are those tools and how do you wield them?

Take a look at the following question. Using the knowledge you gained from Chapters 4 and 5, are there any answer choices that you can eliminate using POE?

> Twenty-two percent of the cars produced in the United States are manufactured in Michigan. If the United States produces a total of 40 million cars, how many of these cars are produced outside of Michigan?
>
> ○   8.8 million
> ○   18 million
> ○   31.2 million
> ○   48.8 million
> ○   62 million

Ballparking

Let's see if we can eliminate any answer choices from this problem quickly and without doing any heavy lifting. The problem is asking for the number of the 40 million cars produced in the United States that are produced outside of Michigan. The problem also states that 22 percent of the cars produced in the United States are produced in Michigan, so you know that 78 percent of the cars produced in the United States are produced outside of Michigan. Even if you're unfamiliar with percentages, are there any answer choices that could be easily eliminated using this information? Well, if there are only 40 million cars produced in the entire United States, is it possible for any combination of states outside Michigan to produce more than 40 million cars? No, it's not, so (D) and (E) can be eliminated because they are greater than the total number of cars.

This tactic is called Ballparking. Ballparking usually involves either making rough comparisons of numbers or rough estimates of the size of an answer. In this case, comparing the answer choices to the total number of cars produced, which is stated in the problem, eliminates two answer choices.

Are there any other answer choices that can be eliminated using Ballparking? Let's try a rough estimate of the size of the answer. If 78 percent of the cars produced in the United States are produced outside of Michigan, then you know that more than three-fourths of the 40 million cars produced in the United States are produced outside of Michigan. Three-fourths of 40 million is 30 million. Two of the answer choices, (A) and (B), are less than half of the total number of cars produced in the United States. Therefore, it is impossible that (A) and (B) represent the number of cars produced outside of Michigan. Choices (A) and (B) can be eliminated. The only answer that remains is (C), which is the correct answer. Note that (C) is also close to our estimate of the answer.

While Ballparking won't usually get you to a single answer, it can often help you to eliminate some answers.

Partial Answers

Let's look at that same problem again, but for a different reason:

> Twenty-two percent of the cars produced in the United States are manufactured in Michigan. If the United States produces a total of 40 million cars, how many of these cars are produced outside of Michigan?
>
> ◯　　8.8 million
> ◯　18 million
> ◯　31.2 million
> ◯　48.8 million
> ◯　62 million

So, let's now assume that you are running low on time for the math section of the test and you come across this question. You're comfortable with percentages, so you decide that you can rush your way through this question. You quickly realize the first step in this problem is to find out how many actual cars are produced in Michigan; in other words, you need to know what 22 percent of 40 million equals. You do the calculation to determine that 8.8 million is 22% of 40 million. Your eye catches (A), which is an exact match for the number you just got, so you select (A) and move on to the next question.

The only problem is that you got the question wrong because you fell for a partial answer.

We discussed partial answers in Chapter 5 in some detail. Partial answers are answer choices that match a correct calculation for part of a question. The GMAT test writers love to include partial answers. Partial answers are particularly tricky when you're in a rush as they are designed to be appealing to test-takers who don't read the full question, or who are in a hurry.

How can you use this information to your advantage? When you are looking to guess on a question, it helps to think critically about the answer choices. Does a certain answer choice look too obvious or easy? If so, there's a good chance it's a partial answer and, absent doing the actual problem, would be a good candidate to be eliminated before you guess.

Many times partial answers also come in the form of answers that can be derived from one step, or answers that contain numbers or variables that are similar to those found in the problem. If you're pressed for time and looking to guess, look for these types of answer choices to eliminate.

Finally, the best way to avoid partial answers is to get into the habit of reading the question stem one more time before selecting your answer. That way, you can be sure that you are answering the question that was asked!

Putting It All Together

Try the following problem and look for ways to eliminate answer choices using Ballparking and partial answers.

The output of a factory is increased by 10% to keep up with rising demand. To handle the holiday rush, this new output is increased by 20%. By approximately what percent would the output of the factory now have to be decreased in order to restore the original output?

○ 20%
○ 24%
○ 30%
○ 32%
○ 70%

Here's How to Crack It

The factory raises its output by 10% and then raises it again by 20%. The problem is asking for the amount the factory will need to lower its output to return to the original level. For this example, don't worry about solving the problem. Just practice eliminating incorrect answer choices using Ballparking or partial answers.

Choice (A) is just a repeat of the numbers in the question, which is a warning sign of a partial answer, so eliminate (A). Choice (C) is the result of adding the two percentages in the question together. This is too easy and a warning sign of a partial answer, so eliminate (C). Choice (E) is significantly greater than the information in the problem would suggest. Even if it's unclear by how much the factory needs to lower its output, the amount by which the factory raised its output is not even close to 70%. Eliminate (E).

The remaining answer choices, (B) and (D), are not as easily eliminated as (A), (C), and (E). Figuring out which answer to eliminate next would require solving the problem. However, if you are in a rush or do not know how to answer this question, you could have eliminated three of the five answer choices and given yourself a 50-50 shot at correctly guessing the answer to the question. Those are better odds than guessing blindly! The correct answer, by the way, is (B).

Look at another example:

A student took 6 courses last year and received an average (arithmetic mean) grade of 100 points. The year before, the student took 5 courses and received an average grade of 90 points. To the nearest tenth of a point, what was the student's average grade for the entire two-year period?

- ○ 79
- ○ 89
- ○ 95
- ○ 95.5
- ○ 97.2

Here's How to Crack It

Again, assume you're running out of time or are unsure how to solve this problem. Can you eliminate any answer choices to improve your odds of correctly guessing the answer? The problem states that the student received average grades of 100 and 90 in a two-year period. The question wants to know the average grade of the student for the entire two-year period. If the least grade the student averaged is 90, it is not possible for the student's average to be less than 90, so (A) and (B) can be eliminated. Choice (C) has all the warning signs of a partial answer as 95 is just the average of 100 and 90, the two numbers found in the problem, so (C) is also a good candidate to be eliminated.

The remaining answer choices are not as easy to eliminate. But again, by applying these POE strategies, you were able to give yourself a 50-50 shot at correctly guessing the answer! The correct answer here is (D).

Summary

○ Process of Elimination allows you to eliminate answer choices even when you don't know how to do a problem or you are running out of time. There are two types of answer choices to look for in these situations: Ballparking and partial answers.

- **Ballparking:** Some GMAC answer choices can be eliminated simply because they are not close enough to what the correct answer choice should be, or can be easily found to be false by rounding the numbers to numbers that are easier to work with.

- **Partial answers:** GMAC likes to include, among the answer choices, answers that are partial completions of the problem. Recognize these answer choices by looking for choices that require little or no work, or are similar to the numbers in the problem.

Chapter 9
Data Sufficiency: Basic Principles

Data Sufficiency is a question type you've never seen before. This chapter will show you how to use basic POE techniques to make this format your new favorite kind of math.

Almost half of the thirty-seven math questions on the GMAT will be Data Sufficiency questions. We're about to show you how to use POE to make this strange question type easy.

WHAT IS DATA SUFFICIENCY?

If you've never heard of Data Sufficiency, that's because this question type is unique to the GMAT, and these questions definitely require some getting used to. If you have already taken a GMAT practice exam, or the actual GMAT, you may have spent several minutes just trying to understand the directions for Data Sufficiency questions.

However, Data Sufficiency questions really just test the same math concepts as Problem Solving questions, but with a twist—a strange question format.

Here's what a Data Sufficiency question looks like on the GMAT:

What is the value of y ?

(1) y is an even integer such that $-1.5 < y < 1.5$.

(2) Integer y is not prime.

○ Statement (1) ALONE is sufficient, but statement (2) alone is not sufficient.
○ Statement (2) ALONE is sufficient, but statement (1) alone is not sufficient.
○ BOTH statements TOGETHER are sufficient, but NEITHER statement ALONE is sufficient.
○ EACH statement ALONE is sufficient.
○ Statements (1) and (2) TOGETHER are not sufficient.

Each Data Sufficiency question consists of a question followed by two statements. There are also five possible answer choices, as shown. The answers are the same for every Data Sufficiency question, so once you learn what each means, you won't need to spend time rereading them. You'll just be able to think about them as answers (A), (B), (C), (D), and (E), which is how we'll refer to them.

Notice that there are two words that the answer choices keep repeating—*alone* and *sufficient*. So, it looks like we're supposed to evaluate the statements on their own—at least at first. Moreover, our task is evidently to determine whether we have sufficient information to answer the question.

That's how Data Sufficiency differs from Problem Solving. In Problem Solving questions, you are asked to give a numerical answer to the question. In fact, the inclusion of five numerical answer choices tells you that you can assume that the question can be solved. For Data

Sufficiency questions, however, you're not being asked to solve the question but to decide WHETHER the question can be solved. It may, in fact, turn out that the statements do not provide sufficient information to answer the question.

Data Sufficiency: How To
Tips and strategies on how to more easily solve complex Data Sufficiency problems. To watch, visit your Student Tools.

Here's How to Crack It

The first answer choice—(A)—indicates that we should first look at Statement (1) by itself to see if it is sufficient to answer the question.

In fact, the best way to work Data Sufficiency problems is to look at *one statement at a time*. So, ignore Statement (2). Here, we've replaced Statement (2) with question marks to indicate that we are looking only at the first statement—almost as though we had covered up the second statement.

What is the value of y ?

(1) y is an even integer such that $-1.5 < y < 1.5$.

(2) ????

Now, we're ready to evaluate Statement (1) alone. There are three integers between –1.5 and 1.5: –1, 0, and 1. Of those, as you may recall from Chapter 7, only 0 is even. So, Statement (1) does provide sufficient information to answer the question.

We're not ready to choose the first answer—(A)—yet, however, because the second part of the answer choice states that Statement (2) alone is not sufficient. Now, forget that you have ever seen Statement (1).

What is the value of y ?

(1) ????

(2) Integer y is not prime.

The second statement only tells us that y is not prime. So, possible values for y include 1, 4, 6, 8, etc. Do we know the value of y? No way. So, Statement (2) is not sufficient. Because (1) is sufficient and (2) is not, the answer to this question is

○ Statement (1) ALONE is sufficient, but statement (2) alone is not sufficient.

Or, in other words, the correct answer is (A).

DATA SUFFICIENCY: GETTING STARTED

Now that you've seen and worked a Data Sufficiency question, it's time to learn how to make this weird question type your own. The first step is to understand what each of the answer choices means.

By making small changes to the example you've just seen, we can provide examples of each of the answer choices. Next to each example, you'll find a graphic that provides a quick and dirty way to understand and remember each answer choice. Here's the example for (A) again:

○ Statement (1) ALONE is sufficient, but statement (2) alone is not sufficient.

What is the value of y ?

(1) y is an even integer such that
$-1.5 < y < 1.5$.

(A) ①❷

(2) Integer y is not prime.

Now, let's make some changes to the statements, to get an example of (B).

○ Statement (2) ALONE is sufficient, but statement (1) alone is not sufficient.

What is the value of y ?

(1) Integer y is not prime.

(B) ✳②

(2) y is an even integer such that
$-1.5 < y < 1.5$.

As you can see from this example, (B) is pretty much the flip side of (A). In this case, the first statement provides no help in determining the value of y, but the second statement tells us that $y = 0$.

A few more changes produce an example of (C).

○ BOTH statements TOGETHER are sufficient, but NEITHER statement ALONE is sufficient.

What is the value of y ?

(1) y is an even integer.

(C) ✳❷

(2) $-1.5 < y < 1.5$

The first statement tells us that y is even, but there are a lot of even integers. The second statement gives us a range of values for y, but, by itself, we don't even know that y is an integer from the second statement. So, neither statement is sufficient on its own. But, when we put them together, we know that $y = 0$.

Now, let's get an example of (D).

○ EACH statement ALONE is sufficient.

What is the value of y ?

(1) y is an even integer such that
$-1.5 < y < 1.5$.

(D)①②

(2) For any integer $a \neq 0$, $ay = 0$.

As pointed out in previous examples, the information in Statement (1) allows us to conclude that $y = 0$. The information in the second statement also tells us that y is 0, because the only way for the product of ay to equal 0 is if either a or y is 0. Since a can't be 0, y must be 0. Note how the statements independently allow us to arrive at the conclusion that $y = 0$ for (D).

Finally, let's look at an example of (E).

○ Statements (1) and (2) TOGETHER are not sufficient.

What is the value of y ?

(1) y is an even integer.

(E) ⊅⊄

(2) Integer y is not prime.

For this example, there's no way to determine the value of y. The first statement doesn't work because y could be any even integer. The second statement also doesn't help because y can be any integer that isn't prime. Even when we combine the statements, we don't know the value of y because any even integer except 2 fits the conditions. So, (E) is the no way, no how answer.

Below, you'll find the full graphic for all of the answers. You may find it helpful to keep the graphic handy until you are completely comfortable with what each answer choice means.

DATA SUFFICIENCY: BASIC POE STRATEGY

One of the reasons the test writers decided to include Data Sufficiency questions on the GMAT is that when this format was first dreamed up they thought these questions would be immune to Process of Elimination (POE). Were they ever wrong! If anything, it's even easier to apply POE to Data Sufficiency questions. Let's see why.

First, however, let's restate one of the most important strategies for working any Data Sufficiency question: *Evaluate the statements one at a time before you think about combining them.* Many people mistakenly pick (C)—you need both statements together—when it would have been possible to answer the question with only the information in the first statement or the second statement. Generally, people make this mistake when they read both statements right after reading the question stem. In fact, this mistake is the most common mistake that test takers make when working Data Sufficiency questions.

To avoid this common mistake, *read the question stem and only the first statement.* Ignore the second statement. Pretend it isn't there. You may even go as far as covering Statement (2) with your finger if you find the temptation to read both statements too overpowering. Once you have evaluated Statement (1), forget it. Ignore it. It doesn't exist anymore. Cover it up if you need to and read and evaluate Statement (2).

Apply POE to Data Sufficiency questions like this one.

What happens when you evaluate the statements one at a time? Something magical, that's what! POE comes roaring back. Consider the following partial example:

What is the value of x ?

(1) $x + 7 = 12$

We don't even have Statement (2), but we can still do a lot with this partial question. (Don't worry. There won't be any partial questions on the real test!) First, you want to see if the statement is sufficient to answer the question. In this case, you could subtract 7 from both sides of the equation to discover that $x = 5$. We'll take this as an opportunity to remind you, however, that you don't really need to solve the equation—you just need to know that you *can* solve the equation. After all, to pick an answer to the problem, you just need to know if you have sufficient information.

Since Statement (1) is sufficient in this case, which answer choices can be eliminated? From the chart, you can see that there are only two answer choices—(A) and (D)— that have Statement (1) circled to indicate that, for that answer choice, Statement (1) is sufficient. So, you no longer need to worry about (B), (C), or (E). They've been eliminated! If the first statement is sufficient, the answer to the problem must be (A) or (D)! You're down to fifty-fifty just based on looking at the first statement!

Now, check out this example:

What is the value of *x* ?

(1) *x* is an integer.

Now, what are the possible answers? If you said (B), (C), or (E), you are well on your way to getting this Data Sufficiency stuff under control. If you said something else, take a look at the steps outlined previously. In this case, the first statement is insufficient to determine the value of *x*. So, you want the answer choices that have 1 crossed off, and that is (B), (C), or (E).

DRILL 1: (AD/BCE)

In the following drill, each question is followed by only one statement. Based on the first statement, decide if you are down to AD or BCE. The answers can be found in Part VI.

1. What is the value of *x* ?

    (1)   *y* = 4

    (2)   ????

2. Is *y* an integer?

    (1)   2*y* is an integer.

    (2)   ????

3. A certain room contains 12 children. How many more boys than girls are there?

    (1)   There are three girls in the room.

    (2)   ????

4. What number is *x* percent of 20 ?

    (1)   10 percent of *x* is 5.

    (2)   ????

From AD or BCE to the Answer

Every time you start a Data Sufficiency question, you should read the question and only the first statement. If the first statement is sufficient, your possible answers are (A) or (D). If the first statement is insufficient, your possible answers are (B), (C), or (E). So, you can always get rid of either two or three answer choices just by evaluating the first statement. The AD/BCE split is so important that you'll want to write down AD or BCE on your noteboard as you work every Data Sufficiency question.

But what happens next? How do you get to the answer? Let's take a look.

———————————◯———————————

If $x + y = 3$, what is the value of xy ?

(1) x and y are integers.

(2) x and y are positive.

◯ Statement (1) ALONE is sufficient, but statement (2) alone is not sufficient.
◯ Statement (2) ALONE is sufficient, but statement (1) alone is not sufficient.
◯ BOTH statements TOGETHER are sufficient, but NEITHER statement ALONE is sufficient.
◯ EACH statement ALONE is sufficient.
◯ Statements (1) and (2) TOGETHER are not sufficient.

Here's How to Crack It

As always, ignore Statement (2) and look only at Statement (1). If x and y are integers and $x + y = 3$, do we know what they are? Not really—x could be 1 and y could be 2 (in which case, xy would be 2). But x could also be 0 (yes, 0 is an integer) and y could be 3 (in which case, xy would be 0). Because Statement (1) alone is not sufficient, we are down to BCE, a one in three shot.

Now, ignore Statement (1) and look at Statement (2). By itself, this statement doesn't begin to give us values for x and y—x could be 1 and y could be 2, but x could just as easily be 1.4 and y could be 1.6. Because there is still more than one possible value for xy, cross off (B).

We're down to (C) or (E). Now it's finally time to look at both statements at the same time. See how late in the process we combine the statements? Get into the habit of physically crossing off (B) before you think about combining the statements. That's how you can avoid making the most common GMAT Data Sufficiency mistake of putting the statements together too early.

Because we know from the first statement that x and y are integers, and from the second statement that they must be positive, do we now know specific values for x and y?

Well, we do know that there are only two positive integers that add up to 3: 2 and 1. (Remember, zero is an integer but it is neither positive nor negative.)

Do we know if $x = 1$ and $y = 2$, or vice versa? Not really, but frankly, it doesn't matter in this case. The question is asking us the value of xy.

Because neither statement by itself is sufficient, but both statements together are sufficient, the answer is (C).

Here's a handy flowchart that shows you what to do for any Data Sufficiency problem. You should keep the flowchart next to you and consult it as you first start practicing Data Sufficiency questions. After you have done ten or twenty questions, you'll probably find that you have learned the basic POE process well enough that you don't need the chart anymore. However, if you ever find yourself having trouble with Data Sufficiency, pull out the chart again and do some more problems, using it as a guide.

Combining the Statements
Notice how late in the process you combine the statements. Remember that one of the most common mistakes on Data Sufficiency is combining the statements before you have properly evaluated each statement on its own.

YES/NO DATA SUFFICIENCY: THE BASICS

If you were going to provide the answer to most Data Sufficiency questions, your response would be a number. However, as many as half of all the Data Sufficiency questions that you will see on your test will ask a yes-or-no question instead.

Leave it to GMAC to come up with a way to give you five different answer choices on a yes-or-no question. Let's look at an example.

Did candidate *x* receive more than half of the 30,000 votes cast in the general election?

(1) Candidate *y* received 12,000 of the votes cast.

(2) Candidate *x* received 18,000 of the votes cast.

Here's How to Crack It

When all is said and done, the answer to this question is either yes or no. Start by ignoring Statement (2) and evaluating Statement (1). Does Statement (1) alone answer the question? If you were in a hurry, you might think so. Many people assume that there are only two candidates in the election. They reason that if candidate *y* got 12,000 votes, then candidate *x* must have received 18,000 votes. However, there's no reason to assume that there are only two candidates. So, Statement (1) is insufficient. Write down BCE. Does Statement (2) alone answer the question? Yes, it's pretty clear that candidate *x* received more than half of the votes. So, the correct answer is (B).

That didn't seem so bad, did it? Yet, you may have heard that yes/no Data Sufficiency questions have a reputation for being hard. Let's change our example to see why.

Did candidate *x* receive more than half of the 30,000 votes cast in the general election?

(1) Candidate *y* received 12,000 of the votes cast.

(2) Candidate *x* received 13,000 of the votes cast.

Here's How to Crack It

As always, start by ignoring Statement (2) so that you can properly evaluate Statement (1) alone. As in our previous example, Statement (1) is insufficient, so be sure to write down BCE. Statement (2) seems pretty straightforward. Candidate *x* received fewer than half of the votes cast. At this point many people say, "Since the guy clearly got fewer than half the votes, this statement doesn't answer the question, either." But those people are wrong!

Just Say No

Broken down to its basics, the question we were asked was, "Did he get more than half of the vote—yes or no?"

Statement (2) *does* answer the question. The answer is, "No, he didn't." So, the answer is the same as that of the first example. The answer is (B).

———————◯———————

On a yes/no Data Sufficiency problem, if the statement answers the question in either the affirmative or the negative, it is sufficient.

Yes/No/Maybe

Yes/no questions really should be called yes/no/maybe questions. Even if that's not their "official" name, it's still worthwhile to think about them in that fashion.

Let's look at one last example to see why.

———————◯———————

Did candidate *x* receive more than half of the 30,000 votes cast in the general election?

(1) Candidate *y* received 12,000 of the votes cast.

(2) Candidate *x* received at least 13,000 of the votes cast.

Here's How to Crack It

Since the first statement of this question is the same as that of the previous two examples, we know that it is insufficient. So, write down BCE. Now, let's tackle Statement (2). Based on Statement (2), candidate *x* could have received exactly 13,000 votes, which would make the answer to the question "No, he did not receive more than half the votes cast." However, he could have also received 16,000 votes, and that would make the answer to the question, "Yes, he did receive more than half the votes cast." So, based on Statement (2), the best we can really say is that candidate *x* may have received more than half the votes. "Maybe" isn't good enough— we need a definitive yes or no answer. So, Statement (2) is insufficient. Cross off (B). What if we combine the statements? We still have the same problem. We've accounted for at least 25,000 of the votes between the two candidates, but we don't know about the other 5,000. All of those votes could have gone to candidate *x*, making the answer to the question "yes." However, there could have been a third candidate who received those 5,000 votes. In that case, *x* would have received only 13,000 votes and the answer to the question is "no." Combining the statements didn't get us to a definitive answer. If the answer is sometimes "yes" and sometimes "no," the statement is not sufficient. Cross off (C). The correct answer is (E).

———————◯———————

MORE ON DATA SUFFICIENCY

Although Data Sufficiency problems test the same material covered by regular Problem Solving questions, some readers find it distracting to learn the more complicated subtleties of this new question type at the same time that they are learning (or relearning) math concepts. That's why we've put our main chapter on Data Sufficiency at the end of our math review.

However, you will find Data Sufficiency problems sprinkled throughout the math drills—and you should feel free at any time to dip into Chapter 14, where you'll find everything in one place, including more advanced strategy, several more drills, and some great techniques to handle the most complicated yes/no questions.

Summary

o   "Data Sufficiency" means just that, sufficiency. These questions are asking you if the data presented is enough to solve the problem.

o   Every Data Sufficiency problem consists of a question followed by two statements. You must decide whether the question can be answered based on the information in the two statements.

o   The best strategy for Data Sufficiency problems is to look at one statement at a time. Cover up the other statement with your hand, so that you can completely focus on one statement at a time.

o   AD or BCE: These are always your options when you first start eliminating. Memorize them.

Chapter 10
Arithmetic

Do you remember all the rules for exponents? This chapter will review rules for those and other important mathematical concepts and teach you how to solve problems involving fractions, proportions, decimals, ratios, percentages, averages, medians, modes, standard deviation, exponents, and radicals.

Although arithmetic is only one of the three types of math tested on the GMAT, arithmetic problems comprise about half of the total number of math questions.

Here are the specific arithmetic topics tested on the GMAT:

1. Axioms and Fundamentals (properties of integers, positive and negative numbers, even and odd). These were covered in Chapter 7.
2. Arithmetic Operations
3. Fractions
4. Decimals
5. Ratios
6. Percentages
7. Averages
8. Exponents and Radicals

In this chapter, we will first discuss the fundamentals of each topic and then show how the test writers construct questions based on that topic.

ARITHMETIC OPERATIONS

There are six arithmetic operations you will need for the GMAT:

1.	**Addition** (2 + 2)	The result of addition is a sum or total.
2.	**Subtraction** (6 − 2)	The result of subtraction is a difference.
3.	**Multiplication** (2 × 2)	The result of multiplication is a product.
4.	**Division** (8 ÷ 2)	The result of division is a quotient.
5.	**Raising to a power** (x^2)	In the expression x^2, the little 2 is called an exponent.
6.	**Finding a square root** $\left(\sqrt{4}\right)$	$\sqrt{4} = \sqrt{2 \times 2} = 2$

Which One Do I Do First?

In a problem that involves several different operations, the operations must be performed in a particular order, and occasionally GMAC likes to see whether you know what that order is. Here's an easy way to remember the order of operations:

Please Excuse My Dear Aunt Sally
or
PEMDAS

The first letters stand for Parentheses, Exponents, Multiplication, Division, Addition, and Subtraction. Do operations that are enclosed in parentheses first; then take care of exponents; then multiply and divide; then add and subtract, going from left to right.

DRILL 2

Just to get you started, solve each of the following problems by performing the indicated operations in the proper order. The answers can be found in Part VI.

1.   74 + (27 − 24) =

2.   (8 × 9) + 7 =

3.   2(9 − (8 ÷ 2)) =

4.   2(7 − 3) + (−4)(5 − 7) =

Here's an easy question that shows how GMAC might test PEMDAS.

5.   4(−3(3 − 5) + 10 − 17) =

   ○ −27
   ○ −4
   ○ −1
   ○ 32
   ○ 84

> **The Drill on Drills**
> - You can't use a calculator on the math section of the GMAT, so please don't use one as you work through the math drills in this book.
> - To mimic the actual conditions of the test, get used to using scratch paper rather than writing in the book directly.

It is not uncommon to see a Data Sufficiency problem like this on the GMAT:

6.   What is the value of x?

   (1) $x^3 = 8$

   (2) $x^2 = 4$

   ○ Statement (1) ALONE is sufficient, but statement (2) alone is not sufficient.
   ○ Statement (2) ALONE is sufficient, but statement (1) alone is not sufficient.
   ○ BOTH statements TOGETHER are sufficient, but NEITHER statement ALONE is sufficient.
   ○ EACH statement ALONE is sufficient.
   ○ Statements (1) and (2) TOGETHER are not sufficient.

There are two operations that can be done in any order, provided they are the only operations involved: *When you are adding or multiplying a series of numbers, you can group or regroup the numbers any way you like.*

> $2 + 3 + 4$ is the same as $4 + 2 + 3$
> and
> $4 \times 5 \times 6$ is the same as $6 \times 5 \times 4$

This is called the **associative law,** but the name will not be tested on the GMAT.

Another law that GMAC likes to test states that

> $a(b + c) = ab + ac$ and $a(b - c) = ab - ac$.

This is called the **distributive law** but, again, you don't need to know that for the test. Sometimes the distributive law can provide you with a shortcut to the solution of a problem. If a problem gives you information in "factored form"—$a(b + c)$—you should distribute it immediately. If the information is given in distributed form—$ab + ac$—you should factor it.

DRILL 3

If the following problems are in distributed form, factor them; if they are in factored form, distribute them. Then do the indicated operations. Answers are in Part VI.

1. $x^2 + x$

2. $(55 \times 12) + (55 \times 88)$

3. $a(b + c - d)$

4. $abc + xyc$

A GMAT problem might look like this:

5. If $x = 6$ what is the value of $\dfrac{2xy - xy}{y}$?

    ◯ −30
    ◯   6
    ◯   8
    ◯ 30
    ◯ It cannot be determined from the information given.

It is not uncommon to see a Data Sufficiency problem like this on the GMAT:

6. If $ax + ay + az = 15$, what is $x + y + z$?

(1) $x = 2$

(2) $a = 5$

○ Statement (1) ALONE is sufficient, but statement (2) alone is not sufficient.
○ Statement (2) ALONE is sufficient, but statement (1) alone is not sufficient.
○ BOTH statements TOGETHER are sufficient, but NEITHER statement ALONE is sufficient.
○ EACH statement ALONE is sufficient.
○ Statements (1) and (2) TOGETHER are not sufficient.

Challenge Question #2

A device calculates the worth of gem stones based on quality such that a gem with a quality rating of $q - 1$ is worth 5 times more than a gem with a quality rating of q. According to this device, the worth of a gem with a quality rating of $p - r$ is how many times greater than that of a gem with a rating of p?

○ $p^5 - r^5$
○ r^5
○ $(p - r)^5$
○ 5^r
○ $5r$

FRACTIONS
Fractions can be thought of in two ways:

- A **fraction** is just another way of expressing division. The expression $\frac{1}{2}$ is exactly the same thing as 1 divided by 2. $\frac{x}{y}$ is nothing more than x divided by y. In the fraction $\frac{x}{y}$, x is known as the **numerator** and y is known as the **denominator**.

- The other important way to think of a fraction is as $\frac{\text{part}}{\text{whole}}$. The fraction $\frac{7}{10}$ can be thought of as 7 parts out of a total of 10 parts.

Adding and Subtracting Fractions with the Same Denominator

To add two or more fractions that have the same denominator, simply add up the numerators and put the sum over the common denominator. For example:

$$\frac{1}{7} + \frac{5}{7} = \frac{(1+5)}{7} = \frac{6}{7}$$

Subtraction works exactly the same way:

$$\frac{6}{7} - \frac{2}{7} = \frac{6-2}{7} = \frac{4}{7}$$

Adding and Subtracting Fractions with Different Denominators

Before you can add or subtract two or more fractions with different denominators, you must give all of them the same denominator. To do this, multiply the numerator and denominator of each fraction by a number that will give it a denominator in common with the others. If you multiplied each fraction by any old number, the fractions wouldn't have their original values, so the number you multiply by has to be equal to 1. For example, if you wanted to change $\frac{1}{2}$ into sixths, you could do the following:

$$\frac{1}{2} \times \frac{3}{3} = \frac{3}{6}$$

We haven't actually changed the value of the fraction, because $\frac{3}{3}$ equals 1.

If we wanted to add:

$$\frac{1}{2} + \frac{2}{3}$$

$$\frac{1}{2} \times \frac{3}{3} + \frac{2}{3} \times \frac{2}{2}$$

$$\frac{3}{6} + \frac{4}{6} = \frac{7}{6}$$

The Bowtie

The Bowtie method has been a staple of The Princeton Review's materials since the company began in a living room in New York City in 1981. It's been around so long because it works so simply.

To add $\frac{3}{5}$ and $\frac{4}{7}$, for example, follow these three steps:

Step One: Multiply the denominators together to form the new denominator.

$$\frac{3}{5}+\frac{4}{7}=\frac{}{5\times 7}=\frac{}{35}$$

Step Two: Multiply the first denominator by the second numerator ($5 \times 4 = 20$) and the second denominator by the first numerator ($7 \times 3 = 21$) and place these numbers above the fractions, as shown below.

See? A bowtie!

Step Three: Add the products to form the new numerator.

$$\frac{3}{5}+\frac{4}{7}=\frac{21+20}{5\times 7}=\frac{41}{35}$$

Subtraction works the same way.

Note that with subtraction, the order of the numerators is important. The new numerator is 21 – 20, or 1. If you somehow get your numbers reversed and use 20 – 21, your answer will be $-\frac{1}{35}$, which is incorrect. One way to keep your subtraction straight is to always multiply **up** from denominator to numerator when you use the Bowtie.

Multiplying Fractions

To multiply fractions, just multiply the numerators and put the product over the product of the denominators. For example:

$$\frac{2}{3} \times \frac{6}{5} = \frac{12}{15}$$

Reducing Fractions

When you add or multiply fractions, you often end up with a big fraction that is hard to work with. You can usually reduce such a fraction. To reduce a fraction, find a factor of the numerator that is also a factor of the denominator. It saves time to find the biggest factor they have in common, but this isn't critical. You may just have to repeat the process a few times. When you find a common factor, cancel it. For example, let's take the product we just found when we multiplied the fractions above:

$$\frac{12}{15} = \frac{4 \times \cancel{3}}{5 \times \cancel{3}} = \frac{4}{5}$$

Get used to reducing all fractions (if they can be reduced) *before* you do any work with them. It saves a lot of time and prevents errors in computation.

For example, in that last problem, we had to multiply two fractions together:

$$\frac{2}{3} \times \frac{6}{5}$$

Before you multiplied 2 × 6 and 3 × 5, you could have reduced $\frac{2}{3} \times \frac{6}{5} = \frac{2 \times \cancel{6}}{\cancel{3} \times 5} = \frac{2 \times 2}{5} = \frac{4}{5}$.

Dividing Fractions

To divide one fraction by another, just invert the second fraction and multiply:

$$\frac{2}{3} \div \frac{3}{4}$$

which is the same thing as...

$$\frac{2}{3} \times \frac{4}{3} = \frac{8}{9}$$

You may see this same operation written like this:

$$\frac{\frac{2}{3}}{\frac{3}{4}}$$

Again, just invert and multiply. This next example is handled the same way:

$$\frac{\frac{6}{2}}{3} = \frac{6}{1} \times \frac{3}{2} = \frac{18}{2} = 9$$

When you invert a fraction, the new fraction is called a **reciprocal**. $\frac{2}{3}$ is the reciprocal of $\frac{3}{2}$. The product of two reciprocals is always 1.

Converting to Fractions

An integer can be expressed as a fraction by making the integer the numerator and 1 the denominator: $16 = \frac{16}{1}$.

The GMAT sometimes gives you numbers that are mixtures of integers and fractions, for example, $3\frac{1}{2}$. It's easier to work with these numbers if you convert them into fractions. Simply multiply the denominator by the integer, then add the numerator, and place the resulting number over the original denominator.

$$3\frac{1}{2} = \frac{(3 \times 2) + 1}{2} = \frac{7}{2}$$

Comparing Fractions

In the course of a problem, you may have to compare two or more fractions and determine which is greater. This is easy to do as long as you remember that you can compare fractions directly only if they have the same denominator. Suppose you had to decide which of these three fractions is greatest:

$$\frac{1}{2}, \frac{5}{9}, \text{ or } \frac{7}{15}$$

To compare these fractions directly, you need a common denominator, but finding a common denominator that works for all three fractions would be complicated and time consuming. It makes more sense to compare these fractions two at a time. We showed you the classical way to find common denominators when we talked about adding fractions earlier.

Let's start with $\frac{1}{2}$ and $\frac{5}{9}$. An easy common denominator for these two fractions is 18 (9×2).

$$\frac{1}{2} \qquad\qquad \frac{5}{9}$$

$$\frac{1}{2} \times \frac{9}{9} \qquad \frac{5}{9} \times \frac{2}{2}$$

$$= \frac{9}{18} \qquad = \frac{10}{18}$$

Because $\frac{5}{9}$ is greater, let's compare it with $\frac{7}{15}$. Here the easiest common denominator is 45. But before we do that...

Two Shortcuts

Comparing fractions is another situation where we can use the Bowtie. The idea is that if all you need to know is which fraction is greater, you just have to compare the new numerators. Again, simply multiply the denominator of the first fraction by the numerator of the second and the denominator of the second by the numerator of the first, as shown here.

$$9 \times 1 = 9 \quad \frac{1}{2} \diagdown\diagup \frac{5}{9} \quad 2 \times 5 = 10$$

$$10 > 9, \text{ therefore } \frac{5}{9} > \frac{1}{2}$$

You could also have saved yourself some time on the last problem by a little fast estimation. Again, which is greater? $\frac{1}{2}$, $\frac{5}{9}$, or $\frac{7}{15}$?

Let's think about $\frac{5}{9}$ in terms of $\frac{1}{2}$. How many ninths equal a half? To put it another way, what is half of 9? 4.5. So $\frac{4.5}{9} = \frac{1}{2}$. That means $\frac{5}{9}$ is *greater* than $\frac{1}{2}$.

Now let's think about $\frac{7}{15}$. Half of 15 is 7.5. $\frac{7.5}{15} = \frac{1}{2}$, which means that $\frac{7}{15}$ is less than $\frac{1}{2}$.

PROPORTIONS

A fraction can be expressed in many ways. $\frac{1}{2}$ also equals $\frac{2}{4}$ or $\frac{4}{8}$, etc. A **proportion** is just a different way of expressing a fraction. Here's an example:

───────────○───────────

If 2 boxes hold a total of 14 shirts, how many shirts are contained in 3 boxes?

Here's How to Crack It
The number of shirts per box can be expressed as a fraction. What you're asked to do is express the fraction $\frac{2}{14}$ in a different way.

$$\frac{2 \,(\text{boxes})}{14 \,(\text{shirts})} = \frac{3 \,(\text{boxes})}{x \,(\text{shirts})}$$

To find the answer, all you need to do is find a value for x such that $\frac{2}{14} = \frac{3}{x}$. The easiest way to do this is to cross-multiply.

$2x = 42$, which means that $x = 21$. There are 21 shirts in 3 boxes.

───────────○───────────

Proportions and Ratios
Proportions are really ratios. Where a proportion question asks about the number of shirts *per* box, a ratio question might ask about the number of red shirts to blue shirts in a box.

DRILL 4

The answers to these questions can be found in Part VI.

1. $5\frac{3}{4} + \frac{3}{8} =$

2. Reduce $\frac{12}{60}$

3. Convert $9\frac{2}{3}$ to a fraction

4. $\frac{9}{2} = \frac{x}{4}$

A relatively easy GMAT fraction problem might look like this:

5. $\dfrac{\left(\dfrac{\dfrac{4}{5}}{\dfrac{3}{5}}\right)\left(\dfrac{\dfrac{1}{8}}{\dfrac{2}{3}}\right)}{\dfrac{3}{4}} =$

   ○ $\frac{3}{100}$

   ○ $\frac{3}{16}$

   ○ $\frac{1}{3}$

   ○ 1

   ○ $\frac{7}{16}$

Fractions: Advanced Principles

Now that you've been reacquainted with the basics of fractions, let's go a little further. More complicated fraction problems usually involve all of the rules we've just mentioned, with the addition of two concepts: $\frac{part}{whole}$, and the rest. Here's a typical medium fraction problem:

A cement mixture is composed of 3 elements. By weight, $\frac{1}{3}$ of the mixture is sand, $\frac{3}{5}$ of the mixture is water, and the remaining 12 pounds of the mixture is gravel. What is the weight of the entire mixture in pounds?

- ○ 4
- ○ 8
- ○ 36
- ○ 60
- ○ 180

Q: There are only roses, tulips, and peonies in a certain garden. There are three roses to every four tulips and every five peonies in the garden. Expressed as a fraction, what part of the flowers in the garden are tulips?

Turn to page 101 for the answer.

Easy Eliminations

Before we even start doing serious math, let's use some common sense. The weight of the gravel alone is 12 pounds. Because we know that sand and water make up the bulk of the mixture—sand $\frac{1}{3}$, water $\frac{3}{5}$ (which is a bit more than half)—the entire mixture must weigh a great deal more than 12 pounds. Choices (A) and (B) are out of the question. Eliminate them.

Here's How to Crack It

The difficulty in solving this problem is that sand and water are expressed as fractions, while gravel is expressed in pounds. At first there seems to be no way of knowing what fractional part of the mixture the 12 pounds of gravel represent; nor do we know how many pounds of sand and water there are.

The first step is to add up the fractional parts that we do have:

$$\frac{1}{3} + \frac{3}{5} = \frac{1}{3}\left(\frac{5}{5}\right) + \frac{3}{5}\left(\frac{3}{3}\right) = \frac{14}{15}$$

Sand and water make up 14 parts out of the whole of 15. This means that gravel makes up what is left over—the rest: 1 part out of the whole of 15. Now the problem is simple. Set up a proportion between parts and weights.

$$\frac{1}{15} = \frac{12}{x} \quad \begin{array}{l} \text{pounds (of gravel)} \\ \text{pounds (total pounds)} \end{array}$$

Cross-multiply: $x = 180$. The answer is (E).

———————————○———————————

DECIMALS ARE REALLY FRACTIONS

A decimal can be expressed as a fraction, and a fraction can be expressed as a decimal.

Decimals or Fractions

Whether you prefer decimals or fractions, you must be able to work with both. The ability to work comfortably and confidently with decimals and fractions is vital to GMAT success.

$$0.6 = \frac{6}{10} \text{, which can be reduced to } \frac{3}{5}$$

$$\frac{3}{5} \text{ is the same thing as } 3 \div 5$$

Which would you rather figure out—the square of $\frac{1}{4}$ or the square of 0.25? There may be a few of you out there who've had so much practice with decimals in your work that you prefer decimals to fractions, but for the rest of us, fractions are infinitely easier to deal with.

Occasionally, you will have to work with decimals. Whenever possible, however, convert decimals to fractions. It will save time and eliminate careless mistakes. In fact, it makes sense to memorize the fractional equivalent of some commonly used decimals:

$$0.2 = \frac{1}{5} \qquad\qquad 0.6 = \frac{3}{5}$$

$$0.25 = \frac{1}{4} \qquad\qquad 0.\overline{66} = \frac{2}{3}$$

$$0.\overline{33} = \frac{1}{3} \qquad\qquad 0.75 = \frac{3}{4}$$

$$0.4 = \frac{2}{5} \qquad\qquad 0.8 = \frac{4}{5}$$

$$0.5 = \frac{1}{2}$$

> A: The relationship between roses, tulips, and peonies was expressed as a ratio. To find the fractional part, first find the *whole*. We know the parts are 3 roses, 4 tulips, and 5 peonies. 3 + 4 + 5 = 12 = the whole. What fractional part of the flowers are tulips? 4 out of a total of 12, otherwise known as $\frac{4}{12}$ or $\frac{1}{3}$.

Adding and Subtracting Decimals

To add or subtract decimals, just line up the decimal points and proceed as usual. Adding 6, 2.5, and 0.3 looks like this:

$$
\begin{array}{r}
6.0 \\
2.5 \\
+\ 0.3 \\
\hline
8.8
\end{array}
$$

Multiplying Decimals

To multiply decimals, simply ignore the decimal points and multiply the two numbers. When you've finished, count all the digits that were to the right of the decimal points in the original numbers you multiplied. Now place the decimal point in your answer so that there are the same number of digits to the right of it. Here are two examples:

$$
\begin{array}{r}
0.3 \\
\times\ 0.7 \\
\hline
0.21
\end{array}
$$

There were a total of two digits to the right of the decimal point in the original numbers, so we place the decimal so that there are two digits to the right in the answer.

$$
\begin{array}{r}
14.3 \\
\times\ 0.232 \\
\hline
3.3176
\end{array}
$$

There were a total of four digits to the right of the decimal point in the original numbers, so we place the decimal such that there are four digits to the right in the answer.

Dividing Decimals

The best way to divide one decimal by another is to convert the number you are dividing by (in mathematical terminology, the **divisor**) into a whole number. You do this simply by moving the decimal point as many places as necessary. This works as long as you remember to move the decimal point in the number that you are *dividing* (in mathematical terminology, the **dividend**) the same number of spaces.

For example, to divide 12 by 0.6, set it up the way you would an ordinary division problem: $0.6\overline{)12}$.

To make 0.6 (the divisor) a whole number, you simply move the decimal point over one place to the right. You must also move the decimal one place to the right in the dividend. Now the operation looks like this:

$$0.6\overline{)12.}$$

$$6\overline{)120}$$

$$\frac{20}{6\overline{)120}}$$

Rounding Decimals

9.4 rounded to the nearest whole number is 9.
9.5 rounded to the nearest whole number is 10.

When GMAC asks you to give an approximate answer on an easy question, it is safe to round numbers. But you should be leery about rounding numbers on a difficult question. If you're scoring in a high percentile, rounding off numbers will be useful to eliminate answer choices that are out of the ballpark, but not to decide between two close answer choices.

Rounding

To round a decimal, look at the digit to the right of the digits place you are rounding to. If that number is 0–4, there is no change. If that number is 5–9, round up.

DRILL 5

The answers to these questions can be found in Part VI.

1.
$$\begin{array}{r} 34.26 \\ -\ 0.96 \\ \hline \end{array}$$

2.
$$\begin{array}{r} 27.3 \\ \times\ 9.75 \\ \hline \end{array}$$

3. $\dfrac{19.6}{3.2} =$

4. $\dfrac{\dfrac{4}{0.25}}{\dfrac{1}{50}} =$

On the GMAT, there might be questions that mix decimals and fractions:

5. $\dfrac{\dfrac{3}{10} \times 4 \times 0.8}{0.32}$

   ○ 0.96
   ○ 0.333
   ○ 3.0
   ○ 30.0
   ○ 96.0

6. If x and y are reciprocals, what is the value of $x + y$ rounded to the nearest hundredth?

   (1) $x = 0.2$

   (2) $y = 5$

   ○ Statement (1) ALONE is sufficient, but statement (2) alone is not sufficient.
   ○ Statement (2) ALONE is sufficient, but statement (1) alone is not sufficient.
   ○ BOTH statements TOGETHER are sufficient, but NEITHER statement ALONE is sufficient.
   ○ EACH statement ALONE is sufficient.
   ○ Statements (1) and (2) TOGETHER are not sufficient.

First Things First
On *all* questions, before you do any serious calculations, take a moment to see whether the answer choices make sense. Eliminate crazy answer choices. Do this first because those "crazy" choices usually reflect the result of a common (but incorrect) approach to the problem. Eliminate first and you won't think (falsely), "Aha, I've got it." Instead, you'll know you took a misstep somewhere.

RATIOS

Ratios are close relatives of fractions. A ratio can be expressed as a fraction and vice versa. The ratio 3 to 4 can be written as $\frac{3}{4}$ as well as in standard ratio format: 3 : 4.

There Is Only One Difference Between a Ratio and a Fraction

A fraction compares a part to whole relationship. A ratio compares a part to part relationship. It's that simple. Check out the box below for a handy visual representation.

Fraction:
$$\frac{\text{part: 3 women}}{\text{whole: 7 people}}$$

Ratio:
$$\frac{\text{part: 3 women}}{\text{part: 4 men}}$$
(The whole is 7.)

Aside from That, All the Rules of Fractions Apply to Ratios

A ratio can be converted to a percentage or a decimal. It can be cross-multiplied, reduced, or expanded—just like a fraction. The ratio of 1 to 3 can be expressed as:

$$\frac{1}{3}$$

$$1 : 3$$

$$\frac{2}{6}$$

$$\frac{3}{9}$$

An Easy Ratio Problem

---○---

The ratio of men to women in a room is 3 to 4. If there are 20 women, what is the number of men in the room?

Here's How to Crack It

No matter how many people are actually in the room, the ratio of men to women will always stay the same: 3 to 4. What you're asked to do is find the numerator of a fraction whose denominator is 20, and which can be reduced to $\frac{3}{4}$. Just set one fraction equal to another and cross-multiply:

$$\frac{3}{4} = \frac{x}{20} \qquad 60 = 4x \qquad x = 15$$

The answer to the question is 15 men. Note that $\frac{15}{20}$ reduces to $\frac{3}{4}$.

---○---

A More Difficult Ratio Problem

---○---

The ratio of women to men in a room is 3 to 4. If there are a total of 28 people in the room, how many are women?

This problem is more difficult because, while we are given the ratio of women to men, we are not given a specific value for either the women or the men. If we tried to set up this problem as we did the previous one, it would look like this:

$$\frac{3}{4} = \frac{x}{y}$$

Of course, you can't solve an equation that has two variables.

Here's How to Crack It

You need a way to see how the total number of people in the room, which you know is 28, can be broken down into groups of 3 women and 4 men.

A good way to solve the problem is to use a ratio box. Here's what that looks like for the information provided by the problem:

	Women	Men	Total
Ratio	3	4	
Multiplier			
Actual Number			28

To use a ratio box, you need a ratio and an actual number. Now, remember that ratios compare parts to parts. So, if you add up the parts, you get a group (or total) of 7 people.

Next, the key idea of a ratio is the multiplier, which allows you to make the group greater or lesser while keeping everything in the same ratio. For this problem, you don't want a group of 7 people. You want a group of 28. So, you multiply $7 \times 4 = 28$.

To keep everything in the same ratio, you just need to remember that whatever you do to one part, you need to do to every part. So, multiply the ratio numbers for both the women and men by 4.

Here's what the box looks like when it is completed:

	Women	Men	Total
Ratio	3	4	7
Multiplier	4	4	4
Actual Number	$12 = (3 \times 4)$	$16 = (4 \times 4)$	$28 = (7 \times 4)$

There are 12 women in the room.

PERCENTAGES

A **percentage** is just a fraction in which the denominator is always equal to 100. Fifty percent means 50 parts out of a whole of 100. Like any fraction, a percentage can be reduced, expanded, cross-multiplied, converted to a decimal, or converted to another fraction: $50\% = \dfrac{1}{2} = 0.5$.

An Easy Percent Problem

5 is what percent of 20 ?

?

Q: What is $\dfrac{1}{4}$ % of 40?

Turn to page 109 for the answer.

Here's How to Crack It

Whenever you see a percent problem, you should be thinking $\dfrac{\text{part}}{\text{whole}}$. In this case, the question asks you to expand $\dfrac{5}{20}$ into another fraction in which the denominator is 100.

$$\frac{\text{part}}{\text{whole}} = \frac{5}{20} = \frac{x}{100}$$

$$500 = 20x$$

$$x = 25$$

$$\frac{x}{100} = 25\%$$

Percent Shortcuts

In the last problem, reducing $\frac{5}{20}$ to $\frac{1}{4}$ would have saved you time if you knew that $\frac{1}{4} = 25\%$.
Here are some fractions and decimals whose percent equivalents you should know:

$$\frac{1}{4} = 0.25 = 25\%$$

$$\frac{1}{2} = 0.50 = 50\%$$

$$\frac{1}{3} = 0.333\ldots \text{ (a repeating decimal)} = 33\frac{1}{3}\%$$

$$\frac{1}{5} = 0.20 = 20\%$$

Some percentages simply involve moving a decimal point: To get 10 percent of any number, you simply move the decimal point of that number over one place to the left:

10% of 6 = 0.6
10% of 60 = 6
10% of 600 = 60

- To get 1 percent of any number, you just move the decimal point of that number over two places to the left:
  1% of 600 = 6
  1% of 60 = 0.6
  1% of 6 = 0.06

- To find a more complicated percentage, it's easy to break the percentage down into easy-to-find chunks:
  20% of 60:   10% of 60 = 6; 20% of 60 is double 10%,
                 so the answer is 2 × 6, or 12.
  30% of 60:   10% of 60 = 6; 30% of 60 is three times 10%,
                 so the answer is 3 × 6, or 18.
  3% of 200:   1% of 200 = 2; 3% of 200 is just three times 1%,
                 so the answer is 3 × 2, or 6.
  23% of 400:   10% of 400 = 40. Therefore, 20% equals 2 × 40, or 80.
                 1% of 400 = 4. Therefore, 3% equals 3 × 4, or 12.
                 Putting it all together, 23% of 400 equals 80 + 12, or 92.

A Medium Percent Problem

Like medium and difficult fraction problems, medium and difficult percent problems often involve remembering the principles of $\frac{\text{part}}{\text{whole}}$ and the rest.

A motor pool has 300 vehicles of which 30 percent are trucks. 20 percent of all the vehicles in the motor pool are diesel, including 15 trucks. What percent of the motor pool is composed of vehicles that are neither trucks nor diesel?

- ○ 165%
- ○ 90%
- ○ 65%
- ○ 55%
- ○ 10%

A: There are a number of ways to calculate the answer, but the simplest is to first calculate 1% of 40 by moving the decimal point two places to the left. This gives 0.4 as a result. Dividing this result by 4 gives us 0.1—the answer.

Here's How to Crack It

Do this problem one sentence at a time.

1. A motor pool has 300 vehicles, of which 30% are trucks. Thirty percent of 300 = 90 trucks, which means that 210 (the rest) are *not* trucks.

2. Twenty percent of all the vehicles are diesel, including 15 trucks. Twenty percent of 300 = 60 diesel vehicles, 15 of which are trucks, which means there are 45 diesel vehicles that are *not* trucks.

3. What percent of the motor pool is composed of vehicles that are neither truck nor diesel? We know from sentence number 1 that there are 210 nontrucks. We know from sentence number 2 that of these 210 nontrucks, 45 are diesel. Therefore, 210 – 45, or 165, are neither diesel nor truck.

The question asks what percent of the entire motor pool these 165 nondiesel nontrucks are.

$$\frac{165}{300} = \frac{x}{100} \qquad 300x = 16{,}500$$

$x = 55$ and the answer is (D).

There's a handy formula for calculating mixed groups. It isn't a priority for you to memorize (you just saw the problem calculated without it), but the formula can be helpful on some questions. Here it is: **Group 1 + Group 2 – both + neither = total.** Here's what that looks like using the numbers from the vehicle problem. 90 trucks + 60 diesel – 15 diesel trucks + x = 300. 135 + x = 300. x = 165, or 55% of 300.

Easy Process of Elimination

1. Because the problem asks us to find a portion of the entire motor pool, it's impossible for that portion to be greater than the motor pool itself. Therefore, (A), 165%, can be eliminated via Ballparking.
2. If the problem simply asked what percent of the motor pool was not made up of trucks, the answer would be 70%. But because there is a further condition (the vehicles must be both nontruck and nondiesel), the answer must be even less than 70%. So, (B) can be eliminated via Ballparking as well.
3. Choice (C) is a partial answer that you can get by simply adding 30 + 20 + 15, all numbers found within the problem. Choice (C) can be reasonably eliminated.

Percent Increase or Decrease

Another type of percent problem you may see on the GMAT has to do with *percent increase* or *percent decrease*. In these problems, the trick is always to put the increase or decrease in terms of the *original* amount. See the following example:

The cost of a one-family home was $120,000 in 1980. In 1988, the price had increased to $180,000. What was the percent increase in the cost of the home?

- ◯ 60%
- ◯ 50%
- ◯ 55%
- ◯ 40%
- ◯ 33.3%

Here's How to Crack It

The actual increase was $60,000. To find the percent increase, set up the following equation:

$$\frac{\text{amount of increase}}{\text{original amount}} = \frac{x}{100}$$

In this case, $\frac{\$60,000}{\$120,000} = \frac{x}{100}$. So, $x = 50$ and the answer is (B).

To solve a percent *decrease* problem, simply put the amount of the decrease over the original amount.

> ### What's the Original Amount?
> GMAT test writers like to see if they can trick you into mistaking which number was the original amount. On percent decrease problems (sometimes called "percent less" problems), the original is the larger number; on percent increase problems (sometimes called "percent greater" problems), the original is the smaller number.

Compound Interest

Another type of percent problem involves **compound interest**. If you kept $1,000 in the bank for a year at 6% simple interest, you would get $60 in interest at the end of the year. Compound interest would pay you slightly more. Let's look at a compound-interest problem:

Ms. Lopez deposits $100 in an account that pays 20% interest, compounded semiannually. How much money will there be in the account at the end of one year?

○ $118.00
○ $120.00
○ $121.00
○ $122.00
○ $140.00

Easy Process of Elimination

How would you work this problem if you were running out of time, or not sure how to find compound interest? Look for answer choices that can be eliminated via POE. The question asks for compound interest but (B) is the calculation of simple interest. Because finding simple interest is how to start a compound interest problem, (B) is a partial answer and can be eliminated. If you know that compound interest is always a *little bit* more than simple interest, you can eliminate (A) and (E) via Ballparking. Solving this problem from here requires knowledge of calculating compound interest. But, if you were having difficulty with this problem or were running out of time, POE can make this a 50-50 guess!

Here's How to Crack It

To find compound interest, divide the interest into as many parts as are being compounded. For example, if you're compounding interest semiannually, you divide the interest into two equal parts. If you're compounding quarterly, you divide the interest into four equal parts.

When Ms. Lopez deposited $100 into her account at a rate of 20% compounded semiannually, the bank divided the interest into two equal parts. Halfway through the year, the bank put the first half of the interest into her account. In this case, because the full rate was 20% compounded semiannually, the bank deposited 10% of $100 (10% of $100 = $10). Halfway through the year, Ms. Lopez had $110.

For the second half of the year, the bank paid 10% interest on the $110 (10% of $110 = $11). At the end of the year, Ms. Lopez had $121.00 in her account. She earned $1 more than she would have earned if the account had paid only simple interest. The answer is (C).

———————○———————

AVERAGES

To find the **average** of a list of n numbers, you simply add the numbers and divide by n. For example:

$$\text{The average of 10, 3, and 5 is } \frac{10+3+5}{3}=6.$$

A good way to handle average problems is to set them up in the same way every time. Whenever you see the word *average*, you should think:

$$\frac{\text{total sum of the items}}{\text{total number of the items}}= \text{average}$$

Reminder!
Averaging problems often have easy eliminations, so be sure to look for them—*before* you solve.

A One-Step Average Problem

In a simple problem, GMAC will give you two parts of this equation, and it will be up to you to figure out the third. Let's warm up those old average skills.

---○---

What is the average (arithmetic mean) of the numbers 3, 4, 5, and 8 ?

Here's How to Crack It

In this case they've given us the actual numbers, which means we know the total sum $(3 + 4 + 5 + 8 = 20)$ and the total number of items (there are four numbers). What we're missing is the average.

$$\frac{\text{total sum of the items}}{\text{total number of the items}} = \text{average} \qquad \frac{20}{4} = x \quad x = 5$$

---○---

Here's another one:

---○---

If the average (arithmetic mean) of 7 numbers is 5, what is the sum of the numbers?

Here's How to Crack It

In this case we know the total number of items and the average, but not the total sum of the numbers.

$$\frac{\text{total sum of the items}}{\text{total number of the items}} = \text{average} \qquad \frac{x}{7} = 5 \quad x = 35$$

---○---

A Two-Step Average Problem

This is the same problem you just did, made a little more difficult:

_____◯_____

The average (arithmetic mean) of 7 numbers is 5. If two of the numbers are 11 and 14, what is the average of the remaining numbers?

Here's How to Crack It

Always set up an average problem the way we showed you above. With more complicated average problems, take things one sentence at a time. The first sentence yields:

$$\frac{\text{total sum of the items}}{\text{total number of the items}} = \text{average} \qquad \frac{x}{7} = 5 \quad x = 35$$

The sum of *all* the numbers is 35. If two of those numbers are 11 and 14, then the sum of the remaining numbers is $35 - (11 + 14)$, or 10. The question asks, "What is the average of the remaining numbers?" Again, let's set this up properly:

$$\frac{\text{total sum of the remaining numbers}}{\text{total number of the remaining numbers}} = \text{average} \qquad \frac{10}{5} = y \quad y = 2$$

Why did we divide the total sum of the remaining numbers by 5? There were only 5 remaining numbers!

_____◯_____

Medians and Modes

Calculating the average of a list of numbers is one way to find the "middle" of these numbers, but there are two other ways that yield slightly different results. To find the **median** of a list of *n* numbers, just reorder the numbers from least to greatest, and pick the middle number.

If *n* is odd, this is a piece of cake:

The median of 4, 7, 12, 14, 20 = 12.

If *n* is even, it's still easy—just add the two middle numbers together and divide by 2:

$$\text{The median of 4, 12, 14, 20} = \frac{12+14}{2} = 13.$$

To find the **mode** of a list of *n* numbers, just pick the number that occurs most frequently…

The mode of 5, 6, 3, 9, 3, 28, 3, 5 = 3.

…but remember that a list of numbers *can* have more than one mode:

The modes of 3, 3, 3, 4, 5, 5, 5 = both 3 and 5.

Here's a relatively easy problem:

────────────────◯────────────────

4, 6, 3, *y*

If the mode of the list of numbers above is 3, then what is the average (arithmetic mean) of the list?

- ◯ 7
- ◯ 3
- ◯ 4
- ◯ 9
- ◯ 12

Here's How to Crack It

The mode of the list of numbers is 3, which means that *y* must also equal 3 (because the mode is the number that occurs most frequently in the list). So now all we have to do is find the average of 4, 6, 3, and 3. The correct answer is (C).

────────────────◯────────────────

> **Mean**
> When a question refers to an average, the words "arithmetic mean" will often follow in parentheses. This is not just to make the problem sound scarier. **Arithmetic mean** is the precise term for the process of finding an average that we've illustrated in the problems above.

RANGE AND STANDARD DEVIATION

To find the **range** of a list of n numbers, take the least number and subtract it from the greatest number. This measures how widely the numbers are dispersed.

The range of 4, 3, 8, 12, 23, 37 = 37 − 3 = 34.

Another way to measure the dispersion of a list of numbers is **standard deviation**, which measures the distance between the arithmetic mean and each of the numbers in that list. Even if you think you've never heard of this concept before, you've actually seen one example of standard deviation in the form of a graph that is near and dear to the test writers' hearts: the bell-shaped curve.

In the graph of approximate score frequencies below, you'll notice that many people's GMAT scores are clustered around the mean (500), with some people's scores below and others above. The standard deviation is a number that expresses the degree to which the list of numbers vary from the mean, either above it or below it. The greater the standard deviation, the greater the degree of variation.

Means, Medians, and Modes, Oh My!

Q: For the list of numbers {3, 2, 5, 8, 2, 16}, find the mean, the mode, the median, and the range.

Turn to page 118 for the answer.

To calculate the standard deviation of a list of n numbers (not that the GMAT is likely to ask you to), first find the average (arithmetic mean) of the numbers. Then find the difference between that average and each number in the set and square each of the differences. And finally, find the average of the squared differences and take the square root of this average. The rather intimidating formula looks like this:

$$\sqrt{\frac{\sum \left(x - \bar{x}\right)^2}{n-1}}$$

But you won't need it.

Standard deviation usually comes down to a single number such as 2.4 or 3.0. Most GMAT questions about standard deviation concern the difference between standard deviation and the mean. Here's a typical problem:

If the average (arithmetic mean) of a list of numbers is 12 and the standard deviation of that list of numbers is 1.3, then which of the following numbers is more than two standard deviations from the mean?

    I.   14.7
   II.   12.3
   III.   9.3

◯ I only
◯ I and II only
◯ II only
◯ III only
◯ I and III only

Here's How to Crack It

One standard deviation above the mean of 12 is 13.3, and two standard deviations is 14.6. So 14.7 (Roman numeral I) is definitely more than two standard deviations. Is the correct answer (A)? We don't know yet—but we can definitely cross off (C) and (D) because they don't include Roman Numeral I. Let's look at Roman Numeral II. 12.3 is definitely less than two standard deviations, so we can cross off (B). Now, you may have wanted to cross off (E) as well, because 9.3 (Roman Numeral III) is much less than 14.6—but remember, standard deviation means a deviation either above *or below* the mean. Two standard deviations below 12 is 9.4, so 9.3 is actually more than two standard deviations from the mean. The correct answer is (E).

EXPONENTS

An **exponent** is a short way of writing the value of a number multiplied several times by itself. $4 \times 4 \times 4 \times 4 \times 4$ can also be written as 4^5. This is expressed as "four to the fifth power." The large number (4) is called the base, and the little number (5) is called the exponent.

There are several rules to remember about exponents:

- **Multiplying numbers with the same base:** When you multiply numbers that have the same base, you simply add their exponents.

$$6^2 \times 6^3 = 6^{(2+3)} = 6^5 \qquad (y^4)(y^6) = y^{(4+6)} = y^{10}$$

- **Dividing numbers with the same base:** When you divide numbers that have the same base, you simply subtract the bottom exponents from the top exponents.

$$\frac{3^6}{3^2} = 3^{(6-2)} = 3^4 \qquad \frac{x^7}{x^4} = x^{(7-4)} = x^3$$

- **Raising a power to a power:** When you raise a number with an exponent to another power, you can simply multiply the exponents.

$$(4^3)^2 = 4^{(3 \times 2)} = 4^6 \qquad (z^2)^4 = z^{(2 \times 4)} = z^8$$

There are several operations that **_seem_** like they ought to work with exponents, but don't.

- Does $x^2 + x^3 = x^5$?   NO!
- Does $x^6 - x^2 = x^4$?   NO!

- Does $\dfrac{\left(x^2 + y^2 + z^2\right)}{\left(x^2 + y^2\right)} = z^2$?   NO!

But note that in the first example, $x^2 + x^3$ can be written in another form, using the distributive property: $x^2 + x^3 = x^2(1 + x)$.

The Strange Powers of Powers

If you raise a positive integer to a power, the result is _greater_ than the original integer. For example, $6^2 = 36$. However, raising a number to a power can sometimes have unexpected results:

- If you raise a positive fraction that is less than 1 to a power, the result is _less_ than the original fraction.

$$\left(\frac{1}{3}\right)^2 = \frac{1}{3} \times \frac{1}{3} = \frac{1}{9}$$

- If you raise a negative number to an odd power, the result is _less_ than the original number.

$$(-3)^3 = (-3)(-3)(-3) = -27$$

(Remember, –27 is smaller than –3.)

- If you raise a negative number to an even power, the result is positive.

$$(-3)^2 = (-3)(-3) = 9$$

(Remember, negative times negative = positive.)

- Any number to the first power = itself.

- Any nonzero number raised to the 0 power = 1.

RADICALS

The **square root** of a positive number x is the number that, when squared, equals x. By definition, you can take the square root of only a nonnegative number and the square root function returns only nonnegative values. The symbol for a square root is $\sqrt{\ }$. A number inside the $\sqrt{\ }$ is called a **radical**. Thus, in $\sqrt{4} = 2$, 4 is the radical and 2 is its square root.

The **cube root** of a positive number x is the number that, when cubed, equals x. For example, the cube root of 8 is 2, because $2 \times 2 \times 2 = 8$. The symbol for a cube root is $\sqrt[3]{\ }$. Thus, the cube root of 27 would be represented as $\sqrt[3]{27} = 3$, because $3 \times 3 \times 3 = 27$. The cube root of -27 would be represented as $\sqrt[3]{-27} = -3$ because $-3 \times -3 \times -3 = -27$.

Even More Strange Powers
A radical can be rewritten as a fractional exponent, and vice versa.
That is: $\sqrt[3]{5} = 5^{\frac{1}{3}}$.

There are several rules to remember about radicals:

1. $\sqrt{x}\sqrt{y} = \sqrt{xy}$. For example, $\sqrt{12}\sqrt{3} = \sqrt{36} = 6$.

2. $\sqrt{\dfrac{x}{y}} = \dfrac{\sqrt{x}}{\sqrt{y}}$. For example, $\sqrt{\dfrac{3}{16}} = \dfrac{\sqrt{3}}{\sqrt{16}} = \dfrac{\sqrt{3}}{4}$.

3. To simplify a radical, try factoring. For example, $\sqrt{32} = \sqrt{16}\sqrt{2} = 4\sqrt{2}$.

4. The square root of a positive fraction less than 1 is actually larger than the original fraction. For example, $\sqrt{\dfrac{1}{4}} = \dfrac{1}{2}$.

DRILL 6

The answers to these questions can be found in Part VI.

1. If 2 men and 1 woman drop out of a certain class, the ratio of men to women in the class would be 8 to 7. If the current ratio of men to women in the class is 6 to 5, then how many men are currently in the class?

   ○ 14
   ○ 16
   ○ 18
   ○ 20
   ○ 22

2. The average (arithmetic mean) of five numbers is 7. If the average of three of the numbers is 5, then what is the average of the other two numbers?

   ◯ 5
   ◯ 10
   ◯ 12
   ◯ 15
   ◯ 20

3. $\dfrac{\left(\frac{1}{3}\right)^6 - \left(\frac{1}{3}\right)^4}{\left(\frac{1}{3}\right)^5} =$

   ◯ $\left(\dfrac{1}{3}\right)^{-3}$

   ◯ $-\dfrac{8}{27}$

   ◯ $-\dfrac{8}{9}$

   ◯ $-\dfrac{8}{3}$

   ◯ $-\left(\dfrac{1}{3}\right)^{-3}$

4. The ratio $\dfrac{\sqrt{147} + \sqrt{75}}{14}$ to $\dfrac{28}{7\sqrt{3}}$ is equal to

   ◯ $\sqrt{74}$ to 2
   ◯ 24 to 7
   ◯ 14 to 9
   ◯ 9 to 14
   ◯ 7 to 24

5. If $5,000 is invested in an account that earns 8% interest compounded semi-annually, then the interest earned after one year would be how much greater than if the $5,000 had been invested at 8% simple yearly interest?

   ◯ $4
   ◯ $8
   ◯ $12
   ◯ $16
   ◯ $432

6. If the average of ten numbers is 10, then which of the following could be the standard deviation of the ten numbers?

   I.   0
   II.   10
   III.   20

   ○ I only
   ○ I and II
   ○ I and III
   ○ II and III
   ○ I, II, and III

7. List I: $\{y, 2, 4, 7, 10, 11\}$
   List II: $\{3, 3, 4, 6, 7, 10\}$

   If the median of List I is equal to the sum of the median of list II and the mode of List II, then y equals

   ○ 5
   ○ 7
   ○ 8
   ○ 9
   ○ 10

Challenge Question #3

A bar over a digit in a decimal indicates an infinitely repeating decimal.

$333{,}333.\overline{3} \times (10^{-3} - 10^{-5}) =$

   ○ $3{,}333.\overline{3}$
   ○ $3{,}330$
   ○ $333.\overline{3}$
   ○ 330
   ○ 0

Summary

o The six arithmetic operations are addition, subtraction, multiplication, division, raising to a power, and finding a square root.

o These operations must be performed in the proper order (**Please Excuse My Dear Aunt Sally**).

o If you are adding or multiplying a group of numbers, you can regroup them in any order. This is called the **associative law.**

o If you are adding or subtracting numbers with common factors, you can regroup them in the following way:

$$ab + ac = a(b + c)$$
$$ab - ac = a(b - c)$$

This is called the **distributive law**.

o A fraction can be thought of in two ways:
  * another way of expressing division
  * as a $\dfrac{\text{part}}{\text{whole}}$

o You must know how to add, subtract, multiply, and divide fractions. You must also know how to raise them to a power and find their roots.

o Always reduce fractions (when you can) before doing a complicated operation. This will reduce your chances of making a careless error.

o In tough fraction problems, always think $\dfrac{\text{part}}{\text{whole}}$ and *the rest*.

o A decimal is just another way of expressing a fraction.

o You must know how to add, subtract, multiply, and divide decimals.

o In general it is easier to work with fractions than with decimals, so convert decimals to fractions.

o   A ratio is a fraction in all ways but one:

- A fraction is a $\dfrac{\text{part}}{\text{whole}}$.

- A ratio is a $\dfrac{\text{part}}{\text{part}}$.

- In a ratio, the whole is the sum of all its parts.

o   A percentage is just a fraction whose denominator is always 100.

o   You must know the percentage shortcuts outlined in this chapter.

o   In tough percent problems, like tough fraction problems, think $\dfrac{part}{whole}$ and *the rest.*

o   In a percentage increase or decrease problem, you must put the amount of the increase or decrease over the *original* amount.

o   In compound interest problems, the answer will always be *a little bit more* than it would be in a similar simple interest problem.

o   To find the average of several values, add the values and divide the total by the number of values.

o   Always set up average problems in the same way:

$$\frac{\text{total sum of the items}}{\text{total number of the items}} = \text{average}$$

o   To find the median of a list of n numbers, reorder the numbers from least to greatest, and pick the middle number if n is odd. Take the average of the two middle numbers if n is even.

o   To find the mode of a list of n numbers, pick the number that occurs most frequently.

o   To find the range of a list of n numbers, subtract the smallest number from the greatest number.

o   Standard deviation measures the distance between a set of numbers and its arithmetic mean. Most GMAT problems about this concept hinge on the difference between the standard deviation and the arithmetic mean.

o An exponent is a shorter way of expressing the result of multiplying a number several times by itself.

o When you multiply numbers with the same base, you simply add the exponents.

o When you divide numbers with the same base, you simply subtract the exponents.

o When you raise a power to a power, you multiply the exponents.

o You *cannot* add or subtract numbers with the same or different bases by adding their exponents.

o The three radical rules you need to know:

- $\sqrt{x}\sqrt{y} = \sqrt{xy}$

- $\sqrt{\dfrac{x}{y}} = \dfrac{\sqrt{x}}{\sqrt{y}}$

- $\sqrt{x^2 y} = x\sqrt{y}$

o There are some unusual features of exponents and radicals:
- The square root of a positive fraction that's less than 1 is larger than the original fraction.
- When you raise a positive fraction that's less than 1 to an exponent, the resulting fraction is smaller.
- When you raise a negative number to an even exponent, the resulting number is positive.
- When you raise a negative number to an odd exponent, the resulting number is still a negative number.

Chapter 11
Algebra

Algebra is usually all about writing equations. In this chapter, we'll show you a foolproof way to write the equations you *need* to write, give you a review of the quadratic formula, and teach you how to do simultaneous equations. Plus, you'll learn two fantastic techniques that will allow you to avoid writing equations on most GMAT questions: *Plugging In* and *Plugging In the Answers* (PITA).

Approximately one-fourth of the problems on the computer-adaptive GMAT Math section involve traditional algebra. Your algebra skills may also be tested by some questions in the Integrated Reasoning section.

In this chapter, we'll show you some powerful techniques that will enable you to solve these problems without using traditional algebra. The first half of this chapter discusses these new techniques. The second half shows you how to do the few algebra problems that must be tackled algebraically.

NOT EXACTLY ALGEBRA: BASIC PRINCIPLES

Algebra is used to come up with general solutions to problems. For example, you might know (for whatever reason) that the price of a new pair of shoes in relation to the cost of a pair of jeans is $3j + 20$, where j is the cost of the jeans. Based on this formula, if you know that the jeans cost \$50, then you know that the shoes cost \$170. But, you also know the cost of the shoes if the jeans cost \$75.

In most algebra problems, you need to find an algebraic expression that matches the description of the relationship given in the problem. For the situation above, the problem might say

> At a certain store, the price of a pair of shoes is twenty dollars more than three times the price of a pair of jeans. If the price of a pair of jeans is j dollars at this store, then what is the price, in dollars, of a pair of shoes, in terms of j ?
>
> ○　$20 - 3j$
> ○　$3j + 20$
> ○　$3j - 20$
> ○　$3j + 60$
> ○　$20j + 3$

You might consider this question a fairly easy algebra question. To solve it, you might just start translating the phrase "the cost of a pair of shoes is twenty dollars more than three times the cost of a pair of jeans." But, you need to be careful while doing that. If you get confused about whether you should add 20 or subtract 20, you'll pick the wrong answer. The test writers have put a lot of thought into the ways that the key statement in the question can be misinterpreted.

Plugging In is a great way to avoid making mistakes when you are manipulating variables.

So, if it's so easy to make a mistake while doing the algebra, is there a more foolproof way to do this question? Of course! Instead of trying to come up with a general solution—the algebraic approach—let's pick a number and come up with a specific solution. Then, we'll just choose the answer that matches.

We call this approach **Plugging In**. It is perhaps our most powerful math technique and will allow you to solve complicated problems more quickly than you might have ever thought possible. Plugging In is easy. There are three steps involved.

Let's look at the same problem again:

———————————○———————————

At a certain store, the price of a pair of shoes is twenty dollars more than three times the price of a pair of jeans. If the price of a pair of jeans is j dollars at this store, then what is the price, in dollars, of a pair of shoes, in terms of j ?

○ $20 - 3j$
○ $3j + 20$
○ $3j - 20$
○ $3j + 60$
○ $20j + 3$

Here's How to Crack It

Let's pick a number for j. Let's say that the jeans cost $10. (We don't need to worry about being realistic!) Write down "$j = 10$". We've now transformed the problem from an algebra problem into an arithmetic problem.

Here's what the problem now asks:

At a certain store, the price of a pair of shoes is twenty dollars more than three times the price of a pair of jeans. If the price of a pair of jeans is **10** dollars at this store, then what is the price, in dollars, of a pair of shoes, ~~in terms of *j*~~?

You'll notice that we've substituted 10 for the variable j in the original problem. You'll also notice that we've crossed out the phrase "in terms of j." Once we put a number into the problem, the phrase "in terms of" has no meaning so we can ignore it.

Using $10 for the price of the jeans, the price of the pair of shoes is $50. All we did was translate the phrase "the price of a pair of shoes is twenty dollars more than three times the price of a pair of jeans." Three times the price of the pair of jeans is 3 × $10 = $30. Twenty dollars more is just $30 + $20 = $50. The numerical answer to our problem is $50. Write that number down on your noteboard and circle it to indicate that it is your target answer.

Now, you just need to find the answer that matches $50 when you substitute 10 for j. You should write down A, B, C, D, E on your noteboard and work out each answer choice. Here's what that looks like:

A) $20 - 3j = 20 - 3(10) = -10$
B) $3j + 20 = 3(10) + 20 = 50$
C) $3j - 20 = 3(10) - 20 = 10$
D) $3j + 60 = 3(10) + 60 = 90$
E) $20j + 3 = 20(10) + 3 = 203$

Choice (B) is the only answer that matches the target answer, so it is the answer to this problem. You'll note that we checked all five answer choices. We did that to be sure we were picking the correct answer.

Scratch Work

The students in our GMAT course learn to automatically do scratch work. When plugging in, always write down the numbers you are plugging in for each variable. Be sure to clearly label the number for each variable by writing down something like $j = 10$. Next, do the work for each step in the problem. When you find the numerical answer to the problem, write that down and circle it. Then, try each of the answer choices, crossing them off as you eliminate them. Here's what your scratch work should have looked like for the last problem:

Why Plug In? Because It Makes Difficult Problems Easy!

You might be thinking, "Wait a minute! It was just as easy to solve this problem algebraically. Why should I Plug In?" To see why, let's take a look at another version of the problem.

At a certain store, the price of a pair of shoes is twenty dollars more than three times the price of a pair of jeans and the price of a sweater is fifty percent more than the price of a pair of shoes. If the price of a pair of jeans is *j* dollars at this store, then what is the price, in dollars, of a pair of shoes, a sweater, and a pair of jeans, in terms of *j* ?

- ◯ 1.5*j* + 10
- ◯ 3*j* + 20
- ◯ 4.5*j* + 30
- ◯ 5.5*j* + 30
- ◯ 8.5*j* + 50

Another Reason to Plug In

Plugging numbers into a problem is a much more natural way to think for most folks than algebra. Has anyone ever asked a bartender, "Say, could I get 6*x* of whiskey, where 6*x* equals a standard shot?" The bartender might comply, but you can be sure he'd ask for your car keys first. Complicate the question with *y*, the ounces of alcohol in a standard shot, and *z*, the number of ice cubes in the glass, and you've got a real headache. Essentially, Plugging In is a matter of putting numbers back into a form that you are used to working with.

Here's How to Crack It

This version of the problem is wordier and that helps to make it more confusing. Let's try Plugging In. As before, we'll start by making *j* = 10. So, the jeans cost $10. Next, we know the relationship between the price of the jeans and the cost of the shoes. The price of the shoes is "twenty dollars more than three times the price of the jeans." So, the price of the shoes is $50. Finally, the sweater costs "fifty percent more than the price of the shoes." So, the sweater is $50 + $25, or $75. So, the cost of all three items is $10 + $50 + $75 = $135. Be sure to circle $135.

Now, it's time to find the answer that equals 135 when *j* = 10. Choice (A) is 25, so cross it off. Choice (B) is 50, so it's wrong. Choice (C) is 75, so it's also wrong. Choice (D) is 85, so it can be eliminated. Finally, (E) is 135. Choice (E) matches the target and is the correct answer.

By the way, (D) is what you get if you misread how to calculate the cost of the sweater. If you were doing the algebra, the cost of the shoes is 3*j* + 20. It would be pretty easy to think that the price of the sweater is then 1.5*j* + 10, which is fifty percent of the cost of the shoes rather than fifty percent *more*. Of course, you could make this mistake while working with the numbers too. But, what's easier—to see that $25 is not more than $50 or to see that 1.5*j* + 10 is not more than 3*j* + 20?

To recap, there are two reasons why you'd want to Plug In even if you are pretty good at algebra.

1. Plugging In can make even the hardest algebra problems much easier to solve.
2. The test writers have thought about all the possible ways you might mess up the algebra while working the problem. If you make one of those mistakes, your answer will be among the answer choices and you'll most likely wind up picking the wrong answer.

What to Plug In
- Numbers that make the math easy!
- Try small simple numbers such as 2, 5, or 10
- Percents? Try 100
- Hours or Minutes? 30 or 120

What NOT to Plug In
- Avoid using 0 or 1
- Numbers in the problem or in the answer choices

What Number Should I Plug In?

While you can plug in any number, you'll find that certain numbers work better than others. Ideally, you want a number that makes it easy to perform the calculations for the problem. For most problems, you can just use small, simple numbers such as 2, 5, or 10. However, you also want numbers that make sense within the context of the problem. For example, for a problem that uses percents, plugging in 100 would be a good idea. Different numbers work for different types of problems. As you practice, you'll get better at picking good numbers—especially if you keep asking yourself "What number will make this problem easy?" You also shouldn't be afraid to change your number if the calculations start to get messy.

Sometimes the best way to select a number is to use a little common sense. Here's an example:

?

Q: If 80% of a certain number x is 50% of y and y is 20% of z, then what is x in terms of z?
A. $5z$
B. $3z$
C. $z/4$
D. $z/5$
E. $z/8$

Turn to page 132 for the answer.

If Jim drives k miles in 50 minutes, how many minutes will it take him to drive 10 miles, at the same rate?

- $\dfrac{500}{k}$
- $\dfrac{k}{500}$
- $60k$
- $10k$
- $\dfrac{50}{k}$

Here's How to Crack It

GMAC would like you to use the formula *distance = rate × time*. There are variables in the answer choices, so we can Plug In. Since it's a good bet that at least a few of the wrong answers are based on using the formula, let's Plug In.

Any number you choose to plug in for k will eventually give you the answer to this problem, but there are some numbers that will make your task even easier.

We need to find a good number for k. Notice that we know that Jim is going to drive 10 miles. Suppose we just made k equal to half of 10? The question now reads as follows:

If Jim drives 5 miles in 50 minutes, how many minutes will it take him to drive 10 miles, at the same rate?

Now the problem is pretty easy. Since Jim is going to drive twice the distance, it's going to take him twice the time. So, the target is 100 minutes. Now, all we need to do is find the answer that matches the target when $k = 5$. Start with (A). Divide 500 by 5 to get 100. Bingo! To double check, plug 5 into the other answer choices as well. None of them match the target.

The answer to this question is (A).

More Times to Plug In

So far, we've been looking at questions that have explicit variables in both the problem and the answer choices. When you see variables in the problem or answer choices, that's one of the signs to Plug In.

However, sometimes GMAC expects you to use algebra to answer a question that doesn't have explicit variables. You can still Plug In on these problems. In fact, *you should consider plugging in whenever you feel the urge to do algebra*. The urge to do algebra is the ultimate sign that the problem can be cracked using some form of Plugging In.

Let's take a look at some other ways to Plug In.

Plugging In with Hidden Variables

Some problems have a hidden variable. For these problems, all the calculations are usually based off one item but you don't know the value of that item. There's a simple solution—just Plug In a value for the item!

Let's look at an example:

A merchant reduces the original price of a coat by 20 percent for a spring sale. Finding that the coat did not sell, the merchant reduces the spring price by a further 15 percent at the start of the summer. The coat's summer price is what percent of its original price?

- ◯ 35%
- ◯ 64%
- ◯ 65%
- ◯ 68%
- ◯ 80%

Here's How to Crack It

You may have noticed that this problem never gave us the coat's original price. You may have felt the urge to do algebra starting to kick in as you read the problem. For example, you might have started to say to yourself "Well, if the price of the coat is *x*, then the spring price is...." That's your sign that you can do this problem as a Plug In! All you need to do is pick a price for the coat.

Let's make the original price of the coat $100. *When you are solving a percent problem, 100 is a great number to Plug In.* The merchant discounts the price of the coat by 20% for the spring sale. Twenty percent of $100 is $20, so the spring price is $80. For the summer, the spring price of the coat is discounted by another 15%. Fifteen percent of $80 is $12, making the summer price $68.

The question asks for the summer price as a percent of the original price. In other words, $68 is what percent of $100? 68%. The answer is (D).

Easy Eliminations

If you were running out of time, you'd need to make a guess. But, you could eliminate some obviously wrong answers first. When you read the problem fast, you might be tempted to think that the overall reduction is 20% + 15% = 35%, but that's too easy. So, cross off (A). Choice (C) is just 100 – 35 = 65. Also, too easy. Finally, (E) is what you get after the first reduction. The answer is probably (B) or (D).

Another way to tell that you can probably solve a question as a hidden Plug In is to look at the answer choices. The answer choices for hidden Plug In questions are typically percents, fractions, or sometimes ratios. How can you tell that this problem is a hidden Plug In?

At College P, one–fourth of the students are seniors and one–fifth of the seniors major in business. If two–fifths of all students at the college major in business, the business majors who are not seniors are what fraction of all business majors?

○ $\dfrac{1}{20}$

○ $\dfrac{1}{8}$

○ $\dfrac{7}{20}$

○ $\dfrac{7}{15}$

○ $\dfrac{7}{8}$

Here's How to Crack It

You may have noticed that while this problem provides lots of fractions to work with, it never reveals how many students attend College P. Of course, knowing the total enrollment at the college would make solving the problem fairly straightforward. So, before you start setting up equations based on x students at College P, let's Plug In a number for the total students.

An easy way to come up with a good number when the problem has fractions is to simply multiply the denominators of the fractions together. In this case, that's $4 \times 5 \times 5 = 100$. Don't worry, by the way, that some of the denominators are not distinct. Multiplying by the extra 5 may help us to avoid getting a result that leads to some fractional part of a student!

So, if there are 100 students at the college, there are 25 seniors and 75 students who are not seniors. Next, you know that one-fifth of the seniors major in business, so that's 5 seniors who are business majors. Since two-fifths of all students are business majors, the college has 40 business majors. Of those 40 business majors, $40 - 5 = 35$ of the business majors are not seniors. So, the fraction of business majors who are not seniors is $\dfrac{35}{40} = \dfrac{7}{8}$. The correct answer is (E).

It Works for Ratios, Too!

You can also Plug In when the answer choices are expressed as ratios. Here's how a similar question would be written as a ratio problem.

At College P, one-fourth of the students are seniors and one-fifth of the seniors major in business. If two-fifths of all students at the college major in business, then what is the ratio of senior business majors to non-senior business majors?

○ 1 : 3
○ 1 : 5
○ 1 : 7
○ 1 : 8
○ 7 : 8

As before, just Plug In 100 for the number of students. There are 5 seniors who are business majors and 35 business majors who are not seniors. The ratio is 5 : 35, which reduces to 1 : 7. The answer is (C).

Plugging In the Answers (PITA)

Some algebra questions ask for a numerical answer. GMAC expects you to write an equation, solve it, and then pick the answer. However, the person who wrote the problem had to do all of that hard work. So, rather than duplicate all of the work the question writer did, why not just test out the answers to see which one works?

We call this method of solving the problem **Plugging In the Answers** (or PITA for short). You'll find that solving problems this way can save you a lot of time and help you to avoid common algebra mistakes. There are three steps involved when you Plug In the Answers.

Let's take a look at an example.

At a certain restaurant, the price of a sandwich is $4.00 more than the price of a cup of coffee. If the price of a sandwich and a cup of coffee is $7.35, including a sales tax of 5%, what is the price of a cup of coffee, EXCLUDING the sales tax?

- ○ $1.50
- ○ $3.00
- ○ $4.00
- ○ $5.50
- ○ $7.00

Here's How to Crack It

If there were no answer choices, you'd be forced to write an equation and solve it. However, because you know the answer must be one of the five provided choices, it will be easier and faster to simply try the answers.

Scratchwork

When you Plug In the Answers, make your scratch work look like an Excel spreadsheet. Label your columns and put your results for each column next to the answer choice you are checking. Doing so will help you to cut down on mistakes and check subsequent answer choices more quickly.

Start by writing down the answers and labeling them as "coffee." Now, start with (C). If the cup of coffee costs $4.00, what can you figure out? The problem states that the sandwich costs $4.00 more than the cup of coffee, so the sandwich is $8.00. Make a column for "sandwich" and write down $8.00 next to (C). You now know that the cost for the sandwich and the cup of coffee is $12.00. Choice (C) is too big because the cost for the sandwich and the cup of coffee is supposed to be only $7.35 including the sales tax. Go ahead and cross off (C).

So far, your work should look like this:

Coffee	Sandwich	Total
A) $1.50		
B) $3.00		
C) $4.00	$8.00	$12.00
D) $5.50		
E) $7.00		

Now, its time to decide if you need a bigger number or a smaller number. It's a pretty easy choice for this problem. Since $4.00 turned out to be too big, it makes sense to try a smaller number. Choices (D) and (E) are out of the question, so cross them off. There's no need to debate over (A) or (B). One of them must be correct, so just try (B). If it works, you're done. If it doesn't, choose (A) and you're still done.

If the cup of coffee costs $3.00, as in (B), then the sandwich is $7.00. That would make the total cost for both items $10.00. That's still too big! The answer must be (A).

Here's what the work should look like at this point:

Coffee	Sandwich	Total
A) $1.50		
B) $3.00	$7.00	$10.00
C) $4.00	$8.00	$12.00
D) $5.50		
E) $7.00		

There's really no need to test (A). However, if the coffee costs $1.50, then the sandwich costs $5.50. Together the two items cost $7.00. The tax on the two items is 5% of $7.00 or $0.35. So, the total with tax is $7.35, which meets the condition stated in the problem. The answer is (A).

Plugging In the Answers
1. Write down the answers, determine what they represent and label them.
2. Start with (C) and work the steps of the problem.
3. Look for some sort of condition that must be met to make the answer correct.

Plugging In the Answers: Advanced Principles

When you solve a problem using Plugging In the Answers (PITA), you'll usually know if you need a bigger or smaller number if (C) didn't work. However, there are times when you won't be sure. Rather than wasting time trying to decide if you need a bigger or smaller number, just pick an answer choice and try it. You'll actually waste less time testing an extra answer choice or two than you will trying to decide which type of number to try next.

Jim is now twice as old as Fred, who is two years older than Sam. Four years ago, Jim was four times as old as Sam. How old is Jim now?

- ◯ 8
- ◯ 12
- ◯ 16
- ◯ 20
- ⬭ 24

Here's How to Crack It

This question has numbers in the answers and you probably started to think "Well, if Jim is x years old, then Fred is…." The urge to do algebra means that it's time to Plug In the Answers. Start with (C).

> ### When to Plug In the Answers
> - There are numbers in the answer choices.
> - The question asks for a specific amount.
> - You have the urge to set up and solve an equation.

The answers represent possible ages for Jim. If Jim is 16 years old, then Fred is 8 because Jim is twice as old as Fred. Next, you know that Fred is two years older than Sam, so Sam is 6. Now, you need to compare Jim's age and Sam's age four years ago. Four years ago, Jim was 12 and Sam was 2. Remember that there's always a condition in the problem that must be met by the correct answer.

In this case, Jim's age four years ago must be four times that of Sam. Is 12 four times 2? No. So, (C) can be eliminated.

Here's what your work should look like up to this point.

	Now			**4 years ago**	
Jim	Fred	Sam		Jim	Sam
A) 8					
B) 12					
C) 16	8	6		12	2
D) 20					
E) 24					

Now, it's time to choose a bigger or smaller number. But, it isn't really clear which direction to go, is it? So, rather than waste a lot of time trying to figure that out, just pick an answer and try it. If Jim is 20 years old now, as in (D), then Fred is 10 and Sam is 8. Four years ago, Jim was 16 and Sam was 4.

Here's what your work should look like.

	Now			4 years ago	
	Jim	Fred	Sam	Jim	Sam
A) 8					
B) 12					
~~C) 16~~	8	6		12	2
D) 20	10	8		16	4
E) 24					

Since $4 \times 4 = 16$, the condition in the problem is met. Choice (D) is the correct answer.

———————◯———————

Most of the time, starting at (C) when doing PITA makes the most sense. By starting at (C), you can usually cut down on the number of answer choices that you need to test. However, there can be times when it makes sense to start with a different answer choice.

———————◯———————

If x is a positive integer such that $x^2 + 5x - 14 = 0$, what is the value of x ?

◯ −7
◯ −5
◯ 0
◯ 2
◯ 5

Here's How to Crack It

Notice that the question states that x is a positive integer. Don't waste time with (A), (B), or (C)—cross them off immediately. For this problem, it makes sense to start with (D). Plug 2 into the equation for x to get $(2)^2 + 5(2) - 14 = 0$. Since the equation is true when $x = 2$, (D) is the correct answer.

———————◯———————

Challenge Question #4

A certain game requires players to collect both blue tokens, which are worth b points each, and red tokens, which are worth r points each. If p percent of Player A's points are from blue tokens and q percent of Player A's tokens are red, which of the following is an expression for the value of p, in terms of b, r, and q ?

$\bigcirc \quad \dfrac{100bq}{bq + 100r - qr}$

$\bigcirc \quad \dfrac{10{,}000b - 100bq}{100b - bq + qr}$

$\bigcirc \quad \dfrac{bq + 100r - qr}{100bq}$

$\bigcirc \quad \dfrac{100b - bq}{100r - 100bq - qr}$

$\bigcirc \quad \dfrac{100b - bq + qr}{10{,}000b - 100bq}$

Plugging In the Answers Advanced Tips

1. If you're not sure whether you need a bigger or smaller number, don't waste time. Just pick another answer choice and try it.
2. You may be able to eliminate some numbers that are too big or too small before you start plugging in. If you can, just start with the middle number that you have left.
3. If you have both easy to work with numbers and messy numbers in the answer choices, try the easy to work with numbers first.

Must Be

Some questions will use the words "must be." For example, the question may ask which of the expressions in the answers must be even or must be divisible by 3. These questions can be solved easily by Plugging In. However, you'll probably need to Plug In at least twice to find the answer.

Here's all you need to do.

Must Be Plugging In
1. Pick numbers for the variables in the problem. Be sure to satisfy any restrictions for the variables.
2. Eliminate any answer choices that don't match what you are looking for.
3. Plug In the most different kind of number you are allowed to try. For example, if you tried an even number, try an odd number.
4. Repeat until only one answer remains.

If n is a positive integer, which of the following must be even?

- ○ $(n - 1)(n + 1)$
- ○ $(n - 2)(n + 1)$
- ○ $(n - 2)(n + 4)$
- ○ $(n - 3)(n + 1)$
- ○ $(n - 3)(n + 5)$

Here's How to Crack It

Start by picking a value for n. How about $n = 2$? Now, evaluate each answer choice. For (A), the expression equals 3, so cross it off. For (B), the expression equals 0. Remember that 0 is an even number, so keep this answer choice. But you aren't done yet. Just because you've found one case where this answer choice is even doesn't mean it will always be even. Keep checking the answers. Choice (C) is also equal to 0, so keep it as well. Choice (D) equals –3. Don't be fooled by the negative sign. Negative integers can also be even or odd. Since –3 is odd, cross this answer off. Choice (E) equals –7 and can also be eliminated.

Next, try a new number. Since this problem is about even and odd numbers, it makes sense to try an odd number next. How about $n = 3$? You need to check only the two answers that remain. Choice (B) equals 4, which is still even. However, (C) now equals 7, so it can be eliminated. The correct answer is (B).

Here's what your work should look like once you have worked through the entire problem.

> **Try the ZONEF Numbers**
> For some "must be" questions, the different number you need is one of the ZONEF numbers. These are the numbers that most people forget to think about.
>
> Zero
> One
> Negatives
> Extremes (like 100)
> Fractions

	$n = 2$	$n = 3$
~~A) $(n - 1)(n + 1)$~~	3	
B) $(n - 2)(n + 1)$	0	4
~~C) $(n - 2)(n + 4)$~~	0	7
~~D) $(n - 3)(n + 1)$~~	–3	
~~E) $(n - 3)(n + 5)$~~	–7	

BASIC ALGEBRA

You can solve most GMAT algebra problems using some form of Plugging In. However, there are some questions that you may need to solve using some relatively basic algebra.

Two Simple Rules

Before we review some very specific types of algebra that GMAC likes to test, let's review the two basic rules that are true for any algebraic situation. These two rules are used pretty much any time that you solve a problem algebraically.

1. Collect like terms. Get all the x's on one side of the equals sign and all the numbers on the other.
2. Whatever you do to one side of an equation, you need to do to the other side of the equation. Did you multiply one side by 5? Then, you need to multiply the other side of the equation by 5, as well.

Solving Equalities

Even the simplest equalities can be solved by Plugging In the Answers, but it's probably easier to solve a simple equation algebraically. If there is one variable in an equation, isolate the variable on one side of the equation and solve it. Let's try an example of this type, although a question this easy wouldn't actually be seen on the GMAT. This one is just for practice.

If $x - 5 = 3x + 2$, then $x =$

- ○ -8
- ○ -7
- ○ $-\dfrac{7}{2}$
- ○ $\dfrac{7}{5}$
- ○ $\dfrac{10}{3}$

Avoiding Common Errors

We'll add a third rule that you won't find written in any math book.

3. Equations cannot become expressions.

If you've ever started working with one side of an equation without writing down both sides of the equation, you've broken this rule. By always writing down both sides of the equation, you can avoid wasting time and making silly mistakes.

Here's How to Crack It

Get all of the x's on one side of the equation. If we subtract x from both sides we have:

$$
\begin{array}{rcl}
x - 5 & = & 3x + 2 \\
-x & & -x \\
\hline
-5 & = & 2x + 2
\end{array}
$$

Now subtract 2 from both sides:

$$
\begin{array}{rcl}
-5 & = & 2x + 2 \\
-2 & & -2 \\
\hline
-7 & = & 2x
\end{array}
$$

Finally, divide both sides by 2:

$$\frac{-7}{2} = \frac{2x}{2}$$

$$x = -\frac{7}{2}$$

The answer is (C).

Solving Inequalities

To solve inequalities, you must be able to recognize the following symbols:

$>$	is greater than
$<$	is less than
$\geq$	is greater than or equal to
$\leq$	is less than or equal to

As with an equation, you can add a number to or subtract a number from both sides of an inequality without changing it; you can collect similar terms and simplify them. In fact, an inequality behaves just like a regular equation except in one way:

> If you multiply or divide both sides of an inequality by a negative number, the direction of the inequality symbol changes.

For example,

$$-2x > 5$$

To solve for x, you would divide both sides by -2, just as you would in an equality. But when you do, the sign flips:

$$\frac{-2x}{-2} < \frac{5}{-2}$$

$$x < -\frac{5}{2}$$

Solving Simultaneous Equations

Simultaneous equations are almost always tested in Data Sufficiency format on the GMAT. It is generally impossible to solve one equation with two variables, and later we will discuss the rare opportunity to do so. But if there are two equations, both of which have the same two variables, then it is possible to solve for both variables. An easy problem might look like this:

$$\text{If } 3x + 2y = 6 \text{ and } 5x - 2y = 10, \text{ then } x = ?$$

To solve simultaneous equations, add or subtract the equations so that one of the variables disappears.

$$
\begin{array}{r}
3x + 2y = 6 \\
+\ 5x - 2y = 10 \\
\hline
8x \quad\ \ = 16
\end{array}
$$

$$x = 2$$

Q: Are the following equations distinct?
(1) $3x + 21y = 12$
(2) $x + 7y = 4$
Go to page 144 for the answer.

In more difficult simultaneous equations, you'll find that neither of the variables will disappear when you try to add or subtract the two equations. In such cases, you must multiply both sides of one of the equations by some number in order to get the coefficient in front of the variable that you want to disappear to be the same in both equations. This sounds more complicated than it is. A difficult problem might look like this:

If $3x + 2y = 6$ and $5x - y = 10$, then $x = ?$

Let's set it up the same way:

$$3x + 2y = 6$$

$$5x - y = 10$$

Unfortunately, in this example, neither adding nor subtracting the two equations gets rid of either variable. But look what happens when we multiply the bottom equation by 2:

$$3x + 2y = 6 \qquad \text{or} \qquad 3x + 2y = 6$$
$$(2)5x - (2)y = (2)10 \qquad \qquad \underline{+\ 10x - 2y = 20}$$
$$13x \qquad = 26 \qquad x = 2$$

Quadratic Equations

On the GMAT, quadratic equations always come in one of two forms: factored or expanded. Here's an example:

$$\underset{\text{factored}}{(x + 2)(x + 5)} = \underset{\text{expanded}}{x^2 + 7x + 10}$$

The first thing to do when solving a problem that involves a quadratic equation is to see which form the equation is in. If the quadratic equation is in an unfactored form, factor it immediately. If the quadratic equation is in a factored form, unfactor it. The test writers like to see whether you know how to do these things.

To unfactor a factored expression, just multiply it out using FOIL (First, Outer, Inner, Last):

$$(x + 2)(x + 5) = (x + 2)(x + 5)$$

$$= (x \text{ times } x) + (x \text{ times } 5) + (2 \text{ times } x) + (2 \text{ times } 5)$$

$$= x^2 + 5x + 2x + 10$$

$$= x^2 + 7x + 10$$

To factor an unfactored expression, put it into the following format and start by looking for the factors of the first and last terms.

$$x^2 + 2x - 15$$
$$= (\quad)(\quad)$$

For the first term of the unfactored expression to be x^2, the first term of each parentheses of the factored expression has to be x.

$$x^2 + 2x - 15$$
$$= (x\quad)(x\quad)$$

For the last term of the unfactored expression to be 15, the last term in each parentheses of the factored expression must be either 5 and 3 or 15 and 1. Since there is no way to get a middle term for the unfactored expression with a coefficient of 2 if the terms were 15 and 1, we are left with

$$x^2 + 2x - 15$$
$$= (x\quad5)(x\quad3)$$

To decide where to put the pluses and minuses in the factored expression, look to see how the inner and outer terms of the factored equation would combine to form the middle term. If we put a minus in front of the 5 and a plus in front of the 3, then the middle term would be $-2x$ (not what we wanted). Therefore, the final factored expression looks like this

$$x^2 + 2x - 15$$
$$= (x + 5)(x - 3)$$

Quadratic equations are usually set equal to 0. Here's an example:

> A: No. Look at what equation #2 looks like multiplied by 3:
> $3(x + 7y) = 3(4)$
> or $3x + 21y = 12$.
> Multiply both sides by 3 and equations #1 and #2 are identical. When one equation can be multiplied to produce the other, the equations are identical, not distinct.

What are all the values of x that satisfy the equation $x^2 + 4x + 3 = 0$?

- ◯ -3
- ◯ -1
- ◯ -3 and -1
- ◯ 3 and 4
- ◯ 4

Here's How to Crack It

This problem contains an unfactored equation, so let's factor it.

$$x^2 + 4x + 3 = 0$$
$$(x\quad)(x\quad) = 0$$
$$(x\quad3)(x\quad1) = 0$$
$$(x + 3)(x + 1) = 0$$

In order for this equation to be correct, x must be either -3 or -1. The correct answer is (C).

Note: This problem would also have been easy to solve by Plugging In the Answers. It asked a specific question, and there were five specific answer choices. One of them was correct. All you had to do was try the choices until you found the right one. Bear in mind, however, that in a quadratic equation there are usually two values that will make the equation work.

Favorites of GMAT Test Writers

There are three types of quadratic equations the GMAT test writers find endlessly fascinating. These equations appear on the GMAT with great regularity in both the Problem Solving format and the Data Sufficiency format:

$$(x + y)^2 = x^2 + 2xy + y^2$$

$$(x + y)(x - y) = x^2 - y^2$$

$$(x - y)^2 = x^2 - 2xy + y^2$$

Memorize all three of these. As with all quadratic equations, if you see the equation in factored form, you should immediately unfactor it; if it's unfactored, factor it immediately. Here's an example:

If $\dfrac{x^2 - 4}{x + 2} = 5$, then $x =$

- ◯ 3
- ◯ 5
- ◯ 6
- ◯ 7
- ◯ 9

Here's How to Crack It

It is unfactored, so let's factor it:

$$\frac{(x + 2)(x - 2)}{(x + 2)} = 5$$

The $(x + 2)$s cancel out, leaving us with $(x - 2) = 5$. So $x = 7$, and the answer is (D).

DRILL 7 (Plugging In)

The answers to these questions can be found in Part VI.

1. 5 years ago, Joe was twice as old as Jessica. If in 4 years Joe will be one and a half times as old as Jessica, then how old is Joe now?

    ○ 23
    ○ 25
    ○ 27
    ○ 29
    ○ 31

2. If $\dfrac{x^2 + 2x - 9}{3} \leq x + 1$, then x could be represented by which of the following?

    ○ $-4 \leq x \leq -3$
    ○ $-4 \leq x \leq 3$
    ○ $-3 \leq x \leq 3$
    ○ $-3 \leq x \leq 4$
    ○ $\ 3 \leq x \leq 4$

3. If $x > 0$ and x percent of a is b, then, in terms of x, a is how many times b ?

    ○ $100x$
    ○ $10x$
    ○ x
    ○ $\dfrac{10}{x}$
    ○ $\dfrac{100}{x}$

4. John has s pairs of shoes, which is $\dfrac{1}{3}$ as many as Shiela and twice as many as James. In terms of s, how many pairs of shoes do the three of them have combined?

    ○ $\dfrac{7}{3}s$

    ○ $\dfrac{10}{3}s$

    ○ $\dfrac{7}{2}s$

    ○ $4s$

    ○ $\dfrac{9}{2}s$

Challenge Question #5

A dealer once sold identical cars at a price of x dollars each (including sales tax). However, the pre-tax price was recently increased by $2,500 such that 18 cars purchased at the old price would cost the same as purchasing three fewer cars at the new price. If the sales tax rate is 8%, what is the new price of the dealer's cars, including sales tax, in dollars?

○ $10,800
○ $12,500
○ $13,500
○ $16,200
○ $16,750

Summary

o Most of the algebra problems on the GMAT are simpler to solve *without* algebra, using two Princeton Review techniques: **Plugging In** and **Plugging In the Answers**.

o Plugging In is easy. There are three steps:
- Pick numbers for the variables in the problem.
- Using your numbers, find an answer to the problem. (Write that answer down and circle it.)
- Plug your numbers into the answer choices to see which choice equals the answer you found in the previous step.

o When you Plug In, try to choose convenient numbers—those that are simple to work with and make the problem easier to manipulate.

o When you Plug In, avoid choosing 0, 1, or a number that already appears in the problem or in the answer choices.

o On problems with variables in the answers that contain the words "must be" or "could be," you may have to Plug In more than once to find the correct answer.

o Plugging In the Answers is easy. There are three steps:
- Always start with (C). Plug that number into the problem and see whether it makes the problem work.
- If (C) is too small, try the next larger number.
- If (C) is too big, try the next smaller number.
- If you're not sure which way to go, don't sweat it. Just pick a direction and try it out!
- If the question asks for the least or greatest number, start with the least or greatest answer choice.

o   If you see a problem with a quadratic equation in factored form, the easiest way to get the answer is to expand the equation immediately. If the equation is expanded, factor it immediately.

o   Memorize the factored and expanded forms of the three most common quadratics on the GMAT:

$$(x + y)^2 = x^2 + 2xy + y^2$$
$$(x + y)(x - y) = x^2 - y^2$$
$$(x - y)^2 = x^2 - 2xy + y^2$$

o   On problems containing inequalities, remember that when you multiply or divide both sides of an inequality by a negative number, the sign flips.

o   In solving simultaneous equations, add or subtract one equation to or from another so that one of the two variables disappears.

Chapter 12
Applied Arithmetic

Applied arithmetic involves knowing how to solve word problems involving rate and work, functions, probability, permutations, and combinations. In this chapter, we cover the important facets of each type of problem and show you how they appear on the GMAT.

It's time to look at some applied arithmetic subjects that the GMAT test writers love to use. In this chapter, we'll cover

1. Rate problems
2. Work problems
3. Function problems
4. Probability problems
5. Permutation and Combination problems

RATE PROBLEMS

Any problem that mentions planes, trains, cars, bicycles, distance, miles per hour, or any other travel-related terminology is asking you to solve a rate problem. You may remember that you can use the formula *distance = rate × time* to solve these types of problems.

We're going to use a **rate pie** to keep track of the information in a rate problem. Here's what it looks like:

Two Out of Three Ain't Bad
For Data Sufficiency problems, as soon as you have two of the pieces of the rate pie, you have sufficient information to find the other piece.

If a problem gives you the rate and time, the pieces on the bottom, you multiply to get the distance. If you have the distance, the piece on the top, and one of the pieces on the bottom, you divide to get the other bottom piece. As soon as you know that you are dealing with a rate problem, draw a rate pie and start filling in what you know.

The rate pie is really just a different way of writing the *distance = rate × time* formula. It works well for GMAT problems, however, because GMAT problems often involve multiple steps. So, the pie helps you to see what information you have and what you need to find.

Let's try a problem:

Pam and Sue drove in the same car to a business meeting that was 120 miles away. Pam drove to the meeting at 60 miles per hour and Sue drove back, along the same route, at 50 miles per hour. How many more minutes did it take Sue to drive the distance than it took Pam?

○ 4
○ 10
○ 20
○ 24
○ 30

Here's How to Crack It

Since the problem deals with rates, you need a rate pie. In fact, since there is rate information for both Pam and Sue, you need two rate pies—one for Pam and one for Sue.

Pam

Sue

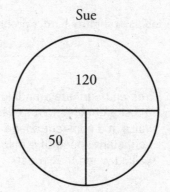

Once you draw the pies, you can transfer the information that you know to each pie. Since Pam and Sue drove along the same route, the distance is 120 miles for each pie. Pam's rate is 60 miles per hour and Sue's rate is 50 miles per hour. Transfer that information to the pies too.

To use the pie, remember that if you have the piece at the top and one of the pieces on the bottom, you divide to find the other piece. So, Pam's time is $120 \div 60 = 2$ and Sue's time is $120 \div 50 = 2\frac{2}{5}$. The pies made it easy to see how to find the time for each driver.

Pam

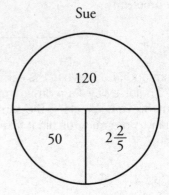

Sue

The problem asks how many more minutes it took Sue to drive the distance than it took Pam.

Start by subtracting $2\frac{2}{5} - 2 = \frac{2}{5}$ to find that it took Sue $\frac{2}{5}$ of an hour longer. Now, just convert to minutes: $60 \times \frac{2}{5} = 24$. The answer is (D).

———○———

Now, let's look at a slightly harder problem:

———○———

Easy Eliminations
Choices (A) and (E) are unlikely because they are numbers in the problem. Choice (B) is just 45 ÷ 5, which is Fred's time to walk the whole distance.

Fred and Sam are standing 45 miles apart and they start walking in a straight line toward each other at the same time. If Fred walks at a constant speed of 4 miles per hour and Sam walks at a constant speed of 5 miles per hour, how many miles has Sam walked when they meet?

○ 5
○ 9
○ 25
○ 30
○ 45

Here's How to Crack It

Since the problem is about rates, draw a rate pie. In this case, you may be wondering if you need one pie or two. You actually need one. Here's why: When dealing with rates, it is often helpful to think about what happens in a certain amount of time such as an hour. In one hour, Fred walks 4 miles and Sam walks 5 miles. Since they are walking toward each other in a straight line, they have covered 9 miles of the distance between them at the end of an hour. Wait! Nine miles in an hour? That means that their combined rate is 9 miles per hour. That's what goes on the pie for the rate.

Here's A Tip!
When two items travel in a straight line toward each other, you can add their rates.

The other piece that you could fill in on the pie from the problem was the distance, 45 miles. Then, use the pie to find that Fred and Sam walk for 5 hours before they meet. (Remember that you divide the top piece of the pie by one of the pieces on the bottom to find the other bottom piece.)

The problem wants to know how many miles Sam had walked when he met Fred. So, set up one more pie. This time you know Sam's rate, 5 miles per hour, and you know that he walked for 5 hours.

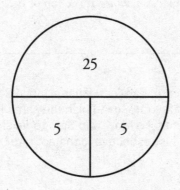

So, Sam walks 25 miles when he meets Fred. The answer is (C).

WORK PROBLEMS

Work problems are a type of rate problem. Rather than asking about a distance, these problems ask about a job or a part of a job. You can use a variation of the rate pie to solve these problems. Here's what it looks like:

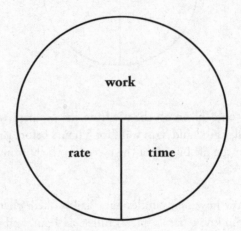

All that changes is that *work* replaces *distance* at the top of the pie. You use the **work pie** in the same way as the rate pie.

———————————○———————————

Working at a constant rate, Sam can finish a job in 3 hours. Mark, also working at a constant rate, can finish the same job in 12 hours. How many hours does it take Mark and Sam to finish the job if they work together each at his respective, constant rate?

○ 1

○ $2\frac{2}{5}$

○ $2\frac{5}{8}$

○ $3\frac{1}{4}$

○ 4

Since the problem mentions a job being completed, you can use a work pie. You'll actually need two pies for the first step of the problem since you'll want to find each worker's individual rate. Once you draw your pies, you can put each worker's time on the pie. You can also put 1 for the work since they each complete 1 job.

Sam

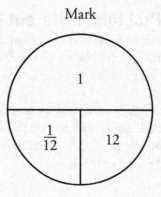 Mark

So, Sam's rate is $\frac{1}{3}$ and Mark's rate is $\frac{1}{12}$. What does that mean? Well, it means that Sam completes $\frac{1}{3}$ of the job every hour, while Mark completes $\frac{1}{12}$ of the job every hour.

To finish the problem, note that Mark and Sam work together. Since they are working together, you can combine their rates to find that they complete $\frac{1}{3} + \frac{1}{12} = \frac{5}{12}$ of the job every hour. When people work together, you can combine their rates. Now, set up one more work pie. Use 1 for the amount of work and $\frac{5}{12}$ for the rate.

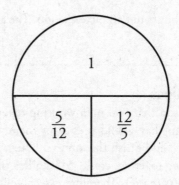

Divide the amount of work by the combined rate to find that the time to complete the job is $1 \div \frac{5}{12} = \frac{12}{5} = 2\frac{2}{5}$ hours. The correct answer is (B).

Same Problem, Different Approach

Another way to look at this problem is to realize that the actual job is never specified. But, wouldn't the problem be much easier to solve if you knew how many of something Sam and Mark needed to make? In other words, this problem can be approached as a Plug In.

Suppose that Sam and Mark were making widgets. Let's say that the complete job is to make 24 widgets. If Sam finishes the job in 3 hours, then he makes 8 widgets per hour. If Mark finishes the job in 12 hours, he makes 2 widgets per hour. Working together, they make 8 + 2 = 10 widgets per hour.

Now, let's set the last step up using a work pie.

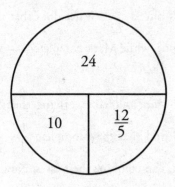

Again, it takes them $\frac{12}{5} = 2\frac{2}{5}$ hours to complete the job. The answer is (B).

Easy Eliminations

It stands to reason that two men working together would take less time to finish a job than they would if each of them worked alone. Because Sam, working alone, could finish the job in 3 hours, it must be true that the two of them, working together, could do it in less time. The answer to this question has to be less than 3. Therefore, we can eliminate (D) and (E).

Here's a slightly harder version of the previous problem:

Working at a constant rate, Sam can finish a job in 3 hours. Mark, also working at a constant rate, can finish the same job in 12 hours. If they work together for 2 hours, how many minutes will it take Sam to finish the job, working alone at his constant rate?

- ⬭　5
- ⬭　20
- ⬭　30
- ⬭　60
- ⬭　120

Here's How to Crack It

This problem starts in the same way so you can use the same work pies to find each worker's rate.

Sam

Mark

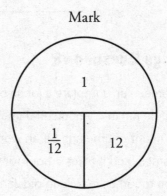

Now, you need a new pie. For this pie, you know the combined rate, $\frac{1}{3} + \frac{1}{12} = \frac{5}{12}$, and that they work together for two hours.

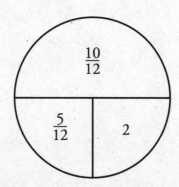

So, you now know that $\frac{5}{12} \times 2 = \frac{10}{12} = \frac{5}{6}$ of the job has been completed when Mark goes home. Sam must finish $\frac{1}{6}$ of the job on his own. Of course, you know Sam's rate, so just set up one last work pie.

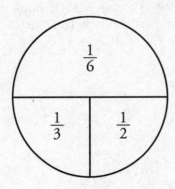

To find the time for Sam to finish the job, use the pie to find that $\frac{1}{6} \div \frac{1}{3} = \frac{1}{2}$, or 30 minutes. The correct answer is (C).

Challenge Question #6

James can complete a job in 6 hours and Sarah can complete the same job in $4\frac{1}{2}$ hours. If James works on the job alone for a certain amount of time and Sarah works on the job alone for half as long as James, and it takes 1 hour for them to complete the remainder of the job together, how long did James work on the job alone?

- ◯ 1 hour, 6 minutes
- ◯ 1 hour, 10 minutes
- ◯ 2 hours, 12 minutes
- ◯ 2 hours, 20 minutes
- ◯ 3 hours, 18 minutes

FUNCTIONS

You know you've hit a function problem by the sensation of panic and fear you get when you see some strange symbol (# or * or Δ) and say, "I studied for two months for this test and somehow managed to miss the part where they told me about # or * or Δ." Relax. Any strange-looking symbol on the GMAT is just a function, and on this test, functions are easy.

A function is basically a set of directions. Let's look at an example:

If $\Delta x = x$ for $x \geq 0$ and $2x$ for $x < 0$, $\dfrac{\Delta 30}{\Delta(-5)} =$

- ○ −12
- ○ −6
- ○ −3
- ○ 6
- ○ 30

Functions?
No Problem
If you can follow a recipe, you can do a GMAT function problem. Because function questions freak so many people out, they often show up in the medium to difficult area of a section. If you can become comfortable with function problems, you'll pick up a point on a question that you might otherwise feel tempted to guess on.

Here's How to Crack It

A function is basically a set of directions. In this case, the directions tell you what to do with the number that comes after the symbol Δ. If the number that follows the symbol is greater than or equal to 0, then the output of the function is just the number x. However, if the number that follows the symbol is negative, the output of the Δ function is $2x$. So, we can evaluate the given expression thus:

$$\frac{\Delta 30}{\Delta(-5)} = \frac{30}{2(-5)} = \frac{30}{-10} \text{ or } -3.$$ The answer is (C).

Mistakes of the Average Test Taker

The average test taker has no idea what to do with Δ, so she just ignores it. Because $\dfrac{30}{-5} = -6$, the average test taker picks (B). On the other hand, the average test taker might also think she can reduce functions. In other words, she might think she can do this:

$$\frac{\Delta 30}{\Delta(-5)} = \Delta(-6)$$

The function of −6 = −12, so she might select also select (A).

You may remember seeing a different notation for functions in school. The standard math notation for functions is $f(x)$—pronounced f of x—and the GMAT test writers will sometimes ask function questions using this notation too.

Let's look at an example.

For which of the following functions does $f(x) = f(-x)$ for all values of x ?

- ◯ $f(x) = x^3 + 3$
- ◯ $f(x) = -x$
- ◯ $f(x) = 2x + 3$
- ◯ $f(x) = -x^2 + 2$
- ◯ $f(x) = 5x - 4$

Here's How to Crack It

Plug in a value for x and use that value to see if $f(x) = f(-x)$ for each of the functions in the answer choices. So, for example, look at (A) if $x = 2$. Does $(2)^3 + 3 = (-2)^3 + 3$? No, so eliminate (A).

Only for (D) does $f(2) = f(-2)$. In this case, $f(2) = -(2)^2 + 2 = -2$ and $f(-2) = -(-2)^2 + 2 = -2$. So, (D) is the correct answer.

Challenge Question #7

For positive integers x, y, and z, the function $x * y * z$ means that $\frac{z}{x^y}$ is an integer, but $\frac{z}{x^{y+1}}$ is not. If $x * 2 * 144$, then which of the following is NOT a possible value of x ?

- ◯ 2
- ◯ 3
- ◯ 4
- ◯ 6
- ◯ 12

PROBABILITY

Probability, Part 1

Just the word is enough to cause math-phobes to run for the exits—but, at least as it appears on the GMAT, probability really isn't all that bad. Check out the easy example below:

> A fair, six-sided die with faces numbered one through six is rolled once. What is the probability that this roll results in a 2 ?

Well, of course, there's only one possibility of this happening, and there are six possible outcomes, so there's a one-in-six chance. In essence, this is all that probability is about. On the GMAT, probability is usually expressed as a fraction: The total number of possibilities is always the denominator. The number of possibilities that match what you want is the numerator. In the example above, that translates to $\frac{1}{6}$.

$$\text{Basic probability formula} = \frac{\text{number of outcomes you want}}{\text{total number of possible outcomes}}$$

Let's make this example a little harder:

> A fair, six-sided die with faces numbered one through six is rolled once. What is the probability that this roll results in either a 2 or a 3 ?

The total number of possible outcomes (the denominator) is still the same: 6. But the numerator is different now. There are two possibilities that would match what we want, so the numerator becomes 2. The probability is $\frac{2}{6}$, or $\frac{1}{3}$.

Let's make the example a little harder still.

> A fair, six-sided die with faces numbered one through six is rolled twice. What is the probability that both rolls result in a 2 ?

Obviously, the odds of this happening are much smaller. How do you figure out the probability of something happening over a series of events? To find the probability of a series of events, you multiply the probabilities of each of the individual events. Let's start with the first roll of the die. We already figured out that the probability of the die landing with its "2" side facing up on a single toss is $\frac{1}{6}$. Now, let's think about the second toss. Well, actually, the probability of this happening on the second toss is exactly the same: $\frac{1}{6}$.

However, to figure out the probability of the "2" side facing upward on *both* tosses, you multiply the first probability by the second probability: $\frac{1}{6} \times \frac{1}{6} = \frac{1}{36}$.

> The probability that A **and** B will both happen:
> p(A and B) = p(A) × p(B)

Here's an example of a moderately difficult GMAT problem.

There are 8 job applicants sitting in a waiting room—4 women and 4 men. If 2 of the applicants are selected at random, what is the probability that both will be women?

- ○ $\frac{1}{2}$
- ○ $\frac{3}{7}$
- ○ $\frac{1}{4}$
- ○ $\frac{3}{14}$
- ○ $\frac{1}{10}$

Let's take the first event in the series. The total number of possibilities for the first selection is 8, because there are 8 applicants in the room. Of those 8 people, 4 are women, so the probability that the first person chosen will be a woman is $\frac{4}{8}$, or $\frac{1}{2}$. You might think that the probability would be exactly the same for the second choice (in which case you would multiply $\frac{1}{2} \times \frac{1}{2}$ and choose (C)), but in fact, that's not true. Let's consider: The first woman has just left the room, and they are about to choose another applicant at random. How many total people are now in the room? Aha! Only 7. And how many of those 7 are women? Only 3. So the probability that the second choice will be a woman is actually only $\frac{3}{7}$, which is (B). But we aren't done yet. We have to figure out the probability that BOTH choices in this series of two choices will be women. The probability that the first will be a woman is $\frac{1}{2}$. The probability that the second will be a woman is $\frac{3}{7}$. The probability that they both will be women is $\frac{1}{2} \times \frac{3}{7}$, or $\frac{3}{14}$. The answer is (D).

Easy Eliminations

The GMAT test writers like to see if they can trick you into picking partial answers—i.e., numbers that you get in the course of solving a problem that are not quite the final answer. The probability that the first choice will be a woman is $\frac{1}{2}$, (A)—but does it feel like you've done enough work to "deserve" to get this problem right yet? Nope—this is only an intermediate step. The probability that the second choice will be a woman is $\frac{3}{7}$, (B). But again, this is just another intermediate step. Don't fall for these trick choices—cross off (A) and (B).

Probability, Part 2: One Thing or Another

So far, we've been dealing with the probability of one event happening and then another event happening (for example, in that last problem, the first event was choosing a female job applicant; the second event was choosing ANOTHER female job applicant). But what if you are asked to find the probability of either one thing OR another thing happening? To solve this type of problem, you simply add the probabilities. Note that pure versions of these "or" problems are incredibly rare on the GMAT. Understanding the idea can be helpful on other problems, however.

> The probability that A or B will happen: p(A or B) = p(A) + p(B).
> This is the formula used if the probabilities are mutually exclusive, that is, if they cannot happen together. Use this formula because **on the GMAT, probabilities are almost always mutually exclusive**. In case you're curious, the formula used to show the probability that A or B will happen, if the events are NOT mutually exclusive, is
> p(A or B) = p(A) + p(B) − p(A and B).

Here's an example:

―――――――――――○―――――――――――

Sally and Sam are watching a magician perform with 16 of their friends. If the magician chooses one audience member at random to assist with a trick, what is the probability that either Sally or Sam is chosen?

Here's How To Crack It

By this point, you should have no problem figuring out that the probability of Sally being chosen is $\frac{1}{18}$. And the probability of Sam being chosen? That's right: $\frac{1}{18}$. So what is the probability of Sally or Sam being chosen?

$$\frac{1}{18} + \frac{1}{18} = \frac{2}{18} \ or \ \frac{1}{9}$$

―――――――――――○―――――――――――

Probability, Part 3:
The Odds That Something Doesn't Happen

But what if you are asked to find the probability that something will NOT happen? Well, think of it this way: If the probability of snow is 70% or $\frac{7}{10}$, what's the probability that it won't snow? That's right: 30% or $\frac{3}{10}$. To figure out the probability that something won't happen, simply figure out the probability that it WILL happen and then subtract that fraction from 1.

$$p(\text{event happens}) + p(\text{event does NOT happen}) = 1$$

Here's an example:

───────────────○───────────────

Sally and Sam are watching a magician perform with 16 of their friends. If one audience member is chosen at random to assist with a trick, what is the probability that neither Sally nor Sam is chosen?

Here's How to Crack It

As we already know, the probability that Sally will be chosen is $\frac{1}{18}$. The probability that Sam will be chosen is also $\frac{1}{18}$. So what is the probability that neither Sally nor Sam will be chosen?

$$1 - \frac{2}{18} = \frac{16}{18} = \frac{8}{9}$$

───────────────○───────────────

Probability, Part 4:
The Odds That at Least One Thing Will Happen

What if the problem asks the probability of something happening at least once? To calculate the probability of at least one thing happening, just use this equation: The probability of what you WANT to happen plus the probability of what you DON'T want to happen equals one. Or, to put it another way:

$$p(\text{event happens}) = 1 - p(\text{event does NOT happen})$$

Here's an example:

Nine boys and nine girls are watching a magician perform. Four times during the performance a child is chosen at random to assist with a trick. If any of the children can be chosen to assist with each of the four tricks, what is the probability that at least one girl is chosen?

Here's How to Crack It

To find out the odds of at least one girl being chosen, let's begin by figuring out the odds that a girl isn't chosen. The magician will make a total of four choices. What are the odds that the magician will not pick a girl in the first round? If you said $\frac{9}{18}$ or $\frac{1}{2}$, you are doing just fine. And what are the odds that the magician will not pick a girl the second, third, and fourth round? Each time, the odds of not picking a girl stay the same, because the children are returned to the pool of possible candidates, so each time the odds will be $\frac{9}{18}$ or $\frac{1}{2}$. The probability of not picking a girl all four times is:

$$\frac{1}{2} \times \frac{1}{2} \times \frac{1}{2} \times \frac{1}{2} = \frac{1}{16}$$

But we aren't done. The probability of a girl being picked at least once is 1 minus the probability that she will not be picked. So the correct answer is:

$$1 - \frac{1}{16} = \frac{15}{16}$$

Challenge Question #8

If there are g girls and b boys on a team, and two members of the team are randomly selected, then what is the probability, in terms of g and b, that at least one selected player is a girl?

○ $\dfrac{g(g-1)}{(b+g)(b+g-1)}$

○ $\dfrac{b(b-1)}{(b+g)(b+g-1)}$

○ $\dfrac{2bg}{(b+g)(b+g-1)}$

○ $\dfrac{g(2b+g-1)}{(b+g)(b+g-1)}$

○ $\dfrac{b(2g+b-1)}{(b+g)(b+g-1)}$

PERMUTATIONS AND COMBINATIONS

In general, permutation and combination problems tend to show up as medium-hard to hard problems on the GMAT.

Here's a very simple example of a combination problem:

At a certain restaurant, a meal consists of one appetizer, one main course, and one dessert. If the restaurant has 2 appetizers, 3 main courses, and 5 desserts, then how many different meals could the restaurant serve?

○ 60
○ 30
○ 10
○ 6
○ 3

Here's How to Crack It

You could just carefully write down all the different combinations:

Shrimp cocktail with meatloaf with cherry pie
Shrimp cocktail with meatloaf with ice cream
Shrimp cocktail with meatloaf with…

You get the idea. But first of all, this is too time consuming, and second of all, there's a much easier way.

> For a problem that asks you to choose a number of items to fill specific spots, when each spot is filled from a different source, all you have to do is multiply the number of choices for each of the spots.

So, because there were 2 appetizers, 3 main courses, and 5 possible desserts, the total number of combinations of a full meal at this restaurant would be 2 × 3 × 5, or 30. The answer is (B).

Permutations: Single Source, Order Matters

The same principle applies when you're choosing from a group of similar items—with one slight wrinkle. Take a look at this easy permutation problem:

Three basketball teams play in a league against each other. At the end of the season, how many different ways could the 3 teams end up ranked against each other?

○ 1
○ 3
○ 6
○ 36
○ 72

Here's How to Crack It

You could just carefully write down all the different combinations. If we call the three teams A, B, and C, then here are the different ways they could end up in the standings:

ABC   ACB   BAC   BCA   CAB   CBA

But again, this approach is time consuming (even more so for more difficult problems). As you probably suspected, there's a simpler and faster way to solve this problem.

> For a problem that asks you to choose from the same source to fill specific spots, all you have to do is multiply the number of choices for each of the spots—but the number of choices keeps getting smaller.

Let's think for a moment about how many teams could possibly end up in first place. If you said 3, you're doing just fine.

Now, let's think about how many teams could finish second. Are there still 3 possibilities? Not really, because one team has already finished first. There are, in fact, only 2 possible teams that could finish second.

And finally, let's think about how many teams could finish third. In fact, there is only 1 team that could finish third.

To find the number of different ways these teams could end up in the rankings, just multiply the number of choices for first place (in this case, 3) times the number of choices for second place (in this case, 2) times the number of choices for third place (in this case, 1).

$$3 \times 2 \times 1 = 6$$

The correct answer is (C).

In general, no matter how many items there are to arrange, you can figure out the number of permutations of a group of n similar objects with the formula:

$$n(n - 1)(n - 2)\ldots \times 3 \times 2 \times 1, \text{ or } n!$$

So if there were 9 baseball teams, the total number of permutations of their standings would be $9 \times 8 \times 7 \times 6 \times 5 \times 4 \times 3 \times 2 \times 1$, also sometimes written as 9! If 4 sailboats sailed a race, the total number of permutations of the orders in which they could cross the finish line would be $4 \times 3 \times 2 \times 1$, also sometimes written as 4!

Single Source, Order Matters but Only for a Selection

The problems we've shown you so far were necessary to show you the concepts behind permutation problems—but were much too easy to be on the GMAT. Here's a problem that would be more likely to appear on the test:

---○---

Seven basketball teams play in a league against each other. At the end of the season, how many different arrangements are there for the top 3 teams in the rankings?

○   6
○   42
○   210
○   5,040
○ 50,450

Easy Eliminations

If you were to see this problem on the computer-adaptive section of the actual GMAT, you should first stop and give yourself a pat on the back, because it means you're doing pretty well—permutation and combination problems usually show up only among the more difficult problems. But after you've congratulated yourself, stop and think for a moment. Could the answer to this difficult problem simply be a matter of finding 7 × 6 × 5 × 4 × 3 × 2 × 1, (D)? Too easy. Because the question is asking for the permutations for only 3 of the 7 slots, the number must be less than that. So get rid of (D) and (E).

Here's How to Crack It

To find all the possible permutations of the top 3 out of 7 baseball teams, simply multiply the number of combinations for each spot in the standings. How many teams are possibilities for the first place slot? If you said 7, you're right. How about for the second slot? Well, one team is already occupying the first place slot, so there are only 6 contenders left. And for the third place slot? That's right: 5.

So, the correct answer is 7 × 6 × 5 = 210, or (C).

---○---

In general, no matter how many items there are to arrange, you can figure out the number of permutations of r objects chosen from a set of n objects with the formula:

$$n(n-1)(n-2) \ldots \times (n-r+1)$$

So if there were 9 baseball teams (n), the total number of permutations of the top 4 teams (r) would be $9 \times 8 \times 7 \times 6$. If 4 sailboats sailed a race (n), the total number of permutations of the first 3 boats to cross the finish line (r) would be $4 \times 3 \times 2$. Here is another way to write this same formula:

$$\frac{n!}{(n-r)!}$$

(where n = total items and r = the number selected)

Because $9 \times 8 \times 7 \times 6$ is the same as $\dfrac{9 \times 8 \times 7 \times 6 \times \cancel{5}!}{\cancel{5}!}$

Combinations: Single Source, Order Doesn't Matter

In the previous problems, the order in which the items are arranged actually matters to the problem. For example, if the order in which the three teams finish a season is Yankees, Red Sox, Orioles—that's entirely different than if the order were Red Sox, Yankees, Orioles, especially if you're from Boston.

But combination problems don't care about the order of the items.

Not Sure If It's a Permutation or a Combination Problem?
Here's a good clue:
Permutation problems usually ask for "arrangements."
Combination problems usually ask for "groups."

Six horses are running in a race. How many different groups of horses could make up the first 3 finishers?

○   6
○   18
○   20
○   120
○   720

Easy Eliminations

If we cared about the order in which the top 3 horses finished the race, then the answer would be the number of permutations: $6 \times 5 \times 4$, or 120. But in this case, we care only about the number of *unique* permutations, and that means the number will be smaller because we don't have to count the set of, for example, (Secretariat, Seattle Slew, and Affirmed) and the set of (Seattle Slew, Secretariat, and Affirmed) as two different permutations. If the correct answer must be smaller than 120, then we can eliminate (D) and (E)—they're too big.

Here's How to Crack It

To find the number of combinations, first find the number of permutations. If 6 horses run in the race, and we are interested in the top 3 finishers, then the number of permutations would be 6 × 5 × 4, or 120. But if we don't care about the order in which they finished, then a bunch of these 120 permutations turn out to be duplicates.

How many? Let's think of one of those permutations. Let's say the first 3 finishers were Secretariat, Seattle Slew, and Affirmed. How many different ways could we arrange these 3 horses? If you said 6, you're thinking like a permutation master. There are 3!, or 3 × 2 × 1 permutations of any 3 objects. So, of those 120 permutations of the top 3 horses, each combination is being counted 3!, or 6 times. To find the number of combinations, we need to divide 120 by 6. The correct answer is (C).

In general, no matter how many items there are to arrange, you can figure out the number of combinations of r objects chosen from a set of n objects with the formula:

$$\frac{n(n-1)(n-2)...\times(n-r+1)}{r!}$$

So if there were 9 baseball teams, the total number of combinations of the top 4 teams would be:

$$\frac{9 \times 8 \times 7 \times 6}{4 \times 3 \times 2 \times 1}$$

Another way to write this same formula is:

$$\frac{n!}{r!(n-r)!}$$

because $\dfrac{9 \times 8 \times 7 \times 6}{4 \times 3 \times 2 \times 1}$ is the same as $\dfrac{9 \times 8 \times 7 \times 6 \times \cancel{5}!}{(4 \times 3 \times 2 \times 1) \times \cancel{5}!}$

Challenge Question #9

On a certain two-part test, a student must choose one of 4 short essays and one of 2 long essays in Part One, and then choose one of x short essays and one of y long essays in Part Two. If there is a total of 144 different lineups of essays that the student could choose, and the ratio of available long essays to short essays remains constant in both parts of the test, then what is the value of x ?

- ○ 3
- ○ 6
- ○ 8
- ○ 9
- ○ 12

DRILL 8 (Applied Arithmetic)

The answers to these questions can be found in Part VI.

1. If Teena is driving at 55 miles per hour and is currently 7.5 miles behind Joe, who is driving at 40 miles per hour in the same direction, then in how many minutes will Teena be 15 miles ahead of Joe ?

- ○ 15
- ○ 60
- ○ 75
- ○ 90
- ○ 105

2. If the operation Δ is defined by $a \, \Delta \, b = \dfrac{(b-a)^2}{a^2}$ for all numbers a and b, and $a \neq 0$, then $-1 \, \Delta \, (1 \, \Delta \, -1) =$

- ○ −1
- ○ 0
- ○ 1
- ○ 9
- ○ 25

3. At a local office, each trainee can stuff $\frac{2}{3}$ as many envelopes per day as a full time worker. If there are $\frac{2}{5}$ as many trainees as there are full time workers, then what fraction of all the envelopes stuffed in a day did the trainees stuff?

   ◯ $\frac{2}{19}$

   ◯ $\frac{2}{17}$

   ◯ $\frac{4}{19}$

   ◯ $\frac{4}{17}$

   ◯ $\frac{4}{15}$

4. A focus group is currently made up of x men and y women. If 2 men and 4 women are added to the group, and if one person is selected at random from the larger focus group, then what is the probability that a man is selected?

   ◯ $\frac{x}{x + 2}$

   ◯ $\frac{x}{x + y}$

   ◯ $\frac{x + 2}{x + y + 2}$

   ◯ $\frac{y + 4}{x + y + 6}$

   ◯ $\frac{x + 2}{x + y + 6}$

Summary

- Rate problems and work problems can be solved using your handy rate or work pies.

- The key to work problems is to think about how much of the job can be done in one hour. But remember, it is often easier to simply Plug In.

- A function problem may have strange symbols like Δ or *, but it is really just a set of directions.

- Probability problems can be solved by putting the total number of possibilities in the denominator and the number of possibilities that match what you are looking for in the numerator.

- Permutation and combination problems ask you to choose or arrange a group of objects.
  - To choose a number of items to fill specific spots, when each spot is filled from a different source, all you have to do is multiply the number of choices for each of the spots.
  - To choose from a set of n objects from the same source to fill specific spots, when order matters, all you have to do is multiply the number of choices for each of the spots—but the number of choices keeps getting smaller, according to the formula:

    $n(n-1)(n-2)\ldots \times 3 \times 2 \times 1$, or $n!$

  - To find the number of permutations of r objects chosen from a set of n objects, when order matters, use the formula: $n(n-1)(n-2)\ldots \times (n-r+1)$, also expressed as $\dfrac{n!}{(n-r)!}$.

  - To find the number of combinations of r objects chosen from a set of n objects, use the formula: $\dfrac{n(n-1)(n-2)\ldots \times (n-r+1)}{r!}$

Chapter 13
Geometry

The geometry tested on the GMAT is but a small fraction of the geometry you probably studied during high school. In this chapter, we cover the geometry the test-makers actually test: angles, triangles, circles, quadrilaterals, volume, surface area, and coordinate geometry.

Fewer than one-quarter of the problems on the computer-adaptive math section of the GMAT will involve geometry. And while this tends to be the math subject most people remember least from high school, the good news is that the GMAT tests only a small portion of the geometry you used to know. It will be relatively easy to refresh your memory.

The bad news is that unlike some standardized tests, such as the SAT, the GMAT does not provide you with the formulas and terms you'll need to solve the problems. You'll have to memorize them.

The first half of this chapter will show you how to eliminate answer choices on certain geometry problems without using traditional geometry. The second half will review all the geometry you need to know in order to answer the problems that must be solved using more traditional methods.

CRAZY ANSWERS

Eliminating choices that don't make sense has already proven to be a valuable technique on arithmetic and algebra questions. On geometry questions, you can develop this technique into an art form. The reason for this is that many geometry problems come complete with a diagram *drawn to scale*.

Most people get so caught up in solving a geometry problem geometrically that they forget to look at the diagram to see whether their answer is reasonable.

Crazy Answers on Easy Questions

How big is angle *x*?

Obviously, you don't know exactly how big this angle is, but it would be easy to compare it with an angle whose measure you *do* know exactly. Let's compare it with a 90-degree angle:

Angle *x* is less than 90 degrees. How much less? It looks as though it's about half of a 90-degree angle, or 45 degrees. Now look at the following problem that asks about the same angle, *x*.

In the figure above, if *BC* = *CD* and angle *ADC* = 90 degrees, then what is the value of *x* ?

○　45
○　50
○　70
○　75
○　100

Easy Eliminations

We've already decided that angle *x* is less than 90 degrees, which means that (E) can be eliminated. How much less is it? Well, we estimated before that it was about half, which rules out (C) and (D) as well.

There is another way to eliminate (C) and (D). We can compare angle *x* with the other marked angle in the problem—angle *DBC*. If the answer to this problem is (C), then angle *x* should look like angle *DBC*. Does it? No. Angle *x* looks a little bit smaller than angle *DBC*, which means that both (C) and (D) can be eliminated.

Eliminating crazy answers will prevent you from making careless mistakes on easy problems.

Crazy Answers on Difficult Questions

If it's important to cross off crazy answer choices on easy questions, it's even more important to eliminate crazy answer choices when you're tackling an average or difficult geometry problem. On these problems, you may not know how to find the answer geometrically, and even if you do, you could still fall victim to one of the traps the test writers have placed in your path. Take a look at the following difficult geometry problem:

In the figure above, the circle with center *O* is inscribed inside square *ABCD* as shown. What is the ratio of the area of circle *O* to the area of square *ABCD* ?

○ $\dfrac{\pi}{2}$

○ $\dfrac{4}{\pi}$

○ $\dfrac{\pi}{3}$

○ $\dfrac{\pi}{4}$

○ $\dfrac{\pi}{5}$

Easy Eliminations

Let's say that you knew how to do this problem, but it's near the end of the section and you don't have enough time to do it. Let's see whether you can eliminate any of the answer choices just by looking at the diagram and using some common sense.

The problem asks you for the ratio of the area of the circle to the area of the square. Just by looking at the diagram, you can tell that the circle is smaller than the square. The correct answer to this question has to be the ratio of a smaller number to a bigger number. Let's look at the answer choices.

In (A), the ratio is π over 2. An approximate value of π is 3, so this really reads $\frac{3}{2}$.

Is this the ratio of a smaller number to a bigger number? Just the opposite. Therefore, (A) is a crazy answer. Eliminate it.

In (B), the ratio is 4 over π. This really reads $\frac{4}{3}$.

Is this the ratio of a smaller number to a bigger number? No. Choice (B) is a crazy answer. Eliminate it.

In (C), the ratio is π over 3. This really reads $\frac{3}{3}$.

Is this the ratio of a smaller number to a bigger number? No. Choice (C) is a crazy answer. Eliminate it.

Choices (D) and (E) both contain ratios of smaller numbers to bigger numbers, so they're both still possibilities. However, we've eliminated three of the answer choices without doing any math. If you know how to solve the problem geometrically, then proceed. If not, guess and move on. (By the way, we will show you how to solve this problem using geometry later in the chapter.)

The Basic Tools

In eliminating crazy answers, it helps to have the following approximations memorized.

$$\pi \approx 3$$
$$\sqrt{1} = 1$$
$$\sqrt{2} \approx 1.4$$
$$\sqrt{3} \approx 1.7$$
$$\sqrt{4} = 2$$

It's also useful to have a feel for the way certain common angles look:

A Note About Measuring:
Remember that measuring a diagram is not considered cheating. If a diagram in the Problem Solving format does not have the words "not drawn to scale," then it's fair game to use a pen or pencil and measure it!

Getting More Precise

When a geometry problem contains a diagram that's drawn to scale, you can get even more precise in eliminating wrong answer choices.

How? By measuring the diagram.

Look at the problem below:

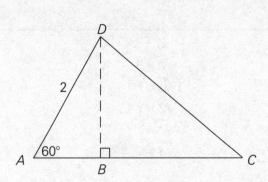

In the figure above, if a line segment connecting points B and D is perpendicular to AC and the area of triangle ADC is $\dfrac{3\sqrt{3}}{2}$, then $BC =$

- ○ $\sqrt{2}$
- ○ $\sqrt{3}$
- ○ 2
- ○ $3\sqrt{3}$
- ○ 6

Here's How to Crack It

Practice measuring the diagram with your pen or pencil. If you measure carefully, you'll notice that the distance between A and D is the same as the distance between B and C—exactly 2. Let's look at the answer choices. Because you memorized the values we told you to memorize earlier, you know that (A) is equal to 1.4. Eliminate it. Choice (B) is equal to 1.7. This is close enough for us to hold on to it while we look at the other choices. Choice (C) is exactly what we're looking for—2. Choice (D) is 3 times 1.7, which equals 5.1. This is much too large. Choice (E) is even larger. Eliminate (D) and (E). We're down to (B) and (C). The correct answer is (C). By the way, we'll show you how to do this problem geometrically later on the chapter.

Three Important Notes

1. Diagrams in questions using the Problem Solving format are drawn to scale (unless otherwise indicated).
2. Diagrams marked "not drawn to scale" cannot be measured. In fact, the drawings in these problems are often purposely misleading to the eye.
3. Data Sufficiency geometry diagrams have their own rules, which we will discuss in Chapter 14.

What Should I Do if There Is No Diagram?

Draw one. It's always difficult to imagine a geometry problem in your head. The first thing you should do with any geometry problem that doesn't have a diagram is sketch it out in your scratch booklet. And when you draw the diagram, try to draw it to scale. That way, you'll be in a position to estimate.

> **Geometry Hint**
> If there's no diagram, draw one yourself.

What Should I Do if the Diagram Is Not Drawn to Scale?

The same thing you would do if there were no diagram at all—draw it yourself. Draw it as accurately as possible so you'll be able to see what a realistic answer should be.

Basic Principles: Fundamentals of GMAT Geometry

The techniques outlined above will enable you to eliminate many incorrect choices on geometry problems. In some cases, you'll be able to eliminate every choice but one. However, there will be some geometry problems in which you will need geometry. Fortunately, GMAC chooses to test only a small number of concepts.

For the sake of simplicity, we've divided GMAT geometry into six basic topics:

1. degrees and angles
2. triangles
3. circles
4. rectangles, squares, and other four-sided objects
5. solids and volume
6. coordinate geometry

> **The 180° Rule, Part I**
> When you see a geometry problem that asks about angles, always look to see if two angles form a line, which tells you that the total of the two angles is 180 degrees. This is often the crucial starting point on the road to the solution. The test writers like to construct problems in such a way that it is very easy to miss this.

DEGREES AND ANGLES

There are 360 degrees in a circle. No matter how large or small a circle is, it still has precisely 360 degrees. If you drew a circle on the ground and then walked a quarter of the distance around it, you would have traveled 90 degrees of that circle. If you walked halfway around the circle, you would have traveled 180 degrees of it.

An angle is formed when two line segments extend from a common point. If you think of that point as the center of a circle, the measure of the angle is the number of degrees enclosed by the lines when they pass through the edge of the circle.

A line is just a 180-degree angle.

ℓ is the symbol for a line. A line can be referred to as ℓ or by naming two points on that line. For example, in the diagram below, both points A and B are on the line ℓ. This line could also be called line AB. Also, the part of the line that is between points A and B is called a line segment. A and B are the end points of the line segment.

If a line is intersected by another line, as in the diagram below, angle *x* and angle *y* add up to one straight line, or 180 degrees. So, for example, if you know that angle *x* equals 120 degrees, you can find the measure of angle *y* by subtracting 120 degrees from 180 degrees. Thus, angle *y* would equal 60 degrees.

Note that in the diagram above, angle *x* could also be called angle *ABC*, with *B* being the point in the middle.

When two lines intersect—as in the diagram below—four angles are formed. The four angles are indicated by letters.

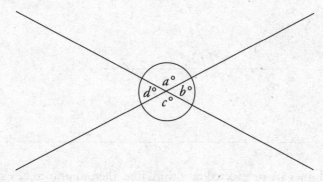

The four angles add up to 360 degrees (remember the circle).

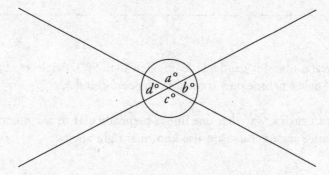

$a° + b° + c° + d° = 360$ degrees. Angle *a* and angle *b*, because they form a straight line, are equal to 180 degrees. Angle *b* and angle *c* also form a straight line, as do *c* + *d* and *d* + *a*. Angles that are opposite each other are called *vertical angles* and have the same number of degrees. For example, in the diagram above, angle *a* is equal to angle *c*. Angle *d* is equal to angle *b*.

Therefore, when two lines intersect, there appear to be four different angles, but there are really only two:

Two lines in the same plane are said to be parallel if they extend infinitely in both directions without intersecting. The symbol for parallel is ∥.

Look at the diagram below:

When two parallel lines are intersected by a third line, there appear to be eight different angle measurements, but there are really only two.

There is a big one (greater than 90°) and a little one (less than 90°). Angle *a* (a big one) is equal to angles *c, e,* and *g*. Angle *b* (a little one) is equal to angles *d, f,* and *h*.

If two lines intersect in such a way that one line is perpendicular to the other, all the angles formed will be 90-degree angles. These are also known as right angles:

Angles *a*, *b*, *c*, and *d* each equal 90 degrees. The little box at the intersection of the two lines is the symbol for a right angle.

Let's practice on a problem:

In the figure above, what is the value of *x* ?

○ 10
○ 15
○ 20
○ 30
○ 40

Here's How to Crack It

On a GMAT geometry problem, you may not know exactly how to solve at first glance, but there is almost always something you can do to get started. Did you notice that 5*y* and *y* together make up a straight line? In other words, 6*y* = 180 degrees. Noticing this is the key to solving the problem. If 6*y* = 180 degrees, then *y* equals 30 degrees. You might be tempted to pick (D), but remember—that we're looking for the value of *x*, not the value for *y*. Opposite angles formed by two straight lines are always equal, so *y* is equal to 3*x*. Therefore, 3*x* also equals 30 degrees, and the correct answer to this problem is (A), 10 degrees.

DRILL 9 (Angles and Lengths)

In the following figures, find numbers for all the variables. The answers to these problems can be found in Part VI.

1.

2.

3.

4.   If a driver has traveled 270 degrees around a circular race track, what fractional part of the track has he driven?

A real GMAT angle problem might look like this:

Note: Figure not drawn to scale.

5.   In the figure above, if $\ell_1 \parallel \ell_2$, then which of the following angles must be equivalent?

    ◯ a and b
    ◯ g and f
    ◯ d and e
    ◯ a and d
    ◯ f and d

You might see a very straightforward Data Sufficiency problem like this on the GMAT:

6.   What is the degree measure of angle x ?

    (1)   Angle $y = 40$ degrees.

    (2)   Angle x and angle y form a straight line.

Challenge Question #10

In the figure above, what is the value of z ?

- ○ 40
- ○ 45
- ○ 50
- ○ 55
- ○ 65

TRIANGLES

A triangle is a three-sided figure that contains three interior angles. The sum of the degree measures of the three angles in a triangle is 180 degrees. Several kinds of triangles appear on the GMAT:

$$AB = BC = CA$$
$$a = b = c = 60°$$

The 180° Rule, Part II
When a question involving angles has a triangle or several triangles in it, remember that the interior angles of a triangle add up to 180 degrees. Apply that rule in every possible way you can. It is one of the things that the GMAT writers love to test most.

An **equilateral triangle** has three sides that are equal in length. Because the angles opposite equal sides are also equal, all three angles in an equilateral triangle are equal.

An **isosceles triangle** has two sides that are equal in length. The angles opposite the two equal sides are also equal.

$$AB = AC$$
$$b = c$$

A **right triangle** has one interior angle that is equal to 90 degrees. The longest side of a right triangle (the one opposite the 90-degree angle) is called the *hypotenuse*.

hypotenuse

Triangles
Triangles are by far the test writers' favorite geometric shape. If you get stuck on a geometry problem that doesn't have triangles in it, ask yourself: Can the figure in this problem be divided into triangles (especially right triangles) that I can work with? This will sometimes be the key to the solution.

Everything Else You Need to Know About Triangles

1. The sides of a triangle are in the same proportion as its angles. For example, in the triangle below, which is the longest side?

The longest side is opposite the largest angle. The longest side in the triangle above is *AB*. The next longest side would be *AC*.

2.   One side of a triangle can never be longer than the sum of the lengths of the other two sides of the triangle, or less than their difference. Why? Look at the diagrams below:

At the point where angle *ACB* = 180 degrees, this figure ceases to be a triangle. Angle *ACB* becomes 180 degrees when side *AB* equals the sum of the other two sides, in this case 6 + 8. Side *AB* can never quite reach 14.

By the same token, if we make angle *ACB* smaller and smaller, at some point, when angle *ACB* = 0 degrees, the figure also ceases to be a triangle. Angle *ACB* becomes 0 degrees when side *AB* equals the difference of the other two sides, in this case 8 – 6. So *AB* can never quite reach 2.

3.   The *perimeter* of a triangle is the sum of the lengths of the three sides.

perimeter = 18

4.   The *area* of a triangle is equal to $\dfrac{height \times base}{2}$. By definition, the base and height must be perpendicular to each other.

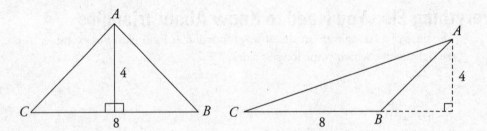

In both of the above triangles, the area = $\dfrac{4 \times 8}{2}$ = 16.

In a right triangle, the height also happens to be one of the sides of the triangle:

5. Don't expect triangles to be right side up:

This is an isosceles triangle.   The area of this triangle is
$$A = \frac{9 \times 4}{2}, \text{ or } 18.$$

6. In a right triangle, the square of the hypotenuse equals the sum of the squares of the other two sides. In the triangle below:

$$a^2 + b^2 = c^2$$

This is called the **Pythagorean Theorem**. The test writers love to test this theorem, but usually you won't actually have to make use of it if you've memorized a few of the most common right-triangle proportions.

The Pythagorean triangle that comes up most frequently on the GMAT is one that has sides of lengths 3, 4, and 5, or multiples of those numbers. Look at the following examples:

Pythagoras's Other Theorem
Pythagoras also developed a theory about the transmigration of souls. So far, this theory has not been proven.

$$3^2 + 4^2 = 5^2$$
$$9 + 16 = 25$$

$$6^2 + 8^2 = 10^2$$
$$36 + 64 = 100$$

Pythagorean Triples

The right triangle in the ratio 3 : 4 : 5 is the most common Pythagorean triple, but it's not the only one that shows up on the GMAT. Here are the three triples you need to know:

$$3 : 4 : 5$$
$$5 : 12 : 13$$
$$7 : 24 : 25$$

There are two other kinds of right triangles that GMAC loves to test. These are a little complicated to remember, but they come up so often that they're worth memorizing.

7. A right isosceles triangle always has proportions in the ratio $x : x : x\sqrt{2}$. This kind of triangle may also be referred to as a 45-45-90 right triangle.

     For example:

8. The second special right triangle is called the **30-60-90** right triangle. The ratio between the lengths of the sides in a 30-60-90 triangle is constant. If you know the length of any of the sides, you can find the lengths of the others. The ratio of the sides is always $x : x\sqrt{3} : 2x$.

How to Label a 30-60-90 Triangle

Remembering how to label the 1, 2, $\sqrt{3}$ sides of a 30-60-90 triangle is easy if you remind yourself that the largest side goes opposite the largest angle and the smallest side opposite the smallest angle, *and* if you remind yourself that $\sqrt{3}$ is roughly 1.7, okay?

That is, if the shortest side is length *x*, then the hypotenuse is 2*x*, and the remaining side is $x\sqrt{3}$.

Try this problem:

In △*ABC* shown above, if ∠*CAB* equals 30°, then what is the area of the triangle?

- ○ 2
- ○ $2\sqrt{2}$
- ○ $2\sqrt{3}$
- ○ $3\sqrt{2}$
- ○ 4

Here's How to Crack It

As with all geometry problems, even if you aren't exactly sure how to solve, there may be something you can do to get started—always half the battle. In this case, since we know that △*ABC* is a right triangle, and the problem tells you that ∠*CAB* equals 30°, do we know the value of ∠*ACB*? We do—it must be 60° (since there are a total of 180 degrees in a triangle). Because this is a 30-60-90 triangle (which always has sides in proportion of *x*, 2*x*, and *x*$\sqrt{3}$), and the diagram gives us the measurement of one of those sides, we actually know the measurement of all sides: 2, 2$\sqrt{3}$, and 4. To find the area, we simply multiply the base times the height and divide by 2:

$A = \dfrac{2 \times 2\sqrt{3}}{2} = 2\sqrt{3}$, and the answer is (C).

DRILL 10 (Triangles)

Find the value of the variables in the following problems. The answers can be found in Part VI.

1.

2.

3.

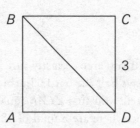

4. What value must *x* be less than in the triangle above? What value must *x* be greater than?

5. In square *ABCD* above, what is the length of line segment *BD* ?

6. In the triangle above, what is the length of the line segment *BC* ?

A real GMAT triangle problem might look like this:

Note: Figure not drawn to scale.

7. In the diagram above, if the area of triangle *LNO* is 32, then what is the area of triangle *LMN* ?

○ 24

○ $24\sqrt{2}$

○ $24\sqrt{3}$

○ 32

○ 48

You might see a Data Sufficiency problem like this on the GMAT:

8. In triangle *ABC* shown above, what is the value of *x* ?

(1) $y = 80$

(2) $AB = BC$

Challenge Question #11

In triangle *RST*, shown above, ∠*RTS* = 30° and ∠*RST* = 15°. What is the length of *ST* ?

- ○ 6
- ○ 12
- ○ 24
- ○ 36
- ○ 72

CIRCLES

A line segment whose endpoints lie on a circle is called a **chord**. The distance from the center of the circle to any point on the circle is called the **radius**. The distance from one point on the circle through the center of the circle to another point on the circle is called the **diameter**. The diameter is equal to twice the radius.

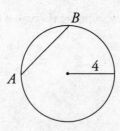

radius = 4

diameter = 8

AB is a chord.

The **circumference** (the length of the entire outer edge of the circle) = $2\pi r$ or πd.

The rounded portion of the circle between points *A* and *B* is called an **arc**.

The **area** of a circle = πr^2.

A circle cut in half by a diameter is called a **semicircle**.

A triangle is said to be **inscribed** inside a semicircle when one of its sides is the diameter of the circle itself, with the two other sides meeting at any point on the circle. A triangle inscribed inside a semicircle is always a **right triangle**.

Let's try a circle problem:

If the circle above has center *Y* and area 4π, then what is the perimeter of triangle *XYZ* ?

○ 2
○ 2π
○ 4
○ 6
○ 6π

Here's How to Crack It

As always, the solution to this problem will probably only become apparent once you've started doing the problem. The only apparent information you've been given: the area of the circle, 4π. Since the formula for the area of a circle is πr^2, set that equal to 4π. Can you figure out what *r* equals? That's right, 2. And since both sides *XY* and *YZ* are radii of the circle, they must both equal 2. To find the perimeter of the triangle, the last thing we need to do is find the length of *XZ*. You might not think that you know what *XZ* equals, but the diagram tells us that angle *XYZ* equals 60 degrees. Since we know sides *xy* and *yz* are equal, that means that this triangle must be equilateral: all three sides have the same length, 2. Therefore, the perimeter of triangle *XYZ* is 6, and the answer is (D).

DRILL 11 (Circles)

Answer the following questions. The answers can be found in Part VI.

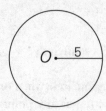

1. In the circle above with center O, what is the area of the circle? What is the circumference?

2. If the area of a circle is 36π, what is the circumference?

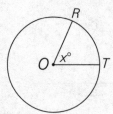

3. In the circle above with center O, if arc RT is equal to $\frac{1}{6}$ of the circumference, what is the value of x ?

A real GMAT circle problem might look like this:

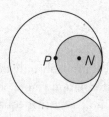

4. In the figure above, P is the center of the larger circle, and N is the center of the smaller, shaded circle. If the radius of the smaller circle is 5, what is the area of the unshaded region?

   ○ 100π
   ○ 75π
   ○ 25π
   ○ 20π
   ○ 10π

You might see a Data Sufficiency problem like this on the GMAT:

5. What is the area of circle *P* ?

   (1)   The diameter of circle *Q* is 6.

   (2)   The radius of circle *Q* is twice the radius of circle *P*.

RECTANGLES, SQUARES, AND OTHER FOUR-SIDED OBJECTS

A four-sided figure is called a **quadrilateral**. The perimeter of any four-sided object is the sum of the lengths of its sides. A **rectangle** is a quadrilateral whose four interior angles are each equal to 90 degrees. Opposite sides of a rectangle are always equal.

perimeter = 22   perimeter = 22

The area of a rectangle is *length* × *width*. The area of the rectangle above is therefore 3 × 8, or 24.

A **square** is a rectangle whose four sides are all equal in length. The *perimeter* of a square is therefore just four times the length of one side. The *area* of a square is the *length* of one of its sides squared. For example:

perimeter = 4 × 5 = 20

area = 5 × 5 = 25

A **parallelogram** is a quadrilateral in which the two pairs of opposite sides are parallel to each other and equal to each other, and in which opposite angles are equal to each other. A rectangle is obviously a parallelogram, but so is a figure like this:

Angle ADC = angle ABC, and angle DAB = angle DCB.

The area of a parallelogram equals *base × height*.

The area of parallelogram $ABCD$ = 8 × 2 = 16. (If you are having trouble picturing this, imagine cutting off the triangular region ADE and sticking it onto the other end of the figure. What you get is a rectangle with dimensions 8 by 2.)

SOLIDS, VOLUME, AND SURFACE AREA

The GMAT will occasionally ask you to find the *volume* or *surface area* of a three-dimensional object.

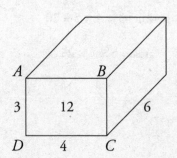

The volume of the *rectangular solid* above is equal to the area of the rectangle *ABCD* times the depth of the solid—in this case, 12 × 6, or 72. Another way to think of it is *length × width × depth* = 3 × 4 × 6, or 72.

The volume of a *cube* is equal to the area of the square *WXYZ* times the depth of the cube, or again, *length × width × depth*. In the case of a cube, the length, width, and depth are all the same, so the volume of a cube is always the length of any side, cubed. The volume of this cube is 4 × 4 × 4, or 64.

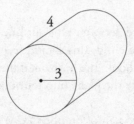

The volume of a *cylinder* is equal to the *area* of the circular base times the *depth*. The area of this circle is 9π. Thus, the volume of the cylinder is 36π.

You may need to find the surface area of a solid. Surface area is just the sum of the areas of all the two-dimensional outer surfaces of the object. So, for example, the surface area of a rectangular solid is the sum of the areas of the solid's six faces. Take a look at how you'd calculate the surface area of the rectangular solid:

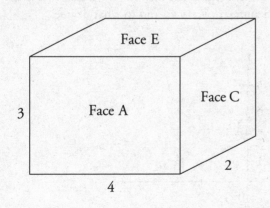

Face A: 3 × 4 = 12

Face B: 3 × 4 = 12
(opposite Face A)

Face C: 3 × 2 = 6

Face D: 3 × 2 = 6
(opposite Face C)

Face E: 4 × 2 = 8

Face F: 4 × 2 = 8
(opposite Face E)

Surface Area: = 52

COORDINATE GEOMETRY

A coordinate plane, like the one above, lets you plot out lines and objects in two dimensions. If you played the game Battleship as a child, this should feel very familiar—even if you don't remember learning about it in high school. The horizontal line is called the *x*-axis. The vertical line is called the *y*-axis. The axes divide the plane into four quadrants, as shown above.

Every point on the plane has an ordered pair of numbers (*x*, *y*) that describes it. For example, in the plane above, point *a* is represented by the ordered pair (2, 1), which simply means, starting from 0, count over 2 to the right along the *x*-axis and then up 1 along the *y*-axis. Point *b* is represented by the ordered pair (−4, 3), which simply means, starting from 0, count over −4 (to the left) along the *x*-axis and up 3 along the *y*-axis.

Any straight line on this plane can be described by the equation $y = mx + b$, where *b* is the *y*-intercept (the point at which the line crosses the *y*-axis) and *m* is the slope of the line, and *x* and *y* are the coordinates of some point on that line. Slope is the measure of steepness of a line, and it defines whether the line is diagonal, horizontal, or vertical, and to what degree.

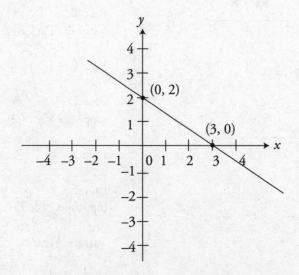

For example, the *y*-intercept of the line shown above is 2 (that's where it crosses the *y*-axis). You can find the slope of any line if you know any two points on that line:

$$\text{slope} = \frac{\text{the difference in the } y\text{-coordinates}}{\text{the difference in the } x\text{-coordinates}}$$

For example, the slope of the line above is

$$\frac{2-0}{0-3} \text{ or } -\frac{2}{3}$$

So the equation of this line can be written as $y = -\frac{2}{3}x + 2$.

Let's see how this might show up in a fairly tough GMAT problem:

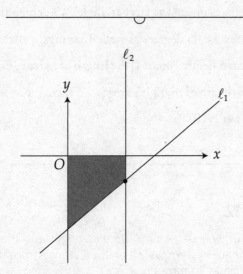

In the coordinate plane above, if the equation of ℓ_1 is $y = x - 3$ and the equation of ℓ_2 is $x = 2$, then what is the area of the shaded region?

- ○ 3
- ○ 4
- ○ $3\sqrt{2}$
- ○ 4.5
- ○ 5

Here's How to Crack It

First, draw your own coordinate axes. The equation for ℓ_1 is $y = x - 3$, which means that the y-intercept is –3 and the slope is 1. That means the bottommost point of the large triangle is point (0, –3), and the rightmost point of the large triangle is (3, 0). What we have here is an upside-down right triangle with base 3 and height 3. The area of this entire triangle is $\frac{b \times h}{2}$ or $\frac{9}{2}$, which is (D), but we aren't done yet. Now we have to find the area of the small triangle and subtract it from the large triangle. What remains will be the shaded region.

The equation for ℓ_2 is $x = 2$, which means that ℓ_2 is a vertical line running parallel to the y-axis. The small triangle therefore must also be an upside-down right triangle. Its base is 1 (from point (2, 0) to point (3, 0)). Eyeballing it, you might decide that its height is 1 too. The way to know for sure is to realize that these two right triangles (the small one and the large one) share an angle formed by the x-axis and ℓ_1. The large triangle is isosceles, so its angles must measure 90-45-45. And since the small triangle shares one of the large triangle's 45-degree angles, we know that the small triangle's third angle must be 45 degrees as well. That means that the small triangle is an isosceles triangle, too, and that its height equals 1, the length of its base. Equipped with this information, we can calculate that the small triangle's area is $\frac{1}{2}$. Thus, the area of the shaded region is $\frac{9}{2} - \frac{1}{2}$, or 4. The correct answer is (B).

Challenge Question #12

A circle with center (h, k), in which $k = 2h$, lies tangent to the y-axis in in the (x, y) coordinate system. What is the distance from the origin to the center of the circle, in terms of k ?

- ○ $\dfrac{k\sqrt{3}}{2}$
- ○ $\dfrac{k\sqrt{5}}{2}$
- ○ k
- ○ $k\sqrt{3}$
- ○ $k\sqrt{5}$

GMAT GEOMETRY: ADVANCED PRINCIPLES

All geometry problems (even easy ones) involve more than one step. Remember the first problem we looked at in this chapter?

In the figure above, if $BC = CD$ and angle ADC = 90 degrees, then what is the value of x ?

- ○ 45
- ○ 50
- ○ 70
- ○ 75
- ○ 100

Here's How to Crack It

Just by looking at the figure, we were able to eliminate (C), (D), and (E). Now let's solve the problem using geometry. The figure includes two—actually three—different triangles: *ABD, BCD,* and *ACD.* The test writers want even this easy problem to be a little challenging; there must be more than one step involved. To find angle *x*, which is part of triangles *ABD* and *ACD*, we must first work on triangle *BCD.*

What do we know about triangle *BCD*? The problem itself tells us that *BC = CD.* This is an isosceles triangle. Because angle *DBC* equals 70, so does angle *BDC*. Angle *BCD* must therefore equal 180 minus the other two angles. Angle *BCD* = 40.

Now look at the larger triangle, *ACD.* We know that angle *ACD* = 40 and that angle *ADC* = 90. What does angle *x* equal? Angle *x* equals 180 minus the other two angles, or 50 degrees. The answer is (B).

Walking and Chewing Gum at the Same Time

Most GMAT geometry problems involve more than one geometric concept. A problem might require you to use both the properties of a triangle and the properties of a rectangle, or you might need to know the formula for the volume of a cube in order to find the dimensions of a cube's surface area. The difficult geometry problems do not test more complicated concepts—they just pile up easier concepts.

Bite-Sized Pieces

With GMAT geometry, you shouldn't expect to see every step a problem involves before you start solving it. Often, arriving at the right answer involves saying, "I have no idea how to get the answer, but because the problem says that $BC = CD$, let me start by figuring out the other angle of that triangle. Now what can I do?" At some point, the answer usually becomes obvious. The main point is not to stare at a geometry problem looking for a complete solution. Just wade in there and start, one bite-sized piece at a time.

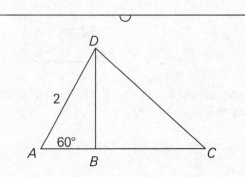

In the figure above, if a line segment connecting points B and D is perpendicular to AC and the area of triangle ADC is $\dfrac{3\sqrt{3}}{2}$, then $BC =$

- ○ $\sqrt{2}$
- ○ $\sqrt{3}$
- ○ 2
- ○ $3\sqrt{3}$
- ○ 6

Here's How to Crack It

You may remember that earlier in this chapter, we already got an approximate answer to this question by measuring; now let's solve it using geometry. If we draw in the line BD (which is perpendicular to line AC), we form a 30-60-90 triangle on the left side of the diagram (triangle ADB). The hypotenuse of this triangle is 2. Using the rules we've learned about 30-60-90 triangles, we can conclude that the measurements of triangle ADB are as follows:

Thus, $BD = \sqrt{3}$. At first you might think we're no closer to the solution, but don't despair. Just look for somewhere else to start. The problem tells us that the area of triangle ADC is $\frac{3\sqrt{3}}{2}$. The area of a triangle is $\frac{\text{base} \times \text{height}}{2}$. BD is the height. Let's find out what the base is. In other words, $\frac{\text{base} \times \sqrt{3}}{2} = \frac{3\sqrt{3}}{2}$, so the base equals 3. We know from the 30-60-90 triangle that $AB = 1$. What is BC? 2. The answer is (C).

○

Plugging In on Geometry?

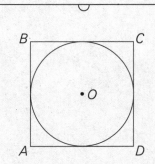

In the figure above, circle O is inscribed inside square $ABCD$ as shown. What is the ratio of the area of circle O to the area of square $ABCD$?

○ $\frac{\pi}{2}$

○ $\frac{4}{\pi}$

○ $\frac{\pi}{3}$

○ $\frac{\pi}{4}$

○ $\frac{\pi}{5}$

Here's How to Crack It
We already saw this problem in the first half of the chapter when we discussed eliminating crazy answers. As you recall, we were able to eliminate (A), (B), and (C) because we determined that the correct answer had to be the ratio of a smaller number to a bigger number.

Now let's solve this problem completely. You may have noticed that the answer choices do not contain *specific numbers* for the areas of the two figures—all we have here are *ratios* in the answer choices. Sound familiar? That's right! This is just another Plugging In problem.

To find the area of the circle, we need a radius. Let's just pick one—3. If the radius is 3, the area of the circle is 9π. Now let's tackle the square. The circle is inscribed inside the square, which means that the diameter of the circle is also the length of a side of the square. Because the radius of the circle is 3, the diameter is 6. Therefore, the side of the square is 6, and the area is 36.

The problem asks for the ratio of the area of the circle to the area of the square:

$$\frac{9\pi}{36} = \frac{\pi}{4}$$

The answer is (D).

Summary

o   While the geometry found on the GMAT is rudimentary, you will have to memorize all of the formulas that you'll need because they are not provided on the test.

o   Always study any problem drawn to scale very closely in order to eliminate crazy answer choices.

o   You must know the following approximate values: $\pi \approx 3$, $\sqrt{2} \approx 1.4$, and $\sqrt{3} \approx 1.7$.

o   You must be familiar with the size of certain common angles:

o   You can estimate Problem Solving diagrams drawn to scale very precisely by using the marker that comes with your scratch booklet.

o   When no diagram is provided, draw your own, and make it to scale.

o   When the diagram is not drawn to scale, redraw it.

o   Degrees and angles:
  - A circle contains 360 degrees.
  - A line is a 180-degree angle.
  - When two lines intersect, four angles are formed, but in reality there are only two pairs of identical angles.
  - When two parallel lines are cut by a third line, eight angles are formed, but in reality there are only two sets of identical angles: a set of big ones and a set of little ones.

o   Triangles:
  - Every triangle contains 180 degrees.
  - An equilateral triangle has three equal sides and three equal angles, each of which measures 60 degrees.
  - An isosceles triangle has two equal sides, and the angles opposite those sides are also equal.
  - A right triangle contains one 90-degree angle.
  - The perimeter of a triangle is the sum of the lengths of its sides.
  - The area of a triangle is $\frac{height \times base}{2}$.
  - In a right triangle, the Pythagorean Theorem states that the square of the hypotenuse equals the sum of the squares of the other two sides, or $a^2 + b^2 = c^2$.
  - Some common right triangles are 3-4-5 triangles and multiples of 3-4-5 triangles, 5-12-13 triangles, and 7-24-25 triangles.
  - Two other triangles that often appear on the GMAT are the right isosceles triangle and the 30-60-90 triangle. Memorize the formulas for these two triangles.
  - The longest side of a triangle is opposite the largest angle; the shortest side is opposite the smallest angle.
  - One side of a triangle can never be as large as the sum of the two remaining sides, nor can it ever be as small as the difference of the two remaining sides.

o   Circles:
  - The circumference of a circle is $2\pi r$ or πd, where r is the radius of the circle and d is the diameter.
  - The area of a circle is πr^2, where r is the radius of the circle.

- Rectangles, squares, and other four-sided objects:
    - Any four-sided object is called a quadrilateral.
    - The perimeter of a quadrilateral is the sum of the lengths of the four sides.
    - The area of a rectangle, or of a square, is equal to *length* × *width*.
    - The area of a parallelogram is equal to *height* × *base*.

- Solids and volume:
    - The volume of most objects is equal to their two-dimensional *area* × their *depth*.
    - The volume of a rectangular solid is equal to *length* × *width* × *depth*.
    - The volume of a cylinder is equal to the *area* of the circular base × *depth*.

- GMAT geometry problems always involve more than one step, and difficult GMAT geometry problems may layer several concepts. Don't be intimidated if you don't see the entire process that's necessary to solve the problem. Start somewhere. You'll be amazed at how often you arrive at the answer.

Chapter 14
Advanced Data Sufficiency

In this chapter, we'll show you how to master Data Sufficiency problems, how to decipher the intermediate and advanced math hidden beneath the unfamiliar format, and how to use POE to eliminate tempting traps.

Now that you've reviewed all the important math concepts covered on the GMAT, it's time to take a second look at how these concepts are used in Data Sufficiency questions.

First, a quick review:

Every Data Sufficiency problem consists of a question followed by two statements:

What is the value of x ?

(1) $x^2 = 4$
(2) x is negative.

You have to decide NOT what the answer is, but WHETHER the question can be answered based on the information in the two statements. There are five possible answer choices:

○ Statement (1) ALONE is sufficient, but statement (2) alone is not sufficient.
○ Statement (2) ALONE is sufficient, but statement (1) alone is not sufficient.
○ BOTH statements TOGETHER are sufficient, but NEITHER statement ALONE is sufficient.
○ EACH statement ALONE is sufficient.
○ Statements (1) and (2) TOGETHER are not sufficient

The best way to answer Data Sufficiency problems is to look at one statement at a time—so ignore Statement (2), and look only at Statement (1). Based on Statement (1), $x^2 = 4$, can we answer the question, "What is x?"

At first glance, you might think so. If $x^2 = 4$, then $x = 2$, right?

AD or BCE

Just by evaluating Statement (1) we have already eliminated several answer choices:

If Statement (1) is sufficient, we are down to (A) or (D).

If Statement (1) is NOT sufficient, we are down to (B), (C), or (E).

AD or BCE. Memorize it; these are always your options. And it makes sense to write it down this way in your scratch book.

Well, not necessarily; x could also equal −2. And when different numbers that satisfy a statement yield different answers to the question, the statement is insufficient. Choices (A) and (D) can be eliminated; the only remaining possible correct choices are (B), (C), and (E).

Now, ignore Statement (1) and look ONLY at Statement (2). Based on Statement (2), "x is negative," can we answer the question, "What is x?"

Nope, x could be any negative number. For instance, x could be −2 or −3. When different numbers that satisfy a statement yield different answers to the question, the statement is insufficient. We are now down to (C) or (E).

Look at both statements together. If $x^2 = 4$ and x is negative, can we answer the question, "What is x?"

Yup! Now there is only one unique number in the world that x could be: –2. The correct answer is (C).

Here's a flowchart that walks you through each step of solving a Data Sufficiency question. If you need more information about how to use the chart or the basic strategy for solving a Data Sufficiency question, check out Chapter 9.

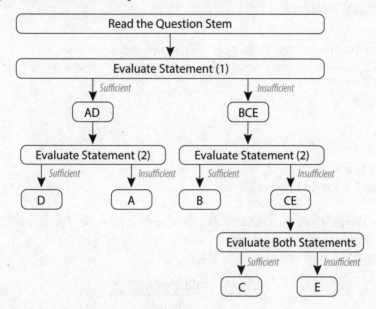

DATA SUFFICIENCY: PIECES OF THE PUZZLE

In terms of mathematical content, Data Sufficiency questions test the same kinds of topics tested by Problem Solving questions (as we told you in Chapter 9). You'll find problems involving integers, percents, averages, ratios, algebra, and geometry. Only the format is different.

Proven Technique:
Pieces of the Puzzle

Your familiarity with the math content, however, can give you an advantage when working a Data Sufficiency question. Most people read the question and then immediately read the statements. But that's not how you would normally work a math problem. Normally, you would read the problem and then ask yourself, "What do I already know?" and "What do I need?"

You should always attempt to do the same thing when working a Data Sufficiency question. Before proceeding to the statements, take stock of the information that you already know. Then, see if you can determine what sort of information the statements need to provide so that you could solve the problem.

We call this approach Pieces of the Puzzle. In a sense, Data Sufficiency questions are just like jigsaw puzzles. When you work a jigsaw puzzle, you know what piece you are looking for based on the shapes of the pieces that fit around it. In a Data Sufficiency question, you'll often know what sort of information you need from the statements based on what you already know from the question stem.

Here's an example:

If a store sold 30 more televisions this month than last month, by what percent has the number of televisions sold increased from last month to this month?

(1) This month the store sold 150 televisions.
(2) Last month the store sold 80% as many televisions as this month.

Here's How to Crack It

Start by asking, "What do I know?"

You know two things. First, the problem asks for a percent increase. That should get you thinking about the formula for percent change:

$$\% \text{ change} = \frac{\text{difference}}{\text{original}} \times 100$$

Next, notice that you already know the change, since the question states that the store sold 30 more televisions this month than last month. So, you can plug the difference into the formula to get:

$$\% \text{ change} = \frac{30}{\text{original}} \times 100$$

Pieces of the Puzzle

What do you know?

The difference is 30.

What do you need?

The sales for last month, the original.

Now, it's time to ask yourself, "What do I need?" By looking at the formula, you can see that you'll be able to answer the question if the statements give you a way to determine the original. So, as soon as you know how many televisions the store sold last month, you have sufficient information.

Now, remember to read only Statement (1). If the store sold 150 televisions this month and that represents an increase of 30 televisions, you know that the store sold 120 televisions last month. So, write down AD.

Now, forget about Statement (1) and read Statement (2). This statement is a little trickier than the first. If last month's sales were 80% of this month's sales, you know that the additional 30 televisions that were sold this month represent 20% of the total. Now, you set up a part-to-whole relationship:

$$\frac{\text{part}}{\text{whole}} = \frac{20}{100} = \frac{30}{x}$$

Can you find the value of x from this equation? Of course. Therefore, Statement (2) is also sufficient and the answer to this question is (D).

———————————○———————————

Let's try the approach again on a difficult question.

———————————○———————————

What is the average (arithmetic mean) of a list of 6 consecutive two-digit integers?

(1) The remainder when the fourth integer is divided by 5 is 3.
(2) The ratio of the largest integer to the smallest integer is 5:4.

Here's How to Crack It

As before, apply the Pieces of the Puzzle approach by asking, "What do I know?"

Since the question asks you to find the average, you should remember that you can find an average if you have the sum of the items being averaged and the number of those items. In this case, you know that there are six integers. You also know that the integers are consecutive. Finally, since the question states that the integers are two-digit, you know that each integer is between 9 and 100.

Now, it's time to ask, "What do I need?" There are lots of possibilities. The statements could give you the sum of the six numbers. Or, the statements could give you the value of one of the integers and its position in the list. For example, if you know that the second integer is 12, you could certainly find the average.

Now, read and evaluate only Statement (1). It's best to think about the information in this statement by plugging in some possible numbers. For example, the fourth integer could be 18 because the remainder when 18 is divided by 5 is 3. If the fourth integer is 18, the first integer is 15. The complete list would be 15, 16, 17, 18, 19, 20 with an average of 17.5. However, the fourth integer could also be 33, making the first integer 30 and the average of the six integers 32.5.

So, Statement (1) does not provide sufficient information to find the average of the six integers. Write down BCE.

Now, forget what you know from the first statement and evaluate only Statement (2). At first, Statement (2) may not seem like much help either. After all, if you are going too quickly, you may be tempted to think that the largest integer could be 15 and the smallest 12 or the largest could be 20 and the smallest 16.

However, here's where you need to remember the puzzle piece that you already have—there are *six* consecutive integers on the list. So, while 12 and 15 may seem to fit the ratio provided in the second statement, those numbers really don't satisfy the statement and the problem because there wouldn't be six numbers for the list.

The only way to satisfy the information in the second statement and in the problem is to make the smallest number 20 and the largest number 25.

Therefore, the answer to this difficult question is (B).

DRILL 12 (Data Sufficiency Parts and Wholes)
The answers can be found in Part VI.

1. If only people who paid deposits attended the Rose Seminar, how many people attended this year?

   (1) 70 people sent in deposits to attend the Rose Seminar this year.
   (2) 60% of the people who sent deposits to attend the Rose Seminar this year actually went.

   ◯ Statement (1) ALONE is sufficient, but statement (2) alone is not sufficient.
   ◯ Statement (2) ALONE is sufficient, but statement (1) alone is not sufficient.
   ◯ BOTH statements TOGETHER are sufficient, but NEITHER statement ALONE is sufficient.
   ◯ EACH statement ALONE is sufficient.
   ◯ Statements (1) and (2) TOGETHER are not sufficient.

2. Luxo paint contains only alcohol and pigment. What is the ratio of alcohol to pigment in Luxo paint?

   (1) Exactly 7 ounces of pigment are contained in a 12-ounce can of Luxo paint.
   (2) Exactly 5 ounces of alcohol are contained in a 12-ounce can of Luxo paint.

   ○ Statement (1) ALONE is sufficient, but statement (2) alone is not sufficient.
   ○ Statement (2) ALONE is sufficient, but statement (1) alone is not sufficient.
   ○ BOTH statements TOGETHER are sufficient, but NEITHER statement ALONE is sufficient.
   ○ EACH statement ALONE is sufficient.
   ○ Statements (1) and (2) TOGETHER are not sufficient.

3. A car drives along a straight road from Smithville to Laredo, going through Ferristown along the way. What is the total distance by car from Smithville to Laredo?

   (1) The distance from Smithville to Ferristown is $\frac{3}{5}$ of the distance from Smithville to Laredo.
   (2) The distance from Ferristown to Laredo is 12 miles.

   ○ Statement (1) ALONE is sufficient, but statement (2) alone is not sufficient.
   ○ Statement (2) ALONE is sufficient, but statement (1) alone is not sufficient.
   ○ BOTH statements TOGETHER are sufficient, but NEITHER statement ALONE is sufficient.
   ○ EACH statement ALONE is sufficient.
   ○ Statements (1) and (2) TOGETHER are not sufficient.

Challenge Question #13

If Angela is twice as old as the combined ages of Bill and Charlie, then how old is Charlie?

(1) Four years from now, the sum of all three people's ages will be 108.
(2) Five years ago, the average (arithmetic mean) of all three people's ages was 27.

Data Sufficiency and Geometry

For Problem Solving questions, the figures are generally drawn to scale. Chapter 13 discussed how you can ballpark by using the figure so long as it isn't marked "not drawn to scale."

For Data Sufficiency questions, however, you should be very careful when using the figure. The figures are drawn so that they represent the information in the question stem, but they need not accurately represent the information in the statements. So, you should base your conclusions about whether you have sufficient information on the statements rather than any figures provided with a Data Sufficiency question.

When Data Sufficiency questions are about geometry, however, you can often make very effective use of the Pieces of the Puzzle approach. The Pieces of the Puzzle approach works very well in situations in which you can use formulas and take stock of facts.

Here's an example of a medium question to illustrate:

In the figure above, arc *QRO* is a semicircle. What is the area of the circle with center *O* ?

(1) The area of triangle *PQO* is 30.
(2) The length of *QRO* is 2.5π.

Here's How to Crack It

Apply the Pieces of the Puzzle approach by asking, "What do I know?"

For this problem, you actually know a lot. You know that arc *QRO* is half a circle and that its diameter is one side of a right triangle. Of course, you also know that triangle *PQO* is a right triangle, so the Pythagorean Theorem applies.

Now, ask, "What do I need?" The question asks for the area of the circle. Since the formula for the area of a circle is $A = \pi r^2$, you'll need a way to find the radius of the circle. If the statements provide either the length of PO or a way to find that length, you'll have sufficient information.

You're ready to look at Statement (1). The formula for the area of a triangle is $A = \frac{base \times height}{2}$. You know the area but neither the base nor the height, so you have insufficient information. Write down BCE.

Next, look only at Statement (2). Now, it's time to remember that QRO is a semicircle. The statement gives you half of the circumference of a circle. You can use the circumference formula to find the diameter, QO. In this case, you actually have half the circumference, so use $2C = \pi d$ or $2(2.5\pi) = \pi d$ and $d = 5$. So, now you know the length of QO, but you still don't have the radius of the circle. (You may think that you recognize a 5-12-13 right triangle, but remember that you need two sides of the triangle to use the Pythagorean Theorem.) Cross off (B).

Finally, put the statements together. Now, you know both the area of the triangle and its height, so you can plug those values into the formula for the area of a triangle to get $30 = \frac{1}{2}(b)(5)$. Can you use this formula to find PO? Yes. So, the answer to the problem is (C).

Challenge Question #14

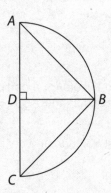

In the figure above, $\overline{AC}$ is the diameter of a circle. Is the area of $\triangle ABD$ equal to the area of $\triangle BCD$?

(1) $\overline{AD} = 2$
(2) $\overline{BD} = 5$

Data Sufficiency and the Strange Powers of Powers

The Data Sufficiency question type is particularly well suited to testing your knowledge of the rules of equations and the strange powers of powers. Let's review this important information:

1. When working with equations, you generally need as many equations as there are variables in those equations.
   - A single equation with two variables cannot be solved,
   - but two distinct equations with the same two variables *can* be solved, using simultaneous equations, as you learned in Chapter 11.

   For example, $x = y + 1$ cannot be solved, but $x = y + 1$ and $2x = -y - 6$ can be added together, eliminating one variable so the other may be solved.

2. Just because there is only one variable doesn't mean that an equation has just one solution.
   - Generally, equations have as many solutions as the greatest exponent in the equation. So, an equation with a squared term will typically have two solutions.
   - Simple equations with a variable raised to an odd power may have only one solution.

   For example, if $x^2 = 4$, then x could equal either 2 or -2. If $x^3 = 8$, then x can only equal 2.

3. But sometimes, it's possible to get an answer even if there is only a single equation with two variables—IF the problem asks for an expression that contains both variables.

4. Sometimes you can also get an answer if there is only a single equation with two variables if both of those variables can only take on integer values.

Let's look at some problems that use these rules.

Mr. Jones spends $25 on movie tickets for a party of adults and children. How many children's tickets did he buy?

(1) Adult movie tickets cost $3 each and children's tickets cost $2 each.
(2) Mr. Jones buys a total of 11 tickets.

Here's How to Crack It

Start by asking, "What do I know?" In this case, you know that Mr. Jones spends $25 and that there are two variables—adult tickets and children's tickets.

Next, ask, "What do I need?" It's time to start thinking "two equations, two unknowns."

Now, evaluate Statement (1). From this statement, you get $3x + 2y = 25$. That's only one equation but two variables, so you do not have sufficient information. So, write down BCE.

Next, evaluate Statement (2), from which you can get the equation $x + y = 11$. Again, there's only one equation and two variables, so cross off (B).

When the statements are combined, you have two distinct equations with two variables, which means that you can solve. So, the answer is (C).

———————————○———————————

Here's a harder example. This example would be an upper-medium problem.

———————————○———————————

What is the value of $\dfrac{a}{b}$?

    (1) $7a - 3b = 0$
    (2) $b = 5$

○ Statement (1) ALONE is sufficient, but statement (2) alone is not
    sufficient.
○ Statement (2) ALONE is sufficient, but statement (1) alone is not
    sufficient.
○ BOTH statements TOGETHER are sufficient, but NEITHER state-
    ment ALONE is sufficient.
○ EACH statement ALONE is sufficient.
○ Statements (1) and (2) TOGETHER are not sufficient.

Here's How to Crack It

You're not going to get much mileage out of the Pieces of the Puzzle approach for this question. All you really know is that there are two variables involved.

So, ignore Statement (2). Based on Statement (1) ALONE, can you answer this question? At first glance, you might think not—because there are two variables in one equation. But the question is not asking you to solve for a and for b, but for $\dfrac{a}{b}$. If you add $3b$ to both sides of the equation in Statement (1), you get $7a = 3b$. If you then divide both sides of the equation by b, you get $\dfrac{7a}{b} = \dfrac{3b}{b}$, which reduces to $\dfrac{7a}{b} = 3$. By dividing both sides by 7, you get $\dfrac{a}{b} = \dfrac{3}{7}$, which answers the question. Statement (1) is sufficient, and you are down to AD. Looking at Statement (2) alone, of course, you can't answer the question, so the correct answer to the problem is (A).

———○———

The problem we just solved made use of the third rule in our review. Notice that (C) was a trap answer for this problem. Sure, you could find the value of *a* and *b* by combining the statements. However, (C) states that you need to put the statements together *because* neither statement provides sufficient information by itself. So, you'll want to remember that it's possible to know the value of an expression without knowing the values of the variables that make up that expression.

Here's one more example. This one doesn't sound that bad, but it's actually a very difficult problem.

———○———

Mr. Jones spends $76 on movie tickets for a group of adults and children. How many children's tickets did he purchase?

(1) Adult movie tickets cost $11 each and children's movie tickets cost $7 each.
(2) Mr. Jones bought two more adult tickets than children's tickets.

Here's How to Crack It

As always, start by asking, "What do I know?" In this case, Mr. Jones spends $76 on movie tickets, and there are two variables. But, notice that there is actually one more thing that you know—movie tickets must be bought in integer quantities.

Next, ask, "What do I need?" You'll probably need two equations, but the fact that the variables can only take on integer values may change things.

Now, it's time to look at Statement (1), which gives you the equation $11x + 7y = 76$. Before dismissing this single equation with two variables as insufficient, remember that both *x* and *y* must be integers. Also, notice that the coefficients, 11 and 7, are large enough to limit the possibilities. Mr. Jones must buy fewer than 7 adult tickets. It's probably worthwhile to investigate how many of those integer values for *x* produce an integer value for *y*. As it happens, *y* is an integer only when *x* = 5. So, Mr. Jones bought 5 adult tickets and 3 children's tickets. So, write down AD.

Statement (2), however, does not provide sufficient information by itself. Remember that you don't even know how much the tickets cost based only on the second statement. So, the answer is (A).

So, how was this problem different from the first problem in which Mr. Jones bought movie tickets? Why didn't we need to worry about the integer quantities on the first problem? Well, actually, we did. However, for the first problem, the first statement gave us the equation $3x + 2y = 25$. Had we taken some time to investigate this equation, we would have quickly discovered that there are several sets of integer solutions. For example, Mr. Jones could have bought 3 adult tickets and 8 children's tickets, or he could have bought 5 adult tickets and 5 children's tickets.

So, how do you know when to look for a single integer solution? Well, first make sure that the variables can only be integers! Since you can't buy half a movie ticket, that was part of the tip-off. Next, if there is going to be only one integer solution, it is likely that at least one of the coefficients will be a larger prime number like 11 or 17 or 29.

Finally, think about your current scoring level. A problem like that last one would show up only in one of the GMAT's most difficult question bins—because the test writers think so few people will get it right. You aren't likely to encounter this problem on your computer-adaptive section of the GMAT unless you are scoring in the mid to high 40s on your practice math tests.

DRILL 13 (Strange Powers of Powers)
The answers can be found in Part VI.

1.   What is the value of x ?

   (1) $x^2 = 4$
   (2) $x < 0$

   ○ Statement (1) ALONE is sufficient, but statement (2) alone is not sufficient.
   ○ Statement (2) ALONE is sufficient, but statement (1) alone is not sufficient.
   ○ BOTH statements TOGETHER are sufficient, but NEITHER statement ALONE is sufficient.
   ○ EACH statement ALONE is sufficient.
   ○ Statements (1) and (2) TOGETHER are not sufficient.

Equation Tricks and Traps
Some equations are not distinct, such as when one equation can be multiplied to equal the other equation.
For example:
$x + y = 4$
$4x + 4y = 16$
These are not distinct equations. There is not enough data yet to solve for x or y.

2. What is the value of xy ?

   (1) $x^2 = 4$
   (2) $y = 0$

   ○ Statement (1) ALONE is sufficient, but statement (2) alone is not sufficient.
   ○ Statement (2) ALONE is sufficient, but statement (1) alone is not sufficient.
   ○ BOTH statements TOGETHER are sufficient, but NEITHER statement ALONE is sufficient.
   ○ EACH statement ALONE is sufficient.
   ○ Statements (1) and (2) TOGETHER are not sufficient.

3. What is the value of xy ?

   (1) $x^2 = 4$
   (2) $y^2 = 9$

   ○ Statement (1) ALONE is sufficient, but statement (2) alone is not sufficient.
   ○ Statement (2) ALONE is sufficient, but statement (1) alone is not sufficient.
   ○ BOTH statements TOGETHER are sufficient, but NEITHER statement ALONE is sufficient.
   ○ EACH statement ALONE is sufficient.
   ○ Statements (1) and (2) TOGETHER are not sufficient.

YES/NO DATA SUFFICIENCY

We covered the basics of Yes/No Data Sufficiency in Chapter 9.

First, let's do a quick review by looking at a problem.

───────────────○───────────────

Is integer x prime?

(1) $47 < x < 53$
(2) $x > 0$

Here's How to Crack It

Notice that this question is phrased so that you would need to respond by saying "yes," "no," or "maybe" rather than by giving a numerical answer. That's why this is a yes/no question.

So, start by evaluating only Statement (1). There are 5 integers between 47 and 53—48, 49, 50, 51, and 52. Are any of these integers prime? No. But, notice that means that you can answer the question. Is x prime? No, it isn't. So, you have sufficient information. (Remember that a statement can be sufficient for a yes/no question if it allows you to answer the question in either the affirmative or the negative.) So, write down AD.

Now, look only at Statement (2). Based on Statement (2), you don't know whether x is prime. If x is 3, for example, the answer to the question is yes. However, if x is 4, the answer to the question is no. The best answer you could give to the question "Is x prime?" based on Statement (2) is "maybe." So, the answer to the problem is (A).

———————◯———————

Plugging In on Yes/No Questions

Because as many as half of the Data Sufficiency problems you'll see on the GMAT will be Yes/No questions, it's a good idea to have a strategy for these questions. When Yes/No questions involve variables, you can plug into the statement and use those numbers to see if you always get the same answer to the question.

In the problem we just looked at, we plugged into the second statement. Because we were able to find examples of numbers that satisfied the statement but that gave different answers to the question, we knew that Statement (2) wasn't sufficient.

Now, let's look at another example.

———————◯———————

Is x an integer?

    (1) $5x$ is a positive integer.
    (2) $5x = 1$

Here's How to Crack It

As always, ignore Statement (2) and look only at Statement (1). Since this question is phrased as a yes/no question and there are variables involved, let's Plug In.

When you Plug In on a yes/no Data Sufficiency question, you start by picking a number that satisfies the statement. For example, we can start with a nice, simple number such as $x = 2$. Notice that we can use $x = 2$ because $5 \times 2 = 10$ and 10 is a positive integer.

Now that we've found a number that satisfies the first statement, it's time to use that number to answer the question. Be sure that you use the value that you picked for

> **Statements Must Be True**
> You can only plug in numbers that make the statement true. The answer to the QUESTION can be "yes" or "no," but the statements themselves must always be true.
> So, for example, if Statement (1) says "$5x$ is a positive integer," then you can't plug -2 in for x. It would make the statement UNTRUE.

x, not the result of the statement. So, the question becomes "Is 2 a positive integer?" and the answer is, of course, yes. Careful! Don't write down AD yet!

All we've done is find one example of a number that satisfies the first statement and used that number to answer the question. Now that we have an answer of yes, we actually want to see if it's possible to get an answer of no to the question based on a number that satisfies the first statement.

What if we make $x = \dfrac{1}{5}$? We've satisfied the statement because $5 \times \dfrac{1}{5} = 1$ and 1 is a positive integer. However, now we need to use our number to get an answer to the question.

Is $\dfrac{1}{5}$ a positive integer? No.

So, some numbers that satisfy the first statement produce an answer of yes to the question, while other numbers that satisfy the statement produce an answer of no. Therefore, we don't have sufficient information to answer the question, "Is x an integer?" Write down BCE.

Now it's time to look at the second statement. In this case, we have an equation that we can solve to find that $x = \dfrac{1}{5}$. So, we ask, "Is $\dfrac{1}{5}$ an integer?" and give a definite answer of no.

The answer to the problem is (B).

Plugging In is your most important strategy for handling yes/no Data Sufficiency questions.

To see how effective Plugging In can be, let's try it on a more difficult question.

Is $3^n > 2^k$?

(1) $k = n + 1$
(2) n is a positive integer.

Here's How to Crack It

This is a yes/no question involving variables, so Plugging In is a good idea.

Start by evaluating Statement (1) alone. Pick an easy number for n. If $n = 2$, then $k = 3$. The numbers satisfy the statement, so it's time to use them to answer the question. Is $3^2 > 2^3$? Yes.

Remember, however, that you can't properly evaluate the statement based on the results from only one set of numbers. Suppose we tried something a little weirder for n? If $n = -1$, then $k = 0$. Is $3^{-1} > 2^0$? No. (Remember that negative exponents are just another way of writing a reciprocal and that any nonzero number raised to 0 is 1.)

So, we don't actually know what the answer to the question is based only on Statement (1). It looks as though the answer depends on the numbers we choose. Write down BCE.

Don't Do the Work in Your Head
To remember that you need to Plug In at least twice for each statement, write down the numbers you plugged in and the answers you get to the questions on your scratch pad.

For Statement (2), we can also Plug In. Notice that the statement doesn't tell us anything about k, however. So, we could say that $n = 2$ and $k = 1$ to get an answer of yes to the question. But, we could also say that $n = 2$ and $k = 4$ to get an answer of no. Cross off (B).

When we combine the statements, we can still use $n = 2$ and $k = 3$, which, as we saw when we looked at Statement (1), gives us an answer of yes to the question. However, we could also use $n = 1$ and $k = 2$ to satisfy the combined statements. Is $3^1 > 2^2$? No. So, the answer to this problem is (E).

Yes or No Plugging In Checklist

- First, try plugging in a normal number for your variable. The number you pick must satisfy the statement itself. If it doesn't, plug in another number. The number will yield an answer to the question—either yes or no. But you're not done yet.
- Now, try plugging in a different number for your variable. This time, you might try one of the "weird" numbers, such as 0, 1, a negative number, or a fraction. If the number still answers the question the same way, then you can begin to suspect that the statement yields a consistent answer and that you're down to AD.
- If you plug in a different number and get a different answer this time (a "yes" after getting a "no," or a "no" after getting a "yes"), then the statement does NOT definitively answer the question, and you're down to BCE.
- Now, repeat this checklist with Statement (2).

DRILL 14 (Yes or No)

The answers can be found in Part VI.

1. If x is a positive number, is $x < 1$?

    (1) $2x < 1$
    (2) $2x \leq 2$

    ○ Statement (1) ALONE is sufficient, but statement (2) alone is not sufficient.
    ○ Statement (2) ALONE is sufficient, but statement (1) alone is not sufficient.
    ○ BOTH statements TOGETHER are sufficient, but NEITHER statement ALONE is sufficient.
    ○ EACH statement ALONE is sufficient.
    ○ Statements (1) and (2) TOGETHER are not sufficient.

2. Is x positive?

    (1) $xy = 6$
    (2) $xy^2 = 12$

    ○ Statement (1) ALONE is sufficient, but statement (2) alone is not sufficient.
    ○ Statement (2) ALONE is sufficient, but statement (1) alone is not sufficient.
    ○ BOTH statements TOGETHER are sufficient, but NEITHER statement ALONE is sufficient.
    ○ EACH statement ALONE is sufficient.
    ○ Statements (1) and (2) TOGETHER are not sufficient.

3. Are x and y integers?

    (1) The product xy is an integer.
    (2) $x + y$ is an integer.

    ○ Statement (1) ALONE is sufficient, but statement (2) alone is not sufficient.
    ○ Statement (2) ALONE is sufficient, but statement (1) alone is not sufficient.
    ○ BOTH statements TOGETHER are sufficient, but NEITHER statement ALONE is sufficient.
    ○ EACH statement ALONE is sufficient.
    ○ Statements (1) and (2) TOGETHER are not sufficient.

More Ways to Plug In

As you have just seen, Plugging In can be a very helpful tool to evaluate whether the statements provide sufficient information to answer the question on Yes/No Data Sufficiency question. Sometimes, however, Plugging In can also help you discover what the question is asking.

Often, test writers make a question harder by writing the question stem in a way that hides the concept being tested. After all, if you're having a hard time understanding the question, you'll almost certainly have a hard time answering the question. You should remember, however, that no matter how confusing the question stem appears when you first read it, GMAT questions really test only fairly straightforward math concepts. Plugging In can help you decipher the question stem.

Here's an example of how the test writers might ask a difficult question:

If l_1 and l_2 are distinct lines in the xy coordinate system such that the equation for l_1 is $y = ax + b$ and the equation for l_2 is $y = cx + d$, is $ac = a^2$?

(1) $d = b + 2$

(2) For each point (x, y) on l_1, there is a corresponding point $(x, y + k)$ on l_2 for some constant k.

Here's How to Crack It

One of the hardest things about this question is understanding the question stem. It's going to be impossible to evaluate the information in the statements before we understand what we're being asked.

Let's try applying the Pieces of the Puzzle approach by first asking, "What do we know?" We know there are two lines. And, since the question tells us that the lines are distinct, we know that they are different. We also sort of have the equations for each line, but we recognize that the equations we're given are really just the general equation for any line— $y = mx + b$.

At this point, it might be a good idea to take stock of what we know about lines. In the equation $y = mx + b$, m is the slope and b is the y-intercept. For our two lines in question, a and c represent the slopes and b and d represent the y-intercepts.

Okay, now we're getting somewhere. The question is asking us something about the slopes of the lines, since a and c represent the slopes. Now ask "What do we need?" We need a way to work with the equations of the two lines. Now, let's Plug In. If we let $a = 2$ and $c = 3$, then $(2)(3) \neq (2)(2)$. How could $ac = a^2$? That could only happen if $a = c$.

Now we've got it. If $a = c$, the slopes of the lines are equal. If the slopes of two lines are equal, the lines are parallel. This question is really just asking, "Is l_1 parallel to l_2?" If the test writers had asked the question this way, the difficulty of the question would have dropped.

Let's check out the statements. If we look only at Statement (1), all we know is that the y-intercept of l_2 is 2 more than the y-intercept of l_1. In that case, the slopes could be the same—producing an answer of Yes to the question—or the slopes could be different—producing an answer of No. So, Statement (1) is insufficient. Write down BCE.

Now, let's look at Statement (2). Plugging In is a good way to evaluate this statement. Start by picking a value of k, which must be a constant. We'll let $k = 2$. Let's say that points (2, 6) and (3, 8) are on line l_1, which would mean that (2, 8) and (3, 10) are on l_2. Using those points, we can calculate that the slope of each line is 2. Since the slopes are the same, the lines are parallel. We have an answer of Yes to the question.

Of course, when you Plug In on Yes/No Data Sufficiency, you shouldn't stop after Plugging In just one set of numbers. This time, let $k = 3$. Let's also say that (2, 8) and (3, 11) are on l_1, which would mean that (2, 11) and (3, 14) are on l_2. Once again, we can calculate the slope of each line. In this case, both slopes turn out to be 3. Again, since the slopes are the same, the lines are parallel. (Don't be thrown by the fact that the slopes are different for each Plug In. We're only trying to see if the slopes of the lines are the same each time we Plug In.)

If you remain unconvinced, you could try Plugging In again, but you'll again find that the slopes of the lines are equal. In effect, the second statement tells us that for each point on l_1 there is a corresponding point on l_2 that is a distance of k units away. That can only happen if the lines are parallel. So, the answer is (B).

If that question left you shaking your head, you're not alone. It's a very difficult question. Only a handful of test takers will wind up getting it right. In effect, the test writers pulled out every trick in their book to make this question difficult. Understanding the various ways that the GMAT test writers make questions difficult can help you improve your score dramatically.

POE PRINCIPLES FOR DATA SUFFICIENCY

Data Sufficiency questions that you find difficult and confusing are a distinct possibility when you take the GMAT, so you need to be prepared for them. After all, if the computer is doing its job properly—and you can pretty much count on that—it will keep feeding you progressively harder questions during the computer-adaptive section, in the hopes that it will find one that you don't know how to do.

In other words, almost every GMAT test taker hits a wall at some point. You've just gotten a string of questions right and suddenly there's a question on your screen that you find confusing. You need to answer it to move on to the next question, but you'd like to do better than a blind guess. In fact, if you narrow your available choices, you may just guess correctly, dodge the bullet, get the next couple of questions right, and wind up with a higher score than if you didn't have a plan for handling those tough, confusing questions. Good test takers always have a good guessing plan in hand.

Part of the key to using a guessing strategy effectively is to know your current GMAT math score. If your current score indicates that you are answering mostly easy questions (a score up to roughly 25), continue to concentrate on mastering the principles that we've already covered. As you master those principles, you'll start to see more questions on practice tests that will make use of the traps that we'll discuss in a minute. To make further improvements, you'll need to learn how to spot and avoid the test writers' favorite traps.

If your score is above 25, you're already seeing Data Sufficiency questions on your practice tests that contain the traps we're about to discuss. The first step to avoiding the traps is to learn to spot them. Learning to avoid the traps can be a very effective way to improve your GMAT score.

Work With What You Know

We've already been using Process of Elimination (POE) throughout this section. On Data Sufficiency questions, a little knowledge can go a long way. Suppose you saw the following Data Sufficiency question:

What is the area of square *ABCD* ?

(1)   The length of the side of square *ABCD* is 2.

(2)   For square *EFGH*, which has sides that are 6 longer than those of square *ABCD*, the ratio of the perimeter to the area is the reciprocal of the corresponding ratio for square *ABCD*.

When we don't know something about a problem, our first impulse is to just skip the whole thing. Or to assume that there's no way to solve it. However, you can't skip questions on the GMAT, and you may not get your best score possible if you assume that everything that looks hard can't be solved.

Obviously, the second statement of this problem is wordy and confusing. You may not be sure what it says or whether it provides sufficient information to answer the question, but that doesn't mean you need to make a random guess.

Let's focus on what you DO know. To find the area of a square, you need to know the length of the side of the square—exactly what the first statement provides. Since the first statement is sufficient, your possible answers are (A) or (D).

In other words, you have a fifty-fifty chance of getting the question right. And you get there even if you find the second statement confusing.

As long as you know *something* about a Data Sufficiency question, you can do some shrewd guessing. Take a look at this variation of the problem we've been discussing:

What is the area of square *ABCD* ?

(1) The length of the side of square *ABCD* is greater than 1.

(2) For square *EFGH*, which has sides that are 6 longer than those of square *ABCD*, the ratio of the perimeter to the area is the reciprocal of the corresponding ratio for square *ABCD*.

You still know that you need the length of the side of the square to find its area. However, now the first statement does not provide that length. If the first statement is insufficient, you can narrow your choices down to (B), (C), or (E).

This time, you have a 1 in 3 chance of getting the question right. As before, you didn't need to tackle the second statement to better your odds of getting the question right.

The Average Test Taker and Data Sufficiency

Understanding the average test taker can help you avoid several types of traps on Data Sufficiency questions. The single most important thing to remember about the average test taker is that he tends to choose his answers very quickly. Any time that you are tempted to answer a Data Sufficiency question in only a few seconds, you may be about to fall for the same sort of trap that sometimes catches the average test taker. That's not to say that you aren't about to pick the correct answer. However, you should take a few more seconds just to make sure that you aren't missing anything.

There are several common traps that the average test taker falls for. Let's take a look at them.

Watch out for these common traps!

Trap #1) Answer Choice E Means "I Don't Know"

Let's revisit that hard question from the More Ways to Plug In section to see how the average test-taker might approach it.

If l_1 and l_2 are distinct lines in the *xy* coordinate system such that the equation for l_1 is $y = ax + b$ and the equation for l_2 is $y = cx + d$, is $ac = a^2$?

(1) $d = b + 2$

(2) For each point (x, y) on l_1, there is a corresponding point $(x, y + k)$ on l_2 for some constant *x*.

Many test takers will find this question confusing. As a result, they have no idea how they are supposed to evaluate the information in the statements. But, these test takers don't want to admit that they don't know what to do. Most people don't like to admit that they don't know how to solve a problem!

Many test takers will pick (E) on questions that they don't understand. They think that (E) means "I don't know how to do this problem." Of course, that's not what (E) means at all. Choice (E) means "I know exactly how to do this problem and that's why I know that the statements don't provide sufficient information."

If you want to pick (E) on a question that you find confusing, make sure that you can explain why don't have enough information. You should be able to state exactly the piece of information that you needed but didn't get. If you can't do that, you may be equating (E) with "I don't know how to do this problem."

Trap #2) The Statements Are Missing Information

Sometimes, test takers pick (E) because the question was designed to make it appear that the statements did not provide sufficient information. This trap is particularly aimed at those test takers who feel pressed for time. It's always necessary to properly evaluate the information provided by the statements.

Consider this example:

What is the value of $r^2 + s$?

(1) $t - u = 8$

(2) $r^2t - su + st - r^2u = 24$

Here's How to Crack It

Many test takers who try to answer this question too quickly will be tempted by (E). There are two variables in the question stem but four variables in the statements. It is unclear what the variables t and u have to do with finding the values of r^2 and s. As a result, many test takers will select (E). Alas, those test takers have reached their conclusion too quickly.

Just because the statements do not appear to provide the required information, it doesn't mean that there is no way to answer the question.

Here's how this one is solved.

There's no way to determine anything about r and s from information about t and u. As a result, Statement (1) is insufficient. So, write down BCE.

Now, let's work with Statement (2). The equation provided does contain the two variables in the question stem. Let's try grouping the expressions differently:

$$r^2t - su + st - r^2u = 24$$

$$(r^2t + st) - (r^2u + su) = 24$$

$$t(r^2 + s) - u(r^2 + s) = 24$$

$$(r^2 + s)(t - u) = 24$$

So, Statement (2) is insufficient. Eliminate (B).

However, if the statements are combined, we can replace the expression $t - u$ with 8 and find that the value of $r^2 + s$ is 3. The correct answer is (C).

———————○———————

How can you avoid this mistake? Make sure that you take the time to fairly evaluate the information in each statement. You may need to do a little algebraic manipulation or Plug In some numbers to see what's going on, but that is time well spent if you can eliminate some answer choices, or even find the correct one.

Trap #3) Confusing Statements Are Not Sufficient

Because the GMAT test writers know that people don't like to pick things that they don't understand, the test writers will sometimes pair a fairly easy statement with one that is difficult to understand. The test writers do this because they know that many test takers will conclude that the difficult to understand statement is insufficient.

———————○———————

What is the volume of a certain rectangular solid?

(1) The solid can be cut into 16 cubes, each of which has a volume of 1.

(2) The base of the rectangular solid is a square, which has a diagonal length of $2\sqrt{2}$, and the ratio of the height of the solid to its length is 2 : 1.

Here's How to Crack It

It's pretty straightforward to conclude that the volume of the solid is 16 from Statement (1). Most test takers will quickly, and correctly, determine that Statement (1) is sufficient.

However, most of these test takers will be confused by the information in Statement (2), So, many test takers will assume that the confusing statement is insufficient and pick (A) as their answer.

However, Statement (2) is also sufficient. Here's how it works:

If the base of the rectangular solid is a square, the diagonal divides the square into two 45-45-90 triangles. For a 45-45-90 triangle, the hypotenuse is $s\sqrt{2}$. In this case, the side of the square turns out to be 2. So, for the rectangular solid, we now know both its length and width. The statement tells us that the ratio of the height of the solid to its length is 2 : 1, which means that the height of the solid is 4. So, we now know all three dimensions of the solid. Since the second statement was also sufficient, the correct answer is (D).

How do you avoid this mistake? This question had a very particular format. An easy to understand statement was matched with a statement that was much harder to understand. Many test takers didn't want to pick an answer that included a statement that they didn't understand. So, these people picked (A). Typically, however, when the test writers match an easy statement with a statement that is wordy and confusing, the harder statement is also sufficient. If the hard statement didn't work, the question would be an easy problem.

Obviously, you need to be careful in employing this guessing strategy. The easy statement needs to be so easy that very few people will evaluate it incorrectly. If that's the case, ask yourself why you're tempted to say that the more confusing statement is insufficient. Do you know what information it doesn't supply? Or are you saying, "I really am not sure what this statement says"? If your reason boils down to not fully understanding the statement, your better bet is to say that the confusing statement probably does supply sufficient information.

Trap #4) Too Many Problems Are Easy

Be wary when you find yourself thinking that many of the questions on the GMAT are easy. GMAT test writers are very good at disguising hard questions as easy ones. They figure that if a problem looks easy, a test taker will be less diligent and less careful than when a problem looks hard.

Now, put GMAC's ability to pass off hard questions as easy questions into the context of the adaptive nature of the test. If you start to do well, the computer will feed you a harder question. But, if you continue to think that all of the questions are pretty easy, you could wind up getting some hard questions wrong!

What was the average (arithmetic mean) attendance for baseball games played at Memorial Stadium during the months of June and July?

(1) The average numbers of people attending baseball games at Memorial Stadium for June and July were 23,100 and 25,200, respectively.

(2) There were 20 baseball games played in June at the stadium and 22 games played in July.

Here's How to Crack It

This question looks pretty easy. Statement (1) gives us the average attendance for June and the average attendance for July. Many test takers think this information is sufficient because they think that they can just average the two averages. (You—having completed our chapter on arithmetic—know better.) The same people look at Statement (2) and don't see any attendance figures at all. They quickly pick (A).

Of course, this reasoning is incorrect. The answer to this question is (C). An average is the total sum of values divided by the *total* number of values. We need to know the number of games in each month in order to find out the total number of people attending.

How do you avoid this mistake? Slow down! If you are purposeful and diligent when evaluating the information in the statements, you will be less likely to fall for this sort of trap.

Trap #5) Making Bad Assumptions

Data Sufficiency questions try to get test takers to make bad assumptions. The test writers know how most people think about math, and they often write the questions to take advantage of the assumptions that people routinely make.

For example, consider the following question:

What is the value of x ?

(1) x > 8

(2) x < 10

Here's How to Crack It

Many test takers assume that the answer is (C) because they assume that numbers are always integers. These test takers probably also chose (C) very quickly.

Of course, the numbers are not always integers. In this case, the value of x could be 9. But, it also could be 8.5. The correct answer is (E).

───────○───────

How can you avoid this mistake? Again, slow down! When a problem seems too easy, go back and reread the information. Are you, for example, assuming anything about the types of numbers that fit the statements? Using the Pieces of the Puzzle approach will also help you to avoid making assumptions about the information provided in the question stem.

Trap #6) Remembering Statement (1) When Evaluating Statement (2)

Test takers will often, unknowingly, use the information from Statement (1) as part of their evaluation of Statement (2).

───────○───────

At a business dinner, people were offered coffee or tea. If all the diners had either coffee or tea, how many of the diners had tea?

(1) Of the 60 people at the dinner, 10% had tea.

(2) Fifty-four people had coffee.

Here's How to Crack It

Choice (D) is the most commonly chosen incorrect answer for this question. From Statement (1), it's pretty easy to conclude that 6 people had tea. With that information in mind, it's also pretty easy to look at the second statement and think "54 people had coffee so that means that 6 had tea. Yeah, that works." So, (D) looks like the answer to pick.

There's only one small problem with this line of reasoning—the second statement does not tell us the number of diners. So, based on the second statement, we have no idea how many people had tea. The correct answer is (A).

───────○───────

How can you avoid this mistake? *Always evaluate the statements independently.*

You should also be careful when the statements seem to agree. If the second statement had said "two people had coffee," it would have been easy to conclude that the second statement was not sufficient. By choosing a number that agreed with the information from the first statement, the test writers made it much easier to fall for the trap. So, remember that just because one statement seems to agree with the other, that doesn't mean that they say the same thing.

Putting It All Together

The biggest reason for falling for any of these traps always boils down to going too fast. We have just run through a list of common ways that test takers make mistakes when answering Data Sufficiency questions, and all of these ways were different. However, these errors invariably happen from thinking that it's okay to answer Data Sufficiency questions quickly. Just because you don't need to compute an answer to a Data Sufficiency question doesn't mean that you can race through the question.

Recognizing the types of errors that the average test taker makes on Data Sufficiency questions can sometimes help you guess your way to the right answer. That can be helpful if you find a question confusing or if you are running short on time close to the end of the section.

Let's look at one last example.

If the perimeter of right triangle *ABC* above is $3 + 3\sqrt{3}$, what is the area of the triangle?

(1) $AC \neq AB$

(2) Angle $ABC = 30°$

Here's How to Crack It

The area of a triangle is $\frac{base \times height}{2}$. The average test taker looks at Statements (1) and (2) and sees neither the base nor the height of the triangle. So, he quickly concludes that the answer is (E) because he doesn't see any way to get the area of the triangle from the information in the statements.

Let's see how close we can get to the answer using Process of Elimination. Ignore Statement (2). The first statement only tells us that the base and height have different lengths. Even with the value for the perimeter, there's no way we're going to get the values of the base or height. So, cross off AD.

Now, let's look at that second statement. From it, we can conclude that this triangle is a 30-60-90 triangle. If the triangle is 30-60-90, that would also mean that the base and the height of the triangle are different—exactly what the first statement told us. It doesn't sound like combining the statements adds anything that we don't know from just the second statement. So, (C) is unlikely to be the correct answer. This leaves only (B) and (E).

If you were running out of time, what answer choice would you choose? What answer choice would the average test taker choose? Choice (E) might appeal to someone who did not describe what information is missing from the problem, so they assume that the statements are not sufficient. To a savvy test-taker, this is a signal that the choice might be incorrect, which could lead to the selection of (B).

And the correct answer *is* (B). If you were running out of time or not exactly sure how to solve this question, you can get to the right answer just by knowing how the average test taker would respond and employing a little deductive reasoning.

———————————————○———————————————

Here's How GMAC Wants You to Crack It

Statement (2) tells us that the right triangle is a 30-60-90 triangle. The side lengths of a 30-60-90 triangle are always in the same proportion: $x : x\sqrt{3} : 2x$. (Remember that the x in the proportion is the side opposite the 30-degree angle.) Therefore, the perimeter of a 30-60-90 triangle is $3x + x\sqrt{3}$. Now use the information in the question stem to solve for the short side of the triangle:

$$3x + x\sqrt{3} = 3 + 3\sqrt{3}$$

Remember that you don't need to solve. You just need to know that you can solve, since this is a Data Sufficiency problem. (Just in case you're curious, $x = \sqrt{3}$). Once you've got the length of the base, you can find the height and then find the area of the triangle.

It is possible to solve this problem. So, Statement (2) is sufficient and the answer is (B).

That Was a Lot of Work

This question was very difficult and very time consuming if you tried to solve it as the test writers wanted you to. Almost every test taker battles the clock on the GMAT. Knowing how to use Process of Elimination can help you make informed guesses when you are stuck on a problem and starting to run out of time.

Need More Practice?
Math Workout for the GMAT contains tons of drills with detailed answer explanations.

Summary

o The instructions for Data Sufficiency questions are very complicated. Memorize them now. Here is a pared-down checklist:
  - The first statement ALONE answers the question.
  - The second statement ALONE answers the question.
  - You need both statements TOGETHER to answer the question.
  - Both statements SEPARATELY answer the question.
  - Neither statement together or separately answers the question.

o Use POE to narrow down the field. If you know that Statement (1) is sufficient, you are already down to a fifty-fifty guess: (A) or (D). If you know that Statement (1) is not sufficient, you are already down to a one-in-three guess: (B), (C), or (E).

o If you are stuck on Statement (1), skip it and look at Statement (2). POE will be just as helpful.

o If Statement (2) is sufficient, you will be down to (B) or (D). If Statement (2) is not sufficient, you will be down to (A), (C), or (E).

o The math content of the Data Sufficiency questions is exactly the same as it is on the regular math questions.

o As you would in the regular math problems, look for the clues that tell you how to solve Data Sufficiency problems.

o When a problem asks a yes-or-no question, remember that the answer can be no.

o In yes-or-no questions, a statement is sufficient if it always gives us the *same* answer: always yes or always no. If the answer is sometimes yes and sometimes no, the statement is insufficient.

- In Data Sufficiency questions, look for opportunities to simplify or restate the question. If a question asks, "Did the foreman reject 40% of the 12,000 computers manufactured?" you could simplify that to ask, "Did the foreman reject 4,800 computers?"

- In intermediate and difficult Data Sufficiency problems, you must be on guard against careless assumptions. Take your time and treat every question the way you would the hardest question on the test.

Part III
How to
Crack the
Verbal GMAT

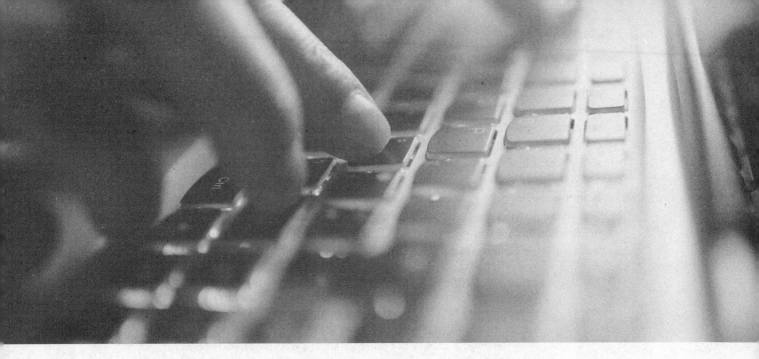

Chapter 15
Sentence Correction

GMAT Sentence Correction involves choosing from among five sentence options the one that is most grammatically correct while maintaining the meaning of the sentence. This chapter will begin with a review of how grammar is tested on the GMAT and then move on to show you the basic approach for handling Sentence Correction questions. Then we'll discuss the different types of grammar errors GMAT loves to test.

Sentence Corrections make up a little more than one-third of the 41 questions on the Verbal portion of the GMAT—approximately 16 questions that will be interspersed throughout the test. A Sentence Correction question consists of one long sentence that is either partially or completely underlined. You have to decide whether the sentence is grammatically correct as it's written, or if it is not, which of the answer choices best replaces the underlined portion.

Before we begin, take a moment to read the following instructions. They are a close approximation of the instructions you'll see on the real GMAT. Be sure you know and understand these instructions before you take the GMAT. If you learn them ahead of time, you won't have to waste valuable seconds reading them on the day of the test.

> Sentence Correction Directions: This question presents a sentence, part of which or all of which is underlined. Beneath the sentence you will find five ways of phrasing the underlined part. The first of these repeats the original; the other four are different. If you think the original is best, choose the first answer; otherwise choose one of the others.
>
> This question tests correctness and effectiveness of expression. In choosing your answer, follow the requirements of standard written English; that is, pay attention to grammar, choice of words, and sentence construction. Choose the answer that produces the most effective sentence; this answer should be clear and exact, without awkwardness, ambiguity, redundancy, or grammatical error.

The Answers Aren't What You Think

It's important to note the directions specifically mention the "best" answer and that the best answer is based on "grammar, word choice, and sentence construction." What this really means is correct answers for Sentence Correction questions on the GMAT are going to be based on grammar rules of the English language.

If you are a native English speaker, this may sound easy—after all, you grew up speaking, reading, and writing the language. The problem is that few people strictly adhere to the grammatical rules when speaking and even when writing. But, GMAT sentence correction questions do strictly use those rules. So, Sentence Correction questions can be challenging for both native and non-native speakers.

It's About What's Correct

Confronted with a poorly constructed sentence, most of us could find a way to fix it so that it makes sense. Of course the writers of Sentence Correction questions know this, so they have studied how to make answers sound correct. In other words, they will make answer choices that sound like something you would expect to hear someone say.

Finding a way to fix a poorly constructed sentence, however, is not good enough for the GMAT. You must be able to find the sentence that is correct based on the rules of the English language. As such, unless you are well versed in the grammatical rules of the English language, there will be times that the correct answer sounds incorrect and an incorrect answer sounds correct.

As a result, to do well on Sentence Correction questions, you'll need to stop trusting your ears and rely on a knowledge of English grammar rules to help differentiate correct from incorrect answers.

The Good News

The people who write the GMAT try to stick to the basics. If they tested a controversial point of grammar, they might be proven wrong. They don't want to have to change their minds after a test is given and mail 20,000 letters explaining why they're changing the answer key (something that has happened from time to time in the past). The easiest way to avoid trouble is to test a handful of the rules of standard written English.

There are huge books devoted exclusively to the correct use of English. You could spend the next six weeks just studying grammar and never even scratch the surface of the subject. The good news is that this won't be necessary. The GMAT concentrates on only a few rules of standard written English. If you are familiar with these rules, then you will be familiar with most of the concepts tested on a given Sentence Correction question.

An Important Note

That the GMAT typically only tests a handful of rules is not to say that those rules comprise the totality of everything the GMAT does test. The truth is, the GMAT can test any English rules it wants. You may encounter a question that does not have an error that fits into the rules we've covered in this chapter and that you are unfamiliar with. If you do, just do your best, use the POE tools, pick an answer, and move on to another question that tests a rule that is more familiar.

However, the rules we outlined here have proven to be the most likely to show up. If you know them, you'll be able to spot the error in the question much more often than not. So, if you know nothing else about the rules of standard written English, know these rules.

Before We Get Started

One final note before we get going. This discussion is not designed to be an all-inclusive discussion of English grammar. This chapter is designed to be a discussion of grammar as it appears on the GMAT. Thus, there will be times that we may oversimplify a point, or ignore an arcane exception to a rule. If we do this, its because we feel that particular point did not warrant more, or any, detail.

Process of Elimination

Most people approach Sentence Correction questions in similar ways. They read the original sentence and then read the entire sentence again with each of the different answer choices. This approach is both laborious and confusing. It's hard to keep five different versions of the same sentence straight, thus increasing the chances that you will make a careless mistake.

The approach we are going to use is based on Process of Elimination. We're going to focus on first identifying any errors in the original sentence, looking to eliminate any obvious repeaters, and then evaluating each remaining answer choice individually.

Answer Choice (A)

Every Sentence Correction question will have five answer choices. However, (A) will always be a repeat of the underlined portion of the original sentence. So, when you evaluate the original sentence you are really evaluating (A). Therefore, if there is an error in the original sentence, you can eliminate (A) without even looking at it.

Basic Approach to Sentence Correction

Spotting grammatical errors is important, but you'll need a strategy to get to the credited answer.

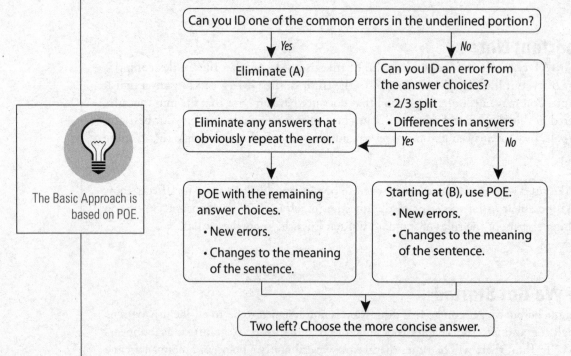

The Basic Approach is based on POE.

Let's explore each of these steps in a little more detail.

Identify any of the common errors in the underlined portion of the sentence

When evaluating a Sentence Correction question, start by looking for one of the common errors tested by the GMAT in the underlined portion of the sentence. Those errors are Pronouns, Misplaced Modifiers, Parallel Construction, Comparison, Verb Tense, Subject-Verb Agreement, and Idioms. We'll go over these, and signs to look for to identify them, in more detail later.

Obvious Repeaters

If you identified an error in the underlined portion of the sentence, eliminate (A). Then, quickly scan the answer choices looking for any answer choice that obviously repeats the error. An obvious repeater is an answer that you don't even need to read to know that it's wrong. Obvious repeater answer choices include errors that can be identified by the inclusion of only one or two words. If the answer has that word, it's wrong. For example, if the original sentence used the verb *is*, which is singular, but the subject of the sentence is plural, then any answer that includes *is* can be eliminated. The answers that include *is* are obvious repeaters. If you need to read the answer choice to evaluate it, then that answer is not an obvious repeater. At this stage, don't spend time evaluating the answer choices. Just look for the obvious repeaters. When you find an answer choice that obviously repeats the error in the underlined portion of the sentence, eliminate that answer choice.

Online Verbal Drills
Visit your Student Tools and get extra practice using these strategies!

Process of Elimination

After you have eliminated any obvious repeaters, move on to working through the remaining answer choices one at a time, looking for reasons to eliminate each.

Begin the Process of Elimination by looking for new errors in the answer choices. Look for the commonly tested errors that you looked for in the underlined portion of the sentence. Start with (B) or the first answer that wasn't eliminated due to the inclusion of obvious repeaters and work your way through the answer choices one at a time. If there were no obvious repeaters, you can first ask whether the answer actually fixes the original error. If it does, then ask whether the answer includes any new errors.

If you do not find a new error in the answer choice, then determine whether the answer choice changes the meaning of the sentence in a substantial way. If the answer choice makes a substantial change to the meaning of the sentence or if the answer choice moves the sentence away from its intended meaning, eliminate it.

If you have two answers left, your final tool is conciseness. In general, the GMAT favors concise language. So, when you have two answers left and neither of them makes a new error or changes the meaning of the sentence, pick the one that's more concise. Recognize that you are essentially making a guess at this point. But, given the GMAT's fondness for concise language, you're making a good guess!

It's important to note here that the first tool you should always use is whether the answer makes a new grammatical error. If you cannot identify a new error, then you should evaluate if the answer choice changes the meaning of the sentence or is not as concise as another.

The No Side of the Chart

What happens if you can't identify an error in the original sentence? If you can't identify an error in the original sentence, try to find an error by working with the answer choices.

In some cases, the answers will have a characteristic referred to as a 2/3 split. For example, two of the answer choices could start with *is* and the other three could start with *are*. This difference could be an indication that the sentence is testing subject verb agreement. So, look back at the original sentence to see if that's the case. If it is, you can eliminate (A) and any obvious repeaters. From there, just follow the steps described above. Really, the split is just another way to use obvious repeaters.

In other cases, the answers may be more complicated. There may not be a 2/3 split. However, if you scan through the answer choices, you may notice a word or phrase that is constructed differently in some or all of the answer choices. Again, these changes could indicate something that you can look for in the original sentence. If you spot an error in this fashion, you can again follow the steps outlined above.

If you can't find an error by examining the answer choices, then start Process of Elimination with (B). Look for answers that include errors that you can identify or answers that make substantial changes to the meaning of the sentence. If an answer includes an error or changes the meaning of the sentence, you can eliminate it.

If you get down to two answers, choose the one that is more concise. If you eliminate all of the answers for good reasons except (A), it likely means that the sentence was correct as written. You should expect to see some sentences that are correct as written.

Let's take a look at a sample question to illustrate the basic approach.

> Registered brokerage firms have been required to record details of all computerized program trades made in the past year so that government agencies <u>will be able to decide whether they should be banned</u>.

○ will be able to decide whether they should be banned
○ should be able to decide whether they should be banned
○ should be able to decide whether they can be banned
○ will be able to decide whether program trades should be able to be banned
○ will be able to decide whether program trades should be banned

Here's How to Crack It

Begin by identifying any of the common errors in the underlined portion of the sentence. We'll go over the common errors later in this chapter, so for now just know that one of the common errors is ambiguous pronouns. In this case, the pronoun *they* in the underlined portion of the sentence is ambiguous as it is unclear whether *they* refers to *registered brokerage firms* or *computerized program trades*. There is an error in the underlined portion of the sentence, so eliminate (A) and look for any obvious repeaters. Choices (B) and (C) also used the ambiguous pronoun *they*, so eliminate (B) and (C) as well. Evaluate the remaining answer choices individually, looking for a reason to eliminate each.

Choice (D) fixes the original error by changing the pronoun *they* to *program trades*. Now, determine whether the answer choice makes any other errors. The verb *able to* modifies the phrase *program trade*, meaning that the *program trades* are *able* to do something. This is a misplaced modifier error, so eliminate (D). Choice (E) fixes the original error by changing the pronoun *they* to *program trades* and creates no new errors, so keep (E).

If it was not apparent that (D) contained the misplaced modifier error, then (D) could have been eliminated because it is not as concise as (E). Either way, the correct answer is (E).

Some Basic Grammar Terminology

While you won't be asked to name the parts of speech on the GMAT, an acquaintance with some of these terms is necessary to understand the techniques we're about to show you.

- A *noun* is a word that's used to name a person, place, thing, or idea.
- A *verb* is a word that expresses action.

Here is a very basic sentence:

   Sue opened the box.

In this sentence, *Sue* and *box* are both nouns, and *opened* is a verb. *Sue* is considered the subject of this sentence because it is the person, place, or thing doing the verb. *Box* is considered the object of the sentence because it receives the action of the verb.

- An *adjective* is a word that modifies a noun.
- An *adverb* is a word that modifies a verb, adjective, or another adverb.
- A *preposition* is a word that notes the relation of a noun to an action or a thing.
- A *phrase* is a group of words acting as a single part of speech. A phrase is missing either a subject, a verb or both.
- A *prepositional phrase* is a group of words beginning with a preposition and containing its object and any of the object's modifiers.

Here's a more complicated version of the same sentence:

   Sue quickly opened the big box of chocolates.

In this sentence, *quickly* is an adverb modifying the verb *opened*. *Big* is an adjective modifying the noun *box*. *Of* is a preposition because it shows a relation between *box* and *chocolates*. *Of chocolates* is a prepositional phrase that acts like an adjective by modifying *box*.

- A *pronoun* is a word that takes the place of a noun.
- A *clause* is a group of words that contains a subject and a verb.

Here's an even more complicated version of the same sentence:

> *Because she was famished, Sue quickly opened the big box of chocolates.*

There are two clauses in this sentence. *Sue quickly opened the big box of chocolates* is considered an *independent clause* because it contains the main idea of the sentence and could stand by itself. *Because she was famished* is also a clause (it contains a subject and a verb), but it cannot stand by itself. This is known as a *dependent clause*. The word *she* is a pronoun referring to the noun *Sue*.

COMMON SENTENCE CORRECTION ERRORS

1. Pronoun Errors

There are two main types of pronoun errors. The first is called *pronoun ambiguity*. You saw an example of this in the sentence about program trading. Take a look at a simple example:

> *Samantha and Jane went shopping, but she couldn't find anything she liked.*

This sentence contains a pronoun ambiguity error. In the example above, the pronoun *she* could refer to either Samantha or Jane. Because it is unclear who *she* is referring to, the sentence is incorrect.

> *Samantha and Jane went shopping, but Samantha couldn't find anything she liked.*

> *Samantha and Jane went shopping, but Jane couldn't find anything she liked.*

> *Samantha and Jane went shopping, but they couldn't find anything they liked.*

The second type of pronoun error is called *pronoun agreement*. Here is a simple example:

> *The average male moviegoer expects to see at least one scene of violence per film, and they are seldom disappointed.*

In this case, the pronoun *they* clearly refers to the average male moviegoer, so there is no pronoun ambiguity. However, *the average male moviegoer* is a singular noun and the pronoun *they* is a plural pronoun. Therefore, the pronoun and noun are not in agreement.

Pronouns and the nouns they refer to must always be in agreement as either singular or plural.

How Do You Spot a Pronoun Error?

Whenever you see a pronoun in the sentence, check to make sure the pronoun could only refer to one other noun in the sentence and that the pronoun is in agreement with the noun. If it is unclear which noun the pronoun refers to, the sentence contains a pronoun ambiguity error. If the pronoun and noun are not both singular or both plural, there is a pronoun agreement error.

A pronoun is a word that replaces a noun. Here's a list of common pronouns. (You don't need to memorize these—just be able to recognize them.)

Singular	Plural	Can Be Singular or Plural Depending on Context
I, me	we, us	some
he, him	they, them	none
she, her	both	ours
it	these	you
each	those	who
another		which
one		what
other		that
mine		
yours		
his, hers		
this		
either		
neither		
each		
everyone		
nobody		
no one		

Let's look at an example.

While Brussels has smashed all Western European tourism revenue records <u>this year, they still lag well behind in exports</u>.

- ○ this year, they still lag well behind in exports
- ○ in the past year, they still lag well behind in exports
- ○ in the past year, it lags still well behind in exports
- ○ this year, they lag still well behind in exports
- ○ this year, it still lags well behind in exports

Here's How to Crack It

Identify any of the common errors in the underlined portion of the sentence. The underlined portion of the sentence contains the pronoun *they,* so check to make sure there are no pronoun ambiguity or pronoun agreement errors. The pronoun *they* clearly refers to *Brussels,* so there is no pronoun ambiguity. However, the pronoun *they* is plural and the noun *Brussels* is singular because it is the name of a single city. Therefore, there is a pronoun agreement error. Eliminate (A) and look for any obvious repeaters. Choices (B) and (D) both use the pronoun *they* to refer to *Brussels,* so eliminate (B) and (D). Evaluate the remaining answer choices individually, looking for reasons to eliminate each.

Choice (C) fixes the original error by changing the pronoun *they* to *it.* Choice (C) is an awkwardly constructed sentence, but there may not be an obvious error with the sentence, so do not eliminate it. Instead, evaluate (E). Choice (E) also fixes the original error and doesn't appear to make any further errors. Because no error may be easily identifiable in either answer choices, look for another reason to eliminate an answer. Choice (E) is more concise than (C), so eliminate (C) and select (E), which is the correct answer.

---

2. Misplaced Modifiers

Misplaced modifiers come in several forms, but the test writers' favorite looks like this:

Coming out of the department store, John's wallet was stolen.

When a sentence begins with a *participial phrase* (just a fancy term for a phrase that starts with a verb), that phrase modifies the noun or pronoun immediately following it.

Remember to use Plans A and B in succession in order to find the correct answer.

So, read literally, this sentence means that *John's wallet* was *coming out of the department store.*

This is a misplaced modifier error. The modifying phrase does not modify the correct noun.

Misplaced modifiers come in other forms as well, such as:

A.   participial phrases preceded by a preposition:
On leaving the department store, John's wallet was stolen.

B.   adjectives:
Frail and weak, the heavy wagon could not be budged by the old horse.

This sentence indicates that *the heavy wagon* is *frail and weak*. The sentence intended to use the modifying phrase *frail and weak* to describe *the old horse*.

(**Correct:** *Frail and weak, the old horse could not budge the heavy wagon.*)

C.   adjectival phrases:
An organization long devoted to the cause of justice, the mayor awarded a medal to the American Civil Liberties Union.

This sentence indicates that *the mayor* is *an organization long devoted to the cause of justice*. The sentence intended to use the modifying phrase to describe *the American Civil Liberties Union*.

In each of these examples, the modifying phrase modified the wrong noun or pronoun.

How Do You Spot a Misplaced Modifier?

Whenever a sentence begins with a modifying phrase that's followed by a comma, the noun or pronoun right after the comma should be what the phrase is referring to. Every single time you see a sentence that begins with a modifying phrase, check to make sure that it modifies the right noun or pronoun. If it doesn't, there is a misplaced modifier error.

Let's look at two examples:

Written in 1961, Joseph Heller scored a literary hit with his comedic first novel, *Catch-22*.

○ Written in 1961, Joseph Heller scored a literary hit with his comedic first novel, *Catch-22*.
○ Written in 1961, Joseph Heller scored a literary hit with *Catch-22*, his comedic first novel.
○ Written in 1961, *Catch-22*, the comedic first novel by Joseph Heller, was a literary hit.
○ *Catch-22*, which was written in 1961 by Joseph Heller, scored a literary hit with his comedic first novel.
○ *Catch-22*, the comedic first novel, scored a literary hit for Joseph Heller by its being written in 1961.

Here's How to Crack It

Begin by identifying any of the common errors in the underlined portion of the sentence. The entire question is underlined, so look for an error anywhere in the text. There is a modifying phrase, so make sure the phrase properly modifies the noun or pronoun directly following it. In this case, the modifying phrase *written in 1961* modifies *Joseph Heller*. This indicates that Joseph Heller was written in 1961, when the modifying phrase intended to modify *Catch-22*. This is a misplaced modifier error. Eliminate (A) and look for any obvious repeaters. Choice (B) repeats the error, so eliminate (B). Evaluate each remaining answer choice individually, looking for reasons to eliminate each.

Choice (C) fixes the original error by correctly placing the noun *Catch-22* immediately following the modifying phrase, and commits no new errors, so keep (C). Choice (D) also contains a misplaced modifier error that results in pronoun ambiguity. The modifying phrase *scored a literary hit with his first comedic novel* is misplaced which creates the error of pronoun ambiguity as it is unclear whether *his* is referring to *Catch-22* or *Joseph Heller*. Eliminate (D). Choice (E) also contains a misplaced modifier error as the answer choice indicates that *Catch-22...scored*, which is an error because a book cannot score. Eliminate (E). The correct answer is (C).

Although not quite as liquid an investment as a money-market account, financial experts recommend a certificate of deposit for its high yield.

○ Although not quite as liquid an investment as
○ Although it is not quite as liquid an investment as
○ While not being quite as liquid an investment as
○ While it is not quite as liquid as an investment
○ Although not quite liquid an investment as

Here's How to Crack It

Begin by identifying any common errors in the underlined portion of the sentence. The underlined portion of the sentence is part of a modifying phrase, so make sure the phrase is correctly modifying the noun or pronoun following it. The modifying phrase *Although not quite as liquid an investment* modifies *financial experts*. This is a misplaced modifier error, so eliminate (A) and look for any obvious repeaters. Despite that some of the answer choices begin with *Although,* none of them qualify as obvious repeaters because it is necessary to evaluate them individually to determine if there is an error. There are no obvious repeaters, so evaluate each answer choice individually, looking for reasons to eliminate each.

Choice (B) fixes the original error by inserting the pronoun *it,* which means that the opening phrase is no longer a modifying phrase, and does not appear to create any new errors, so keep (B). Choice (C) does not fix the original error as the modifying phrase still modifies the noun *financial experts.* Eliminate (C). Choice (D) fixes the original error but creates a new error. Choice (D) moves the word *as,* which changes the meaning of the sentence to indicate that the *certificate of deposit* referred to by the pronoun *it* is not *as liquid as an investment,* as opposed to *as liquid an investment as a money-market account.* Eliminate (D). Choice (E) does not fix the original error as the modifying phrase still modifies the noun *financial experts* and creates a new error by eliminating the word *as* from the idiom *as...as.* Eliminate (E). The correct answer is (B).

Remember, while (B) may not sound like a sentence you would speak, the object of Sentence Correction questions is to find the grammatical errors, not to find the sentences that sound correct.

3. Parallel Construction

Parallel Construction errors on the GMAT can show up in many different formats, so we're going to focus on the general premise of Parallel Construction and how they most frequently show up.

Parallel Construction errors on the GMAT exist mostly with verbs. In a Sentence Correction question, the verbs in that sentence must have the same grammatical status. For verbs, that could mean that all the verbs need to be in the same tense. But it could also mean that all the verbs need to have the same form, such as a list of infinitives.

To illustrate this idea for verbs, take a look at the following example:

The results of the pharmaceutical company's studies reveal that the screening technique may be capable of recognizing the presence of an illness, to identify the appropriate prescription, and monitoring the progress of recovery with subsequent screenings.

Look at the verbs in that sentence—are all the verbs in the same form? The verbs are in the form *recognizing the presence*, *to identify*, and *monitoring the progress*. Two of the verbs are in the same form (*recognizing* and *monitoring*), but the other is in the infinitive form *to identify*. As a result the verbs are not parallel, so this is a parallel construction error.

There are a number of ways to fix this error, but all of them require that the verbs be constructed the same way. So, a potential way to fix this sentence is to write:

The results of the pharmaceutical company's studies reveal that the screening technique may be capable of recognizing the presence of an illness, identifying the appropriate prescription, and monitoring the progress of recovery with subsequent screenings.

Again, this is not the only way this sentence could be fixed. But the sentence is now correct because all the verbs are constructed in the same way.

Take a look at another example:

To say that the song patterns of the common robin are less complex than those of the indigo bunting is doing a great disservice to both birds.

Are the verbs in this sentence constructed in the same way? The first verb, *To say,* is an infinitive but the second verb, *is doing,* is not an infinitive, so this is a parallel construction error.

As before, there are many ways to fix the parallel construction error in the sentence. As long as the verbs are constructed the same way, the parallel construction error is fixed. Here is one way that the sentence could be fixed:

To say that the song patterns of the common robin are less complex than those of the indigo bunting is to do a great disservice to both birds.

How Do You Spot Parallel Construction?

When a sentence has words, usually verbs, that are in a list or related to each other, check to make sure that the words are constructed the same way.

Here's an example:

In a recent survey, the Gallup poll discovered that the average American speaks 1.3 languages, buys a new car every 5.2 years, <u>drinks 14 gallons of alcoholic beverages every year, and forgot to pay at least one bill per quarter</u>.

○ drinks 14 gallons of alcoholic beverages every year, and forgot to pay at least one bill per quarter

○ drinks 14 gallons of alcoholic beverages every year, and forgets to pay at least one bill per quarter

○ can drink 14 gallons of alcoholic beverages every quarter and forgot to pay at least one bill per quarter

○ drinks 14 gallons of alcoholic beverages every year, and forgets at least to pay one bill per quarter

○ drank 14 gallons of alcoholic beverages every year, and forgets to pay at least one bill per quarter

Here's How to Crack It

Begin by identifying any common errors in the underlined portion of the sentence. The underlined portion of the sentence contains verbs that are in a list, so make sure that they are constructed similarly. The verbs in the list begin with the non-underlined verb *buys* and then includes the underlined verbs *drinks* and *forgot*. These verbs are not in the same form, so this is a parallel construction error. Because the verb *buys* is in the non-underlined portion of the sentence, the correct construction of the verbs in the list need to be in the same form as *buys*. The verb *forgot* is not in the same form, so eliminate (A) and look for any obvious repeaters. Choice (C) also uses the verb *forgot,* so it is an obvious repeater. Eliminate (C). Evaluate each of the remaining answer choices individually, looking for reasons to eliminate each.

Choice (B) fixes the original error by changing the verb *forgot* into *forgets* and makes no new errors, so keep (B). Choice (D) fixes the original error, but changes the meaning of the sentence by putting the adjectival phrase *at least* in front of *to pay,* so eliminate (D). Choice (E) also contains a parallel construction error by changing the word *drinks* to *drank,* so eliminate (E). The correct answer is (B).

Challenge Question #15

There are many skills Karishma wishes to learn, but her parents have reluctantly agreed <u>to buying rock climbing gear, providing sailing lessons, and join a chess club, if she continues to keep up with her schoolwork.</u>

- ○ to buying rock climbing gear, providing sailing lessons, and join a chess club, if she continues to keep up with her schoolwork.
- ○ with buying rock climbing gear, providing lessons for learning to sail, and to join a chess club, if she keeps up with schoolwork.
- ○ having rock climbing gear bought, providing lessons for sailing, and joining a chess club would be allowed if she continues her schoolwork.
- ○ to buy rock climbing gear, provide sailing lessons, and allow her to join a chess club, if she continues to keep up with her schoolwork.
- ○ to having bought rock climbing gear, provided sailing lessons, and allowed her joining of a chess club, if she had continued to keep up with her schoolwork.

4. Comparison

Comparison errors are similar to parallel construction errors in that things that are being compared must be the same. Here's an example:

The people in my office are smarter than other offices.

Taken literally, this sentence compares *the people in my office* with *other offices*. Therefore, it's an example of faulty comparison—it compares two dissimilar things (in this case, *people* and *offices*). When comparing things within a sentence, the things being compared have to be the same. Because people and offices are not the same, this is a comparison error.

Parallel comparison problems also come up when you compare two actions. Take a look at the following example:

Synthetic oils burn less efficiently than natural oils.

While this sentence may not seem to contain an error, and certainly does not sound like it contains an error, there is a comparison error. The first item being compared is how *synthetic oils burn* and the second item being compared is *natural oils*.

There are many ways to fix this comparison error, but the fix will ultimately always be the same—the things being compared have to be similar. The GMAT will often employ pronouns or verb to indicate back to the thing or action to fix comparison errors. So, for example, the comparison error in the sentence above is fixed by writing the following:

Synthetic oils burn less efficiently than do natural oils.

In this case, the verb *do* refers to the action *burn*, thus eliminating the comparison error.

How Do You Spot Parallel Comparison?

Look for sentences that make comparisons. These sentences often include words such as *than*, *as*, *similar to*, and *like*. When you find one of these comparison words, check to see whether the two things compared are really comparable.

Let's look at an example:

Doctors sometimes have difficulty diagnosing viral pneumonia because the early symptoms of this potentially deadly illness <u>are often quite similar to the common cold</u>.

○ are often quite similar to the common cold
○ often resemble that of the common cold
○ are often quite similar to those of the common cold
○ are often quite similar to the common cold's symptom
○ quite often are, like the common cold, similar

Q: What is an indication of a parallel comparison error?
Turn to page 271 for the answer.

Here's How to Crack It

Begin by identifying any of the common errors in the underlined portion of the sentence. The underlined portion of the sentence contains the comparison word *similar* so look for comparison errors. The first item being compared in the non-underlined portion of the sentence is the *symptoms* of *viral pneumonia*. The second item being compared is *the common cold*. This is a comparison error as the *symptoms* are not being compared to other *symptoms*. Eliminate (A) and look for obvious repeaters. Choice (E) does not compare *symptoms* to other symptoms, so eliminate (E). Evaluate the remaining answer choices, looking for reasons to eliminate each.

Choice (B) fixes the original error by introducing the pronoun *that*. However, the noun *symptoms* is plural and the pronoun *that* is singular, so there is a pronoun agreement error. Eliminate (B). Choice (C) fixes the original error and makes no new errors so keep (C). Choice (D) appears to fix the original error, but actually compares *symptoms* to *symptom*, which is both a parallel construction and comparison error. Eliminate (D). The correct answer is (C).

Extra Practice
Visit your Student Tools to download a free excerpt from *Verbal Workout for the GMAT*.

Challenge Question #16

Unlike Edgar Allen Poe, <u>whose poems have gained recognition over the years as portraying a foreboding tone, Homer's epic volumes of poetry are</u> valued more for the expansive tales they portray.

○ whose poems have gained recognition over the years as portraying a foreboding tone, Homer's epic volumes of poetry are

○ with poems that are recognized portraying a foreboding tone over the years, the epic volumes of poetry written by Homer are

○ the poems of which have been recognized as portraying a foreboding tone, in the example of Homer, his epic volumes of poetry are

○ whose poems have gained recognition over the years for their foreboding tone, Homer produced epic volumes of poetry that are

○ for whom recognition has been gained over the years for poems in a foreboding tone, Homer's epic volumes of poetry are

5. Verb Tense

Verb tense problems happen when two verbs in the same sentence are in different tenses, or when a sentence starts in one tense and then shifts to a different tense.

When he was younger, he walked three miles every day and has lifted weights too.

The clause *when he was younger* puts the entire sentence firmly in the past. Thus, the two verbs that follow should be in the past tense as well. You may not have known the technical term for *has lifted* (the present perfect tense), but you probably noticed that it was inconsistent with *walked* (the simple past tense). This is a verb tense error.

Here are the tenses that often appear on the GMAT:

Tense	Example
present	He *walks* three miles a day.
simple past	When he was younger, he *walked* three miles a day.
present perfect	He *has walked* three miles a day for the last several years.
past perfect	He *had walked* three miles a day until he bought his motorcycle.
future	He *will walk* three miles a day, starting tomorrow.

It isn't important that you know the names of these tenses as long as you understand how they're used. For example, a sentence that begins in the present perfect (which describes an action that has happened in the past, but is potentially going on in the present as well) should stay in the present perfect.

> *He has walked three miles a day for the last several years and has never complained.*

One exception to this rule is a sentence that contains the past perfect (in which one action in the past happened before another action in the past). By definition, any action set in the past perfect must have another action that comes after it, set in the simple past.

> *He had ridden his motorcycle for two hours when it ran out of gas.*

The only other exceptions to this rule come up when one action in a sentence clearly precedes another.

> *The dinosaurs are extinct now, but they were once present on the earth in large numbers.*

In this case, the sentence clearly refers to two different time periods: *now*, which requires the present tense, and a period long ago, which requires the past tense.

How Do You Spot Tense Errors?

When the underlined portion of a sentence contains a verb, check to make sure that the verb is in the same tense as the non-underlined portion of the sentence.

Try the following problem:

> A doctor at the Amsterdam Clinic maintains that if children eat a diet high in vitamins and <u>took vitamin supplements, they will be less likely to catch</u> the common cold.

○ took vitamin supplements, they will be less likely to catch
○ took vitamin supplements, they are less likely to catch
○ take vitamin supplements, they were less likely of catching
○ take vitamin supplements, they will be less likely of catching
○ take vitamin supplements, they are less likely to catch

A: A comparison! Check that the two things being compared are really comparable.

If you read through this book, you might be able to avoid tense errors!

Here's How to Crack It

Begin by identifying any common errors in the underlined portion of the sentence. The underlined portion of the sentence contains the verb *took,* so make sure there are no verb tense errors. The verb *took* is in the past tense while the verb *eat* in the non-underlined portion of the sentence is in the present tense. This is a verb tense error, so eliminate (A) and look for any obvious repeaters. Choice (B) also uses the verb *took,* so eliminate (B). Evaluate the remaining answer choices individually, looking for reasons to eliminate each.

Choice (C) fixes the original error by changing the verb *took* to *take* but creates a new error by using the past tense verb *were,* thus creating a new verb tense error. Eliminate (C). Choice (D) fixes the original error, by using the future tense verb *will be.* This is a verb tense error, so eliminate (D). Choice (E) fixes the original error and commits no new errors, so keep (E). The correct answer is (E).

You may have noticed that the original sentence contained another error in addition to *took.* The verb form *will be* is in the future tense. This is also a verb tense error. GMAT sentence correction questions will sometimes contain more than one error. If you noticed the other error, that is fine—the process for handling the remaining answer choices remains the same.

---

6. Subject-Verb Agreement Errors

A singular verb needs to be in agreement with a singular noun or pronoun. If a singular verb is paired with a plural noun or pronoun, there is a subject-verb agreement error.

Take a look at the following example:

> *The number of arrests of drunken drivers are increasing every year.*

The subject of the sentence above is *number,* which is singular. The phrase *of arrests of drunken drivers* modifies the subject. The verb of this sentence is *are,* which is plural. This is a subject-verb agreement error.

If the test writers had written the sentence *The number are increasing every year,* identifying the subject-verb agreement error would be easy. However, the test writers will often separate the subject and the verb by using several prepositional phrases to describe or modify the subject. Do not be thrown off by these phrases. Find the subject of the verb and then make sure that they are in agreement.

How to Spot Subject-Verb Agreement Errors

Find the verb and trace it back to its subject and determine if they are in agreement.

One of the common ways that test writers will make these questions harder is by using nouns that sound plural but are actually singular.

> **Nouns That Sound Plural (But Aren't)**
> - The Netherlands (the name of any city, state, or country)
> - Tom or John (any two singular nouns connected by *or*)
> - the family
> - the audience
> - politics
> - measles
> - the number
> - the amount

Sometimes pronouns can be the subject of a sentence, in which case the verb has to agree with the pronoun. There are some pronouns that people tend to think are plural when they are in fact singular:

> **Pronouns That Sound Plural (But Aren't)**
>
> | | | | |
> |---|---|---|---|
> | everyone | no one | anyone | none |
> | everybody | nobody | anybody | each |
> | everything | nothing | anything | |

Let's look at an example of a subject-verb error as it might appear on the GMAT:

Many political insiders now believe that the dissension in Congress over health issues <u>decrease the likelihood for significant action being</u> taken this year to combat the rising costs of healthcare.

○ decrease the likelihood for significant action being
○ decrease the likelihood that significant action will be
○ decrease the likelihood of significant action to be
○ decreases the likelihood for significant action being
○ decreases the likelihood that significant action will be

Here's How to Crack It
Begin by identifying any common errors in the underlined portion of the sentence. The underlined portion of the sentence contains the plural verb *decrease,* so trace that verb back to its subject. The subject of *decrease* is *the dissension*, which is singular, so there is a subject-verb agreement error. Eliminate (A) and look for any obvious repeaters. Choices (B) and (C) repeat the error, so eliminate both choices. Evaluate the remaining answer choices individually, looking for reasons to eliminate each.

Choice (D) fixes the original error with the use of the verb *being* and the unidiomatic expression *likelihood for*. Eliminate (D). Choice (E) fixes the original error and makes no new errors, so keep (E). The correct answer is (E).

---

7. Idiom

Idioms, or idiomatic expressions, are expressions, words, or phrases that have commonly understood meanings and constructions. Most idioms tested on the GMAT are pairs of words that must be used together. Often the first word is a verb that needs to be followed by a specific preposition. For example, *I plan to attend business school* is idiomatically correct, while *I plan on attending business school* is not. The biggest problem with idioms is that there are really no rules governing idiomatic errors—you simply must know them—and there are too many to list.

The good news is that in comparison to the other common errors, the GMAT tests idioms less than the other errors. Additionally, if you are familiar with common English constructions, then you know many idioms already.

How Do You Spot Idiomatic Errors?

Idiomatic errors will appear in sentences that appear to have nothing else wrong with them. Be on the lookout for awkward constructions of sentences or phrases. These could be the sign of an idiom error.

Idioms should also be the last thing that you look for as an error. If the sentence in question has any other error, use that error to work through the Process of Elimination.

Here's an example of what an idiom question on the GMAT may look like:

The administration of a small daily dose of aspirin has not only been shown to lower the risk of heart attack, <u>and it has also been shown to help</u> relieve the suffering of arthritis.

- ⭘ and it has also been shown to help
- ⭘ and it has also been shown helpful to
- ⭘ but it has also been shown to help
- ⭘ but it has been shown helpful in addition for
- ⭘ in addition it has also been shown helping

Here's How to Crack It

Begin by identifying any common errors in the sentence. The sentence contains the phrase *not only* to introduce one example and then introduces another example. However, when the construction *not only* is used to introduce an example, the next example must be introduced by the phrase *but also*. Therefore, the correct idiomatic construction is *not only...but also*. Choice (A) is an idiom error, so eliminate (A) and look for any obvious repeaters. Because *not only* appears in the non-underlined portion of the sentence, the underlined portion of the sentence must contain *but also*. Choices (B), (D), and (E) do not have the phrase *but also*, so these choices are unidiomatic and can be eliminated. Choice (C) is the only answer choice that uses the proper *not only...but also* construction. The correct answer is (C).

The Idioms Most Commonly Tested on the GMAT

There are, of course, thousands of idiomatic expressions that could be tested on the GMAT. But here are a handful that appear most often.

not only...but also...	according to
not so much...as...	agree with
defined as	appear to
regard as	because of
neither...nor...	choose from
modeled after	conclude that
based on	contribute to
a result of	depend on
to result in	due to
a debate over	in order to
a dispute over	instead of
a responsibility to	rather than
responsible for	subject to
different from	worry about
a consequence of	think of...as
so...as to be...	see...as
so (adjective) that	target...as
depicted as	prohibit from
define as	distinguish between...and...
as great as	distinguish...from...
as good as, or better than	attributed to
credited with	

MINOR GRAMMAR ERRORS ON THE GMAT

The seven errors you've just learned to spot will enable you to answer most of the Sentence Correction problems that come up on the GMAT. However, there is one more error that shows up often enough that you will probably want to be looking out for it.

8. Quantity Words

GMAC likes to see if you know how to indicate quantity. Here's an example:

> *On the flight to Los Angeles, Nancy had to choose among two dinner entrees.*

If there were more than two items being compared, then "among" would be correct. However, if there are only two choices available, the correct quantity word would be "between."

> *On the flight to Los Angeles, Nancy had to choose* between *two dinner entrees.*

Below are the comparison quantity words that come up on the GMAT most frequently:

If two items	If more than two items
between	among
more	most
better	best
less	least

Another type of quantity word that shows up on the GMAT from time to time involves things that can be counted as opposed to things that can't. For example, if you were standing in line at a buffet, and you didn't want as big a serving of soup as the person in front of you received, which of the following would be correct?

> *Could I have* fewer *soup, please?*

or

> *Could I have* less *soup, please?*

If an item can't be counted, the correct adjective would be "less." However, if we were talking about french fries (which can be counted), the correct adjective would be "fewer."

Countable items	Uncountable items
fewer	less
number	amount, quantity
many	much

How Do You Spot Quantity Word Errors?

Look for quantity words. Whenever you see a "between," check to see if there are only two items discussed in the sentence. (If there are more, you'll need an "among.") Whenever you see an "amount," make sure that whatever is discussed cannot be counted. (If the sentence is talking about the "amount" of people, then you'll need to change it to "number.")

Here's what a "between–among" quantity word error might look like on the GMAT:

---○---

Of the many decisions facing the energy commission as it meets to decide on new directions for the next several decades, the question of the future of nuclear energy <u>is for certain the more perplexing</u>.

- ○ is for certain the more perplexing
- ○ is certainly the most perplexing
- ○ it seems certain, is the most perplexed
- ○ is certainly the more perplexing
- ○ it seems certain, is perplexing the most

Here's How to Crack It

Begin by identifying any common errors in the sentence. The sentence uses the word *more*, which is a quantity word, so make sure this use is correct. The sentence says there are *many decisions facing the energy commission*, so the use of the word *more* is incorrect. More can be used to decide between two things, but not three or more. Eliminate (A) and look for any obvious repeaters. Choice (D) also uses the word *more*, so eliminate (D). Evaluate the remaining answer choices individually, looking for reasons to eliminate each.

Choice (B) fixes the original error by using the correct quantity word *most* and makes no new errors, so keep (B). Choice (C) fixes the original error, but changes the tense of the verb *perplexing* to *perplexed*, which changes the meaning of the sentence to indicate that the question is itself *perplexed*. Eliminate (C). Choice (E) fixes the original error but moves the modifying phrase the most so that it now modifies *perplexing*, indicating a volume of things that are perplexed. Eliminate (E). The correct answer is (B).

The foresight <u>that was evident in the court's selection of an independent trustee</u> to oversee the provisions of the agreement will probably go unremarked by the press.

- ○ that was evident in the court's selection of an independent trustee
- ○ that was evident by the court's selection of an independent trustee
- ○ evidenced with the court's selection of an independent trustee
- ○ evidenced of the court's selection of an independent trustee
- ○ that was evident of the court's selection of an independent trustee

Here's How to Crack It

The sentence is correct as written.

The construction *that was evident* is consistent with the tense of the remainder of the sentence, and the idiom *evident in* is used correctly, so there appears to be no errors in this sentence. Because there appear to be no errors, there are no obvious repeaters. Evaluate the answer choices individually, looking for reasons to eliminate each.

Choice (B) used the unidiomatic construction *evident by*, so eliminate (B). Choice (C) changes the tense of the verb to *evidenced* which is not parallel to the rest of the sentence and also used the unidiomatic construction *evidenced with*, so eliminate (C). Choice (D) commits the same verb tense error as (C) and also uses the unidiomatic construction *evidenced of*, so eliminate (D). Choice (E) uses the unidiomatic construction *evident of*, so eliminate (E). The correct answer is (A).

If You're Really Gung Ho

You can expand your checklist to include as many types of errors as you like. Obviously, the more types of errors you can identify, the better prepared you'll be to take the test. But you should bear in mind that while there are other types of errors that we haven't discussed, these errors don't come up very often on the GMAT. Some of the errors to consider: redundant words, misuse of the subjunctive mood, and the use of the passive voice when the active voice is possible. If you're seriously gunning to get every Sentence Correction question correct, you should dig out your old grammar book from high school and study it carefully. You should also do as many of the real GMAT Sentence Correction questions in *The Official Guide for GMAT Review* as you can; pay special attention to the idiomatic expressions that come up in these sections, because these are sometimes repeated.

Summary

o   Sentence Correction questions test only a handful of rules. Once you learn them, you will be able to score quite well on this type of question.

o   Follow the basic approach and flow chart for Sentence Correction questions.

o   Make a checklist of errors to look for when you read a Sentence Correction question. The most common are:

- **Pronouns:** If a sentence contains a pronoun, check to see whether it clearly refers to the noun it is replacing; also check to see whether the pronoun agrees in number with the noun to which it refers.
- **Misplaced modifiers:** If the sentence begins with a modifying phrase, check to make sure that the noun it modifies comes directly after the modifying phrase.
- **Parallel construction:** If a sentence contains a list of things, or actions, or is broken up into two halves, check to make sure the parts of the sentence are parallel.
- **Comparisons:** When a sentence makes a comparison, check to see whether the two things compared are really comparable.
- **Verb Tense:** If the answer choices contain different verb tenses, make sure that the tense of the verb or verbs in the original sentence is correct. For the most part, verb tense should be consistent throughout a sentence.
- **Subject-verb agreement:** GMAT test writers sometimes put extraneous prepositional phrases between the subject and the verb. Cover up or ignore these phrases so that you can see whether the subject and the verb of each clause in the sentence agree with each other.
- **Idiom:** If a sentence contains an idiomatic expression that seems wrong to you, try taking the expression out of the sentence and creating a sentence of your own with the suspect expression.
- **Quantity words:** Whenever you see a quantity word (countable vs. uncountable; two vs. three or more), check to see if it is used correctly.

- If you've spotted the error, go through the answer choices and eliminate any that contain the same error. Then look at the remaining answer choices and find the one that fixes the sentence.

- About one-fifth of the sentences are correct as they are. When a sentence is correct, the answer is (A), which simply repeats the sentence word for word.

- Once you've gained confidence in your ability to spot the major errors, you should expand your checklist to include other types of errors.

Chapter 16
Reading
Comprehension

Reading Comprehension questions make up approximately one-third of the questions in the Verbal section. Reading passages occur at any point in the Verbal section, but all questions related to a passage will be presented together.

READING COMPREHENSION OVERVIEW

In most cases, you'll see four reading passages on the test. There are usually three short passages, which average around 250 words and are typically followed by three questions, and one long passage, which averages around 350 words and is typically followed by four questions. It is possible that you may get two short and two long passages, which means that the total number of questions you will see is most likely either 13 or 14 out of 41 total questions.

Reading Comprehension passages can be intimidating to test takers, as there is a sudden rush of information on the screen and the test taker prepares for the task of reading and answering questions on a passage that is often dense, wordy, and boring. During Reading Comprehension passages, it is not uncommon for test takers to feel rushed, which makes it hard to pay attention to a passage that covers a topic area that most find dry. However, contrary to popular belief, everything you need to know to crack Reading Comprehension questions can be found in the text. This chapter is going to teach you how to crack the passages and questions, leading you to the correct answers.

MORE INFORMATION ON READING COMPREHENSION PASSAGES

GMAT passages cover a variety of topics but typically come from four primary areas.

- *Social Science*: social or historical issues, such as the civil rights movement or World War I.
- *Physical Sciences*: natural science topics, such as photosynthesis or black holes.
- *Biological Sciences:* topics related to living organisms and how they interact with their environment.
- *Business*: business-related topics, such as management strategies or the loosening of international trade restrictions.

The passage appears on the left side of the screen. The passage may be too long to fit in the window, so you may have to use the scroll bar to read it completely. The questions appear on the right side of the screen, one at a time. After you answer the first question, another appears in its place. The passage remains unchanged and in place so you can always refer to it. As with any other type of question on the GMAT, you must answer Reading Comprehension questions in the order that they appear on your screen. So, if a question that asks for the main idea appears first, that's the question you must answer first.

THE BASIC APPROACH TO CRACKING GMAT READING COMPREHENSION

Before we begin to crack the Reading Comprehension passages and questions, it is important to establish The Basic Approach. The Basic Approach allows you to:

- actively read the passages and seek out the most important information
- understand the different types of questions and what they require you to do
- quickly find the credited response by eliminating incorrect answers

Don't Be Predictable

The typical test taker is predictable and approaches questions on the test in a certain way. The people who write the GMAT create questions and passages that are designed with those people in mind. They will make questions that trick and confuse test takers who follow the typical approach. However, if you approach the test in a better way, you improve your chance of getting a better score. One hard-and-fast rule of test taking is that whenever you do what the test writers expect, you don't get the best score that you could. When you do things in a different way, you increase your chances of getting a better score. So, our approach to reading needs to be that "different way." The different ways you are going to learn are the Basics of Cracking the Passage, The Basics of Cracking the Questions, and The Basics of Cracking the Answer Choices. These combine to form the foundation that is used for the Basic Approach to Cracking Reading Comprehension.

The Basics of Cracking the Passage

Let's start with the approach to cracking the passage. The typical test taker reads the passage without a plan. So to crack the passage, you need to have a plan for reading the passage. The typical test taker concentrates on the facts in the passage rather than why those facts are there. So to crack the passage, you also need to read for the main idea of the passage.

The Basics of Cracking the Questions

The typical test taker reads the question but doesn't identify the question task. To crack the questions, you must learn to locate both the subject and the task of the question. The **subject** of the question is what you need to find in the passage. The **question task** tells you what type of information you need to find about the subject of the question. For example, do you need to locate what the author said about the subject or do you need to find out why the author mentioned the subject?

The Basics of Cracking the Answer Choices

The typical test taker is focused on simply finding the correct answer. While that may seem a reasonable goal, it's actually a more effective strategy to utilize Process of Elimination (POE) and eliminate wrong answers. Cracking the answer choices is all about understanding how the

GMAC constructs incorrect answer choices. If you can learn to identify common trap answer choices, you can often eliminate them with confidence.

Additionally, the typical test taker relies a lot on memory and only reads parts of sentences that are referenced by the question or answer choices. Reading only parts of sentences makes it easy to misconstrue the context of the sentence. Flipping this behavior around by not only reading full sentences but also reading sentences before and after it is crucial to cracking both the question and the answer choices. Remember, the correct answer is always found in the text. Always refer back to the passage and always read full sentences when you do so.

THE STEPS OF THE BASIC APPROACH TO CRACKING GMAT READING COMPREHENSION

Here are the steps of the Basic Approach:

1. **Work the Passage**

   This is where you apply The Basics of Cracking the Passage. You must have a plan for reading the passage and you must learn to read actively. As you read, always be on the lookout for the main idea of the passage. To find the main idea, ask yourself questions such as what does the author want you to remember or believe about the topic under discussion? What's the author's conclusion? How is that conclusion supported?

2. **Understand the Question Task**

   This is where you apply The Basics of Cracking the Questions. Try to break the question down. First, look for the subject of the question. Then, find the words that indicate the task.

3. **Find the Information in the Passage That Addresses the Task of the Question**

   Refer back to the passage. GMAC needs to be able to justify its credited responses by referring to specific information mentioned in the passage. When you understand the task of the question, it becomes easier to find this information. Once you locate the information in the passage that addresses the question task, you're ready to look at the answer choices.

4. **Use POE to Find the Answer.**

   This is where you use The Basics of Cracking the Answer Choices. Approach each answer choice with a healthy level of suspicion. Since there are four incorrect answers for every question, you are more likely to be reading a wrong answer than a right answer. Look for signs that are more likely to make an answer wrong, such as the answer sounding too much like the passage. Don't be afraid to just pick the answer that remains if you can find good reasons to eliminate the other four answer choices. An overview of common trap answer choices can be found in the next chapter.

STEP 1: WORK THE PASSAGE

Overview

Working the passage is the first step of The Basic Approach to Cracking GMAT Reading Comprehension Passages. By following the recommendations here on how to Work The Passage, you will be able to follow a strategic plan for reading the passage, avoid wasting time by actively reading the passage, learn a little about common passage structures, and map the passage to glean all the relevant information from the passage which enables you to answer the questions later on. All in all, you will know what it takes the Crack the Passage. From there on, it's time to practice!

How Do You Plan To Read?

Before we talk about how to Crack the Passage, let's quickly explore how you can plan to read. You saw the idea of planning to read a handful of times in the previous chapter, but what does it mean? Let's first explore how the typical test taker handles the passage. Typical test takers approach the Reading Comprehension passage in the same way they would approach any reading assignment. They read as quickly as possible, only barely scratching the surface of the major points of the passage that the author was trying to express. Often about halfway through the passage, they realize they have not retained a single major point of the passage. The test taker is now either forced to reread the entire passage, or move on to the answer choices without a full comprehension of the material. This strategy is ineffective and wastes a lot of time!

A better way to approach the passage is to plan to read! Central to the plan is the test taker's ability to comprehend the passage by Active Reading. Active Reading keeps you engaged with the passage, fights off the tendency to let your mind wander away from the task at hand, and leaves you with a better understanding of the author's main point once you are finished. But what is Active Reading and how do you do it?

The Basics of Cracking the Passage

Active Reading

The easiest way to define "Active Reading" is to define the opposite, or "Passive Reading." During passive reading, you look at the words but the content just isn't registering. You may remember some of the details from the passage but you probably missed why the author told you about those details. This is common on GMAT passages, as the content is often thick and boring.

Active reading, on the other hand, means that you follow the author's argument. Put another way, you try to separate the author's claims from the facts and other evidence used to back up those claims. This is an essential ingredient for Cracking the Passage.

Effective active reading involves:

- *Asking questions as you read:* Asking questions helps to engage your mind. For example, ask yourself key questions about the passage and its author. What is the author's purpose for writing the passage? What are the big ideas? Where in the passage are the big ideas located? What kind of tone is the author adopting (scholarly, friendly, critical, objective, biased)? At the end of a paragraph, try to predict where the author takes the argument next. These practices help to create a full understanding of the passage.

- *Identifying the Structure of the Passage*: The structure of a passage is an undervalued hint to deciphering the intentions of the author and the main point of the passage. Passages written in a conventional manner usually proceed from the general to the specific and then return to the general. Individual paragraphs are also usually written that way. Authors may open with a topic sentence, elaborate on the topic with explanations and examples, and then conclude the paragraph with a general statement that transitions to the next paragraph. Be on the lookout for pivotal words or phrases in the middle of a paragraph (*however, on the contrary, on the other hand*). These words are indicators of the author's perspective of the topic of the passage. Often the author follows up one of these pivotal words with the perspective they are trying to convince you to adopt.

- *Look for Topic Sentences*: Topic sentences usually can be found at the start of each paragraph and are not only a great tool to keep you engaged in the passage but also a way to easily find your way back to the appropriate point in the passage when you need to consult the passage to answer a question. A bit further in the paragraph you usually find explanations and examples of that topic. Like before, be on watch for pivotal words mid-paragraph. Note how each new paragraph follows the one that precedes it, and look to the end of a paragraph for clues about the next idea. Use the noteboard to record the flow of ideas from one paragraph to the next. Sometimes two or more paragraphs may act as a "chunk" of the passage. Ideas can flow between these chunks in the same way they flow from paragraph to paragraph.

The Main Idea

One of the central goals of Active Reading is to find the main idea and try to follow it. The main idea of the passage is what the author wants you to believe about the issue being presented in the passage.

Note here that this does not mean that the topic of the passage is the main idea. The topic of the passage—which is usually on one of the four primary areas of GMAT passages outlined in the previous chapter as social science, physical science, biological science, or business—is the overarching theme of the entire passage. The main idea is what the author wants you to believe about the topic. So, if you find yourself agreeing or disagreeing with the author, or noticing the author pushing an opinion or arguing a point, chances are that is the main idea of the passage.

By identifying the main idea of the passage, you can quickly and easily determine the purpose of the passage, which is one of the key components of successfully Cracking the Passage.

The Purpose of the Passage

The purpose of the passage is what the author wants you to believe after reading the passage. The purpose of most passages is to persuade the reader to accept their main point. However, there are other reasons an author may write a passage. Broadly, the purpose behind a passage falls into one of three categories.

- *To Persuade*: The most common purpose for a GMAT passage is to persuade. As stated earlier, the author typically tries to convince you that his or her viewpoint (the main idea) is correct. In that sense, the main idea and the purpose are intimately connected.

- *To Criticize or Evaluate*: The second most common passage purpose is criticism or evaluation. The author may favor a new view over an existing one, or may criticize someone else's ideas. But criticism need not be negative; authors may play up the merits of a particular theory, book, technique, or other idea.

  When the author's purpose is to criticize or evaluate an idea, the passage almost always starts with a review of that idea. The author generally gives a quick overview in a neutral tone. The author's tone changes from neutral to critical (or perhaps complimentary) shortly after the main conclusions of the theory or idea are presented.

- *To Explain or Analyze*: While most passages involve some explanations and some analysis, passages that only explain or analyze are infrequent on the GMAT. Most authors have a point of view about the topic under discussion. However, a passage that deals with some sort of problem or puzzle may be purely explanatory in nature.

Mapping the Passage

Mapping the Passage is the final tool in learning how to Crack the Passage. By Mapping the Passage you can easily identify the main idea and purpose of the passage, and doing so will keep you engaged and save you time as you move on to the questions. But, to successfully map the passage, you must do something that a typical test taker never does. You must write things down. Just because you reach a reading comprehension passage does not give you an excuse to stop writing things down. In fact, as a time saving tactic alone, writing things down while working on a reading comprehension passage is worth the effort. Writing things down also helps you get a better understanding on the topic being presented, which yields a more complete appreciation for the passage and makes answering the questions a lot more manageable!

The best strategy for Mapping the Passage is called Key Sentences. In this approach, read the passage one paragraph at a time. At the end of each paragraph, stop and try to identify the one sentence that seems the most like an opinion, recommendation, conclusion, or reason. Write a short summary of that sentence down on the note board. You don't need to write the entire sentence, but you do want to write more than one or two words. It's also a good idea to label the sentence as either a claim (a primary or secondary conclusion of the passage) or a reason that supports a previous claim. The idea of mapping the passage in this fashion is to uncover the author's original outline for the passage. When you are finished mapping the passage, you should be able to string together your key sentences to produce the main idea of the passage.

STEP 2: UNDERSTAND THE QUESTION TASK

Overview

Understanding the question task is important to Cracking GMAT Reading Comprehension and it is largely overlooked by the average test taker. The Basics of Cracking the Questions can be broken down into two parts: identifying the subject and understanding the task.

The Basics of Cracking the Questions

Part 1: Identifying the Subject

When cracking GMAT Reading Comprehension questions, it's crucial to identify the subject of the question. For example, in the question "The author mentions land management policy in order to," the subject is *land management policy*. The subject helps you locate what you need to read *about* to answer the question.

By identifying the subject, know what the question writer is testing you on. This is important for two reasons. First, by knowing the content that the question writer is testing you on you are able to locate that information in the passage more easily. This is outlined in Step 3 of the Basic Approach. Secondly, without identifying the subject, you may struggle to eventually answer the question and are susceptible to some of the common trap incorrect answer choices. Identifying the subject is critical to Cracking the Questions, but equally as important is understanding the task of the question.

Part 2: Understanding the Task

If you have been actively reading, you may have been able to predict that the second part of Cracking the Questions is understanding the task of the question. The task of the question is what you need to find out about the subject. For example, is the question asking for a detail from the passage, or is it asking why that detail is in the passage? Are you required merely to describe something, or does the question expect you to analyze it? Meanwhile, you should also be on the lookout for words such as EXCEPT, LEAST, and NOT.

In the example question given earlier, "The author mentions land management policy in order to," the task words are *in order to*. The tasks that questions can ask about are diverse and can be categorized as *general*, *specific*, or *complex* tasks.

Specific: Specific tasks reference a small part of the passage. There are four different ways specific questions can be asked. They are retrieval, inference, purpose, and vocab-in-context.

- **Retrieval** questions ask you to find information in the passage and may make reference to a detail or fact (a person's name, a theory, a time period). The answer is typically just a paraphrase of this information in the passage. These questions are highlighted by phrases such as *According to the passage,* and any reference to things that are mentioned by the author.

- **Inference** questions make test takers nervous because they appear to suggest that the answer has to be figured out using knowledge about the author. Remember that all answer choices are found directly in the passage. In fact, inference tasks are a lot like retrieval tasks, particularly since a good portion of inference questions ask about a small detail that is easily overlooked. Keywords that identify a question as an inference include *infer, suggest, conclude,* or *imply,* among others. Because of the nature of these questions, it's easy to go wrong by drawing on outside information or making assumptions. Many wrong answers are based on the ways that people read into or interpret the information in the passage.

- **Purpose** questions ask *why* the author included the subject or some particular piece of information. Typically, the answer to these questions are closely related to the main point of the subject of the question. These questions can be identified by phrases such as *in order to,* and *serves which of the following functions.* To answer these questions, identify what the author said about the subject of the question and find an answer choice that reflects that idea.

- **Vocabulary-in-Context** questions ask you to state what the author means by a certain word or phrase. They are very similar to inference questions, because they usually ask what the author is suggesting or implying by the use of a particular term. The correct answer must fit the context of its sentence and the paragraph containing that sentence and match the main point of the passage.

General: General tasks ask about the passage as a whole. General questions can be asked in four different ways as well. Those ways are primary purpose, main idea, tone, and structure.

- **Primary Purpose** questions may seem similar to Main Idea questions, but they differ in one critical way. Primary Purpose questions ask *why* the author wrote the passage. Therefore, the answers are typically more general than those for Main Idea questions. The subject of Primary Purpose questions is usually the whole passage. These questions can be identified by the phrase *primary purpose,* and *chiefly concerned.* Not to be confused with Purpose questions, Primary Purpose questions test very broad ideas. This is an instance where, if you have carefully Cracked the Passage, you should be able to answer these questions easily.

- The task of **Main Idea** questions is to figure out what the author wants you to believe. The main idea is the overall claim, supported by the evidence contained in the rest of the text, in other words what does the author want you to accept as true? Main Idea questions differ from Primary Purpose questions in that the former deal with *what* the passage is about rather than *why* the author wrote it. These questions can be identified by any phrase that indicates a need for a general understanding of the passage, such as *overall claims* and *main point*. However, much like Primary Purpose questions, these questions are easily answerable if you have successfully Cracked the Passage.

- **Tone** questions ask you to evaluate how strongly or negatively the author feels about the subject of the question. Find the subject in the passage and look for words that reveal the author's feelings. Examples of such words and phrases include *misrepresenting, unlikely, considerable importance, unfortunately,* and *a poor grasp,* among others. Questions that ask about the authors tone generally use the words *tone* or *attitude.*

- Some **structure** questions ask about the overall sequence of the passage, while others ask about a smaller piece of it, such as a single paragraph. Either way, these questions test the general flow of the passage. If you can describe the flow of ideas—a task made easier by Mapping the Passage on the note board—you'll be able to narrow down the answer choices, crossing off answers that describe things that didn't happen in the passage.

Complex: Complex tasks require a good understanding of the main idea, so Cracking the Passage is essential. Complex questions also can be asked in four different ways. Those ways are evaluation, weaken/strengthen, analogy, and application.

- **Evaluation** questions on the GMAT are pretty rare, but they do exist. These questions test your ability to compare or analyze information from the passage. For example, you may be asked to assess the relationship between two pieces of information from the passage. There aren't many common forms of questions like this, so an example of this type of question would be *Which of the following most accurately summarizes the relationship between nineteenth century American women and eighteenth century American women in the highlighted text?*

- Slightly more common than evaluation questions, **Weaken/Strengthen** questions ask the test taker to weaken or strengthen an assertion made in the passage. These questions can be identified by the presence of the word *weaken* or *strengthen* in the question.

- **Analogy** questions typically use the answer choices to draw comparisons to information discussed in the passage. The correct answer is the one that completes a reasonable analogy. Mostly, these questions can be identified by the key phrase *most similar.*

- Sometimes questions ask you to apply information from the passage to a new scenario. These are **Application** questions and can be easily spotted when the question stem refers to the answer choices as either "scenarios," "situations," or "assertions."

STEP 3: FIND INFORMATION IN THE PASSAGE THAT ADDRESSES THE TASK

Overview

Step 3 of the Basic Approach to Cracking the GMAT Reading Comprehension is finding the information in the passage that addresses the question task. After you have Cracked the Question by identifying the subject and the task, look for the subject in the passage. Once you locate the subject, find the information about the subject that addresses the task of the question.

This is when Cracking the Passage from Step 1 of The Basic Approach is invaluable. Use your notes to find the appropriate place in the passage that addresses the subject and start reading. Try to read eight to ten lines. Then make sure you understand what you have read. It is important for you to not attempt to answer the question in your own words. Attempting to do so may cause you to interpret the passage, which is not your goal. Your goal is to find the information from the passage that addresses the task of the question. And, as always, the answers to the questions can always be found in the passage.

It is important for this step to use the **Active Reading** strategies from Step 1 again. After you have found the appropriate place to begin reading, keep the task of the question in the back of your mind and be on constant lookout for any information that addresses the task of the question. After you have found this information, and have taken measures to ensure you truly understand the information, you are ready to move on to Step 4 of The Basic Approach to Cracking GMAT Reading Comprehension—examining and eliminating the answer choices.

STEP 4: USE POE TO FIND THE ANSWER

Overview

The final step of The Basic Approach to Cracking GMAT Reading Comprehension is using POE to find the answer. If you have followed all of the steps up to this point, then you have worked the passage and have a thorough understanding of it through Active Reading, analyzed and achieved understanding of the question subject and task, and located and read the information about the question subject and task in the passage. Now, it's time to look at the answer choices and find the correct answer by using POE (Process of Elimination).

As discussed throughout this entire book thus far, POE is one of the most powerful tools at your disposal on test day. Reading Comprehension is no different as POE is the best tool to help you find the correct answer by eliminating the incorrect ones. Once you understand the task of the question and have been able to locate its information in the passage, eliminating wrong answer choices is the most effective way to answer the question correctly.

Many test takers do exactly what the writers of the test want them to do—they answer questions based on memory or what sounds correct. However, if you learn how test takers create incorrect answer choices, you can eliminate answers quickly and stand your best chance at achieving the highest score possible for you.

In light of that, the final step in learning how to crack GMAT Reading Comprehension is learning about the different ways that the test writers create wrong answer choices. Once you know their methodology, you can learn how to spot wrong answers and then confidently eliminate the offending answer choices.

The Basics of Cracking the Answer Choices

Knowing the types of answer choices that test writers use to create wrong answers is the key to being prepared to use POE on test day. Test writers use certain kinds of answer choices to make an answer choice look attractive. The problem is, even if you have read the passage and followed the steps, a lot of times the incorrect answer choices still look correct! The test writers have to write hard answer choices like this or else the questions are too easy. Your job is to become familiar with the ways by which they create these wrong answers so that when you read an answer choice constructed in a certain way it raises suspicion. The more skeptical you are of the answer choices, the more likely you are to be able to eliminate them.

The following are the ways in which test writers create wrong answers. They are:

Watch out for these
tricks and traps!

- Recycled Language and Memory Traps
- Extreme Language
- No Such Comparison
- Reversals
- Emotional Appeals
- Outside Knowledge

Become familiar with these and you are one step closer to cracking GMAT Reading Comprehension.

Recycled Language and Memory Traps

One of the easiest and most common ways that test writers create wrong answer choices is by repeating memorable words or phrases from the passage. The correct answers for GMAT Reading Comprehension questions are generally paraphrases of the passage. So the presence of words or phrases that are very reminiscent of the passage is a reason to be skeptical of the answer choice.

Recycled language is one of the most common forms of memory traps. Recycled language in an answer choice is easily identified because recycled language is words or phrases that are direct quotes from the text. If you see words or phrases that fit the description of recycled language, you should be very skeptical of the answer choice. Did the passage say exactly what the answer choice says regarding the recycled language? If it doesn't, the answer choice is incorrect.

More commonly, memory traps are words or phrases that evoke a strong memory from the passage. These answer choices are designed to make the average test taker think "Oh, I remember reading that in the passage" and, because of that, make for very appealing answer choices. Memory traps evoke a stronger memory than actual correct answers do, so if you find yourself attracted to an answer choice because of the mention of something you remember, be wary! Make sure that the answer choice hasn't taken that piece of information out of context or confused it with another part of the passage.

Extreme Language

Another common way to create wrong answer choices is by using language that is too "powerful" or overt. Common ways to do that are by using words such as *must, always, never, only, best,* and other very strong words, or by answers that use verbs that are really strong, such as *prove* or *fail.*

For instance, a primary purpose question may have answer choices that use a powerful verb such as *defend* or *criticize.* If the passage does not explicitly defend or criticize the main idea, this answer choice is incorrect because it contains the extreme language. Below is a chart of common words that should cause skepticism for extreme language.

Common Extreme Words			
Never	Not	Defend	Contradict
Always	No	Attack	Failure
Only	Must	Denounce	
None	Prove	Counter	

No Such Comparison

Comparison words such as *better, more, reconcile, less, decide,* or *more than* are used by test writers to make answer choices more appealing by drawing a comparison between two items referenced in the passage. If you see them, you should be skeptical. As with every answer choice, make sure to reference against the information in the passage. Often the ideas being compared in the answer choices were discussed in the passage but not explicitly compared.

Reversals

Reversal answer choices seek to confuse the test taker by saying the opposite of the main idea or a detail from the passage. These answer choices are more difficult to spot because there isn't a list of common words. However, if you have successfully Cracked the Passage and found the information in the passage that references the task of the question, then identifying reversals of the answer choices becomes a lot more manageable.

Emotional Appeals

This answer choice type is fairly rare on the GMAT. However, it is still worth mentioning. Some answer choices may try to appeal to the beliefs of the test taker. For instance, a political passage may contain an answer choice that values one political stance over another even if the passage made no such claim. If you have successfully followed the steps to Crack the Passage and identified the main idea and the task of the question, these answer choices are easily eliminated.

Outside Knowledge

Much like emotional appeal answer choices, outside knowledge answer choices are also fairly rare on the GMAT. Correct answer choices on the GMAT contain information that is only found in the passage. However, these answer choices can be very tempting to the test taker because you may know a piece of information that is not mentioned in the passage but is reflected in an answer choice. Remember, you should rely only on the information in the passage only to answer questions on the GMAT.

Summary

○ Most likely you will see four Reading Comprehension passages. There are usually 3 short passages, followed by 3 questions each, and 1 long passage, followed by 4 questions.

○ GMAT Reading Comprehension passage topics are usually from 4 areas: social sciences, biological science, physical science, and business.

○ GMAT test writers create questions in a certain way. For you to be successful, follow the steps of The Basic Approach to Cracking GMAT Reading Comprehension:
   • Step 1: Work the Passage
   • Step 2: Understand the Question Task
   • Step 3: Find Info in Passage That Addresses Task
   • Step 4: Use POE to Find the Answer

○ The Basics of cracking the passage start with Active Reading. Active Reading enables you to gain a greater understanding of the passage by asking questions, identifying the structure of the passage, and looking for topic sentences.

○ Crack the passage by identifying the main point and the purpose of the passage. The main point is what the author wants you to believe about something, and the purpose is why the author wrote the passage (to persuade, to criticize or evaluate, or to explain or analyze).

○ Mapping the passage is an effective tool in keeping yourself organized in order to work efficiently while cracking the passage.

○ Test writers deliberately create wrong answer using recycled language and memory traps, extreme language, no such comparison, reversals, emotional appeals, and outside knowledge.

Chapter 17
Critical Reasoning

To perform well on Critical Reasoning questions, you need to know how GMAT arguments are constructed and how they are commonly reasoned. It is also helpful to know how incorrect answer choices are typically created so you can recognize them on test day. In this chapter, we will show you how to recognize and master the eight types of argument questions that appear on the GMAT.

CRITICAL REASONING OVERVIEW

Critical Reasoning questions comprise just over one-quarter of the GMAT's Verbal section—approximately 11 of 41 questions are in this format. Each question consists of a short reading passage, followed by a single question and 5 multiple choice answers. Critical Reasoning passages are based on a short argument, a set of statements, or a plan of action. For each question, select the best answer from among the choices provided.

The Passage

Critical Reasoning passages tend to be short (usually 20–100 words) and oftentimes take the form of an argument. The subjects they consider don't often fall into neat categories, and the scenarios they present are commonly hypothetical. Read your passages carefully, pay attention to the language employed, and interpret that language literally. It is important to be precise when reading the passage for Critical Reasoning questions. As you'll see in the pages to come, the difference between getting a Critical Reasoning question correct and falling for a trap answer often lies in the particulars of the passage's wording.

The Question

There are eight types of Critical Reasoning question, each of which involves a different task with respect to the passage. Most questions test your ability to evaluate the reasoning employed in an argument, but some test your ability to reason on the basis of information. This chapter will outline the different types of questions you will see, how to identify them, and what to look for in the passage based on the type of question. So much of your evaluation of the passage depends on what the question is asking for you identify in the passage. Because of this, you should read the question first, and then read the passage.

The Answer Choices

All things verbal come down to Process of Elimination, and Critical Reasoning is no exception. Each question type for Critical Reasoning questions has its own set of POE tools. These tools are based off the common trap answers constructed by the test makers. Because the question types all vary, the common trap answers and POE tools to employ also vary based on question type. After mastering the different types of questions, you'll learn how answer choices for those question types are constructed and, with enough practice, you'll be able to spot a bad answer choice with confidence.

HOW GMAT ARGUMENTS ARE CONSTRUCTED

Most Critical Reasoning passages take the form of *arguments* in which the writer tries to convince the reader of something. Here's an example:

> During the past 10 years, advertising revenues for the magazine *True Investor* have fallen by 30 percent. The magazine has failed to attract new subscribers, and newsstand sales are at an all-time low. Thus, sweeping changes to the editorial board will be necessary for the magazine to survive.

GMAT arguments consist of three connected parts:

- Conclusion—what the author tries to persuade the reader to accept
- Premise—evidence provided in support of a conclusion
- Assumption—unstated ideas upon which an argument's validity rests

Conclusions

A conclusion is the primary claim made in an argument. The easiest way to identify the conclusion is to ask yourself what its author wants you to believe. In the argument above, the conclusion is found in the last sentence, where the author attempts to persuade the reader that *sweeping changes to the editorial board will be necessary for the magazine to survive*.

In some cases, indicator words can help you to find the conclusion. These include:

Therefore	Hence
Clearly	Consequently
Thus	So

Indicator words can help you to identify the parts of an argument, but not every argument uses them. However, almost every argument will have a conclusion of some kind. A conclusion can be a plan or course of action, an argument, a statement of supposed truth, or any number of resolutions to the contents of the passage.

Learning to identify the conclusion is the first important step in evaluating the passage. Once you've identified the conclusion, the remaining information in the passage should reveal evidence that is used in support of the conclusion.

Premises

The premises of an argument include any reasons, statistics, or other evidence provided in support of the conclusion. In the case of GMAT arguments, you must accept the truth of the premises, whether you agree with them or not. The easiest way to identify the premises is to ask what information the author has provided to justify the truth of the conclusion.

In the argument above, the premises can be found in the first two sentences, where the author provides three pieces of evidence in support of the conclusion: *advertising revenues have fallen by 30 percent*, *the magazine has failed to attract new subscribers*, and *sales are at an all-time low*.

Sometimes you'll see indicator words that can help you to find the premises. These include:

Because	In view of
Given that	Since
As a result of	Supposing that

Assumptions

Assumptions are unstated premises on which the author relies to prove his or her conclusion. Even well-reasoned arguments rest on assumptions; because it's impossible to say everything, some things must go unsaid. Therefore, assumptions play a crucial role in the structure of an argument, bridging gaps in reasoning from the premises to the conclusion.

The argument above assumes that the editorial board *caused* the problems now attributed to the magazine. If something other than the editorial board were responsible—had the local population declined by 30 percent, for example—then sweeping changes to the board might do little to improve the magazine's financial situation. In this case, the connection between the premises (the magazine's problems) and the conclusion (changes to the editorial board) falls apart. The reader is no longer persuaded that *changes to the editorial board will be necessary for the magazine to survive*. The argument collapses.

The easiest way to identify an assumption is to distinguish an argument's conclusion from its premises. Then, ask what additional information is required to link the conclusion to the premises.

Gaps

In many cases, gaps in reasoning are indicated by gaps in language. Look for words or phrases in the conclusion that do not come from the premises. Identify an assumption in the following example:

> Cream cheese contains half as many calories per tablespoon as does butter or margarine. Therefore, a bagel with cream cheese is more healthful than is a bagel with butter.

First, find the conclusion. The word "therefore" gives the conclusion away: *a bagel with cream cheese is more healthful than is a bagel with butter.*

Second, find the premises. What information does the author provide to support the conclusion? The premise states that *cream cheese contains half as many calories per tablespoon.*

Third, look for shifts in language between the premise and conclusion. The premise compares the calorie content of a tablespoon of cream cheese to that of a tablespoon of butter or margarine. The conclusion introduces the word "healthful," which does not appear in the premise. This shift in the argument's language is indicative of a gap in reasoning—the argument leaps from a thing that *has fewer calories per tablespoon* to a thing that *is more healthful*. Therefore, this argument rests on the assumption that a food with *fewer calories* is a food that is *more healthful*.

Although most Critical Reasoning passages consist of three basic parts—conclusions, premises, and assumptions—some passages also include extraneous ideas, background information, or opposing points of view. The efficiency with which you identify assumptions depends in large part on the accuracy with which you identify conclusions and premises, so don't be distracted by nonessential information.

COMMON REASONING PATTERNS

Like the other question formats on the GMAT, Critical Reasoning questions tend to be predictable. While you'll never see the same question twice, many Critical Reasoning passages employ similar patterns of reasoning. Learning to recognize these patterns provides you with another means of identifying assumptions.

Not every GMAT argument models one of the common reasoning patterns, so you'll sometimes still need to look for shifts in language. However, when one of the common reasoning patterns is present, it can help you to locate information needed to strengthen or weaken an argument. Each of the five common patterns involves its own standard assumption or assumptions. Learning to recognize these patterns, and the assumptions they incorporate, will help you to identify unstated presuppositions and pinpoint an argument's flaws.

Causal Patterns

Causal reasoning is the most common type of reasoning you'll encounter in GMAT arguments. Test writers are fond of causal arguments, and you're likely to see several of them on the GMAT. In a causal argument, the premises usually state that two things happened, from which the author concludes that one thing caused the other. Consider the following simple example:

> A study indicated that adults who listen to classical music regularly are less likely to have anxiety disorders. Clearly, classical music calms the nerves and reduces anxiety.

The author of this argument concludes that *classical music calms the nerves and reduces anxiety*. This conclusion is based on a study indicating that *adults who listen to classical music regularly are less likely to have anxiety disorders*. Thus, the premise posits a correlation between two things—exposure to classical music and reduced likelihood of anxiety disorders—and the conclusion makes a leap from correlation to causation.

Every causal argument involves two standard assumptions:

- There's no other cause.
- It's not a coincidence.

Our argument assumes that it's not a coincidence that adults who listened to classical music were less likely to have anxiety disorders, and that makes sense because it also assumes that nothing other than classical music caused study participants to experience fewer anxiety disorders.

The first standard assumption suggests that classical music, and only classical music, caused participants in the study to experience fewer anxiety disorders. But what if something else was responsible? The passage doesn't rule out the possibility that study participants used anxiety-reducing medication, or that they simply happened to be calm people to begin with. In neither of these cases would it follow that *classical music calms the nerves and reduces anxiety*. Thus, the argument must assume that a causal relationship exists.

The second standard assumption denies that the correlation between classical music and anxiety is a coincidence. But what if a different study indicated that adults who listen to classical music regularly were more likely to have anxiety disorders? In that case, it no longer follows that classical music calms the nerves and reduces anxiety—on the contrary, the counterexample suggests that the first study's results were coincidental. Thus, the argument must assume that the correlation between classical music and lower anxiety is not a coincidence.

When you spot an argument that employs a causal reasoning pattern, remember that the argument relies on two assumptions: first, there's no other cause; and second, it's not a coincidence.

Planning Patterns

Many GMAT arguments introduce plans that are designed to solve problems: a municipal government's plan to improve water quality, a transit authority's plan to reduce traffic congestion, or a town board's plan to increase voter turnout. The premises of planning arguments describe what the plan is supposed to accomplish and how it is supposed to work. For example:

> During the past 5 years, Meridian Township has seen a dramatic rise in crime. As a result, Meridian's police force plans to install video surveillance cameras at major intersections in neighborhoods that suffer the worst crime rates. Clearly, the crime rate in Meridian Township will drop.

Consider this argument in terms of its parts. Meridian Township has a problem: *a dramatic rise in crime*. To address this problem, the police force plans to *install video surveillance cameras*. These are the premises of the argument because they outline the plan for addressing the problem. The argument concludes that, as a result of instituting the plan, the crime rate will drop. In general, the conclusion of an argument that employs the planning pattern can simply be expressed: *do the plan*.

Every planning argument involves one standard assumption:

- There's no problem with the plan.

Evaluating an argument with a planning reasoning pattern will revolve around the plan itself. For instance, what if there *is* a problem with the plan to reduce crime by installing video cameras at major intersections? After all, crime is not limited to major intersections. Perhaps the cameras will malfunction or produce poor quality images. Perhaps criminals will simply relocate to neighborhoods without cameras. In these cases, our confidence in the conclusion is shaken. On the basis of the premises alone, it no longer seems to follow that *the crime rate will drop*. Thus, in order for the argument to "work," its author must assume that installing the cameras really will reduce crime, or that there's no problem with the plan. A question could ask to identify a potential problem with the plan, or to strengthen the plan with the addition of some other fact.

No matter what the question asks, when you encounter an argument that employs a planning pattern, remember the standard assumption at play: there's no problem with the plan.

Sampling Patterns

Arguments that exhibit a sampling pattern are less common than causal or planning arguments. In a sampling argument, the author reaches a general conclusion about a population based on evidence about some members of the population. Sampling arguments assume that a smaller group is typical of a larger group and accurately reflects the relevant characteristics or feelings of the larger group. Here is an example:

> Contrary to popular belief, football fans overwhelmingly approve of the decisions made by the administrative staffs of their local teams. We know this to be true because a large group of fans leaving a stadium expressed admiration for their teams' coaches and coordinators in an interview last week.

The author of this argument concludes that *football fans overwhelmingly approve of the decisions made by the administrative staffs of their local teams*. This conclusion is based on the premise that *a large group of fans leaving a stadium expressed admiration for their teams' coaches and coordinators in an interview last week*. Thus, the conclusion makes a leap from the opinion of one group of fans at a particular moment to the opinion of football fans in general.

Every sampling argument involves one standard assumption:

- The sample is representative.

When you encounter a sampling reasoning pattern, look for reasons why the sample itself is either representative or not. What if the opinion of the interviewed group of football fans isn't representative of the opinions of football fans in general? Perhaps the interviewed fans attended a game their team won, and perhaps their local team has long enjoyed a winning record. It does not follow from this that fans of every team approve of the decisions made by their team's administrative staff. To properly link the argument's conclusion to its premise, the author must assume that the opinions of interviewed fans accurately reflect those of football fans in general.

When you run into an argument that employs a sampling pattern, remember that the argument relies on the assumption that a sample is representative of a larger population.

Interpretation of Evidence Patterns

In some GMAT arguments, the author understands the conclusion to be synonymous with one or more of the premises. In other words, information in the premises is interpreted to mean information in the conclusion. These arguments exhibit the interpretation of evidence pattern.

One particularly common instance of this pattern involves the misinterpretation of statistical data. Not every argument that incorporates statistics is an interpretation of evidence argument, but arguments that exhibit this pattern frequently involve statistics. Most often, the argument confuses percentages with actual values. Consider the following example:

> Local grocer: Ninety percent of customers bought store brand soup last winter, but only eighty percent bought store brand soup this winter. Obviously, more customers bought store brand soup last winter.

The author concludes that *more customers bought store brand soup last winter*. This conclusion is based on the premise that *ninety percent of customers bought soup last winter, but only eighty percent bought soup this winter*. The premise describes a change in the percentage of customers who bought store brand soup, and the conclusion leaps from percentages to actual numbers.

Every interpretation of evidence argument involves one standard assumption:

- There's no other way to interpret the evidence.

What if there's another way to interpret the data? If 100 customers visited the grocer last winter, and ninety percent bought soup, then 90 bought soup last winter. But if 200 customers visited the grocer this winter, and eighty percent bought soup, then 160 bought soup this winter. In this case, it no longer follows that more people bought soup last winter—the author misinterprets the statistical data.

When you come across an interpretation of evidence pattern, the argument most likely relies on the standard assumption that there's no other way to interpret the evidence.

Analogy Patterns

Reasoning by analogy is relatively rare on the GMAT, but that doesn't mean you won't see arguments by analogy. These arguments characteristically assume that what is appropriate in one case is also appropriate in another. They typically rely on the assumption that two things are similar enough to sustain a comparison. Here is a simple example:

> Using this line of products has been shown to cause cancer in laboratory animals. Therefore, you should stop using this line of products.

The author concludes that *you should stop using this line of products*. This conclusion is based on the premise that *this line of products has been shown to cause cancer in laboratory animals*. The premise concerns lab animals, and the conclusion leaps to humans. Thus, the argument relies on the assumption that humans and lab animals are similar: what causes cancer in laboratory animals also causes cancer in humans.

Arguments by analogy involve one standard assumption:

- One thing is similar to another.

What if humans are significantly different from laboratory animals? For example, if a feature of human physiology not shared by lab animals prevented the growth of cancers in humans who used the products, it would no longer follow that you should stop using the products.

When you encounter an argument that employs an analogy pattern, it probably relies on the assumption that one thing is similar to another in some relevant way.

THE BASIC APPROACH TO CRITICAL REASONING QUESTIONS

Critical Reasoning questions come in eight flavors. The majority of the questions as either *assumption*, *weaken*, *strengthen*, or *inference* questions. However, there are some minor question types, such as *resolve/explain*, *evaluate*, *identify the reasoning*, or *flaw* questions, of which you should be aware. Each of these question types has its own unique task and common trap answers.

Most Critical Reasoning questions will present you with an argument, but not all questions involve arguments. In fact, some Critical Reasoning passages don't look like arguments at all. In order to master the Critical Reasoning format, you need a basic approach that can be applied to any Critical Reasoning question you encounter, no matter what kind of question it is.

Here are the steps of the Basic Approach:

1. **Identify the Question**

   Look for words or phrases in the question stem that can be used to identify the question type. Your knowledge of the question type informs your approach to the passage, so always read the question stem before you read the passage.

2. **Work the Passage**

   For most question types, begin working an argument by distinguishing its conclusion from its premises. Then, look for shifts in language or reasoning patterns that can help you to identify the argument's assumption.

3. **Predict What the Answer Should Do**

   While it's often difficult to predict the answer, it's usually easier to predict what the answer should do. Before turning to the answer choices, use your knowledge of the question and the information in the passage to determine what the correct answer needs to accomplish.

4. **Use POE to Find the Answer**

   It's often easier to identify incorrect answers than it is to identify correct answers, so use POE aggressively. The POE tools changed based on the question type, which is why it is critically important for you to become familiar with the different types of questions and how answer choices are constructed for them.

Step 1: Identify the Question

The surest way to improve performance and boost confidence in your Critical Reasoning ability is to take control of your approach to Critical Reasoning questions. Every question includes a word or phrase that can help you to identify what kind of question it is, and each question type involves a unique task with respect to the passage. Not all tasks are created equally, so it's important to know what's required of you.

Your knowledge of the question type should inform your approach, suggesting what kind of information to look for in the passage and what kind of answers to avoid. For now, we'll introduce the different question types, saving a more detailed discussion for later in the chapter.

Assumption Questions

Assumptions are necessary but invisible parts of an argument that bridge gaps in reasoning between its premises and conclusion. Here's where all that practice identifying the parts of an argument really begins to pay off. Simply put, assumption questions ask you to identify an unstated premise on which an argument depends.

Assumption questions typically ask:

- The argument above assumes which of the following?
- The author of the argument above presupposes which of the following to be true?
- Which of the following is an assumption on which the truth of the author's conclusion depends?

Different forms of the words *presupposition*, *expectation*, and *assumption* can alert you to the fact that you've encountered an assumption question.

Weaken Questions

Weaken questions ask to find a reason why the information in the passage could be wrong, or is incomplete. The vast majority of weaken questions require you to undermine the conclusion by attacking one of the argument's assumptions. Most commonly, the real job when answering weaken questions is not to attack the conclusion, but to attack *the way the conclusion follows from the premises*.

Weaken questions typically ask:

- Which of the following, if true, most seriously weakens the argument above?
- Which of the following casts the most doubt on the author's conclusion?
- Which of the following calls into question the reasoning above?

Indicator words such as *weaken*, *undermine*, and *cast doubt* can help you to spot a weaken question.

Strengthen Questions

Strengthen questions require you to reinforce an argument's conclusion. This is usually accomplished by strengthening one of the argument's assumptions. In order to answer a strengthen question with confidence, therefore, you must first identify an assumption. Once the pivotal assumption has been found, your job is to strengthen it—support the conclusion by strengthening the assumption.

Strengthen questions typically ask:

- Which of the following provides the best support for the claims made above?
- Which of the following statements, if true, most strengthens the argument's conclusion?
- Which of the following, if true, increases the likelihood that the author's claim is also true?

Words such as *strengthen*, *support*, and *justify* can help you to recognize a strengthen question.

Inference Questions

In one sense, an inference question is like a strengthen question in reverse. In a strengthen question, the correct answer strengthens the passage, but in an inference question, the passage strengthens the correct answer. As a result, many indicator words associated with strengthen questions—words such as *strengthen*, *support*, and *bolster*—are also associated with inference questions. Distinguish an inference question from a strengthen question by determining the direction of support.

In another sense, inference questions are unlike any of the question types we've discussed so far, because they don't require you to break an argument into its parts. In fact, inference passages tend not to resemble arguments at all. Instead, they merely present you with information—usually a collection of facts or opinions that lead to a particular conclusion. Once you're clear on the facts, your job is to select the answer that necessarily follows from them.

Inference questions typically ask:

- Which of the following can be inferred from the information above?
- On the basis of the statements above, which of the following must be true?
- With which of the following statements would the author of the passage most agree?

Words such as *inference*, *support*, and *strengthen* can help you spot an inference question.

Resolve/Explain Questions

Some Critical Reasoning questions ask you to resolve an apparent discrepancy or explain a paradoxical situation. The passages that accompany these questions almost never resemble arguments. Like inference passages, they merely present you with information. Resolve/explain questions ask how two seemingly incongruous statements can be true at the same time. Clearly state the two ideas that seem to be opposed, and then select the answer that allows both ideas to be true.

Resolve/Explain questions typically ask:

- Which of the following, if true, resolves the paradox outlined above?
- Which of the following best explains the apparent contradiction?
- Which of the following statements goes farthest in explaining the situation above?

Resolve/Explain questions are easy to recognize because they include the word *resolve* or *explain*. Words such as *paradox* and *discrepancy* can also help you identify resolve/explain questions.

Evaluate Questions

Evaluate questions target your ability to spot a question (or test) that could be answered (or performed) to *evaluate* or *assess* an argument. Your job is to identify the question that, if answered, would allow you to test the argument's key assumption. Thus, evaluate questions are similar to strengthen and weaken questions in that they first require you to identify an unstated premise.

However, once the key assumption has been found, your task is not to weaken or strengthen it, but to identify the test that could help determine whether the argument is weak or strong.

Evaluate questions typically ask:

- The answer to which of the following questions would most likely yield information that could be used to assess the author's claim?
- Which of the following experiments would be most useful in evaluating the argument above?
- Which of the following tests could be performed to determine the truth of the argument's conclusion?

Indicator words such as *evaluate* and *assess* can help you to recognize an evaluate question.

Identify the Reasoning Questions

Occasionally, a Critical Reasoning question will ask you to identify the method, technique, or strategy used by the author of an argument, or to describe the roles played by bolded phrases in an argument. Identify the reasoning questions concern the relationships that exist between an argument's parts. Before you can answer a question about that relationship, you must first identify those parts. Distinguish the argument's conclusion from its premises, and then select the answer that accurately describes the structure of the argument.

Identify the reasoning questions typically ask:

- The author provides support for the argument above by…
- Which of the following methods of reasoning does the argument above exhibit?
- The bolded phrases play which of the following roles in the argument above?

Words such as *technique*, *strategy*, *method*, and *by* can help you to spot an identify the reasoning question.

Flaw Questions

Flaw questions ask you to describe what went wrong in an argument. The question stem already acknowledges that you're dealing with a bad argument. Your job is to identify its vulnerability. Flaw questions tend to resemble a blend of the identify the reasoning and weaken question types. Select the answer that accurately describes a vulnerability in the argument's reasoning.

Flaw questions typically ask:

- Which of the following statements describes a flaw in the argument above?
- The argument above is vulnerable to criticism for which of the following reasons?

To identify a flaw question, look for the words *vulnerable*, *criticism*, and *flaw*.

Step 2: Work the Argument

After you've read a Critical Reasoning question, read the accompanying passage. Allow your knowledge of the question type to guide you to relevant information.

Most Critical Reasoning questions—assumption, weaken, strengthen, evaluate, flaw, and identify the reasoning questions—provide you with an argument, and then ask you to perform a task related to the reasoning that argument employs.

- **Assumption questions** ask for an assumption required to make the argument valid. The correct answer will bridge a gap in an argument's reasoning from premise to conclusion, so begin by distinguishing the conclusion from the premises that support it. Then, identify the assumption that links the conclusion to the premises, choosing the answer that bridges the gap. Shifts in language and reasoning patterns can help you to spot assumptions.

- **Weaken questions**: Weakening a GMAT argument is almost always accomplished by attacking one of the argument's key assumptions. Therefore, begin a weaken question the same way you begin an assumption question, by using the argument's premises and conclusion to identify unstated information on which the argument depends. Once you've spotted the pivotal assumption, choose the answer that offers good reason to believe it isn't true.

- **Strengthen questions**: Strengthening a GMAT argument is almost always accomplished by reinforcing one of the argument's key assumptions. Begin a strengthen question by identifying the argument's premises and conclusion, as well as any gaps in reasoning between them. Once you've found the pivotal assumption, choose the answer that suggests it's true.

- **Evaluate questions** are similar to weaken and strengthen questions in that they ask you to consider the unstated piece of information that, if you knew it, would tell you whether you're looking at a weak argument or a strong argument. Evaluating a GMAT argument is almost always accomplished by identifying a test you could perform or a question you could answer to determine the truth or falsity of an assumption.

- **Identify the Reasoning questions** ask you to describe the structure of an argument or how it works. Some identify the reasoning questions concern the logical function of bolded phrases in the passage. For any identify the reasoning question, determine which part of the argument functions as its claim and which parts function as evidence. Choose the answer that accurately describes the structure of the argument. There's no need to worry about assumptions.

- **Flaw questions** combine the tasks involved in identify the reasoning and weaken questions. You're looking for the answer that accurately describes the structure of the argument (identify the reasoning), usually by exposing the weakness of an assumption made by the author (weaken). Begin by distinguishing the argument's conclusion from its premises. Use shifts in language or reasoning patterns to identify the faulty assumption.

- **Inference questions**: Passages that accompany inference questions tend to look like collections of facts without any logical progression from premises to conclusion. There's usually no way to differentiate claims from evidence, so don't bother. In fact, you may feel as though the question gives you the evidence and asks you to provide the conclusion. Begin an inference question by familiarizing yourself with the information provided; if it helps, use your whiteboard to create a list of facts. Then, choose the answer that must be true on the basis of the facts.

- **Resolve/Explain questions**: Like inference passages, the passages that accompany resolve/explain questions tend not to exhibit the structural elements of an argument. Instead, they present two ideas that seem to be opposed. Rather than looking for premises and conclusions, begin by using your whiteboard to clarify the apparent conflict: "On the one hand, *X*, but on the other, *Y*." Indicator words such as *but*, *yet*, and *however* can draw your attention to opposing ideas and help you to articulate the apparent conflict. Choose the answer that explains how *X* and *Y* might both be true at the same time.

Step 3: Predict What the Answer Should Do

Just as your knowledge of the question type can help you to identify relevant information in a Critical Reasoning passage, your knowledge of the question type can help you to recognize the characteristics of the answer you're looking for.

Predicting the answer to a Critical Reasoning question is often quite difficult. Predicting what the answer should do is usually easier. Before turning to the answers, think about what the correct answer needs to accomplish based on the question type and information in the argument. In this way, you continue to exercise control over a question as you move from information gathering to answer selection.

- **Assumption questions:** Good answers to assumption questions bridge a gap in reasoning between the premises of an argument and its conclusion. For this reason, they often employ words or phrases that appear in the premises, as well as language from the conclusion. A good answer links the author's claim to evidence that supports it, or rules out obstacles to that link.

- **Weaken questions:** Good answers to weaken questions widen a gap in reasoning between the premises of an argument and its conclusion. In order to do so, they often introduce new information that attacks one of the argument's assumptions. A good answer makes the truth of an author's claim seem less likely by disrupting the link between that claim and the evidence that supports it.

- **Strengthen questions:** Good answers to strengthen questions are very similar to those for assumption questions. That's because both question types require you to find an assumption that supports the argument's conclusion. A good answer will confirm the pivotal assumption or introduce new information that rules out obstacles to it.

- **Inference questions:** Like inference questions in the Reading Comprehension format, inference questions in the Critical Reasoning format don't really ask you to make an inference beyond the scope of the information provided. It can be difficult to come up with your own answer to an inference question, so let the test writers worry about the phrasing. Simply keep in mind that you want the answer best supported by the facts. An answer that paraphrases a fact from the passage is often the credited response.

- **Resolve/Explain questions:** Passages that accompany resolve/explain questions introduce a pair of facts or ideas that seem to oppose one another. Once you've clarified the apparent conflict, look for answer choices that allow both facts to be true simultaneously. Good answers address both sides of the issue, rather than ignoring one side or the other.

- **Evaluate questions:** Evaluate questions require you to select a test you could perform, or a question you could ask, to assess the validity of an argument. If the answer choices are phrased as questions, try answering each question "Yes" and "No" to see whether different answers change your belief in the argument's conclusion. If so, you're probably dealing with the credited response. Good answers make it possible to determine the truth or falsity of an assumption made in the argument.

- **Identify the Reasoning questions:** Once you've identified the premises and conclusion of an identify the reasoning passage, look for answer choices that accurately describe the relationships between an argument's parts. There's no reason to look for gaps or assumptions; the task is purely descriptive. Keep an eye out for answers that focus on the structure of the argument rather than its content. Good answer choices accurately mirror the argument's structure.

- **Flaw questions:** Good answers to flaw questions accurately reflect the structure of the argument. They differ from good answers to identify the reasoning questions only because they invariably describe flaws in reasoning. The correct answer most often articulates a faulty assumption.

Step 4: Use POE to Find the Answer

This is the last step in the basic approach to Critical Reasoning questions. You've done most of the work required to answer the question. All that remains is to select and confirm your answer. You're already armed with a sense of what the correct answer needs to accomplish. Now, supplement that understanding with an efficient, effective process for weeding out bad answers and avoiding traps—tempting answers that are nevertheless incorrect.

Just as your knowledge of question types can help you find relevant information in a passage and predict what the correct answer should do, it can help you to narrow your search for the correct answer by enabling you to quickly eliminate answers that are flawed. You've read about the characteristics of good answers. It's time to consider the characteristics of poor answers. Each Critical Reasoning question type has its own set of attractor answers that you will learn to anticipate. GMAT arguments are often quite specific, so read them carefully and interpret them literally. Pay close attention to the language used in arguments and answer choices.

Assumption questions ask you for the unstated premise in the argument. Correct answers link conclusions to the premises that support them, so ask how each answer affects the author's claim. When you think you've found the correct answer, apply the **Negation Test**. Negate your preferred answer, and if your belief in the argument's conclusion isn't affected, the answer is incorrect. Avoid answers that:

- are out of scope
- use extreme language

Weaken questions ask you to select the answer that disrupts the link between the premises and the conclusion. Ask yourself how each choice affects the author's claim. Eliminate answers that:

- are out of scope
- use extreme language
- strengthen the argument

Strengthen questions ask you to select the answer that reinforces the link between the premises and the conclusion. Ask yourself how each choice affects the author's claim. Eliminate answers that:

- are out of scope
- use extreme language
- weaken the argument

Inference questions ask for the answer choice that follows necessarily from the facts in the passage. The answers to inference questions generally don't stray far from the information provided, so look to eliminate answers that require additional assumptions. Avoid answers that:

- are out of scope
- use extreme language

Resolve/Explain questions for the answer that resolves an apparent conflict between two ideas, or that explains the conflict away. When you consider the answer choices, adhere closely to the opposing ideas. Avoid answers that:

- are out of scope
- make the conflict worse
- address only one side of the conflict

Evaluate questions ask you to select the answer that allows the strength or weakness of an argument to be determined. Incorrect answers offer new information that does not connect the argument's conclusion to its premises in a meaningful way. Eliminate answers that:

- are out of scope

Identify the Reasoning questions ask you to find the answer that accurately describes the structure of an argument. Avoid answers that:

- do not match the structure of the argument
- only partially match the structure

Flaw questions ask you to choose the answer that accurately describes a flaw in the structure of an argument. Watch out for answers that describe the argument faithfully, but neglect to mention a flaw. Eliminate answers that:

- are out of scope
- cannot be matched to the argument or are only partial matches

PRACTICE QUESTIONS

Now that you've been introduced to the parts of a GMAT argument, the reasoning patterns typical of GMAT arguments, and the basic approach to Critical Reasoning questions, work through some example questions to bolster your understanding of the Critical Reasoning question format.

Here is an example of an **Assumption question.**

Most people believe that gold and platinum are the most valuable commodities. To the true entrepreneur, however, gold and platinum are less valuable than is the knowledge of opportunities. Thus, in the world of high finance, information is the most valuable commodity.

The author of the passage above makes which of the following assumptions?

- ○ Gold and platinum are not the most valuable commodities.
- ○ Entrepreneurs are not like most people.
- ○ The value of information is incalculably high.
- ○ Information about business opportunities is accurate and leads to increased wealth.
- ○ Only entrepreneurs feel that information is the most valuable commodity.

Here's How to Crack It

The question asks for the *assumption* made by the author, so this is an assumption question.

An assumption supports the conclusion of an argument, so when you read the passage, look for the conclusion. The word "thus" in the passage's final sentence gives it away: *in the world of high finance, information is the most valuable commodity.*

Now determine what information in the passage is in support of the conclusion. Two pieces of information are provided in support of the conclusion. One group of people—*most people*—believe that *gold and platinum are the most valuable commodities*. Another group—*true entrepreneurs*—believe that *gold and platinum are less valuable than is the knowledge of opportunities*.

From the opinions of two groups of people, the author concludes that the opinion of one group is to be preferred, but the passage doesn't say why. Therefore, it's likely that the correct answer will explain why the opinion of *the true entrepreneur* is to be preferred. With that in mind, you're ready to attack the answer choices:

◯ Gold and platinum are not the most valuable commodities.

This answer appears to support the conclusion. If *gold and platinum are not the most valuable commodities*, there's a chance that *information is*. By itself, however, the idea that gold and platinum *are not* the most valuable commodities doesn't mean information *is* the most valuable commodity. This assumption provides no reason why the author should agree with *the true entrepreneur*; it doesn't link the argument's premises to its conclusion. Eliminate (A).

◯ Entrepreneurs are not like most people in other careers.

This answer choice doesn't tell you anything you don't already know: if the true entrepreneur doesn't share the opinion of most people, then entrepreneurs aren't like most people (at least not in the way they value commodities). In any case, this answer doesn't provide a reason to favor the opinion of the true entrepreneur. Eliminate (B).

◯ The value of information is incalculably high.

Be wary of the extreme language in this answer choice. The author needn't assume the value of information is incalculable in order to believe that it's the most valuable commodity. On the other hand, the value of many commodities might be incalculable; it doesn't follow from this that information is most valuable. Eliminate (C).

◯ Information about business opportunities is accurate and leads to increased wealth.

This answer links the argument's conclusion to its premises by providing a reason to side with the true entrepreneur. To check whether this assumption is required by the argument, apply the Negation Test. If information *isn't* accurate and *doesn't* lead to increased wealth, it's unclear why the author believes it to be most valuable. Negating this answer disrupts the argument, so keep (D).

◯ Only entrepreneurs feel that information is the most valuable commodity.

This answer is out of scope. It doesn't matter *who* believes information to be most valuable. What matters is *why* the author believes it to be most valuable. Eliminate (E).

The correct answer is (D).

――――――――――――――― ◯ ―――――――――――――――

Here is an example of a **Weaken question.**

Given the current economic climate, universal healthcare is an impossibility in the United States. More than half of all U.S. households report feeling overwhelmed by expenses, and many people are struggling to find additional sources of income. Funding such a massive program would require significant tax increases, adding to the financial burden of many individuals. The employer-sponsored healthcare system currently in place keeps taxes low, protecting our nation's economy.

Which of the following, if true, would most weaken argument above?

○ Many U.S. citizens enjoy sizeable tax breaks for medical expenses.
○ Universal healthcare would reduce the financial burden on employers, resulting in significant job growth and wage increases.
○ A majority of profitable, private health insurers have indicated that they expect to increase their payrolls in the coming quarter.
○ Pharmaceutical companies have fewer incentives to innovate new drugs in a universal healthcare system.
○ Most U.S. citizens depend on their employers for health coverage and could not afford comparable coverage under the current system.

Here's How to Crack It

The question asks you to *weaken* the argument, so this is a weaken question.

Let's break this argument down into its core components. The author concludes that *universal healthcare represents an impossibility in the United States.* Why? Because *funding such a program would require significant tax increases*, and *more than half of all US households already report feeling overwhelmed by expenses....*

Did you spot the gap in the argument's reasoning? The premises refer to the financial burden faced by Americans and to the costs associated with universal healthcare. The conclusion leaps from the cost of such a system to its impossibility. This shift in language exposes a gap in the author's reasoning. Bridging this gap requires an assumption that links the cost of universal healthcare to its impossibility. We know what the correct answer needs to do, and we have a good idea how it might get done. Let's turn to the answer choices.

○ Many U.S. citizens enjoy sizeable tax breaks for medical expenses.

Under the current healthcare system, many people are compensated for medical expenses via tax breaks. However, there's no information about what will happen to these tax breaks under a universal healthcare system. This answer touches on the financial problem mentioned in the premises, but because it doesn't link this problem to the impossibility of instituting universal healthcare, it can't be used to weaken the argument. This choice is out of scope, so eliminate it.

    ○ Universal healthcare would reduce the financial burden on employers, resulting in significant job growth and wage increases.

This answer suggests that universal healthcare might lead to positive financial outcomes. If the benefits of universal healthcare outweigh its costs, then those costs don't contribute to the impossibility of universal healthcare. This choice breaks the link between the cost of universal healthcare and its impossibility, so keep (B).

    ○ A majority of profitable, private health insurers have indicated that they expect to increase their payrolls in the coming quarter.

Are the plans of private health insurers to increase their payrolls relevant to the argument we identified? No, what private insurers do with their payrolls has no bearing on the argument that universal healthcare is impossible because it's expensive. Choice (C) is out of scope. Eliminate it.

    ○ Pharmaceutical companies have fewer incentives to innovate in a universal healthcare system.

If drug companies have fewer incentives to innovate, then there's evidence to suggest universal healthcare might be a bad idea. This answer addresses the impossibility of universal healthcare by introducing another reason not to pursue it, but that reason doesn't link the impossibility of universal healthcare to its cost. Eliminate (D).

    ○ Most U.S. citizens depend on their employers for health coverage and could not afford comparable coverage under the current system.

This answer acknowledges the high cost of healthcare under the current system. However, the argument concerns the cost of instituting a universal healthcare system, not the cost of the current system, which is out of scope. Eliminate (E).

The correct answer is (B).

———————————○———————————

Challenge Question #17

In an effort to stimulate economic growth, the parliament of Sapland is promoting new legislation which halves the corporate tax rate. Members of parliament claim the move will lead to job creation and investment by the impacted corporations. Critics disagree vocally, pointing to a plethora of studies indicating that such tax savings tend to be kept as profit rather than reinvested, and therefore are unlikely to spur job creation or corporate investment.

Which of the following, if true, most undermines the critics objection to the tax plan promoted by parliament to spur job creation and corporate investment by halving the corporate tax rate?

○ The legislation halving the corporate tax rate includes a stipulation that funds equal to those owed in the form of taxes must be used by the impacted corporation to promote its primary business purpose.

○ The tax savings will induce the shareholders of many impacted corporations to increase their personal investment portfolios significantly.

○ Many corporate shareholders consider their respective corporations' performance to be more than sufficient, and see no reason to expand either their workforces or capital investments.

○ The majority of the tax revenue lost due to the corporate tax rate reduction can be reclaimed by raising property taxes on large estates.

○ Sapland currently suffers from high unemployment, brought on by years of government-mandated anti-discrimination policies and environmental regulations.

Here is an example of a **Strengthen question**.

It has recently been proposed that Country X adopt an all-volunteer army. This policy was tried on a limited basis several years ago and was a miserable failure. The level of education of the volunteers was unacceptably low, while levels of drug use and crime soared among army personnel. Can Country X trust its national defense to a volunteer army? The answer is clearly "No."

Which of the following statements, if true, provides the most support for the claim that an all-volunteer army should not be implemented?

○ The population's level of education has risen since the first time an all-volunteer army was tried.

○ The proposal was made by an organization called Citizens for Peace.

○ The first attempt to create a volunteer army was carried out according to the same plan now under proposal and under the same conditions as those that exist today.

○ A volunteer army would be less expensive than an army that relies on the draft.

○ Armies are smaller today than they were when a volunteer army was last proposed.

Here's How to Crack It

The question asks for the statement that *provides the most support for the claim*, so this is a strengthen question. Begin by distinguishing the argument's conclusion from its premises, and then find the assumption.

The conclusion of the argument is easy to identify because it's stated in the question stem: *an all-volunteer army should not be implemented*. As you read the passage, be on the lookout for premises that support the author's claim.

The author provides only one piece of evidence to suggest that an all-volunteer army shouldn't be implemented: it was *tried on a limited basis several years ago and was a miserable failure*. According to the argument, Country X shouldn't implement an all-volunteer army now because it didn't work out then. This argument exhibits the analogy pattern; it assumes that the current attempt to institute an all-volunteer army will be like the previous attempt.

Because this is a strengthen question, look for answer choices that suggest the two attempts are similar. The more similar they are, the more likely the current attempt will end in failure, and the easier it is to conclude that Country X shouldn't implement an all-volunteer army.

○ The population's level of education has risen since the first time an all-volunteer army was tried.

This answer choice introduces a difference between the current attempt to implement an all-volunteer army and the past attempt. If the education level of the population increased, there's reason to expect a different result this time around. Rather than strengthen the argument against an all-volunteer army, this answer weakens it. Eliminate (A).

○ The proposal was made by an organization called Citizens for Peace.

The identity of the group that made the proposal is out of scope. The relevant question asks whether there's good reason to believe that acting on the proposal will end in failure. Eliminate (B).

○ The first attempt to create a volunteer army was carried out according to the same plan now under proposal and under the same conditions as those that exist today.

Eureka! This answer introduces a relevant similarity between the two attempts to institute an all-volunteer army. If the last attempt ended in disaster, and the current attempt follows the same plan under the same conditions, there's reason to believe the outcome will be similar. Choice (C) strengthens the argument against an all-volunteer army, so keep it.

○ A volunteer army would be less expensive than an army that relies on the draft.

The cost of a volunteer army is out of scope. The argument concerns the trustworthiness of such an army, not its cost. Eliminate (D).

○ Armies are smaller today than they were when a volunteer army was last proposed.

Like (A), choice (E) introduces a dissimilarity between the two attempts to institute a volunteer army. For that reason, it's unlikely to be the correct answer. More importantly, like (B) and (D), it's out of scope. It doesn't matter how big the army is or was, but whether it's staffed by trustworthy people or fools and criminals. Eliminate (E).

The correct answer is (C).

○

Here is an example of an **Inference question.**

In film and television, it's possible to induce viewers to project their feelings onto characters on the screen. In one study, a camera shot of a woman's face was preceded by images of a baby. The audience thought the woman's face registered contentment. When the same woman's face was preceded by images of a shark attack, the audience thought the woman's face registered fear. Television news teams must be careful to avoid such manipulation of their viewers.

Which of the following is best supported by the information in the passage?

○ Television news teams have abused their position of trust in the past.
○ The expression on the woman's face was, in actuality, blank.
○ Images of a baby engendered feelings of happiness in the audience.
○ Audiences should strive to be less gullible.
○ The technique for manipulating audiences described in the passage would also work in a radio program that played dramatic music.

Here's How to Crack It

The question asks for the answer *best supported by the information in the passage*. The direction of support is from the passage to the answer choices, so this is an inference question. Begin by getting clear on the facts.

> Fact 1: *In film and television, it's possible to induce viewers to project their feelings onto characters on the screen, making it possible for news teams to manipulate viewers.*

> Fact 2: *When a camera shot of a woman's face was preceded by images of a baby, the audience thought the woman's face registered contentment.*

> Fact 3: *When the same woman's face was preceded by images of a shark attack, the audience thought the woman's face registered fear.*

Once you're clear on the facts, look for the answer that must be true on their basis. Be wary of extreme language and eliminate answers that are beyond the scope of the information provided. The correct answer is likely to paraphrase information in the passage.

> ○ Television news teams have abused their position of trust in the past.

This answer goes well beyond the scope of the passage. We have no idea what news teams did in the past based on the information provided. Eliminate (A).

> ○ The expression on the woman's face was, in actuality, blank.

Like the previous choice, this answer is out of scope. Based on the information provided, we simply don't know whether the woman's face was expressionless. Eliminate (B).

○ Images of a baby engendered feelings of happiness in the audience.

Images of a baby led the audience to believe the woman's face registered contentment. If audience members projected their feelings onto the woman, then audience members must have experienced contentment, and it's likely the images of a baby were responsible. Keep (C).

○ Audiences should strive to be less gullible.

Of course, we should all strive to be less gullible, but we know that simply because we know what "gullible" means, not because of the information provided. Nothing in the passage suggests that audience members were gullible. Eliminate (D).

○ The technique for manipulating audiences described in the passage would also work in a radio program that played dramatic music.

It's possible that the information in this answer choice is true, but possible isn't good enough. We need an answer that *must be* true, and the passage provides no information about the projection of emotion in the medium of sound. Eliminate (E).

The correct answer is (C).

―――――――――――― ○ ――――――――――――

Challenge Question #18

Glacial ablation is the term for a loss of glacial mass in terms of ice. Ablation rates vary based on a wide number of factors, one of which is submarine melt: ice loss due to contact between the glacier and seawater. While factors such as air temperature, precipitation, and snow accumulation play significant roles, glacial ablation along coastlines tends to proceed at its greatest rate when warm ocean currents come into contact with the base of the glacier and produce a high degree of submarine melt. Warm ocean currents along glacial coastline areas increase in frequency as overall ocean temperatures rise.

Which of the following can be most readily inferred from the information in the passage?

○ Regions with the greatest rate of glacial ablation have the greatest proximity to the strongest warm ocean currents.
○ Very few glaciers in regions without warm ocean currents suffer from high rates of glacial ablation.
○ Glacial ablation due to submarine melt rates was lower on average during periods of lower overall ocean temperatures.
○ Submarine melt rates have become an important factor to glacial ablation only with the onset of global climactic shifts.
○ The lower the overall ocean temperature, the more likely that factors such as snow accumulation are to play a significant role in glacial ablation.

Here is an example of a **Resolve/Explain question.**

In 2008, the world's airlines reported an increase in the total number of passengers carried, but a decrease in total revenues, even though prices for airline tickets on all routes remained unchanged from the year before.

Which of the following resolves the paradox described above?

○ The airline industry was a victim of the recession in 2008.
○ Total passenger miles were up in 2008.
○ Fuel costs remained constant from 2007 to 2008.
○ Passengers traveled shorter distances on less expensive flights in 2008.
○ No new aircraft were purchased by any carrier in 2008.

Here's How to Crack It

The question asks for the answer that *resolves the paradox*, so this is a resolve/explain question. Your knowledge of question types suggests that the accompanying passage will present two pieces of information, which seem to be in conflict. State that opposition as clearly as possible.

On the one hand, more passengers traveled by air.

On the other, airline revenues decreased, even though ticket prices remained unchanged.

The correct answer to a resolve/explain question will allow both pieces of information to be true simultaneously. Eliminate answers that are out of scope, address only one side of the conflict, or make the conflict worse.

○ The airline industry was a victim of the recession in 2008.

A recession might account for the decrease in revenue, but if ticket prices remained the same, it's unclear how the number of passengers could have increased. Choice (A) addresses only one side of the conflict, so eliminate it.

○ Total passenger miles were up in 2008.

If passengers flew farther in 2008 and ticket prices remained the same, it's unclear how revenues could have decreased. Like (A), this answer addresses only one side of the conflict. Eliminate (B).

○ Fuel costs remained constant from 2007 to 2008.

Fuel costs are out of scope. An increase in fuel costs might have affected airline profits, but profits are not revenues. This answer has no bearing on either side of the conflict. Eliminate (C).

○ Passengers traveled shorter distances on less expensive flights in 2008.

This answer looks promising. If the increase in passengers was offset by passengers taking cheaper flights, then revenues could have decreased even as the number of passengers increased. Keep (D).

○ No new aircraft were purchased by any carrier in 2008.

New aircraft are out of scope. The purchase of new aircraft might have affected airline profits, but if no new aircraft were purchased, then new aircraft affected neither profits nor revenues, and this answer has no relevance at all. Eliminate (E).

The correct answer is (D).

───────────────○───────────────

Here is an example of an **Evaluate question.**

───────────────○───────────────

During a period of low growth after a recent and remarkable boom in the solar energy sector, Company X, a major manufacturer of solar-powered generators, attributed its success during the boom to the sale of excess inventory it had discovered in one of its warehouses.

Which of the following tests would most help to evaluate the company's hypothesis as to the cause of its success?

○ Comparing the length of the low-growth period to the length of the preceding boom
○ Comparing the boom experienced by Company X to those experienced by similarly-sized manufacturers of solar-powered generators that did not have inventory on hand
○ Calculating average sales increases within the individual divisions of Company X
○ Comparing the total number of generators sold by Company X during the boom to the total number sold by Company X during the period of low growth
○ Using economic theory to predict the next economic boom for Company X

Here's How to Crack It

The question asks for the test that would most help to *evaluate* the company's hypothesis, so this is an evaluate question. According to the question stem, the hypothesis concerns the cause of Company X's success. As you begin to work the argument, look for claims that provide a reason company X succeeded.

The passage's final sentence states that Company X *attributed its success during the boom to the sale of excess inventory,* but how does Company X come to believe that? The only other piece of information we get from the passage is that there was a *boom in the solar energy sector,* followed by a *period of low growth.*

Without additional information, it's unclear how changes in the solar energy sector relate to the company's claim about its own success. However, if you noticed the word *cause* in the question stem, then you probably recognized that Company X makes a causal argument.

Take advantage of the causal reasoning pattern by recalling its standard assumptions: there's no other cause, and it's not a coincidence. The former assumption seems more relevant here, because Company X assumes the sale of excess inventory alone was responsible for its success.

Evaluate the answer choices one at a time, looking for the test that would allow you to determine whether there isn't another reason for Company X's success.

○ Comparing the length of the low-growth period to the length of the preceding boom

Executing this comparison would tell us how long each of the periods lasted, but connecting that information to the sale of excess inventory would require inferences beyond the scope of the information provided. Eliminate (A).

○ Comparing the boom experienced by Company X to those experienced by similarly-sized manufacturers of solar-powered generators that did not have inventory on hand

This answer choice is tempting. We're looking for a way to determine whether something other than the sale of excess inventory might have caused Company X's success. If competitors without excess inventory to sell experienced booms comparable to that of Company X, then the company's claim might be incorrect. On the other hand, if competitors didn't experience as big a boom, it appears more likely that the sale of excess inventory was responsible for Company X's success. Keep (B).

○ Calculating average sales increases within the individual divisions of Company X

Individual divisions of Company X are out of scope. We already know that the company sold excess inventory; which divisions saw sales increases is irrelevant. Eliminate (C).

○ Comparing the total number of generators sold by Company X during the boom to the total number sold by Company X during the period of low growth

At first glance, this answer choice looks appealing. The comparison described here would allow us to determine how many generators were sold during each period. If more generators were sold during the boom than during the low-growth period, it might seem as though Company X's success during the boom resulted from the sale of excess inventory. However, the passage states that the period of low growth *followed* the boom. If more generators were sold during the boom, then at best, we could infer that a *decline* in sales led to *decreased* success. To determine whether the sale of excess inventory *caused* Company X's success during the boom, we'd need sales numbers from the period *before* the boom, not the period *after* it. Eliminate (D).

○ Using economic theory to predict when the next economic boom for Company X will occur

Of the five answer choices, this one is most obviously out of scope. An estimate of the time that will elapse before the next boom needn't have any relevance to the cause of the last boom. Eliminate (E).

The correct answer is (B).

Here is an example of an **Identify the Reasoning question.**

Although measuring the productivity of outside consultants is a complex endeavor, **Company K, which relies heavily on consultants, must find ways to assess the performance of these workers.** The risks to a company that does not review the productivity of its human resources are simply too great. **Last year, Company L was forced into receivership after its productivity declined for three consecutive quarters.**

The bolded clauses play which of the following roles in the argument above?

○ The first bolded clause states the author's conclusion, and the second introduces unrelated information.
○ The first bolded clause provides background information, and the second offers evidence to contradict that information.
○ The first bolded clause states one of the author's premises, while the second states the author's conclusion.
○ The first bolded clause expresses a position, and the second warns against the adoption of that position.
○ The first bolded clause represents the author's conclusion, and the second supports the conclusion with an analogy.

Here's How to Crack It

The bolded clauses in the passage immediately indicate that this is an identify the reasoning question, so begin by distinguishing the argument's conclusion from the premises that support it. Don't worry about finding assumptions.

The phrase *must find ways to assess* is strong language, making the first bolded phrase a good candidate for the argument's conclusion. Why must Company K find ways to assess the performance of its outside consultants? Because companies that don't review the productivity of human resources face risks—just look at Company L! Both of the passage's remaining sentences operate in support of the first bolded phrase. The second bolded clause supports the conclusion by offering the example of a company that was *forced into receivership after its productivity declined.*

Now that you've got a good sense of the argument's structure, look for the answer that correctly mirrors it.

    ○ The first bolded clause states the author's conclusion, and the second introduces unrelated information.

The first part of this answer looks good, because the first bolded clause *does* state the author's conclusion. However, the second bolded clause supports the conclusion; it does not introduce unrelated information. Choice (A) only partially matches the argument's structure, so eliminate it.

    ○ The first bolded clause provides background information, and the second offers evidence to contradict that information.

Part of the first bolded clause states that Company K *relies heavily on consultants*, which does resemble background information. However, nothing in the second bolded clause contradicts that information. Choice (B) is a partial match. Eliminate it.

    ○ The first bolded clause states one of the author's premises, while the second states the author's conclusion.

This answer choice reverses the roles played by the bolded clauses. Since it doesn't match the structure of the argument, eliminate (C).

    ○ The first bolded clause expresses a position, and the second warns against the adoption of that position.

Like (A) and (B), (D) is a partial match. The first bolded clause expresses a position, but the second doesn't warn against the adoption of that position. Eliminate (D).

    ○ The first bolded clause represents the author's conclusion, and the second supports the conclusion with an analogy.

This answer accurately reflects the relationship between the bolded clauses: the first is the author's conclusion, and the second supports the conclusion by offering the example of analogous Company L. Keep (E).

The correct answer is (E).

Here is an example of a **Flaw question.**

A telephone poll conducted in two states asked respondents whether their homes were cold during the winter months. Ninety-nine percent of respondents said their houses were always warm during the winter. The pollsters published their findings, concluding that ninety-nine percent of all homes in the United States have adequate heating.

Which of the following most accurately describes a questionable technique employed by the pollsters in drawing their conclusion?

- ○ The poll wrongly ascribes the underlying causes of the problem.
- ○ The poll assumes conditions in the two states are representative of the entire country.
- ○ The pollsters conducted the poll by telephone, thereby relying on the veracity of respondents.
- ○ The pollsters didn't visit respondents' houses in person, so no measure of the temperature in a subject's home was actually made.
- ○ The pollsters never defined the term "cold" in terms of a specific temperature.

Here's How to Crack It

The question asks for a *questionable technique* used by the pollsters, so this is a flaw question.

You already know from the question stem that the argument has a serious problem. Your job is to figure out what that problem is. Begin by identifying the argument's premises and conclusion. Then, use a gap in the reasoning to hone in on the assumption. Because this is a flaw question, be on the lookout for common reasoning patterns.

The word *concluding* in the last sentence of the passage gives away the conclusion: *ninety-nine percent of all homes in the United States have adequate heating.* Why did the pollsters conclude this? Their findings were based on the results of *a telephone poll conducted in two states,* in which *ninety-nine percent of respondents said their houses were always warm during the winter.*

Did you recognize the pattern of reasoning in this argument? Information about one group of people (the poll was conducted in two states) is used to make a claim about a much larger group (all households in the United States). This argument employs the sampling pattern. The standard assumption involved in the sampling pattern is that the sample is representative of the larger population. Look for answers that call attention to this assumption.

- ○ The poll wrongly ascribes the underlying causes of a problem.

Underlying causes are out of scope. The pollsters ask whether people's homes are cold. The reason they might be cold is irrelevant. Eliminate (A).

○ The poll assumes conditions in the two states are representative of the entire country.

This answer expresses the standard assumption involved in the sampling pattern. Nothing in the passage suggests that the households surveyed are representative of U.S. householders in general. Keep (B).

○ The pollsters conducted the poll by telephone, thereby relying on the veracity of respondents.

The information in this answer might betray a weakness in the pollsters' methodology, but it isn't a weakness in the pollsters' reasoning. Eliminate (C).

○ The pollsters didn't visit respondents' houses in person, so no measurement of the temperature in a subject's home was actually made.

Like (C), this answer describes a problem with the poll, not with the argument. Eliminate (D).

○ The pollsters never defined the term "cold" in terms of a specific temperature.

It's true that the pollsters never defined the term "cold," but does that represent a flaw in the pollsters' reasoning? The flaw identified here concerns the poll itself, not the argument. Eliminate (E).

The correct answer is (B).

———————○———————

Now that you know how to identify and approach each of the eight Critical Reasoning question types, the best way to proceed is to practice. The more you experience through preparation, the less likely you are to be surprised on test day.

As you complete Critical Reasoning drills and exercises, force yourself to follow the basic approach. Your knowledge of the question type informs every step of the basic approach to Critical Reasoning questions, from reading the passage to eliminating incorrect answers, so always read the question first. Memorize the common reasoning patterns and the assumptions that go with them, develop a familiarity with the characteristics of good and bad answers, and you'll be well on your way to mastering the Critical Reasoning format.

DRILL 15 (Spotting Critical Reasoning Question Types)

The answers to questions in this drill can be found in Part VI.

For each of the questions below, decide which question type it belongs to. For extra credit, list what you should look for in the passage that would normally precede the question.

1. Which of the following, if true, gives the most support to the recommendations above?
2. Which of the following statements can properly be inferred on the basis of the statements above?
3. The answer to which of the following questions would most help the CEO to evaluate the manager's claim?
4. The argument in the passage depends on which of the following assumptions?
5. The argument above is vulnerable to criticism for which of the following reasons?
6. The author's argument would be most seriously weakened if it were true that...
7. The senator responds to the constituent's assertion by...
8. Which of the following statements best explains the apparent discrepancy described above?

Summary

o Critical Reasoning is made up of short passages. Each of these passages is followed by one question, for a total of roughly 11 questions.

o There are three parts to an argument.
   • Conclusion
   • Premises
   • Assumptions

o Critical Reasoning is **not** like Reading Comprehension.
   • You should never skim; each word is important.
   • Most of the Reading Comprehension techniques we have shown you are inappropriate for Critical Reasoning.

o Follow the basic approach and make sure to read the question first.

o Learn to identify the common reasoning patterns in argument passages:
   • Causal patterns
   • Planning patterns
   • Sampling patterns
   • Interpretation of Evidence patterns
   • Analogy patterns

o There are eight question types. Each type has its own strategy.
   • **Assumption questions**
     Assumptions are unstated premises that support the conclusion.

   • **Strengthen questions**
     Look for an answer choice with information that supports the conclusion.

   • **Weaken questions**
     These questions ask you to find the answer choice that provides information that weakens the conclusion.

- **Inference questions**

  Like Reading Comprehension inference questions, these questions do not actually want you to infer. Unlike most Critical Reasoning questions, these questions typically concern the *premises,* not the conclusion.

- **Resolve/explain questions**

  This type of question asks you to pick an answer choice that explains an apparent contradiction between two incompatible facts.

- **Evaluate questions**

  This type of question asks you to pick an answer choice that would help to evaluate an unspoken assumption about the argument.

- **Identify the Reasoning questions**

  This type of question asks you to pick an answer choice that identifies the purpose of a word or phrase or the type of reasoning used in an argument.

- **Flaw questions**

  Flaw questions ask you to choose the answer that accurately describes a flaw in the structure of an argument.

Part IV
How to Crack the Integrated Reasoning GMAT

Chapter 18
Integrated
Reasoning: Basics

This chapter provides an overview of the section. The following chapter provides some specific strategies. We have also included some practice questions to help you prepare.

This chapter reviews the basics of the Integrated Reasoning section, including a run down on all four question types. We've also included a chapter that explains some strategies that will help you handle these questions. Finally, this book includes two complete Integrated Reasoning sections with explanations so that you can practice.

MEET THE INTEGRATED REASONING SECTION

The Integrated Reasoning section is 30 minutes long. You'll see it as the second section of your test. Officially, there are only 12 questions, which sounds pretty great. However, most of those questions have multiple parts. So, for example, a Table Analysis question—one of the question types we'll discuss—usually has three statements that you need to evaluate. So, your answer to the question really consists of three separate responses. For the entire section, you'll actually need to select approximately 28 different responses.

Integrated Reasoning Is Not Adaptive

Unlike the Quantitative and Verbal sections, the Integrated Reasoning section is not adaptive. So, you won't see harder questions if you keep answering questions correctly. That's good news because it means that you'll more easily be able to focus your attention on the current question rather than worrying whether you got the previous question right!

Test writers refer to non-adaptive sections as linear. Pacing for a linear section is different from the pacing that we reviewed for the adaptive Quantitative and Verbal sections.

For Integrated Reasoning, pacing is motivated by two general principles.

Following these guidelines can save you time.

> Pacing Guidelines
> 1. Work the easier parts of each question first. As you'll see, many Integrated Reasoning questions call for more than one response per question. Work the easier parts of each question first.
>
> 2. Don't get stubborn. With so many questions to answer in only 30 minutes, the Integrated Reasoning section can seem very fast paced. Spending too much time on one question means that you may not get to see all of the questions. Sometimes it's best to guess and move on.

Integrated Reasoning Scores

The Integrated Reasoning section is scored on a scale from 1 to 8 in one-point increments. While GMAC has not released too many details about the way in which they calculate the score for this section of the test, there are two key facts to keep in mind.

- **Scoring is all or nothing.** Most Integrated Reasoning questions include multiple parts. To get credit for the question, you must select the correct response for each part. For example, Table Analysis questions generally include three statements that you must evaluate. If you select the wrong response for even one of these statements, you get no credit for the entire question.
- **There are experimental questions.** GMAC has stated that the Integrated Reasoning section contains experimental questions that do not count toward your score. They have not, however, stated how many experimental questions there are in the section. It's likely that two or three of the twelve questions in the section are experimental. If you find a question particularly difficult or time consuming, it is worthwhile to remember that the question could be experimental.

To score the section, GMAC first calculates a raw score. You get one point for each non-experimental question that you get completely correct. Then, your raw score is converted to the 1 to 8 Integrated Reasoning scaled score.

There's a Calculator

There's an onscreen calculator available for the Integrated Reasoning section. The calculator is not available, however, for the Quantitative section. For the Quantitative section, you still need to perform any necessary calculations by hand.

The calculator for the Integrated Reasoning section is relatively basic. There are buttons to perform the four standard operations: addition, subtraction, multiplication, and division. In addition, buttons to take a square root, find a percent, and take a reciprocal round out the available functions. There are also buttons to store and recall a value in the calculator's memory.

To use the calculator, you'll need to open it by clicking on the "calculator" button in the upper left corner of your screen. The calculator will generally open in the middle of your screen but you can move it around so that you can see the text of the problem or the numbers on any charts or graphs that are part of the question. The calculator is available for all Integrated Reasoning questions. You can enter a number into the calculator either by clicking on the onscreen number buttons or by typing the number using the keyboard.

Here's what the calculator looks like:

For the most part, the keys on the onscreen calculator work as you might expect. However, a few keys may not work as expected. Oddly enough, that's particularly true if you are used to using a more sophisticated calculator. So, here are few tips about using some of the calculator keys:

MC   MC is the memory clear key. Use this key to wipe out any values that you have stored in the calculator's memory.

MR   MR is the memory recall key. Use this key to return any value that you have stored in the memory to the calculation area. For example, if you want to divide the number currently on your screen by the number in the memory, you would enter the key sequence / MR =.

MS   MS is the memory store key. Use this key to store the number currently on the screen in the calculator's memory.

M+   M+ is the memory addition key. Use this key to add the current onscreen number to the number in the calculator's memory. For example, if 2 is stored in the calculator's memory and 3 is on screen, then clicking M+ will result in 5 being stored in the calculator's memory.

Backspace   Backspace is used to clear the last digit entered. Use this key to correct mistakes when entering numbers without clearing the entire number. For example, if you entered 23 but meant to enter 25, click backspace then enter 5.

CE   CE is the clear entry button. Use this button to correct a mistake when entering a longer calculation without starting over. For example, suppose you entered 2*3+5 but you meant to enter 2*3+9. If you click on CE right after you enter 5, your screen will show 6, the result of 2*3, and you can now enter +9= to finish your intended calculation.

C   C is the clear key. Use this key when you want to start a calculation over. In our previous example, if you click C after you enter 5, the intermediate result, 6, is not retained.

sqrt   sqrt is the square root key. Click this key after you enter the number for which you want to take the square root. For example, if you enter 4 sqrt, the result 2 will display on your screen.

%   % is the key used to take a percentage without entering a decimal. For example, if you want to take 20% of 400, enter 400*20%. The result 80 will now show on your screen. Note that you do not need to enter = after you click %.

1/x   1/x is used to take a reciprocal. Click this key after you enter the number for which you want to take the reciprocal. For example, the keystrokes 2 followed by 1/x produces the result 0.5 on your screen. Again, note that you do not need to enter = after you click 1/x.

Calculator Practice Tip
When you practice for the Integrated Reasoning section, use a calculator similar to the calculator provided by GMAC. If you are doing online practice, use the onscreen calculator. If you are working problems from this book, use a basic calculator rather than that fancy calculator that you might still have from your high school or college math classes.

Be sure that you thoroughly understand the way the keys for the onscreen calculator work so as to avoid errors and wasted time when you take your GMAT.

THE QUESTION TYPES

There are four question types in the Integrated Reasoning section. While some of these questions test Critical Reasoning skills similar to those tested on the Verbal section, these question types are also used to test the same type of content that is tested in the Quantitative section. So, expect to calculate percents and averages. You'll also be asked to make a lot of inferences based on the data presented in the various charts, graphs, and tables that accompany the questions. So, the format of these questions may take some getting used to but the content will probably seem familiar.

Let's take a more detailed look at each of the question types.

Table Analysis

Table Analysis questions present data in a table. If you've ever seen a spreadsheet—and really, who hasn't?—you'll feel right at home. Most tables have 5 to 10 columns and anywhere from 6 to 25 rows. You'll be able to sort the data in the table by each column heading. The sort function is fairly basic, however. If you're used to being able to sort first by a column such as state and then a column such as city to produce an alphabetical list of cities by state, you can't do that sort of sorting for these questions. You can sort only one column at a time.

Here's what a Table Analysis question looks like:

Sort By Select... ▼ **1**

National Park		Visitors			Area	
Name	State	Number	% change	Rank	Acres	Rank
Grand Canyon	AZ	4,388,386	0.9	2	1,217,403	11
Yosemite	CA	3,901,408	4.4	3	791,266	16
Yellowstone	WY	3,640,185	10.5	4	2,219,791	8
Rocky Mtn.	CO	2,955,821	4.7	5	265,828	26
Zion	UT	2,665,972	-2.5	8	145,598	35
Acadia	ME	2,504,208	12.4	9	47,390	47
Bryce	UT	1,285,492	5.7	15	35,835	50
Arches	UT	1,014,405	1.8	19	76,519	42
Badlands	SD	977,778	4.7	22	242,756	28
Mesa Verde	CO	559,712	1.7	30	52,122	46
Canyonlands	UT	435,908	-0.1	36	337,598	23

The table above gives information for 2010 on total visitors and total acreage for 11 US National Parks. In addition to the numbers of total visitors and total acreage for each National Park, the table also provides the percent increase or decrease over the total visitors for 2009 and the rank of the National Park for total visitors and total acreage in 2010. **4**

2 Each column of the table can be sorted in ascending order by clicking on the word "Select" above the table and choosing, from the drop-down menu, the heading of the column on which you want the table to be sorted.

3 Consider each of the following statements about these National Parks. For each statement indicate whether the statement is true or false, based on the information provided in the table.

True False **5**

○ ○ The park that experienced the greatest percent increase in visitors from 2009 to 2010 also had the least total acreage.

○ ○ The park with the median rank by the number of visitors is larger than only one other park by acreage.

○ ○ The total number of visitors at Arches in 2009 was fewer than 1,000,000.

Answers for this Question

We'll discuss how you can solve this Table Analysis question—including which strategies you can apply—in our second chapter devoted to the Integrated Reasoning section.

One thing you won't see on your screen when you take the Integrated Reasoning section are the circled numbers. We've added those so we can talk about different parts of a Table Analysis question. Here's what each circled number represents:

1 This is the Sort By drop-down box. When opened, you'll see all the different ways that you can sort the data in the table. In this table, for example, the possibilities are National Park Name, National Park State, Visitors Number, Visitors % change, Visitors Rank, Area Acreage, and Area Rank. You can always sort by every column.

2 These are the standard directions for a Table Analysis question. These directions are the same for every Table Analysis question. So, once you've read these directions once, you don't really need to bother reading them again.

3 These lines are additional directions. These additional directions are slightly tailored to the question. However, they'll always tell you to base your answers on the information in the table. They always tell you which type of evaluation you are to make for each statement: true/false, yes/no, agree/disagree, etc. Again, you can probably get by without reading these most of the time.

4 These lines explain the table. Mostly, this information will recap the column headings from the table. Occasionally, you can learn some additional information by reading this explanatory text. For example, the explanatory text for this table states that the Visitors Number column is for 2010 and that % change column shows the change from 2009 to 2010.

5 These statements are the questions. Typically, there are four statements and you need to evaluate and select an answer for each. The good news is that you can answer these in any order. However, if you try to move to the next question without selecting a response for one or more statements, a pop up window opens to inform you that you have not selected an answer for all statements. You cannot leave any part of the question blank.

If you've read through the statements, you may have noticed that the questions asked you to do things such as calculate a percentage or find a median. That's typical for Table Analysis questions. You've probably also realized just how helpful the sorting function can be in answering some questions.

Graphics Interpretation

Graphics Interpretation questions give you one chart, graph, or image and ask you to answer two questions based on that information. The questions are statements that include one drop-down box. You select your answer from the drop-down box to complete the statement.

Here's an example of a Graphics Interpretation question:

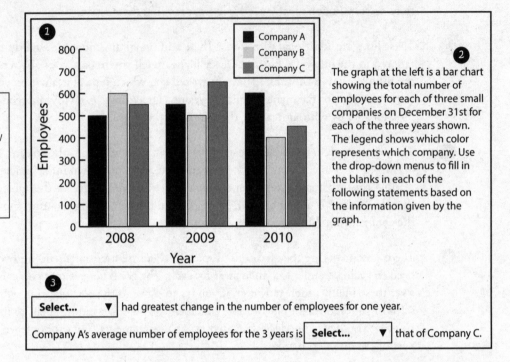

Want to See What's in the Drop-Downs?
We'll be discussing how to answer this question in the strategy chapter. We'll expand the drop-down boxes there!

The graph at the left is a bar chart showing the total number of employees for each of three small companies on December 31st for each of the three years shown. The legend shows which color represents which company. Use the drop-down menus to fill in the blanks in each of the following statements based on the information given by the graph.

Select... ▼ had greatest change in the number of employees for one year.

Company A's average number of employees for the 3 years is Select... ▼ that of Company C.

As with the Table Analysis questions, we've added the circled numbers so we can point out the different things that you'll see on your screen for a Graphics Interpretation question. Here's what each circled number represents:

1   The chart, graph, or image is always in the upper left of the screen. As shown here, the chart will take up a good deal of the screen. It will certainly be large enough that you can clearly extract information from it. You can expect to see a variety of different types of charts or graphs including scatterplots, bar charts, line graphs, and circle (or pie) charts. For the most part, you'll see fairly standard types of graphs, however. Be sure to check out any labels on the axes as well as any sort of included legend.

2   These lines provide an explanation of the graph or chart. Mostly, you'll be told what the chart represents as well as what the individual lines, bars, or sectors may represent. Sometimes, you'll be given some additional information such as when measurements were made. For example, here you are told that the bars show the numbers of employees for each firm on December 31st of the year in question. This information is typically extraneous to answering the questions. The explanatory information always ends with the same line about selecting your answers from the drop-down menu.

③ These are the questions. Graphics Interpretation questions typically include two statements. You don't have to answer them in order, but you must answer them both to move on to the next question. Each statement is typically a single sentence with one drop-down menu. Each drop-down menu typically includes three to five answer choices. Choose that answer choice that makes the statement true.

Graphics Interpretation questions mostly ask you to find relationships and trends for the data. You can also be asked to calculate percentage increases or decreases, averages, and medians.

Two-Part Analysis

Next up is the Two-Part Analysis question. In many ways, the Two-Part Analysis question is most similar to a standard math question. You'll typically be presented with a word problem that essentially has two variables in it. You'll need to pick an answer for each variable that makes some condition in the problem true.

Here's an example of a Two-Part Analysis question:

Two families buy new refrigerators using installment plans. Family A makes an initial payment of $750. Family B makes an initial payment of $1200. Both families make five additional payments to pay off the balance. Both families pay the same amount for their refrigerators including all taxes, fees, and finance charges. ①

In the table below, identify a monthly payment, in dollars, for Family A and a monthly payment, in dollars, for Family B that are consistent with the installment plan described above. Make only one selection in each column. ②

Family A	Family B	Monthly payment (in dollars)
○	○	50
○	○	80
○	○	120 ③
○	○	160
○	○	250
○	○	300

What's the Answer?
Be sure to read our second chapter on the Integrated Reasoning section to find out!

As you might have surmised, we have once again added the circled numbers so we can described the different parts of the question. Here's what each circled number represents:

① This first block of text is the actual problem. Here, you'll find the description of the two variables in the problem. You'll also find the condition that needs to be made true. As with any word problem, make sure that you read the information carefully. For these problems, you'll also want to make sure that you are clear about which information goes with the first variable and which information goes with the second.

② This part of the problem tells you how to pick your answers. Mostly this part tells you to pick a value for column A and a value for column B based on the conditions of the problem. This part is mostly boilerplate text that varies slightly from problem to problem.

③ These are the answer choices. Two-Part Analysis questions generally have five or six answer choices. You choose only one answer choice for each column. It is possible that the same number is the answer for both columns. So, if that's what your calculations indicate, go ahead and choose the same number for both columns.

Most Two-Part Analysis questions can be solved using math that is no more sophisticated than simple arithmetic. There is one exception to that, however. While most Two-Part Analysis questions are math problems, you may see one that looks like a Critical Reasoning question. For these, you'll be given an argument and you'll need to do something like pick one answer that strengthens and one answer that weakens the argument. For these questions, just use the methods from our Critical Reasoning chapter.

Multi-Source Reasoning

Finally, we come to the Multi-Source Reasoning question. Multi-Source Reasoning questions present information on tabs. The information can be text, charts, graphs, or a combination. In other words, GMAC can put almost anything on the tabs! The layout looks a little bit like Reading Comprehension because the tabbed information is on the left side of your screen while the right side shows the questions.

Here's an example of a Multi-Source Reasoning question:

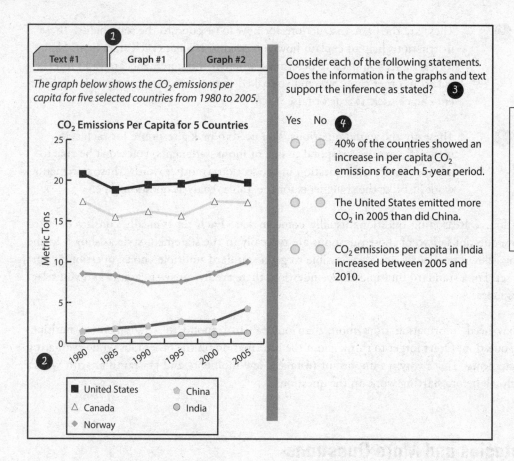

The graph below shows the CO₂ emissions per capita for five selected countries from 1980 to 2005.

CO₂ Emissions Per Capita for 5 Countries

Legend:
- ■ United States
- △ Canada
- ◆ Norway
- ⬠ China
- ○ India

Consider each of the following statements. Does the information in the graphs and text support the inference as stated?

Yes   No

○   ○   40% of the countries showed an increase in per capita CO_2 emissions for each 5-year period.

○   ○   The United States emitted more CO_2 in 2005 than did China.

○   ○ CO_2 emissions per capita in India increased between 2005 and 2010.

What's on those Other Tabs?

We'll show you the other tabs and the answers to these questions in our other chapter on the Integrated Reasoning section.

Again, we've added circled numbers to indicate the different parts of the question. Here's what each circled number represents:

1. The tabs appear across the top left of the screen. Some questions have two tabs and some, as in this example, have three. The tabs typically give you some sort of indication about what's on the tab. The currently selected tab is white, while the unselected tabs are grey. GMAC can put almost anything on each tab including graphs, tables, charts, text, or some combination. It's a good idea to take a few seconds and get your bearings before attempting the questions. Make sure you know what is on each tab and how the information on one tab relates to information on the other tab or tabs.

2. The information for each tab appears on the left of the screen. In this case, the information is a graph. When you see a chart or graph, be sure to check out the axes. You'll also want to look for a legend or other information to help explain the information shown by the graph or chart. For tables, check out the column headings so as to better understand the table. Finally, don't neglect to read any supplied headings for the chart, graph, or table. Sometimes, that's all you need for the chart to make sense.

(3) These are the basic instructions for how to respond to the statements. These instructions help to explain how you need to evaluate each statement. Here, for example, you need to determine whether the statements are valid inferences. In other cases, you may be asked to evaluate the statements for a different choice such as true or false.

(4) These are the actual questions. You need to pick a response for each statement. If you fail to respond to one or more statements, you won't be able to advance to the next question in the section. In other words, these statements work just like the statements for the Table Analysis question type.

Multi-Source Reasoning questions usually come in sets. Each set typically consists of three separate questions. Two of those questions are typically in the statement style as shown in the example shown previously. It's also possible to get a standard multiple choice question as part of the set. For a standard multiple-choice question, there are five answer choices and you select one response.

You may need information from more than one tab to respond to a statement or multiple-choice question. Don't forget to think about the information on the other tabs while evaluating the statements. That's why it's important to take a few moments and get familiar with what's on each tab before starting work on the questions.

Strategies and More Questions

Now, that you understand the basics of the new question types, it's time to start thinking about the best ways to solve these questions. You can find strategies and more practice questions in Chapters 19 and 20.

Summary

o   The Integrated Reasoning section is 30 minutes long and contains 12 questions, each with multiple parts. This section is not adaptive and you may use an onscreen calculator.

o   Work the easier questions first, then tackle the tougher ones. Sometimes your best bet is simply to guess and move along.

o   There are four question types. Be sure that you familiarize yourself with these.
  • Table Analysis
  • Graphics Interpretation
  • Two-Part Analysis
  • Multi-Source Reasoning

o   Check out these new question types on www.mba.com and practice with the full-length practice GMAT exams available to you once you've registered your book at **PrincetonReview.com**.

Chapter 19
Integrated Reasoning: Strategies

GMAC has devised four question types for the Integrated Reasoning section. As with any section on a standardized test, doing well requires a blend of content knowledge and strategy. Test takers who approach the Integrated Reasoning section with a firm grasp of strategy will do better than those who haven't thought about strategies for the section.

We'll be looking at two types of strategies in this chapter. Some strategies apply to most or all of the question types that you'll see. Other strategies apply to specific questions types. We'll start by reviewing strategies and pointers for the entire section and then move on to examine some methods for the individual question types.

GENERAL STRATEGIES

Some strategies apply to the entire section, and you'll use these methods on almost every question. The more consistently you apply these pointers, the better you'll do and the more efficiently you'll use your time.

Get Your Bearings

What Do the Questions Look Like?

If you aren't sure what the Integrated Reasoning questions look like, you should reread Chapter 18, Integrated Reasoning: Basics. We introduced the four question types there.

Before you can use a chart, graph, or table to answer questions, you need to understand the information on it. So, before you evaluate any statements or answer any questions, take a few moments to review the charts, graphs, and tables.

For charts and graphs, make sure you look at the axes. You'll want to take note of what each axis measures and the units used to make the measurements. You'll also want to read any headings or titles because those can provide valuable insight into the purpose of the graph. There may be a legend. If there is, take a moment to identify the different items that the chart or graph compares. For tables, make sure that you look at each column heading. This sort of review is essential before you start working on evaluating the statements or answering the questions that go with Table Analysis and Graphics Interpretation questions.

For Multi-Source Reasoning questions, you need to review the information that is on each tab. It's also a good idea to look for connections between the charts on one tab and those on the others. One way that you can do so is to think about what quantities you'd be able to calculate if you used the information from two charts. For example, if one chart shows the number of cars per day that several factories produce and another chart shows the number of days those factories were active in a year, you know that you could calculate the total number of cars each factory produced that year.

Read What You Need When You Need It

Both Table Analysis and Graphics Interpretation questions include a blurb of text that explains the table or chart. While GMAC includes this information to help you to understand the table or chart, you may not need to take the time to read it.

Most of the charts and tables are understandable without the explanatory text. So, if your review of the chart or table doesn't turn up any unusual quantities or units that need further explanation, you're most likely ready to get to work on the actual questions. You can also be guided by the questions. If something about the question or statement isn't making sense, then you can always go back and read the explanatory information.

Integrated Reasoning Strategies
Having a solid grasp of the strategies outlined in this chapter will give you an edge. This video highlights one of the most important— pacing. To watch, visit your Student Tools.

Valid Inferences

Both Table Analysis and Multi-Source Reasoning items include statement style questions. (Reread Chapter 18 to see examples of statement style questions.) In some cases, you'll be asked to decide whether the statement is true or false. In other cases, you'll be asked whether the information supplied supports the inference as stated and then respond yes or no. That's a little different from asking whether the statement is true or false. After all, there's the possibility that there is insufficient information to conclude whether the statement is true or false. If that's the case, you need to pick "no" as your answer.

It's also important to remember that a valid inference is something that you know to be true. You know something is true if you can support it with evidence. GMAC knows, however, that most people start thinking "interpret" or "read into" when they see the word "infer." So, some statements provided on Table Analysis and Multi-Source Reasoning questions attempt to get you to read too much into the information on the chart or table to come up with a conclusion. For example, there may be a clear trend on a chart showing that a company has increased its sales for every year between 2000 and 2008. The statement may try to get you to conclude that the company also increased its sales in 2009 even though 2009 is not shown on the chart. That's not a valid inference! Be careful that you don't mix up "true" and "very likely" when evaluating what can be inferred from the data.

What's an Inference?
An inference is a statement that you can prove true using supplied facts or other evidence.

TABLE ANALYSIS

Table Analysis questions always include one table to display data. You'll be asked to evaluate four statements. You may be asked whether the statements are true or false based on the data in the table. You may also be asked whether the statements represent valid inferences based on the table.

While you won't be called upon to provide numerical answers as part of Table Analysis questions, you may need to perform some calculations to evaluate the statements. For example, you may be asked to verify that a certain percentage of the items in the table have a certain characteristic.

The Sort Function

The sort function allows you to sort the data in the table by any column. However, the sort function will sort only one column at a time. So, forget all those fancy multiple column sorts that you can do with Excel.

To see how the sort function works for Table Analysis questions, let's look at a very simple table. This table is really too simple for a GMAT question, but it will help us to illustrate how the sort function works.

When you first see the table, it is typically sorted by one key statistic from the table. All numerical sorts are always smallest to largest. This table, for example, is sorted by Median Household Income (2014) and represents the original sort for this table.

City	State	Median Household Income (2014)
Rochester	NY	$51,086
Philadelphia	PA	$62,171
Salt Lake City	UT	$62,642
New York	NY	$67,066

Now, here's what you'll see if you sort by State.

City	State	Median Household Income (2014)
Rochester	NY	$51,086
New York	NY	$67,066
Philadelphia	PA	$62,171
Salt Lake City	UT	$62,642

If you sort next by City, you might expect that Rochester and New York would exchange positions. That's particularly true if you are used to the way that Excel lets you sort by multiple columns.

Question Order

In general, you should just evaluate the statements in order for Table Analysis questions. Of course, if you get stuck on one statement, skip over it, evaluate the other statements, and come back to the one that gave you trouble.

However, what you'll really get is an alphabetical listing by City. Here's what the sort by City looks like.

City	State	Median Household Income (2014)
New York	NY	$67,066
Philadelphia	PA	$62,171
Rochester	NY	$51,086
Salt Lake City	UT	$62,642

To Sort or Not To Sort

While the sort feature can be a huge help when answering some questions, you may not need to use it to answer every question. In some cases, you may need to find only one piece of information on the table. In other cases, the table may not have that many rows. Table Analysis questions can have as few as six rows of data. It may be faster to simply scan the table for the information that you need.

On the other hand, remember that sorting the table takes only a few seconds. If you think sorting will help, do it! One thing you shouldn't do, however, is spend time trying to organize the statements so that you do as little sorting as possible. You're actually likely to waste more time trying to come up with the perfect order in which to evaluate the statements than you would if you wind up sorting the same way twice in evaluating the statements.

Let's look at a sample Table Analysis question. Here's the question that we discussed in Chapter 18.

Sort By [Select... ▼]

National Park		Visitors			Area	
Name	State	Number	% change	Rank	Acres	Rank
Grand Canyon	AZ	4,388,386	0.9	2	1,217,403	11
Yosemite	CA	3,901,408	4.4	3	791,266	16
Yellowstone	WY	3,640,185	10.5	4	2,219,791	8
Rocky Mtn.	CO	2,955,821	4.7	5	265,828	26
Zion	UT	2,665,972	-2.5	8	145,598	35
Acadia	ME	2,504,208	12.4	9	47,390	47
Bryce	UT	1,285,492	5.7	15	35,835	50
Arches	UT	1,014,405	1.8	19	76,519	42
Badlands	SD	977,778	4.7	22	242,756	28
Mesa Verde	CO	559,712	1.7	30	52,122	46
Canyonlands	UT	435,908	-0.1	36	337,598	23

Each column of the table can be sorted in ascending order by clicking on the word "Select" above the table and choosing, from the drop-down menu, the heading of the column on which you want the table to be sorted.

Consider each of the following statements about these National Parks. For each statement indicate whether the statement is true or false, based on the information provided in the table.

True False
- ○ ○ The park that experienced the greatest percent increase in visitors from 2009 to 2010 also had the least total acreage.

- ○ ○ The park with the median rank by the number of visitors is larger than only one other park by acreage.

- ○ ○ The total number of visitors at Arches in 2009 was fewer than 1,000,000.

The table above gives information for 2010 on total visitors and total acreage for 11 U.S. National Parks. In addition to the numbers of total visitors and total acreage for each National Park, the table also provides the percent increase or decrease over the total visitors for 2009 and the rank of the National Park for total visitors and total acreage in 2010.

> **Get Your Bearings**
> Step one for any Table Analysis question is to review the information presented by the table.

Here's How To Crack It:

As with any Table Analysis question, the first step is to make sure that you take a moment to understand the information presented by the table. While it might be tempting to jump straight to the statements, you'll be able to evaluate the statements more efficiently when you first take a moment to understand the information on the table. Looking at the column headings can also help you to decide whether you need to read the explanatory information under the table.

The first two columns of this table—National Park Name and National Park State—are self-explanatory. More importantly, however, the first column—National Park Name—tells you that this table provides information about national parks. Next, you get information about visitors to the national parks included in the table. The third column heading—Visitors Number—is pretty clear. However, you don't know the time period for the visitation numbers. The next column—Visitors % Change—shows increases or decreases from some previous time period. Again, you don't know the time period just by looking at the table. Do the time periods matter? Probably not. You'll probably learn the time period from the statements. If the statements seem to indicate that the time periods matter, you can read the explanatory text at that time.

The next column—Visitors Rank—is potentially more confusing, however. Does the rank refer to the number of visitors or the percent change? That's an important distinction for understanding the information in the table. There are two ways to figure out what's being ranked. You could scan the table looking for evidence. Of course, that could be time consuming. Or, you could scan the explanatory text beneath the table. *If you don't understand one of the column headings shown in the table, that's when you want to read the explanatory text.* The explanation indicates that the rank refers to the total number of visitors. As a bonus, you now also know that the visitation numbers are for 2010.

> **Step 2**
> Decide the best way to sort the table. For some statements, you may be able to sort in more than one way. Sort by the column with the larger numbers or more complex data.

The last two column headings—Area Acres and Area Rank—are also pretty clear. Note that the inclusion of Area Rank means that you won't need to deal with the larger number in the Area Acres column if all you need to do is compare the size of one park to another. The same is also true of the inclusion of the Visitors Rank column. The inclusion of these columns makes it much easier to make some types of comparisons about the parks in the table. That's definitely something to make note of as you finish reviewing the information presented by the chart.

We'll just evaluate the statements in order. First, we'll evaluate:

> The park that experienced the greatest percent increase in visitors from 2009 to 2010 also had the least total acreage.

This statement is typical of the sorts of statements that you are called upon to evaluate for Table Analysis questions. Note that there are two possible sorts that you could perform to evaluate this question. First, you could sort by Visitors % Change. But, you could also sort by Area Acres. So, what's the best? Sort by only one of those columns? Sort by both? Sort by neither?

With 11 rows of data, you'll probably find it safer to sort by at least one of the columns. But, which one? Well, note that the table provides you with ranking information for the areas of the parks. The smaller numbers used to rank the parks by area make it easier to identify the smallest park by area without sorting.

However, you might reasonably be worried about missing which park had the greatest percent increase by visitors. So, sort by Visitors % Change.

Here's what the sorted table looks like:

National Park		Visitors			Area	
Name	State	Number	% Change	Rank	Acres	Rank
Zion	UT	2,556,972	-2.5	8	145,598	35
Canyonlands	UT	435,908	-0.1	36	337,598	23
Grand Canyon	AZ	4,388,386	0.9	2	1,217,403	11
Mesa Verde	CO	559,712	1.7	30	52,122	46
Arches	UT	1,014,405	1.8	19	76,519	42
Yosemite	CA	3,901,408	4.4	3	791,266	16
Rocky Mtn.	CO	2,955,821	4.7	5	265,828	26
Badlands	SD	977,778	4.7	22	242,756	28
Bryce	UT	1,285,492	5.7	15	35,835	50
Yellowstone	WY	3,640,185	10.5	4	2,219,791	8
Acadia	ME	2,504,208	12.4	9	47,390	47

Now, it's clear that Acadia had the greatest percent increase in the number of visitors from 2009 to 2010. Acadia was ranked 47th in terms of overall acreage. You could sort the chart by Area Acres or by Area Rank at this point to finish evaluating the statement. However, since you know Acadia's rank for acreage, it's probably slightly faster to simply scan to see if any park had a higher rank for area. In this case, Bryce was ranked 50th, so this first statement is false.

Now, let's take a look at the second statement, which states:

> The park with the median rank by the number of visitors is larger than only one other park by acreage.

Again, you may be considering several different ways to sort the chart. So, start by asking yourself "What's hardest to see right now?" Remember that your chart will still be sorted as shown above, which is the sort that you did to evaluate the first statement. This sort makes it pretty hard to see which park had the median rank for visitors, so it makes sense to sort by Visitors Rank.

> **Medians, Modes, Percents**
> Medians, modes, and percents are all frequently used in Integrated Reasoning questions. If you need a review, read through Chapters 10 and 12.

Here's what the sorted chart looks like:

| National Park | | Visitors | | | Area | |
Name	State	Number	% Change	Rank	Acres	Rank
Grand Canyon	AZ	4,388,386	0.9	2	1,217,403	11
Yosemite	CA	3,901,408	4.4	3	791,266	16
Yellowstone	WY	3,640,185	10.5	4	2,219,791	8
Rocky Mtn.	CO	2,955,821	4.7	5	265,828	26
Zion	UT	2,665,972	-2.5	8	145,598	35
Acadia	ME	2,504,208	12.4	9	47,390	47
Bryce	UT	1,285,492	5.7	15	35,835	50
Arches	UT	1,014,405	1.8	19	76,519	42
Badlands	SD	977,778	4.7	22	242,756	28
Mesa Verde	CO	559,712	1.7	30	52,122	46
Canyonlands	UT	435,908	-0.1	36	337,598	23

With the table sorted by Visitors Rank, it's now fairly easy to find the park with the median rank. To find a median, you start by putting the items on a list into numerical order, which we just did by sorting the list. Then, you can just choose the middle number. In this case, Acadia is the park in the middle position since there are 5 parks ranked before it and 5 parks ranked after it.

Use Your Noteboards
For more complicated statements, you may want to make a list of the items that satisfy a condition in the statement.

Note that you could have also sorted the list by Visitors Number. Since data is always sorted from least to greatest, Canyonlands would have been the first row of the table and Grand Canyon would have been the last row. But, Acadia still would have been in the middle. We chose to sort by Visitors Rank because that term was mentioned in the question and it's easier to work with smaller numbers.

Having identified Acadia as the park with the median rank, you now need to decide whether to sort the table again. Since the table provides ranks for the total acreage of the parks on the list, you likely don't need to sort again. Acadia is 47th by acreage. One park, Bryce, with a rank of 50, is smaller. So, Acadia, the median park by visitation, is larger than only one other park on the list. The second statement is true.

Note, however, that if the table had not provided ranks for the parks by total area, then you most likely would have wanted to sort by Area Acres. After all, it's a lot easier to see that only one number is greater than 47 than to see that only one number is less than 47,390. Remember that sorting takes only a few seconds and you should sort whenever you think doing so will help you to accurately find what you need on the table.

Now, it's time to finish the question by evaluating the third statement. The third statement claims:

The total number of visitors at Arches in 2009 was fewer than 1,000,000.

Because this statement involves only a single data point, you don't really need to worry about doing any sorting. Even the most involved GMAT tables will have fewer than 30 rows of data. So, it will never be an issue to quickly scan the table, no matter how it is currently sorted, to find one data point. Just use the current sort which has Arches in the 8th row.

Next, you need some information about Arches to evaluate the statement. The table shows that Arches had 1,014,405 visitors in 2010. The table also shows that the number of visitors in 2010 was 1.8% greater than it was in 2009. To find the number of visitors in 2009, use the percent change formula:

Calculations Required
Expect to do some calculations such as computing an average or a percent change to evaluate one or two of the statements in a Table Analysis question.

$$\% \text{ change} = \frac{\text{difference}}{\text{original}} \times 100$$

Next, put the numbers that you know into the formula to get:

$$1.8 = \frac{(1,014,405 - x)}{x} \times 100$$

We've called the 2009 number that we're trying to find x. A little rearranging gives:

$$101.8x = 101,440,500$$

Finally, just divide through by 101.8 to find that x, the 2009 visitation at Arches, was 996,469 rounded to the nearest integer. So, statement three is true.

Here's what your answers should look like just before you click next to move onto the next question in the Integrated Reasoning section:

Calculator Time!
Don't forget that you can use the onscreen calculator to perform messy calculations such as dividing through by 101.8!

Sort By	Select...	▼					

National Park		Visitors			Area	
Name	State	Number	% change	Rank	Acres	Rank
Grand Canyon	AZ	4,388,386	0.9	2	1,217,403	11
Yosemite	CA	3,901,408	4.4	3	791,266	16
Yellowstone	WY	3,640,185	10.5	4	2,219,791	8
Rocky Mtn.	CO	2,955,821	4.7	5	265,828	26
Zion	UT	2,665,972	-2.5	8	145,598	35
Acadia	ME	2,504,208	12.4	9	47,390	47
Bryce	UT	1,285,492	5.7	15	35,835	50
Arches	UT	1,014,405	1.8	19	76,519	42
Badlands	SD	977,778	4.7	22	242,756	28
Mesa Verde	CO	559,712	1.7	30	52,122	46
Canyonlands	UT	435,908	-0.1	36	337,598	23

Each column of the table can be sorted in ascending order by clicking on the word "Select" above the table and choosing, from the drop-down menu, the heading of the column on which you want the table to be sorted.

Consider each of the following statements about these National Parks. For each statement indicate whether the statement is true or false, based on the information provided in the table.

True False
- ○ ● The park that experienced the greatest percent increase in visitors from 2009 to 2010 also had the least total acreage.
- ● ○ The park with the median rank by the number of visitors is larger than only one other park by acreage.
- ● ○ The total number of visitors at Arches in 2009 was fewer than 1,000,000.

The table above gives information for 2010 on total visitors and total acreage for 11 US National Parks. In addition to the numbers of total visitors and total acreage for each National Park, the table also provides the percent increase or decrease over the total visitors for 2009 and the rank of the National Park for total visitors and total acreage in 2010.

GRAPHICS INTERPRETATION

Graphics Interpretation questions provide you with one chart, graph, or image. Each chart is followed by two statements. The statements each contain one drop-down list from which you choose one answer. Your job is to pick the answer that makes the statement true. Each drop-down list typically contains between three to five answer choices.

You'll find a few sentences of explanatory text to the right of the chart or graph. As with Table Analysis questions, you may not need to read this explanatory information. Just as with Table Analysis questions, you can be guided by how well you understand the chart or graph. If you understand the chart or graph, then you probably don't need to read the explanatory text.

So, what should you look for when you review the chart or graph? Start by looking at any labels on the axes. Are quantities being measured in common, easily understood units? You should also look to see if the chart or graph has any titles that help to explain the data it shows. Finally, see if there's any sort of legend that helps to differentiate different types of data.

Let's take a look at the sample Graphics Interpretation question that we discussed in Chapter 18.

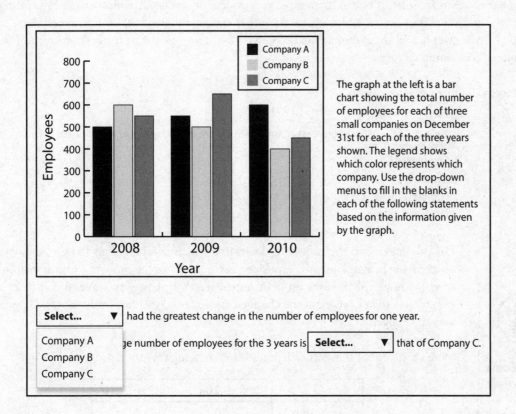

The graph at the left is a bar chart showing the total number of employees for each of three small companies on December 31st for each of the three years shown. The legend shows which color represents which company. Use the drop-down menus to fill in the blanks in each of the following statements based on the information given by the graph.

| Select...   ▼ | had the greatest change in the number of employees for one year.

| Company A |
| Company B | number of employees for the 3 years is | Select...   ▼ | that of Company C.
| Company C |

Here's How To Crack It:

Before we get started discussing this question, note that we've expanded the drop down list for the first statement. When the question first appears on the screen, none of the drop-downs are expanded. Here, we just wanted to show what the expanded drop-downs look like in the context of a question.

The first step in answering any Graphics Interpretation question is to review the chart or graph. In this case, there's a bar chart. The vertical axis shows the number of employees, which seems fairly easy to understand. The horizontal axis shows results for three years. The different colored bars are explained by the legend—there are three companies. So, this chart seems fairly straightforward. It shows the number of employees for three companies for three different years.

With everything on the chart so clearly marked, there's little reason to read the explanatory text to the right of the chart. Note that the only piece of information that the explanatory text really adds is that the number of employees for each company was tallied on December 31 of each year. That's the sort of detail that often turns out to be irrelevant in answering the questions. Remember that you can always go back and read the explanatory text if it seems like you need to know something that wasn't clearly reflected on the chart or graph.

Let's take a look at the questions. As with Table Analysis questions, it's best to just evaluate the statements in order. If one of them gives you trouble or seems particularly time consuming, you can always skip over it and evaluate the other statements first. Of course, you'll need to pick an answer for all three statements before you can move to the next question in the Integrated Reasoning section.

Here's the first statement again:

For this statement, the task is to determine which company had the greatest overall changes in employees in any one-year period. You'll probably find it helpful to write down the changes on your noteboard. You may even want to construct a rough table to keep track of the changes. In that way, you can easily spot the largest overall change.

Here's a table that shows the changes for each company:

	2008 to 2009	2009 to 2010
Company A	50	50
Company B	−100	−100
Company C	100	−200

Avoid Common Errors
Be careful when you read the chart. Are you looking at the right item? It's also a good idea to write down the data before performing any calculations with the data.

For this statement, it's important to note that the question asked for the greatest change. So, you need to include overall decreases in looking for the greatest change. Employment at Company C declined by 200 between 2009 and 2010. The correct answer to statement one is "Company C."

Here's the second statement showing the possible answers:

To evaluate this statement, you need to calculate the average number of employees for Companies A and C. Questions that ask you to perform calculations such as finding an average are fairly common for Graphics Interpretation questions. Just be sure to read the information from the chart carefully. Common errors for questions such as this one usually involve reading the information for the wrong company or mixing the information for two companies.

For Company A, the total number of employees for each year was 500, 550, and 600. To find the average, take the sum of the three numbers to get 1,650. Now, just divide by 3 because you want the average over three years. So, the average number of employees for Company A is 550.

For Company C, the total number of employees for each year was 550, 650, and 450. The average number of employees per year for Company C is also 550. So, the correct answer for the second statement is "the same as."

Here's what your answers should look like just before you click next to move on to the next question in the Integrated Reasoning section:

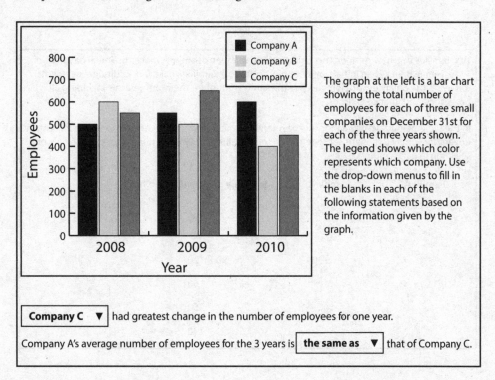

The graph at the left is a bar chart showing the total number of employees for each of three small companies on December 31st for each of the three years shown. The legend shows which color represents which company. Use the drop-down menus to fill in the blanks in each of the following statements based on the information given by the graph.

| **Company C** ▼ | had greatest change in the number of employees for one year.

Company A's average number of employees for the 3 years is | **the same as** ▼ | that of Company C.

TWO-PART ANALYSIS

Most Two-Part Analysis questions will remind you of the word problems that are part of the Quantitative section of the GMAT. The only difference is that you'll need to pick two answers rather than one! It's likely that you'll need to do some calculations to solve most Two-Part Analysis questions. For the most part, the math you'll need to do will be fairly straightforward arithmetic. You may find that it's faster to do the calculations without the calculator. However, remember that the calculator is available. Just remember to set up your calculations before entering them into the calculator.

For most Two-Part Analysis questions, the two answers that you need to pick are related or linked in some way. When that's the case, you may be able to identify one part as easier to solve than the other. If so, do the easier part first. It's also important to remember that working with the answer choices is often easier for these questions. While some Two-Part Analysis questions can be solved algebraically, it's very often faster to just test out the answer choices. In other words, you'll be able to use a form of PITA (Plugging In the Answers, discussed in our Algebra Chapter) to solve most of these questions. Let's take a look at how to solve the question we saw in Chapter 18.

Two families buy new refrigerators using installment plans. Family A makes an initial payment of $750. Family B makes an initial payment of $1200. Both families make five additional payments to pay off the balance. Both families pay the same amount for their refrigerators including all taxes, fees, and finance charges.

In the table below, identify a monthly payment, in dollars, for Family A and a monthly payment, in dollars, for Family B that are consistent with the installment plan described above. Make only one selection in each column.

Family A	Family B	Monthly payment (in dollars)
○	○	50
○	○	80
○	○	120
○	○	160
○	○	250
○	○	300

Here's How to Crack It

For this problem, one of the first things to notice is that there is a connection between the payments that each family makes. Since Family B's initial payment is $450 more than that of Family A, Family A's monthly payment is larger than that of Family B. That can help when you start testing the answer choices. Moreover, you can also see that the answer for Family A cannot be either $50 or $80. If Family A's monthly payment were $80, then they would have paid only an additional $400 after 5 months. That's not even enough to make Family A's total payment equal to Family B's initial payment. Of course, Family B makes monthly payments too.

The other thing to notice in this question is that there is a crucial piece of information missing: the cost of the refrigerator. In this case, Plugging In the Answers will enable us to verify that the cost of that fridge is the same for both families. You can set the problem up just like you would a PITA question with one change. So that you can keep track of your Process of

Elimination, write the answer choices down twice leaving some space between the answers to show any quantities that you needed to calculate. Of course, you'll label your answer choices just as you would with any other PITA question. For this problem, you can label your columns of numbers as "A's payment" and "B's payment." Here's what your initial setup should look like:

A's payment		B's payment	
~~50~~		50	
~~80~~		80	
120		120	
160		160	
250		250	
300		300	

Note that we've already crossed off 50 and 80 as possible payments for Family A. As discussed, these answers are too small for A's payment. As with any other PITA question, it makes sense to start with a number in the middle. We'll start with $160 for Family A's payment.

If Family A's payment is $160, what can you find? The problem states that Family A makes 5 payments, so the total of those 5 payments is $800. Moreover, the problem also states that Family A made an initial payment of $750. So, if Family A made payments of $160, then the refrigerator cost $750 + $800 = $1,550. That's what goes into the next column for Family A.

What about Family B? If Family A makes payments of $160, then Family B's payments must be less than that amount. So, Family B could make payments of $50, $80, or $120. For each of those numbers, calculate how much Family B would have paid for the refrigerator. Here's what your table should look like at this step:

A's payment	A's Total	B's payment	B's Total
~~50~~		50	$1450
~~80~~		80	$1600
120		120	$1800
160	$1550	160	
250		250	
300		300	

So, how do you know if you've found the correct answers? Remember that the problem states that both families pay the same amount for their refrigerators. Since Family B cannot pay $1,550 for their refrigerator, you can eliminate 160 as an answer for Family A.

It's not that clear whether Family A's payment needs to be larger or smaller. So, just pick a direction and try it. Let's try $250 for Family A's payment. If Family A's payment is $250, then their refrigerator costs $750 + (5 × $250) = $2,000. For Family B, none of the answers we've already worked out make their refrigerator cost $2,000. However, we can also check what happens if Family B makes monthly payments of $160. In that case, Family B's refrigerator costs $1,200 + (5 × $160) = $2,000. So, the answers are 250 for Family A and 160 for Family B.

Here's what your completed table looks like:

A's payment	A's Total	B's payment	B's Total
~~50~~		50	$1,450
~~80~~		80	$1,600
120		120	$1,800
~~160~~	$1,550	160	$2,000
250	$2,000	250	
300		300	

Here's what your answers should look like just before you click next to move on to the next question in the Integrated Reasoning section:

Check Your Answers
Always double check your answers for a Two-Part Analysis question. Flipping your answers is a very common mistake for these questions. Make sure you have the correct answer for each column.

Two families buy new refrigerators using installment plans. Family A makes an initial payment of $750. Family B makes an initial payment of $1200. Both families make five additional payments to pay off the balance. Both families pay the same amount for their refrigerators including all taxes, fees, and finance charges.

In the table below, identify a monthly payment, in dollars, for Family A and a monthly payment, in dollars, for Family B that are consistent with the installment plan described above. Make only one selection in each column.

Family A	Family B	Monthly payment (in dollars)
○	○	50
○	○	80
○	○	120
○	⦿	160
⦿	○	250
○	○	300

We used a form of Plugging In the Answers (PITA) to solve the previous question. You can use that approach for most of the Two-Part Analysis questions that you see. Here's a recap of the steps.

PITA for Two-Part Analysis Questions

1. Write down the answer choices on your noteboard. Make two columns and leave some space between.

2. Decide which variable is easier to work with. For example, you might be able to eliminate some answers for one variable because those answers are too big or too small.

3. Write a label over each column of numbers. Label the first column as the easier variable to work with.

4. Starting with an answer in the middle for the first column, work the steps of the problem. For the second column, remember that you may need to test only the answers that are bigger or smaller than the number you worked with in the first column.

5. Check for a match between the first and second column that makes a condition in the problem true.

For some Two-Part Analysis questions, however, you won't be able to use PITA. For the problem we just discussed, the two monthly payments were linked because both families needed to pay the same amount for a refrigerator. For some Two-Part Analysis questions, however, the variables are either unlinked or, at least, less linked.

Let's look at an example:

Jack divides $30,000 between two investments. He invests 35% of the money in Investment A, which pays 4% simple interest annually for 5 years. He invests the remainder of the money in Investment B, which pays 2% interest compounded semiannually for 4 years.

In the table below, identify the total interest earned, in dollars, for Investment A and the total interest earned, rounded to the nearest dollar, for Investment B that are consistent with the investments described above. Make only one selection in each column.

Investment A	Investment B	Interest Earned (in dollars)
○	○	392
○	○	870
○	○	1560
○	○	1616
○	○	2100
○	○	3347

Here's How to Crack It

For this question, note that there's no common condition that needs to be satisfied. Rather, there are two independent calculations. That's how you know that you can't use PITA to solve this question.

The solution to this question starts with calculating how Jack divides the $30,000 between the two investments. Start by calculating 35% of $30,000. Remember that you can just use the onscreen calculator: $30,000 \times 0.35 = 10,500$. So, $10,500 is invested in Investment A and the rest, or $19,500, is invested in Investment B.

Next, it's time to calculate the interest earned on each investment. Investment A earns simple interest at a rate of 4% per year for 5 years. To find simple interest, you multiply the principal amount, $10,500, by the interest rate, 0.04, by the time period, 5 years. Here's what the calculation looks like:

$$\$10,500 \times 0.04 \times 5 = \$2,100$$

The onscreen calculator makes doing the calculation an easy, one-step operation. Just make sure that you use the right numbers from the problem!

For Investment B, the interest is compounded semiannually. That means that every six months the interest is added to the principal so that interest can be earned on the combined amount. There are several ways to calculate compound interest. One of the easiest is to divide the yearly interest rate by the compounding period. For this problem, the investment pays 2% per year, but the interest is compounded twice per year.

So, that's 1% every six months. In four years, there are 8 compounding periods. So, to find the account balance at the end of 4 years, you'd calculate the interest for the first six months by multiplying by 0.01. Then, you'd add that amount to the principal and repeat the calculation. Keep calculating until you've done all 8 compounding periods. Of course, since you are multiplying each time, there's a shorter way. Here's what the overall calculation looks like.

$$\$19,500 \times (1.01)^8 = \$21,115.71$$

Now, to find the interest just subtract $19,500 from the account balance. The interest earned is $1,616 rounded to the nearest dollar.

Here's what your answers should look like just before you click next to move onto the next question in the Integrated Reasoning section:

Jack divides $30,000 between two investments. He invests 35% of the money in Investment A, which pays 4% simple interest annually for 5 years. He invests the remainder of the money in Investment B, which pays 2% interest compounded semiannually for 4 years.

In the table below, identify the total interest earned, in dollars, for Investment A and the total interest earned, rounded to the nearest dollar, for Investment B that are consistent with the investments described above. Make only one selection in each column.

Investment A	Investment B	Interest Earned (in dollars)
○	○	392
○	○	870
○	○	1560
○	●	1616
●	○	2100
○	○	3347

MULTI-SOURCE REASONING

For Multi-Source Reasoning questions, you'll be given a variety of information that can include text, charts, tables, and graphs. The information is arranged on 2 or 3 tabs. Multi-Source Reasoning questions typically come in sets. So, you'll probably get two sets of statement style questions and perhaps one standard multiple-choice question.

When a new Multi-Source question appears on your screen, you should take a minute to review the information on each tab. As usual, you'll want to check out things like the axes on graphs and any headings for the charts. But, for Multi-Source Reasoning questions, you also want to see how the information on one tab relates to the information on the other tabs.

Let's look at the example that we saw in the previous Integrated Reasoning chapter. This time, we'll take a look at the information on all three tabs. We'll also discuss how to evaluate statements and answer questions.

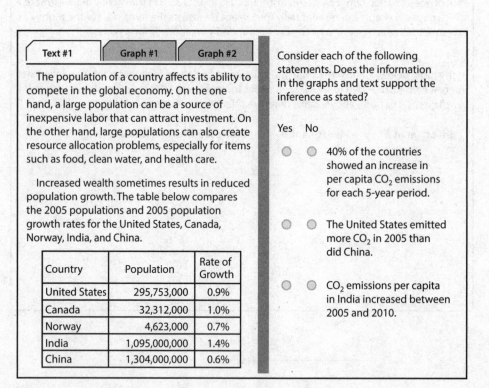

| Text #1 | Graph #1 | Graph #2 |

The population of a country affects its ability to compete in the global economy. On the one hand, a large population can be a source of inexpensive labor that can attract investment. On the other hand, large populations can also create resource allocation problems, especially for items such as food, clean water, and health care.

Increased wealth sometimes results in reduced population growth. The table below compares the 2005 populations and 2005 population growth rates for the United States, Canada, Norway, India, and China.

Country	Population	Rate of Growth
United States	295,753,000	0.9%
Canada	32,312,000	1.0%
Norway	4,623,000	0.7%
India	1,095,000,000	1.4%
China	1,304,000,000	0.6%

Consider each of the following statements. Does the information in the graphs and text support the inference as stated?

Yes No

○ ○ 40% of the countries showed an increase in per capita CO_2 emissions for each 5-year period.

○ ○ The United States emitted more CO_2 in 2005 than did China.

○ ○ CO_2 emissions per capita in India increased between 2005 and 2010.

Here's How to Crack It

We'll review the information one tab at a time before we start evaluating the statements. The first tab, Text #1, provides some background information about the ways in which a country's population can affect its participation in the global economy. This tab also presents a table with population and growth rates for five countries. Notice that you need to read the included information on this tab to determine that the table displays data from 2005. Unlike the other question types that we've discussed, you should always read any text that's included on a tab in a Multi-Source Reasoning question.

Now, here's the information for the second tab:

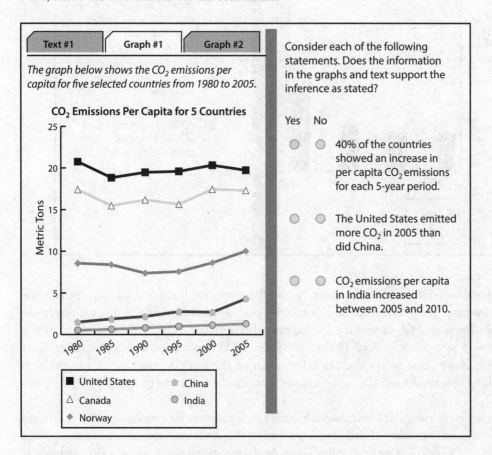

This tab shows CO_2 emissions for five countries over a 25-year period. Notice that the countries on this tab are the same as the countries on the first tab. It's also important to note that the CO_2 emissions on this tab are per capita emissions. Since the first tab provided information about populations for 2005, it would be possible to calculate approximate total CO_2 emissions for these five countries for 2005. While you don't necessarily need to consider all the calculations you could perform, thinking about what you could calculate is an excellent way to notice connections between the data provided on the tabs.

Next, let's take a look at the information on the third tab:

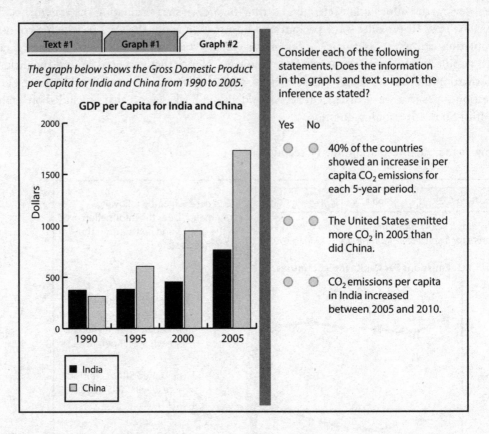

This tab provides GDP information about two of the countries, India and China, discussed on the first two tabs. The information on this tab is provided for a subset of the timespan from the second tab. The second tab showed the 25-year range from 1980 to 2005, while this information is only for the 15-year timespan from 1990 to 2005. The GDP information is provided as per capita information. Again, that means that the information on the first tab could be used to calculate the overall GDP for India and China. Of course, that calculation can be completed only for 2005.

Now that we've reviewed the information on each tab, it's time to start evaluating the statements. But first, we need to consider the directions carefully. The directions state that you are supposed to consider the question "Does the information in the graphs and text support the inference as stated?" Remember our discussion of valid inferences. An inference is a statement that you know to be true because you can back it up with proof.

There are really three cases to consider when evaluating these statements. If the graphs and other information on the tabs are sufficient to show that the statement is true, answer "yes." If the graphs and other information on the tabs are sufficient to show that the statement is false, answer "no." But, what if there is simply insufficient information to conclusively show that the statement is either true or false? In that case, you answer "no" because the information did not support the inference. In other words, the task here is a little different from simply evaluating whether the statements are true or false. After all, GMAC could have made the answer choices True and False rather than Yes and No.

Remember, however, that most GMAC statements won't try to trick you that way. But, it is important to remember that you need proof to claim that something can be inferred. You will see statements that try to get you to read into or interpret the information. Such activities do not lead to valid inferences!

Let's take a look at the first statement:

> 40% of the countries showed an increase in per capita CO_2 emissions for each 5-year period.

The first step in evaluating a statement for a Multi-Source Reasoning question is to determine which tab or tabs contain the information that you need. For this statement, the second tab contains information about per capita CO_2 emissions so select that tab. Next, start checking out the trend lines on the graph. We've reprinted the chart from the second tab below.

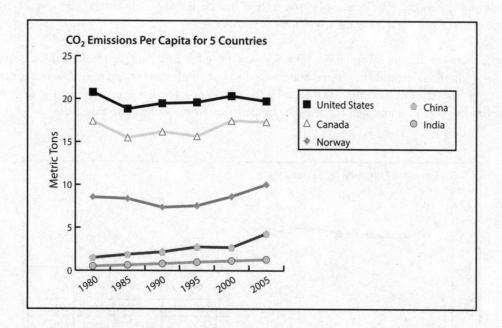

The trend lines for the United States, Canada, and Norway clearly show both increases and decreases between five year periods. So, none of those countries fit the requirements of the statement. The trend line for China needs to be examined carefully. China's CO_2 emissions per capita increase for four out of the five five-year periods shown. However, China's emissions decreased slightly between 1995 and 2000. So, China also does not fit the requirements of the statement. Only India's trend line shows an increase for every five-year period depicted on the graph. But, that means that only 1 out of 5 or 20% of the countries showed an increase in CO_2 emissions for each five-year period. So, the answer to the first statement is "no."

Next, let's take a look at the second statement:

The United States emitted more CO_2 in 2005 than did China.

Evaluating this statement is a little trickier than evaluating the first statement. First, be careful of the wording. The statement is about total CO_2 emissions rather than the per capita emissions that are shown by the chart on the second tab. So, while the emissions chart does show that per capita emissions for the United States were greater than those for China in 2005, you cannot base your answer only on that piece of information. Remember that the test writers will try to get you to make hasty conclusions so always check out the wording of the statement carefully.

Since none of the provided charts allows you to simply look up the information for this statement, you need to determine if you have sufficient information to evaluate the statement. To go from per capita CO_2 emissions in 2005 to total CO_2 emissions in 2005, you need to know the populations for China and the United States in 2005. That information is provided by the table on the first tab. As discussed before, if there had been insufficient information, you could have clicked "no" right away for your answer.

Since there is sufficient information, however, you'll need to calculate the total 2005 CO_2 emissions for both China and the United States. To do so, multiply the per capita emissions for each country from the chart on the second tab by the population for that country from the table on the first tab. We've duplicated the relevant information from the first two tabs below.

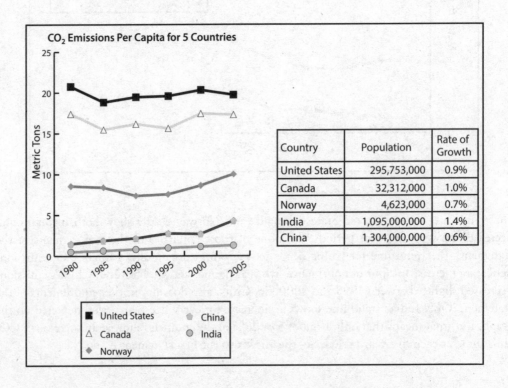

Of course, you won't be able to split the view on your computer screen this way. So, you'll need to write down some of the relevant information on your noteboards. You should use your noteboards to take notes whenever you need information from two different tabs. Simply trying to remember the numbers can cause errors and waste time. For example, to evaluate this statement, you might jot down the 2005 per capita CO_2 emissions for the United States and China. Then, go to the first tab to get the population numbers for each country.

For the United States, per capita CO_2 emissions in 2005 were approximately 20 metric tons. The U.S. population in 2005 was 295,753,000. So, the total 2005 CO_2 emissions for the United States was 20 × 295,753,000 = 5,915,060,000 metric tons. For China, the per capita CO_2 emissions are approximately 4.8 and the population was 1,304,000,000. So, China's total CO_2 emissions for 2005 were 4.8 × 1,304,000,000 = 6,259,200,000, greater than those of the United States. Therefore, the answer to the second statement is "no."

It's time to tackle the third statement:

CO_2 emissions per capita in India increased between 2005 and 2010.

In contrast with the second statement, evaluating this statement is certainly less time consuming. However, as we'll see, you'll need to remember what is necessary for a valid inference. The necessary information is displayed on the graph on the second tab. Again, we've duplicated the necessary information below.

Use Your Noteboards
If the information you need is on two different tabs, use your noteboards to keep track of the information from one of the tabs.

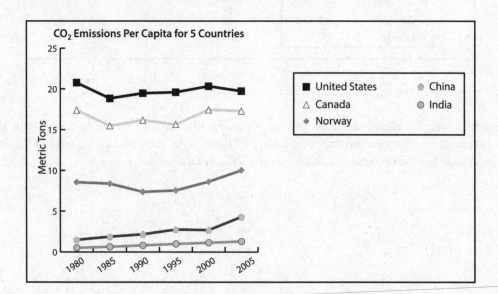

Now it's time to be careful. Notice that the chart only displays data up to 2005. While India's per capita CO_2 emissions have shown a steady increase over the 25-year period shown on the chart, that's not sufficient for a valid inference. Since the chart does not display the actual numbers for 2010, the answer to the third statement is "no."

Here's what your answers should look like just before you click next to move on to the next question in the Integrated Reasoning section:

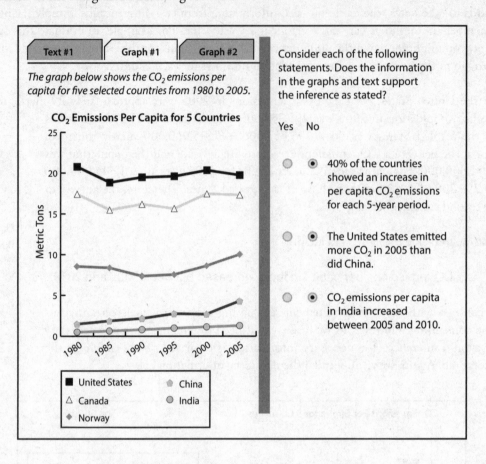

As mentioned, Multi-Source Reasoning questions usually come in sets. Typically, you'll get two statement style questions and one multiple-choice style question. The questions on the right change but the tabbed information on the left stays the same.

Let's take a look at a multiple-choice question for the tabbed information that we just used to evaluate a statement style question.

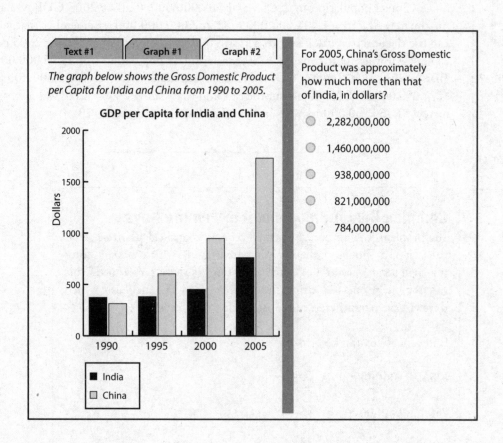

Here's How to Crack It

As with any other Multi-Source Reasoning question, your first step is to determine which chart or charts contain the relevant data. For this question, you certainly need the bar chart on the third tab because that chart shows information about GDP. The bar chart is shown above. However, the bar chart displays data about GDP per capita and the question asks about overall Gross Domestic Product. So, you'll also need the 2005 population numbers from the table on tab one. We've reproduced the relevant table below.

Country	Population	Rate of Growth
United States	295,753,000	0.9%
Canada	32,312,000	1.0%
Norway	4,623,000	0.7%
India	1,095,000,000	1.4%
China	1,304,000,000	0.6%

To answer the question, you need to multiply each country's GDP per capita from 2005 by its population from 2005. Then, subtract India's GDP from that of China.

Need More Practice?
Check out *1,138 GMAT Practice Questions, 3rd Edition* for access to 100 more Integrated Reasoning questions!

Based on the bar chart, China's 2005 per capita GDP was approximately $1,750. Since China's population in 2005 was 1,304,000,000, China's 2005 GDP was approximately $1,750 × 1,304,000,000 = $2,282,000,000,000. (Remember that you can use the onscreen calculator to perform the calculation.) For India, the 2005 per capita GDP was approximately $750, while India's population was 1,095,000,000. That means that India's GDP was approximately $750 × 1,095,000,000 = $821,250,000,000. Now, just subtract to find that China's 2005 GDP was approximately $1,460,750,000 more than that of India. That's closest to (B).

Complex Calculations and the Memory Keys

The problem just discussed featured several longer calculations. Your calculator at home probably has parentheses, which makes entering such a calculation a one-step operation. Is there a way to do this calculation in one-step using the onscreen GMAT calculator which doesn't have parentheses? Sure, use the memory keys!

Enter the following keystrokes:

1750 * 1304000000 = | MS |

750 * 1095000000 = | +/– | | M+ | | MR |

These keystrokes will minimize the number of times you need to enter the large numbers, which helps to avoid errors.

Summary

o Before you jump into the Integrated Reasoning questions, get your bearings and peruse each tab or piece of information.

o On Table Analysis questions, know that you can sort only by one column at a time. If you think that sorting will help, go for it. But don't waste time devising the perfect order to evaluate statements.

o On Graphics Interpretation questions, start by looking for labels on the axes and finding the legend if there is one.

o On Two-Part Analysis questions, do some algebra or PITA to get to the right answer. Careful that you select the right button in the right column when answering these questions.

o On Multi-Source Reasoning questions, take a minute to review the information on each tab before you jump in. Think about how the information on one tab relates to the information on other tabs.

Chapter 20
Integrated
Reasoning: Drills

PRACTICE INTEGRATED REASONING: SECTION 1

12 Items

Time limit: 30 minutes

This section is a full practice Integrated Reasoning section. Please note that some questions are laid out slightly differently in this book versus what you'll see on the GMAT. Many of the new question formats are interactive. Hence, only approximations can be printed. Specifically,

- Table Analysis questions are shown with a main sort and several alternate sorts. You may not need every sort.
- Graphics Interpretation questions include drop down boxes. In this book, the box is shown as a fill-in blank and the answers are printed below the blank.
- For Multi-Source Reasoning questions, we've printed what's on each tab consecutively on the page.
- For some questions, you'll see (A), (B), (C), (D), and (E) next to the answer choices. These are included only to make it easier to check your work. These do not appear on the real GMAT.

We've included answers to this section starting on page 445.

Item 1:

Subway Station	Riders	% Change	Connecting Subway Lines
Times Square/42nd St.	58,422,597	0.6%	11
Grand Central/42nd St.	41,903,210	−0.2%	5
34th St./Herald Square	37,769,752	2.2%	7
14th St./Union Square	34,730,692	1.4%	7
34th St./Penn Station (Red Lines)	26,892,243	−1.1%	3
34th St./Penn Station (Blue Lines)	24,265,016	0.3%	3
59th St/Columbus Circle	20,711,058	1.4%	5
Lexington Ave/59th St	19,553,597	3.3%	6
86th St. (Green Lines)	19,147,021	1.4%	3

The table above gives information on the ridership in 9 subway stations in New York City for the year 2010. The subway stations were chosen for inclusion in the table because they were the busiest stations in 2010, based on the number of passengers entering the station. In addition to annual ridership (number of passengers) for each station in 2010, the table also gives the percent increase or decrease in ridership from 2009 to 2010 and the number of subway lines that connect to the station.

Each column of the table can be sorted in ascending order by clicking on the word "Select" above the table and choosing, from the drop-down menu, the heading of the column on which you want the table to be sorted.

Alternate Sort 1: *% Change*

Subway Station	Riders	% Change	Connecting Subway Lines
34th St./Penn Station (Red Lines)	26,892,243	−1.1%	3
Grand Central/42nd St.	41,903,210	−0.2%	5
34th St./Penn Station (Blue Lines)	24,265,016	0.3%	3
Times Square/42nd St	58,422,597	0.6%	11
14th St./Union Square	34,730,692	1.4%	7
59th St/Columbus Circle	20,711,058	1.4%	5
86th St. (Green Lines)	19,147,021	1.4%	3
34th St./Herald Square	37,769,752	2.2%	7
Lexington Ave/59th St	19,553,597	3.3%	6

Alternate Sort 2: *Connecting Subway Lines*

Subway Station	Riders	% Change	Connecting Subway Lines
34th St./Penn Station (Red Lines)	26,892,243	−1.1%	3
34th St./Penn Station (Blue Lines)	24,265,016	0.3%	3
86th St. (Green Lines)	19,147,021	1.4%	3
Grand Central/42nd St.	41,903,210	−0.2%	5
59th St/Columbus Circle	20,711,058	1.4%	5
Lexington Ave/59th St	19,553,597	3.3%	6
14th St./Union Square	34,730,692	1.4%	7
34th St./Herald Square	37,769,752	2.2%	7
Times Square/42nd St	58,422,597	0.6%	11

Consider each of the following statements about the subway stations. For each statement indicate whether the statement is true or false, based on the information provided in the table.

	True	False	
Question 1-1	O	O	The station with the median rank based on annual ridership is also the station with the greatest decrease in annual ridership from 2009 to 2010.
Question 1-2	O	O	The ratio of the average (arithmetic mean) number of riders in 2010 for those subway stations having 5 connecting lines to those having 3 connecting lines is approximately 4:3.
Question 1-3	O	O	The station with the greatest percent increase in riders from 2009 to 2010 had the least annual ridership in 2010.

Item 2:

Frank researched the 45 doctors in his local area and found that 8 of them graduated from medical school with honors, but that the services of only 3 of those 8 doctors are covered by his medical plan. He also found that 27 doctors whose services are covered by his medical plan graduated from medical school without honors.

In the table below, for the doctors in Frank's local area, identify the total number of doctors whose services are not covered by Frank's medical plan, and identify the number of doctors who both graduated from medical school without honors and whose services are not covered by Frank's health plan. Make only one selection in each column.

	Services Not Covered by Medical Plan	Graduated Without Honors and Services Not Covered by Medical Plan	Total Number
(A)	○	○	10
(B)	○	○	15
(C)	○	○	18
(D)	○	○	30
(E)	○	○	37
(F)	○	○	40

Item 3:

A flower market sells orchids for $1.35 and dahlias for $1.80. Faustino spends $18.00 on orchids and dahlias.

In the table below, choose the number of orchids and the number of dahlias that are consistent with the amount spent by Faustino. Make only one selection in each column.

	Orchids	Dahlias	Number Purchased
(A)	○	○	0
(B)	○	○	2
(C)	○	○	4
(D)	○	○	5
(E)	○	○	6
(F)	○	○	8

Item 4:

At a certain archery school, each of five students shot a single arrow at the end of each day of training, as well as one arrow before the first day of training. The graph above is a scatterplot, in which each of the 30 points represents the distance from the center of the target to each student's arrow and the number of days the student had been in training at the time the arrow was shot. The solid line is the regression line. Use the drop-down menus to fill in the blanks in each of the following statements based on the information given by the graph.

Question 4-1:

The slope of the regression line is closest to _____.

        (A) −2.6
        (B) −1.3
        (C) −0.8
        (D) 1.2
        (E) 2.9

Question 4-2:

The number of students within 11 inches of the center of the target is _____ after day 2 of training than before any training.

        (A)   50% less
        (B)   25% less
        (C)   50% greater
        (D) 100% greater
        (E) 200% greater

Item 5:

The earliest known evidence of seafaring by human ancestors dates to approximately 130,000 years ago. However, in 2010, archaeologists discovered stone tools on the coast of a Mediterranean island that date to the Paleolithic age (about 2.6 million years ago). Because more than 40 miles of open sea separate the island from Greece, the archaeologists theorized that some human ancestors developed nautical skills millions of years earlier than previously discovered.

Question 5-1:

In the table below, identify which statement, if true, most strengthens the argument above, and which statement, if true, most seriously weakens the argument above.

Strengthen	Weaken	Statement
(A) ○	○	In the same area of the island, archaeologists discovered pieces of ancient harpoons and spears used for fishing.
(B) ○	○	The stone tools resemble those made and used by *Homo erectus* and *Homo heidelbergensis*, human ancestors in the Paleolithic era who lived on the mainland of Greece.
(C) ○	○	The stone tools were probably used primarily for skinning animals.
(D) ○	○	It would be impossible to construct a seaworthy boat solely from the tools discovered by the archaeologists.
(E) ○	○	Approximately 5 million years ago, during the Messinian Salinity Crisis of the late Miocene era, the Mediterranean Sea dried up.
(F) ○	○	The stone tools were likely used for purposes other than construction of boats or rafts.

There is no testing material on this page.

Data for Items 6, 7, and 8:

This table provides the standard interest rates offered by Central Bank for CDs, listed according to term offering and purchase amount. The interest rates listed are annual rates, compounded annually, to be paid when the CD comes to term. No bonuses or other adjustments are included.

CD Options and Standard Interest Rates

General memo to employees of Central Bank:

January 15th

In order to improve and stabilize our bank's investment opportunities, we are seeking to shift the balance of our customers' CD accounts towards those with longer maturity terms. We have begun testing two incentive programs. All CDs purchased with terms of at least 5 years now receive, as a bonus, an additional 0.1% interest during the first year to be added to the standard rate. More-over, preferred customers (those who have previously bought CDs of any term length in amounts of $10,000 or more) will receive a bonus of 0.2% during the first year when they purchase a CD with a term of 5 or 10 years in the amount of at least $10,000. Other CDs continue at the standard rates.

We have also revised the schedule of penalties for early withdrawal and made these applicable to all new CDs. The penalties are as follows: For any CD, early withdrawal less than a year after the CD is purchased results in a loss of all interest. For 2-year CDs, early withdrawal after the first year results in the loss of one year of interest. For 5-year and 10-year CDs, withdrawal after the first year results in the loss of two years of interest and of any accrued bonus interest.

Item 6:

Determine whether each of the following investments will earn at least $250 of interest in its first year.

	Yes	No	
Question 6-1	◯	◯	$11,000 invested by a new customer in a 1-year CD
Question 6-2	◯	◯	$9,500 invested by a preferred customer in a 5-year CD
Question 6-3	◯	◯	$9,500 invested by a new customer in a 10-year CD

Item 7:

Determine whether each of these transactions will, according to the new rules and rates described, yield a total interest payment of between $500 and $600.

	Yes	No	
Question 7-1	◯	◯	A new customer's $20,000 1-year CD held for the complete term
Question 7-2	◯	◯	A new customer's $4,000 5-year CD held for the complete term
Question 7-3	◯	◯	A preferred customer's $10,000 2-year CD held for the complete term

Item 8:

Consider each of the following statements. Does the information in the memo and the table support the inference as stated?

	Yes	No	
Question 8-1	◯	◯	Prior to the policy changes described, there were no penalties for early CD withdrawals.
Question 8-2	◯	◯	Certain bank policies are designed to reward preferred customers for their loyalty.
Question 8-3	◯	◯	If the bank accomplishes its stated intentions, it will likely pay a higher average (arithmetic mean) interest rate to customers than if it does not.

Item 9:

Year of Election	President	Political Party	Popular Vote (millions)	% of Popular Vote	Electoral Vote	% of Electoral Vote
1960	John Kennedy	Democratic	34.2	49.72%	303	56.40%
1964	Lyndon Johnson	Democratic	43.1	61.05%	486	90.30%
1968	Richard Nixon	Republican	31.8	43.42%	301	55.90%
1972	Richard Nixon	Republican	47.2	60.67%	520	96.70%
1976	James Carter	Democratic	40.8	50.08%	297	55.20%
1980	Ronald Reagan	Republican	43.9	50.75%	489	90.90%
1984	Ronald Reagan	Republican	54.5	58.77%	525	97.60%
1988	George Bush	Republican	48.9	53.37%	426	79.20%
1992	William Clinton	Democratic	44.9	43.01%	370	68.80%
1996	William Clinton	Democratic	47.4	49.23%	379	70.40%
2000	George W. Bush	Republican	50.5	47.87%	271	50.40%
2004	George W. Bush	Republican	62.0	50.73%	286	53.20%
2008	Barack Obama	Democratic	69.5	52.87%	365	67.80%

The table above gives information about the voting patterns in United States presidential elections from 1960 to 2008. In addition to giving the name and the political party of the President elected in each year, the table provides the total popular vote and electoral vote that the winner received in that election, as well as the percentage of the total vote that each figure represents.

Each column of the table can be sorted in ascending order by clicking on the word "Select" above the table and choosing, from the drop-down menu, the heading of the column on which you want the table to be sorted.

Alternate Sort 1: *Electoral Vote*

Year of Election	President	Political Party	Popular Vote (millions)	% of Popular Vote	Electoral Vote	% of Electoral Vote
2000	George W. Bush	Republican	50.5	47.87%	271	50.40%
2004	George W. Bush	Republican	62.0	50.73%	286	53.20%
1976	James Carter	Democratic	40.8	50.08%	297	55.20%
1968	Richard Nixon	Republican	31.8	43.42%	301	55.90%
1960	John Kennedy	Democratic	34.2	49.72%	303	56.40%
2008	Barack Obama	Democratic	69.5	52.87%	365	67.80%
1992	William Clinton	Democratic	44.9	43.01%	370	68.80%
1996	William Clinton	Democratic	47.4	49.23%	379	70.40%
1988	George Bush	Republican	48.9	53.37%	426	79.20%
1964	Lyndon Johnson	Democratic	43.1	61.05%	486	90.30%
1980	Ronald Reagan	Republican	43.9	50.75%	489	90.90%
1972	Richard Nixon	Republican	47.2	60.67%	520	96.70%
1984	Ronald Reagan	Republican	54.4	58.77%	525	97.60%

Alternate Sort 2: *Percent of Popular Vote*

Year of Election	President	Political Party	Popular Vote (millions)	% of Popular Vote	Electoral Vote	% of Electoral Vote
1992	William Clinton	Democratic	44.9	43.01%	370	68.80%
1968	Richard Nixon	Republican	31.8	43.42%	301	55.90%
2000	George W. Bush	Republican	50.5	47.87%	271	50.40%
1996	William Clinton	Democratic	47.4	49.23%	379	70.40%
1960	John Kennedy	Democratic	34.2	49.72%	303	56.40%
1976	James Carter	Democratic	40.8	50.08%	297	55.20%
2004	George W. Bush	Republican	62.0	50.73%	286	53.20%
1980	Ronald Reagan	Republican	43.9	50.75%	489	90.90%
2008	Barack Obama	Democratic	69.5	52.87%	365	67.80%
1988	George Bush	Republican	48.9	53.37%	426	79.20%
1984	Ronald Reagan	Republican	54.4	58.77%	525	97.60%
1972	Richard Nixon	Republican	47.2	60.67%	520	96.70%
1964	Lyndon Johnson	Democratic	43.1	61.05%	486	90.30%

Consider each of the following statements about the Presidential election data. For each statement indicate whether the statement is true or false, based on the information provided in the table.

	True	False	
Question 9-1	O	O	Of those Presidents elected for two terms, William Clinton had the smallest percent increase in popular vote between the two years.
Question 9-2	O	O	The average (arithmetic mean) number of electoral votes received by Democratic presidents was greater than the average number of electoral votes received by Republican presidents.
Question 9-3	O	O	The same President was elected in the two election years in which the winner's percentage of the popular vote and percentage of the electoral vote were most nearly equal.

Data for Items 10, 11, and 12:

| Memo #1 | Memo #2 | Email #1 |

MEMORANDUM
To: Regional Office Managers
From: Chief Operations Officer
RE: Travel planning

Once again, our annual management retreat will be held in Bloomsbury. In preparation for this year's retreat, all Regional Office Managers (ROMs) will be responsible for arranging the travel reservations for all Level 2 managers within his or her Region. You may delegate that task should you wish.

ROMs will receive a research memorandum from the Logistics Division providing the average (arithmetic mean) airfare from the 6 Regions to Bloomsbury. While ROMs should use that average airfare as a guide, we anticipate that there may be some variation in ticket prices based upon the specifics of travel arrangements. As such, Regional offices will be reimbursed for the full cost of any plane ticket priced within 1 (one) standard deviation of the average airfare from its region to Bloomsbury, inclusive. For any ticket priced more than 1 (one) standard deviation above the mean, regional offices will be reimbursed up to the average airfare from your region to Bloomsbury. For any ticket priced 1 (one) standard deviation or more below average, in addition to full reimbursement of the ticket cost, regional offices will receive a "Budget Bonus" of 50% of the difference between the ticket price and the average airfare from your region to Bloomsbury.

| Memo #1 | Memo #2 | Email #1 |

MEMORANDUM
To: Regional Office Managers
From: Logistics Division
RE: Airfare Research

The attached chart lists the average (arithmetic mean) airfare from the listed Regions to Bloomsbury. The mean airfare was calculated based upon taking a normally distributed sample of airfares. The standard deviation and size of each sample is also listed in the chart.

(See the next page for additional information)

Email from Marco Roland, Human Resources Manager, West Region to Marisa Cortland, Regional Office Manager, West Region

Dear Marisa,

Tickets have been purchased for all of the Level 2 Managers in the West Region. Below is a summary:

Airfare	Number of Tickets Purchased
$150	18
$210	4
$230	8

Best,

Marco

Item 10:

Consider each of the following statements. Select *Yes* if the information contained in the two memoranda and the email support the inference as stated. Otherwise, select *No*.

Yes No

Question 10-1 ○ ○ No region had a lower average (arithmetic mean) airfare to Bloomsbury than the Midwest.

Question 10-2 ○ ○ Only Level 2 managers will attend the management retreat.

Question 10-3 ○ ○ The Regional Office Manager need not make the reservations personally.

Item 11:

Consider each of the following statements. Based upon the information contained in the two memoranda and the email, determine whether each statement is true or false as stated.

True False

Question 11-1 ○ ○ The West Region will receive a "Budget Bonus" of $450.

Question 11-2 ○ ○ The two regions with the least sample size also had the least difference between the most and least expensive airfare found during research.

Question 11-3 ○ ○ The combined mean airfare of all the researched regions is less than the mean airfare for three of the regions individually.

Item 12:

If one of the tickets purchased by the West Region's Level 2 managers were selected at random, what is the probability that it is eligible to be fully reimbursed?

(A) $\dfrac{4}{15}$

(B) $\dfrac{9}{15}$

(C) $\dfrac{11}{15}$

(D) $\dfrac{12}{15}$

(E) $\dfrac{14}{15}$

PRACTICE INTEGRATED REASONING: SECTION 2

12 Items

Time limit: 30 minutes

This section is a full practice Integrated Reasoning section. Please note that some questions are laid out slightly differently in this book versus what you'll see on the GMAT. Many of the new question formats are interactive. Hence, only approximations can be printed. Specifically,

- Table Analysis questions are shown with a main sort and several alternate sorts. You may not need every sort.
- Graphics Interpretation questions include drop down boxes. In this book, the box is shown as a fill-in blank and the answers printed below the blank.
- For Multi-Source Reasoning questions, we've printed what's on each tab consecutively on the page.
- For some questions, you'll see (A), (B), (C), (D), and (E) next to the answer choices. These are included only to make it easier to check your work. These do not appear on the real GMAT.

We've included answers to this section starting on page 452.

Item 1:

The graph above gives the daily output for five days at a certain clock factory. Use the drop-down menus to fill in the blanks in each of the following statements based on the information given by the graph.

Question 1-1:

The ratio of the number of clocks produced on Tuesday to those produced on Wednesday is approximately _____.

        (A) 15 to 8
        (B) 12 to 7
        (C) 10 to 9
        (D)   8 to 11
        (E)   5 to 13

Question 1-2:

The total number of clocks produced on Monday and Wednesday is approximately _____ of the number of clocks produced for all five days.

        (A) 16%
        (B) 20%
        (C) 28%
        (D) 36%
        (E) 45%

Item 2:

Company X: Our company's computer technology is out of date. We will be unable to compete effectively in the modern economy if we are not using current computer technology. We have decided to purchase new computers that run Portals 8, the newest version of the world's best-selling operating system, throughout the entire company.

Technology Consultant: We agree that Company X needs to purchase new computers, but instead of installing Portals 8, Company X should purchase GreenCap, our consulting firm's proprietary operating system. The initial purchase of a GreenCap operating system costs substantially less than does Portals 8, and it provides the same functionality with current computer technology. With the money saved, Company X will be better able to compete effectively in the modern economy.

In the table below, identify which statement, if true, most weakens Company X's argument, and which statement, if true, most weakens the Technology Consultant's argument.

Weakens Company X	Weakens Technology Consultant	Statement
(A) ○	○	GreenCap makes more efficient use of computer resources than does Portals 8.
(B) ○	○	GreenCap is not the most cutting-edge software available on the market.
(C) ○	○	Although Portals 8 was released this year, GreenCap has been available for three years.
(D) ○	○	GreenCap requires purchase of an annual maintenance agreement, making it more expensive overall than Portals 8.
(E) ○	○	Portals 8 is available in several different versions with different price levels, depending on the proposed use of the operating system.
(F) ○	○	Portals 8, which was newly released, contains bugs and design flaws that will impair Company X's ability to compete in the modern economy.

There is no testing material on this page.

Item 3:

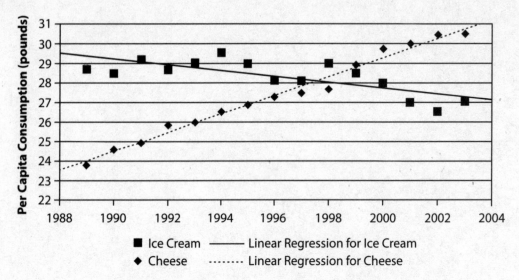

The graph above is a scatterplot with 30 points, each representing the per capita consumption, in pounds, of ice cream and cheese for the years 1989 through 2003 in the United States. The solid line is a regression line for the points representing the per capita consumption of ice cream. The dashed line is a regression line for the points representing the per capita consumption of cheese. Use the drop-down menus to fill in the blanks in each of the following statements based on the information given by the graph.

Question 3-1:

For the year with the lowest total per capita consumption of both ice cream and cheese combined, the ratio of per capita ice cream consumption to per capita cheese consumption is approximately _____ .

(A) 2 to 3
(B) 3 to 2
(C) 6 to 5
(D) 5 to 6

Question 3-2:

The slope of the regression line for ice cream is _____ the slope of the regression line for cheese.

(A) greater than
(B) less than
(C) equal to

Item 4:

XM Representative: Your federal committee thoroughly reviews all of the geo-engineering industry's planned projects and approves only those that meet your guidelines for safety and environmental impact. Since less than two percent of XM projects have ever been rejected, the costly and time-consuming review should be waived so that our latest project can be passed and implemented quickly.

Committee Member: Your request fails to consider that the decisions of our board affect not only the corporation involved, but also the entire field. If we fail to review your project, we also fail to observe innovations in geo-engineering that may need guidelines drafted for the safety of subsequent projects throughout the industry.

In the table below, please identify the additional evidence that most strengthens and the additional evidence that most weakens the committee member's response to the XM representative.

	Strengthens Committee Member's Response	Weakens Committee Member's Response	Additional Evidence
(A)	◯	◯	XM's latest project is nearly identical to a previous project by XM that had successfully passed the committee review process.
(B)	◯	◯	The geo-engineering corporation CL, which is XM's biggest competitor, has had less than one percent of its projects rejected by the committee.
(C)	◯	◯	Once a geo-engineering innovation has been passed by the committee, the same innovation is automatically approved in all subsequent projects, without further review.
(D)	◯	◯	Many of XM's geo-engineering projects are peer-reviewed within the industry before they are submitted to the federal committee.
(E)	◯	◯	Geo-engineering is a hazardous field that deserves careful monitoring.
(F)	◯	◯	The federal committee has had to reverse some of its decisions on past projects.

Item 5:

A group of entomologists estimates that the population of Insect Species X is decreasing at a constant rate of 10% per year, while the population of Insect Species Y is decreasing at a constant rate of 15% per year. Based on these estimates, in four years, the two species will have equal populations, rounded to the nearest million.

In the table below, identify a number for the current population of Insect Species X, in millions, and a number for the current population of Insect Species Y, in millions, that is consistent with the entomologists' estimates.

	Insect Species X	Insect Species Y	Current Populations (in millions)
(A)	○	○	450
(B)	○	○	525
(C)	○	○	565
(D)	○	○	600
(E)	○	○	625
(F)	○	○	770

Data for Items 6, 7, and 8:

| Email #1 | Email #2 | Memo #1 |

Email from Marketing Director to Marketing Researcher on October 4, 2011.

As you know, our revenues have declined for each of the past three quarters. To address this issue, I suggest that we initiate a massive advertising buy. On three separate occasions, in 1978, 1987, and 1993, we responded to revenue decreases by increasing our advertising expenditures by 30%. On all three occasions, our revenues began to increase again within one quarter. Therefore, if we increase the number of advertisements targeted at our top consumers by 30%, we will once again increase our revenues.

Since our top consumers are females aged 15–25, determine the top two television programs watched by that group. Also, research the prices for a 30-second commercial for each television program.

| Email #1 | Email #2 | Memo #1 |

Email from Marketing Researcher to Marketing Director on October 10, 2011.

We've hit a slight complication in our research. While we've had no problem determining the top two programs and advertising prices for each, we've realized that there is a fair amount of overlap between the viewers of the two programs. We've found that 80% of the viewers who are females aged 15–25 for *Hart Attack* also watch *Blonde Fury*.

I'll send you the chart summarizing the audience size and advertising prices tomorrow.

| Email #1 | Email #2 | Memo #1 |

MEMORANDUM
TO: Marketing Director
FROM: Marketing Researcher
DATE: October 11, 2011
RE: Market Research Results

The attached chart presents the results from our research on the top 2 television programs watched by females aged 15–25.

Market Research Results

■ Price of 30-Second Commercial (in thousands of dollars)
■ Percent of Females aged 15–25 who are viewers

Item 6:

Consider each of the following statements. Select *Yes* if the information contained in the two emails and the memorandum support the inference as stated. Otherwise, select *No*.

	Yes	No	
Question 6-1	○	○	No age and gender group watches *Blonde Fury* more frequently than do females aged 15–25.
Question 6-2	○	○	Thirty second advertisements are more expensive for programs with larger audiences.
Question 6-3	○	○	The ratio of female viewers aged 15 to 25 to dollars spent on advertising for *Hart Attack* is greater than that for *Blonde Fury*.

Item 7:

If there are 20,000,000 females aged 15–25, then how many females aged 15–25 (in millions) watch neither *Blonde Fury* nor *Hart Attack*?

(A) 1.4
(B) 4.0
(C) 5.6
(D) 9.6
(E) 11.2

Item 8:

Consider each of the following statements. Based on the information contained in the two emails and the memoranda, select *Yes* if the statement is an assumption made by the Marketing Director. Otherwise, select *No*.

	Yes	No	
Question 8-1	○	○	It is possible for a strategy that succeeded in the past to succeed again.
Question 8-2	○	○	The previous increases in revenues were attributable at least in part to the effect of increased advertising.
Question 8-3	○	○	Increasing the number of advertisements has a similar effect on revenues, to increasing the amount of money spent on advertising expenditures.

Item 9:

Name	Population 2010	Population 2050	% of Population Foreign-Born
Andorra	84,000	75,000	77.25
Australia	22,729,000	29,013,000	19.93
Barbados	273,000	282,000	9.31
Brazil	190,733,000	260,692,000	0.34
Canada	34,611,000	41,136,000	18.76
China	1,399,725,000	1,303,723,000	0.29
Egypt	80,942,000	137,873,000	0.22
France	65,822,000	69,768,000	10.18
India	1,210,193,000	1,656,554,000	0.52
Indonesia	237,556,000	313,021,000	0.07
Kazakhstan	16,518,000	15,100,000	16.88
Laos	6,230,000	10,069,000	0.42
Nauru	10,000	12,000	38.45
Portugal	10,637,000	9,933,000	7.2
Republic of the Congo	4,043,000	9,599,000	7.2
Russia	142,914,000	109,187,000	8.48
Suriname	525,000	617,000	1.11
United Kingdom	62,436,000	71,154,000	8.98
United States	312,399,000	439,010,000	21.81

The table above gives 2010 populations based on UN estimates and 2050 populations based on UN projections for 19 selected countries. The table also gives the UN estimates of the percentage of the population that is foreign-born for each country in 2010.

Each column of the table can be sorted in ascending order by clicking on the word "Select" above the table and choosing, from the drop-down menu, the heading of the column on which you want the table to be sorted.

Alternate Sort 1: *Population 2010*

Name	Population 2010	Projected Population 2050	% of Population Foreign-Born
Nauru	10,000	12,000	38.45
Andorra	84,000	75,000	77.25
Barbados	273,000	282,000	9.31
Suriname	525,000	617,000	1.11
Republic of the Congo	4,043,000	9,599,000	7.2
Laos	6,230,000	10,069,000	0.42
Portugal	10,637,000	9,993,000	7.2
Kazakhstan	16,518,000	15,100,000	16.88
Australia	22,729,000	29,013,000	19.93
Canada	34,611,000	41,136,000	18.76
United Kingdom	62,436,000	71,154,000	8.98
France	65,822,000	69,768,000	10.18
Egypt	80,942,000	137,873,000	0.22
Russia	142,914,000	109,187,000	8.48
Brazil	190,733,000	260,692,000	0.34
Indonesia	237,556,000	313,021,000	0.07
United States	312,399,000	439,010,000	21.81
India	1,210,193,000	1,656,554,000	0.52
China	1,399,725,000	1,303,723,000	0.29

Consider each of the following statements about these countries. For each statement indicate whether the statement is supported based on the information provided in the table.

	Supported	Unsupported	
Question 9-1	○	○	Of the countries with a population greater than 150 million in 2010, the country with the median number of foreign-born inhabitants is China.
Question 9-2	○	○	The total population of Laos is projected to be about 8 million in 2030.
Question 9-3	○	○	Andorra's rank for the number of foreign-born inhabitants is greater than that for all other countries listed.

Data for Items 10, 11, and 12:

The following emails come from the Public Relations division of a large non-profit organization.

Email #1 | **Email #2**

Hello Gloria!

We have to choose a caterer for our upcoming gala. Two caterers under consideration are DoxySource and BrightRight. Although DoxySource has delivered satisfactory service in the past, our First Annual Sponsors Gala promises to be the largest event we have ever hosted, and BrightRight is known for large event planning and production. However, I'd like more information before switching from a tried and true contractor. Also, I'd like to consider how to justify any over-budget costs from using BrightRight, if that comes up. I am committed to using only one provider. Please work up a comparison of costs of services and rentals for BrightRight and DoxySource. We require: tables, audio, food, and a punch fountain or fountains (a dessert fountain would be a lovely addition). Our budget is $6,000.00, and we plan for a maximum of 400 people.

Thanks!

Evelyn Schott

Gala Coordinator

Email #1 | **Email #2**

Hello Evelyn,

I've broken out the data in the following chart:

	DoxySource		BrightRight	
	Description	Price	Description	Price
AUDIO	200 Watt P.A. System (up to 40 people)	$65.00	Party Sound System	$650.00
	500 Watt P.A. System (up to 120 people)	$90.00	Marquee Sound System	$850.00
CATERING	Choice of appetizers (shrimp or spring roll)	$2.00 per piece	The Classic Western BBQ	$14.00 per person
	Choice of entree (chicken or beef w/ rice)	$6.25 per piece	The Greek Feast	$17.50 per person
	Choice of dessert (cupcakes or lemon bars)	$3.40 per piece	The Far East Extravaganza	$19.50 per person
TABLES	Trestle Table (seats 8)	$15.50 each	Classroom (seats 8)	$20.00 each
	Circular Table (seats 7)	$17.00 each	Bistro/Hightop (seats 6)	$22.00 each
FOUNTAINS	Chocolate Fountain (supplies not included)	$105.00	Chocolate Fountain (supplies included)	$500.00
	Punch Fountain (7 gallons, provided, serves approx. 70)	$47.00	Punch Fountain, waterfall tier (40 gallons, provided)	$350.00

BrightRight offers packages that are generally more elegant and comprehensive, and more expensive. For instance, we can choose a single full meal set, such as "The Greek Feast," for the entire gala. Using Doxy Source, while more economical and flexible in the catering, does mean more hands-on involvement on our end.

The biggest price difference comes in the audio systems. BrightRight, which consistently hosts events with attendance of several hundred people, offers complex systems that include lights and sound effects, in addition to high-definition audio reproduction. DoxySource offers two standard, large public address systems. I am not sure whether the Gala will need all the flash and sizzle of the high-end sound system; but the projected attendance is above the recommended usage for DoxySource's P.A. systems. Due to electrical concerns, we can only have one P.A. system at the gala.

Gloria Welch

Administrative Assistant, Public Relations

Item 10:

If the maximum number of guests attend the gala, determine if each of the statements is true or false based on the information in the two emails.

	True	False	
Question 10-1	○	○	If the coordinator uses DoxySource and orders one appetizer, one entrée, and one dessert per person, then the least amount that can be spent on tables to seat all guests is approximately 16.6% of the cost of food.
Question 10-2	○	○	If the large punch fountain from BrightRight is sufficient for 400 guests, then using smaller fountains from DoxySource to serve the same number of guests would cost at least 20% less per gallon.
Question 10-3	○	○	If BrightRight is used, the project will go over its present budget by at least 15%.

Item 11:

Suppose the Gala Coordinator uses DoxySource for the maximum number of guests. If she wants to use at least one of each type of table, what is the least possible cost for the tables?

(A) $775.00
(B) $787.00
(C) $792.00
(D) $873.21
(E) $971.43

Item 12:

Based on the information in the messages between the Gala Coordinator and the Administrative Assistant, select *Yes* if the statement can be inferred. Otherwise, select *No*.

	Yes	No	
Question 12-1	○	○	The Gala Coordinator is willing to ask for a budgetary increase, if necessary.
Question 12-2	○	○	According to the Administrative Assistant, audio costs are not the only determining factor in choosing one event planning service over another.
Question 12-3	○	○	Fountains are an optional element of the gala.

Part V
How to Crack the Analytical Writing Assessment

Chapter 21
Analytical Writing Assessment

Writing a coherent essay in 30 minutes might seem daunting, but in this chapter, you will learn techniques of pre-construction and pre-structuring that will make the process easy. You will also learn how the essay is scored and the *key factor* the readers are told to look for. (*Hint*: It isn't originality.)

The very first thing you will be asked to do on the GMAT is to write an essay using a word-processing program. You will have 30 minutes for your essay. You will not be given the essay topic in advance, nor will you be given a choice of topics. However, there is a complete list of most the possible writing assessment topics available for you to review on the GMAC website. Simply go to **www.mba.com/us/the-gmat-exam/gmat-exam-format-timing**, select the link for the Analytical Writing Assessment section, and follow the directions to download a list of current topics. Oh, and just in case you are wondering, it's free!

Practice writing an essay when you take a full-length GMAT at PrincetonReview.com. You'll have the option of selecting free LiveGrader™ essay scoring.

Why Have an Essay on the GMAT?

The business schools themselves asked for the essay. Recent studies have indicated that success in business (and in business school) actually depends more on verbal skills than has been traditionally thought.

The business schools have also had to contend with a huge increase in the number of applicants from overseas. Admissions officers at the business schools were finding that the application essays they received from outside the United States did not always accurately reflect the abilities of the students who were supposed to have written them. To put it more bluntly, some of these applicants were paying native English speakers to write their essays for them.

The GMAT Analytical Writing Assessment (AWA) is thus at least partly a check on the writing ability of foreign applicants who now make up more than one-third of all applicants to American business schools.

At the business schools' request, all schools to which you apply now receive, in addition to your AWA score, a copy of the actual essay you wrote.

How Do the Schools Use the Analytical Writing Assessment?

If you are a citizen of a non-English-speaking country, you can expect the schools to look quite closely at both the score you receive on the essay you write and the essay itself. If you are a native English speaker with reasonable Verbal scores and English grades in college, then the AWA is not likely to be a crucial part of your package.

On the other hand, if your verbal skills are *not* adequately reflected by your grades in college, or in the other sections of the GMAT, then a strong performance on the AWA could be extremely helpful.

How Is the Essay Scored?

When you get your GMAT score back from GMAC, you will also receive a separate score for the AWA. Your essay is read by two readers, each of whom will assign your writing a grade from 0 to 6, in half-point increments (6 being the highest score possible). If the two scores are within a point of each other, they will be averaged. If there is more than a one-point spread, the essay will be read by a third reader, and scores will be adjusted to reflect the third scorer's evaluation.

The essay readers use the "holistic" scoring method to grade essays; your writing will be judged not on small details but rather on its overall impact. The readers are supposed to ignore small errors of grammar and spelling. Considering that these readers are going to have to plow through more than 600,000 essays each year, this is probably just as well.

Who Are These Readers Anyway?

We'll put this in the form of a multiple-choice question:

Your essay will be read by:

(A)   captains of industry
(B)   leading business school professors
(C)   college TAs working part time

If you guessed (C), you're doing just fine. Each essay will be read by part-time employees of the testing company, mostly culled from graduate school programs.

How Much Time Do They Devote to Each Essay?

The graders get two minutes, tops. They work in eight-hour marathon sessions (nine to five, with an hour off for lunch), and are each required to read 30 essays per hour. Obviously, these poor graders do not have time for an in-depth reading of your essay. They probably aren't going to notice how carefully you thought out your ideas or how clever your analysis was. Under pressure to meet their quota, they are simply going to be giving it a fast skim. By the time your reader gets to your essay, she will probably have already seen more than a hundred essays—and no matter how ingenious you were in coming up with original ideas, she's already seen them.

So How Do You Score High on the AWA Essays?

On the face of it, you might think it would be pretty difficult to impress these jaded readers, but it turns out that there are some very specific ways to persuade them of your superior writing skills.

What GMAC Doesn't Want You to Know

In a 1982 internal study, two researchers from one of the big testing companies analyzed a group of essays written by actual test takers and the grades that those essays received. The most successful essays had one thing in common. Which of the following characteristics do you think it was?

- o   Good organization
- o   Proper diction
- o   Noteworthy ideas
- o   Good vocabulary
- o   Sentence variety
- o   Length
- o   Number of paragraphs

What Your Essay Needs in Order to Look Like a Successful Essay

Those researchers discovered that the essays that received the highest grades from the essay graders had one single factor in common: length.

To ace the AWA, you need to take one simple step: *Write as much as you possibly can.* Each essay should include at least four indented paragraphs.

How Does the Word-Processing Program Work?

The test makers have created a simple word-processing program to allow students to compose their essays on the screen.

Admissions Insight No. 9: Financial Aid, Part 2

The best kind of student loans: low-cost Stafford loans (which don't have to be repaid until the student has graduated or left the program and which generally have much lower rates than regular, unsecured loans). If necessary, borrow the rest through private educational loans.

Here's what your screen will look like during the essay portion of the test:

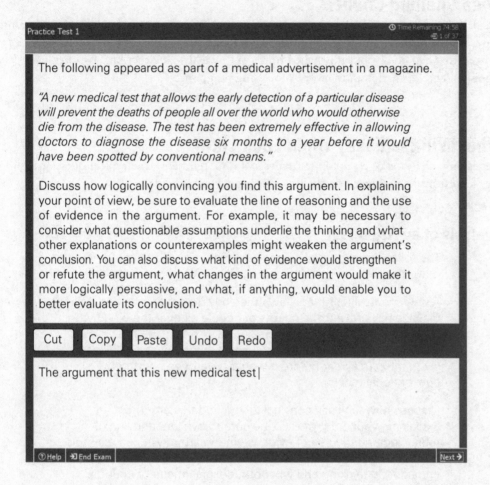

The following appeared as part of a medical advertisement in a magazine.

"A new medical test that allows the early detection of a particular disease will prevent the deaths of people all over the world who would otherwise die from the disease. The test has been extremely effective in allowing doctors to diagnose the disease six months to a year before it would have been spotted by conventional means."

Discuss how logically convincing you find this argument. In explaining your point of view, be sure to evaluate the line of reasoning and the use of evidence in the argument. For example, it may be necessary to consider what questionable assumptions underlie the thinking and what other explanations or counterexamples might weaken the argument's conclusion. You can also discuss what kind of evidence would strengthen or refute the argument, what changes in the argument would make it more logically persuasive, and what, if anything, would enable you to better evaluate its conclusion.

The question always appears at the top of your screen. Below it, in a box, will be your writing area (where you can see a partially completed sentence). When you click inside the box with your mouse, a winking cursor will appear, indicating that you can begin typing. The program supports the use of many of the normal computer keys, plus the following shortcuts:

Cut: Ctrl + X and Alt + T
Copy: Ctrl + C and Alt + C
Paste: Ctrl + V and Alt + A
Undo: Ctrl + Z and Alt + U
Redo: Ctrl + Y and Alt + R

You can also use the icons above the writing area to copy and paste words, sentences, or paragraphs and to undo and redo actions.

Obviously, this small box is not big enough to display your entire essay. However, you can see your entire essay by using the scroll bar, the up and down arrows, or the Page Up and Page Down keys.

Does Spelling Count?

Officially, no. Essay readers are supposed to ignore minor errors of spelling and grammar. However, the readers wouldn't be human (so to speak) if they weren't influenced favorably by an essay that had no obvious misspelled words or unwieldy constructions. Unfortunately, there is no spell-check function in the word-processing program.

What Will the Essay Topic Look Like?

There's only one type of essay topic: Analysis of an Argument. The typical question will look like the text inside the screen on the previous page. Here it is again:

Analysis of an Argument

The following appeared as part of a medical advertisement in a magazine.

"A new medical test that allows the early detection of a particular disease will prevent the deaths of people all over the world who would otherwise die from the disease. The test has been extremely effective in allowing doctors to diagnose the disease six months to a year before it would have been spotted by conventional means."

Discuss how logically convincing you find this argument. In explaining your point of view, be sure to evaluate the line of reasoning and the use of evidence in the argument. For example, it may be necessary to consider what questionable assumptions underlie the thinking and what other explanations or counter-examples might weaken the argument's conclusion. You can also discuss what kind of evidence would strengthen or refute the argument, what changes in the argument would make it more logically persuasive, and what, if anything, would enable you to better evaluate its conclusion.

THE AWA: BASIC PRINCIPLES

You might think that there is really no way to prepare for the AWA (other than by practicing writing over a long period of time and by practicing your typing skills). After all, you won't find out the topic of the essay they'll ask you to write until you get there, and there is no way to plan your essay in advance.

However, it turns out there are some very specific ways to prepare for the GMAT essay. Let's take a look.

Create a Template

When a builder builds a house, the first thing he does is construct a frame. The frame supports the entire house. After the frame is completed, he can nail the walls and windows to the frame. We're going to show you how to build the frame for the perfect GMAT essay. Of course, you won't know the exact topic of the essay until you get there (just as the builder may not know what color his client is going to paint the living room), but you will have an all-purpose frame on which to construct a great essay no matter what the topic is.

We call this frame the *template*.

Preconstruction

Just as a builder can construct the windows of a house in his workshop weeks before he arrives to install them, so too can you pre-build certain elements of your essay.

We call this *preconstruction*.

In the rest of this chapter, we'll show you how to prepare *ahead of time* to write essays on two topics you won't see until they appear on your screen.

ANALYSIS OF AN ARGUMENT

The Analysis of an Argument essay must initially be approached just like a logical argument in the Critical Reasoning section.

An Analysis of an Argument topic requires the following steps:

Step 1: Read the topic and separate out the conclusion from the premises.

Step 2: Because they're asking you to critique (i.e., weaken) the argument, concentrate on identifying its assumptions. Brainstorm as many different assumptions as you can think of. It helps to write or type these out.

Step 3: Look at the premises. Do they actually help to prove the conclusion?

Step 4: Choose a template that allows you to attack the assumptions and premises in an organized way.

Step 5: At the end of the essay, take a moment to illustrate how these same assumptions could be used to make the argument more compelling.

Step 6: Read over the essay and do some editing.

Opinions vs. Arguments

The most common mistake our students make is offering an opinion on the topic presented in the argument. For the Analysis of an Argument essay, you need to analyze the reasoning rather than explain why you agree or disagree.

What the Readers Look For

An Analysis of an Argument topic presents you with an argument. Your job is to critique the argument's line of reasoning and the evidence supporting it and suggest ways in which the argument could be strengthened. You aren't required to know more about the subject than would any normal person—but you must be able to spot logical weaknesses. This should start to remind you of Critical Reasoning.

The essay readers will look for four things as they skim through your Analysis of an Argument essay at the speed of light. According to GMAC, "an outstanding argument essay…

- clearly identifies and insightfully analyzes important features of the argument;
- develops ideas cogently, organizes them logically, and connects them smoothly with clear transitions;
- effectively supports the main points of the critique; and
- demonstrates superior control of language, including diction, syntactic variety, and the conventions of standard written English. There may be minor flaws."

To put it more simply, the readers look for good organization, good analysis based on a cursory understanding of the rules of logic, and reasonable use of the English language.

Critical Reasoning in Essay Form

In any GMAT argument, the first thing to do is to separate the conclusion from the premises.

Let's see how this works with an actual essay topic. Check out the Analysis of an Argument topic you saw before.

Topic:

The following appeared as part of a medical advertisement in a magazine.

"A new medical test that allows the early detection of a particular disease will prevent the deaths of people all over the world who would otherwise die from the disease. The test has been extremely effective in allowing doctors to diagnose the disease six months to a year before it would have been spotted by conventional means."

Discuss how logically convincing you find this argument. In explaining your point of view, be sure to evaluate the line of reasoning and the use of evidence in the argument. For example, it may be necessary to consider what questionable assumptions underlie the thinking and what other explanations or counterexamples might weaken the argument's conclusion. You can also discuss what kind of evidence would strengthen or refute the argument, what changes in the argument would make it more logically persuasive, and what, if anything, would enable you to better evaluate its conclusion.

The conclusion in this argument comes in the first line:

A new medical test that allows the early detection of a particular disease will prevent the deaths of people all over the world who would otherwise die from that disease.

The premises are the evidence in support of this conclusion.

The test has been extremely effective in allowing doctors to diagnose the disease six months to a year before it would have been spotted by conventional means.

The assumptions are the *unspoken* premises of the argument—without which the argument would fall apart. Remember that assumptions are often causal, analogical, or statistical. What are some assumptions of *this* argument? Let's brainstorm.

Brainstorming for Assumptions

You can often find assumptions by looking for a gap in the reasoning:

Medical test → early detection: According to the conclusion, the medical test leads to the early detection of the disease. There doesn't seem to be a gap here.

Early detection → nonfatal: In turn, the early detection of the disease allows patients to survive the disease. Well, hold on a minute. Is this necessarily true? Let's brainstorm:

1. First of all, do we know that early detection will necessarily lead to survival? We don't even know if this disease is *curable*. Early detection of an incurable disease is not going to help someone survive it.
2. Second, will the test be widely available and cheap enough for general use? If the test is expensive or available only in certain parts of the world, people will continue to die from the disease.
3. Will doctors and patients interpret the tests correctly? The test may be fine, but if doctors misinterpret the results or if patients ignore the need for treatment, then the test will not save lives.

The Use of the Evidence

Okay, we've uncovered some assumptions. Now, the essay graders also want to know what we thought of the argument's "use of evidence." In other words, did the premises help to prove the conclusion? Well, in fact, no, they didn't. The premise here (the fact that the test can *spot* the disease six months to a year earlier than conventional tests) does not really help to prove the conclusion that the test will save *lives*.

B-School Lingo

three Cs: the primary forces considered in marketing—Customer, Competition, Company

Source: *The Best 294 Business Schools*

Organizing the Analysis of an Argument Essay

We're ready to put this into a ready-made template. In any Analysis of an Argument essay, the template structure will be pretty straightforward: You're simply going to reiterate the argument, attack the argument in three different ways (one to a paragraph), summarize what you've said, and mention how the argument could be strengthened. From an organizational standpoint, this is pretty easy. Try to minimize your use of the word "I." *Your* opinion is not really the point in an Analysis of an Argument essay.

A Sample Template

Of course, you will want to develop your *own* template for the Analysis of an Argument essay, but to get you started, here's one possible structure:

The argument that __(restatement of the conclusion)__ is not entirely logically convincing, because it ignores certain crucial assumptions.

First, the argument assumes that _____

_____.

Second, the argument never addresses _____

_____.

Finally, the argument omits _____

_____.

Thus, the argument is not completely sound. The evidence in support of the conclusion

_____.

Ultimately, the argument might have been strengthened by _____

_____.

How Would Our Brainstorming Fit Into the Template?

Here's how the assumptions we came up with for this argument would have fit into the template:

The Analysis of an Argument Essay in Six Steps

Step 1: Read the topic. Isolate the conclusion and premises.

Step 2: Identify its assumptions. Brainstorm for five minutes.

Step 3: Look at the assumptions. Do they help to prove the conclusion?

Step 4: Choose a template that allows you to attack the assumptions in an organized way.

Step 5: Illustrate how these same assumptions could be used to make the argument more compelling.

Step 6: Do some editing to correct spelling or grammar mistakes.

The argument that the new medical test will prevent deaths that would have occurred in the past is not entirely logically persuasive, because it ignores certain crucial assumptions.

First, the argument assumes that early detection of the disease will lead to a reduced mortality rate. There are a number of reasons this might not be true. For example, the disease might be incurable [etc.].

Second, the argument never addresses the point that the existence of this new test, even if totally effective, is not the same as the widespread use of the test [etc.].

Finally, even supposing the ability of early detection to save lives and the widespread use of the test, the argument still depends on the doctors' correct interpretation of the test and the patients' willingness to undergo treatment. [etc.]

Thus, the argument is not completely sound. The evidence in support of the conclusion (further information about the test itself) does little to prove the conclusion—that the test will save lives—because it does not address the assumptions already raised. Ultimately, the argument might have been strengthened by making it plain that the disease responds to early treatment, that the test will be widely available around the world, and that doctors and patients will make proper use of the test.

Customizing Your Analysis of an Argument Template

Your organizational structure may vary in some ways, but it will always include the following elements:

- The *first paragraph* should sum up the argument's conclusion.
- In the *second, third, and fourth paragraphs*, you should attack the argument and the supporting evidence.
- In the *last* paragraph, you should summarize what you've said and state how the argument could be strengthened. Here are some alternate ways of organizing your essay.

Q: What are the most important aspects of writing a good Analysis of an Argument essay? *Turn to page 428 for the answer.*

Variation 1:

1st paragraph: Restate the argument.

2nd paragraph: Discuss the link (or lack of one) between the conclusion and the evidence presented in support of it.

3rd paragraph: Show three holes in the reasoning of the argument.

4th paragraph: Show how each of the three holes could be plugged up by explicitly stating the missing assumptions.

Variation 2:

1st paragraph: Restate the argument and say it has three flaws.

2nd paragraph: Point out a flaw and show how it could be plugged up by explicitly stating the missing assumption.

3rd paragraph: Point out a second flaw and show how it could be plugged up by explicitly stating the missing assumption.

4th paragraph: Point out a third flaw and show how it could be plugged up by explicitly stating the missing assumption.

5th paragraph: Summarize and conclude that because of these three flaws, the argument is weak.

Analysis of an Argument: Final Thoughts

You've separated the conclusion from the premises. You've brainstormed for the gaps that weaken the argument. You've noted how the premises support (or don't support) the conclusion. Now it's time to write your essay. Start typing, indenting each of the four or five paragraphs. Use all the tools you've learned in this chapter. Remember to keep an eye on the time.

If you have a minute at the end, read over your essay and do any editing that's necessary.

PRECONSTRUCTION

The readers will look for evidence of your facility with standard written English. This is where preconstruction comes in. It's amazing how a little elementary preparation can enhance an essay. We'll look at two tricks that almost instantly improve the appearance of a person's writing.

- Structure words
- Sentence variety

Structure Words

In our Reading Comprehension chapter, we brought up a problem that most students encounter when they get to the Reading Comprehension section: There isn't enough time to read the passages carefully and answer all the questions. To get around this problem, we showed you some ways to spot the overall organization of a dense reading passage in order to understand the main idea and to find specific points quickly.

When you think about it, the essay readers face almost the identical problem: They have less than two minutes to read your essay and figure out if it's any good. There's no time to appreciate the finer points of your argument. All they want to know is whether it's well organized and reasonably lucid—and to find out, they will look for the *same* structural clues you have learned to look for in the Reading Comprehension passages. Let's mention them again:

- If you have three points to make in a paragraph, it helps to point this out ahead of time:

    There are three reasons why I believe that the Grand Canyon should be preserved for all eternity. First…Second…Third…

- If you want to clue the reader in to the fact that you are about to support the main idea with examples or illustrations, the following words are useful:

    for example
    to illustrate
    for instance
    because

- To add yet another example or argument in support of your main idea, you can use one of the following words to indicate your intention:

    furthermore
    in addition
    similarly
    just as
    also
    moreover

- To indicate that the idea you're about to bring up is important, special, or surprising in some way, you can use one of these words:

  surely
  truly
  undoubtedly
  clearly
  certainly
  indeed
  as a matter of fact
  in fact
  most important

- To signal that you're about to reach a conclusion, you might use one of these words:

  therefore
  in summary
  consequently
  hence
  in conclusion
  in short

The Appearance of Depth

You may have noticed that much of the structure we have discussed thus far has involved contrasting viewpoints. Nothing will give your writing the *appearance* of depth faster than learning to use this technique. The idea is to set up your main idea by first introducing its opposite.

It is a favorite ploy of incoming presidents to blame the federal bureaucracy for the high cost of government, but I believe that bureaucratic waste is only a small part of the problem.

You may have noticed that this sentence contained a "trigger word." In this case, the trigger word *but* tells us that what was expressed in the first half of the sentence is going to be contradicted in the second half. We discussed trigger words in the Reading Comprehension chapter of this book. Here they are again:

but	*however*
on the contrary	*although*
yet	*while*
despite	*in spite of*
rather	*nevertheless*
instead	

By using these words, you can instantly give your writing the appearance of depth.

Key to Analysis of an Argument
Critique the weaknesses in the argument clearly.

How It Works

Here's a paragraph that consists of a main point and two supporting arguments:

> *I believe he is wrong. He doesn't know the facts. He isn't thinking clearly.*

Watch how a few structure words can make this paragraph classier and clearer at the same time:

> *I believe he is wrong.* **For one thing**, *he doesn't know the facts.* **For another**, *he isn't thinking clearly.*

> *I believe he is wrong.* **Obviously**, *he doesn't know the facts.* **Moreover**, *he isn't thinking clearly.*

> *I believe he is wrong* **because, first**, *he doesn't know the facts, and* **second**, *he isn't thinking clearly.*

> **Certainly**, *he doesn't know the facts, and he isn't thinking clearly* **either**. **Consequently**, *I believe he is wrong.*

Example:

Main thought: *I believe that television programs should be censored.*

While many people believe in the sanctity of free speech, I believe that television programs should be censored.

Most people believe in the sanctity of free speech, but I believe that television programs should be censored.

In addition to trigger words, here are a few other words or phrases you can use to introduce the view you are eventually going to decide *against*:

admittedly	*true*
certainly	*granted*
obviously	*of course*
undoubtedly	*to be sure*
one cannot deny that	*it could be argued that*

Also, don't forget about yin-yang words, which can be used to point directly to two contrasting ideas:

on the one hand/on the other hand

the traditional view/the new view

Contrasting Paragraphs

Trigger words can be used to signal the opposing viewpoints of entire paragraphs. Suppose you saw an essay that began:

Many people believe that youth is wasted on the young. They point out that young people never seem to enjoy, or even think about, the great gifts they have been given but will not always have: physical dexterity, good hearing, good vision. However…

What do you think is going to happen in the second paragraph? That's right, the author is now going to disagree with the *many people* of the first paragraph.

Setting up one paragraph in opposition to another lets the reader know what's going on right away. The organization of the essay is immediately evident.

Sentence Variety

Many people think good writing is a mysterious talent that you either have or don't have, like good rhythm. In fact, good writing has a kind of rhythm to it, but there is nothing mysterious about it. Good writing is a matter of mixing up the different kinds of raw materials that you have available to you—phrases, dependent and independent clauses—to build sentences that don't all sound the same.

The graders won't have time to savor your essay, but they will look for variety in your writing. Here's an example of a passage in which all the sentences sound alike:

Movies cost too much. Everyone agrees about that. Studios need to cut costs.
No one is sure exactly how to do it. I have two simple solutions. They can cut
costs by paying stars less. They can also cut costs by reducing overhead.

Why do all the sentences sound alike? Well, for one thing, they are all about the same length. For another thing, the sentences are all made up of independent clauses with the same exact setup: subject, verb, and sometimes object. There are no dependent clauses, almost no phrases, no structure words, and, frankly, no variety at all.

Now let's take a look at the same passage, with some minor modifications.

Everyone agrees that movies cost too much. Clearly, studios need to cut
costs, but no one is sure exactly how to do it. I have two simple solutions:
They can cut costs by paying stars less and by reducing overhead.

In this version of the passage, we've combined some clauses and used conjunctions. This helped to add variety in both sentence structure and sentence length. We also threw in a few structure words as well. As you can see, simple techniques like these can make your writing appear stronger and more polished.

The AWA

Few people are rejected by a business school based on their writing score, so don't bother feeling intimidated. Think of it this way: The essays represent an opportunity if your Verbal score is low, or if English is your second language. For the rest of you, the essay is as good a way as any to warm up (and wake up) before the sections that count.

Summary

- The GMAT AWA section consists of one essay, written in 30 minutes, using a basic word-processing program and the computer keyboard. The essay will be given scores that range from 0 to 6 in half-point increments.

- Each essay will be evaluated by at least two underpaid, overworked college teaching assistants.

- To score high on the AWA:
  - Write as many words as possible.
  - Use a prebuilt template to organize your thoughts.
  - Use structure words and vary your sentence structure and length to give the appearance of depth to your writing.
  - If possible, refer to a well-known work of literature or nonfiction.

- For the Analysis of an Argument topic:
  - **Step 1:** Read the topic and separate out the conclusion from the premises.
  - **Step 2:** Because they ask you to critique (i.e., weaken) the argument, concentrate on identifying its assumptions. Brainstorm as many different assumptions as you can think of and write them down.
  - **Step 3:** Look at the premises. Do they actually help to prove the conclusion?
  - **Step 4:** Choose a template that allows you to attack the assumptions and premises in an organized way.
  - **Step 5:** At the end of the essay, take a moment to illustrate how these same assumptions could be used to make the argument more compelling.
  - **Step 6:** Read over the essay and edit your work.

Part VI
Answer Key to Drills

DRILL 1 (AD/BCE)

1. **BCE** Statement (1) gives a value for y but no information on the value of x. Since the problem asks for a value of x, Statement (1) is insufficient.

2. **BCE** Statement (1) states that $2y$ is an integer. Consider what values of y are possible. y could be an integer, such as 2, but it could also be a fraction, such as $\frac{1}{2}$. Statement (1) is insufficient.

3. **AD** The question states that there are 12 children in the room. Statement (1) provides the number of girls, so both the number of boys and the difference between the number of boys and the number of girls can be determined. Since the difference can be determined, Statement (1) is sufficient.

4. **AD** Statement (1) can be rewritten as the equation $\left(\frac{10}{100}\right)x = 5$, which can be used to solve for x. If the value of x is known, then the question can be answered. Statement (1) is sufficient.

DRILL 2

1. **77** $74 + (27 - 24) = 74 + 3 = 77$

2. **79** $(8 \times 9) + 7 = 72 + 7 = 79$

3. **10** $2(9 - (8 \div 2)) = 2(9 - 4)$, which simplifies to $2(5) = 10$.

4. **16** $2(7 - 3) + (-4)(5 - 7) = 2(4) + (-4)(-2)$, which simplifies to $8 + 8 = 16$.

5. **B** $4(-3(3 - 5) + 10 - 17) = 4(-3(-2) + 10 - 17)$, which simplifies to $4(6 + 10 - 17) = 4(-1)$, or -4.

6. **A** Statement (1) states that $x^3 = 8$. If $x^3 = 8$, then x equals 2. Since there is only one possible value of x that satisfies the equation, Statement (1) is sufficient. Write down AD. Statement (2) states that $x^2 = 4$. In this case, x could be 2 or -2. Statement (2) is therefore insufficient. The correct answer is (A).

DRILL 3

1. $x^2 + x = x(x + 1)$

2. $(55 \times 12) + (55 \times 88) = 55(12 + 88)$, which simplifies to $55(100) = 5,500$.

3. $a(b + c - d) = ab + ac - ad$

4. $abc + xyc = c(ab + xy)$

5. **B** If $x = 6$, then $\dfrac{2xy - xy}{y} = \dfrac{2(6)y - (6)y}{y}$, which simplifies to $\dfrac{12y - 6y}{y} = \dfrac{6y}{y}$, and reduces to 6.

6. **B** Statement (1) provides a value for x, but provides no information about y and z, so Statement (1) is insufficient. Write down BCE. Statement (2) provides a value for a. Factor the equation given to yield $a(x + y + z) = 15$. If $a = 5$, then $x + y + z = 3$, and Statement (2) is sufficient. The correct answer is (B).

DRILL 4

1. $\dfrac{49}{8}$ or $6\dfrac{1}{8}$

$5\dfrac{3}{4}+\dfrac{3}{8}=\dfrac{23}{4}+\dfrac{3}{8}$, which may be rewritten as $\dfrac{46}{8}+\dfrac{3}{8}=\dfrac{49}{8}$.

2. $\dfrac{1}{5}$ $\quad$ $\dfrac{12}{60}=\dfrac{12\times1}{12\times5}$, which reduces to $\dfrac{1}{5}$.

3. $\dfrac{29}{3}$ $\quad$ $9\dfrac{2}{3}=\dfrac{9\times3}{3}+\dfrac{2}{3}$, which yields $\dfrac{27}{3}+\dfrac{2}{3}=\dfrac{29}{3}$

4. 18 $\quad$ Cross-multiply to get $2x=36$. Divide both sides of the equation by 2 to get $x=18$.

5. C $\quad$ $\dfrac{\left(\dfrac{\frac{4}{5}}{\frac{3}{5}}\right)\left(\dfrac{\frac{1}{8}}{\frac{2}{3}}\right)}{\dfrac{3}{4}}=\dfrac{\left(\dfrac{4}{5}\times\dfrac{5}{3}\right)\left(\dfrac{1}{8}\times\dfrac{3}{2}\right)}{\dfrac{3}{4}}$, which yields $\dfrac{\dfrac{4}{3}\times\dfrac{3}{16}}{\dfrac{3}{4}}=\dfrac{\dfrac{4}{16}}{\dfrac{3}{4}}$, which further yields $\dfrac{1}{4}\times\dfrac{4}{3}=\dfrac{4}{12}$,

or $\dfrac{1}{3}$.

DRILL 5

1. **33.30** $\quad$ Since the numbers are lined up, just subtract down, remembering to borrow when dealing with the tenths digit.

2. **266.175** $\quad$ Multiply 273 by 975 as normal and then move the decimal point over 3 spots.

3. **6.125** $\quad$ Set up to do long division: $3.2\,\overline{)19.6}$. Move the decimal point over one to the right to get $32\,\overline{)196}$.

32 goes into 196 6 times, so $32\,\overline{)196}$. Next, multiply 6 by 32 to get 192 and subtract 192 from 196

to get 4. Then add a decimal point and a 0, bring that 0 down, and see that 32 goes into 40 one

time, so multiply 1 by 32 and then subtract 32 from 40 to get 6.1. Add another 0, bring it down, and see that 32 goes into 80 two times, so multiply 32 by 2 to get 64 and then subtract that from

80. Finally, add one more 0 an see that 32 goes into 160 exactly 5 times:

$$
\begin{array}{r}
6.125 \\
32\overline{)196.000} \\
192 \\
\hline
40 \\
32 \\
\hline
80 \\
64 \\
\hline
160 \\
160 \\
\hline
0
\end{array}
$$

The correct answer is 6.125.

4. **800** $\dfrac{\dfrac{4}{0.25}}{\dfrac{1}{50}} = \dfrac{\dfrac{4}{1}}{\dfrac{1}{50}}$, which may be rewritten as $\dfrac{4 \times \dfrac{4}{1}}{\dfrac{1}{50}} = \dfrac{\dfrac{16}{1}}{\dfrac{1}{50}}$, and yields $16 \times \dfrac{50}{1} = 800$.

5. **C** $\dfrac{\dfrac{3}{10} \times 4 \times 0.8}{0.32} = \dfrac{\dfrac{3}{10} \times \dfrac{4}{1} \times \dfrac{8}{10}}{\dfrac{32}{100}}$, which yields $\dfrac{\dfrac{96}{100}}{\dfrac{32}{100}} = \dfrac{96}{100} \times \dfrac{100}{32}$, which reduces to $\dfrac{96}{32} = 3$.

6. **D**   The question states that x and y are reciprocals, which means that determining the value of either variable provides the value of the other. Therefore, Statement (1) provides the values of both x and y, which allows the question to be answered. Write down AD. Statement (2) also provides the values of both y and x, so the correct answer is (D).

DRILL 6

1. **C**   The question involves ratios, so set up a ratio box. Since there are 2 ratios given, set up 2 ratio boxes—the current situation and the hypothetical if the students drop out.

Current:

	Men	Women	Total
Ratio	6	5	11
Multiplier			
Actual			

After drop outs:

	Men	Women	Total
Ratio	8	7	15
Multiplier			
Actual			

Since the algebra seems somewhat complicated, Plug In the Answers. Start with (C). The answers represent the number of men currently in the class. Plugging 18 in gives

Current

	Men	Women	Total
Ratio	6	5	11
Multiplier	3	3	3
Actual	18	15	33

The problem then states that 2 men and 1 woman drop out, so subtract 2 from the total men and 1 from the total women and check if that fits a 8 to 7 ratio in the After drop outs box:

After drop outs:

	Men	Women	Total
Ratio	8	7	15
Multiplier			
Actual	16	14	

16 to 14 is an 8 to 7 ratio. Since the condition is met, the correct answer is (C).

2. **B**   If the average of 5 numbers is 7, then the numbers must add up to 35. If three of those numbers average 5, then those 3 numbers must add up to 15. The sum of the two numbers left is therefore $35 - 15 = 20$. If the sum of the two numbers is 20, then the average of those two numbers is 10. The correct answer is (B).

3. **D** $\dfrac{\dfrac{1}{3}^6 - \dfrac{1}{3}^4}{\left(\dfrac{1}{3}\right)^5}$ may be factored to yield $\dfrac{\left(\dfrac{1}{3}\right)^4\left(\left(\dfrac{1}{3}\right)^2 - 1\right)}{\left(\dfrac{1}{3}\right)^5} = \dfrac{\left(\dfrac{1}{3}\right)^4\left(\left(\dfrac{1}{3}\right)^2 - 1\right)}{\left(\dfrac{1}{3}\right)^4\left(\dfrac{1}{3}\right)}$, which reduces to

$\dfrac{\left(\dfrac{1}{3}\right)^2 - 1}{\dfrac{1}{3}} = \dfrac{\dfrac{1}{9} - 1}{\dfrac{1}{3}}$, which yields $\dfrac{-\dfrac{8}{9}}{\dfrac{1}{3}} = -\dfrac{8}{9} \times \dfrac{3}{1}$, which results in $-\dfrac{8 \times 3}{3 \times 3} = -\dfrac{8}{3}$.

4. **D**   Factor $\dfrac{\sqrt{147} + \sqrt{75}}{14}$ as $\dfrac{\sqrt{7 \times 7 \times 3} + \sqrt{5 \times 5 \times 3}}{14} = \dfrac{7\sqrt{3} + 5\sqrt{3}}{14}$, which simplifies to

$\dfrac{12\sqrt{3}}{14} = \dfrac{6\sqrt{3}}{7}$. The second expression simplifies to $\dfrac{28}{7\sqrt{3}} = \dfrac{4}{\sqrt{3}}$. In order to evaluate the

ratio between the expressions, express them as the fraction $\dfrac{\dfrac{6\sqrt{3}}{7}}{\dfrac{4}{\sqrt{3}}} = \dfrac{6\sqrt{3}}{7} \times \dfrac{\sqrt{3}}{4}$, which yields

$\dfrac{6\sqrt{3 \times 3}}{28} = \dfrac{6 \times 3}{28}$, and reduces to $\dfrac{9}{14}$, or a 9 to 14 ratio.

5. **B**   Determine the two amounts of interest. $5,000 earning 8% interest, compounded semi-annually, earns 4% interest compounded every 6 months. 4% of 5,000 is $5,000 \times \dfrac{4}{100} = 200$. 4% of the new $5,200 balance is $5,200 \times \dfrac{4}{100} = 208$, and the account contains $5,408 at the end of one year. For the other account, 8% of 5,000 is $5,000 \times \dfrac{8}{100} = 400$, so the account contains $5,400 at the end of one year. The difference is $5,408 − $5,400 = $8. The correct answer is (B).

6. **E**   If the average of ten numbers is 10, then the numbers have to add up to 100. However, the numbers could be anything. For example, if all ten numbers are 10, then the standard deviation is 0. However, since standard deviation is defined as the spread of numbers away from the average, the standard deviation could be anything—as the numbers could be negative numbers, really big numbers, and so on—as long as the sum is 100. So, 0, 10, and 20 could all be standard deviations. The correct answer is (E).

7. **D**   Start by figuring out the median and mode of List II. The mode is 3 and the median is 5. Their sum is 8. So, the median of List I must also be 8. Since there are 6 elements in List I, the median will be the average of the 3rd and 4th numbers. Therefore, those two numbers must add up to 16. Since 7 is already listed, the only possible way to get a median of 8 is if y is 9. The correct answer is (D).

DRILL 7

1. **A**   There are numbers in the answer choices, so Plug In the Answers. Start with (C) and label the columns as Joe's current age. Draw a new column for Joe's age 5 years ago, which is 27 − 5 = 22. Draw a new column for Jessica's age 5 years ago, which is 22 ÷ 2 = 11. Draw a new column for Jessica's current age, which is 11 + 5 = 16. Draw a new column for Jessica's age in 4 years, which is 16 + 4 = 20. Draw a new column for Joe's age in 4 years, which is 27 + 4 = 31. Finally, evaluate the condition that Joe's age in 4 years *will be one and half times as old* as Jessica's age in 4 years, which is incorrect for (C). Eliminate (C). Because Joe's age in 4 years is greater than *one and a half times* that of Jessica, try (B). If Joe's current age is 25, then Joe's age 5 years ago is 25 − 5 = 20, Jessica's age 5 years ago is 20 ÷ 2 = 10, Jessica's current age is 10 + 5 = 15, Jessica's age in 4 years is 15 + 4 = 19, and Joe's age in 4 years is 25 + 4 = 29. Joe's age in 4 years is still greater than *one and half times* that of Jessica, so eliminate (B) and check (A) to confirm that it is the correct answer. If Joe's current age is 23, then Joe's age 5 years ago is 23 − 5 = 18, Jessica's age 5 years ago is 18 ÷ 2 = 9, Jessica's current age is 9 + 5 = 14, Jessica's age in 4 years is 14 + 4 = 18, and Joe's age in 4 years is 27. 27 is *one and a half times* 18, so (A) meets the condition. The correct answer is (A).

2. **D** $\dfrac{x^2 + 2x - 9}{3} \le x + 1$ can be rewritten as $x^2 + 2x - 9 \le 3(x + 1)$ or $x^2 + 2x - 9 \le 3x + 3$. Subtract $3x$ and 3 from both sides to yield $x^2 + 2x - 3x - 9 - 3 \le 0$, or $x^2 - x - 12 \le 0$. Factor the quadratic expression to yield $(x - 4)(x + 3) \le 0$. Thus, the parabola defined by the quadratic expression has x-intercepts of (4, 0) and (−3, 0). Because the term x^2 is positive, the y-value of

the parabola is negative between its x-intercepts, and the values of x which satisfy the inequality are those values from –3 to 4, inclusive, which may be represented as $-3 \leq x \leq 4$. The correct answer is (D).

3. **E**   There are variables in the answer choices, so Plug In. Let $x = 20$ and $a = 100$. 20% of 100 is 20, so $b = 20$. 100 is 5 times 20, so the target is 5. Now, Plug In $x = 20$ into the answer choices, looking for the target of 5. Only (E) matches. The correct answer is (E).

4. **E**   There are variables in the answer choices, so Plug In. Let $s = 6$. John has 6 pairs of shoes, so Shiela has 18 and James has 3. The *three of them combined* have 27 pairs of shoes, and 27 is the target. Now, Plug In $s = 6$ into the answer choices, looking for a target of 27. Only (E) matches. The correct answer is (E).

DRILL 8

1. **D**   When objects move in the same direction, the difference in their rates may be calculated by subtraction. Teena's rate of 55 miles per hour minus Joe's rate of 40 miles per hour yields $55 - 40 = 15$ miles per hour. Thus, Teena travels 15 miles further than Joe every hour. Because Teena is currently 7.5 miles behind Joe, and the question asks in how many minutes she will be 15 miles ahead of Joe, Teena needs to cover a relative distance of $15 + 7.5 = 22.5$ miles. Use $D = RT$, and solve for T. $22.5 = 15 \times T$ yields that $T = \dfrac{22.5}{15}$, or $T = 1.5$ hours. Because there are 60 minutes in each hour, multiply 1.5 by 60 to determine the number of minutes. $1.5 \times 60 = 90$ minutes. The correct answer is (D).

2. **E**   The problem provides the definition of the function $a \triangle b$ and asks for the value of $-1 \triangle (1 \triangle - 1)$, so evaluate the expression in the parenthesis first. $(1 \triangle - 1) = \dfrac{(-1 - 1)^2}{1^2}$, which simplifies to $\dfrac{(-2)^2}{1} = 4$. Now, evaluate $-1 \triangle 4$. $-1 \triangle 4 = \dfrac{(4 - (-1))^2}{(-1)^2}$, which simplifies to $\dfrac{(5)^2}{1} = 25$. The correct answer is (E).

3. **C**   The problem does not specify the number of workers or envelopes each worker can stuff, so Plug In. Let the number of full-time workers be 5. There are $\dfrac{2}{5}$ as many trainees as there are full-time workers, so there are $\dfrac{2}{5} \times 5 = 2$ trainees. Let the number of envelopes each full-time worker can

stuff per day be 3. Each trainee can stuff $\frac{2}{3}$ as many envelopes as can a full-time worker, so each

trainee can stuff $\frac{2}{3} \times 3 = 2$ envelopes per day. Thus, each day the full-time workers stuff

$5 \times 3 = 15$ envelopes, the trainees stuff $2 \times 2 = 4$ envelopes, and together the two groups stuff

$15 + 4 = 19$ envelopes. The trainees stuff 4 envelopes, so they stuffed $\frac{4}{19}$ of the envelopes. The

correct answer is (C).

4. **E**   There are variables in the answer choices, so Plug In. Let $x = 3$ and $y = 5$. The larger group con-

sists of $3 + 2 = 5$ men and $5 + 4 = 9$ women, for a total of $5 + 9 = 14$ members. The probability

of selecting a man from the larger group is $\frac{5}{14}$, and that is the target. Plug In $x = 3$ and $y = 5$

into the answer choices, looking for the target of $\frac{5}{14}$. The correct answer is (E).

DRILL 9 (Angles and Lengths)

1. $x = 110°$ There are 180 degrees in a line, so $180 - 70 = 110$.

2. $x = 50°$; $y = 130°$; $z = 130°$
    There are 180 degrees in a line, and y and z each form lines with the 50° angle, so they
    each have a value of $180 - 50 = 130°$. x forms a line with either y or z, so x has a value of
    $180 - 130 = 50°$.

3. $x = 60°$; $y = 120°$; $z = 120°$
    x forms a line with the 120 degree angle, so it equals 60. Then, with parallel lines, all the small
    angles are equal and all the big angles are equal. y and z are both big angles, so they both equal
    120.

4. $\frac{3}{4}$ There are 360 degrees in a circle. Since the driver has traveled 270 degrees, he has traveled
    $\frac{270}{360}$ of the track. Reduce to get $\frac{3}{4}$.

5. **D**   The questions states that l_1 and l_2 are parallel, so redraw the figure twice, each time with just
    one of the lines intersecting l_1 and l_2. When looking at the line that goes down from left to
    right, notice that both a and d are "big" angles created as that line crosses l_1 and l_2 and there-
    fore a and d must be equal. The correct answer is (D).

6. **C**   Statement (1) provides the measure of y, but provides no information about angle x, so State-
    ment (1) is insufficient. Write down BCE. Statement (2) indicates that $x + y = 180°$, but it
    provides no information to determine the value of either angle, so Statement (2) is insuffi-
    cient. Eliminate (B). The statements together provide the relationship between the angles and
    the value of y, so the statements together are sufficient. The correct answer is (C).

DRILL 10 (Triangles)

1. **8**   The legs of a 45-45-90 triangle are the same. Since the other leg is 8, x must also be 8.

2. **60**   Because all three sides of the triangle are equal, the angles of the triangle must also be equal. There are 180° in a triangle, so $x = 180 \div 3$, or 60°.

3. **5**   Notice that this is a 3-4-5 right triangle, so $x = 5$. Alternately, by the Pythagorean Theorem, $3^2 + 4^2 = x^2$ yields $9 + 16 = x^2$, which simplifies to $25 = x^2$, or $x = 5$.

4. **$3 < x < 11$**   The third side of a triangle is less than the sum and greater than the difference of the other two sides. Thus, x must be less than $7 + 4 = 11$ and greater than $7 - 4 = 3$.

5. **$3\sqrt{2}$**   Since the figure is a square and line AC is the diagonal of the square, then the two triangles formed must be 45-45-90 triangles. The relationship for the sides of a 45-45-90 triangle is $x : x : x\sqrt{2}$. Since one of the sides is 3, then the diagonal must be $3\sqrt{2}$.

6. **$2\sqrt{3}$**   The triangle is a 30-60-90 triangle, so the relationship of its sides is $x : x\sqrt{3} : 2x$. 4 aligns with the $2x$ side, so the x side equals 2. Line segment BC is opposite the 60° angle, so BC aligns with the $x\sqrt{3}$ side, so BC is $2\sqrt{3}$.

7. **B**   The area of a triangle is given by $\frac{1}{2}bh$, so $32 = \frac{1}{2}(LO)8$, which simplifies to $32 = 4LO$, and $LO = 8$. Because triangle LNO is a right triangle with equal length legs, it is a 45-45-90 triangle, with a side length relationship of $x : x : x\sqrt{2}$. Because NO aligns with an x side and has a length of 8, LN has a length of $8\sqrt{2}$. The area of a triangle may be calculated from any base and height lines which form a 90° angle, so use LN as the base of triangle LMN, and the line with a length of 6 as its height. Thus, $\frac{1}{2}bh = \frac{1}{2}\left(8\sqrt{2}\right)6$, which simplifies to $3\left(8\sqrt{2}\right) = 24\sqrt{2}$. The correct answer is (B).

8. **C**   Recognize that the figure may not be drawn to scale. Statement (1) provides that the measure of angle y, but it does not provide any way to solve for the value of x, so Statement (1) is insufficient. Write down BCE. Statement (2) indicates that $AB = BC$, which provides that x and y are equal, but it provides no means to determine their values, so Statement (2) is insufficient. Eliminate (B). Together, the statements provide that $x = y = 80$. The correct answer is (C).

DRILL 11 (Circles)

1. Area = 25π, Circumference = 10π

    The formula for area is πr^2, and the formula for circumference is $2\pi r$. The radius is shown as 5, so area = 25π and circumference = 10π.

2. 12π The area of circle is given by $A = \pi r^2$, so the radius is $36\pi = \pi r^2$, which simplifies to $36 = r^2$, or $r = 6$. The circumference of a circle is given by $C = 2\pi r$, so the circumference is $2\pi(6) = 12\pi$.

3. 60   The relationship between arc and circumference is equal to relationship between a central angle which describes the arc and 360°. Thus, since $\dfrac{\text{arc}}{\text{circumference}} = \dfrac{1}{6}$, $\dfrac{x}{360} = \dfrac{1}{6}$, which yields that $x = 60$.

4. B   The area of the unshaded region is determined by subtracting the shaded region from the total region. The radius of the circle with center N is 5, so the area of the circle with center N is $\pi r^2 = \pi(5)^2$, or 25π. The radius of the circle with center P is equal to the diameter of the circle with center N, which is $2 \times 5 = 10$, so the area of the circle with center P is $\pi r^2 = \pi(10)^2$, or 100π. Thus, the area of the unshaded region is $100\pi - 25\pi = 75\pi$. The correct answer is (B).

5. C   Statement (1) provides information about circle Q, but it provides no means by which to relate this information to circle P, so Statement (1) is insufficient. Write down BCE. Statement (2) provides a relationship between circles Q and P, but no values, so Statement (2) is insufficient. The statements together provide that the radius of circle Q is $6 \div 2 = 3$, and that the radius of circle P is $3 \div 2 = 1.5$, which allows the question to be answered. The correct answer is (C).

DRILL 12 (Data Sufficiency Parts and Wholes)

1. C   Statement (1) provides the number of people who *paid deposits*, which may seem sufficient, but the question allows for the possibility that a person may pay a deposit and yet not attend, so Statement (1) is insufficient. Write down BCE. Statement (2) provides the percent of people who attended after paying a deposit, but it does not indicate the number of people who paid a deposit, so Statement (2) is insufficient. Eliminate (B). The statements together indicate that 60% of the 70 people who paid deposits attend, which allows the question to be answered. The correct answer is (C).

2. D   Statement (1) provides an amount of pigment and a total volume, which allows solving for the amount of alcohol and subsequently the ratio of alcohol to pigment, as there are only two ingredients in the paint. Statement (1) is sufficient. Write down AD. Similarly, Statement (2) provides an amount of alcohol and a total volume, which also allows solving for the ratio of alcohol to pigment. Statement (2) is sufficient. The correct answer is (D).

3. C   Statement (1) provides the proportional distances between the three towns, but no specific values, so Statement (1) is insufficient. Write down BCE. Statement (2) provides the distance from Ferristown to Laredo, but it provides no information about the distance from Smithville to Ferristown, so Statement (2) is insufficient. Eliminate (B). Together, the statements provide that Ferristown to Laredo is 12 miles, which is $\dfrac{2}{5}$ of the distance from Smithville to Laredo, and allows the question to be answered. The correct answer is (C).

DRILL 13 (Strange Powers of Powers)

1. **C**   Statement (1) provides that $x^2 = 4$, which indicates that x is equal to either 2 or –2. Statement (1) is insufficient. Write down BCE. Statement (2) provides only that $x < 0$, so Statement (2) is insufficient. Eliminate (B). Together the statements indicate that $x = -2$. The correct answer is (C).

2. **B**   Statement (1) provides that $x^2 = 4$, which indicates that x is equal to either 2 or –2, and provides no information about y. Statement (1) is insufficient. Write down BCE. Statement (2) provides that $y = 0$. While no information is provided about the value of x, any value multiplied by 0 is equal to 0, so Statement (2) is sufficient. The correct answer is (B).

3. **E**   Statement (1) provides that $x^2 = 4$, which indicates that x is equal to either 2 or –2, and provides no information about y. Statement (1) is insufficient. Write down BCE. Statement (2) provides that $y^2 = 9$, which indicates that y is equal to either 3 or –3, and provides no information about x. Statement (2) is insufficient. Eliminate (B). Together the statements provide possible values for both x and y, but allow for both 6 and –6 as possible values of xy, so the statements together are insufficient. Eliminate (C). The correct answer is (E).

DRILL 14 (Yes or No)

1. **A**   Statement (1) states that $2x < 1$. Divide by 2 to yield that $x < \frac{1}{2}$. The answer to the question is "Yes." Statement (1) is sufficient. Write down AD. Statement (1) states that $2x \leq 2$. Divide by 2 to yield that $x \leq 1$. x can equal 1, and the answer to the question is "No." x can also equal $\frac{1}{2}$, and the answer to the question is "Yes." When two values that satisfy a statement yield different answers to the question, the statement is insufficient. The correct answer is (A).

2. **B**   Statement (1) states that $xy = 6$. Let $x = 2$ and $y = 3$. These values satisfy the statement and the answer to the question is "Yes." Try to arrive at an answer of "No." Let $x = -2$ and $y = -3$. These values satisfy the statement and the answer to the question is "No." When two values that satisfy a statement yield different answers to the question, the statement is insufficient. Write down BCE. Statement (2) states that $xy^2 = 12$. Let $x = 3$ and $y = 2$. These values satisfy the statement and the answer to the question is "Yes." Try to arrive at an answer of "No." Because the product is not equal to 0, y^2 must be positive. Thus, x must also be positive in order to yield a product of positive 12. Statement (2) is sufficient. The correct answer is (B).

3. **E**   Statement (1) states that xy is an integer. Let $x = 2$ and $y = 3$. These values satisfy the statement and the answer to the question is "Yes." Try to arrive at an answer of "No." Let $x = \frac{1}{2}$ and $y = 2$. These values satisfy the statement and the answer to the question is "No." When two values that satisfy a statement yield different answers to the question, the statement is insufficient. Write down BCE. Statement (2) states that $x + y$ is an integer. Let $x = 2$ and $y = 3$. These values satisfy the statement and the answer to the question is "Yes." Try to arrive at an answer of "No." Let

$x = \dfrac{1}{2}$ and $y = \dfrac{1}{2}$. These values satisfy the statement and the answer to the question is "No."

Statement (2) is insufficient. Eliminate (B). Together, the statements may seem to be sufficient, and the values of $x = 2$ and $y = 3$ will allow a "Yes" answer, but let $x = \sqrt{2}$ and $y = -\sqrt{2}$. These values satisfy the statements and the answer to the question is "No." The statements together are insufficient. Eliminate (C). The correct answer is (E).

DRILL 15 (Spotting Critical Reasoning Question Types)

1. **Strengthen question.**
   Look for the conclusion and premise in the question. The correct answer will strengthen a premise that supports the conclusion.

2. **Inference question.**
   Look for information in the passage that pertains to the subject of the question.

3. **Evaluate question.**
   Look for assumptions in the passage.

4. **Assumption question.**
   To find the correct answer, look for the gap in the argument.

5. **Flaw question.**
   The passage should contain information that can be disputed. Find that information and anything that contradicts it.

6. **Weaken question.**
   Look for the conclusion and premise in the argument. The correct answer will weaken a premise that supports the conclusion.

7. **Identify the reasoning question.**
   The passage will provide a response to an assertion and the correct answer will reveal how the response was made.

8. **Resolve/Explain question.**
   Look for two incongruent facts in the passage and find a way to explain why both facts could be simultaneously true.

How to Score Your Integrated Reasoning Section

Integrated Reasoning sections are scored on a scale from 1 to 8. Use the chart below to approximate your score.

Please note that Integrated Reasoning items are scored all or nothing. For example, Table Analysis items have three parts. You must have picked the correct answer for each part to count the item as correct.

Please also note that Integrated Reasoning sections on the GMAT contain experimental questions that do not count toward your score. The chart below has been adjusted to compensate for the fact that these sections do not contain experimental questions.

Number Correct	Approximate Score
0–1	1
2	2
3–4	3
5–6	4
7–8	5
9–10	6
11	7
12	8

INTEGRATED REASONING DRILLS: Section 1

Item 1: Table Analysis

1-1. True   Read the text blurb to learn that *% Change* refers to the time period from 2009 to 2010. Sort the table by *Riders* to identify the station with the median annual number of riders: *34th Street/ Penn Station (Red Lines)*. Note that *Grand Central/42nd Street* is the only other station that experienced a decrease in ridership from 2009 to 2010. Determine the actual decrease in ridership for these two stations.

Approximately 27,000,000 riders visited *34th Street/Penn Station (Red Lines)* in 2010. The number of riders who visited this station decreased by 1.1% from 2009, so 2010 ridership was 98.9% of 2009 ridership. Set up a proportion, $\frac{98.9}{100} = \frac{27,000,000}{x}$, where *x* represents 2009 ridership.

Use the calculator to find that $x \approx 27,300,000$. The actual decrease in ridership for *34th Street/ Penn Station (Red Lines)* was approximately 27,300,000 – 27,000,000 = 300,000 riders.

Calculate the actual decrease in ridership at the *Grand Central/42nd Street* station in the same manner. Approximately 85,000 fewer riders visited *Grand Central/42nd Street* in 2010 than had visited the station in 2009. Since the actual decrease was greater at *34th Street/Penn Station (Red Lines)*, the statement is true.

1-2. True   Sort the table by *Connecting Subway Lines* to quickly identify which stations have 3 connecting lines and which have 5. Use the calculator to determine that the average number of riders at stations with 5 connecting lines is 31,307,134, and that the average number of riders at stations with 3 connecting lines is 23,434,760. Use the calculator again to determine that the average at stations with 5 connecting lines is approximately 1.34 times the average at stations with 3 connecting lines. Expressed as a fraction, $1.34 \approx \frac{4}{3}$, so the statement is true.

1-3. False   Sort the table by *% Change* to quickly identify the station with the greatest percent increase in riders: *Lexington Ave/59th Street*. Now, sort the table by *Riders* to quickly identify the station with the least number of riders: *86th Street (Green Lines)*. Since *Lexington Ave/59th Street* does not have the least number of riders, the statement is false.

Item 2: Two-Part Analysis

Column 1: Services Not Covered by Medical Plan—Choice (B)

The passage identifies mutually exclusive groups of doctors: doctors who either graduated with honors or who did not, and doctors who are either covered by Frank's medical plan or who are not. Use a group grid to represent the information provided. Since all of the information refers to the same population of doctors, the two columns are linked; a single group grid can be used to find the answer in both columns.

	Services Covered by Medical Plan	Services Not Covered by Medical Plan	Total
Graduated With Honors	3		8
Graduated Without Honors	27		
Total			45

Complete the bottom row of the grid to determine the number of doctors whose services are not covered by Frank's medical plan. If 3 doctors whose services are covered graduated with honors, and 27 doctors whose services are covered graduated without honors, then the services of 3 + 27 = 30 doctors are covered by Frank's plan. If there are 45 doctors in Frank's area, then the services of 45 − 30 = 15 doctors are not covered by Frank's plan. The correct answer is (B).

Column 2: Graduated Without Honors and Services Not Covered by Medical Plan—Choice (A)

Complete the middle row of the grid to determine the number of doctors who didn't graduate with honors and aren't covered by Frank's medical plan. If 8 of the 45 local doctors graduated with honors, then 45 − 8 = 37 doctors graduated without honors. Of those 37 doctors, 27 of them are covered by Frank's plan. Therefore, 37 − 27 = 10 doctors without honors aren't covered by Frank's plan. The correct answer is (A).

	Services Covered by Medical Plan	Services Not Covered by Medical Plan	Total
Graduated With Honors	3		8
Graduated Without Honors	27		
Total	30	15	45

Item 3: Two-Part Analysis

Column 1: Orchids—Choice (F)

Column 2: Dahlias—Choice (C)

The first column asks for the number of orchids purchased, and the second asks for the number of dahlias purchased. Translate the information provided into an algebraic equation, $1.35o + 1.8d = 18$, where o and d represent the number of orchids and dahlias purchased, respectively. Since o and d are related by a single equation, the two columns are linked.

The number of each type of flower must be an integer. Therefore, if Faustino spends $18 on orchids and dahlias, and each orchid costs $1.35, Faustino must buy an even number of orchids (an odd number of orchids would never yield an integer value for the price of the flowers). Eliminate (D) in the first column because it is odd. Plug In the remaining answers to determine the numbers of flowers purchased. Begin with (C), 4 orchids.

If $o = 4$, then $1.35(4) + 1.8d = 18$. Simplify the equation, so that $1.8d = 12.60$. Divide both sides of this equation by 1.8, so that $d = 7$. Since 7 is not an answer choice, eliminate (C) in the first column.

The more orchids Faustino purchases, the fewer dahlias he purchases. Plug In $o = 6$, so that $1.35(6) + 1.8d = 18$. Simplify the equation, so that $1.8d = 9.90$. Dividing both sides of this equation by 1.8 yields a non-integer value of d, so eliminate (E) in the first column.

Plug In $o = 8$, so that $1.35(8) + 1.8d = 18$. Simplify the equation, so that $1.8d = 7.2$. Divide both sides of this equation by 1.8, so that $d = 4$. The correct answer in the first column is (F), and the correct answer in the second column is (C).

Item 4: Graphics Interpretation

4-1. **B** The graph is clearly labeled, so there's no reason to read the text blurb. The first question asks for the slope of the regression line. Open the drop-down box and review the answer choices. The line's slope is negative, so eliminate (D) and (E). The line clearly passes through points (1, 10) and (4, 6), so the slope of the line is approximately equal to $\frac{y - y_1}{x - x_1} = \frac{6 - 10}{4 - 1}$, or $-\frac{4}{3}$. Expressed as a decimal, $-\frac{4}{3}$ is approximately equal to –1.3. The correct answer is (B).

4-2. **D** The question asks for the percent by which the number of students within 11 inches of the target's center after day 2 is greater or less than it was before any training. Open the drop-down box and review the answer choices. More students were within 11 inches of the target after 2 days of training, so eliminate (A) and (B). Before any training, 2 students were within 11 inches of the target's center. After 2 days of training, 4 students were within 11 inches of the target's center. Use the percent change formula, $\frac{difference}{original} \times 100$, to calculate the percent increase, which is equal to $\frac{4 - 2}{2} \times 100$, or 100%. The correct answer is (D).

Item 5: Two-Part Analysis

Column 1: Strengthen—Choice (B)

Column 2: Weaken—Choice (E)

The first column asks for the statement that most strengthens the argument, and the second column asks for the statement that most weakens the argument. Since the questions involve opposite tasks with respect to the same argument, the two columns are linked. Treat this as you would a Critical Reasoning question. Find the argument's premises and conclusion, and then use them to find an assumption.

The archaeologists conclude that *some human ancestors developed nautical skills millions of years earlier than previously discovered*. This conclusion is based on the discovery, on an island *40 miles from Greece*, of *stone tools* dating to *the Paleolithic age*. The argument assumes the tools were brought to the island by boat from mainland Greece.

Beginning with (A), evaluate the answers one at a time. Whether the tools were *used for fishing* is out of scope. What matters is how the tools got to the island, so eliminate (A). Choice (B) likens the tools to those used by Paleolithic human ancestors who lived on the mainland, reinforcing the assumption that the tools were brought to the island by boat. Keep (B) for the first column. Choices (C) and (D) are out of scope, as how the tools may have been used is irrelevant so eliminate (C) and (D). Choice (E) suggests that the Mediterranean Sea didn't exist 5 million years ago, weakening the assumption that the tools were brought to the island by boat, so keep (E) for the second column. Choice (F) is out of scope. Whether the tools were *used for purposes other than the construction of boats* is irrelevant. The correct answer in the first column is (B), and the correct answer in the second column is (E).

Item 6: Multi-Source Reasoning

6-1. **No** The *CD Offerings* tab relates the cost and length of an investment to the interest rate it earns. The *Memo* tab explains how the bank uses rewards and penalties to encourage longer-term investment. According to the *CD Offerings* tab, a 1-year, $11,000 investment earns 2.2% interest in the first year. According to the *Memo* tab, a 1-year investment doesn't qualify for bonus interest. Use the calculator to determine that 2.2% of $11,000 is $242. Since $242 < $250, the answer to the first question is "No."

6-2. **No** According to the *CD Offerings* tab, a 5-year, $9,500 investment earns 2.5% interest, compounded annually. According to the *Memo* tab, a 5-year investment earns an additional 0.1% interest in the first year. Use the calculator to determine that 2.6% of $9,500 is $247. Since $247 < $250, the answer to the second question is "No."

6-3. **Yes** According to the *CD Offerings* tab, a 10-year, $9,500 investment earns 2.8% interest, compounded annually. According to the *Memo* tab, CDs with 10-year terms earn an additional 0.1% interest in the first year. Use the calculator to determine that 2.9% of $9,500 is $275.50. Since $275.50 > $250, the answer to the third question is "Yes."

Item 7: Multi-Source Reasoning

7-1. **No**   The *CD Offerings* tab relates the cost and length of an investment to the interest rate it earns. The *Memo* tab explains how the bank uses rewards and penalties to encourage longer-term investment. According to the *CD Offerings* tab, a 1-year, $20,000 investment earns 2.2% interest, compounded annually. According to the *Memo* tab, a 1-year investment doesn't qualify for bonus interest. Use the calculator to determine that 2.2% of $20,000 is $440. Since $440 isn't between $500 and $600, the answer is "No."

7-2. **Yes**   According to the *CD Offerings* tab, a 5-year, $4,000 investment earns 2.5% interest, compounded annually. According to the *Memo* tab, a 5-year investment earns an additional 0.1% interest during the first year. Use the calculator to determine that the CD is worth $1.026 \times \$4,000 = \$4,104$ at the end of the first year. Similarly, the investment is worth $(1.025)4 \times \$4,104 = \$4,530.05$ at the end of the fifth year. Thus, the total interest earned is $4,530.05 − $4,000 = $530.05, and the answer is "Yes."

7-3. **No**   According to the *CD Offerings* tab, a 2-year, $10,000 investment earns 2.4% interest, compounded annually. According to the *Memo* tab, a 2-year investment doesn't qualify for bonus interest. Use the calculator to determine that the CD is worth $(1.024)2 \times \$10,000 = \$10,485.76$ at the end of the second year. Thus, the total interest earned is $10,485.76 − $10,000 = $485.76, and the answer is "No."

Item 8: Multi-Source Reasoning

8-1. **No**   The *CD Offerings* tab relates the cost and length of an investment to the interest rate it earns. The *Memo* tab explains how the bank uses rewards and penalties to encourage longer-term investment. According to the *Memo* tab, the schedule of penalties has been *revised*, so penalties for early withdrawals must have existed prior to the policy changes. The statement cannot be inferred from the information provided, so the answer is "No."

8-2. **No**   According to the *Memo* tab, the bank policies described are designed to *shift the balance of customers' CD accounts towards those with longer maturity terms.* Although preferred customers receive a bonus that new customers do not receive, there's no indication that the bonus rewards them for their loyalty. The statement cannot be inferred from the information provided, so the answer is "No."

8-3. **Yes**   According to the *Memo* tab, the bank intends to steer customers toward CDs with *longer maturity terms.* As an incentive, the bank will reward longer-term investments with bonus interest. If the bank successfully shifts even one customer to a longer-term CD, then it will pay a higher average interest rate to customers. The statement can be inferred from the information provided, so the answer is "Yes."

Item 9: Table Analysis

9-1. **True** Read the text blurb to learn that *Popular Vote (Millions)* refers to the number of votes earned by the winning candidate. Sort the table by *President* to quickly identify Nixon, Reagan, Clinton, and Bush as the presidents who served two terms. The question asks for the two-term president with the smallest percent increase in *Popular Vote* from one term to the next, so use the percent change formula, $\frac{difference}{original} \times 100$. Compare $\frac{difference}{original}$ for the two-term presidents. William Clinton's $\frac{2.5}{40} \times 100 = 6.25$ percent increase in *Popular Vote* was the smallest percent increase for the two-term presidents, so the statement is true.

9-2. **False** Sort the table by *Political Party* to quickly determine that there are 6 Democratic presidents and 7 Republican presidents listed in the table. Use the calculator to determine that the 6 Democratic presidents earned 2,200 electoral votes, averaging $2{,}200 \div 6 \approx 367$ electoral votes per candidate, and the 7 Republican presidents earned a total of 2,818 electoral votes, averaging $2{,}818 \div 7 \approx 403$ per candidate. Since $403 > 367$, the statement is false.

9-3. **True** Sort the table by *% of Popular Vote* to help identify the presidents for whom the difference between *% of Popular Vote* and *% of Electoral Vote* is least. In both 2000 and 2004, the difference between the two percentages is less than 3, much less than the difference for any other president. In both years, George W. Bush was president, so the statement is true.

Item 10: Multi-Source Reasoning

10-1. **Yes** *Memo #1* explains the company's airfare reimbursement policy, *Memo #2* details the average, standard deviation, and sample size for flights from each region to Bloomsbury, and *Email #1* describes the number of tickets purchased at various prices in the West region. According to the *Memo #2* tab, the West and Midwest regions had the same average ticket price, but no other region had a ticket price lower than that of the Midwest. The statement can be inferred from *Memo #2*, so the answer is "Yes."

10-2. **No** According to *Memo #1*, *Regional Office Managers will be responsible for arranging the travel reservations for all Level 2 managers....* However, no information is provided about who will attend the annual management retreat in addition to Level 2 managers. The statement cannot be inferred from the information in any of the tabs, so the answer is "No."

10-3. **Yes** According to *Memo #1*, Regional Office Managers may *delegate the task* as they wish. Therefore, ROMs *need not make the reservations personally*. The statement can be inferred from *Memo #1*, so the answer is "Yes."

Item 11: Multi-Source Reasoning

11-1. **True**   *Memo #1* explains the company's airfare reimbursement policy, *Memo #2* details the average, standard deviation, and sample size for flights from each region to Bloomsbury, and *Email #1* describes the number of tickets purchased at various prices in the West region. According to *Memo #1, any ticket priced 1 standard deviation or more below average* will be reimbursed a "Budget Bonus" of *50% of the difference between the ticket price and the average airfare* from that region. According to *Memo #2*, airfare from the West region averages $200 with a standard deviation of $25. Therefore, the West region will receive a "Budget Bonus" for any flight costing $175 or less. According to *Email #1*, the West region bought 18 tickets at $150 per ticket. Thus, the West region will receive $25 for each one of these 18 tickets. Use the calculator to determine that 18 × $25 = $450, which matches the information in the statement. The statement is True.

11-2. **False**   Standard deviation is the measure of the spread, or range, of the numbers within a set. Based on *Memo #2*, this may suggest that it is true that the two regions with the least sample size also had the least difference between the most and least expensive airfare found during research, the information provided in the question gives no insight into how many standard deviations were required to encompass all the data points. Therefore, it is impossible to know the distance between the greatest and least values for the information. The statement is False.

11-3. **True**   This question asks about the averages of the researched airfare prices, so look at *Memo #2*. Determine the combined mean airfare of the researched regions by finding the sum of total amount for each of the regions individually, and then dividing that number by the total number of the sample size. The combined mean airfare for the researched regions is $271.42. This is less than the mean airfare for the Northeast, Mid-Atlantic, and Plains regions. The statement is True.

Item 12: Multi-Source Reasoning

Choice C   *Memo #1* explains the company's airfare reimbursement policy, *Memo #2* details the average, standard deviation, and sample size for flights from each region to Bloomsbury, and *Email #1* describes the number of tickets purchased at various prices in the West region. According to *Memo #1*, any ticket priced at or below one standard deviation above the mean is eligible for reimbursement. According to *Memo #2*, airfare from the West region averages $200 per ticket with a standard deviation of $25. Therefore, any ticket priced at or below $225 is fully reimbursed. According to *Email #1*, 22 of the 30 tickets purchased in the West region are priced within this range. Thus, the probability a randomly selected ticket is eligible to be fully reimbursed is $\frac{22}{30}$, which reduces to $\frac{11}{15}$. The correct answer is (C).

INTEGRATED REASONING DRILLS: Section 2

Item 1: Graphics Interpretation

1-1. **A** Open the drop-down menu and review the answer choices. More clocks are produced on Tuesday than on Wednesday, so eliminate (D) and (E). According to the histogram, 75 clocks are produced on Tuesday and 40 are produced on Wednesday. Express the ratio as a fraction, $\frac{75}{40}$, which can be reduced to $\frac{15}{8}$. The correct answer is (A).

1-2. **D** According to the histogram, 90 clocks are produced on Monday and Wednesday, and 250 clocks are produced during the week, so that $\frac{9}{25}$ of the clocks are produced on Monday and Wednesday. To convert this fraction into a percentage, multiply the numerator and denominator by 4, so that $\frac{36}{100} = 36\%$ of the clocks are produced on Monday and Wednesday. The correct answer is (D).

Item 2: Two-Part Analysis

Column 1: Weakens Company X—Choice (F)

Column 2: Weakens Technology Consultant—Choice (D)

The first column asks for the statement that most weakens Company X's argument, and the second column asks for the statement that most weakens the Consultant's argument. Since the tasks involve different arguments, the columns are not linked. Treat these questions as Critical Reasoning questions. Begin with the first column.

Company X concludes that it will *purchase new computers that run Portals 8*, basing its decision on the desire to *compete effectively in the modern economy* and the fact that its *computer technology is out of date*. This argument exhibits the planning pattern, so Company X assumes that there's no problem with its plan to purchase Portals 8. Because this is a weaken question, look for an answer that introduces a problem with the plan.

Choices (A), (B), and (D) are out of scope. Whether GreenCap is *more efficient, the most cutting-edge*, or *more expensive* is irrelevant, since Company X has decided to purchase Portals 8. Choice (C) is also out of scope. Company X bases its decision on its desire to compete in the economy. *When* the operating systems were released is irrelevant. Choice (E) states that Portals 8 is available in *different versions with different price levels*, strengthening Company X's argument by making Portals 8 more appealing. Choice (F) weakens Company X's argument. If Portals 8 *contains bugs and design flaws that will impair its ability to compete in the modern economy*, then there's a problem with Company X's plan to buy Portals 8. The correct answer in the first column is (F).

Now, consider the second column. The Consultant concludes that Company X should *purchase GreenCap* instead of Portals 8, basing the decision on Company X's desire to *complete effectively in the modern economy* and the fact that GreenCap *costs substantially less than does Portals 8.* This argument, too, exhibits the planning pattern. Because this is a weaken question, look for an answer that introduces a problem with the Consultant's plan.

Choices (A), (B), and (C) are out of scope. Whether GreenCap is *more efficient, the most cutting-edge,* or *has been available for three years* is irrelevant. What matters is whether GreenCap will better allow Company X to compete in the economy. Choice (D) weakens the Consultant's argument by challenging the premise that GreenCap *costs substantially less.* If GreenCap *requires an annual maintenance agreement that makes it more expensive overall,* then there's a problem with the Consultant's plan to save Company X money. Choice (E) weakens the Consultant's argument indirectly by making Portals 8 seem more appealing. However, without information describing how *price levels* for Portals 8 will affect Company X, the extent to which this answer weakens the Consultant's argument is unclear. Eliminate (E). Choice (F) strengthens the Consultant's argument by suggesting a reason for Company X to purchase GreenCap instead of Portals 8. The correct answer in the second column is (D).

Item 3: Graphics Interpretation

3-1. **C** A quick glance at the graph reveals that ice cream consumption is relatively consistent when compared to cheese consumption, which tends to increase over time. Thus, the year with the lowest total consumption will be the year with the lowest cheese consumption, 1989.

Open the drop-down menu to review the answer choices. In 1989, ice cream consumption exceeded cheese consumption, so eliminate (A) and (D). Per capita ice cream consumption was roughly 29 pounds, while per capita cheese consumption was roughly 24 pounds. Express the ratio as a fraction, $\frac{29}{24}$. Since $\frac{29}{24}$ is closer to $\frac{30}{25}$, or $\frac{6}{5}$, than it is to $\frac{36}{24}$, or $\frac{3}{2}$, the correct answer is (C).

3-2. **B** The question asks for the relationship between the slopes of the two regression lines. A quick glance at the graph reveals that the regression line for ice cream slopes downward while the regression line for cheese slopes upward. Open the drop-down menu to review the answer choices. Eliminate (A) and (C), because the slope of the regression line for ice cream is less than the slope of the regression line for cheese. The correct answer is (B).

Item 4: Two-Part Analysis

Column 1: Strengthens Committee Member's Response—Choice (C)

Column 2: Weakens Committee Member's Response—Choice (A)

The first column asks for the statement that most strengthens the committee member's response, and the second column asks for the statement that most weakens the committee member's response. Since the questions involve opposite tasks with respect to the same argument, the two columns are linked. Treat this as you would a Critical Reasoning question. Begin with the first column.

The XM representative argues that *the costly and time-consuming review should be waived*, because *less than two percent of XM projects have ever been rejected*. The committee member counters that the review should not be waived, because failing to review the project entails failing *to observe innovations in geo-engineering that may need guidelines drafted for the safety of subsequent projects*. Thus, the committee member is concerned with *safety throughout the industry* and seems to assume that reviews are the only way to observe innovations that can lead to the drafting of guidelines. Because this is a strengthen question, look for answers that reinforce this assumption.

Choice (A) weakens the committee member's response by breaking the link between the review and the observation of innovations. If XM's current project is nearly identical to a project that already passed review, then the committee can expect to see nothing new from a review. Choice (B) is out of scope. The percentage of CL's projects which have been rejected is irrelevant to the argument that XM's project should be reviewed. Choice (C) strengthens the argument that XM's project should be reviewed by suggesting that opportunities for review are limited. If new innovations are reviewed only once, then all new innovations should be reviewed. Choices (D), (E), and (F) are out of scope. Whether *XM's projects are peer-reviewed*, *Geo-engineering deserves careful monitoring*, or *the committee has had to reverse some of its decisions* is irrelevant to the argument that innovation can be observed, and guidelines drawn up, only when projects are reviewed by the committee. The correct answer in the first column is (C), and the correct answer in the second column is (A).

Item 5: Two-Part Analysis

Column 1: Insect Species X—Choice (A)

Column 2: Insect Species Y—Choice (C)

The first column asks for the current population of insect species X, and the second column asks for the current population of insect species Y. The passage provides the constant rate at which the population of each species changes, and states that in four years, the populations will be equal. Since the information provided can be used to write a single equation relating the current populations of species X and Y, the two columns are linked. Translate the information into an algebraic equation.

The population of species X decreases at a rate of 10% per year, so each year, only 90% of the population survives. The population of species Y decreases at a rate of 15% per year, so each year, only 85% of the population survives. After 4 years, the two populations will be equal, so $x(0.9)^4 = y(0.85)^4$, where x and y represent the current populations of species X and Y, respectively. Note that, because the population of species Y decreases faster than the population of species X, the current population of Y must be greater than that of X.

Manipulate the equation so that the ratio $\dfrac{x}{y}$ can be determined. Divide both sides of the equation by $y(0.9)^4$, so that $\dfrac{x}{y} = \dfrac{0.85^4}{0.9^4}$. Use the calculator to determine that $\dfrac{x}{y} \approx 0.796$.

In the *Current Population* column, look for two values whose ratio is just under 0.8. Since $\dfrac{500}{600} = 0.8$, try $\dfrac{450}{600}$. Expressed as a decimal, $\dfrac{450}{600} = 0.75$, which is too less than 0.8. To increase the ratio, either increase the numerator or decrease the denominator. The next least possible numerator is 525. Since $\dfrac{525}{600} > 0.8$, try decreasing the denominator. Expressed as a decimal, $\dfrac{450}{565} \approx 0.796$. The correct answer in the first column is (A), and the correct answer in the second column is (C).

Item 6: Multi-Source Reasoning

6-1. **No**   *Email #1* describes the company's plan to increase revenue by ramping up advertising to females aged 15–25. *Email #2* identifies the two most popular programs among females aged 15–25. *Memo #1* presents advertising and viewership data for the two programs. According to *Memo #1*, 45% of females aged 15–25 watch *Blonde Fury*. However, none of the tabs provide information about other age and gender groups. Since the statement cannot be inferred from the information provided, the answer is "No."

6-2. **No**   According to *Memo #1*, a greater percentage of females aged 15–25 watches *Blonde Fury* than watches Hart Attack. However, none of the tabs provide information sufficient to determine the size of the audience for either program. On the basis of the information provided, it cannot be inferred that thirty-second ads are more expensive for programs with larger audiences. The answer is "No."

6-3. **No**   According to *Memo #1*, 45% of females aged 15–25 watch *Blonde Fury*, during which a 30-second commercial costs $70,000, and 35% of females aged 15–25 watch Hart Attack, during which a 30-second commercial costs $55,000. However, none of the tabs provides information sufficient to determine how much money was actually spent on advertising. The statement cannot be inferred from the information provided, so the answer is "No."

Item 7: Multi-Source Reasoning

Choice D   *Email #1* describes the company's plan to increase revenue by ramping up advertising to females aged 15–25. *Email #2* identifies the two most popular programs among females aged 15–25. *Memo #1* presents advertising and viewership data for the two programs.

According to *Memo #1*, 45% of females aged 15–25 watch *Blonde Fury* and 35% of females aged 15–25 watch *Hart Attack*. If there are 20,000,000 females aged 15–25, then 0.45 × 20,000,000 = 9,000,000 watch *Blonde Fury*, and 0.35 × 20,000,000 = 7,000,000 watch *Hart Attack*. According to *Email #2*, 80% of female viewers aged 15–25 who watch *Hart Attack* also watch *Blonde Fury*. If 7,000,000 females aged 15–25 watch *Hart Attack*, then 0.80 × 7,000,000 = 5,600,000 who watch *Hart Attack* also watch *Blonde Fury*.

Use the group formula to answer the question, *group 1 + group 2 + neither – both = total*. Substitute the calculated values into the formula, so that $7,000,000 + 9,000,000 + neither – 5,600,000 = 20,000,000$. Simplify the equation, so that *neither* = 9,600,000. The correct answer is (D).

Item 8: Multi-Source Reasoning

8-1.   **Yes**   *Email #1* describes the company's plan to increase revenue by ramping up advertising to females aged 15–25. *Email #2* identifies the two most popular programs among females aged 15–25. *Memo #1* presents advertising and viewership data for the two programs. In *Email #1*, the Marketing Director writes that *in 1978, 1987, and 1993, we responded to revenue decreases by increasing our advertising expenditures by 30%. On all three occasions, our revenues began to increase again within one quarter.* Since the Director attributes success on all three occasions to increased advertising expenditures, the Director must assume that *it is possible for a strategy that succeeded in the past to succeed again.* The correct answer is "Yes."

8-2.   **Yes**   In *Email #1*, the Marketing Director writes that *in 1978, 1987, and 1993, we responded to revenue decreases by increasing our advertising expenditures by 30%. On all three occasions, our revenues began to increase again within one quarter.* Since the Director now wants to increase revenue by increasing the number of advertisements by 30%, the Director must assume that *the previous increases in revenues were attributable at least in part to the effect of increased advertising.* The correct answer is "Yes."

8-3.   **Yes**   In *Email #1*, the Marketing Director states that *in 1978, 1987, and 1993, we responded to revenue decreases by increasing our advertising expenditures by 30%. On all three occasions, our revenues began to increase again within one quarter.* Since the Director now wants to increase revenue by increasing the number of advertisements by 30%, the Director must assume that *increasing the number of advertisements and increasing advertising expenditures have similar effects on revenue.* The correct answer is "Yes."

Item 9: Table Analysis

9-1.   **Supported**

Sort the table by *Population 2010* to quickly identify countries with a population greater than 150 million: Brazil, Indonesia, United States, India, and China. For each of these five countries, use the calculator to determine the number of foreign-born inhabitants.

In Brazil, 0.34% of 190,733,000 inhabitants are foreign-born, so $0.0034 \times 190,733,000 = 648,492$ inhabitants are foreign born. In Indonesia, 0.07% of 237,556,000 inhabitants are foreign-born, so $0.0007 \times 237,556,000 = 166,289$ inhabitants are foreign-born. In the United States, 21.81% of 312,399,000 inhabitants are foreign-born, so $0.2181 \times 312,399,000 = 68,134,222$ inhabitants are foreign-born. In India, 0.52% of 1,210,193,000 inhabitants are foreign-born, so $0.0052 \times 1,210,193,000 = 6,293,004$ inhabitants are foreign-born. In China, 0.29% of 1,399,725,000 inhabitants are foreign-born, so $0.0029 \times 1,399,725,000 = 4,059,203$ inhabitants are foreign-born. The country with the median number of foreign-born inhabitants is China, so the statement is supported by the table.

9-2. **Unsupported**

The table doesn't include any information about projected populations for the year 2030, so the statement is not supported by the table.

9-3. **Supported**

Sort the table by *% of Population Foreign-Born* to quickly identify the country with the greatest percentage of foreign-born inhabitants. Of the countries listed, Andorra has the greatest percentage of inhabitants who are foreign-born, so the statement is supported by the table.

Item 10: Multi-Source Reasoning

10-1. **True**   *Email #1* describes what the organization requires for the gala and mentions two catering companies it might hire. *Email #2* compares costs and services for the two companies. According to *Email #1*, the organization expects *a maximum of 400 people*. If 400 people attend a gala catered by DoxySource, then according to *Email #2*, the appetizers cost $2 × 400 = $800, the entrees cost $6.25 × 400 = $2,500, and the desserts cost $3.40 × 400 = $1,360. In this case, the total cost of food is $4,660. DoxySource charges $15.50 per 8-person table. Since 50 tables are needed to seat 400 guests, the least amount that can be spent on seating is $15.50 × 50 = $775. Finally, seating costs are $\frac{\$775}{\$4,660} \times 100 \approx 16.6\%$ of food costs, so the statement is true.

10-2. **True**   According to *Email #2*, BrightRight charges $350 for a 40-gallon punch fountain, or $350 ÷ 40 = $8.75 per gallon. DoxySource charges $47 for a 7-gallon punch fountain, or $47 ÷ 7 ≈ $6.72 per gallon. Use the percent change formula, $\frac{difference}{original} \times 100$, to determine whether DoxySource punch costs at least 20% less per gallon than BrightRight punch. Substitute the costs-per-gallon into the percent change formula, $\frac{8.75 - 6.72}{8.75} \times 100$. Simplify the expression, so that DoxySource punch costs $\frac{2.03}{8.75} \times 100 = 23.2\%$ less per gallon than BrightRight punch. DoxySource fountains cost at least 20% less per gallon, so the statement is true.

10-3. **True**   According the *Email #1*, the organization requires *tables, audio, food, and a punch fountain*. The organization's budget is $6,000. To determine whether the organization will go over budget by at least 15%, calculate the cheapest possible cost of using BrightRight.

According to *Email #2*, BrightRight's 8-person tables cost $20 each. Since 50 tables are needed to seat 400 people, the total cost of tables is $20 × 50 = $1,000. *The Classic Western BBQ* costs $14 per person, so the total cost of food is $14 × 400 = $5,600. The *Party Sound System* costs

$650, and the *Punch Fountain* costs $350. Therefore, the cheapest possible cost of hiring Bright-Right to cater the gala is $1,000 + $650 + $5,600 + $350 = $7,600. In this case, the project will go over budget by $1,600, or by $\dfrac{\$1,600}{\$6,000} \times 100 \approx 27\%$. Since the project will go over budget by at least 15%, the statement is true.

Item 11: Multi-Source Reasoning

Choice C   *Email #1* describes what the organization requires for the gala and mentions two catering companies it might hire. *Email #2* compares costs and services for the two companies. According to *Email #2*, 8-person DoxySource tables cost $15.50 each, and 7-person tables cost $17 each. The cheapest way to seat 400 people, using at least one of each table type, would be to use only one of the more expensive tables, leaving 393 people to sit at 8-person tables. Seating 393 people requires 393 ÷ 8 = 49.125 of the cheaper tables. Since the number of tables should be an integer, and more than 49 cheaper tables are required, the Coordinator should use fifty 8-person tables and one 7-person table, for a total cost of $17 + 50($15.50) = $792. The correct answer is (C).

Item 12: Multi-Source Reasoning

12-1. Yes   *Email #1* describes what the organization requires for the gala and mentions two catering companies it might hire. *Email #2* compares costs and services for the two companies. In *Email #1*, the Gala Coordinator states: *I'd like to consider how to justify any over-budget costs from using BrightRight.* If the Coordinator is considering how to justify over-budget costs, then it can be inferred that the Coordinator is willing to ask for a budgetary increase. The answer is "Yes."

12-2. Yes   In *Email #2*, the Assistant mentions the *price difference* between services offered by the two companies. In addition, the Assistant refers to BrightRight packages as *more elegant and comprehensive*, and to DoxySource packages as *more flexible* and requiring *more hands-on involvement on our end*. Thus, costs are not the only determining factor in choosing one event planning service over the other. The answer is "Yes."

12-3. No   In *Email #1*, the Coordinator states that *tables, audio, food, and a punch fountain or fountains* are required. Therefore, fountains are not an optional element of the gala. The answer is "No."

ANSWERS TO CHALLENGE QUESTIONS

Page 63—Challenge Question #1

C Begin by considering the possible values of x and y. Prime numbers with squares less than 60 are 2, 3, 5, and 7, for squares of 4, 9, 25, and 49, respectively. Therefore, possible sums of distinct pairs of squares are $4 + 9 = 13$, $4 + 25 = 29$, $4 + 49 = 53$, $9 + 25 = 34$, and $9 + 49 = 58$. Thus, x can be 13, 29, 34, 53, or 58. For y, multiples of 17 less than 60 are 17, 34, and 51. Now consider the answer choices. Choice (A) is –19, so look for combinations of answer choices that could result in –19. The only possible values that are close are $13 - 34 = -21$, $29 - 51 = -22$, and $34 - 51 = -17$. None of these values match –19, so eliminate (A). Choice (B) is –7, so consider whether that values might be used. $13 - 17 = -4$ and $29 - 34 = -5$, none of which match –7, so eliminate (B). Choice (C) is 0, and $34 - 34 = 0$. The correct answer is (C).

Page 91—Challenge Question #2

D The question asks for the factor by which the value of a gem with a rating of p would have to be multiplied to equal the value of a gem with a rating of $p - r$. According to the rating system described by the question stem, the value of a gem with a rating of $q - 1$ is 5 times greater than the value of a gem with a rating of q. Subtracting 1 from the rating corresponds to a 5-fold increase in value.

Following the pattern suggested by the question stem, the value of a gem with a $q - 2$ rating is greater than the value of a gem with a q rating by a factor of 25, or 5^2. Similarly, the value of a gem with a $q - 3$ rating is greater than the value of a gem with a q rating by a factor of 125, or 53.

Apply this pattern to gems rated $p - r$ and p. The easiest way to do this is to Plug In values of p and r. Let $p = 5$ and $r = 2$. In this case, the gems to be compared are rated '5 – 2' and '5'. Based on the pattern above, the value of the gem rated '5 – 2' is greater than the value of the gem rated '5' by a factor of 25. Substitute $p = 5$ and $r = 2$ into the answer choices, looking for the answer that equals 25.

Choice (A) is $(5)^5 - (2)^5$, a number much greater than 25. Eliminate (A). Choice (B) is $(2)^5$, or 32. Eliminate (B). Choice (C) is $(5 - 2)^5$, or 243. Eliminate (C). Choice (D) is 5^2, or 25. Keep (D). Choice (E) is $5^{5×2}$, or 5^{10}, a number much greater than 25. The correct answer is (D).

Page 121—Challenge Question #3

D The question asks for the value of $333{,}333.\overline{3} \times \left(10^{-3} - 10^{-5}\right)$. Rewrite the expression without the

negative exponents, yielding $333{,}333.\overline{3} \times \left(\dfrac{1}{10^3} - \dfrac{1}{10^5}\right)$. Use the distributive property of multipli-

cation to rewrite the expression, $\dfrac{333{,}333.\overline{3}}{10^3} - \dfrac{333{,}333.\overline{3}}{10^5}$. Eliminate the fractions by shifting the

decimal places in the numerators the appropriate number of places to the left, resulting in a subtrac-

tion problem, $333.\overline{3} - 3.\overline{3} = 330$. The correct answer is (D).

Page 138—Challenge Question #4

B There are variables in the answer choices, so Plug In values for b, r and q. However, there is information in the question stem that should first be considered. The question asks for the value of p in terms of b, r, and q, where b and r represent the point values of blue tokens and red tokens, respectively, and q represents the number of red tokens acquired by Player A expressed as a percentage of all Player A's tokens. Had the question provided the total number of tokens acquired by Player A, then plugging in values of b, r, and q would have allowed for the calculation of p, the percentage of points earned from blue tokens. The question does not provide the number of tokens acquired by Player A, so not only is this a Plug In question, it's also a Hidden Plug In question. Let Player A acquire 10 tokens, and let $b = 5$, $r = 2$, and $q = 80$.

If Player A acquired 10 tokens during the game, and $q = 80\%$ of the tokens were red, then Player A acquired 8 red tokens and 2 blue tokens. If each blue token is worth 5 points and each red token is worth 2 points, then Player A earned $2 \times 5 = 10$ points from blue tokens and $8 \times 2 = 16$ points from red tokens, for a total of $10 + 16 = 26$ points. In this case, the percentage of points that were earned from blue tokens is $p = \dfrac{10}{26} \times 100$. Circle the target answer, $\dfrac{1,000}{26}$.

Now, Plug In $b = 5$, $r = 2$, and $x = 80$ for each of the answer choices, looking for the choice that equals $\dfrac{1,000}{26}$. Choice (A) is $\dfrac{100(5)(80)}{(5)(80)+100(2)-(80)(2)} = \dfrac{40,000}{440}$, which reduces to $\dfrac{4,000}{44}$, or $\dfrac{1,000}{11}$. Eliminate (A). Choice (B) is $\dfrac{10,000(5)-100(5)(80)}{100(5)-(5)(80)+(80)(2)} = \dfrac{10,000}{260}$, which reduces to $\dfrac{1,000}{26}$. Keep (B). Choice (C) is $\dfrac{(5)(80)+100(2)-(80)(2)}{100(5)(80)} = \dfrac{440}{40,000}$. Eliminate (C). Choice (D) is $\dfrac{100(5)-(5)(80)}{100(2)-100(5)(80)+(80)(2)} = \dfrac{100}{-39,640}$. Eliminate (D). Choice (E) is $\dfrac{100(5)-(5)(80)+(80)(2)}{10,000(5)-100(5)(80)} = \dfrac{260}{10,000}$. Eliminate (E). The correct answer is (B).

Page 147—Challenge Question #5

D   The answer choices represent the information directly asked for by the question, so Plug In the Answers. Begin with (C). If the new after-tax price of a car is \$13,500, then the new pre-tax price is $\dfrac{\$13,500}{1.08} = \$12,500$, the old pre-tax price is \$12,500 – \$2,500 = \$10,000, and the old after-tax price is \$10,000 × 1.08 = \$10,800. In this case, the cost of 18 cars at the old after-tax price is 18 × \$10,800 = \$194,400, and the cost of 15 cars at the new after-tax price is 15 × \$13,500 = \$202,500. Since these costs should be equal, eliminate (C).

When the new after-tax price of a car was \$13,500, the cost of 15 cars at the new after-tax price was too great, and the cost of 18 cars at the old after-tax price was less than necessary. Two factors contributed to the unwanted gap between these values. First, fewer cars were purchased at the new price than at the old price. Nothing can be done about this, since the quantities purchased are built into the question. Second, the difference between the new pre-tax price and the old pre-tax price is \$2,500. This difference was too great relative to a new after-tax price of \$13,500. To lessen the impact of the \$2,500 pre-tax price difference, therefore, increase the new after-tax price of per car. Try (D).

If the new after-tax price of a car is \$16,200, then the new pre-tax price is $\dfrac{\$16,200}{1.08} = \$15,000$, the old pre-tax price is \$15,000 – \$2,500 = \$12,500, and the old after-tax price is \$12,500 × 1.08 = \$13,500. In this case, the cost of 18 cars at the old after-tax price is 18 × \$13,500 = \$243,000, and the cost of 15 cars at the new after-tax price is 15 × \$16,200 = \$243,000. The correct answer is (D).

Page 160—Challenge Question #6

C   If James can complete the job in 6 hours, then James' rate is $\dfrac{1}{6}$ of a job per hour. If Sarah can complete the job in 4.5 hours, then Sarah's rate is $\dfrac{1}{4.5}$ or $\dfrac{2}{9}$ of a job per hour.

Together, James and Sarah work at a rate of $\dfrac{1}{6} + \dfrac{2}{9}$ or $\dfrac{3}{18} + \dfrac{4}{18} = \dfrac{7}{18}$ of a job per hour.

During the hour that James and Sarah work together, they complete $\dfrac{7}{18}$ of the job, leaving $\dfrac{11}{18}$ of the job unfinished. James will complete some of the unfinished work at a rate of $\dfrac{1}{6}$ per hour, and Sarah will finish the rest at a rate of $\dfrac{2}{9}$ per hour, such that Sarah works by herself half as long as James does. Translate this information into an algebraic equation. If t represents the number of hours during which James works alone, then $t \times \dfrac{1}{6} + \dfrac{t}{2} \times \dfrac{2}{9} = \dfrac{11}{18}$. Multiply both sides of the equation by 18 and simplify to find that $3t + 2t = 11$. Simplify the equation further so that $5t = 11$. Divide both sides of the equation by 5, so that $t = 2.2$ hours, or 2 hours and 12 minutes. The correct answer is (C).

Page 162—Challenge Question #7

A First, Plug In the values from the question stem. Plug In 2 for y and 144 for z to get that $\dfrac{144}{x^2}$ is an integer, while $\dfrac{144}{x^3}$ is not, which means that x^2 divides evenly into 144, but x^3 does not. To easily determine if a number divides evenly into another, find the prime factors. In this case, the prime factorization of 144 is $144 = 2^4 * 3^2$. Now Plug In the Answer choices for the value of x and determine if $\dfrac{144}{x^2}$ is an integer, while $\dfrac{144}{x^3}$ is not. Choice (A) is 2 and 2^2 and 2^3 are factors of 144. Because the question asks which answer choice is NOT a factor of 144, keep (A). Because the answer choices were used to determine the factors and there can be only one answer choice that works, there is no need to test other answer choices. In fact, if the remaining answer choices are all taken down to their prime factors and Plugged In for x, they will all abide by the rules in the problem that $\dfrac{144}{x^2}$ is an integer, while $\dfrac{144}{x^3}$ is not. The correct answer is (A).

Page 169—Challenge Question #8

D There are variables in the answer choices, so Plug In values for g and b. Let $g = 2$ and $b = 3$. The question asks for the probability that at least one of two randomly selected players is a girl, which is equivalent to 1 minus the probability that both of the selected players are boys. The probability that the first player selected is a boy is $\dfrac{3}{5}$, and the probability that the second player selected is a boy is $\dfrac{2}{4}$. Therefore, the probability that both selected players are boys is $\dfrac{3}{5} \times \dfrac{2}{4} = \dfrac{6}{20}$, and the probability that at least one of the players is a girl is $1 - \dfrac{6}{20} = \dfrac{14}{20}$. Plug $g = 2$ and $b = 3$ into each of the answer choices, looking for the answer that equals $\dfrac{14}{20}$.

Choice (A) is $\dfrac{2(2-1)}{(3+2)(3+2-1)} = \dfrac{2}{20}$, so eliminate (A). Choice (B) is $\dfrac{3(3-1)}{(3+2)(3+2-1)} = \dfrac{6}{20}$, so eliminate (B). Choice (C) is $\dfrac{2(3)(2)}{(3+2)(3+2-1)} = \dfrac{12}{20}$, so eliminate (C). Choice (D) is

$\dfrac{2(2 \times 3 + 2 - 1)}{(3+2)(3+2-1)} = \dfrac{14}{20}$, so keep (D). Choice (E) is $\dfrac{3(2 \times 2 + 3 - 1)}{(3+2)(3+2-1)} = \dfrac{18}{20}$, so eliminate (E). The

correct answer is (D).

Page 175—Challenge Question #9

B The answer choices represent the information directly asked for by the question, so Plug In the Answers. However, there is information in the question that should first be considered. Variables x and y represent the number of short and long essays available in Part Two of the test, respectively. The ratio of available long essays to short essays remains a constant in both parts of the test, and the ratio of short to long essays in Part One is 2:1. Therefore, the ratio of short to long essays in Part Two is 2:1, and the value of x must be twice the value of y. Eliminate (A) and (D), in which x is an odd number, because they entail non-integer values of y. Now, Plug In the Answers, beginning with (C).

If $x = 8$, then there are 8 short essays and 4 long essays available in Part Two, and $8 \times 4 = 32$ ways to select these essays. In this case, because there are $4 \times 2 = 8$ ways to select essays in Part One, there are $8 \times 32 = 256$ different lineups of essays a student can choose. This does not match the criterion in the question stem, which states that there are 144 different lineups. Since the number of essays in Part One is fixed, there must be fewer essays available in Part Two. Try (B).

If $x = 6$, then there are 6 short essays and 3 long essays available in Part Two, and $6 \times 3 = 18$ ways to select these essays. In this case, because there are 8 ways to select essays in Part One, there are $8 \times 18 = 144$ different lineups of essays a student can choose. This matches the criterion in the question stem, so the correct answer is (B).

Page 194—Challenge Question #10

A The problem asks for the value of z, so begin manipulating the information in the question to work towards z. The sum of the angles in a triangle is 180°, so the equation of the smaller triangle that contains z is $z + 85 + (x + 15) = 180$. Simplify the equation to find that $z + x + 100 = 180$ and $z + x = 80$. Because the larger triangle contains a value of x, solve for x, so $x = 80 - z$. Now, write the equation for the larger triangle and solve the equation for x. The equation for the larger triangle is $z + (2x - 5) + 65 = 180$, which simplifies to $z + 2x + 60 = 180$ and $z + 2x = 120$. Solve for x, so $2x = 120 - z$ and $x = \dfrac{120 - z}{2}$. Next, set the equations equal to each other, so $80 - z = \dfrac{120 - z}{2}$. Finally, solve for z, so $160 - 2z = 120 - z$ and $160 = 120 + z$, so $40 = z$. The correct answer is (A).

Page 202—Challenge Question #11

B   Begin by drawing the figure. Drawing the triangle with angles consistent with the information in the problem yields a scalene triangle. When solving for side lengths of unfamiliar triangles, always look for ways to create a more familiar shape. Recognize that the length of $6\sqrt{2}$ for SR indicates the possible presence of a 45°-45°-90° triangle. Draw lines vertically down from point S and horizontally left from point R. Label the new point Z for reference.

Solving for the measure of angle SRT yields 180 − 30 − 15 = 135°. Because the straight line created by the extension of the figure left from point R has to have a degree measure of 180°, the degree measure of angle ZRS is 180° − 135° = 45°. Because $\angle SZT$ is 90°, triangle ZRS is a 45°-45°-90° triangle. The problem provides that angle RST is 15°, which means that angle ZST is 45° + 15° = 60°. Therefore, triangle ZST is a 30°-60°-90° triangle, with sides in a ratio of $x : x\sqrt{3} : 2x$. Because triangle ZSR is a 45°-45°-90° triangle, with sides in a ratio of $x : x : x\sqrt{2}$, and SR is $6\sqrt{2}$, SZ is 6. SZ relates to the x side of the 30°-60°-90° triangle, so ST, which relates to the $2x$ side of the 30°-60°-90° triangle, is 12. The correct answer is (B).

Page 210—Challenge Question #12

B   There are variables in the answer choices, so Plug In values for h and k. The value of k must be twice the value of h, so let $h = 2$ and $k = 4$. Draw a circle with center (2, 4) that is tangent to the y-axis. Create a right triangle by drawing lines from the center of the circle to the y-axis and the origin, such that the vertices of the triangle lie at points (0, 0), (0, 4), and (2, 4). Use the Pythagorean Theorem, $a^2 + b^2 = c^2$, to determine the length of the triangle's hypotenuse, c. The shorter sides of the triangle are of lengths 2 and 4, so $2^2 + 4^2 = c^2$. Simplify the equation, so that $c^2 = 20$. Take the positive square root of both sides of the equation, so that the distance from the origin to the center of the circle is $2\sqrt{5}$. Now, Plug In $k = 4$ for each of the answer choices, looking for the answer that equals $2\sqrt{5}$.

Choice (A) is $\dfrac{4\sqrt{3}}{2}=2\sqrt{3}$, so eliminate (A). Choice (B) is $\dfrac{4\sqrt{5}}{2}=2\sqrt{5}$, so keep (B). Choice (C) is 4, so eliminate (C). Choice (D) is $4\sqrt{3}$, so eliminate (D). Choice (E) is $4\sqrt{5}$, so eliminate (E). The correct answer is (B).

Page 225—Challenge Question #13

E   This is a value data sufficiency question, so begin by determining what is known and what is needed to answer the question. What is known is that Angela is twice as old as the sum of Bill's and Charlie's ages. This information can be expressed algebraically: let a be Angela's age, b be Bill's age, and c be Charlie's age. Thus, $a = 2(b + c)$. To solve this equation, what is needed are values for both a and b or two more distinct equations with all three variables.

Now, evaluate Statement (1). In four years, each of the people will have aged, so make sure to include this information in an algebraic equation: $(a + 4) + (b + 4) + (c + 4) = 108$. This equation simplifies into $a + b + c = 96$. This statement gives another equation with all 3 variables. However, there are still 3 variables and only 2 equations. This statement is therefore insufficient. Write down BCE.

Now, evaluate Statement (2). Remember that an average is calculated by adding the values and dividing by the number of values. Also, five years ago will affect each person's age, so make sure this information is included in the algebraic expression: $\dfrac{(a - 5) + (b - 5) + (c - 5)}{3} = 27$, which simplifies to: $a + b + c - 15 = 81$ or $a + b + c = 96$. This statement gives an equation with all 3 variables. But, there are still 3 variables and only 2 equations. This statement is therefore insufficient. Eliminate (B).

Finally, evaluate the two statements combined. The rules for simultaneous equations require that each of the three equations be distinct. Since the equation for Statement (1) is identical to that of Statement (2), the combination of the two statements still only gives 2 equations and 3 variables. The two statements together are therefore insufficient. The correct answer is (E).

Page 227—Challenge Question #14

C   This is a Yes/No Data Sufficiency question. However, there is information in the question stem that should be considered, so use the Pieces of the Puzzle approach to assess the question. The question asks whether the area of triangle ABD is equal to the area of triangle BCD. Since the two triangles share a common height, BD, their areas will be equal only if their bases, AD and DC, are the same length. Therefore, in order to answer the question, the statements must provide information sufficient to determine whether $AD = DC$. The task of a Yes/No Data Sufficiency question is to determine whether the information in the statements produces a consistent "Yes" or "No" answer to the question. Evaluate the statements one at a time.

Evaluate Statement (1). The length of AD is 2. However, Statement (1) does not provide the length of DC, so it is insufficient to determine whether $AD = DC$. Write down BCE.

Now, evaluate Statement (2). The length of *BD* is 5. However, Statement (2) does not provide the lengths of *AD* and *DC*, so it is insufficient to determine whether *AD* = *DC*. Eliminate (B).

Now, evaluate both statements together. Recognize that triangles *ABD* and *BCD* together form a larger triangle, triangle *ABC*. The Inscribed Angle Theorem dictates that angle *ABC* must be 90°, so triangle *ABC* is a right triangle, and $(AB)^2 + (BC)^2 = (AC)^2$. From Statement (1), *AD* = 2. Therefore, *AC* = *DC* + 2. Substitute this value of *AC* into the equation above, so that $(AB)^2 + (BC)^2 = (DC + 2)^2$. If the values of $(AB)^2$ and $(BC)^2$ can be determined, then the length of *DC* can be determined. Determine the value of $(AB)^2$. If *AD* = 2 and *BD* = 5, then $2^2 + 5^2 = (AB)^2$. Simplify the equation, so that $(AB)^2 = 29$. Substitute this value of $(AB)^2$ into the equation above, so that $29 + (BC)^2 = (DC + 2)^2$. Now, determine the value of $(BC)^2$. If *BD* = 5, then $(DC)^2 + 5^2 = (BC)^2$. Simplify the equation, so that $(BC)^2 = (DC)^2 + 25$. Substitute this value of $(BC)^2$ into the equation above, so that $29 + (DC)^2 + 25 = (DC + 2)^2$. Simplify the equation, so that $(DC)^2 + 54 = (DC)^2 + 4(DC) + 4$. Combine like terms, so that 50 = 4(*DC*). Divide both sides of the equation by 4, so that (*DC*) = 12.5. Since (*DC*) ≠ (*AD*), the areas of triangles *ABD* and *BCD* are not the same, and the answer is "No." Together, both statements are sufficient to answer the question, so eliminate (E). The correct answer is (C).

Page 268—Challenge Question #15

D   The sentence as written contains a parallel construction error in the list *buying…providing…join,* so eliminate (A) and any obvious repeaters. Choice (B) adds the word *to* before *join,* but commits the same error as (A), so eliminate (B). Consider the remaining choices. Choice (C) alters the meaning of the original sentence by stating that the parents will [have] *climbing gear bought,* so eliminate (C). Choice (D) fixes the parallel construction error and creates no new errors, so keep (D). Choice (E) contains a parallel construction error in the list *having bought…provided…allowed,* so eliminate (E). The correct answer is (D).

Page 270—Challenge Question #16

D   The sentence as written contains an invalid comparison between *Edgar Allen Poe* and *Homer's… poetry.* Eliminate (A) and any obvious repeaters. Choices (B) and (E) repeat the invalid comparison and may be eliminated. Consider the remaining choices. Choice (C) creates the phrase, *Unlike Edgar Allen Poe…in the example of Homer,* which incorrect compares *Edgar Allen Poe* to *the example of Homer,* so eliminate (C). Choice (D) fixes the invalid comparison by comparing *Edgar Allen Poe* to *Homer* and makes no new errors. The correct answer is (D).

Page 318—Challenge Question #17

A   The task of the question is to weaken the objection, which means to provide a reason that the proposed tax plan might work despite the objection. The objection is that *such tax savings tend to be kept as profit rather than reinvested.* This objection is significant, because if the savings are not reinvested, there will be no *job creation or corporate investment* as a result of the savings. Thus, the correct answer needs to change something about what happens to the tax savings. Choice (A) indicates that the savings are required to be reinvested, which addresses the objection. Keep (A). Choice (B) is out of scope, as it discusses *personal* investments, so eliminate (B). Choice (C) is reversal—it strengthens the objection, so eliminate (C). Choice (D) is out of scope. It provides a mechanism by which the lower tax rate may not significantly hurt overall government revenue, which is irrelevant to whether the tax plan will produce *job creation or corporate investment,* so eliminate (D). Choice (E) is out of scope, as it discusses reasons for economic issues that cannot be directly tied to a reason that tax savings would be used to create jobs, so eliminate (E). The correct answer is (A).

Page 322—Challenge Question #18

C   Treat the passage as a series of facts and consider whether each answer choice can be proven. Choice (A) is out of scope. Proximity to the strongest warm ocean currents may not mean that any warm ocean currents impact that portion of coastline directly. Eliminate (A). Choice (B) is extreme language, as the other factors of glacial ablation may lead to *high rates* of ablation without warm ocean currents, so eliminate (B). Choice (C) matches the information in the passage. If a rise in ocean temperatures leads to a rise in warm ocean currents along glacial coasts, those currents will cause a rise in submarine melt rates. Thus, submarine melt rates are higher in the presence of warm ocean currents than they are in the absence of warm ocean currents. Keep (C). Choice (D) is extreme. While global climactic shifts may increase the occurrence of submarine melt rates, submarine melt may still have been an important factor in prior periods, so eliminate (D). Choice (E) is extreme language. Lower ocean temperatures may lead to a reduction in submarine melt rates, but that doesn't prove that snow accumulation will be a more significant factor. Eliminate (E). The correct answer is (C).

Part VII
The Princeton Review GMAT Math and Verbal Warm-Up Test and Explanations

Chapter 22
GMAT Math and Verbal Warm-Up Test

The purpose of this 60-minute test is to get a rough idea of your current scoring range on the Math and Verbal sections of the GMAT and rough percentiles. Using these scores as a guide, you can then select from the bins of practice questions that follow to improve your performance.

According to the test makers, the computer-adaptive sections of the GMAT hone in on your approximate scoring level after only a few questions. You then spend the rest of the test time answering questions from around that level of difficulty, chosen by the computer from bins of potential questions.

To further refine your assessment of where you are right now, we recommend that you take one of The Princeton Review computer-adaptive tests (available for free online). See the Get More (Free) Content section at the beginning of this book for details. We also highly recommend that you take an actual computer-adaptive GMAT, downloadable for free from the GMAT website at **www.mba.com**.

Math Test
Time—30 Minutes
20 Questions

This test is composed of both problem solving questions and data sufficiency questions.

<u>Problem Solving Directions</u>: Solve each problem and choose the best of the answer choices provided.

<u>Data Sufficiency Directions</u>: Each <u>data sufficiency</u> problem consists of a question and two statements, labeled (1) and (2), which contain certain data. Using these data and your knowledge of mathematics and everyday facts (such as the number of days in July or the meaning of *counterclockwise*), decide whether the data given are sufficient for answering the question and then indicate one of the following answer choices:

- ○ Statement (1) ALONE is sufficient, but statement (2) alone is not sufficient.
- ○ Statement (2) ALONE is sufficient, but statement (1) alone is not sufficient.
- ○ BOTH statements TOGETHER are sufficient, but NEITHER statement ALONE is sufficient.
- ○ EACH statement ALONE is sufficient.
- ○ Statements (1) and (2) TOGETHER are not sufficient.

---

1. If $(16)(3^2) = x(2^3)$, then $x =$

   - ○ 81
   - ○ 72
   - ⊘ 18
   - ○ 16
   - ○ 8

2. By how many dollars is the price of a certain portable tape recorder reduced during a sale?

   (1) The price of the portable tape recorder is reduced by 25% during the sale.

   (2) The sale price of the portable tape recorder is $36.

   - ○ Statement (1) ALONE is sufficient, but statement (2) alone is not sufficient.
   - ○ Statement (2) ALONE is sufficient, but statement (1) alone is not sufficient.
   - ⊘ BOTH statements TOGETHER are sufficient, but NEITHER statement ALONE is sufficient.
   - ○ EACH statement ALONE is sufficient.
   - ○ Statements (1) and (2) TOGETHER are not sufficient.

GO ON TO THE NEXT PAGE.

3. Of the 720 players who participated in a softball tournament, 65 percent traveled more than 200 miles to play. What is the difference between the number of participants who traveled more than 200 miles and the number of participants who traveled 200 miles or less?

- ○ 108
- ● 216
- ○ 252
- ○ 468
- ○ 655

handwritten: 720 −468 → 152

handwritten: 720 ×.65 ... 468 468 −152 316

4. If $r - s = 240$, does $r = 320$?

(1) $r = 4s$

(2) $s = 80$

- ○ Statement (1) ALONE is sufficient, but statement (2) alone is not sufficient.
- ● Statement (2) ALONE is sufficient, but statement (1) alone is not sufficient.
- ○ BOTH statements TOGETHER are sufficient, but NEITHER statement ALONE is sufficient.
- ○ EACH statement ALONE is sufficient.
- ○ Statements (1) and (2) TOGETHER are not sufficient.

handwritten: $r = 320$

5. If a heavy-load trailer travels 7 miles in 1 hour and 10 minutes, what is its speed in miles per hour?

- ○ 6
- ● 6.5
- ○ 8
- ○ 8.5
- ○ 10

handwritten: $7 \times \frac{7}{6} = \frac{49}{6}$

6. If Bob purchases 18 cans of soda, how many of the cans do not contain diet soda?

(1) The number of cans Bob purchases that contain diet soda is equal to the number that do not contain diet soda.

(2) Bob purchases an odd number of cans of diet soda.

- ○ Statement (1) ALONE is sufficient, but statement (2) alone is not sufficient.
- ○ Statement (2) ALONE is sufficient, but statement (1) alone is not sufficient.
- ○ BOTH statements TOGETHER are sufficient, but NEITHER statement ALONE is sufficient.
- ○ EACH statement ALONE is sufficient.
- ● Statements (1) and (2) TOGETHER are not sufficient.

GO ON TO THE NEXT PAGE.

7. If y is an odd integer, which of the following must be an even integer?

   ○ $y + 2$
   ○ $y + 6$
   ● $2y - 1$
   ○ $3y$
   ● $3y + 1$

8. At Perry High School, the ratio of students who participate in either the band program or the choral program to students who participate in neither program is 3 to 8. If 220 students attend Perry High School, how many of them participate in neither program?

   ○ 40
   ○ 60
   ○ 100
   ● 160
   ○ 180

   $$220 \times \frac{5}{3} = \frac{1100}{3}$$

   $$220 \times \frac{8}{11} = \frac{1760}{11}$$

   $$\frac{220}{8}$$
   $$\overline{1760}$$

9. The quadrants of the xy-plane are shown in the figure above. Does line d (not shown) pass through Quadrant III ?

   (1) Line d has a negative x-intercept.

   (2) Line f, which is parallel to line d, has a negative y-intercept.

   ● Statement (1) ALONE is sufficient, but statement (2) alone is not sufficient.
   ○ Statement (2) ALONE is sufficient, but statement (1) alone is not sufficient.
   ○ BOTH statements TOGETHER are sufficient, but NEITHER statement ALONE is sufficient.
   ○ EACH statement ALONE is sufficient.
   ○ Statements (1) and (2) TOGETHER are not sufficient.

GO ON TO THE NEXT PAGE.

10. A $240 interest-free loan is to be paid back in equal monthly payments. If a total of $2\frac{1}{2}$ percent of the original amount of the loan is paid back semi-annually, then how many months will it take to pay back $21.00 ?

- ○ 6
- ● 7
- ○ 18
- ○ 21
- ○ 24

$240 \times 2.5\%$

$1\% = 2.4$
$.5\% = 1.2$
$2.5\% = 6$

$\frac{21}{6} = 3.5$

11. If x and y are positive integers, is x a factor of 12 ?

(1) xy is a factor of 12.

(2) $y = 3$

- ● Statement (1) ALONE is sufficient, but statement (2) alone is not sufficient.
- ○ Statement (2) ALONE is sufficient, but statement (1) alone is not sufficient.
- ○ BOTH statements TOGETHER are sufficient, but NEITHER statement ALONE is sufficient.
- ○ EACH statement ALONE is sufficient.
- ○ Statements (1) and (2) TOGETHER are not sufficient.

12. If a zebra can only get water from either a stream or a pond, which of the two sources of water is closer to the zebra's current position?

(1) Moving at a constant rate from its current position, the zebra reaches the stream in 2 hours.

(2) Moving at a constant rate from the stream, the zebra takes 2 hours to reach the pond.

- ○ Statement (1) ALONE is sufficient, but statement (2) alone is not sufficient.
- ○ Statement (2) ALONE is sufficient, but statement (1) alone is not sufficient.
- ● BOTH statements TOGETHER are sufficient, but NEITHER statement ALONE is sufficient.
- ○ EACH statement ALONE is sufficient.
- ○ Statements (1) and (2) TOGETHER are not sufficient.

13. What is the value of $x^2 - y^2$?

(1) $x - y = 0$

(2) $x + y = 4$

- ● Statement (1) ALONE is sufficient, but statement (2) alone is not sufficient.
- ○ Statement (2) ALONE is sufficient, but statement (1) alone is not sufficient.
- ○ BOTH statements TOGETHER are sufficient, but NEITHER statement ALONE is sufficient.
- ○ EACH statement ALONE is sufficient.
- ○ Statements (1) and (2) TOGETHER are not sufficient.

GO ON TO THE NEXT PAGE.

14. If the remainder when a certain integer x is divided by 5 is 2, then each of the following could also be an integer, EXCEPT

- ○ $\dfrac{x}{17}$
- ○ $\dfrac{x}{11}$
- ○ $\dfrac{x}{10}$
- ○ $\dfrac{x}{6}$
- ○ $\dfrac{x}{3}$

15. A mixture of ground meat consists of 2 pounds of veal that costs x dollars per pound, and 5 pounds of beef that costs y dollars per pound. What is the cost of the mixture in dollars per pound?

- ⬤ $2x + 5y$
- ○ $\dfrac{2x + 5y}{xy}$
- ○ $5(2x + 5y)$
- ○ $x + y$
- ⬤ $\dfrac{2x + 5y}{7}$

16. Is $0 < y < 1$?

(1) $0 < \sqrt{y} < 1$

(2) $y^2 = \dfrac{1}{4}$

- ○ Statement (1) ALONE is sufficient, but statement (2) alone is not sufficient.
- ○ Statement (2) ALONE is sufficient, but statement (1) alone is not sufficient.
- ○ BOTH statements TOGETHER are sufficient, but NEITHER statement ALONE is sufficient.
- ⬤ EACH statement ALONE is sufficient.
- ○ Statements (1) and (2) TOGETHER are not sufficient.

17. If a and b are positive integers, is ab odd?

(1) $b = 3$

(2) a and b are consecutive integers.

- ○ Statement (1) ALONE is sufficient, but statement (2) alone is not sufficient.
- ⬤ Statement (2) ALONE is sufficient, but statement (1) alone is not sufficient.
- ○ BOTH statements TOGETHER are sufficient, but NEITHER statement ALONE is sufficient.
- ○ EACH statement ALONE is sufficient.
- ○ Statements (1) and (2) TOGETHER are not sufficient.

GO ON TO THE NEXT PAGE.

18. Last year, an appliance store sold an average (arithmetic mean) of 42 microwave ovens per month. In the first 10 months of this year, the store sold an average of only 20 microwaves per month. What is the average number of microwaves sold per month for the entire 22-month period?

ADVANCE PURCHASE DISCOUNTS FOR AIRLINE TRAVEL	
Days Prior to Departure	**Percentage Discount**
0–6 days	0%
7–13 days	10%
14–29 days	25%
30 days or more	40%

○ 29
○ 30
● 31
○ 32
○ 42

19. If *AB* is the diameter of the circle with center *X* and *C* is a point on the circle such that *AC* = *AX* = 3, what is the perimeter of triangle *ABC* ?

20. The table above shows the discount structure for advance purchase of tickets at a particular airline. A passenger bought a ticket at this airline for $1,050. Had she purchased the ticket one day later, she would have paid $210 more. How many days before her departure did she purchase her ticket?

○ 6 days
○ 7 days
○ 13 days
○ 14 days
○ 29 days

○ $\dfrac{9\sqrt{3}}{2}$

○ 9

● $6 + 3\sqrt{3}$

○ $9 + 3\sqrt{3}$

○ $9\sqrt{3}$

GO ON TO THE NEXT PAGE.

Verbal Test
Time—30 Minutes
20 Questions

This test is made up of sentence correction, critical reasoning, and reading comprehension questions.

<u>Sentence Correction Directions</u>: Each of the <u>sentence correction</u> questions presents a sentence, part or all of which is underlined. Beneath the sentence you will find five ways of phrasing the underlined part. The first of these repeats the original; the other four are different. Follow the requirements of standard written English to choose your answer, paying attention to grammar, word choice, and sentence construction. Select the answer that produces the most effective sentence; your answer should make the sentence clear, exact, and free of grammatical errors. It should also minimize awkwardness, ambiguity, and redundancy.

<u>Reading Comprehension Directions</u>: Each of the <u>reading comprehension</u> questions is based on the content of a passage. After reading the passage, answer all questions pertaining to it on the basis of what is <u>stated</u> or <u>implied</u> in the passage. For each question, select the best answer of the choices given.

<u>Critical Reasoning Directions</u>: Each of the <u>critical reasoning</u> questions is based on a short argument, a set of statements, or a plan of action. For each question, select the best answer of the choices given.

---

21. Unseasonable weather in the months before a wine harvest can cool vineyards in the Bordeaux region enough <u>to affect the overall size of the grapes themselves, create</u> unwanted moisture that can cause mold in some grape varieties and deterioration in others.

- ⊘ to affect the overall size of the grapes themselves, create
- ● to affect the overall size of the grapes themselves and create
- ⊘ that the overall size of the grapes themselves are affected, create
- ⊘ that it affects the overall size of the grapes themselves, creates
- ○ that the size of the grapes are affected and creates

22. It is posited by some scientists that the near extinction of the sap-eating gray bat of northwestern America was caused by government-sponsored logging operations in the early 1920s that greatly reduced the species' habitat.

Which of the following, if true, most strongly weakens the scientists' claims?

- ○ Logging operations in the 1920s are widely held responsible for the near extinction of other species that lived in the same area.
- ○ A boom in new home construction in the early 1920s led congress to open federal lands to logging operations.
- ● A 5-year drought in the early 1920s severely reduced the output of sap in trees in northwestern America.
- ○ Numbers of sightings of sap-eating gray bats fell to their lowest numbers in 1926.
- ○ Sightings of sap-eating gray bats in Europe stayed roughly the same during the same period.

GO ON TO THE NEXT PAGE.

23. Upset by the recent downturn in production numbers during the first half of the year, <u>the possibility of adding worker incentives was raised by the board of directors at its quarterly meeting</u>.

- the possibility of adding worker incentives was raised by the board of directors at its quarterly meeting
- the addition of worker incentives was raised as a possibility by the board of directors at its quarterly meeting
- added worker incentives was raised by the board of directors at its quarterly meeting as a possibility
- the board of directors raised at its quarterly meeting the possibility of worker incentives being added
- the board of directors, at its quarterly meeting, raised the possibility of adding worker incentives

24. Whenever a major airplane accident occurs, there is a dramatic increase in the number of airplane mishaps reported in the media, a phenomenon that may last for as long as a few months after the accident. Airline officials assert that the publicity given the gruesomeness of major airplane accidents focuses media attention on the airline industry, and the increase in the number of reported accidents is caused by an increase in the number of news sources covering airline accidents, not by an increase in the number of accidents.

Which of the following, if true, would seriously weaken the assertions of the airline officials?

- The publicity surrounding airline accidents is largely limited to the country in which the crash occurred.
- Airline accidents tend to occur far more often during certain peak travel months.
- Media organizations do not have any guidelines to help them decide how severe an accident must be for it to receive coverage.
- Airplane accidents receive coverage by news sources only when the news sources find it advantageous to do so.
- Studies by government regulators show that the number of airplane flight miles remains relatively constant from month to month.

GO ON TO THE NEXT PAGE.

Questions 25–28 are based on the following passage:

The function of strategic planning is to position a company for long-term growth and expansion in a variety of markets by analyzing its strengths and weaknesses and examining current and
(5) potential opportunities. Based on this information, the company develops a strategy for itself. That strategy becomes the basis for supporting strategies for the company's various departments.

This implementation strategy is where all too
(10) many strategic plans go astray. Recent business management surveys show that most CEOs who have a strategic plan are concerned with the potential breakdown in the implementation of the plan. Unlike corporations in the 1980s that blindly
(15) followed their 5-year plans, even when they were misguided, today's corporations tend to second-guess their long-term plans.

Outsiders can help facilitate the process, but in the final analysis, if the company does not make
(20) the plan, the company will not follow the plan. This was one of the problems with strategic planning in the 1980s. In that era, strategic planning was an abstract, top-down process involving only a few top corporate officers and hired guns. Number
(25) crunching experts came into a company and generated tome-like volumes filled with a mixture of abstruse facts and grand theories that had little to do with the day-to-day realities of the company. Key middle managers were left out of planning
(30) sessions, resulting in lost opportunities and ruffled feelings.

However, more hands-on strategic planning can produce startling results. A recent survey queried more than a thousand small-to-medium sized
(35) businesses to compare companies with a strategic plan to companies without one. The survey found that companies with strategic plans had annual revenue growth of 6.2 percent as opposed to 3.8 percent for the other companies.
(40) Perhaps most important, a strategic plan helps companies anticipate—and survive—change. New technology and the mobility of capital means that markets can shift faster than ever before. Some financial analysts wonder why companies
(45) should bother planning two years ahead when market dynamics might be transformed by next quarter. However, it is this pace of change that makes planning so crucial. Now, more than ever, companies have to stay alert to the marketplace.
(50) In an environment of continual and rapid change, long-range planning expands options and organizational flexibility.

25. The primary purpose of the passage is to

○ refute the idea that change is bad for a corporation's long-term health
● describe how long-term planning, despite some potential pitfalls, can help a corporation to grow
○ compare and contrast two styles of corporate planning
○ evaluate the strategic planning goals of corporate America today
○ defend a methodology that has come under sharp attack

26. It can be inferred from the passage that strategic planning during the 1980s had all of the following shortcomings EXCEPT

○ a reliance on outside consultants who did not necessarily understand the nuts and bolts of the business
○ a dependence on theoretical models that did not always perfectly describe the workings of the company
● an inherent weakness in the company's own ability to implement the strategic plan
○ an excess of information and data that made it difficult to get to key concepts
○ the lack of a forum for middle managers to express their ideas

GO ON TO THE NEXT PAGE.

27. The author most likely mentions the results of the survey of 1,000 companies in order to

    ○ put forth an opposing view on strategic plans which is later refuted
    ○ illustrate that when strategic planning is "hands-on," it produces uninspiring results
    ○ give a concrete example of why strategic planning did not work during the 1980s
    ● support the contention that strategic planning can be very successful when done correctly
    ○ give supporting data to prove that many companies have implemented strategic plans

28. The passage suggests which of the following about the "financial analysts" mentioned in lines 44–47 ?

    ○ They believe that strategic planning is the key to weathering the rapid changes of the marketplace.
    ○ They are working to understand and anticipate market developments that are two years ahead.
    ○ Their study of market dynamics has led them to question the reliability of short-term planning strategies.
    ● They might not agree with the author that one way to survive rapidly changing conditions comes from long-range planning.
    ○ They consider the mobility of capital to be a necessary condition for the growth of new technology.

29. The Internal Revenue Service has directed that taxpayers who generate no self-employment income can no longer deduct home offices, home office expenses, <u>or nothing that was already</u> depreciated as a business expense the previous year.

    ○ or nothing that was already
    ○ or that was already
    ● or anything that was already
    ○ and anything
    ○ and nothing that already was

30. Informed people generally assimilate information from several divergent sources before coming to an opinion. However, most popular news organizations view foreign affairs solely through the eyes of our State Department. In reporting the political crisis in a foreign country, news organizations must endeavor to find alternative sources of information.

    Which of the following inferences can be drawn from the argument above?

    ○ To the degree that a news source gives an account of another country that mirrors that of our State Department, that reporting is suspect.
    ○ To protect their integrity, news media should avoid the influence of State Department releases in their coverage of foreign affairs.
    ○ Reporting that is not influenced by the State Department is usually more accurate than are other accounts.
    ● The alternative sources of information mentioned in the passage might not share the same views as the State Department.
    ○ A report cannot be seen as influenced by the State Department if it accurately depicts the events in a foreign country.

GO ON TO THE NEXT PAGE.

31. When automatic teller machines were first installed in the 1980s, bank officials promised <u>they would be faster, more reliable, and less prone to make errors</u> than their human counterparts.

○ they would be faster, more reliable, and less prone to make errors

○ they would be faster, more reliable, and that they would be less prone for making errors

● the machines would be faster, more reliable, and less prone to errors

○ the machines were faster, more reliable, and errors would occur much less

○ faster, more reliable machines, and that errors would be less prone

32. With its plan to create a wildlife sanctuary out of previously unused landfill, Sweden is but one of a number of industrialized nations that <u>is accepting its responsibility to protect endangered species and promote</u> conservation.

○ is accepting its responsibility to protect endangered species and promote

○ is accepting its responsibility for protecting endangered species and promoting

○ are accepting its responsibility to protect endangered species and promoting

● are accepting of their responsibility to protect endangered species and to promote

○ are accepting their responsibility to protect endangered species and promote

33. A decade after a logging operation in India began cutting down trees in a territory that serves as a sanctuary for Bengal tigers, the incidence of tigers attacking humans in nearby villages has increased by 300 percent. Because the logging operation has reduced the number of acres of woodland per tiger on average from 15 acres to approximately 12 acres, scientists have theorized that tigers must need a minimum number of acres of woodland in order to remain content.

Which of the following statements, if true, would most strengthen the scientists' hypothesis?

● In other wildlife areas in India where the number of acres of woodland per tiger remains at least 15 acres, there has been no increase in the number of tiger attacks on humans.

○ Before the logging operation began, there were many fewer humans living in the area.

○ The largest number of acres per tiger before the logging operation began was 32 acres per tiger in one area of the sanctuary, whereas the smallest number of acres per tiger after the logging operation was 9 acres.

○ Other species of wild animals have begun competing with the Bengal tigers for the dwindling food supply.

○ The Bengal tiger has become completely extinct in other areas of Asia.

GO ON TO THE NEXT PAGE.

34. The machine press union and company management were not able to communicate effectively, and it was a major cause of the 1999 strike in Seattle.

    ○ The machine press union and company management were not able to communicate effectively, and it

    ○ Communications between the machine press union and company management were not effective, and it

    ○ For the machine press union and company management, to be unable to communicate effectively

    ● The inability of the machine press union and company management to communicate effectively

    ○ The machine press union, being unable to communicate effectively with company management,

35. A greater number of fresh vegetables are sold in City X than in City Y. Therefore, the people in City X have better nutritional habits than those in City Y.

    Each of the following, if true, weakens the conclusion above EXCEPT:

    ○ City X has more people living in it than City Y.

    ○ Most of the people in City Y work in City X and buy their vegetables there.

    ○ The people in City X buy many of their vegetables as decorations, not to eat.

    ● The per capita consumption of junk food in City X is three times that of City Y.

    ● The average price per pound of vegetables in City Y is lower than the average price per pound of vegetables in City X.

36. Heavy metals, toxic waste by-products that can cause tumors in fish, are generally found in the waters off industrial shorelines, but have been discovered in trace amounts even in the relatively pristine waters of the South Pacific.

    ● are generally found in the waters off industrial shorelines, but have been discovered in trace amounts even

    ○ are generally to be found in the waters off industrial shorelines, and have even been discovered in trace amounts

    ○ can, in general, be found in the waters off industrial shorelines, and have been discovered in trace amounts even

    ○ had generally been found in the waters off industrial shorelines, but have even been discovered in trace amounts

    ○ are found generally in the waters off industrial shorelines, but have been discovered in a trace amount even

GO ON TO THE NEXT PAGE.

Questions 37–40 are based on the following passage:

In Roman times, defeated enemies were generally put to death as criminals for having offended the emperor of Rome. In the Middle
Line Ages, however, the practice of ransoming, or
(5) returning prisoners in exchange for money, became common. Though some saw this custom as a step toward a more humane society, the primary reasons behind it were economic rather than humanitarian.
(10) In those times, rulers had only a limited ability to raise taxes. They could neither force their subjects to fight nor pay them to do so. The promise of material compensation in the form of goods and ransom was therefore the only way of inducing
(15) combatants to participate in a war. In the Middle Ages, the predominant incentive for the individual soldier was the expectation of spoils. Although collecting ransom clearly brought financial gain, keeping a prisoner and arranging for his exchange
(20) had its costs. Consequently, procedures were devised to reduce transaction costs.
One such device was a rule asserting that the prisoner had to assess his own value. This compelled the prisoner to establish a value without
(25) too much distortion; indicating too low a value would increase the captive's chances of being killed, while indicating too high a value would either ruin him financially or create a prohibitively expensive ransom that would also result in death.

37. The primary purpose of the passage is to

- ⬤ discuss the economic basis of the medieval practice of exchanging prisoners for ransom
- ◯ examine the history of the treatment of prisoners of war
- ◯ emphasize the importance of a warrior's code of honor during the Middle Ages
- ◯ explore a way of reducing the costs of ransom
- ◯ demonstrate why warriors of the Middle Ages looked forward to battles

38. It can be inferred from the passage that a medieval soldier

- ◯ was less likely to kill captured members of opposing armies than was a soldier of the Roman Empire
- ⬤ operated on a basically independent level and was motivated solely by economic incentives
- ◯ had few economic options and chose to fight because it was the only way to earn an adequate living
- ◯ was motivated to spare prisoners' lives by humanitarian rather than economic ideals
- ◯ had no respect for his captured enemies since captives were typically regarded as weak

GO ON TO THE NEXT PAGE.

Which of the following best describes the change in policy from executing prisoners in Roman times to ransoming prisoners in the Middle Ages?

○ The emperors of Rome demanded more respect than did medieval rulers, and thus Roman subjects went to greater lengths to defend their nation.

○ It was a reflection of the lesser degree of direct control medieval rulers had over their subjects.

○ It became a show of strength and honor for warriors of the Middle Ages to be able to capture and return their enemies.

● Medieval soldiers were not as humanitarian as their ransoming practices might have indicated.

○ Medieval soldiers demonstrated more concern about economic policy than did their Roman counterparts.

40. The author uses the phrase "without too much distortion" (lines 24–25) in order to

● indicate that prisoners would fairly assess their worth

○ emphasize the important role medieval prisoners played in determining whether they should be ransomed

○ explain how prisoners often paid more than an appropriate ransom in order to increase their chances for survival

○ suggest that captors and captives often had understanding relationships

○ show that when in prison a soldier's view could become distorted

END OF WARM-UP TEST

Chapter 23
GMAT Math and Verbal Warm-Up Test: Answers and Explanations

GMAT WARM-UP TEST SCORING GUIDE

Detailed explanations to these answers can be found on page 490.

ANSWER KEY

MATH		VERBAL	
1.	C	21.	B
2.	C	22.	C
3.	B	23.	E
~~4.~~	D	~~24.~~	B
~~5.~~	A	25.	B
~~6.~~	A	26.	C
7.	E	27.	D
8.	D	28.	D
9.	A	29.	C
~~10.~~	D	30.	D
11.	A	31.	C
~~12.~~	E	~~32.~~	E
13.	A	33.	A
~~14.~~	C	34.	D
~~15.~~	E	35.	E
~~16.~~	A	36.	A
17.	B	37.	A
~~18.~~	D	~~38.~~	A
~~19.~~	D	~~39.~~	B
~~20.~~	D	~~40.~~	A

$$\frac{10}{20} \qquad \frac{16}{20} = \frac{26}{40}$$

The Math Score

If you got 6 or fewer math questions correct: Your percentile rank is in the lower one-third of the testing group and you should begin by practicing the problems in Math Bin 1. Once you've mastered the material in Math Bin 1, you should move on to the questions in Math Bin 2 of our practice test.

If you got between 6 and 13 math questions correct: Your percentile rank is in the middle one-third of the testing group and you should begin by practicing the problems in Math Bin 2 of our practice test. Once you've mastered the material in Math Bin 2, you should move on to the questions in Math Bin 3.

If you got 14 or more math questions correct: Your percentile rank is in the top one-third of the testing group and you should begin by practicing the problems in Math Bins 3 and 4 of our practice test.

The Verbal Score

If you got 6 or fewer verbal questions correct: Your percentile rank is in the lower one-third of the testing group and you should begin by practicing the problems in Verbal Bin 1 of our practice test. Once you've mastered the material in Verbal Bin 1, you should move on to the questions in Verbal Bin 2.

If you got between 6 and 13 verbal questions correct: Your percentile rank is in the middle one-third of the testing group and you should begin by practicing the problems in Verbal Bin 2 of our practice test. Once you've mastered the material in Verbal Bin 2, you should move on to the questions in Verbal Bin 3 of our practice test.

If you got 14 or more verbal questions correct: Your percentile rank is in the top one-third of the testing group and you should begin by practicing the problems in Verbal Bin 3 of our practice test.

(If you want additional practice for either the Math or the Verbal section, you may find it helpful to do the problems in a bin with a lower number than the one suggested. So if your math diagnostic score indicates that you should do the questions in Math Bin 2, you might want to do the questions in Math Bin 1 as well.)

The Combined Score

If you got 12 or fewer of the 40 total questions correct: Your combined score at the moment is less than 450.

If you got between 12 and 31 of the 40 total questions correct: Your combined score at the moment is between 450 and 550.

If you got 32 or more of the 40 total questions correct: Your combined score at the moment is more than 550.

1. If $(16)(3^2) = x(2^3)$, then $x =$

   ○ 81
   ○ 72
   ○ 18
   ○ 16
   ○ 8

1. **C** Rather than multiply out each side of the equation, recognize that 16 is really 2^4. Divide 2^3 from each side of the equation to get $2(3)^2 = x$. The correct answer is 18, or (C).

2. By how many dollars is the price of a certain portable tape recorder reduced during a sale?

   (1) The price of the portable tape recorder is reduced by 25% during the sale.

   (2) The sale price of the portable tape recorder is $36.

   ○ Statement (1) ALONE is sufficient, but statement (2) alone is not sufficient.
   ○ Statement (2) ALONE is sufficient, but statement (1) alone is not sufficient.
   ○ BOTH statements TOGETHER are sufficient, but NEITHER statement ALONE is sufficient.
   ○ EACH statement ALONE is sufficient.
   ○ Statements (1) and (2) TOGETHER are not sufficient.

2. **C** Statement (1) gives the percent reduction, but the actual price or sale price is not given. Statement (1) is insufficient. Write BCE.
   Statement (2) gives the sale price, but no information is given about the original amount or percent reduction. Cross off (B).
   Statements (1) and (2) together give both the percent reduction and the sale price, so the original price could be figured out and therefore so could the amount that the price is reduced. The two statements together are sufficient. The correct answer is (C).

3. Of the 720 players who participated in a softball tournament, 65 percent traveled more than 200 miles to play. What is the difference between the number of participants who traveled more than 200 miles and the number of participants who traveled 200 miles or less?

   ○ 108
   ○ 216
   ○ 252
   ○ 468
   ○ 655

3. **B** This is a percent problem, so start by finding the number of players who traveled more than 200 miles: 65% of 720 is 468. The number of players who traveled 200 miles or less, then, is 720 − 468 = 252 (or, alternatively, 35% of 720 is 252). Although both 468 and 252 are answer choices, the question asks for the difference between the two types of participants: 468 − 252 = 216. Alternately, the question can be solved using difference of the percentages rather than that of the actual numbers of people: 65% traveled more than 200 miles so 35% had to travel less than 200 miles. The difference is 30%. 30% of 720 is 216.

| QUESTIONS | MATH EXPLANATIONS |

QUESTIONS

4. If $r - s = 240$, does $r = 320$?

   (1) $r = 4s$

   (2) $s = 80$

   ○ Statement (1) ALONE is sufficient, but statement (2) alone is not sufficient.
   ○ Statement (2) ALONE is sufficient, but statement (1) alone is not sufficient.
   ○ BOTH statements TOGETHER are sufficient, but NEITHER statement ALONE is sufficient.
   ○ EACH statement ALONE is sufficient.
   ○ Statements (1) and (2) TOGETHER are not sufficient.

5. If a heavy-load trailer travels 7 miles in 1 hour and 10 minutes, what is its speed in miles per hour?

   ○ 6
   ○ 6.5
   ○ 8
   ○ 8.5
   ○ 10

6. If Bob purchases 18 cans of soda, how many of the cans do not contain diet soda?

   (1) The number of cans Bob purchases that contain diet soda is equal to the number that do not contain diet soda.

   (2) Bob purchases an odd number of cans of diet soda.

   ○ Statement (1) ALONE is sufficient, but statement (2) alone is not sufficient.
   ○ Statement (2) ALONE is sufficient, but statement (1) alone is not sufficient.
   ○ BOTH statements TOGETHER are sufficient, but NEITHER statement ALONE is sufficient.
   ○ EACH statement ALONE is sufficient.
   ○ Statements (1) and (2) TOGETHER are not sufficient.

MATH EXPLANATIONS

 4. D Evaluate Statement (1). If $r = 4s$, then substitute $4s$ into r in the original equation to find that $4s - s = 240$. Therefore, $3s = 240$ and $s = 80$. So, $r = 320$. Write down AD. Statement (2) provides a value for s that can be used in the original equation to solve and find that $r = 320$. The correct answer is (D).

 5. A The question mentions distances and rates, so make a rate pie. The distance is 7 miles. The time is 1 hour and 10 minutes. Convert 1 hour and 10 minutes to hours. 10 minutes is $\frac{1}{6}$ of an hour. So, the time is $1\frac{1}{6}$. Divide to find time: $\frac{7}{1\frac{1}{6}} = \frac{7}{\frac{7}{6}} = 7 \times \frac{6}{7} = 6$. The correct answer is (A).

6. A The question states that Bob purchases a total of 18 cans of soda. Statement (1) states there is an equal number of diet and non-diet cans, which means that there must be 9 of each. Statement (1) is sufficient. Write AD.
Statement (2) states that there are an odd number of cans of diet soda, but that could be 5 cans or 11 cans. Statement (2) is insufficient.

QUESTIONS

7. If y is an odd integer, which of the following must be an even integer?

   ○ $y + 2$
   ○ $y + 6$
   ○ $2y - 1$
   ○ $3y$
   ○ $3y + 1$

8. At Perry High School, the ratio of students who participate in either the band program or the choral program to students who participate in neither program is 3 to 8. If 220 students attend Perry High School, how many of them participate in neither program?

   ○ 40
   ○ 60
   ○ 100
   ○ 160
   ○ 180

MATH EXPLANATIONS

7. **E** This question is a must be question with variables, so Plug In (possibly more than once). Since y must be odd, try $y = 3$. If $y = 3$, then (A) is 5, which is not even, so eliminate (A). Choice (B) is 9, which is also not even, so eliminate (B). Choice (C) is 5, which is again not even. Eliminate (C). Choice (D) is 9, which is not even. Eliminate (D). Choice (E) is 10. Since (E) is the only answer choice to give an even integer, it must be the correct answer.

8. **D** The question involves ratios, so set up a ratio box. The ratio of the students who participate to those who don't is 3 to 8 and the total number of students is 220. Filling those into the box gives a multiplier of 20. Then, multiply 8 by 20 to get 160 students who don't participate in either program. The ratio box looks like this:

	Participate	Don't Participate	Total
Ratio	3	8	11
Multiplier	20	20	20
Actual	60	160	220

The correct answer is (D).

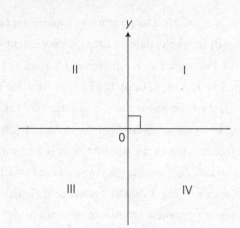

9. The quadrants of the *xy*-plane are shown in the figure above. Does line *d* (not shown) pass through Quadrant III ?

    (1) Line *d* has a negative *x*-intercept.

    (2) Line *f*, which is parallel to line *d*, has a negative *y*-intercept.

    ○ Statement (1) ALONE is sufficient, but statement (2) alone is not sufficient.
    ○ Statement (2) ALONE is sufficient, but statement (1) alone is not sufficient.
    ○ BOTH statements TOGETHER are sufficient, but NEITHER statement ALONE is sufficient.
    ○ EACH statement ALONE is sufficient.
    ○ Statements (1) and (2) TOGETHER are not sufficient.

9. A   Statement (1) states that line *d* has a negative *x*-intercept. The *x*-intercept is where the line passes through the *x*-axis. If the *x*-intercept is negative, then the line must pass through both Quadrants II and III. Statement (1) is sufficient. Write AD. Statement (2) states that line *f* has a negative *y*-intercept (where it crosses the *y*-axis) and that line *f* is parallel to line *d*. Even though the lines are parallel and must have the same slope, line *d* could have a negative *y*-intercept and pass through Quadrant III, or it could have a positive *y*-intercept and a negative slope and therefore not pass through Quadrant III. Statement (2) is insufficient. The correct answer is (A).

10. A $240 interest-free loan is to be paid back in equal monthly payments. If a total of $2\frac{1}{2}$ of the original amount of the loan is paid back semi-annually, then how many months will it take to pay back $21.00 ?

    ○ 6
    ○ 7
    ○ 18
    ○ 21
    ○ 24

10. D   Start by finding $2\frac{1}{2}$ percent of $240, which is $\frac{2.5}{100} \times 240 = 6$. The word semi-annually indicates every 6 months, so every 6 months a total of $6 is repaid. If these amounts are paid back in equal monthly payments, then each month $1 is paid toward the loan. So, to pay back $21.00 would take 21 months, and the correct answer is (D).

11. If x and y are positive integers, then is x a factor of 12 ?

    (1) xy is a factor of 12.

    (2) $y = 3$

    ○ Statement (1) ALONE is sufficient, but statement (2) alone is not sufficient.
    ○ Statement (2) ALONE is sufficient, but statement (1) alone is not sufficient.
    ○ BOTH statements TOGETHER are sufficient, but NEITHER statement ALONE is sufficient.
    ○ EACH statement ALONE is sufficient.
    ○ Statements (1) and (2) TOGETHER are not sufficient.

11. A This is a Yes/No Data Sufficiency question, so Plug In for the variables. Evaluate Statement (1). If the product of xy is a factor of 12, then xy is equal to 1, 2, 3, 4, 6, or 12. Plug In. If $x = 2$ and $y = 3$, then the answer to the question is "Yes." Plug In again to try and get an answer of "No." In fact, as long as the product of xy is a factor of 12, and x and y are integers, x is a factor of 12. Write down AD. Evaluate Statement (2). This statement provides no information about the value of x. Therefore, it is impossible to know if x is a factor of 12. The correct answer is (A).

12. If a zebra can only get water from either a stream or a pond, which of the two sources of water is closer to the zebra's current position?

    (1) Moving at a constant rate from its current position, the zebra reaches the stream in 2 hours.

    (2) Moving at a constant rate from the stream, the zebra takes 2 hours to reach the pond.

    ○ Statement (1) ALONE is sufficient, but statement (2) alone is not sufficient.
    ○ Statement (2) ALONE is sufficient, but statement (1) alone is not sufficient.
    ○ BOTH statements TOGETHER are sufficient, but NEITHER statement ALONE is sufficient.
    ○ EACH statement ALONE is sufficient.
    ○ Statements (1) and (2) TOGETHER are not sufficient.

12. E Statement (1) gives the time it takes the zebra to reach the stream from its current position; however, it gives no information about the time required to reach the pond. Statement (1) is insufficient, and we're down to BCE. Similarly, Statement (2) only gives the time it takes the zebra to get from the pond to the stream—and doesn't mention the zebra's current position. Statement (2) is insufficient. Cross off (B).

Statements (1) and (2) together give how long it takes for the zebra to reach the stream and then how long it takes the zebra to reach the pond from the stream. However, no information is given about the direction. For example, the zebra, pond, and stream might be in a straight line, they could form many different triangles, or the zebra could even double back from the stream to the pond. The two statements together are insufficient. The correct answer to this question is (E).

13. What is the value of $x^2 - y^2$?

(1) $x - y = 0$

(2) $x + y = 4$

○ Statement (1) ALONE is sufficient, but statement (2) alone is not sufficient.
○ Statement (2) ALONE is sufficient, but statement (1) alone is not sufficient.
○ BOTH statements TOGETHER are sufficient, but NEITHER statement ALONE is sufficient.
○ EACH statement ALONE is sufficient.
○ Statements (1) and (2) TOGETHER are not sufficient.

13. **A** Start by noticing that $x^2 - y^2$ is the common quadratic $(x + y)(x - y)$. Statement (1) gives that $x - y = 0$. If $x - y = 0$, the the value of $(x + y)(x - y)$ will also always be 0. Alternatively, plug in some values and the result will still always be 0. Statement (1) is sufficient. Write AD.
Statement (2) gives that $x + y = 4$. No information is given about $x - y$. For example, x and y could both be 2 or x could be 3 and y could be 1, which will give a different value for $x^2 - y^2$. Statement (2) is insufficient. The correct answer is (A).

14. If the remainder when a certain integer x is divided by 5 is 2, then each of the following could also be an integer, EXCEPT

○ $\dfrac{x}{17}$

○ $\dfrac{x}{11}$

○ $\dfrac{x}{10}$

○ $\dfrac{x}{6}$

○ $\dfrac{x}{3}$

 14. **C** As always, when there are variables in the answer choices, the easiest thing to do is Plug In. To get a remainder of 2 when x is divided by 5, x must be a multiple of 5 plus 2 more. In other words, x could be 7 or 12 or 17 or 22, etc. Now, go through the answer choices, plugging in numbers for x that allow them to be integers as well. For example, if $x = 17$, then (A) is $\dfrac{17}{17}$, which is an integer. Cross off (A).
In (B), if $x = 22$, then the result is $\dfrac{22}{11}$, which is an integer. Cross off (B). In (D) and (E), plugging in the number 12 makes both choices integers. Only (C) is never an integer as long as x divided by 5 has a remainder of 2. The correct answer is (C).

15. A mixture of ground meat consists of 2 pounds of veal that costs x dollars per pound, and 5 pounds of beef that costs y dollars per pound. What is the cost of the mixture in dollars per pound?

○ $2x + 5y$

○ $\dfrac{2x + 5y}{xy}$

○ $5(2x + 5y)$

○ $x + y$

○ $\dfrac{2x + 5y}{7}$

15. **E** There are variables in the answer choices, so Plug In. The question asks for the cost of the mixture in dollars per pound, so since there are 7 total pounds of meat, try numbers divisible by 7, such as $x = 14$ and $y = 7$. In that case, the total cost of the mixture is $(2)(14) + (5)(7) = 63$. Divide by 7 to get the cost per pound, which is $9 and is thus the target answer. Plug $x = 14$ and $y = 7$ into the answers. Only (E) matches the target answer.

16. Is $0 < y < 1$?

(1) $0 < \sqrt{y} < 1$

(2) $y^2 = \dfrac{1}{4}$

○ Statement (1) ALONE is sufficient, but statement (2) alone is not sufficient.
○ Statement (2) ALONE is sufficient, but statement (1) alone is not sufficient.
○ BOTH statements TOGETHER are sufficient, but NEITHER statement ALONE is sufficient.
○ EACH statement ALONE is sufficient.
○ Statements (1) and (2) TOGETHER are not sufficient.

16. **A** Statement (1) states that $0 < \sqrt{y} < 1$, so test out possible values of y. The only values of y that will satisfy $0 < \sqrt{y} < 1$ are fractions (such as $\dfrac{1}{4}, \dfrac{1}{2}, \dfrac{4}{9}$, etc.) and the answer to the question will always be a "yes." Statement (1) is sufficient. Write AD.

Statement (2) states that $y^2 = \dfrac{1}{4}$, so y could be either $\dfrac{1}{2}$ or $-\dfrac{1}{2}$. In one case, the answer to the question is a "yes" and in the other it is a "no." Statement (2) is insufficient. The correct answer is (A).

17. If *a* and *b* are positive integers, is *ab* odd?

    (1) $b = 3$

    (2) *a* and *b* are consecutive integers.

    ○ Statement (1) ALONE is sufficient, but statement (2) alone is not sufficient.
    ○ Statement (2) ALONE is sufficient, but statement (1) alone is not sufficient.
    ○ BOTH statements TOGETHER are sufficient, but NEITHER statement ALONE is sufficient.
    ○ EACH statement ALONE is sufficient.
    ○ Statements (1) and (2) TOGETHER are not sufficient.

17. **B** Statement (1) states that $b = 3$. Plug In different values for *a*. If $a = 2$, then $ab = 6$ and the answer to the question is "no." If $a = 3$, the $ab = 9$ and the answer to the question is a "yes." Statement (1) is insufficient. Write BCE.
Statement (2) states that *a* and *b* are consecutive integers. Plug in some values for *a* and *b*. If $a = 2$ and $b = 3$, then $ab = 6$ and the answer to the question is "no." If $a = 3$ and $b = 4$, then $ab = 12$ and the answer is still "no." The product of any two consecutive integers is even and will give a definitive "no." Statement (2) is sufficient. The correct answer is (B).

18. Last year, an appliance store sold an average (arithmetic mean) of 42 microwave ovens per month. In the first 10 months of this year, the store sold an average of only 20 microwaves per month. What is the average number of microwaves sold per month for the entire 22-month period?

    ○ 21
    ○ 30
    ○ 31
    ○ 32
    ○ 44

18. **D** If the appliance store sold an average of 42 microwaves per month last year, then the total microwaves sold for the year was $42 \times 12 = 504$. For the first 10 months of this year, the total sold was $20 \times 10 = 200$. So, the total sold for the 22-month period is 704. Divide 704 by 22 to get the average. $704 \div 22 = 32$. The correct answer is (D).

QUESTIONS

19. If *AB* is the diameter of the circle with center *X* and *C* is a point on the circle such that *AC* = *AX* = 3, what is the perimeter of triangle *ABC* ?

○ $\dfrac{9\sqrt{3}}{2}$

○ 9

○ $6 + 3\sqrt{3}$

○ $9 + 3\sqrt{3}$

○ $9\sqrt{3}$

MATH EXPLANATIONS

19. **D** First, draw the picture. It looks something like this:

The problem states that *AB* is the diameter of the circle and that *X* is center of the circle. *ABC* is the triangle that connects the 3 points. *AC* and *AX* can be labeled as 3—as can *BX*, since, like *AX*, it's a radius.

To find the 3rd side, recognize that triangle *ABC*, because it's inscribed in a semicircle, is a right triangle, with the right angle at point *C*.

Now use the Pythagorean Theorem—recognize *ABC* as a 30-60-90 triangle—to determine that *BC* is $3\sqrt{3}$. The perimeter is $6 + 3 + 3\sqrt{3}$, or $9 + 3\sqrt{3}$. The correct answer is (D).

ADVANCE PURCHASE DISCOUNTS FOR AIRLINE TRAVEL	
Days Prior to Departure	**Percentage Discount**
0–6 days	0%
7–13 days	10%
14–29 days	25%
30 days or more	40%

20. The table above shows the discount structure for advanced purchase of tickets at a particular airline. A passenger bought a ticket at this airline for $1,050. Had she purchased the ticket one day later, she would have paid $210 more. How many days before her departure did she purchase her ticket?

  ○ 6 days
  ○ 7 days
  ○ 13 days
  ○ 14 days
  ○ 29 days

20. D The algebra is complicated here, so Plug In the Answers. Start with (C). If the passenger bought a ticket 13 days in advance versus 12 days in advance (one day later), then there would be no savings (discount is the same for 13 days and 12 days), so eliminate (C). Try (D). If the passenger bought a ticket 14 days in advance, then the discount would be 25%. So, the cost of the ticket would be 75% of the undiscounted cost. Set up an equation to find the undiscounted cost (called x in the equation): $\frac{75}{100}x = 1,050$. Solving for x gives an undiscounted cost of $1,400. The discount if the ticket had been bought one day later is 10%. 10% of $1,400 is $140, so the cost of the ticket would be $1,260. The difference in cost is $1,260 − $1,050 = $210, which meets the condition of a $210 savings. The correct answer is (D).

21. Unseasonable weather in the months before a wine harvest can cool vineyards in the Bordeaux region enough <u>to affect the overall size of the grapes themselves, create</u> unwanted moisture that can cause mold in some grape varieties and deterioration in others.

   ○ to affect the overall size of the grapes themselves, create
   ○ to affect the overall size of the grapes themselves and create
   ○ that the overall size of the grapes themselves are affected, create
   ○ that it affects the overall size of the grapes themselves, creates
   ○ that the size of the grapes are affected and creates

21. **B** Go through your checklist of potential errors. Is there a misplaced modifier here? No. Is there a pronoun problem? No. Is there a parallel construction problem? Yes! At first it seems as if this sentence contains a list of three actions: to affect… create…and deteriorate—but wait! The third action is not an action, it's a noun: deterioration. However, since *deterioration* is not underlined, we can't fix this. Going back to the original sentence, it becomes clear that, in fact, there are only two main actions: to affect the overall size of the grapes and (to) create unwanted moisture. To correctly use this compound verb, the original sentence would need an "and" between the verbs. Only (B) gives you this option. Choices (C), (D), and (E) use the idiomatic expression "enough that" which is not necessarily wrong, but which would require the word "creating."

22. It is posited by some scientists that the near extinction of the sap-eating gray bat of northwestern America was caused by government-sponsored logging operations in the early 1920s that greatly reduced the species' habitat.

   Which of the following, if true, most strongly weakens the scientists' claims?

   ○ Logging operations in the 1920s are widely held responsible for the near extinction of other species that lived in the same area.
   ○ A boom in new home construction in the early 1920s led congress to open federal lands to logging operations.
   ○ A 5-year drought in the early 1920s severely reduced the output of sap in trees in northwestern America.
   ○ Numbers of sightings of sap-eating gray bats fell to their lowest numbers in 1926.
   ○ Sightings of sap-eating gray bats in Europe stayed roughly the same during the same period.

22. **C** This is a causal argument. The scientists claim that the bat's near extinction was caused by logging. How do we weaken this argument? By presenting an alternate cause—another reason why the bat almost became extinct. Choices (A) and (B) actually strengthen the argument. Choice (A) says that other species were also threatened with extinction by logging, and (B) gives us a reason the government might have been tempted to agree to logging on federal lands. Choice (D) is outside the scope of the argument since "sightings" are irrelevant. Choice (E) also goes outside the scope of the argument by telling us about the bat population on another continent. But (C) gives us an alternate cause for the near extinction of these bats: The sap they depended on for nourishment was severely reduced at the time in question by a five-year drought.

23. Upset by the recent downturn in production numbers during the first half of the year, <u>the possibility of adding worker incentives was raised by the board of directors at its quarterly meeting</u>.

- ○ the possibility of adding worker incentives was raised by the board of directors at its quarterly meeting
- ○ the addition of worker incentives was raised as a possibility by the board of directors at its quarterly meeting
- ○ added worker incentives was raised by the board of directors at its quarterly meeting as a possibility
- ○ the board of directors raised at its quarterly meeting the possibility of worker incentives being added
- ○ the board of directors, at its quarterly meeting, raised the possibility of adding worker incentives

24. Whenever a major airplane accident occurs, there is a dramatic increase in the number of airplane mishaps reported in the media, a phenomenon that may last for as long as a few months after the accident. Airline officials assert that the publicity given the gruesomeness of major airplane accidents focuses media attention on the airline industry, and the increase in the number of reported accidents is caused by an increase in the number of news sources covering airline accidents, not by an increase in the number of accidents.

Which of the following, if true, would seriously weaken the assertions of the airline officials?

- ○ The publicity surrounding airline accidents is largely limited to the country in which the crash occurred.
- ○ Airline accidents tend to occur far more often during certain peak travel months.
- ○ News organizations do not have any guidelines to help them decide how severe an accident must be for it to receive coverage.
- ○ Airplane accidents receive coverage by news sources only when the news sources find it advantageous to do so.
- ○ Studies by government regulators show that the number of airplane flight miles remains relatively constant from month to month.

23. **E** This is a misplaced modifier question. Who was "upset by the recent downturn"? It was the board of directors. This eliminates (A), (B), and (C). Choice (E) correctly positions the prepositional phrase "at its quarterly meeting" and avoids the passive phrase "being added" in (D).

24. **B** This is a statistical argument. The officials assert that there is in fact no increase in actual mishaps during the months after an accident, but an increase in the number of news sources *reporting* the mishaps—in other words, they argue that the statistics are not representative. To weaken this assertion, we would have to show that the statistics are in fact representative. Choice (B) does this by implying that certain months are more likely to have more frequent accidents due to high volume of flights. Choice (A) is outside the scope of the argument. Choices (C), (D), and (E) would all *strengthen* the assertions of the officials.

<u>Questions 25–28</u> are based on the following passage:

The function of strategic planning is to position a company for long-term growth and expansion in a variety of markets by analyzing its strengths
Line and weaknesses and examining current and
(5) potential opportunities. Based on this information, the company develops a strategy for itself. That strategy becomes the basis for supporting strategies for the company's various departments.

This implementation stage is where all too
(10) many strategic plans go astray. Recent business management surveys show that most CEOs who have a strategic plan are concerned with the potential breakdown in the implementation of the plan. Unlike corporations in the 1980s that blindly
(15) followed their 5-year plans, even when they were misguided, today's corporations tend to second-guess its long-term plans.

Outsiders can help facilitate the process, but in the final analysis, if the company does not make
(20) the plan, the company will not follow the plan. This was one of the problems with strategic planning in the 1980s. In that era, strategic planning was an abstract, top-down process involving only a few top corporate officers and hired guns. Number
(25) crunching experts came into a company and generated tome-like volumes filled with a mixture of abstruse facts and grand theories that had little to do with the day-to-day realities of the company. Key middle managers were left out of planning
(30) sessions, resulting in lost opportunities and ruffled feelings.

However, more hands-on strategic planning can produce startling results. A recent survey queried more than a thousand small-to-medium sized
(35) businesses to compare companies with a strategic plan to companies without one. The survey found that companies with strategic plans had annual revenue growth of 6.2 percent as opposed to 3.8 percent for the other companies.
(40) Perhaps most important, a strategic plan helps companies anticipate—and survive—change. New technology and the mobility of capital means that markets can shift faster than ever before. Some financial analysts wonder why companies
(45) should bother planning two years ahead when market dynamics might be transformed by next quarter. However, it is this pace of change that makes planning so crucial. Now, more than ever, companies have to stay alert to the marketplace.
(50) In an environment of continual and rapid change, long-range planning expands options and organizational flexibility.

25. The primary purpose of the passage is to

- ○ refute the idea that change is bad for a corporation's long-term health
- ○ describe how long-term planning, despite some potential pitfalls, can help a corporation to grow
- ○ compare and contrast two styles of corporate planning
- ○ evaluate the strategic planning goals of corporate America today
- ○ defend a methodology that has come under sharp attack

26. It can be inferred from the passage that strategic planning during the 1980s had all of the following shortcomings EXCEPT

- ○ a reliance on outside consultants who did not necessarily understand the nuts and bolts of the business
- ○ a dependence on theoretical models that did not always perfectly describe the workings of the company
- ○ an inherent weakness in the company's own ability to implement the strategic plan
- ○ an excess of information and data that made it difficult to get to key concepts
- ○ the lack of a forum for middle managers to express their ideas

25. **B** Most Reading Comprehension passages ask some form of this question characterized by the phrase "primary purpose." Choice (B) best summarizes the main idea of the passage: that despite some potential problems, strategic planning can allow a company to expand and grow.

26. **C** According to the passage, the difficulty in implementation of strategic plans is a more modern phenomenon, not related to the weaknesses of the 1980s.

27. The author most likely mentions the results of the survey of 1,000 companies in order to

   ○ put forth an opposing view on strategic plans which is later refuted
   ○ illustrate that when strategic planning is "hands-on," it produces uninspiring results
   ○ give a concrete example of why strategic planning did not work during the 1980s
   ○ support the contention that strategic planning can be very successful when done correctly
   ○ give supporting data to prove that many companies have implemented strategic plans

27. D Skim the passage quickly to find the survey, then read that portion carefully. According to the passage, the survey shows that companies with strategic plans outperformed companies without strategic plans.

28. The passage suggests which of the following about the "financial analysts" mentioned in lines 44–47 ?

   ○ They believe that strategic planning is the key to weathering the rapid changes of the marketplace.
   ○ They are working to understand and anticipate market developments that are two years ahead.
   ○ Their study of market dynamics has led them to question the reliability of short-term planning strategies.
   ○ They might not agree with the author that one way to survive rapidly changing conditions comes from long-range planning.
   ○ They consider the mobility of capital to be a necessary condition for the growth of new technology.

28. D It's always a good idea to read a few lines above and below the cited lines, just to make sure you understand the context. The financial analysts mentioned in the passage seem to say that it is not worth trying to plan when the market is changing so rapidly. The author mentions their views in order to refute them.

29. The Internal Revenue Service has directed that taxpayers who generate no self-employment income can no longer deduct home offices, home office expenses, <u>or nothing that was already</u> depreciated as a business expense the previous year.

- ○ or nothing that was already
- ○ or that was already
- ○ or anything that was already
- ○ and anything
- ○ and nothing that already was

29. **C** The underlined portion of the sentence the idiom *or nothing* so check for idiom errors. The idiom *no...nothing* is an incorrect idiom. Eliminate (A) and look for obvious repeaters. Choice (E) also contains the incorrect idiom *no...nothing*, so eliminate (E) as well. Evaluate the remaining answer choices individually looking for reasons to eliminate each.

Choice (B) eliminates the noun *nothing* which creates a parallel construction error as the list *home offices, home office expenses,* or *that* is not parallel. Eliminate (B) for a parallel construction error. Choice (C) fixes the original error by using the proper idiom *no...anything,* and commits no new errors, so keep (C). Choice (D) fixes the original error by using the proper idiom *no...anything,* but commits another error with the use of the word *and* which is a clauses and connectors error. Eliminate (D).

30. Informed people generally assimilate information from several divergent sources before coming to an opinion. However, most popular news organizations view foreign affairs solely through the eyes of our State Department. In reporting the political crisis in a foreign country, news organizations must endeavor to find alternative sources of information.

Which of the following inferences can be drawn from the argument above?

○ To the degree that a news source gives an account of another country that mirrors that of our State Department, that reporting is suspect.

○ To protect their integrity, news media should avoid the influence of State Department releases in their coverage of foreign affairs.

○ Reporting that is not influenced by the State Department is usually more accurate than are other accounts.

○ The alternative sources of information mentioned in the passage might not share the same views as the State Department.

○ A report cannot be seen as influenced by the State Department if it accurately depicts the events in a foreign country.

30. D To get an inference question correct, just look for an answer that you know to be true. Choice (A) implies that the State Department's views are always likely to diverge from other news sources, which is an extreme answer, and extreme answers are almost always incorrect. Choice (B) implies that the State Department should never be used as a news source, which is also extreme. Choice (C) is never mentioned; therefore, it is out of scope. Choice (E) is wrong because the answer is too extreme. Choice (D) is the credited answer because the argument makes it clear that the "alternative" sources of information would provide the "divergent" opinions mentioned in the first sentence.

31. When automatic teller machines were first installed in the 1980s, bank officials promised they would be faster, more reliable, and less prone to make errors than their human counterparts.

○ they would be faster, more reliable, and less prone to make errors

○ they would be faster, more reliable, and that they would be less prone for making errors

○ the machines would be faster, more reliable, and less prone to errors

○ the machines were faster, more reliable, and errors would occur much less

○ faster, more reliable machines, and that errors would be less prone

31. C Go through your checklist of potential errors. Is there a misplaced modifier here? No. Is there a pronoun problem? There certainly is a pronoun here, so be sure to check it out. Is it possible that the "they" could be ambiguous? As a matter of fact, "they" is obviously supposed to refer to the automatic teller machines, but it also could refer to the bank officials. Replacing "they" with "the machines" clarifies the sentence, which means we are down to (C), (D), or (E), but (C) is correct because (D) and (E) are not parallel.

QUESTIONS

32. With its plan to create a wildlife sanctuary out of previously unused landfill, Sweden is but one of a number of industrialized nations that <u>is accepting its responsibility to protect endangered species and promote</u> conservation.

- ○ is accepting its responsibility to protect endangered species and promote
- ○ is accepting its responsibility for protecting endangered species and promoting
- ○ are accepting its responsibility to protect endangered species and promoting
- ○ are accepting of their responsibility to protect endangered species and to promote
- ○ are accepting their responsibility to protect endangered species and promote

33. A decade after a logging operation in India began cutting down trees in a territory that serves as a sanctuary for Bengal tigers, the incidence of tigers attacking humans in nearby villages has increased by 300 percent. Because the logging operation has reduced the number of acres of woodland per tiger on average from 15 acres to approximately 12 acres, scientists have theorized that tigers must need a minimum number of acres of woodland in order to remain content.

Which of the following statements, if true, would most strengthen the scientists' hypothesis?

- ○ In other wildlife areas in India where the number of acres of woodland per tiger remains at least 15 acres, there has been no increase in the number of tiger attacks on humans.
- ○ Before the logging operation began, there were many fewer humans living in the area.
- ○ The largest number of acres per tiger before the logging operation began was 32 acres per tiger in one area of the sanctuary, whereas the smallest number of acres per tiger after the logging operation was 9 acres.
- ○ Other species of wild animals have begun competing with the Bengal tigers for the dwindling food supply.
- ○ The Bengal tiger has become completely extinct in other areas of Asia.

VERBAL EXPLANATIONS

32. **E** This is a subject-verb question. The verb *is* in the underlined portion seems to agree with the subject of the sentence, *Sweden*, but in fact, the noun *is* must agree with *nations*, which is plural. We're down to (C), (D), or (E). Choice (C) keeps the singular pronoun *its,* so we can eliminate that. Choice (D) contains the clunky phrase "accepting of." The "of" is an unnecessary preposition and, some might say, unidiomatic, making (E) the credited answer.

33. **A** In this causal argument, the decrease in the number of acres of woodland per tiger is said to cause the increasing number of tiger attacks on humans. To strengthen this argument, it would help if the Bengal tigers in areas with a normal number of acres of woodland per tiger have NOT increased their attacks on humans. That's what (A) tells us. Choice (B) gives us an alternate cause for the increase in tiger attacks—in other words, it weakens the argument instead of strengthening it. Choice (C) adds details without really strengthening the argument. Choice (D) weakens the scientists' hypothesis by presenting a possible alternate cause for the tigers' attacks on humans. Choice (E) emphasizes the seriousness of the problem without shedding light on its cause.

34. <u>The machine press union and company management were not able to communicate effectively, and it</u> was a major cause of the 1999 strike in Seattle.

   ○ The machine press union and company management were not able to communicate effectively, and it
   ○ Communications between the machine press union and company management were not effective, and it
   ○ For the machine press union and company management, to be unable to communicate effectively
   ○ The inability of the machine press union and company management to communicate effectively
   ○ The machine press union, being unable to communicate effectively with company management,

34. **D** The tip-off here is the pronoun *it*. To what does *it* refer? Not the union nor the management. Really what *it* seems to refer to is the inability of the two sides to communicate. We can eliminate (A) and (B) for that reason. Choice (C) seems to indicate that it was effective communication that led to the strike. Choice (E) is both awkward and unidiomatic. Choice (D) is the correct response.

35. A greater number of fresh vegetables are sold in City *X* than in City *Y*. Therefore, the people in City *X* have better nutritional habits than those in City *Y*.

   Each of the following, if true, weakens the conclusion above EXCEPT:

   ○ City *X* has more people living in it than City *Y*.
   ○ Most of the people in City *Y* work in City *X* and buy their vegetables there.
   ○ The people in City *X* buy many of their vegetables as decorations, not to eat.
   ○ The per capita consumption of junk food in City *X* is three times that of City *Y*.
   ○ The average price per pound of vegetables in City *Y* is lower than the average price per pound of vegetables in City *X*.

35. **E** We are looking for an answer that does NOT weaken the argument. You might think that means the correct answer would *strengthen* the argument, but while that COULD be the case, it doesn't have to be. The correct answer might simply be irrelevant to the argument. In this causal argument, more fresh vegetable sales in City *X* are said to mean that City *X* has better nutritional habits than City *Y*. Each of the answer choices pokes holes in that argument, except for (E). It suggests that if vegetables are cheaper in City *Y*, and yet more vegetables are being sold in City *X*, then the argument that *X* has better nutritional habits might be right.

36. Heavy metals, toxic waste by-products that can cause tumors in fish, <u>are generally found in the waters off industrial shorelines, but have been discovered in trace amounts even</u> in the relatively pristine waters of the South Pacific.

   ⬭ are generally found in the waters off industrial shorelines, but have been discovered in trace amounts even

   ⬭ are generally to be found in the waters off industrial shorelines, and have even been discovered in trace amounts

   ⬭ can, in general, be found in the waters off industrial shorelines, and have been discovered in trace amounts even

   ⬭ had generally been found in the waters off industrial shorelines, but have even been discovered in trace amounts

   ⬭ are found generally in the waters off industrial shorelines, but have been discovered in a trace amount even

36. **A**   In both (B) and (C), the conjunction *and* wrongly gives the impression that the second half of the sentence is merely an added thought, instead of a new and dangerous development that goes beyond what *generally* happens. Choice (D) needlessly changes the verb tense. Choice (E)'s *in a trace amount* does not agree with the plural *heavy metals*.

Questions 37–40 are based on the following passage:

In Roman times, defeated enemies were generally put to death as criminals for having offended the emperor of Rome. In the Middle *Line* Ages, however, the practice of ransoming, or (5) returning prisoners in exchange for money, became common. Though some saw this custom as a step toward a more humane society, the primary reasons behind it were economic rather than humanitarian.

(10) In those times, rulers had only a limited ability to raise taxes. They could neither force their subjects to fight nor pay them to do so. The promise of material compensation in the form of goods and ransom was therefore the only way of inducing (15) combatants to participate in a war. In the Middle Ages, the predominant incentive for the individual soldier was the expectation of spoils. Although collecting ransom clearly brought financial gain, keeping a prisoner and arranging for his exchange (20) had its costs. Consequently, procedures were devised to reduce transaction costs.

One such device was a rule asserting that the prisoner had to assess his own value. This compelled the prisoner to establish a value without (25) too much distortion; indicating too low a value would increase the captive's chances of being killed, while indicating too high a value would either ruin him financially or create a prohibitively expensive ransom that would also result in death.

37. The primary purpose of the passage is to

○ discuss the economic basis of the medieval practice of exchanging prisoners for ransom

○ examine the history of the treatment of prisoners of war

○ emphasize the importance of a warrior's code of honor during the Middle Ages

○ explore a way of reducing the costs of ransom

○ demonstrate why warriors of the Middle Ages looked forward to battles

37. **A** Choice (A) best summarizes the main idea of the first paragraph. While (D) reflects a part of the passage, it does not encompass the main idea of the passage.

QUESTIONS

38. It can be inferred from the passage that a medieval soldier

 ○ was less likely to kill captured members of opposing armies than was a soldier of the Roman Empire
 ○ operated on a basically independent level and was motivated solely by economic incentives
 ○ had few economic options and chose to fight because it was the only way to earn an adequate living
 ○ was motivated to spare prisoners' lives by humanitarian rather than economic ideals
 ○ had no respect for his captured enemies since captives were typically regarded as weak

39. Which of the following best describes the change in policy from executing prisoners in Roman times to ransoming prisoners in the Middle Ages?

 ○ The emperors of Rome demanded more respect than did medieval rulers, and thus Roman subjects went to greater lengths to defend their nation.
 ○ It was a reflection of the lesser degree of direct control medieval rulers had over their subjects.
 ○ It became a show of strength and honor for warriors of the Middle Ages to be able to capture and return their enemies.
 ○ Medieval soldiers were not as humanitarian as their ransoming practices might have indicated.
 ○ Medieval soldiers demonstrated more concern about economic policy than did their Roman counterparts.

VERBAL EXPLANATIONS

38. **A** The first paragraph gives us the information to answer this question. Note the trigger word *however* that underscores the difference between the Roman era and the Middle Ages.

39. **B** The best answer can be found in the first line of the second paragraph. Ransom was one of the few ways a ruler could give his subjects what they wanted to get them to do something *he* wanted.

40. The author uses the phrase "without too much distortion" (lines 24–25) in order to

- ○ indicate that prisoners would fairly assess their worth
- ○ emphasize the important role medieval prisoners played in determining whether they should be ransomed
- ○ explain how prisoners often paid more than an appropriate ransom in order to increase their chances for survival
- ○ suggest that captors and captives often had understanding relationships
- ○ show that when in prison a soldier's view could become distorted

40. A To get the answer, we have to understand the meaning of the quoted words, but it also helps to read the rest of the paragraph. The paragraph describes a ransom value that was neither too low nor too high, therefore making (A) the best answer choice.

Part VIII
The Princeton
Review GMAT
Math and Verbal
Practice Bins and
Explanations

Chapter 24
GMAT Math and Verbal Practice Bins

Once you know your current scoring level from taking the Warm-Up Test, use the "bins" in the following pages to improve your performance.

If you got six or fewer math questions correct on the Warm-Up Test, start by practicing with the problems in Math Bin 1. If you got 6–13 math questions correct on the Warm-Up Test, start by practicing with the problems in Math Bin 2. If you got 14 or more math questions correct, practice with the problems in Math Bins 3 and 4.

If you got six or fewer verbal questions correct on the Warm-up Test, start by practicing with the problems in Verbal Bin 1. If you got 6–13 verbal questions correct on the Warm-Up Test, start by practicing with the problems in Verbal Bin 2. If you got 14 or more verbal questions correct, practice with the problems in Verbal Bin 3.

Math Test
Bin 1—Easier Questions
26 Questions

This test is composed of both problem solving questions and data sufficiency questions.

<u>Problem Solving Directions</u>: Solve each problem and choose the best of the answer choices provided.

<u>Data Sufficiency Directions</u>: Each <u>data sufficiency</u> problem consists of a question and two statements, labeled (1) and (2), which contain certain data. Using these data and your knowledge of mathematics and everyday facts (such as the number of days in July or the meaning of *counterclockwise*), decide whether the data given are sufficient for answering the question and then indicate one of the following answer choices:

- ◯ Statement (1) ALONE is sufficient, but statement (2) alone is not sufficient.
- ◯ Statement (2) ALONE is sufficient, but statement (1) alone is not sufficient.
- ◯ BOTH statements TOGETHER are sufficient, but NEITHER statement ALONE is sufficient.
- ◯ EACH statement ALONE is sufficient.
- ◯ Statements (1) and (2) TOGETHER are not sufficient.

---

1. What percent of 112 is 14 ?

   - ◯ 0.125%
   - ◯ 8%
   - ◯ 12.5%
   - ◯ 125%
   - ◯ 800%

2. The number of flights leaving a certain airport doubles during every one-hour period between 9 A.M. and noon; after noon, the number of flights leaving from the airport doubles during every two-hour period. If 4 flights left from the airport between 9 and 10 A.M., how many flights left the airport between 2 and 4 P.M. ?

   - ◯ 32
   - ◯ 48
   - ◯ 64
   - ◯ 128
   - ◯ 256

3. If both *ABDC* and *CDFE* are parallelograms, what is $q + r$?

   (1) $r = 70$

   (2) $p = 110$

   - ◯ Statement (1) ALONE is sufficient, but statement (2) alone is not sufficient.
   - ◯ Statement (2) ALONE is sufficient, but statement (1) alone is not sufficient.
   - ◯ BOTH statements TOGETHER are sufficient, but NEITHER statement ALONE is sufficient.
   - ◯ EACH statement ALONE is sufficient.
   - ◯ Statements (1) and (2) TOGETHER are not sufficient.

GO ON TO THE NEXT PAGE.

4. Chris's convertible gets gas mileage that is 40 percent greater than that of Stan's SUV. If Harry's hatchback gets gas mileage that is 15 percent greater than that of Chris's convertible, then Harry's hatchback gets gas mileage that is what percent greater than that of Stan's SUV?

○ 25%
○ 46%
○ 55%
○ 61%
○ 66%

5. If x is equal to 1 more than the product of 3 and z, and y is equal to 1 less than the product of 2 and z, then $2x$ is how much greater than $3y$ when z is 4 ?

○ 1
○ 2
○ 3
○ 5
○ 6

6. In 2005, did Company A have more than twice the number of employees that Company B did?

(1) In 2005, Company A had 11,500 more employees than did Company B.

(2) In 2005, the 3,000 employees with advanced degrees at Company A made up 12.5 percent of that company's total number employees, and the 2,500 employees with advanced degrees at Company B made up 20 percent of that company's total number of employees.

○ Statement (1) ALONE is sufficient, but statement (2) alone is not sufficient.
○ Statement (2) ALONE is sufficient, but statement (1) alone is not sufficient.
○ BOTH statements TOGETHER are sufficient, but NEITHER statement ALONE is sufficient.
○ EACH statement ALONE is sufficient.
○ Statements (1) and (2) TOGETHER are not sufficient.

7. Is x^3 equal to 125 ?

(1) $x > 4$

(2) $x < 6$

○ Statement (1) ALONE is sufficient, but statement (2) alone is not sufficient.
○ Statement (2) ALONE is sufficient, but statement (1) alone is not sufficient.
○ BOTH statements TOGETHER are sufficient, but NEITHER statement ALONE is sufficient.
○ EACH statement ALONE is sufficient.
○ Statements (1) and (2) TOGETHER are not sufficient.

8. Bob leaves point A and drives due west to point B. From point B, he drives due south to point C. How far is Bob from his original location?

(1) Point A is 24 miles from point B.

(2) Point B is 18 miles from point C.

○ Statement (1) ALONE is sufficient, but statement (2) alone is not sufficient.
○ Statement (2) ALONE is sufficient, but statement (1) alone is not sufficient.
○ BOTH statements TOGETHER are sufficient, but NEITHER statement ALONE is sufficient.
○ EACH statement ALONE is sufficient.
○ Statements (1) and (2) TOGETHER are not sufficient.

GO ON TO THE NEXT PAGE.

9. The formula $M = \sqrt{l^2 + w^2 + d^2}$ describes the relationship between the length of M, which is the longest line that can be drawn in a rectangular solid, and the length, l, width, w, and depth, d, of that rectangular solid. The longest line that can be drawn in a rectangular solid with a length of 12, a width of 4, and a depth of 3 is how much longer than the longest line that can drawn in a rectangular solid with a length of 6, a width of 3, and a depth of 2 ?

   ○ 5
   ○ 6
   ○ 7
   ○ 9
   ○ 13

10. Is the average (arithmetic mean) of a, b, and c equal to 8 ?

   (1) Three times the sum of a, b, and c is equal to 72.

   (2) The sum of $2a$, $2b$, and $2c$ is equal to 48.

   ○ Statement (1) ALONE is sufficient, but statement (2) alone is not sufficient.
   ○ Statement (2) ALONE is sufficient, but statement (1) alone is not sufficient.
   ○ BOTH statements TOGETHER are sufficient, but NEITHER statement ALONE is sufficient.
   ○ EACH statement ALONE is sufficient.
   ○ Statements (1) and (2) TOGETHER are not sufficient.

11. $\sqrt{\sqrt{\left(1 + \dfrac{17}{64}\right)}} =$

   ○ $\dfrac{\sqrt{34}}{8}$
   ○ $\dfrac{3\sqrt{2}}{4}$
   ○ $\dfrac{9}{8}$
   ○ $\dfrac{\sqrt{68}}{4}$
   ○ $\dfrac{3\sqrt{2}}{2}$

12. A certain stadium is currently full to $\dfrac{13}{16}$ of its maximum seating capacity. What is the maximum seating capacity of the stadium?

   (1) If 1,250 people were to enter the stadium, the stadium would be full to $\dfrac{15}{16}$ of its maximum seating capacity.

   (2) If 2,500 people were to leave the stadium, the stadium would be full to $\dfrac{9}{16}$ of its maximum seating capacity.

   ○ Statement (1) ALONE is sufficient, but statement (2) alone is not sufficient.
   ○ Statement (2) ALONE is sufficient, but statement (1) alone is not sufficient.
   ○ BOTH statements TOGETHER are sufficient, but NEITHER statement ALONE is sufficient.
   ○ EACH statement ALONE is sufficient.
   ○ Statements (1) and (2) TOGETHER are not sufficient.

GO ON TO THE NEXT PAGE.

13. Andre has already saved $\frac{3}{7}$ of the cost of a new car, and he has calculated that he will be able to save $\frac{2}{5}$ of the remaining amount before the end of the summer. What fraction of the cost of the new car will he still need to save after the end of the summer?

○ $\frac{6}{35}$

○ $\frac{8}{35}$

○ $\frac{12}{35}$

○ $\frac{23}{35}$

○ $\frac{29}{35}$

$\{1, 4, 6, y\}$

14. If the average (arithmetic mean) of the set of numbers above is 6, then what is the median?

○ 5
○ 6
○ 7
○ 13
○ 24

15. A store sells a six-pack of soda for $2.70. If this represents a savings of 10 percent of the individual price of cans of soda, then what is the price of a single can of soda?

○ $ 0.35
○ $ 0.40
○ $ 0.45
○ $ 0.50
○ $ 0.55

16. If Beth spent $400 of her earnings last month on rent, how much did Beth earn last month?

(1) Beth saved $\frac{1}{3}$ of her earnings last month and spent half of the remainder on rent.

(2) Beth earned twice as much this month as last month.

○ Statement (1) ALONE is sufficient, but statement (2) alone is not sufficient.
○ Statement (2) ALONE is sufficient, but statement (1) alone is not sufficient.
○ BOTH statements TOGETHER are sufficient, but NEITHER statement ALONE is sufficient.
○ EACH statement ALONE is sufficient.
○ Statements (1) and (2) TOGETHER are not sufficient.

17. If n is an integer, is n even?

(1) $2n$ is an even integer.

(2) $n - 1$ is an odd integer.

○ Statement (1) ALONE is sufficient, but statement (2) alone is not sufficient.
○ Statement (2) ALONE is sufficient, but statement (1) alone is not sufficient.
○ BOTH statements TOGETHER are sufficient, but NEITHER statement ALONE is sufficient.
○ EACH statement ALONE is sufficient.
○ Statements (1) and (2) TOGETHER are not sufficient.

GO ON TO THE NEXT PAGE.

18. At apartment complex Z, 30 percent of the residents are men over the age of 18, and 40 percent are women over the age of 18. If there are 24 children living in the complex, how many total residents live in apartment complex Z?

   - ○ 32
   - ○ 80
   - ○ 94
   - ○ 112
   - ○ 124

19. Over the course of a soccer season, 30 percent of the players on a team scored goals. What is the ratio of players on the team who scored goals to those who did not?

   - ○ 3 to 10
   - ○ 1 to 3
   - ○ 3 to 7
   - ○ 1 to 1
   - ○ 3 to 1

20. At a restaurant, Luis left a tip for his waiter equal to 20 percent of his entire dinner check, including tax. What was the amount of the dinner check?

   (1) The sum of the dinner check and the tip was $16.80.

   (2) Luis's tip consisted of two bills and four coins.

   - ○ Statement (1) ALONE is sufficient, but statement (2) alone is not sufficient.
   - ○ Statement (2) ALONE is sufficient, but statement (1) alone is not sufficient.
   - ○ BOTH statements TOGETHER are sufficient, but NEITHER statement ALONE is sufficient.
   - ○ EACH statement ALONE is sufficient.
   - ○ Statements (1) and (2) TOGETHER are not sufficient.

21. Which sport utility vehicle has a higher list price, the Touristo or the Leisure?

   (1) The list price of the Leisure is $\frac{5}{6}$ the list price of the Touristo.

   (2) The list price of the Touristo is 1.2 times the list price of the Leisure.

   - ○ Statement (1) ALONE is sufficient, but statement (2) alone is not sufficient.
   - ○ Statement (2) ALONE is sufficient, but statement (1) alone is not sufficient.
   - ○ BOTH statements TOGETHER are sufficient, but NEITHER statement ALONE is sufficient.
   - ○ EACH statement ALONE is sufficient.
   - ○ Statements (1) and (2) TOGETHER are not sufficient.

GO ON TO THE NEXT PAGE.

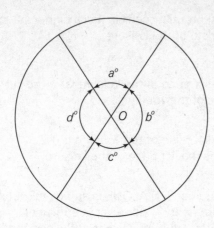

22. In the circle above, center O is intersected by 2 straight lines, and $3a = b$. What is the value of $b - a$?

    ○ 2
    ○ 30
    ○ 45
    ○ 90
    ○ 135

23. What is the value of integer w ?

  (1) w is a multiple of 3.

  (2) $420 < w < 425$

    ○ Statement (1) ALONE is sufficient, but statement (2) alone is not sufficient.
    ○ Statement (2) ALONE is sufficient, but statement (1) alone is not sufficient.
    ○ BOTH statements TOGETHER are sufficient, but NEITHER statement ALONE is sufficient.
    ○ EACH statement ALONE is sufficient.
    ○ Statements (1) and (2) TOGETHER are not sufficient.

24. What is the quotient when 0.25% of 600 is divided by 0.25 of 600 ?

    ○ 10
    ○ 1
    ○ 0.1
    ○ 0.01
    ○ 0.001

25. A certain town's economic development council has 21 members. If the number of females on the council is 3 less than 3 times the number of males on the council, then the town's economic development council has how many male members?

    ○ 5
    ○ 6
    ○ 7
    ○ 9
    ○ 15

26. Roger can chop down 4 trees in an hour. How long does it take Vincent to chop down 4 trees?

  (1) Vincent spends 6 hours per day chopping down trees.

  (2) Vincent takes twice as long as Roger to chop down trees.

    ○ Statement (1) ALONE is sufficient, but statement (2) alone is not sufficient.
    ○ Statement (2) ALONE is sufficient, but statement (1) alone is not sufficient.
    ○ BOTH statements TOGETHER are sufficient, but NEITHER statement ALONE is sufficient.
    ○ EACH statement ALONE is sufficient.
    ○ Statements (1) and (2) TOGETHER are not sufficient.

END OF BIN.

Math Test
Bin 2—Medium Questions
27 Questions

This test is composed of both problem solving questions and data sufficiency questions.

Problem Solving Directions: Solve each problem and choose the best of the answer choices provided.

Data Sufficiency Directions: Each <u>data sufficiency</u> problem consists of a question and two statements, labeled (1) and (2), which contain certain data. Using these data and your knowledge of mathematics and everyday facts (such as the number of days in July or the meaning of *counterclockwise*), decide whether the data given are sufficient for answering the question and then indicate one of the following answer choices:

⚬ Statement (1) ALONE is sufficient, but statement (2) alone is not sufficient.

⚬ Statement (2) ALONE is sufficient, but statement (1) alone is not sufficient.

⚬ BOTH statements TOGETHER are sufficient, but NEITHER statement ALONE is sufficient.

⚬ EACH statement ALONE is sufficient.

⚬ Statements (1) and (2) TOGETHER are not sufficient.

---

1. If $x = \dfrac{\dfrac{5}{9} + \dfrac{15}{27} + \dfrac{45}{81}}{3}$, then $\sqrt{1-x} =$

⚬ $\dfrac{\sqrt{5}}{9}$

⚬ $\dfrac{5}{9}$

⚬ $\dfrac{2}{3}$

⚬ $\dfrac{\sqrt{5}}{3}$

⚬ $\dfrac{15}{9}$

2. Steven has run a certain number of laps around a track at an average (arithmetic mean) time per lap of 51 seconds. If he runs one additional lap in 39 seconds and reduces his average time per lap to 49 seconds, how many laps did he run at an average time per lap of 51 seconds?

⚬ 2
⚬ 5
⚬ 6
⚬ 10
⚬ 12

3. $200^2 - 2(200)(199) + 199^2 =$

⚬ $-79{,}201$
⚬ -200
⚬ 1
⚬ 200
⚬ $79{,}999$

GO ON TO THE NEXT PAGE.

4. If $x \neq \dfrac{1}{2}$, then $\dfrac{6x^2 + 11x - 7}{2x - 1} =$

   ○ $3x + 7$
   ○ $3x - 7$
   ○ $3x + 1$
   ○ $x + 7$
   ○ $x - 7$

5. If Amy drove the distance from her home to the beach in less than 2 hours, was her average speed greater than 60 miles per hour?

   (1) The distance that Amy drove from her home to the beach was less than 125 miles.

   (2) The distance that Amy drove from her home to the beach was greater than 122 miles.

   ○ Statement (1) ALONE is sufficient, but statement (2) alone is not sufficient.
   ○ Statement (2) ALONE is sufficient, but statement (1) alone is not sufficient.
   ○ BOTH statements TOGETHER are sufficient, but NEITHER statement ALONE is sufficient.
   ○ EACH statement ALONE is sufficient.
   ○ Statements (1) and (2) TOGETHER are not sufficient.

6. If $x = m - 1$, which of the following is true when $m = \dfrac{1}{2}$?

   ○ $x^0 > x^2 > x^3 > x^1$
   ○ $x^0 > x^2 > x^1 > x^3$
   ○ $x^0 > x^1 > x^2 > x^3$
   ○ $x^2 > x^0 > x^3 > x^1$
   ○ $x^3 > x^2 > x^1 > x^0$

7. If a comedian plays two shows and twice as many tickets are available for the evening show as for the afternoon show, what percentage of the total number of tickets available for both shows have been sold?

   (1) A total of 450 tickets are available for both shows.

   (2) Exactly $\dfrac{3}{5}$ of the tickets available for the afternoon show have been sold, and exactly $\dfrac{1}{5}$ of the tickets available for the evening show have been sold.

   ○ Statement (1) ALONE is sufficient, but statement (2) alone is not sufficient.
   ○ Statement (2) ALONE is sufficient, but statement (1) alone is not sufficient.
   ○ BOTH statements TOGETHER are sufficient, but NEITHER statement ALONE is sufficient.
   ○ EACH statement ALONE is sufficient.
   ○ Statements (1) and (2) TOGETHER are not sufficient.

8. If $\dfrac{1}{y} = 2\dfrac{2}{3}$, then $\left(\dfrac{1}{y+1}\right)^2 =$

   ○ $\dfrac{9}{64}$
   ○ $\dfrac{3}{8}$
   ○ $\dfrac{64}{121}$
   ○ $\dfrac{121}{64}$
   ○ $\dfrac{64}{9}$

GO ON TO THE NEXT PAGE.

9. An operation $\sim$ is defined by $a \sim b = \dfrac{a+b}{(ab)^2}$ for all numbers a and b such that $ab \neq 0$. If $c \neq 0$ and $a \sim c = 0$, then $c =$

○ $-a$

○ 0

○ $\sqrt{a}$

○ a

○ a^2

10. If x is a positive integer, is the greatest common factor of 150 and x a prime number?

(1) x is a prime number.

(2) $x < 4$

○ Statement (1) ALONE is sufficient, but statement (2) alone is not sufficient.
○ Statement (2) ALONE is sufficient, but statement (1) alone is not sufficient.
○ BOTH statements TOGETHER are sufficient, but NEITHER statement ALONE is sufficient.
○ EACH statement ALONE is sufficient.
○ Statements (1) and (2) TOGETHER are not sufficient.

$$X = \{9, 10, 11, 12\}$$

$$Y = \{2, 3, 4, 5\}$$

11. If one number is chosen at random from each of the sets above and the number from Set X is divided by the number from Set Y, what is the probability that the result is an integer?

○ $\dfrac{1}{16}$

○ $\dfrac{3}{8}$

○ $\dfrac{1}{2}$

○ $\dfrac{3}{4}$

○ $\dfrac{15}{16}$

12. If p and q are integers, is $\dfrac{p+q}{2}$ an integer?

(1) $p < 17$

(2) $p = q$

○ Statement (1) ALONE is sufficient, but statement (2) alone is not sufficient.
○ Statement (2) ALONE is sufficient, but statement (1) alone is not sufficient.
○ BOTH statements TOGETHER are sufficient, but NEITHER statement ALONE is sufficient.
○ EACH statement ALONE is sufficient.
○ Statements (1) and (2) TOGETHER are not sufficient.

GO ON TO THE NEXT PAGE.

13. A perfectly spherical satellite with a radius of 4 feet is being packed for shipment to its launch site. If the inside dimensions of the rectangular crates available for shipment, when measured in feet, are consecutive even integers, then what is the volume of the smallest available crate that can be used? (Note: the volume of a sphere is given by the equation $V = \frac{4}{3}\pi r^3$.)

- ○   48
- ○   192
- ○   480
- ○   960
- ○ 1,680

14. Richard is 6 years older than David, and David is 8 years older than Scott. In 8 years, if Richard will be twice as old as Scott, then how old was David 4 years ago?

- ○   8
- ○ 10
- ○ 12
- ○ 14
- ○ 16

15. What is the value of x ?

(1) $x^2 - 5x + 4 = 0$

(2) x is not prime.

- ○ Statement (1) ALONE is sufficient, but statement (2) alone is not sufficient.
- ○ Statement (2) ALONE is sufficient, but statement (1) alone is not sufficient.
- ○ BOTH statements TOGETHER are sufficient, but NEITHER statement ALONE is sufficient.
- ○ EACH statement ALONE is sufficient.
- ○ Statements (1) and (2) TOGETHER are not sufficient.

16. Sam and Jessica are invited to a dance. If there are 7 men and 7 women in total at the dance, and one woman and one man are chosen to lead the dance, what is the probability that Sam and Jessica will NOT be the pair chosen to lead the dance?

- ○ $\dfrac{1}{49}$
- ○ $\dfrac{1}{7}$
- ○ $\dfrac{6}{7}$
- ○ $\dfrac{47}{49}$
- ○ $\dfrac{48}{49}$

17. What is the surface area of rectangular solid Y ?

(1) The dimensions of one face of rectangular solid Y are 2 by 3.

(2) The volume of rectangular solid Y is 12.

- ○ Statement (1) ALONE is sufficient, but statement (2) alone is not sufficient.
- ○ Statement (2) ALONE is sufficient, but statement (1) alone is not sufficient.
- ○ BOTH statements TOGETHER are sufficient, but NEITHER statement ALONE is sufficient.
- ○ EACH statement ALONE is sufficient.
- ○ Statements (1) and (2) TOGETHER are not sufficient.

GO ON TO THE NEXT PAGE.

18. A six-sided die with faces numbered one through six is rolled three times. What is the probability that the face with the number 6 on it will NOT be facing upward on all three rolls?

    ○ $\dfrac{1}{216}$

    ○ $\dfrac{1}{6}$

    ○ $\dfrac{2}{3}$

    ○ $\dfrac{17}{18}$

    ○ $\dfrac{215}{216}$

19. What is the sum of x, y, and z ?

(1) $2x + y + 3z = 45$

(2) $x + 2y = 30$

    ○ Statement (1) ALONE is sufficient, but statement (2) alone is not sufficient.
    ○ Statement (2) ALONE is sufficient, but statement (1) alone is not sufficient.
    ○ BOTH statements TOGETHER are sufficient, but NEITHER statement ALONE is sufficient.
    ○ EACH statement ALONE is sufficient.
    ○ Statements (1) and (2) TOGETHER are not sufficient.

20. A department store receives a shipment of 1,000 shirts, for which it pays $9,000. The store sells the shirts at a price 80 percent above cost for one month, after which it reduces the price of the shirts to 20 percent above cost. The store sells 75 percent of the shirts during the first month and 50 percent of the remaining shirts afterward. How much gross income did sales of the shirts generate?

    ○ $10,000
    ○ $10,800
    ○ $12,150
    ○ $13,500
    ○ $16,200

21. David has three credit cards: a Passport card, an EverywhereCard, and an American Local card. He owes balances on all three cards. Does he owe the greatest balance on the EverywhereCard?

(1) The sum of the balances on his EverywhereCard and American Local card is $1,350, which is three times the balance on his Passport card.

(2) The balance on his EverywhereCard is $\dfrac{4}{3}$ of the balance on his Passport card and $\dfrac{4}{5}$ of the balance on his American Local card.

    ○ Statement (1) ALONE is sufficient, but statement (2) alone is not sufficient.
    ○ Statement (2) ALONE is sufficient, but statement (1) alone is not sufficient.
    ○ BOTH statements TOGETHER are sufficient, but NEITHER statement ALONE is sufficient.
    ○ EACH statement ALONE is sufficient.
    ○ Statements (1) and (2) TOGETHER are not sufficient.

GO ON TO THE NEXT PAGE.

22. Automobile A is traveling at two-thirds the speed that Automobile B is traveling. At what speed is Automobile A traveling?

(1) If both automobiles increased their speed by 10 miles per hour, Automobile A would be traveling at three-quarters the speed that Automobile B would be traveling.

(2) If both automobiles decreased their speed by 10 miles per hour, Automobile A would be traveling at half the speed that Automobile B would be traveling.

○ Statement (1) ALONE is sufficient, but statement (2) alone is not sufficient.
○ Statement (2) ALONE is sufficient, but statement (1) alone is not sufficient.
○ BOTH statements TOGETHER are sufficient, but NEITHER statement ALONE is sufficient.
○ EACH statement ALONE is sufficient.
○ Statements (1) and (2) TOGETHER are not sufficient.

23. a and b are nonzero integers such that 0.35a = 0.2b. What is the value of b in terms of a ?

○ 0.07a
○ 0.57a
○ 0.7a
○ 1.75a
○ 17.5a

24. The Binary Ice Cream Shoppe sells two flavors of cones, vanilla and chocolate. On Friday, the ratio of vanilla cones sold to chocolate cones sold was 2 to 3. If the store sold 4 more vanilla cones, the ratio of vanilla cones sold to chocolate cones sold would have been 3 to 4. How many vanilla cones did the store sell on Friday?

○ 32
○ 35
○ 42
○ 48
○ 54

25. Is integer a a prime number?

(1) 2a has exactly three factors.

(2) a is an even number.

○ Statement (1) ALONE is sufficient, but statement (2) alone is not sufficient.
○ Statement (2) ALONE is sufficient, but statement (1) alone is not sufficient.
○ BOTH statements TOGETHER are sufficient, but NEITHER statement ALONE is sufficient.
○ EACH statement ALONE is sufficient.
○ Statements (1) and (2) TOGETHER are not sufficient.

26. Renee rides her bicycle 20 miles in m minutes. If she rides x miles in 10 minutes at the same rate, which of the following is an expression for x, in terms of m ?

○ $\dfrac{m}{200}$

○ $\dfrac{m}{20}$

○ $\dfrac{m}{2}$

○ $2m$

○ $\dfrac{200}{m}$

27. If s and w are integers, is $\dfrac{w}{5}$ an integer?

(1) 4s + 2 is divisible by 5.

(2) w + 3 = 4s

○ Statement (1) ALONE is sufficient, but statement (2) alone is not sufficient.
○ Statement (2) ALONE is sufficient, but statement (1) alone is not sufficient.
○ BOTH statements TOGETHER are sufficient, but NEITHER statement ALONE is sufficient.
○ EACH statement ALONE is sufficient.
○ Statements (1) and (2) TOGETHER are not sufficient.

END OF BIN.

Math Test
Bin 3—Medium-Hard Questions
26 Questions

This test is composed of both problem solving questions and data sufficiency questions.

Problem Solving Directions: Solve each problem and choose the best of the answer choices provided.

Data Sufficiency Directions: Each <u>data sufficiency</u> problem consists of a question and two statements, labeled (1) and (2), which contain certain data. Using these data and your knowledge of mathematics and everyday facts (such as the number of days in July or the meaning of *counterclockwise*), decide whether the data given are sufficient for answering the question and then indicate one of the following answer choices:

○ Statement (1) ALONE is sufficient, but statement (2) alone is not sufficient.

○ Statement (2) ALONE is sufficient, but statement (1) alone is not sufficient.

○ BOTH statements TOGETHER are sufficient, but NEITHER statement ALONE is sufficient.

○ EACH statement ALONE is sufficient.

○ Statements (1) and (2) TOGETHER are not sufficient.

---

1. An electronics store normally sells all its merchandise at a 10 percent to 30 percent discount from the suggested retail price. During a sale, if the store were to deduct an additional 20 percent from the discounted price, what is the lowest price possible for an item with a suggested retail price of $260 ?

   ○ $130.00
   ○ $145.60
   ○ $163.80
   ○ $182.00
   ○ $210.00

2. A certain gas station discounts the price per gallon of all gasoline purchased after the first 10 gallons by 10 percent. The total per gallon discount for 25 gallons of gas purchased at this station is what percent of the total per gallon discount for 20 gallons of gas?

   ○ 80%
   ○ 100%
   ○ 116.7%
   ○ 120%
   ○ 140%

GO ON TO THE NEXT PAGE.

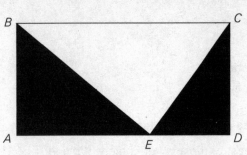

3. What is the area of the shaded region in the figure shown above?

(1) The area of rectangle *ABCD* is 54.

(2) $AE = 2ED$

○ Statement (1) ALONE is sufficient, but statement (2) alone is not sufficient.
○ Statement (2) ALONE is sufficient, but statement (1) alone is not sufficient.
○ BOTH statements TOGETHER are sufficient, but NEITHER statement ALONE is sufficient.
○ EACH statement ALONE is sufficient.
○ Statements (1) and (2) TOGETHER are not sufficient.

4. For the triangle shown above, does $p = q = 60$?

(1) $r = 180 - (p + r)$

(2) $p = 60$

○ Statement (1) ALONE is sufficient, but statement (2) alone is not sufficient.
○ Statement (2) ALONE is sufficient, but statement (1) alone is not sufficient.
○ BOTH statements TOGETHER are sufficient, but NEITHER statement ALONE is sufficient.
○ EACH statement ALONE is sufficient.
○ Statements (1) and (2) TOGETHER are not sufficient.

5. During a certain two-week period, a video rental store rented only comedies, dramas, and action movies. If 70 percent of the movies rented were comedies, and of the remaining movies rented, 5 times as many dramas as action movies were rented and *A* action movies were rented, then, in terms of *A*, how many of the movies rented were comedies?

○ $\dfrac{A}{14}$

○ $\dfrac{5A}{7}$

○ $\dfrac{7A}{5}$

○ $14A$

○ $35A$

6. x, y, and z are consecutive positive integers such that $x < y < z$. If the units digit of x^2 is 6 and the units digit of y^2 is 9, what is the units digit of z^2 ?

○ 0
○ 1
○ 2
○ 4
○ 5

GO ON TO THE NEXT PAGE.

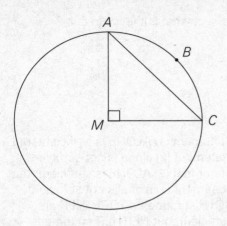

7. What is the area of the circle with center M shown above?

(1) The length of AC is $8\sqrt{2}$.

(2) The length of arc ABC is 4π.

○ Statement (1) ALONE is sufficient, but statement (2) alone is not sufficient.
○ Statement (2) ALONE is sufficient, but statement (1) alone is not sufficient.
○ BOTH statements TOGETHER are sufficient, but NEITHER statement ALONE is sufficient.
○ EACH statement ALONE is sufficient.
○ Statements (1) and (2) TOGETHER are not sufficient.

8. If 70 percent of the female and 90 percent of the male students in the senior class at a certain school are going on the senior trip and the senior class is 60 percent female, what percent of the senior class is going on the senior trip?

○ 82%
○ 80%
○ 78%
○ 76%
○ 72%

9. If P is a set of integers and 3 is in P, is every positive multiple of 3 in P?

(1) For any integer in P, the sum of 3 and that integer is also in P.

(2) For any integer in P, that integer minus 3 is also in P.

○ Statement (1) ALONE is sufficient, but statement (2) alone is not sufficient.
○ Statement (2) ALONE is sufficient, but statement (1) alone is not sufficient.
○ BOTH statements TOGETHER are sufficient, but NEITHER statement ALONE is sufficient.
○ EACH statement ALONE is sufficient.
○ Statements (1) and (2) TOGETHER are not sufficient.

10. A certain seafood restaurant gets a delivery of fresh seafood every day of the week. If the delivery company charges d dollars per delivery and c cents per delivered item and the restaurant has an average (arithmetic mean) of x items delivered per day, then which of the following is an expression for the total cost, in dollars, of one week's deliveries?

○ $\dfrac{7cdx}{100}$

○ $d + \dfrac{7cx}{100}$

○ $7d + \dfrac{xc}{100}$

○ $7d + \dfrac{7xc}{100}$

○ $7cdx$

11. Which of the following contains the interval two standard deviations from the mean of a set of data with an arithmetic mean of 46 and a standard deviation of 4 ?

   ○ 38 to 46
   ○ 38 to 54
   ○ 42 to 50
   ○ 44 to 48
   ○ 46 to 50

12. If a and b are positive integers, is a a multiple of b ?

   (1) Every distinct prime factor of b is also a distinct prime factor of a.

   (2) Every factor of b is also a factor of a.

   ○ Statement (1) ALONE is sufficient, but statement (2) alone is not sufficient.
   ○ Statement (2) ALONE is sufficient, but statement (1) alone is not sufficient.
   ○ BOTH statements TOGETHER are sufficient, but NEITHER statement alone is sufficient.
   ○ EACH statement ALONE is sufficient.
   ○ Statements (1) and (2) TOGETHER are NOT sufficient.

13. If Set X contains 10 consecutive integers and the sum of the 5 least members of the set is 265, then what is the sum of the 5 greatest members of the set?

   ○ 290
   ○ 285
   ○ 280
   ○ 275
   ○ 270

14. If $a - b = c$, what is the value of b ?

   (1) $c + 6 = a$

   (2) $a = 6$

   ○ Statement (1) ALONE is sufficient, but statement (2) alone is not sufficient.
   ○ Statement (2) ALONE is sufficient, but statement (1) alone is not sufficient.
   ○ BOTH statements TOGETHER are sufficient, but NEITHER statement ALONE is sufficient.
   ○ EACH statement ALONE is sufficient.
   ○ Statements (1) and (2) TOGETHER are not sufficient.

$$\{3, 5, 9, 13, y\}$$

15. If the average (arithmetic mean) and the median of the set of numbers shown above are equal, then what is the value of y ?

   ○ 7
   ○ 8
   ○ 10
   ○ 15
   ○ 17

16. For a certain foot race, how many different arrangements of medal winners are possible?

   (1) Medals will be given for 1st, 2nd, and 3rd place.

   (2) There are 10 runners in the race.

   ○ Statement (1) ALONE is sufficient, but statement (2) alone is not sufficient.
   ○ Statement (2) ALONE is sufficient, but statement (1) alone is not sufficient.
   ○ BOTH statements TOGETHER are sufficient, but NEITHER statement ALONE is sufficient.
   ○ EACH statement ALONE is sufficient.
   ○ Statements (1) and (2) TOGETHER are not sufficient.

GO ON TO THE NEXT PAGE.

17. For the set of measurements 3, x_2, x_3, what is the value of x_3?

    (1) The range of the set of measurements is 0.

    (2) The standard deviation of the set of measurements is 0.

    ○ Statement (1) ALONE is sufficient, but statement (2) alone is not sufficient.
    ○ Statement (2) ALONE is sufficient, but statement (1) alone is not sufficient.
    ○ BOTH statements TOGETHER are sufficient, but NEITHER statement ALONE is sufficient.
    ○ EACH statement ALONE is sufficient.
    ○ Statements (1) and (2) TOGETHER are not sufficient.

18. An employer has 6 applicants for a programming position and 4 applicants for a manager position. If the employer must hire 3 programmers and 2 managers, what is the total number of ways the employer can make the selection?

    ○ 1,490
    ○ 132
    ○ 120
    ○ 60
    ○ 23

19. On Monday, an animal shelter housed 55 cats and dogs, and by Friday exactly $\frac{1}{5}$ of the cats and $\frac{1}{4}$ of the dogs had been adopted. If no new cats or dogs were brought to the shelter during this period, what is the greatest possible number of pets that could have been adopted from the animal shelter between Monday and Friday?

    ○ 11
    ○ 12
    ○ 13
    ○ 14
    ○ 20

20. If x is an integer, then which of the following statements about $x^2 - x - 1$ is true?

    ○ It is always odd.
    ○ It is always even.
    ○ It is always positive.
    ○ It is even when x is even and odd when x is odd.
    ○ It is even when x is odd and odd when x is even.

21. During a five-day period, Monday through Friday, the average (arithmetic mean) high temperature was 86 degrees Fahrenheit. What was the high temperature on Friday?

    (1) The average high temperature for Monday through Thursday was 87 degrees Fahrenheit.

    (2) The high temperature on Friday reduced the average high temperature for the five-day period by 1 degree Fahrenheit.

    ○ Statement (1) ALONE is sufficient, but statement (2) alone is not sufficient.
    ○ Statement (2) ALONE is sufficient, but statement (1) alone is not sufficient.
    ○ BOTH statements TOGETHER are sufficient, but NEITHER statement ALONE is sufficient.
    ○ EACH statement ALONE is sufficient.
    ○ Statements (1) and (2) TOGETHER are not sufficient.

GO ON TO THE NEXT PAGE.

22. What is the value of $x^2 - y^2$?

    (1) $x + y = 0$

    (2) $x - y = 2$

    ○ Statement (1) ALONE is sufficient, but statement (2) alone is not sufficient.
    ○ Statement (2) ALONE is sufficient, but statement (1) alone is not sufficient.
    ○ BOTH statements TOGETHER are sufficient, but NEITHER statement ALONE is sufficient.
    ○ EACH statement ALONE is sufficient.
    ○ Statements (1) and (2) TOGETHER are not sufficient.

23. If P is the perimeter of an equilateral triangle, which of the following represents the height of the triangle?

    ○ $\dfrac{P}{3}$

    ○ $\dfrac{P\sqrt{3}}{3}$

    ○ $\dfrac{P}{4}$

    ○ $\dfrac{P\sqrt{3}}{6}$

    ○ $\dfrac{P}{6}$

24. If 75 percent of all Americans own an automobile, 15 percent of all Americans own a bicycle, and 20 percent of all Americans own neither an automobile nor a bicycle, then what percent of Americans own *both* an automobile and a bicycle?

    ○   0%
    ○   1.33%
    ○   3.75%
    ○   5%
    ○   10%

25. Triangle *ABC* above is an isosceles right triangle and triangle *DEF* above is an equilateral triangle with height *EG*. What is the ratio of the area of *ABC* to the area of *DEF* ?

    (1) The ratio of *BC* to *EG* is 1:1.

    (2) The ratio of *AC* to *DF* is $\sqrt{3}:2$.

    ○ Statement (1) ALONE is sufficient, but statement (2) alone is not sufficient.
    ○ Statement (2) ALONE is sufficient, but statement (1) alone is not sufficient.
    ○ BOTH statements TOGETHER are sufficient, but NEITHER statement ALONE is sufficient.
    ○ EACH statement ALONE is sufficient.
    ○ Statements (1) and (2) TOGETHER are not sufficient.

26. What is the value of integer x ?

    (1) $\sqrt[x]{64} = 4$

    (2) $x^2 = x + 6$

    ○ Statement (1) ALONE is sufficient, but statement (2) alone is not sufficient.
    ○ Statement (2) ALONE is sufficient, but statement (1) alone is not sufficient.
    ○ BOTH statements TOGETHER are sufficient, but NEITHER statement ALONE is sufficient.
    ○ EACH statement ALONE is sufficient.
    ○ Statements (1) and (2) TOGETHER are not sufficient.

    END OF BIN.

Math Test
Bin 4—Hard Questions
25 Questions

This test is composed of both problem solving questions and data sufficiency questions.

Problem Solving Directions: Solve each problem and choose the best of the answer choices provided.

Data Sufficiency Directions: Each <u>data sufficiency</u> problem consists of a question and two statements, labeled (1) and (2), which contain certain data. Using these data and your knowledge of mathematics and everyday facts (such as the number of days in July or the meaning of *counterclockwise*), decide whether the data given are sufficient for answering the question and then indicate one of the following answer choices:

○ Statement (1) ALONE is sufficient, but statement (2) alone is not sufficient.

○ Statement (2) ALONE is sufficient, but statement (1) alone is not sufficient.

○ BOTH statements TOGETHER are sufficient, but NEITHER statement ALONE is sufficient.

○ EACH statement ALONE is sufficient.

○ Statements (1) and (2) TOGETHER are not sufficient.

---

1. A rectangular garden with dimensions 20 feet by 30 feet is surrounded by a rectangular brick walkway of uniform width, as shown by the figure above. If the area of the walkway equals the area of the garden, what is the width of the walkway?

○ 1 foot
○ 3 feet
○ 5 feet
○ 8 feet
○ 10 feet

2. If a fair two-sided coin is flipped 6 times, what is the probability that tails is the result at least twice but at most 5 times?

○ $\dfrac{5}{8}$

○ $\dfrac{3}{4}$

○ $\dfrac{7}{8}$

○ $\dfrac{57}{64}$

○ $\dfrac{15}{16}$

GO ON TO THE NEXT PAGE.

3. The new recruits of a military organization who score in the bottom 16 percent on their physical conditioning tests are required to retest. If the test scores are normally distributed and have an arithmetic mean of 72, what is the score at or below which the recruits are required to retest?

   (1) There are 500 new recruits.

   (2) 10 new recruits scored at least 82 on the physical conditioning test.

   ○ Statement (1) ALONE is sufficient, but statement (2) alone is not sufficient.
   ○ Statement (2) ALONE is sufficient, but statement (1) alone is not sufficient.
   ○ BOTH statements TOGETHER are sufficient, but NEITHER statement ALONE is sufficient.
   ○ EACH statement ALONE is sufficient.
   ○ Statements (1) and (2) TOGETHER are not sufficient.

4. Each of the integers from 1 to 20 is written on a separate index card and placed in a box. If the cards are drawn from the box at random without replacement, how many cards must be drawn to ensure that the product of all the integers drawn is even?

   ○ 19
   ○ 12
   ○ 11
   ○ 10
   ○ 3

5. The average (arithmetic mean) of integers r, s, t, u, and v is 100. Are exactly two of the integers greater than 100 ?

   (1) Three of the integers are less than 50.

   (2) None of the integers is equal to 100.

   ○ Statement (1) ALONE is sufficient, but statement (2) alone is not sufficient.
   ○ Statement (2) ALONE is sufficient, but statement (1) alone is not sufficient.
   ○ BOTH statements TOGETHER are sufficient, but NEITHER statement ALONE is sufficient.
   ○ EACH statement ALONE is sufficient.
   ○ Statements (1) and (2) TOGETHER are not sufficient.

6. Paul jogs along the same route every day at a constant rate for 80 minutes. What distance does he jog?

   (1) Yesterday, Paul began jogging at 5:00 P.M.

   (2) Yesterday, Paul had jogged 5 miles by 5:40 P.M. and 8 miles by 6:04 P.M.

   ○ Statement (1) ALONE is sufficient, but statement (2) alone is not sufficient.
   ○ Statement (2) ALONE is sufficient, but statement (1) alone is not sufficient.
   ○ BOTH statements TOGETHER are sufficient, but NEITHER statement ALONE is sufficient.
   ○ EACH statement ALONE is sufficient.
   ○ Statements (1) and (2) TOGETHER are not sufficient.

GO ON TO THE NEXT PAGE.

7. The diagram above shows two wheels that drive a conveyor belt. The larger wheel has a diameter of 40 centimeters, and the smaller wheel has a diameter of 32 centimeters. If each wheel must rotate the exact same number of centimeters per minute, and the larger wheel makes r revolutions per minute, then, in terms of r, how many revolutions does the smaller wheel make per hour?

○ $\dfrac{1{,}280\pi}{3}$

○ $75r$

○ $48r$

○ $24r$

○ $\dfrac{64\pi}{3}$

8. An automobile dealership sells only sedans and coupes. It sells each in only two colors: red and blue. Last year, the dealership sold 9,000 vehicles, half of which were red. How many coupes did the dealership sell last year?

(1) The dealership sold three times as many blue coupes as red sedans last year.

(2) The dealership sold half as many blue sedans as blue coupes last year.

○ Statement (1) ALONE is sufficient, but statement (2) alone is not sufficient.
○ Statement (2) ALONE is sufficient, but statement (1) alone is not sufficient.
○ BOTH statements TOGETHER are sufficient, but NEITHER statement ALONE is sufficient.
○ EACH statement ALONE is sufficient.
○ Statements (1) and (2) TOGETHER are not sufficient.

9. At a college football game, $\dfrac{4}{5}$ of the seats in the lower deck of the stadium were sold. If $\dfrac{1}{4}$ of all the seats in the stadium are located in the lower deck, and if $\dfrac{2}{3}$ of all the seats in the stadium were sold, what fraction of the unsold seats in the stadium are in the lower deck?

○ $\dfrac{3}{20}$

○ $\dfrac{1}{6}$

○ $\dfrac{1}{5}$

○ $\dfrac{1}{3}$

○ $\dfrac{7}{15}$

10. At Company R, the average (arithmetic mean) age of executive employees is 54 years old and the average age of non-executive employees is 34 years old. What is the average age of all the employees at Company R ?

(1) There are 10 executive employees at Company R.

(2) The number of non-executive employees at Company R is four times the number of executive employees at Company R.

○ Statement (1) ALONE is sufficient, but statement (2) alone is not sufficient.
○ Statement (2) ALONE is sufficient, but statement (1) alone is not sufficient.
○ BOTH statements TOGETHER are sufficient, but NEITHER statement ALONE is sufficient.
○ EACH statement ALONE is sufficient.
○ Statements (1) and (2) TOGETHER are not sufficient.

GO ON TO THE NEXT PAGE.

11. If a, b, c, d, and x are all nonzero integers, is the product $ax \cdot (bx)^2 \cdot (cx)^3 \cdot (dx)^4$ negative?

(1) $a < c < x < 0$

(2) $b < d < x < 0$

○ Statement (1) ALONE is sufficient, but statement (2) alone is not sufficient.
○ Statement (2) ALONE is sufficient, but statement (1) alone is not sufficient.
○ BOTH statements TOGETHER are sufficient, but NEITHER statement ALONE is sufficient.
○ EACH statement ALONE is sufficient.
○ Statements (1) and (2) TOGETHER are not sufficient.

12. A four character password consists of one letter from the English alphabet and three different digits from 0 to 9. If the letter is the second or third character of the password, how many different passwords are possible?

○ 5,040
○ 18,720
○ 26,000
○ 37,440
○ 52,000

13. If x is a positive integer, is x divisible by 48 ?

(1) x is divisible by 8.

(2) x is divisible by 6.

○ Statement (1) ALONE is sufficient, but statement (2) alone is not sufficient.
○ Statement (2) ALONE is sufficient, but statement (1) alone is not sufficient.
○ BOTH statements TOGETHER are sufficient, but NEITHER statement ALONE is sufficient.
○ EACH statement ALONE is sufficient.
○ Statements (1) and (2) TOGETHER are not sufficient.

$$\begin{array}{r} FGF \\ \times\ G \\ \hline HGG \end{array}$$

14. In the multiplication problem above, F, G, and H represent distinct odd digits. What is the value of the three-digit number FGF ?

○ 151
○ 161
○ 171
○ 313
○ 353

15. A group of 20 friends formed an investment club, with each member contributing an equal amount to the general fund. The club then invested the entire fund, which amounted to d dollars, in Stock X. The value of the stock subsequently increased 40 percent, at which point the stock was sold and the proceeds divided evenly among the members. In terms of d, how much money did each member of the club receive from the sale? (Assume that transaction fees and other associated costs were negligible.)

○ $800d$

○ $\dfrac{7d}{5}$

○ $\dfrac{d}{20}+40$

○ $\dfrac{d}{2}$

○ $\dfrac{7d}{100}$

GO ON TO THE NEXT PAGE.

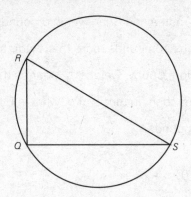

16. Triangle *QRS* is inscribed in a circle as shown above. Is *QRS* a right triangle?

(1) *RS* is a diameter of the circle.

(2) *QR* = 3 and *RS* = 5

○ Statement (1) ALONE is sufficient, but statement (2) alone is not sufficient.
○ Statement (2) ALONE is sufficient, but statement (1) alone is not sufficient.
○ BOTH statements TOGETHER are sufficient, but NEITHER statement ALONE is sufficient.
○ EACH statement ALONE is sufficient.
○ Statements (1) and (2) TOGETHER are not sufficient.

17. Square *G* has sides of length 4 inches. Is the area of Square *H* exactly one half the area of Square *G* ?

(1) The length of the diagonal of Square *H* equals the length of one side of Square *G*.

(2) The perimeter of Square *H* is twice the length of the diagonal of Square *G*.

○ Statement (1) ALONE is sufficient, but statement (2) alone is not sufficient.
○ Statement (2) ALONE is sufficient, but statement (1) alone is not sufficient.
○ BOTH statements TOGETHER are sufficient, but NEITHER statement ALONE is sufficient.
○ EACH statement ALONE is sufficient.
○ Statements (1) and (2) TOGETHER are not sufficient.

18. In a certain state, 70 percent of the counties received some rain on Monday, and 65 percent of the counties received some rain on Tuesday. No rain fell either day in 25 percent of the counties in the state. What percent of the counties received some rain on Monday and Tuesday?

○ 12.5%
○ 40%
○ 50%
○ 60%
○ 67.5%

GO ON TO THE NEXT PAGE.

19. *ABCD* is a rectangle with sides of length *x* centimeters and width *y* centimeters and a diagonal of length *z* centimeters. What is the perimeter, in centimeters, of *ABCD* ?

(1) $x - y = 7$

(2) $z = 13$

○ Statement (1) ALONE is sufficient, but statement (2) alone is not sufficient.
○ Statement (2) ALONE is sufficient, but statement (1) alone is not sufficient.
○ BOTH statements TOGETHER are sufficient, but NEITHER statement ALONE is sufficient.
○ EACH statement ALONE is sufficient.
○ Statements (1) and (2) TOGETHER are not sufficient.

20. Together, Andrea and Brian weigh *p* pounds and Brian weighs 10 pounds more than Andrea. If Andrea's dog, Cubby, weighs $\frac{p}{4}$ pounds more than Andrea then, in terms of *p*, what is Cubby's weight in pounds?

○ $\dfrac{p}{2} - 10$

○ $\dfrac{3p}{4} - 5$

○ $\dfrac{3p}{2} - 5$

○ $\dfrac{5p}{4} - 10$

○ $5p - 5$

21. A first-grade teacher uses ten flash cards, numbered 1 through 10, to teach her students to order numbers correctly. She has students choose four flash cards at random, then arrange the cards in ascending order. If she removes the cards numbered 2 and 4, how many different correctly ordered arrangements of the four selected cards are possible?

○   70
○   210
○   336
○   840
○ 1,680

GO ON TO THE NEXT PAGE.

22. If *A* and *B* are two-digit integers that share the same digits, except in reverse order, then what is the sum of *A* and *B* ?

(1) $A - B = 45$

(2) The difference between the two digits in each number is 5.

○ Statement (1) ALONE is sufficient, but statement (2) alone is not sufficient.
○ Statement (2) ALONE is sufficient, but statement (1) alone is not sufficient.
○ BOTH statements TOGETHER are sufficient, but NEITHER statement ALONE is sufficient.
○ EACH statement ALONE is sufficient.
○ Statements (1) and (2) TOGETHER are not sufficient.

23. A university awarded grants in the amount of either $7,000 or $10,000 to selected incoming freshmen. If the total amount of all such awards is $2,300,000, did the university award more $7,000 grants than $10,000 grants to the selected incoming freshmen?

(1) A total of 275 freshmen received grants in one of the two amounts.

(2) The amount of money awarded in $10,000 grants was $200,000 more than the amount of money awarded in $7,000 grants.

○ Statement (1) ALONE is sufficient, but statement (2) alone is not sufficient.
○ Statement (2) ALONE is sufficient, but statement (1) alone is not sufficient.
○ BOTH statements TOGETHER are sufficient, but NEITHER statement ALONE is sufficient.
○ EACH statement ALONE is sufficient.
○ Statements (1) and (2) TOGETHER are not sufficient.

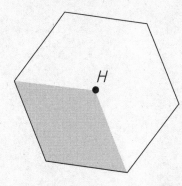

24. The figure shown above is a regular hexagon with center *H*. The shaded area is a parallelogram that shares three vertices with the hexagon and its fourth vertex is the center of the hexagon. If the length of one side of the hexagon is 8 centimeters, what is the area of the unshaded region?

○ $16\sqrt{3}$ cm²
○ 96 cm²
○ $64\sqrt{3}$ cm²
○ $96\sqrt{3}$ cm²
○ 256 cm²

25. A fish tank contains a number of fish, including 5 Fantails. If two fish are selected from the tank at random, what is the probability that both will be Fantails?

(1) The probability that the first fish chosen is a Fantail is $\frac{1}{2}$.

(2) The probability that the second fish chosen is a Fantail is $\frac{4}{9}$.

○ Statement (1) ALONE is sufficient, but statement (2) alone is not sufficient.
○ Statement (2) ALONE is sufficient, but statement (1) alone is not sufficient.
○ BOTH statements TOGETHER are sufficient, but NEITHER statement ALONE is sufficient.
○ EACH statement ALONE is sufficient.
○ Statements (1) and (2) TOGETHER are not sufficient.

END OF BIN.

Verbal Test
Bin 1—Easy Questions
25 Questions

This test is made up of sentence correction, critical reasoning, and reading comprehension questions.

Sentence Correction Directions: Each of the <u>sentence correction</u> questions presents a sentence, part or all of which is underlined. Beneath the sentence you will find five ways of phrasing the underlined part. The first of these repeats the original; the other four are different. Follow the requirements of standard written English to choose your answer, paying attention to grammar, word choice, and sentence construction. Select the answer that produces the most effective sentence; your answer should make the sentence clear, exact, and free of grammatical errors. It should also minimize awkwardness, ambiguity, and redundancy.

Reading Comprehension Directions: Each of the <u>reading comprehension</u> questions is based on the content of a passage. After reading the passage, answer all questions pertaining to it on the basis of what is <u>stated</u> or <u>implied</u> in the passage. For each question, select the best answer of the choices given.

Critical Reasoning Directions: Each of the <u>critical reasoning</u> questions is based on a short argument, a set of statements, or a plan of action. For each question, select the best answer of the choices given.

_____

1. As its reputation for making acquisitions of important masterpieces has grown, the museum has increasingly turned down gifts of lesser-known paintings <u>they would in the past have accepted gratefully</u>.

   - they would in the past have accepted gratefully
   - they would have accepted gratefully in the past
   - it would in the past have accepted gratefully
   - it previously would have accepted gratefully in the past
   - that previously would have been accepted in the past

2. Over the past few decades, despite periodic attempts to reign in spending, currencies in South America <u>are devalued</u> by rampant inflation.

   - are devalued
   - are becoming more devalued
   - which have lost value
   - have become devalued
   - have since become devalued

3. A fashion designer's fall line for women utilizing new soft fabrics broke all sales records last year. To capitalize on her success, the designer plans to launch a line of clothing for men this year that makes use of the same new soft fabrics.

   The designer's plan assumes that

   - other designers are not planning to introduce new lines for men utilizing the same soft fabrics
   - men will be as interested in the new soft fabrics as women were the year before
   - the designer will have time to develop new lines for both men and women
   - the line for men will be considered innovative and daring because of its use of fabrics
   - women who bought the new line last year will continue to buy it this year

GO ON TO THE NEXT PAGE.

4. The standard lamp is becoming outmoded, and <u>so too is the incandescent light bulb, it is Edison's miraculous invention to use</u> so much more energy than the new low-wattage halogen bulbs.

  ○ so too is the incandescent light bulb, it is Edison's miraculous invention to use
  ○ so too is the incandescent light bulb, Edison's miraculous invention that uses
  ○ so too the incandescent light bulb, Edison's miraculous invention using
  ○ also the incandescent light bulb, it is Edison's miraculous invention that uses
  ○ also the incandescent light bulb, which is Edison's miraculous invention to use

5. Over the last 20 years, <u>the growth of information technology has been more rapid than any other business field</u>, but has recently begun to lag behind as newly emerging fields seem more enticing to new graduates.

  ○ the growth of information technology has been more rapid than any other business field
  ○ the growth of information technology has been more rapid than any other fields of business
  ○ information technology's growth has been more rapid than any other fields of business
  ○ the growing of information technology has been more rapid than that of any other business field
  ○ the growth of information technology has been more rapid than that of any other business field

6. According to mutual fund sales experts, a successful year for a stock fund should result not only in increased investor dollars flowing into the fund, but also in increased investor dollars flowing into other mutual stock funds offered by the same company. However, while last year the Grafton Mutual Company's "Growth Stock Fund" beat average market returns by a factor of two and recorded substantial new investment, the other stock funds offered by Grafton did not report any increase whatsoever.

Which of the following conclusions can properly be drawn from the statements above?

  ○ When one of the mutual funds offered by a company beats average market returns, the other mutual funds offered by that company will beat average market returns.
  ○ The mutual fund sales experts neglected to consider bond funds in formulating their theory.
  ○ The performance of the Grafton "Growth Stock Fund" was a result of a wave of mergers and acquisitions that year.
  ○ Investors currently dislike all stock mutual funds because of market volatility.
  ○ The success of one mutual fund is not the only factor affecting whether investors will invest in other mutual funds run by the same company.

7. With <u>less than thirty thousand dollars in advance ticket sales and fewer</u> acceptances by guest speakers than expected, the one-day symposium on art and religion was canceled for lack of interest.

  ○ less than thirty thousand dollars in advance ticket sales and fewer
  ○ fewer than thirty thousand dollars in advance ticket sales and less
  ○ fewer than thirty thousand dollars in advance ticket sales and fewer
  ○ lesser than thirty thousand dollars in advance ticket sales and fewer
  ○ less than thirty thousand dollars in advance ticket sales and as few

GO ON TO THE NEXT PAGE.

8. New technology now makes it feasible for computer call-in help desk services to route calls they receive to almost anywhere, theoretically allowing employees to work from home, without the need for a daily commute.

   The adoption of this policy would be most likely to increase productivity if employees did not _____.

   ○ commute from a distance of fewer than 10 miles
   ○ commute by car as opposed to by rail
   ○ live in areas with dependable phone service
   ○ need to consult frequently with each other to solve callers' problems
   ○ have more than one telephone line

9. The port cities of England in the 19th century saw a renaissance of ship construction, with some innovative designs breaking new ground, stretching the limits of ship-building theory, and <u>received</u> acclaim from around the world.

   ○ received
   ○ it received
   ○ receiving
   ○ would receive
   ○ it had received

10. According to a consumer research group survey, the majority of kitchen appliances purchased in the United States are purchased by men. This appears to belie the myth that women spend more time in the kitchen than men.

    The argument is flawed primarily because the author _____.

    ○ fails to differentiate between buying and using
    ○ does not provide information about the types of kitchen appliances surveyed
    ○ depends on the results of one survey
    ○ does not give exact statistics to back up his case
    ○ does not provide information on other appliances such as washers and dryers

11. <u>A contribution to a favorite charity being sent instead</u> of flowers when a colleague dies is becoming more the rule than the exception when it comes to funeral etiquette.

    ○ A contribution to a favorite charity being sent instead
    ○ A contribution being sent to a favorite charity as opposed
    ○ To send a contribution for a favorite charity instead
    ○ Sending a contribution to a favorite charity instead
    ○ Sending a contribution to a favorite charity as opposed

GO ON TO THE NEXT PAGE.

Questions 12–15 are based on the following passage:

As a business model, the world of publishing has always been a somewhat sleepy enclave, but now all that seems poised to change. Several
Line companies have moved aggressively into a new
(5) business endeavor whose genesis comes from the question: Who owns the great works of literature?

Text-on-demand is not a completely new idea, of course. In the 1990s, the Gutenberg project sought volunteers to type literary classics that had
(10) expired copyrights into word processing files so that scholars would have searchable databases for their research. Most of the works of Shakespeare, Cervantes, Proust, and Molière were to be found free online by as early as 1995.
(15) However, now large-scale companies have moved into the market, with scanners and business plans, and are looking for bargain basement content. These companies are striking deals with libraries, and some publishers, to
(20) be able to provide their content, for a price, to individual buyers over the Internet.

At stake are the rights to an estimated store of 30 million books, most of which are now out of print. Many of these books are now also in the
(25) public domain, giving any company the right to sell them online. Still, a good portion of the books a general audience might actually want to buy is still under copyright. The urgent question: Who owns those copyrights? In the case of all too
(30) many books put out more than 20 years ago by now-defunct publishing companies, the answer is unclear—a situation the new text-on-demand companies are eager to exploit. An association of publishers has sued, claiming massive copyright
(35) infringement. The case is several years away from trial.

12. The primary purpose of the passage is to

○ present the results of a statistical analysis and propose further study
○ explain a recent development and explore its consequences
○ identify the reasons for a trend and recommend measures to address it
○ outline several theories about a phenomenon and advocate one of them
○ describe the potential consequences of implementing a new policy and argue in favor of that policy

13. It can be inferred from the passage that the works of Shakespeare, Cervantes, and Molière

○ are some of the most popular works of literature
○ are no longer copyrighted
○ are among the works for which the association of publishers is suing text-on-demand companies
○ do not currently exist as searchable databases
○ were owned by now-defunct publishing companies

14. Which of the following is an example of a book that a text-on-demand company would not have to acquire the rights to?

○ A book still under copyright
○ A book more than 20 years old
○ A book in the public domain
○ A book a general audience might want to buy
○ A book not already owned by publishers the company has a deal with

15. It can be inferred from the passage that a common practice of text-on-demand companies is to

○ use scanners to find books they want to acquire
○ create business plans well before they have any actual business
○ buy content at premium prices
○ acquire the rights to books for as little as possible
○ attempt to supplant the role of traditional publishers

GO ON TO THE NEXT PAGE.

16. Exit polls, conducted by an independent organization among voters at five polling locations during a recent election, suggested that the incumbent mayor—a Democrat—was going to lose the election by a wide margin. But, in fact, by the time the final results were tabulated, the incumbent had won the election by a narrow margin.

Which of the following, if true, would explain the apparent contradiction in the results of the exit polls?

○ The people chosen at random to be polled by the independent organization happened to be Democrats.

○ The exit poll locations chosen by the independent organization were in predominantly Republican districts.

○ The exit polls were conducted during the afternoon, when most of the districts' younger voters, who did not support the incumbent mayor, were at work.

○ The incumbent mayor ran on a platform that promised to lower taxes if elected.

○ An earlier poll, conducted the week before the election, had predicted that the incumbent mayor would win.

17. The spread of Avian flu from animals to humans has been well-documented, but less understood is the mechanism by which it is spread from one bird species to another. **In order to avoid a worldwide epidemic of Avian flu, scientists must make that study a first priority.** To solely tackle the human dimension of this possible pandemic is to miss half of the problem: its spread from one hemisphere to another.

The bolded phrase plays which of the following roles in the argument above?

○ The bolded phrase states a premise of the argument.

○ The bolded phrase contradicts the author's main point.

○ The bolded phrase makes a statement that the author is about to contradict.

○ The bolded phrase states the author's conclusion.

○ The bolded phrase states an assumption the author is making.

18. Successful business leaders not only anticipate potential problems and have contingency plans <u>ready, instead proceeding as if they are likely to occur at any time</u>.

○ ready, instead proceeding as if they are likely to occur at any time

○ ready, but also proceed as if such problems are likely to occur at any time

○ ready, but also proceeding as if the occurrence of them is at any time likely

○ ready; they instead proceed as if their occurrence is likely at any time

○ ready; such problems are likely to occur at any time, is how they proceed

19. An artist who sells her paintings for a fixed price decides that she must increase her income. Because she does not believe that customers will pay more for her paintings, she decides to cut costs by using cheaper paints and canvases. She expects that, by cutting costs, she will increase her profit margin per painting and thus increase her annual net income.

Which of the following, if true, most weakens the argument above?

○ Other area artists charge more for their paintings than the artist charges for hers.

○ The artist has failed to consider other options, such as renting cheaper studio space.

○ The artist's plan will result in the production of inferior paintings which, in turn, will cause a reduction in sales.

○ If the economy were to enter a period of inflation, the artist's projected increase in income could be wiped out by increases in the price of art supplies.

○ The artist considered trying to complete paintings more quickly and thus increase production, but concluded that it would be impossible.

GO ON TO THE NEXT PAGE.

20. Although tapirs reared in captivity are generally docile and have even been kept as pets by South American villagers, <u>it is nonetheless a volatile creature</u> prone to unpredictable and dangerous temper tantrums.

○ it is nonetheless a volatile creature
○ it is nonetheless volatile creatures
○ being nonetheless volatile creatures
○ they are nonetheless a volatile creature
○ they are nonetheless volatile creatures

21. According to a recent report, the original tires supplied with the Impressivo, a new sedan-class automobile, wore much more quickly than tires conventionally wear. The report suggested two possible causes: (1) defects in the tires and (2) improper wheel alignment of the automobile.

Which of the following would best help the authors of the report determine which of the two causes identified was responsible for the extra wear?

○ A study in which the rate of tire wear in the Impressivo is compared to the rate of tire wear in all automobiles in the same class
○ A study in which a second set of tires, manufactured by a different company from the one that made the first set, is installed on all Impressivos and the rate of wear is measured
○ A study in which the level of satisfaction of workers in the Impressivo manufacturing plant is measured and compared to that of workers at other automobile manufacturing plants
○ A study that determines how often improper wheel alignment results in major problems for manufacturers of other automobiles in the Impressivo's class
○ A study that determines the degree to which faulty driving techniques employed by Impressivo drivers contributed to tire wear

<u>Questions 22–25</u> are based on the following passage:

Founded at the dawn of the modern industrial era, the nearly forgotten Women's Trade Union League (WTUL) played an instrumental role
Line in advancing the cause of working women
(5) throughout the early part of the twentieth century. In the face of considerable adversity, the WTUL made a contribution far greater than did most historical footnotes.

The organization's successes did not come
(10) easily; conflict beset the WTUL in many forms. During those early days of American unions, organized labor was aggressively opposed by both industry and government. The WTUL, which represented a largely unskilled labor force, had
(15) little leverage against these powerful opponents. Also, because of the skill level of its workers as well as inherent societal gender bias, the WTUL had great difficulty finding allies among other unions. Even the large and powerful American
(20) Federation of Labor (AFL), which nominally took the WTUL under its wing, kept it at a distance. Because the AFL's power stemmed from its highly skilled labor force, the organization saw little economic benefit in working with the WTUL. The
(25) affiliation provided the AFL with political cover, allowing it to claim support for women workers; in return, the WTUL gained a potent but largely absent ally.

The WTUL also had to overcome internal
(30) discord. While the majority of the group's members were working women, a sizeable and powerful minority consisted of middle- and upper-class social reformers whose goals extended beyond labor reform. While workers argued that
(35) the WTUL should focus its efforts on collective bargaining and working conditions, the reformers looked beyond the workplace, seeking state and national legislation aimed at education reform and urban poverty relief as well as workplace issues.
(40) Despite these obstacles, the WTUL accomplished a great deal. The organization was instrumental in the passage of state laws mandating an eight-hour workday, a minimum wage for women, and a ban on child labor. It
(45) provided seed money to women who organized workers in specific plants and industries, and it also established strike funds and soup kitchens to support striking unionists. After the tragic Triangle Shirtwaist Company fire of 1911, the
(50) WTUL launched a four-year investigation whose

GO ON TO THE NEXT PAGE.

conclusions formed the basis of much subsequent workplace safety legislation. The organization also offered a political base for all reform-minded women, and thus helped develop the next
(55) generation of American leaders. Eleanor Roosevelt was one of many prominent figures to emerge from the WTUL.

The organization began a slow death in the late 1920s, when the Great Depression choked
(60) off its funding. The organization limped through the 1940s; the death knell eventually rang in 1950, at the onset of the McCarthy era. A turn-of-the-century labor organization dedicated to social reform, one that during its heyday was regarded by
(65) many as "radical," stood little chance of weathering that storm. This humble ending, however, does nothing to diminish the accomplishments of an organization that is yet to receive its historical due.

22. The primary purpose of this passage is to

○ describe the barriers confronting women in the contemporary workplace

○ compare and contrast the methods of two labor unions of the early industrial era

○ critique the methods employed by an important labor union

○ rebuke historians for failing to cover the women's labor movement adequately

○ call readers' attention to an overlooked contributor to American history

23. Which of the following best characterizes the American Federation of Labor's view of the Women's Trade Union League, as it is presented in the passage?

○ The WTUL was an important component of the AFL's multifront assault on industry and its treatment of workers.

○ Because of Eleanor Roosevelt's affiliation with the organization, the WTUL was a vehicle through which the AFL could gain access to the White House.

○ The WTUL was to be avoided because the radical element within it attracted unwanted government scrutiny.

○ The WTUL offered the AFL some political capital but little that would assist it in labor negotiations.

○ The WTUL was weakened by its hesitance in pursuing widespread social reform beyond the workplace.

24. Each of the following is cited in the passage as an accomplishment of the Women's Trade Union League EXCEPT

○ it organized a highly skilled workforce to increase its bargaining power

○ it contributed to the development of a group of leaders in America

○ it provided essential support to striking women

○ it helped fund start-up unions for women

○ it contributed to the passage of important social and labor reform legislation

GO ON TO THE NEXT PAGE.

25. The passage suggests which of the following about the "middle- and upper-class social reformers" mentioned in lines 32–33 ?

○ They did not understand, nor were they sympathetic to, the plight of poor women workers.

○ Their naive interest in Communism was ultimately detrimental to the Women's Trade Union League.

○ It was because of their social and political power that the Women's Trade Union League was able to form an alliance with the American Federation of Labor.

○ They represented only an insignificant fraction of the leadership of Women's Trade Union League.

○ They sought to advance a broad political agenda of societal improvement.

END OF BIN.

Verbal Test
Bin 2—Medium Questions
27 Questions

This test is made up of sentence correction, critical reasoning, and reading comprehension questions.

Sentence Correction Directions: Each of the sentence correction questions presents a sentence, part or all of which is underlined. Beneath the sentence you will find five ways of phrasing the underlined part. The first of these repeats the original; the other four are different. Follow the requirements of standard written English to choose your answer, paying attention to grammar, word choice, and sentence construction. Select the answer that produces the most effective sentence; your answer should make the sentence clear, exact, and free of grammatical errors. It should also minimize awkwardness, ambiguity, and redundancy.

Reading Comprehension Directions: Each of the reading comprehension questions is based on the content of a passage. After reading the passage, answer all questions pertaining to it on the basis of what is stated or implied in the passage. For each question, select the best answer of the choices given.

Critical Reasoning Directions: Each of the critical reasoning questions is based on a short argument, a set of statements, or a plan of action. For each question, select the best answer of the choices given.

---

1. As its performance has risen on all the stock indexes, the bio-tech start-up has branched out into new markets to look for opportunities they would previously have had to ignore.

   ○ they would previously have had to ignore
   ○ they would have had to ignore previously
   ○ that previously they would have had to ignore
   ○ it previously would have had to ignore in past years
   ○ it would previously have had to ignore

2. Scientists wishing to understand the kinetic movements of ancient dinosaurs are today studying the movements of modern day birds, which many scientists believe are descended from dinosaurs. A flaw in this strategy is that birds, although once genetically linked to dinosaurs, have evolved so far that any comparison is effectively meaningless.

   Which of the following, if true, would most weaken the criticism made above of the scientists' strategy?

   ○ Birds and dinosaurs have a number of important features in common that exist in no other living species.
   ○ Birds are separated from dinosaurs by 65 million years of evolution.
   ○ Our theories of dinosaur movements have recently undergone a radical reappraisal.
   ○ The study of kinetic movement is a relatively new discipline.
   ○ Many bird experts do not study dinosaurs to draw inferences about birds.

GO ON TO THE NEXT PAGE.

3. A factory in China has two options to improve efficiency: adding robotic assembly lines and subcontracting out certain small production goals that could be done more efficiently elsewhere. Adding robotic assembly lines will improve efficiency more than subcontracting some small production goals. Therefore, by adding robotic assembly lines, the factory will be doing the most that can be done to improve efficiency.

Which of the following is an assumption on which the argument depends?

○ Adding robotic assembly lines will be more expensive than subcontracting some small production goals.
○ The factory has a choice of robotic assembly lines, some of which might be better suited to this factory than others.
○ The factory may or may not decide to choose either alternative.
○ Efficiency cannot be improved more by using both methods together than by adding robotic assembly lines alone.
○ This particular factory is already the third most efficient factory in China.

4. Just as the early NASA space explorers attempted on each flight to push the frontiers of our knowledge, so too are the new private-consortium space explorers seeking to add to man's general understanding of the cosmos.

○ Just as the early NASA space explorers attempted on each flight to push the frontiers of our knowledge, so too
○ The early NASA space explorers attempted on each flight to push the frontiers of our knowledge, and in the same way
○ Like the case of the early NASA space explorers who attempted on each flight to push the frontiers of our knowledge, so too
○ As in the early NASA space explorers' attempts on each flight to push the frontiers of our knowledge, so too
○ Similar to the early NASA space explorers attempted on each flight to push the frontiers of our knowledge, so too

5. A proposal for a new building fire safety code requires that fire-retardant insulation no longer be sprayed on steel girders in the factory, but be sprayed on once the girders have arrived at the building site. This will eliminate the dislodging of the insulation in transit and reduce fatalities in catastrophic fires by an estimated 20%.

Which of the following, if true, represents the strongest challenge to the new proposal?

○ The fire-retardant insulation will also be required to be one inch thicker than in the past.
○ Studies have shown that most dislodgement of insulation occurs after the girders arrive on site.
○ Catastrophic fires represent only 4% of the fires reported nationally.
○ The proposed safety code will add considerably to the cost of new construction.
○ In most of Europe, spraying fire-retardant insulation onto steel girders at the building site has been required for the past ten years.

6. An effort to control the crippling effects of poverty in Brazil's interior cities, begun almost thirty years ago, has been partially successful, despite the setback of a major drought and the interruption of aid during an extended economic crisis.

○ to control the crippling effects of poverty in Brazil's interior cities, begun almost thirty years ago,
○ begun almost thirty years ago for controlling the crippling effects of poverty in Brazil's interior cities,
○ begun for controlling the crippling effects of poverty in Brazil's interior cities almost thirty years ago,
○ at controlling the crippling effects of poverty in Brazil's interior cities begun almost thirty years ago,
○ that has begun almost thirty years ago to control the crippling effects of poverty in Brazil's interior cities,

GO ON TO THE NEXT PAGE.

7. A newly discovered disease is thought to be caused by a certain bacterium. However, recently released data note that the bacterium thrives in the presence of a certain virus, implying that it is actually the virus that causes the new disease.

Which of the following pieces of evidence would most support the data's implication?

○ In the absence of the virus, the disease has been observed to follow infection by the bacterium.
○ The virus has been shown to aid the growth of bacteria, a process which often leads to the onset of the disease.
○ The virus alone has been observed in many cases of the disease.
○ In cases where the disease does not develop, infection by the bacterium is usually preceded by infection by the virus.
○ Onset of the disease usually follows infection by both the virus and the bacterium.

8. The company was not even publicly traded until 1968, when the owner and founder sold it to David P. Markham, a private investor, who took the company public and established a long and generous policy of stock options for valued employees.

○ who took the company public and established a long and generous policy of stock options for
○ who, taking the company public, established a long and generous policy of stock options to
○ who, when he took the company public, established a long and generous policy of stock options to
○ who had taken the company public, establishing a long and generous policy of stock options as
○ taking the company public and establishing a long and generous policy of stock options for

9. Because of a quality control problem, a supplier of flu vaccines will not be able to ship any supplies of the vaccine for the upcoming flu season. This will create a shortage of flu vaccines and result in a loss of productivity as workers call in sick.

Which of the following, if true, most seriously weakens the argument above?

○ The quality control problem of the supplier is not as severe as some experts had initially predicted.
○ Other suppliers of flu vaccine have not been affected by the quality control problem.
○ Last year there was also a shortage of flu vaccine available.
○ The price of flu vaccines is expected to fall in the next ten years.
○ The flu season is expected to last longer than usual this year.

10. Never before had the navy defeated so many foes at once as it had in the battle of Trafalgar in 1805.

○ so many foes at once as it had in
○ at once as many foes as
○ at once as many foes that there were in
○ as many foes at once as it did in
○ so many foes at once as that it defeated in

11. The changes that may be part of a general global warming trend include an increase in the frequency and severity of hurricanes, a gradual rise in sea level, depleting the ozone layer, and raising the temperature of the earth.

○ depleting the ozone layer, and raising the temperature of the earth
○ depleting the ozone layer, and a rise in the earth's temperature
○ a depletion of the ozone layer, and raising the earth's temperature
○ a depletion of the ozone layer, and a raise of the temperature of the earth
○ a depletion of the ozone layer, and a rise in the temperature of the earth

GO ON TO THE NEXT PAGE.

Questions 12–16 are based on the following passage:

It has long been a tenet of business theory that the best decisions are made after careful review and consideration. Only after weighing all
Line the options and studying projections, say most
(5) professors of business, can a practical decision be made.

Now, that model is being questioned by some business thinkers in the light of the theories of Malcolm Gladwell, who states that human beings
(10) often make better decisions in the blink of an eye.

It is, at first glance, a theory so counter-intuitive as to seem almost ludicrous. Behind any decision, Gladwell posits, there is a behind-the-scenes subconscious process in which the brain
(15) analyzes; ranks in order of importance; compares and contrasts vast amounts of information; and dismisses extraneous factors, seemingly almost instantaneously, often arriving at a conclusion in less than two seconds. Citing a multitude of
(20) studies and examples from life, Gladwell shows how that split-second decision is often better informed than a drawn-out examination.

Evanston and Cramer were the first to apply this theory to the business world. Evanston
(25) videotaped the job interviews of 400 applicants at different firms. He then played only 10 seconds of each videotape to independent human resources specialists. The specialists were able to pick out the applicants who were hired with an accuracy of
(30) over 90%.

Cramer took the experiment even further, using only five seconds of videotape, without sound. To his astonishment, the rate of accuracy with which the HR specialists were able to predict the
(35) successful applicants fell only to 82%.

Critics argue that these results illustrate a problem with stereotyping that impedes human resources specialists from hiring the best candidates even when they have the time to
(40) get below the surface: going for the candidate who "looks the part." Gladwell argues that, on the contrary, the human mind is able to make complicated decisions quickly and that intuition often trumps an extended decision-making
(45) process.

12. The primary purpose of the passage is to

○ discuss reasons an accepted business theory is being reexamined
○ present evidence that resolves a contradiction in business theory
○ describe a tenet of business practices and how that tenet can be tested in today's economic environment
○ argue that a counter-intuitive new business idea is, in the final analysis, incorrect
○ present evidence that invalidates a new business model

13. According to the passage, all of the following are examples of the subconscious processes by which the brain makes a decision EXCEPT

○ analysis of information
○ ranking of information
○ comparison and contrast of information
○ rejecting information that is not pertinent
○ consulting a multitude of studies and examples

14. The author's attitude toward the long-held view that decisions should be made carefully over time expressed in lines 1–5 can best be described as

○ dismissive and scornful
○ respectful but questioning
○ admiring and deferential
○ uncertain but optimistic
○ condescending and impatient

GO ON TO THE NEXT PAGE.

15. The author most likely mentions the results of Cramer's extension of Evanston's experiment in order to

   ○ show that Cramer's hypothesis was correct, while Evanston's hypothesis turned out to be incorrect
   ○ show that Evanston's hypothesis was correct, while Cramer's hypothesis turned out to be incorrect
   ○ demonstrate that while both experiments were scientifically rigorous, neither ended up being scientifically valid
   ○ illustrate that the principle of subconscious decisions continues to work even when less information is available
   ○ demonstrate that Cramer's experiment was 8% more accurate than Evanston's, even though his subjects had less information to work with

16. It can be inferred that the critics referred to in line 36 believed the results of the two experiments had less to do with the innate decision-making of the subjects than with

   ○ the excellent decision-making of Evanston and Cramer
   ○ the expertise of Malcolm Gladwell, who originated the theory
   ○ not choosing candidates who "looked the part"
   ○ the use of videotape as a method of choosing candidates
   ○ their unconscious use of visual stereotypes in making their selections

17. The women's volleyball team at a local college finished fifth in its division, prompting the college to fire the team's general manager. The manager responded by suing the college, saying that the team's performance put it among the top teams in the country.

   Which of the following statements, if true, would support the claim of the team's manager, and resolve the apparent contradiction?

   ○ The team won all of its "away" games during the season in question.
   ○ Attendance at the volleyball team's games was up 35% from the year before.
   ○ Of the starting team, three team members were unable to play for at least half the season because of injuries.
   ○ There are 80 teams in this particular volleyball team's division.
   ○ The team lost more games this year than it did the year before.

18. Country A recently broke off diplomatic relations with Country B when it was reported that Country B had been running a covert intelligence operation within the borders of Country A. While a spokesperson for Country B admitted the charge, the spokesperson said that it was common knowledge that all countries do this, and that Country A was no exception.

   Which of the following inferences can be drawn from the argument above?

   ○ Country B should apologize and dismantle its intelligence operation in Country A.
   ○ The spokesperson for Country B claims that Country A engages in intelligence gathering too.
   ○ Because all countries engage in this practice, Country A's outrage was disingenuous.
   ○ Relations between Country A and Country B will be strained for some time.
   ○ Country B would be just as outraged if it was reported that Country A was running a covert intelligence operation with Country B's borders.

GO ON TO THE NEXT PAGE.

19. Because cellular telephones emit signals that can interfere with cockpit-to-control-tower transmissions, airplane passengers' use of these instruments <u>at all times that the airplane is in motion, even while on the ground, are</u> prohibited.

○ at all times that the airplane is in motion, even while on the ground, are

○ at all times during which the airplane, even while on the ground, is in motion, are

○ during airplane motion, even when it is on the ground, are

○ during times of the airplane being in motion, even on the ground, is

○ when the airplane is in motion, even while on the ground, is

20. In contrast to classical guitars, whose owners prefer the dulcet, rounded tones produced by nylon strings, <u>folk guitar owners prefer the bright and brassy sound</u> that only bronze or steel can create.

○ folk guitar owners prefer the bright and brassy sound

○ folk guitar owners prefer to get a sound that is bright and brassy

○ with a folk guitar, the owner gets the preferably bright and brassy sound

○ folk guitars produce a bright and brassy sound, which their owners prefer,

○ folk guitars produce a preferred bright and brassy sound for their owners

Questions 21–22 are based on the following passage:

A system-wide county school anti-smoking education program was instituted last year. The program was clearly a success. Last year, the incidence of students smoking on school premises decreased by over 70 percent.

21. Which of the following assumptions underlies the argument in the passage?

○ Cigarettes are detrimental to one's health; once people understand this, they will quit smoking.

○ The doubling of the price of a pack of cigarettes last year was not the only cause of the students' altered smoking habits.

○ The teachers chosen to lead the anti-smoking education program were the most effective teachers in the school system.

○ The number of cigarettes smoked each day by those students who continued to smoke last year did not greatly increase.

○ School policy enforcers were less vigilant in seeking out smokers last year than they were in previous years.

22. Which of the following, if true, would most seriously weaken the argument in the passage?

○ The author of this statement is a school system official hoping to generate good publicity for the anti-smoking program.

○ Most students who smoke stopped smoking on school premises last year continued to smoke when away from school.

○ Last year, another policy change made it much easier for students to leave and return to school grounds during the school day.

○ The school system spent more on anti-smoking education programs last year than it did in all previous years.

○ The amount of time students spent in anti-smoking education programs last year resulted in a reduction of in-class hours devoted to academic subjects.

GO ON TO THE NEXT PAGE.

23. Mild exercise throughout pregnancy <u>may reduce the discomfort associated with pregnancy and result in</u> a speedier, easier birth, according to a recent study.

○ may reduce the discomfort associated with pregnancy and result in

○ may reduce the discomfort associated with pregnancy, with the result

○ may cause a reduction in the discomfort associated with pregnancy and as a result

○ might lead to a reduction in the discomfort associated with pregnancy and as a result

○ might reduce the discomfort associated with pregnancy and resulting in

<u>Questions 24–27</u> are based on the following passage:

What is it that keeps the developing world in an apparent state of perpetual poverty? Poor education, lack of basic medical care, and the
Line absence of democratic structures all certainly
(5) contribute to these nations' plight. However, according to Peruvian economist Hernando de Soto, the overriding cause is the overwhelming prevalence of black market activity, well outside the formal economy, in these countries. The losses
(10) incurred from this condition are twofold. First, they deny the government tax revenues which could be used to improve education, medical treatment, and government efficiency. More important, however, they deny earners the chance to accumulate assets
(15) recognized by law and thus prevent them from leveraging those assets to borrow. Reforming these nations' legal systems in order to confer ownership through titling, De Soto argues, would help the poor there access the assets their work
(20) should be generating. These assets could then be used to buy homes and construct businesses, thus building a more stable and prosperous economy. De Soto estimates the value of these assets, which he terms "dead capital," at nearly $10 trillion
(25) worldwide.

De Soto is not the first to locate the developing world's problems in the domain of property rights. Others have tried property rights reform and failed. According to de Soto, this is because
(30) his predecessors attempted to model their plans on existing, successful property rights systems. In other words, they tried to transplant American and British property law to an inhospitable host. De Soto argues that within many of the extralegal
(35) markets of the developing world, mutually agreed upon rules for distributing assets and recognizing property rights already exist. Rather than force these markets to adjust to a new, foreign system of property titling, reformers should focus on
(40) codifying the existing systems wherever it is practical to do so. This would facilitate a quicker, more natural transition to an economy that builds wealth rather than squanders it.

GO ON TO THE NEXT PAGE.

24. The author's primary goal in the passage is to

    ○ compare several failed attempts to
      address a problem
    ○ respond to criticism of a new theory
    ○ identify the problems inherent in a
      new economic theory
    ○ describe a novel approach to an old
      problem
    ○ compare different property rights
      systems in the industrial world

25. According to the passage, de Soto believes
    that the quickest way to address poverty in the
    developing world is to

    ○ increase funding for education
    ○ build the infrastructure to support
      lending
    ○ ensure medical care for all citizens
    ○ aggressively root out corruption in
      government
    ○ increase tax rates on all citizens in
      developing countries

26. The author's assertion that "reformers should
    focus on codifying the existing systems wherever
    it is practical to do so" (lines 39–41) suggests that

    ○ in some instances, current systems
      are inadequate to meet the needs of a
      market economy
    ○ these systems are already written
      down and need only be enacted as
      law
    ○ where it is impractical to codify
      existing systems, countries should
      adopt American property law
    ○ the existing systems are superior
      to those currently in use in modern
      industrialized countries
    ○ improving education and medical care
      in these countries should take priority
      over reforming property laws

27. The term "dead capital" (line 24) refers to

    ○ loans that are never repaid
    ○ failed investments in new businesses
    ○ cities ruined by over-industrialization
    ○ the proceeds of extralegal commerce
    ○ property passed from generation to
      generation

END OF BIN.

Verbal Test
Bin 3—Hard Questions
26 Questions

This test is made up of sentence correction, critical reasoning, and reading comprehension questions.

Sentence Correction Directions: Each of the <u>sentence correction</u> questions presents a sentence, part or all of which is underlined. Beneath the sentence you will find five ways of phrasing the underlined part. The first of these repeats the original; the other four are different. Follow the requirements of standard written English to choose your answer, paying attention to grammar, word choice, and sentence construction. Select the answer that produces the most effective sentence; your answer should make the sentence clear, exact, and free of grammatical errors. It should also minimize awkwardness, ambiguity, and redundancy.

Reading Comprehension Directions: Each of the <u>reading comprehension</u> questions is based on the content of a passage. After reading the passage, answer all questions pertaining to it on the basis of what is <u>stated</u> or <u>implied</u> in the passage. For each question, select the best answer of the choices given.

Critical Reasoning Directions: Each of the <u>critical reasoning</u> questions is based on a short argument, a set of statements, or a plan of action. For each question, select the best answer of the choices given.

---

1. Unlike <u>Franklin D. Roosevelt's bootstrap program that helped</u> to restart economic growth in the 1930s through public works, Ronald Reagan proposed a program of trickle-down economics to restart the economy.

   ○ Franklin D. Roosevelt's bootstrap program that helped
   ○ Franklin D. Roosevelt and his bootstrap program which helped
   ○ Franklin D. Roosevelt, whose bootstrap program helped
   ○ the bootstrap program of Franklin D. Roosevelt that has helped
   ○ Franklin D. Roosevelt and his bootstrap program helping

2. In the 1970s, it became evident <u>that writing about someone else's research was much easier for social scientists who wanted to make a quick name for themselves</u> than it was to do their own research.

   ○ that writing about someone else's research was much easier for social scientists who wanted to make a quick name for themselves
   ○ that for social scientists who wanted to make a quick name for themselves, it was much easier to write about someone else's research
   ○ that for social scientists wanting to make a quick name for themselves, writing about someone else's research was much easier
   ○ for social scientists who wanted to make a quick name for themselves that writing about someone else's research was much easier
   ○ for social scientists who wanted to make a quick name for themselves, writing about someone else's research was much easier

GO ON TO THE NEXT PAGE.

Questions 3–4 are based on the following passage:

To improve the town's overcrowded school system, the town council has proposed an ambitious education plan to reduce classroom size and make capital improvements—a plan they intend to pay for with an increase in property taxes for homes valued over $500,000. Although the school system desperately needs improving, the town council's plan should be defeated because the majority of the people who would end up paying for the improvements receive no benefit from them.

3. Which of the following, if true, most strengthens the argument above?

   ○ The town's school system is currently ranked among the worst in the state.
   ○ Other towns nearby that have made similar capital improvements did not find that the improvements translated to a better quality of education.
   ○ The town will need to spend additional money on an architect's plans for the capital improvements.
   ○ An examination of the tax rolls shows that most homeowners in this category no longer have school-age children.
   ○ Some homeowners will delay home improvement projects in order to keep the value of their homes below $500,000.

4. Which of the following, if true, provides the town council with the strongest counter to the objection that its plan is unfair?

   ○ Even with the proposed increase, property taxes in the town are well below the national average.
   ○ Paying for the school system improvements using existing town funds will result in shortfalls that will force the town into arrears.
   ○ The teachers in the town's school system receive some of the lowest salary packages in the immediate area, which is a major cause of attrition.
   ○ Smaller class sizes and capital improvements in a school system tend to increase property values in the surrounding community.
   ○ A feasibility study has shown that the cost of the improvements will likely be 20% higher than projected.

5. The rules of engagement under which a border patrol station can decide to use deadly force <u>includes responding to an invasionary incursion and the return of</u> hostile fire.

   ○ includes responding to an invasionary incursion and the return of
   ○ includes responding to an invasionary incursion and returning
   ○ include responding to an invasionary incursion and the return of
   ○ include a response to an invasionary incursion and the return of
   ○ include a response to an invasionary incursion and returning

6. Although the word "phonetician" is popularly associated with Henry Higgins's task of improving the diction of Eliza Doolittle in *My Fair Lady*, in linguistics, <u>it is someone who studies</u> the formation of language.

   ○ it is someone who studies
   ○ it is a person studying
   ○ it refers to someone who studies
   ○ they are people who study
   ○ it is in reference to people who study

GO ON TO THE NEXT PAGE.

7. Experts studying patterns of shark attacks on humans have noted that attacks tend to diminish when the water temperature drops below 65 degrees Fahrenheit. Until recently, researchers believed this was because sharks prefer warmer water, and thus are present in fewer numbers in colder water. However, new research shows that sharks are present in equal numbers in cold and warm water.

Which of the following, if true, best explains the apparent paradox?

○ In general, humans prefer warm water.

○ Sharks' keen sense of smell is enhanced in cold water.

○ In the Pacific, shark attacks tend to occur more frequently in the daytime.

○ Of the more than 200 types of sharks present in the ocean, only three attack humans.

○ The average temperature of the earth's oceans is 55 degrees.

8. As a result of surging economic indicators, most analysts upgraded the company's stock to a strong "buy," ignoring the advice of the head of a watchdog organization <u>who warned that the company's product would prove not only dangerous but</u> ineffective in the long run.

○ who warned that the company's product would prove not only dangerous but

○ warning that the company's product would prove not only dangerous and also

○ warning that the company's product would prove itself to be both dangerous and

○ who warned that the company's product would prove to be both dangerous and

○ who was warning that the company's product would prove not only dangerous but

9. MoviesNow! streaming service is projected to buy more licenses to stream more movies in the next 5 years than in any previous 5-year window. This is because MoviesNow!'s board of directors has encouraged the pursuit of subscribers who are parents of children under the age of 12 and the current selection of movies to stream in the MoviesNow! database is targeted at subscribers ages 18–35.

Which of the following, if true, would most strengthen the argument from MoviesNow!'s board of directors that they should pursue subscribers who are parents of children under the age of 12?

○ The board monitors the demographic targets of large advertising companies and chooses target audiences for their streaming service based off those trends.

○ A population study conducted by an independent research group has uncovered a large uptick in the number of parents who are raising children under the age of 12.

○ People aged 18–35 generally have less disposable income than other age demographics.

○ The licensing agreement MoviesNow! has with the largest movie production company is set to expire within the next 5 years.

○ The board of MoviesNow! is comprised of parents of children under the age of 12.

GO ON TO THE NEXT PAGE.

10. A new influx of unprecedented private investment should create a bright new future for manned space exploration, <u>making the possibility of commercial space tourism much more viable than 10 years ago</u>.

- ⬭ making the possibility of commercial space tourism much more viable than 10 years ago
- ⬭ and make the possibility of commercial space tourism much more viable than 10 years ago
- ⬭ making the possibility of commercial space tourism much more viable than it was 10 years ago
- ⬭ and make the possibility of commercial space tourism much more viable than it was 10 years in the past
- ⬭ making the possibility of commercial space tourism much more viable than 10 years in the past

Questions 11–15 are based on the following passage:

As the American workforce gets grayer, age discrimination will likely become a more prominent issue in the courts. It is, of course, illegal to
Line discriminate against an employee because of his or
(5) her age, and yet it is not illegal to dismiss a worker because he has a high salary and expensive health care.

This apparent contradiction is at the heart of a raft of cases now making their way through the
(10) courts. The outcome of these cases will have broad implications for the workplace in the coming years. By 2020, the Bureau of Labor Statistics has projected that more than half of all workers will be over 40—many of whom, by dint of seniority and
(15) promotions, will be earning higher than median salaries, eligible for more stock options, and carrying higher health care costs as a result of a larger number of dependents and the increased cost of health care for older workers.

(20) Is it any wonder that a bottom-line oriented business might want to shed these workers, whose productivity is likely to plummet in the next few years, even as they become more expensive employees?

(25) Still, the legal challenges of implementing this policy are daunting. Businesses have the right to rate workers on their productivity and to rank them against their peers. But they are not allowed to prejudge individuals based on their sex, race, or
(30) age. Each worker must be treated on his or her own merits, rather than by how they fit into a larger profile of the group they belong to.

For companies looking to lay off these workers, the cost of making a mistake is high; while only
(35) one in three age discrimination suits are won by the plaintiff, the awards tend to be steep and the political fall-out harsh.

GO ON TO THE NEXT PAGE.

11. The primary purpose of the passage is to

    ○ advocate on behalf of the older American worker who could soon face dismissal
    ○ describe the origin of two theories of labor law and their effects on the workplace
    ○ present an overview of the legal ramifications of a practice some call discriminatory
    ○ describe the process by which America's workforce is getting older
    ○ describe the methods by which a company could reduce its bottom line

12. Which of the following best describes the organization of the second paragraph of the passage?

    ○ An assertion is made and then briefly contradicted.
    ○ A contradiction is stated and then quickly resolved.
    ○ A new theory is described and then qualified.
    ○ An apparent inconsistency is stated and its consequences outlined.
    ○ A conventional model is described and an alternative is introduced.

13. Which of the following, if true, would most effectively weaken the author's assertion that a "bottom-line oriented business" might want to lay off older workers?

    ○ A new study shows that, on average, younger workers earn less and have lower associated medical costs than older workers.
    ○ Older workers have a higher rate of absenteeism than younger workers.
    ○ A new study shows that older workers are in fact more productive and have fewer medical expenses compared to younger workers.
    ○ A forecasted downturn in the economy will erode profits in may American businesses.
    ○ A new bill scheduled to become law will make it easier for employers to employ illegal aliens.

14. It can be inferred from the passage regarding the relationship between American companies and older Americans that

    ○ what is good for American companies is not necessarily good for older Americans
    ○ American companies are prohibited by law from practices that discriminate based on age
    ○ large monetary judgments from age discrimination suits might prove more expensive than paying older employees' salaries
    ○ by the year 2030, the percentage of older employees will be even higher than in the year 2020
    ○ some older employees may well be more productive than some younger employees

15. The author mentions all of the following as driving up the cost to employers for employing workers over the age of 40 EXCEPT

    ○ the cost of out-placement services
    ○ a larger number of dependents
    ○ increased cost of health care
    ○ higher median salaries
    ○ the cost of employee stock options

GO ON TO THE NEXT PAGE.

16. A pharmaceutical company claims that its new drug promotes learning in children. To back up its claims, the company points to a study of 300 children who were given the drug, along with a control group of 300 children who were given a placebo. The 300 children who were given the drug reported that they were able to retain new information much more easily.

Which of the following statements, if true, would most tend to weaken the claims of the pharmaceutical company?

- ○ The 300 children in the control group also reported that they were able to retain new information much more easily.
- ○ The drug has also been shown to prevent common skin rashes.
- ○ The drug has been proven to have severe side-effects.
- ○ The children in the study were not given any other medications during the study.
- ○ The children who were given the drug did better on cognitive measurement tests after the drug therapy than before.

17. In order to understand the dangers of the current real-estate bubble in Country Y, one has only to look to the real-estate bubble of the last decade in Country Z. In that country, incautious investors used the inflated value of their real estate as collateral in risky margin loans. When the real-estate market collapsed, many investors went bankrupt, creating a major recession. Country Y is in real danger of a similar recession if more-stringent laws restricting margin loans are not enacted promptly.

The answer to which of the following questions would be most useful in evaluating the significance of the author's claims?

- ○ Was the real estate in Country Z located principally in rural areas or was it located in more urban communities?
- ○ Could the bankruptcies in Country Z have been prevented by a private bailout plan by the nation's banks?
- ○ Does Country Y currently have any laws on its books regarding margin loans?
- ○ Are there business ties and connections between Country Y and Country Z?
- ○ Were there other factors in the case of Country Y that would make the comparison with Country Z less meaningful?

18. Rules governing participation in a new extreme sports fantasy camp require <u>that applicants should be physically fit enough to endure the demanding</u> activities in which they will be engaging.

- ○ that applicants should be physically fit enough to endure the demanding
- ○ that applicants be physically fit enough to endure the demanding
- ○ applicants should have enough physical fitness to allow enduring the demands of
- ○ applicants are physically fit enough as to endure the demands of
- ○ physical fitness in applicants, enough for endurance of demanding

GO ON TO THE NEXT PAGE.

19. During the summer of 2002, the Outer Banks <u>suffered a massive toad infestation, discouraging</u> many vacationers from visiting the area.

- ○ suffered a massive toad infestation, discouraging
- ○ suffered from a massive toad infestation and discouraged
- ○ suffered a massive infestation of toads, which discouraged
- ○ was suffering a massive infestation of toads and discouraging
- ○ had suffered from a massive toad infestation and this discouraged

20. A prolonged period of low mortgage rates resulted in a period of the most robust home sales ever. At the same time, the average sale price of resale homes actually dropped, when adjusted for inflation.

Which of the following, if true, would explain the apparent contradiction between the robust home sales and the drop in the average sale price of resale homes?

- ○ The inflation rate during this period exceeded the increase in the average salary, thus preventing many buyers from securing mortgages.
- ○ Resale homes represent the best value on the real estate market.
- ○ Without the adjustment for inflation, the price of resale homes actually increased by a very slight amount.
- ○ The decrease in mortgage rates was accompanied by a widening of the types of mortgages from which borrowers could choose.
- ○ The increase in home sales was due entirely to an increase in the sale of new homes.

21. Luis is taller than Rei. Kiko is taller than Marcus. Therefore, Kiko is taller than Rei.

The conclusion drawn above is not supported by the argument; however, the addition of one additional piece of information would make the conclusion logically sound. All of the following could be that additional piece of information EXCEPT

- ○ Kiko is taller than Luis.
- ○ Luis is taller than Marcus.
- ○ Luis and Marcus are the same height.
- ○ Marcus and Rei are the same height.
- ○ Marcus is taller than Rei.

22. It has been estimated that <u>an increase in average regional temperature of even 0.5 degrees Fahrenheit could cost the southern United States more than $10 billion in lost agricultural income annually</u>.

- ○ an increase in average regional temperature of even 0.5 degrees Fahrenheit could cost the southern United States more than $10 billion in lost agricultural income annually
- ○ every year, $10 billion in agricultural income could be the cost to the southern United States as a result of an increase in the average temperature of the region of even 0.5 degrees Fahrenheit
- ○ the cost to the southern United States could be more than $10 billion in income from agriculture that results from a regional increase in average temperature of even 0.5 degrees Fahrenheit annually
- ○ annual income losses in agriculture of more than $10 billion could be the cost from increasing average temperatures in the southern United States of even 0.5 degrees Fahrenheit
- ○ annual income losses to the southern United States from the increase in average regional temperature of even 0.5 percent costing more than $10 billion in agricultural income each year

GO ON TO THE NEXT PAGE.

23. Within the Green Party, an internal debate is raging <u>among those who believe in compromising with mainstream politicians in order to achieve some goals with those who believe the party must not abandon any of its principles</u>.

    ○ among those who believe in compromising with mainstream politicians in order to achieve some goals with those who believe the party must not abandon any of its principles

    ○ among those who believe that achieving some goals requires compromise with mainstream politicians and those believing that none of the party's principles must be abandoned

    ○ between those believing in compromising with mainstream politicians in order to achieve some goals with those who believe the party must not abandon any of its principles

    ○ between those who believe in compromising with mainstream politicians in order to achieve some goals and those who believe the party must not abandon any of its principles

    ○ between those believing that achieving some goals means compromising with mainstream politicians and those who believe that the principles of the party must not be abandoned

24. In comparison to the drivers who live in Mountainview, a greater proportion of the drivers who live in Oak Valley exceed the speed limit regularly. This explains why there are more accidents each year in Oak Valley than in Mountainview.

    All of the following statements, if true, weaken the conclusion drawn above EXCEPT:

    ○ Oak Valley has a greater proportion of blind intersections and sharp turns than has Mountainview.

    ○ There is a greater number of drivers in Oak Valley than in Mountainview.

    ○ Drivers in Mountainview must travel to Oak Valley to shop and work.

    ○ Per capita, there are fewer police officers monitoring traffic in Oak Valley than there are in Mountainview.

    ○ The roads are icier for a greater portion of the year in Oak Valley than in Mountainview.

GO ON TO THE NEXT PAGE.

25. A study showed that only ten percent of American dog owners enroll their dogs in formal obedience training classes. More than twenty percent of these dog owners, the study also showed, participate in dog shows. Thus, it is obvious that people who train their dogs are more likely to participate in dog shows than are people who do not train their dogs.

The conclusion above is correct provided which of the following statements is also true?

○ It is impossible for a dog to compete in a dog show if the dog has not completed at least one formal obedience training class.

○ The proportion of dog owners who enroll their dogs in formal obedience training classes is representative of the proportion who train their dogs outside such classes.

○ Dog owners who participate in dog shows only train their dogs by enrolling them in formal obedience training lessons.

○ Participation in dog shows is a reliable indicator of how much attention a dog owner pays to his dog.

○ Only purebred dogs can participate in dog shows, so many owners who enroll their dogs in formal obedience training classes are excluded from this activity.

26. A bullet train travels in excess of 150 miles per hour. Therefore, if a train travels slower than 150 miles per hour, it is not a bullet train.

Which of the following most closely parallels the reasoning used in the argument above?

○ An orange ripens only on the vine. If it ripens on the vine, then it is not an orange.

○ Newspapers are often read by more than one person. Therefore, magazines are also likely to be read by more than one person.

○ An earthquake of 5.0 or above on the Richter scale causes massive damage. If there is not massive damage, then the earthquake did not attain a 5.0 or above.

○ A supersonic plane travels at speeds in excess of Mach 1. If it is not supersonic, then it will travel at speeds below Mach 1.

○ Fluoride generally prevents cavities. If there are no cavities, then there was no fluoride used.

END OF EXAMINATION

Chapter 25
GMAT Math and Verbal Practice Bins: Answers and Explanations

If you really want to improve your score, then you should read *all* the explanations for *all* the questions on the pages that follow, not just the ones you got wrong. It's important to make sure you're getting questions correct for the right reasons and even more important that you are recognizing opportunities to use The Princeton Review techniques, which can save you time and eliminate the possibility of careless errors.

ANSWER KEY

	MATH				VERBAL	
Bin 1	**Bin 2**	**Bin 3**	**Bin 4**	**Bin 1**	**Bin 2**	**Bin 3**
1. C	1. C	1. B	1. C	1. C	1. E	1. C
2. C	2. B	2. D	2. C	2. D	2. A	2. B
3. D	3. C	3. A	3. C	3. B	3. D	3. D
4. D	4. A	4. C	4. C	4. B	4. A	4. D
5. D	5. B	5. D	5. E	5. E	5. B	5. D
6. B	6. A	6. D	6. B	6. E	6. A	6. C
7. E	7. B	7. D	7. B	7. A	7. C	7. A
8. C	8. C	8. C	8. C	8. D	8. A	8. D
9. B	9. A	9. A	9. A	9. C	9. B	9. B
10. D	10. C	10. D	10. B	10. A	10. D	10. C
11. B	11. B	11. B	11. A	11. D	11. E	11. C
12. D	12. B	12. B	12. D	12. B	12. A	12. D
13. C	13. D	13. A	13. E	13. B	13. E	13. C
14. A	14. B	14. A	14. A	14. C	14. B	14. B
15. D	15. E	15. G	15. E	15. D	15. D	15. A
16. A	16. E	16. C	16. A	16. B	16. E	16. A
17. B	17. C	17. D	17. D	17. D	17. D	17. E
18. B	18. E	18. C	18. D	18. B	18. B	18. B
19. C	19. C	19. C	19. C	19. C	19. E	19. C
20. A	20. D	20. A	20. B	20. E	20. D	20. E
21. D	21. B	21. D	21. A	21. B	21. B	21. B
22. D	22. D	22. A	22. E	22. E	22. C	22. A
23. C	23. D	23. D	23. D	23. D	23. A	23. D
24. D	24. A	24. E	24. C	24. A	24. D	24. D
25. B	25. A	25. D	25. D	25. E	25. B	25. B
26. B	26. E	26. A			26. A	26. C
	27. C				27. D	

MATH BIN 1

QUESTIONS

1. What percent of 112 is 14 ?

   ○ 0.125%
   ○ 8%
   ○ 12.5%
   ○ 125%
   ○ 800%

2. The number of flights leaving a certain airport doubles during every one-hour period between 9 A.M. and noon; after noon, the number of flights leaving from the airport doubles during every two-hour period. If 4 flights left from the airport between 9 and 10 A.M., how many flights left the airport between 2 and 4 P.M. ?

   ○ 32
   ○ 48
   ○ 64
   ○ 128
   ○ 256

3. If both *ABDC* and *CDFE* are parallelograms, what is $q + r$?

   (1) $r = 70$

   (2) $p = 110$

   ○ Statement (1) ALONE is sufficient, but statement (2) alone is not sufficient.
   ○ Statement (2) ALONE is sufficient, but statement (1) alone is not sufficient.
   ○ BOTH statements TOGETHER are sufficient, but NEITHER statement ALONE is sufficient.
   ○ EACH statement ALONE is sufficient.
   ○ Statements (1) and (2) TOGETHER are not sufficient.

EXPLANATIONS

1. **C** Since this is a percent problem, you can solve it by thinking in terms of $\frac{part}{whole}$. In this case,

   $\frac{part}{whole} = \frac{14}{112} = \frac{x}{100}$; cross-multiply to get

   $112x = 1,400$, so $x = \frac{1,400}{112}$, and $x = 12.5$.

   Like most percent questions on the GMAT, you can also find the answer using POE. 14 is a little bigger than $\frac{1}{10}$, or 10%, of 112—11.2 is exactly 10%—so the answer can only be (C).

2. **C** Rather than try to rely on high school-style exponential growth formulas, let's just count this one out. If 4 flights left the airport between 9 and 10 A.M., then 8 left between 10 and 11 A.M., and 16 left between 11 A.M. and noon. Starting at noon, the flights begin to double every *two* hours, so 32 left between noon and 2 P.M. and 64 left between 2 P.M. and 4 P.M. The correct answer is (C). If you chose (E), you may have forgotten to account for the afternoon change in the rate of increase, and the test writers, of course, made sure that the answer you came up with was there waiting for you.

3. **D** Since we have parallelograms, we really have only two angles, big ones and small ones, and we know that a big angle plus a small one equals 180. Statement (1) tells us the value of *r; q*, like *r*, is a small angle, so $q + r = 70 + 70$, or 140. We're down to AD.
   Statement (2) gives us the value of a big angle, which we can subtract from 180 to get the value of a small angle. We now have the same information we had in Statement (1) and our answer is (D).

MATH BIN 1

QUESTIONS

4. Chris's convertible gets gas mileage that is 40% greater than that of Stan's SUV. If Harry's hatchback gets gas mileage that is 15% greater than that of Chris's convertible, then Harry's hatchback gets gas mileage that is what percent greater than that of Stan's SUV?

- ◯ 25%
- ◯ 46%
- ◯ 55%
- ◯ 61%
- ◯ 66%

5. If x is equal to 1 more than the product of 3 and z, and y is equal to 1 less than the product of 2 and z, then $2x$ is how much greater than $3y$ when z is 4 ?

- ◯ 1
- ◯ 2
- ◯ 3
- ◯ 5
- ◯ 6

EXPLANATIONS

4. **D** This is a Plugging In problem. Since it's a percent problem, too, and the question asks us to find a percentage greater than the mileage of Stan's SUV, let's make Stan's mileage 100. Chris's mileage is therefore 140; 15% of 140 is 21, so Harry's mileage is 161. 161 is 61% greater than 100, and the correct answer is (D).

   Choices (A) and (C) are both traps, since they're simple addition and subtraction, respectively, of the numbers in the problem. If you got (B), you probably increased Chris's mileage by 15% of 40, rather than 15% of 140.

5. **D** Start by translating the two original equations: $x = 3z + 1$ and $y = 2z - 1$. If z is 4, then $x = 13$ and $y = 7$. $2x$ is thus 26 and $3y$ is 21. The difference between the two values is 5, so the correct answer is (D).

   If you chose (A), you may have mistakenly added when the problem asked for a product. If you got (E), you may have solved for $x - y$ when the problem asked for $2x - 3y$. And if you got (C), you may have done both.

MATH BIN 1

QUESTIONS

EXPLANATIONS

6. In 2005, did Company A have more than twice the number of employees that Company B did?

   (1) In 2005, Company A had 11,500 more employees than did Company B.

   (2) In 2005, the 3,000 employees with advanced degrees at Company A made up 12.5% of that company's total number employees, and the 2,500 employees with advanced degrees at Company B made up 20% of that company's total number of employees.

   ○ Statement (1) ALONE is sufficient, but statement (2) alone is not sufficient.
   ○ Statement (2) ALONE is sufficient, but statement (1) alone is not sufficient.
   ○ BOTH statements TOGETHER are sufficient, but NEITHER statement ALONE is sufficient.
   ○ EACH statement ALONE is sufficient.
   ○ Statements (1) and (2) TOGETHER are not sufficient.

6. **B** Statement (1) tells us the difference between the numbers of employees at the two companies. Without the actual number of employees at either company, though, this information isn't sufficient to answer this yes-or-no question, so we're down to BCE.

Statement (2), on the other hand, gives us the part-to-whole relationship we need to solve for the actual number of employees at each of the companies. We therefore know we can answer the question with a definitive "yes" or "no"—it doesn't matter which one is actually correct—so the answer is (B).

(If you really want to crunch the numbers, that 12.5% at Company A is the same as $\frac{1}{8}$, and Company A had 24,000 employees; that 20% at Company B is the same as $\frac{1}{5}$, and Company B had 12,500 employees. The answer to the original question is "no"; Company A did not have more than twice the number of employees as did Company B.)

7. Is x^3 equal to 125 ?

   (1) $x > 4$

   (2) $x < 6$

   ○ Statement (1) ALONE is sufficient, but statement (2) alone is not sufficient.
   ○ Statement (2) ALONE is sufficient, but statement (1) alone is not sufficient.
   ○ BOTH statements TOGETHER are sufficient, but NEITHER statement ALONE is sufficient.
   ○ EACH statement ALONE is sufficient.
   ○ Statements (1) and (2) TOGETHER are not sufficient.

7. **E** The question "Is x^3 equal to 125?" can be rewritten as "Is $x = 5$?" This is a yes-or-no question, and the best way to tackle it is to Plug In twice. In Statement (1), we can Plug In 5, in which case the answer to the question "Is x^3 equal to 125?" is "yes." Or, we can Plug In 6, in which case the answer is "no." Thus, because we get two different answers depending on the numbers we Plug In, Statement (1) is not sufficient. We're down to BCE.

In Statement (2), we can Plug In 5, in which case the answer is "yes," or 4, in which case the answer is "no." Eliminate (B).

QUESTIONS

EXPLANATIONS

To see if the answer is (C), we must choose a number that satisfies the conditions of both Statements (1) and (2) at the same time. We can plug in 5, in which case the answer is "yes." You might have been tempted to choose (C) at this point because no other integer will satisfy the two equations at the same time, but does this problem limit us to picking integers? Nope. What about 4.5? Or 5.2? In either of these cases, the answer is "no." Because we get two different answers depending on what numbers we plug in, the combination of Statements (1) and (2) is not sufficient either, and the correct answer is (E).

8. Bob leaves point A and drives due west to point B. From point B, he drives due south to point C. How far is Bob from his original location?

   (1) Point A is 24 miles from point B.

   (2) Point B is 18 miles from point C.

   ○ Statement (1) ALONE is sufficient, but statement (2) alone is not sufficient.
   ○ Statement (2) ALONE is sufficient, but statement (1) alone is not sufficient.
   ○ BOTH statements TOGETHER are sufficient, but NEITHER statement ALONE is sufficient.
   ○ EACH statement ALONE is sufficient.
   ○ Statements (1) and (2) TOGETHER are not sufficient.

8. **C** When a geometry problem comes without a diagram, always start by drawing one of your own. In this case, your diagram should look like this:

Statement (1) tells us the length of one side of our triangle, the distance from A to B. Since we know we have a right triangle (because Bob drove due west and due south), any two sides would be enough to find the remaining side. And *if* we knew that we had a "special" right triangle, one side might be enough. Neither of these cases applies, though, so we're down to BCE. Statement (2) gives us, again, a single side. Remember, though, that we can no longer consider the information from Statement (1), so this statement alone is also insufficient. We're down to (C) or (E).

MATH BIN 1

When we put the 2 statements together, we know we *could* solve for the remaining side using the Pythagorean Theorem—although, since this is a Data Sufficiency question, there's no reason we would. The correct answer is (C). Incidentally, if we did want to solve for the third side, we could save a lot of unnecessary calculation by recognizing this as a multiple of the old GMAT favorite, the 3-4-5 triangle. The two shorter sides of the triangle are multiplied by 6, so the remaining side must be 30.

9. The formula $M = \sqrt{l^2 + w^2 + d^2}$ describes the relationship between the length of M, which is the longest line that can be drawn in a rectangular solid, and the length, l, width, w, and depth, d, of that rectangular solid. The longest line that can be drawn in a rectangular solid with a length of 12, a width of 4, and a depth of 3 is how much longer than the longest line that can drawn in a rectangular solid with a length of 6, a width of 3, and a depth of 2 ?

○ 5
○ 6
○ 7
○ 9
○ 13

9. **B** Although the relationship provided in the problem is based on geometry, this isn't really a geometry problem for us: We can simply plug the given numbers into the formula. Starting with the larger rectangular solid, $\sqrt{12^2 + 4^2 + 3^2}$ $= \sqrt{144 + 16 + 9} = \sqrt{169} = 13$. For the smaller rectangular solid, $\sqrt{6^2 + 3^2 + 2^2} = \sqrt{36 + 9 + 4} = \sqrt{49} = 7$. Both 13 and 7 are, of course, answer choices, but the problem asked us for the *difference* between the two values, so the correct answer is 6, (B).

MATH BIN 1

QUESTIONS

10. Is the average (arithmetic mean) of *a, b,* and *c* equal to 8 ?

 (1) Three times the sum of *a, b,* and *c* is equal to 72.

 (2) The sum of 2*a,* 2*b,* and 2*c* is equal to 48.

 ○ Statement (1) ALONE is sufficient, but statement (2) alone is not sufficient.
 ○ Statement (2) ALONE is sufficient, but statement (1) alone is not sufficient.
 ○ BOTH statements TOGETHER are sufficient, but NEITHER statement ALONE is sufficient.
 ○ EACH statement ALONE is sufficient.
 ○ Statements (1) and (2) TOGETHER are not sufficient.

EXPLANATIONS

10. **D** This is a yes-or-no question, and we need to recognize that it's not asking about the individual values of *a, b,* and *c*—it's asking only about the average of those values. Of course, we could easily find the average if we knew the individual values. But, we can also find the average if we know the sum of the values, since the average of any group of values is their sum divided by the number of values in the group. Therefore, the question is asking us whether $\frac{a+b+c}{3} = 8$. To simplify this equation, multiply both sides by 3 to get $a + b + c = 24$. If the sum is 24, then the average is 8.

Statement (1) tells us that $3(a + b + c) = 72$. We can divide both sides by 3 to find out that the sum is, indeed, 24; the average is 8; and the answer to the question is "yes." Since this is a Data Sufficiency problem, though, we can stop as soon as we know that we can find the sum of *a, b,* and *c,* and we're down to AD.

Statement (2) tells us that $2a + 2b + 2c = 48$. If we factor a 2 out of the left side of the equation, we get $2(a + b + c) = 48$ and once again see that we can find the sum. The correct answer is (D).

MATH BIN 1

QUESTIONS

11. $\sqrt{\sqrt{\left(1 + \dfrac{17}{64}\right)}} =$

- ◯ $\dfrac{\sqrt{34}}{8}$

- ◯ $\dfrac{3\sqrt{2}}{4}$

- ◯ $\dfrac{9}{8}$

- ◯ $\dfrac{\sqrt{68}}{4}$

- ◯ $\dfrac{3\sqrt{2}}{2}$

EXPLANATIONS

11. **B** Since we should always calculate things inside the parentheses first—don't forget PEMDAS!—start by adding 1 and $\dfrac{17}{64}$ to get $\dfrac{81}{64}$. Those are both perfect squares, so the inner root sign will be easy to handle: $\sqrt{\dfrac{81}{64}} = \dfrac{\sqrt{81}}{\sqrt{64}} = \dfrac{9}{8}$. Don't grab (C), though—we still need to work the outer sign: $\sqrt{\dfrac{9}{8}} = \dfrac{\sqrt{9}}{\sqrt{8}} = \dfrac{3}{2\sqrt{2}}$. Like in high school, we can't leave a radical on the bottom of a fraction, so we'll need to multiply our answer by $\dfrac{\sqrt{2}}{\sqrt{2}}$ to get our final answer of (B), $\dfrac{3\sqrt{2}}{4}$.

If you're comfortable estimating fractions and roots, you can apply POE to this question.

$1 + \dfrac{17}{64}$ is a little greater than 1; the square root of something a little greater than 1 is also something a little greater than 1; and the square root of that number is, again, something a little greater than 1. Only (B) and (C) are a little greater than 1.

MATH BIN 1

QUESTIONS

12. A certain stadium is currently full to $\frac{13}{16}$ of its maximum seating capacity. What is the maximum seating capacity of the stadium?

   (1) If 1,250 people were to enter the stadium, the stadium would be full to $\frac{15}{16}$ of its maximum seating capacity.

   (2) If 2,500 people were to leave the stadium, the stadium would be full to $\frac{9}{16}$ of its maximum seating capacity.

   ○ Statement (1) ALONE is sufficient, but statement (2) alone is not sufficient.
   ○ Statement (2) ALONE is sufficient, but statement (1) alone is not sufficient.
   ○ BOTH statements TOGETHER are sufficient, but NEITHER statement ALONE is sufficient.
   ○ EACH statement ALONE is sufficient.
   ○ Statements (1) and (2) TOGETHER are not sufficient.

EXPLANATIONS

12. **D** This is a fraction problem, so the key is to convert fractions to actual numbers. Statement (1) tells us that 1,250 people will take the stadium from $\frac{13}{16}$ full to $\frac{15}{16}$ full; that's a difference of $\frac{2}{16}$, or $\frac{1}{8}$, so we know that 1,250 represents $\frac{1}{8}$ of the total seating capacity of the stadium. The stadium must, therefore, hold 8 × 1,250, or 10,000 people, and we're down to AD.

Statement (2) allows us to find a similar equivalence: a change of 2,500 represents the difference between $\frac{9}{16}$ and $\frac{13}{16}$, that is, $\frac{4}{16}$, or $\frac{1}{4}$ of the stadium's total seating capacity. So we know we can find the total seating capacity (4 × 2,500, or 10,000 people) with Statement (2) as well, making (D) the correct answer.

MATH BIN 1

QUESTIONS

13. Andre has already saved $\frac{3}{7}$ of the cost of a new car, and he has calculated that he will be able to save $\frac{2}{5}$ of the remaining amount before the end of the summer. What fraction of the cost of the new car will he still need to save after the end of the summer?

○ $\frac{6}{35}$

○ $\frac{8}{35}$

○ $\frac{12}{35}$

○ $\frac{23}{35}$

○ $\frac{29}{35}$

$\{1, 4, 6, y\}$

14. If the average (arithmetic mean) of the set of numbers above is 6, then what is the median?

○ 5
○ 6
○ 7
○ 13
○ 24

EXPLANATIONS

13. **C** Because there are fractions in the answer choices, and they're fractions of an unspecified amount, the quickest way to solve this problem is to Plug In. Let's make the price of Andre's dream car $35—the denominators of the fractions in the problem are 7 and 5 (both factors of 35) and, moreover, 35 is in the denominator of *all* of the answer choices.

If the car costs $35, and Andre has already saved $\frac{3}{7}$ of that, or $15, he currently has $20 left to save. Before the end of the summer, he'll be able to save $\frac{2}{5}$ of that remaining $20, or $8. That will give him a total of $23 saved toward his car, leaving him $12 to go. Expressed as a fraction of the cost of the car, that's $\frac{12}{35}$, and the correct answer is (C).

As always, watch those trap answers. Choice (D) is the fraction of the cost that Andre will have saved by the end of the summer. Choice (A) is what you'd get if you calculated Andre's summer earnings as two-fifths of the total cost of the car instead of two-fifths of what Andre has left to save. Choice (E) is what you'd get if you made both mistakes.

14. **A** The average of all four numbers is 6, so the numbers must add up to 6 times 4, or 24. That means y must equal 13. And if y equals 13, the median must be 5—that is, the average of the two middle numbers in the set. Even if y is very large, the middle numbers will still be 4 and 6, so (D) and (E) are much too large.

MATH BIN 1

QUESTIONS

15. A store sells a six-pack of soda for $2.70. If this represents a savings of 10 percent of the individual price of cans of soda, then what is the price of a single can of soda?

- ◯ $ 0.35
- ◯ $ 0.40
- ◯ $ 0.45
- ◯ $ 0.50
- ◯ $ 0.55

16. If Beth spent $400 of her earnings last month on rent, how much did Beth earn last month?

(1) Beth saved $\frac{1}{3}$ of her earnings last month and spent half of the remainder on rent.

(2) Beth earned twice as much this month as last month.

- ◯ Statement (1) ALONE is sufficient, but statement (2) alone is not sufficient.
- ◯ Statement (2) ALONE is sufficient, but statement (1) alone is not sufficient.
- ◯ BOTH statements TOGETHER are sufficient, but NEITHER statement ALONE is sufficient.
- ◯ EACH statement ALONE is sufficient.
- ◯ Statements (1) and (2) TOGETHER are not sufficient.

EXPLANATIONS

15. **D** If a six-pack sells for $2.70, then each can costs 45 cents when purchased together. When purchased individually, the price is higher than 45 cents, so cross off (A), (B), and (C). Let's Plug In (D). Choice (D) says the price of an individual can is 50 cents. 10% of 50 cents is 5 cents, so the price per can of a six-pack would be 50 − 5 = 45 cents. Therefore, (D) is correct.

16. **A** Covering up Statement (2) and looking only at Statement (1), we see that Beth saved one-third of her earnings and spent half of the two-thirds that remained on rent. Half of two-thirds is one-third. So we can set up the equation:

$$\frac{1}{3} = \frac{400}{x}$$

And x equals $1,200. Note that we didn't actually need to find out how much Beth earned. We just needed to know that we *could* find out. We're down to AD.

Now, looking at Statement (2) we see that it tells us how Beth did THIS month. But do we care? Nope. The question asks us about LAST month. The correct answer is (A).

MATH BIN 1

QUESTIONS

17. If *n* is an integer, is *n* even?

(1) 2*n* is an even integer.

(2) *n* – 1 is an odd integer.

○ Statement (1) ALONE is sufficient, but statement (2) alone is not sufficient.
○ Statement (2) ALONE is sufficient, but statement (1) alone is not sufficient.
○ BOTH statements TOGETHER are sufficient, but NEITHER statement ALONE is sufficient.
○ EACH statement ALONE is sufficient.
○ Statements (1) and (2) TOGETHER are not sufficient.

18. At apartment complex *Z*, 30 percent of the residents are men over the age of 18, and 40 percent are women over the age of 18. If there are 24 children living in the complex, how many total residents live in apartment complex *Z* ?

○ 32
○ 80
○ 94
○ 112
○ 124

EXPLANATIONS

17. **B** To answer this yes-or-no question, you must plug in values that make the statements true. Starting with Statement (1), let's Plug In 4 for *n*, which makes the statement "2*n* is an even integer" true, and gives us a "yes" to our overall question. Now, let's Plug In 3 for *n*, which still makes the statement true, but gives us a "no" to our overall question. Because the answer is sometimes "yes" and sometimes "no," we're down to BCE. Looking at Statement (2) only, let's Plug In values that make the statement true. If *n* = 2, the statement is true, and the answer to our overall question is a tentative "yes." Now, if we can find even one case where we can plug a number into this statement that makes the statement true but answers the question "no," then we'll be down to CE. But as you try different numbers, you'll realize that in order to make Statement (2) true, *n* has to be even. So the answer to this question is (B).

18. **B** Altogether, the percentages of men and women add up to 70%, so that means 30% of the residents at this complex are children. Just set up an equation:

$$\frac{30}{100} = \frac{24}{x}$$

Solving for *x*, the total number of residents is 80. The answer is (B).

You could also Plug In the Answers. Choice (C) seems difficult, so why not start with (B), which has an easy number to work with? 30% of 80 = 24. 40% of 80 = 32. So there are a total of 24 + 32 = 56 adults. If (B) is correct, there should be 24 kids. And guess what? That's just what the problem says.

MATH BIN 1

QUESTIONS

19. Over the course of a soccer season, 30 percent of the players on a team scored goals. What is the ratio of players on the team who scored goals to those who did not?

   ○ 3 to 10
   ○ 1 to 3
   ○ 3 to 7
   ○ 1 to 1
   ○ 3 to 1

20. At a restaurant, Luis left a tip for his waiter equal to 20 percent of his entire dinner check, including tax. What was the amount of the dinner check?

   (1) The sum of the dinner check and the tip was $16.80.

   (2) Luis's tip consisted of two bills and four coins.

   ○ Statement (1) ALONE is sufficient, but statement (2) alone is not sufficient.
   ○ Statement (2) ALONE is sufficient, but statement (1) alone is not sufficient.
   ○ BOTH statements TOGETHER are sufficient, but NEITHER statement ALONE is sufficient.
   ○ EACH statement ALONE is sufficient.
   ○ Statements (1) and (2) TOGETHER are not sufficient.

EXPLANATIONS

19. **C** If 30% of the players on the soccer team scored goals during the season, then 70% did not score goals. The ratio of those who scored to those who did not is 30 to 70, which reduces to 3 to 7. Some will find that Plugging In is the easiest way to solve this problem. Plug In 10 for the number of players on the team (choose this number because it is easy to work with in a percentage problem). 30% of the 10 players—that is to say, 3 players—scored goals. The other 7, it then follows, did not score goals. The ratio of those who scored to those who did not is 3 to 7. The correct answer is (C).

20. **A** Because Luis tipped the waiter 20%, we know that the sum of the check and tip equals 1.2 times the amount of the check. Thus, we can write the equation

$$1.2x = 16.80$$

and solve for x to determine both the amount of the check and the amount of Luis's tip. The answer must be (A) or (D).
Statement (2) is insufficient because it does not identify either the bills or the coins. The correct answer is (A).

MATH BIN 1

QUESTIONS

21. Which sport utility vehicle has a higher list price, the Touristo or the Leisure?

   (1) The list price of the Leisure is $\frac{5}{6}$ the list price of the Touristo.

   (2) The list price of the Touristo is 1.2 times the list price of the Leisure.

   ○ Statement (1) ALONE is sufficient, but statement (2) alone is not sufficient.
   ○ Statement (2) ALONE is sufficient, but statement (1) alone is not sufficient.
   ○ BOTH statements TOGETHER are sufficient, but NEITHER statement ALONE is sufficient.
   ○ EACH statement ALONE is sufficient.
   ○ Statements (1) and (2) TOGETHER are not sufficient.

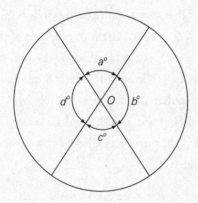

22. In the circle above, center O is intersected by 2 straight lines, and $3a = b$. What is the value of $b - a$?

   ○ 2
   ○ 30
   ○ 45
   ○ 90
   ○ 135

EXPLANATIONS

21. **D** According to Statement (1), the list price of the Leisure is $\frac{5}{6}$ the list price of the Touristo. The list price of the Touristo is therefore greater than the list price of the Leisure. Statement (1) is sufficient; the answer must be (A) or (D). Statement (2) tells you that the list price of the Touristo is 1.2 times the list price of the Leisure. So Statement (2) also tells you that the list price of the Touristo is greater than the list price of the Leisure. The correct answer is (D).

22. **D** If you look carefully at the drawing, you should notice that a and b are supplementary angles; that is, together they make up a line. The sum of these angles, therefore, is 180°. Or, to put this in math-speak:

   $$a + b = 180$$

   Now, return to the equation in the question stem, $3a = b$. We can use this information to rewrite the equation $a + b = 180$ as

   $$a + 3a = 180$$
   $$4a = 180$$
   $$a = 45$$

MATH BIN 1

Because $a + b = 180$, and $a = 45$, b must equal 135, which is (E). Wait, though, you're not done yet: The question asks for the solution $b - a$. Because $b - a = 135 - 45$, the answer to this question is 90. The correct answer is (D).

23. What is the value of integer w ?

(1) w is a multiple of 3.

(2) $420 < w < 425$

○ Statement (1) ALONE is sufficient, but statement (2) alone is not sufficient.
○ Statement (2) ALONE is sufficient, but statement (1) alone is not sufficient.
○ BOTH statements TOGETHER are sufficient, but NEITHER statement ALONE is sufficient.
○ EACH statement ALONE is sufficient.
○ Statements (1) and (2) TOGETHER are not sufficient.

23. **C** Because there are an infinite number of multiples of 3, it is clear that Statement (1) is not sufficient to answer the question. The answer must be (B), (C), or (E). Statement (2) narrows the range of possible answers to 421, 422, 423, or 424. However, because it does not narrow the answer to a single solution, it is not sufficient. Eliminate (B). When you put the two statements together, you know that w is a multiple of 3 that is either 421, 422, 423, or 424. Because only one of these values, 423, is a multiple of 3, the two statements together are sufficient. (A quick way to test whether an integer is divisible by 3 is to add its digits; if the sum of the digits is divisible by 3, then the number is divisible by 3.) The correct answer is (C).

24. What is the quotient when 0.25% of 600 is divided by 0.25 of 600 ?

○ 10
○ 1
○ 0.1
○ 0.01
○ 0.001

24. **D** Before we worry about the division, let's solve for the two values. The second one is easier, so let's start there: "of" means multiply, so $0.25 \times 600 = 150$. With the first value, we have to be sure to take into account both the decimal *and* the percent sign: 0.25% can be represented as $\frac{0.25}{100}$, or 0.0025. Either way, when you multiply by 600, the result is 1.5. The quotient is thus 1.5 divided by 150, or 0.01. The answer is (D).

If you're really comfortable with manipulating fractions, you can save yourself a lot of math. The whole question translates into $\dfrac{\dfrac{0.25}{100} \times 600}{0.25 \times 600}$, which easily cancels down to $\dfrac{1}{100}$, or 0.01.

25. A certain town's economic development council has 21 members. If the number of females on the council is 3 less than 3 times the number of males on the council, then the town's economic development council has how many male members?

- ⚪ 5
- ⚪ 6
- ⚪ 7
- ⚪ 9
- ⚪ 15

25. **B** Although you could solve this by writing a pair of algebraic equations ($f + m = 21$ and $f = m - 3$), it's simpler to Plug In the Answers. Start with (C), 7 men. The number of women would be 3 less than 3 times that number, or $21 - 3 = 18$ women. That's a total of 25 council members altogether, and we're looking for 21. Now that we know that (C) is too big, we can eliminate (C), (D), and (E). If we try (B), 6 men, then we have $18 - 3 = 15$ women. This gives us our desired total of 21 council members, so the correct answer is (B). If you got (E), by the way, you solved for the number of *female* members on the board.

26. Roger can chop down 4 trees in an hour. How long does it take Vincent to chop down 4 trees?

(1) Vincent spends 6 hours per day chopping down trees.

(2) Vincent takes twice as long as Roger to chop down trees.

- ⚪ Statement (1) ALONE is sufficient, but statement (2) alone is not sufficient.
- ⚪ Statement (2) ALONE is sufficient, but statement (1) alone is not sufficient.
- ⚪ BOTH statements TOGETHER are sufficient, but NEITHER statement ALONE is sufficient.
- ⚪ EACH statement ALONE is sufficient.
- ⚪ Statements (1) and (2) TOGETHER are not sufficient.

26. **B** Statement (1) tells you how many hours Vincent spends chopping down trees in a day, but it provides no data to help you determine how long it takes him to chop down 4 trees. This statement is clearly insufficient to answer the question. The answer must be (B), (C), or (E).

Statement (2) tells you that Vincent takes twice as long as Roger to chop down trees. Because the question stem tells you that Roger chops down 4 trees per hour, you can deduce that Vincent chops down 4 trees every 2 hours. Thus, Statement (2) is sufficient to answer the question. The correct answer is (B).

MATH BIN 2

QUESTIONS

1. If $x = \dfrac{\dfrac{5}{9} + \dfrac{15}{27} + \dfrac{45}{81}}{3}$, then $\sqrt{1-x} =$

- ○ $\dfrac{\sqrt{5}}{9}$
- ○ $\dfrac{5}{9}$
- ○ $\dfrac{2}{3}$
- ○ $\dfrac{\sqrt{5}}{3}$
- ○ $\dfrac{15}{9}$

2. Steven has run a certain number of laps around a track at an average (arithmetic mean) time per lap of 51 seconds. If he runs one additional lap in 39 seconds and reduces his average time per lap to 49 seconds, how many laps did he run at an average time per lap of 51 seconds?

- ○ 2
- ○ 5
- ○ 6
- ○ 10
- ○ 12

EXPLANATIONS

1. **C** You could start by converting all the fractions to their least common denominator of 81—an understandable temptation. However, in this case, it's quicker and simpler to reduce the fractions instead. They all reduce to $\dfrac{5}{9}$, so $x = \dfrac{\dfrac{5}{9} + \dfrac{5}{9} + \dfrac{5}{9}}{3}$, or $\dfrac{3\left(\dfrac{5}{9}\right)}{3}$ ...or $\dfrac{5}{9}$. Now that we know the value of x, we can solve for $\sqrt{(1-x)}$:

$$\sqrt{\left(1 - \frac{5}{9}\right)} = \sqrt{\frac{4}{9}} = \frac{\sqrt{4}}{\sqrt{9}} = \frac{2}{3}.$$ The correct answer is (C). Choice (B), of course, is x itself, and (D) is $\sqrt{x}$.

2. **B** This is a multistep average problem involving an unknown quantity—in short, a perfect place to Plug In the Answers! Start with (C): If Steven has already run 6 laps, then we know that he has run for a total of 6×51, or 306, seconds. One more lap in 39 seconds gives him a total of 7 laps in 345 seconds, and the average works out to be a little greater than 49 seconds ($49\dfrac{2}{7}$, to be exact). Close, but not quite. Fewer laps will reduce Steven's average speed, so (B) is the next logical choice to try. Five laps in 51 seconds means Steven has run 5×51, or 255, seconds so far, and the additional 39-second lap gives a total of 6 laps run in 294 seconds. The average is now $\dfrac{294}{6} = 49$ seconds, and (B) is the correct answer.

MATH BIN 2

3. $200^2 - 2(200)(199) + 199^2 =$

- ○ −79,201
- ○ −200
- ○ 1
- ○ 200
- ○ 79,999

3. **C** Although you could solve this problem with lots of tedious multiplication, it's much faster to recognize the common quadratic hidden in the numbers: $x^2 - 2xy + y^2 = (x - y)(x - y)$. That means this calculation can be rewritten as $(200 - 199)(200 - 199)$, or $(1)(1)$. The correct answer is (C).

Since the answer choices vary so widely, you could have applied some POE to the most extreme answer choices, (A) and (E). The product of 200 and 199, which we have to double, is not too different from either 200^2 or 199^2. Thus, the negative value in the equation is roughly equal to the sum of the two positive values in the equation. If you did the math, by the way, and *got* one of those answers, you must have reversed an addition or subtraction sign.

4. If $x \neq \dfrac{1}{2}$, then $\dfrac{6x^2 + 11x - 7}{2x - 1} =$

- ○ $3x + 7$
- ○ $3x - 7$
- ○ $3x + 1$
- ○ $x + 7$
- ○ $x - 7$

4. **A** Since this problem has variables in the answer choices, the simplest way to solve it is to Plug In. If $x = 2$, the equation becomes $\dfrac{6(2)^2 + 11(2) - 7}{2(2) - 1} = \dfrac{24 + 22 - 7}{4 - 1} = \dfrac{39}{3} = 13$. Now Plug In 2 for x in the answer choices—only (A) gives us 13, so it must be the correct answer. You could also try Plugging In the Answers. Try multiplying the answer choices by the expression in the denominator of the fraction and see which one yields the expression in the numerator. Only (A) does, so it is the correct answer.

MATH BIN 2

QUESTIONS

5. If Amy drove the distance from her home to the beach in less than 2 hours, was her average speed greater than 60 miles per hour?

 (1) The distance that Amy drove from her home to the beach was less than 125 miles.

 (2) The distance that Amy drove from her home to the beach was greater than 122 miles.

 ○ Statement (1) ALONE is sufficient, but statement (2) alone is not sufficient.
 ○ Statement (2) ALONE is sufficient, but statement (1) alone is not sufficient.
 ○ BOTH statements TOGETHER are sufficient, but NEITHER statement ALONE is sufficient.
 ○ EACH statement ALONE is sufficient.
 ○ Statements (1) and (2) TOGETHER are not sufficient.

6. If $x = m - 1$, which of the following is true when $m = \dfrac{1}{2}$?

 ○ $x^0 > x^2 > x^3 > x^1$
 ○ $x^0 > x^2 > x^1 > x^3$
 ○ $x^0 > x^1 > x^2 > x^3$
 ○ $x^2 > x^0 > x^3 > x^1$
 ○ $x^3 > x^2 > x^1 > x^0$

EXPLANATIONS

5. **B** Take a moment to translate what this question is really asking: Is the distance Amy drove greater than 120 miles? This rate problem is also a yes-or-no question, so we don't need to know Amy's exact speed, just whether her average speed was greater than 60 miles per hour. The simplest way to find out whether Statement (1) is sufficient is to try different possible times and distances. If her total driving time was, for instance, 1 hour, a distance of 61 miles yields an answer of "yes." Meanwhile, a distance of 59 miles yields an answer of "no." That means the possible answers are BCE.

Regardless of what times and distances you Plug In for Statement (2), you will always get an answer of "yes." Even if Amy were to have driven the *full* 2 hours and gone *only* 122 miles, she would be driving at a rate of 61 miles per hour; since she actually drove a greater distance in less time, her rate must be greater than 61. Since Statement (2) always gives us the same answer, it is sufficient, and the answer is (B).

6. **A** Once you've solved for x, which equals $-\dfrac{1}{2}$, this question is just a matter of putting the four values in order. Even better, you already know two of them: $x = -\dfrac{1}{2}$ and $x^0 = 1$. With the other two values, be especially careful about the negative sign: $x^2 = \dfrac{1}{4}$ and $x^3 = -\dfrac{1}{8}$. The correct order is $x^0 > x^2 > x^3 > x^1$, and the answer is (A).

MATH BIN 2

QUESTIONS

7. If a comedian plays two shows and twice as many tickets are available for the evening show as for the afternoon show, what percentage of the total number of tickets available for both shows have been sold?

(1) A total of 450 tickets are available for both shows.

(2) Exactly $\frac{3}{5}$ of the tickets available for the afternoon show have been sold, and exactly $\frac{1}{5}$ of the tickets available for the evening show have been sold.

○ Statement (1) ALONE is sufficient, but statement (2) alone is not sufficient.
○ Statement (2) ALONE is sufficient, but statement (1) alone is not sufficient.
○ BOTH statements TOGETHER are sufficient, but NEITHER statement ALONE is sufficient.
○ EACH statement ALONE is sufficient.
○ Statements (1) and (2) TOGETHER are not sufficient.

8. If $\frac{1}{y} = 2\frac{2}{3}$, then $\left(\frac{1}{y+1}\right)^2 =$

○ $\frac{9}{64}$

○ $\frac{3}{8}$

○ $\frac{64}{121}$

○ $\frac{121}{64}$

○ $\frac{64}{9}$

EXPLANATIONS

7. **B** The information in Statement (1), along with that in the question itself, is enough for us to find the number of tickets issued for each show. Without any information about the number of tickets that were sold, though, we can't answer the question, and we're down to BCE.

Statement (2), along with the information in the question, is sufficient—even without the information in Statement (1). If we have the fraction of each type of ticket that was sold, and the ratio of one type of ticket to the other, we can figure out the overall percentage of tickets sold. The correct answer is (B).

Want to prove it? Try Plugging In. In Statement (2), the denominator of both fractions is 5, so let's say that 25 tickets have been issued for the afternoon show and 50 have been issued for the evening show. That means 15 tickets have been sold for the afternoon show and 10 have been sold for the evening show, for a total of 25 tickets sold out of a total of 75 tickets issued. The answer is $\frac{1}{3}$, as it will always be if we meet the requirements of Statement (2) and the question itself.

8. **C** First, solve for y. Since $2\frac{2}{3} = \frac{8}{3}$, $\frac{1}{y} = \frac{8}{3}$ and thus $y = \frac{3}{8}$. Now plug the value for y into the expression:

$$\left(\frac{1}{\frac{3}{8}+1}\right)^2 = \left(\frac{1}{\left(\frac{11}{8}\right)}\right)^2 = \frac{1^2}{\left(\frac{11}{8}\right)^2} = \frac{1}{\frac{121}{64}} = \frac{64}{121}.$$

The correct answer is (C).
Choice (B), of course, is the value of y. Choice (D) is the reciprocal of the correct answer, which

MATH BIN 2

QUESTIONS

EXPLANATIONS

could indicate that you didn't do the last step of the calculation. If you chose (A), you forgot to add 1 when you put the value for y into the expression. And if you chose (E), you did both.

9. An operation $\sim$ is defined by $a \sim b = \dfrac{a+b}{(ab)^2}$ for all numbers a and b such that $ab \neq 0$. If $c \neq 0$ and $a \sim c = 0$, then $c =$

- $\bigcirc$ $-a$
- $\bigcirc$ 0
- $\bigcirc$ $\sqrt{a}$
- $\bigcirc$ a
- $\bigcirc$ a^2

9. **A** Answering a function problem on the GMAT is simply a matter of following the directions provided by the definition of the function. In this case, the operation signified by two numbers with the $\sim$ between them is defined as the sum of the numbers on either side of the $\sim$ sign divided by the square of the product of the two numbers. If $a \sim c = 0$, then $\dfrac{a+c}{(ac)^2} = 0$; since the numerator must be zero in order for the fraction itself to equal zero, we know that $a + c = 0$. Subtract a from both sides and $c = -a$. The answer is (A).

10. If x is a positive integer, is the greatest common factor of 150 and x a prime number?

(1) x is a prime number.

(2) $x < 4$

- $\bigcirc$ Statement (1) ALONE is sufficient, but statement (2) alone is not sufficient.
- $\bigcirc$ Statement (2) ALONE is sufficient, but statement (1) alone is not sufficient.
- $\bigcirc$ BOTH statements TOGETHER are sufficient, but NEITHER statement ALONE is sufficient.
- $\bigcirc$ EACH statement ALONE is sufficient.
- $\bigcirc$ Statements (1) and (2) TOGETHER are not sufficient.

10. **C** The easiest way to determine whether Statement (1) by itself is sufficient is to plug in different values for x. If $x = 2$, the greatest common factor is 2, and the answer to this yes-or-no question is "yes." If $x = 7$, on the other hand, the greatest common factor is 1, and since 1 is not prime, the answer is "no." The possible answers are BCE.

Statement (2) by itself is also not sufficient. If x is equal to 1, 2, or 3, then the greatest common factor of x and 150 is x itself. But since 2 and 3 are prime, and 1 is not, the possible answers are (C) and (E).

MATH BIN 2

When we put the statements together, the only possible values for x are 2 and 3. With either one, the greatest common factor is equal to x itself and is, therefore, prime. The correct answer is (C).

$$X = \{9, 10, 11, 12\}$$
$$Y = \{2, 3, 4, 5\}$$

11. If one number is chosen at random from each of the sets above and the number from Set X is divided by the number from Set Y, what is the probability that the result is an integer?

- ○ $\dfrac{1}{16}$
- ○ $\dfrac{3}{8}$
- ○ $\dfrac{1}{2}$
- ○ $\dfrac{3}{4}$
- ○ $\dfrac{15}{16}$

11. B As with all probability problems, we'll have to find a fraction that has the total number of possibilities in the denominator and the number of those possibilities that meet a certain requirement in the numerator. The denominator is the easy part: Because there are 4 members of each set, there are $4 \times 4 = 16$ total possibilities for the quotient when one member of X is divided by one member of Y. Now we just have to figure out how many of those possibilities meet the requirement.

The requirement, in this case, is that the quotient is an integer—in other words, that the member chosen from X is divisible by the member chosen from Y—and we can count out all of the combinations that meet that requirement quickly and easily. The first member of Set X, 9, is divisible by only one member of Set Y, 3, so that's one. Then, working through Set X: 10 is divisible by both 2 and 5, so there are another two possibilities; 11 is prime, so it's not divisible by any members of Set Y; and 12 gives us another three possibilities, because it's divisible by 2, 3, and 4. Thus, 6 of our total of 16 possibilities meet our requirement, and our probability is $\dfrac{6}{16}$, or $\dfrac{3}{8}$. The answer is (B).

MATH BIN 2

QUESTIONS

12. If p and q are integers, is $\dfrac{p+q}{2}$ an integer?

   (1) $p < 17$

   (2) $p = q$

   ○ Statement (1) ALONE is sufficient, but statement (2) alone is not sufficient.
   ○ Statement (2) ALONE is sufficient, but statement (1) alone is not sufficient.
   ○ BOTH statements TOGETHER are sufficient, but NEITHER statement ALONE is sufficient.
   ○ EACH statement ALONE is sufficient.
   ○ Statements (1) and (2) TOGETHER are not sufficient.

13. A perfectly spherical satellite with a radius of 4 feet is being packed for shipment to its launch site. If the inside dimensions of the rectangular crates available for shipment, when measured in feet, are consecutive even integers, then what is the volume of the smallest available crate that can be used? (The volume of a sphere is $V = \dfrac{4}{3}\pi r^3$.)

   ○   48
   ○   192
   ○   480
   ○   960
   ○ 1,680

EXPLANATIONS

12. **B**   Since Statement (1) doesn't tell us anything about the value of q, and very little about the value of p, it is, by itself, insufficient to answer this yes-or-no question. Statement (2), though, while it gives us no new specifics about the values of p or q, gives enough information to know the answer to the question. If $p = q$, then $\dfrac{p+q}{2} = \dfrac{p+p}{2} = \dfrac{2p}{2} = p$ since we know from the question that p is an integer, the answer to the question is "yes," and our answer is (B). Of course, we can easily show the sufficiency of Statement (2) by plugging in values for p and q: as long as the values are equal integers, the answer is always "yes."

13. **D**   Although this may seem like a volume question, it's really about being able to fit the diameter of the satellite inside the crate—we can entirely disregard the formula for the volume of a sphere. Let's start with what we know: Since the radius of the sphere is 4, the diameter is 8. Therefore, every dimension in our crate must be at least 8 and the smallest available crate will measure $8 \times 10 \times 12$. The volume of that crate is 960, and the correct answer is (D).

   In fact, if we try to use the volume formula we can easily go astray. Using a rough value of 3 for π, we can approximate the value of the sphere to be a little greater than 250 (replacing π with 3 in the formula gives a value of 256, and the exact value is a little greater than 268). We might be tempted, therefore, to select (C), but we can't: The only set of three consecutive integers that yields a volume of 480 is $6 \times 8 \times 10$, and we can't put a spherical object with a diameter of 8 feet into a crate that's only 6 feet across in one direction.

MATH BIN 2

14. Richard is 6 years older than David, and David is 8 years older than Scott. In 8 years, if Richard will be twice as old as Scott, then how old was David 4 years ago?

- ⭕ 8
- ⭕ 10
- ⭕ 12
- ⭕ 14
- ⭕ 16

14. **B** This problem could be an algebraic nightmare, so let's Plug In the Answers. We'll start with (C), 12. If David was 12 years old 4 years ago, he's 16 now, and that means Richard is 22 and Scott is 8. In 8 years, then, Richard will be 30 and Scott will be 16; since Richard won't be twice as old as Scott at that point, this can't be the answer.

Now try (B), 10, using the same process. If David was 10 years old 4 years ago, he's 14 now, so Richard is 20 and Scott is 6. In 8 years, then, Richard will be 28 and Scott will be 14; since Richard will then be twice as old as Scott, the answer is (B).

15. What is the value of x ?

(1) $x^2 - 5x + 4 = 0$

(2) x is not prime.

- ⭕ Statement (1) ALONE is sufficient, but statement (2) alone is not sufficient.
- ⭕ Statement (2) ALONE is sufficient, but statement (1) alone is not sufficient.
- ⭕ BOTH statements TOGETHER are sufficient, but NEITHER statement ALONE is sufficient.
- ⭕ EACH statement ALONE is sufficient.
- ⭕ Statements (1) and (2) TOGETHER are not sufficient.

15. **E** Statement (1) is a quadratic equation, so let's factor it and see what the options are for x:
$x^2 - 5x + 4 = 0$ factors into $(x - 4)(x - 1) = 0$, so x could be 4 or 1. Since there's more than one value for x, Statement (1) alone is insufficient, and we're down to BCE.

Statement (2) alone leaves us with the vast majority of all numbers—this statement is *definitely* not sufficient, so we're down to (C) or (E). When we combine the statements, they're still not sufficient. Be careful not to fall for one of the classic GMAT traps: 1 is *not* prime. Because 4 is also not prime, we're left with both values, and the correct answer is (E).

QUESTIONS

EXPLANATIONS

16. Sam and Jessica are invited to a dance. If there are 7 men and 7 women in total at the dance, and one woman and one man are chosen to lead the dance, what is the probability that Sam and Jessica will NOT be the pair chosen to lead the dance?

○ $\frac{1}{49}$

○ $\frac{1}{7}$

○ $\frac{6}{7}$

○ $\frac{47}{49}$

○ $\frac{48}{49}$

16. E The probability that Sam will be chosen is $\frac{1}{7}$. The probability that Jessica will be chosen is also $\frac{1}{7}$. The probability that they will both be chosen is $\frac{1}{7} \times \frac{1}{7} = \frac{1}{49}$ This is (A), but we aren't done yet. The question asks for the probability that they will NOT both be chosen. The probability that an event does NOT happen can be expressed as 1 minus the probability that the event DOES happen. So $1 - \frac{1}{49} = \frac{48}{49}$, or (E).

17. What is the surface area of rectangular solid *Y* ?

(1) The dimensions of one face of rectangular solid *Y* are 2 by 3.

(2) The volume of rectangular solid *Y* is 12.

○ Statement (1) ALONE is sufficient, but statement (2) alone is not sufficient.
○ Statement (2) ALONE is sufficient, but statement (1) alone is not sufficient.
○ BOTH statements TOGETHER are sufficient, but NEITHER statement ALONE is sufficient.
○ EACH statement ALONE is sufficient.
○ Statements (1) and (2) TOGETHER are not sufficient.

17. C Whenever you see a geometry problem without a diagram, it's a good idea to make one. Statement (1) tells us only two of the three dimensions we need to find the surface area. We're down to BCE.

Statement (2) tells us the the volume of the rectangular solid. By itself, the volume does not give us any of the three dimensions that we need to find the surface area, so we're down to (C) and (E). Putting the two statements together, we have all three dimensions. Statement (1) tells us that two of the dimensions are 2 and 3. Since the formula for the volume of a rectangular solid is $V = lwh$, the third dimension of the solid is 2. With all three dimensions, the surface area can be calculated. The answer is (C).

MATH BIN 2

QUESTIONS

18. A six-sided die with faces numbered 1 through 6 is rolled three times. What is the probability that the face with the number 6 on it will NOT face upward on all three rolls?

- ○ $\dfrac{1}{216}$
- ○ $\dfrac{1}{6}$
- ○ $\dfrac{2}{3}$
- ○ $\dfrac{17}{18}$
- ○ $\dfrac{215}{216}$

EXPLANATIONS

18. **E** Before you start calculating, it is always helpful to think about what is reasonable. The probability that the number 6 is going to come up three times in a row is pretty low, which is another way of saying that the probability that 6 is NOT going to come up three times in a row is pretty high. So we can eliminate (A), (B), and (C). Now, let's figure out the problem. The probability that the first roll yields the number 6 is $\dfrac{1}{6}$. The probability that the second roll yields the number 6 is also $\dfrac{1}{6}$. The probability that the third roll yields the number 6? You guessed it: $\dfrac{1}{6}$. To find the probability of the series of these three events happening, you multiply the probabilities of each of the individual events: $\dfrac{1}{6} \times \dfrac{1}{6} \times \dfrac{1}{6} = \dfrac{1}{216}$. That's (A), but we aren't done yet. $\dfrac{1}{216}$ is the probability that the number 6 WILL land face up on all three rolls. The probability that an event does NOT happen can be expressed as 1 minus the probability that the event DOES happen. $1 - \dfrac{1}{216} = \dfrac{215}{216}$. The correct answer is (E).

MATH BIN 2

QUESTIONS	EXPLANATIONS

19. What is the sum of x, y, and z ?

(1) $2x + y + 3z = 45$

(2) $x + 2y = 30$

○ Statement (1) ALONE is sufficient, but statement (2) alone is not sufficient.
○ Statement (2) ALONE is sufficient, but statement (1) alone is not sufficient.
○ BOTH statements TOGETHER are sufficient, but NEITHER statement ALONE is sufficient.
○ EACH statement ALONE is sufficient.
○ Statements (1) and (2) TOGETHER are not sufficient.

19. C Gut instinct may lead to you select (E) on this one; after all, Statement (1) provides a three-variable equation, which does not have an unique solution. Statement (2) refers to only two of the three variables mentioned in the question stem, so clearly it cannot be sufficient. At first glance, it may be hard to imagine how the two statements together could be any more helpful than each is on its own.

Statement (1) is, in fact, insufficient on its own, for the reason stated above. The possible answers are BCE. Statement (2) is also insufficient, again for the reason stated above. Eliminate (B). The answer is (C) or (E).

Now, add the two equations provided by Statements (1) and (2) to get $3x + 3y + 3z = 75$. Factor a 3 out of both sides of the equation and you end up with $x + y + z = 25$. Thus, the two statements together *are* sufficient to answer the question. The correct answer is (C).

20. A department store receives a shipment of 1,000 shirts, for which it pays $9,000. The store sells the shirts at a price 80 percent above cost for one month, after which it reduces the price of the shirts to 20 percent above cost. The store sells 75 percent of the shirts during the first month and 50 percent of the remaining shirts afterward. How much gross income did sales of the shirts generate?

○ $10,000
○ $10,800
○ $12,150
○ $13,500
○ $16,200

20. D To answer this question, break the problem down into small, manageable steps. The first job at hand is to determine the selling price of the shirt, both during the first month they were on sale and then during subsequent months. Because the store bought 1,000 shirts for $9,000, the cost of each shirt was $9.00. The store sold the shirts at an 80% markup during the first month. $1.8 \times \$9.00 = \$16.20$, so during the first month, the shirts sold for $16.20 each. After the first month, the selling price was 20% above cost. $1.20 \times \$9.00 = \$10.80$, so that was the selling price after the first month.

The store sold 75% of the shirts during the first month. 75% of 1,000 is 750; the store sold 750 shirts at $16.20 each. $750 \times \$16.20 = \$12,150$. Note that this partial answer is (C). Test takers who only half-finish their work will choose this incorrect answer. The store then sold 50% of its remaining stock at $10.80 per shirt. The remaining stock is 250 shirts (1,000 – 750), half of which is 125. The store, then, sold 125 shirts at $10.80 each. 125 × $10.80 = $1,350. The store's gross income from the sale of these shirts, then, is $12,150 + $1,350 = $13,500. The correct answer is (D).

21. David has three credit cards: a Passport card, an EverywhereCard, and an American Local card. He owes balances on all three cards. Does he owe the greatest balance on the EverywhereCard?

(1) The sum of the balances on his EverywhereCard and American Local card is $1,350, which is three times the balance on his Passport card.

(2) The balance on his EverywhereCard is $\frac{4}{3}$ of the balance on his Passport card and $\frac{4}{5}$ of the balance on his American Local card.

○ Statement (1) ALONE is sufficient, but statement (2) alone is not sufficient.
○ Statement (2) ALONE is sufficient, but statement (1) alone is not sufficient.
○ BOTH statements TOGETHER are sufficient, but NEITHER statement ALONE is sufficient.
○ EACH statement ALONE is sufficient.
○ Statements (1) and (2) TOGETHER are not sufficient.

21. **B** Statement (1) provides information only about the sum of the balances on David's EverywhereCard and his American Local card. Therefore, the statement is insufficient to determine whether the balance on David's EverywhereCard is his highest balance, because it does not provide any information that allows you to compare the balance on the EverywhereCard to the balances on the other two cards. The possible answers are BCE.

Statement (2) tells you that the balance on David's EverywhereCard is greater than the balance on his Passport card and less than the balance on his American Local card. Thus, it provides enough information to answer the question. The correct answer is (B).

There are a couple of places where you can go wrong on this question. The first involves the fact that Statement (2) answers the question this way: "No, he does not owe the greatest balance on the EverywhereCard." Some test takers get confused and use a "no" answer to decide that a statement is insufficient. Remember, it doesn't matter how you answer a yes-or-no question, just so long as you can answer it conclusively.

Some test takers might realize that Statements (1) and (2) together provide enough information to calculate the exact balance on each credit card, and thus may choose (C). But because Statement (2) is sufficient on its own, (C) cannot be the correct answer to this question.

MATH BIN 2

QUESTIONS

22. Automobile A is traveling at two-thirds the speed that Automobile B is traveling. At what speed is Automobile A traveling?

   (1) If both automobiles increased their speed by 10 miles per hour, Automobile A would be traveling at three-quarters the speed that Automobile B would be traveling.

   (2) If both automobiles decreased their speed by 10 miles per hour, Automobile A would be traveling at half the speed that Automobile B would be traveling.

   ○ Statement (1) ALONE is sufficient, but statement (2) alone is not sufficient.
   ○ Statement (2) ALONE is sufficient, but statement (1) alone is not sufficient.
   ○ BOTH statements TOGETHER are sufficient, but NEITHER statement ALONE is sufficient.
   ○ EACH statement ALONE is sufficient.
   ○ Statements (1) and (2) TOGETHER are not sufficient.

23. a and b are nonzero integers such that $0.35a = 0.2b$. What is the value of b in terms of a ?

   ○ 0.07a
   ○ 0.57a
   ○ 0.7a
   ○ 1.75a
   ○ 17.5a

EXPLANATIONS

22. **D** To solve this problem, we need to write some equations. Let's call Automobile A's current speed A and Automobile B's current speed B. The question stem tells us that $A = \frac{2}{3}B$. Statement (1) tells us that $A + 10 = \frac{3}{4}(B + 10)$. Thus, between the question stem and Statement (1), we have two distinct equations, which means we can solve for the two variables. The possible answers are (A) or (D). Statement (2) tells us that $A - 10 = \frac{1}{2}(B - 10)$. Once again, we have two distinct equations and two variables. Statement (2) is sufficient, and the correct answer is (D).

23. **D** What makes this problem tricky is the presence of decimals, so the best thing to do is to convert the decimals to integers. Multiply both sides of the equation by 100 to produce the equation $35a = 20b$. (If you don't multiply both sides carefully, you could end up with (E).) Now, simply solve for b by dividing both sides by 20 to get $b = \frac{35}{20}a$. Convert the fraction to a decimal by dividing 35 by 20 to yield $b = 1.75a$. The correct answer is (D).

MATH BIN 2

QUESTIONS

24. The Binary Ice Cream Shoppe sells two flavors of cones, vanilla and chocolate. On Friday, the ratio of vanilla cones sold to chocolate cones sold was 2 to 3. If the store sold 4 more vanilla cones, the ratio of vanilla cones sold to chocolate cones sold would have been 3 to 4. How many vanilla cones did the store sell on Friday?

- ○ 32
- ○ 35
- ○ 42
- ○ 48
- ○ 54

25. Is integer a a prime number?

(1) $2a$ has exactly three factors.

(2) a is an even number.

- ○ Statement (1) ALONE is sufficient, but statement (2) alone is not sufficient.
- ○ Statement (2) ALONE is sufficient, but statement (1) alone is not sufficient.
- ○ BOTH statements TOGETHER are sufficient, but NEITHER statement ALONE is sufficient.
- ○ EACH statement ALONE is sufficient.
- ○ Statements (1) and (2) TOGETHER are not sufficient.

EXPLANATIONS

24. **A** Plug In the Answers! Start with (C). If this is the correct answer, then the Binary Ice Cream Shoppe sold 42 vanilla cones on Friday. Because vanilla cones sold at a 2-to-3 ratio to chocolate cones, this means that the shop sold 63 chocolate cones $\left(\frac{2}{3} = \frac{42}{63} \right)$. If this is the correct answer, then the ratio of 46, the result of adding 4 to the number of vanilla cones sold, to 63 is 3 to 4. It is not, so this answer is incorrect.

You must decide next whether the correct answer is more or less than 42. Since the situation is complicated, you may not be sure which direction to go so just pick a direction; you'll find the correct answer soon enough. Note that the answer cannot be (B) because 35 is not divisible by 2, thus it cannot be the number of vanilla cones sold. Choice (A) is the correct answer. 32 to 48 is a 2-to-3 ratio; add 4 more vanilla cones to get a ratio of 36 to 48, which reduces to 3 to 4.

25. **A** In order to answer this yes-or-no question correctly, you must remember that 2 is a prime number. Statement (1) tells us that $2a$ has exactly 3 distinct factors. Let's plug in some numbers. If you choose 3 for a, then $2a = 6$. What are the factors of 6? 1, 6, 2, and 3. In other words, there are 4 factors. Is there any number we can plug in for a that gives us only 3 factors for the number $2a$? As a matter of fact, there is only one: 2. Only 2 times 2, or 4, has exactly three factors: 1, 2, and 4. This tells us that a is 2; any other multiple of 2 has at least 4 factors (itself, 1, 2, and the product of itself and 2.) So if a can only be 2, can we definitely answer this yes-or-no question? Yes, 2 is a prime number.

MATH BIN 2

Statement (2) is tempting for several reasons. If you forgot that 2 is prime, you would incorrectly conclude that this statement alone is sufficient to answer the question "No." If you figured out that $a = 2$ from Statement (1), you may be tempted to choose this because it confirms the information given in Statement (1). However, because it is not sufficient to answer the question on its own, you must resist temptation. The correct answer is (A).

26. Renee rides her bicycle 20 miles in m minutes. If she rides x miles in 10 minutes at the same rate, which of the following is an expression for x, in terms of m ?

- ○ $\dfrac{m}{200}$
- ○ $\dfrac{m}{20}$
- ○ $\dfrac{m}{2}$
- ○ $2m$
- ○ $\dfrac{200}{m}$

26. **E** Solve this problem by Plugging In. Set m equal to a value that turns the question into an easy arithmetic problem. For example, $m = 40$ is a good, easy value. It tells us that Renee can ride 1 mile every 2 minutes. How many miles, then, can she ride in 10 minutes? She can ride 5 miles in 10 minutes.

Now, Plug In 40 for m in each of the answer choices. The correct answer will calculate to 5, the value of x when $m = 40$. Because (E) is the only answer that equals 5, (E) is the correct answer.

27. If s and w are integers, is $\dfrac{w}{5}$ an integer?

(1) $4s + 2$ is divisible by 5.

(2) $w + 3 = 4s$

- ○ Statement (1) ALONE is sufficient, but statement (2) alone is not sufficient.
- ○ Statement (2) ALONE is sufficient, but statement (1) alone is not sufficient.
- ○ BOTH statements TOGETHER are sufficient, but NEITHER statement ALONE is sufficient.
- ○ EACH statement ALONE is sufficient.
- ○ Statements (1) and (2) TOGETHER are not sufficient.

27. **C** Since this question is a yes-no question, Plug In to evaluate the statements. Note that Statement (1) does not provide any information about w. So, while we can say that $s = 2$ is a value that satisfies Statement (1), we can pick any value for w. If $s = 2$ and $w = 5$, the answer to the question is "yes." However, if $s = 2$ and $w = 7$, the answer to the question is "no." So, as we suspected, Statement (1) is insufficient. The possible answers are BCE.

For Statement (2), $s = 2$ and $w = 5$ satisfy the statement and produce an answer of "yes" to the question. However, $s = 4$ and $w = 13$ also satisfy the statement and produce an answer of "no" to the question. The possible answers are (C) or (E). Now, pick numbers that satisfy both statements. Start by using a pair that we've already used: $s = 2$ and $w = 5$. These numbers satisfy both statements and produce an answer of "yes" to the question. Now, try $s = 7$ and $w = 25$. These numbers also satisfy both statements and produce an answer of "yes" to the question. If you keep trying to pick numbers that satisfy both statements, you'll discover that you must pick values for w that are divisible by 5. The correct answer is (C).

You might also note the algebraic reason the combined statements ensure that w is divisible by 5. Statement (2) provides an expression for $4s$ that can be substituted into the expression in Statement (1): $w + 3 + 2 = w + 5$ is divisible by 5. Both parts of this expression must be divisible by 5 for $w + 5$ to be divisible by 5. So, w is divisible by 5.

MATH BIN 3

QUESTIONS

1. An electronics store normally sells all its merchandise at a 10 percent to 30 percent discount from the suggested retail price. During a sale, if the store were to deduct an additional 20 percent from the discounted price, what is the lowest price possible for an item with a suggested retail price of $260 ?

- ○ $130.00
- ○ $145.60
- ○ $163.80
- ○ $182.00
- ○ $210.00

2. A certain gas station discounts the price per gallon of all gasoline purchased after the first 10 gallons by 10 percent. The total per gallon discount for 25 gallons of gas purchased at this station is what percent of the total per gallon discount for 20 gallons of gas?

- ○ 80%
- ○ 100%
- ○ 116.7%
- ○ 120%
- ○ 140%

EXPLANATIONS

1. **B** We don't need to worry about that range for the initial discount: Since we want the *lowest* possible price, we want the *greatest* possible discount. Thirty percent of 260 is 78, so the price after the initial discount is $260 – $78, or $182. The additional 20% discount amounts to $36.40—remember, the 20% discount is 20% of the already-discounted price. $182 – $36.40 = $145.60, and the correct answer is (B).

2. **D** This problem never specifies the cost of a gallon of gas, so let's Plug In $1. If the price per gallon is $1 for the first 10 gallons, then the price for every subsequent gallon is $0.90. Now calculate the per gallon discount for 20 gallons. First, calculate the total cost for 20 gallons. The cost is $10 for the first 10 gallons and 10 × $0.90 = $9 for the next 10 gallons, for a total of $19 and an average price per gallon of $0.95. So the per gallon discount is 5 cents. Repeat this process to calculate the per gallon discount for 25 gallons. The total price for 25 gallons is $23.50, for an average per gallon price of $0.94 and a discount of 6 cents. The question asks us to relate the per gallon discounts as a percentage, so 6 is 120% of 5 and the correct answer is (D).

QUESTIONS

3. What is the area of the shaded region in the figure shown above?

(1) The area of rectangle *ABCD* is 54.

(2) *AE* = 2*ED*

- ◯ Statement (1) ALONE is sufficient, but statement (2) alone is not sufficient.
- ◯ Statement (2) ALONE is sufficient, but statement (1) alone is not sufficient.
- ◯ BOTH statements TOGETHER are sufficient, but NEITHER statement ALONE is sufficient.
- ◯ EACH statement ALONE is sufficient.
- ◯ Statements (1) and (2) TOGETHER are not sufficient.

EXPLANATIONS

3. A Statement (1) is sufficient, by itself, to answer the question. Although we can't determine, from Statement (1), the individual areas of the two triangular shaded regions, when combined they equal 27 (half of the total area of rectangle *ABCD*). The easiest way to see this is to draw a vertical line through point *E*, cutting the rectangle into two smaller ones. Now we have two rectangles that are divided by diagonals, and diagonals, by definition, cut rectangles in half. If half of the two smaller rectangles are shaded, then so is half of the larger rectangle. We're down to AD.

Statement (2) gives us the relationship between the two smaller shaded regions, but it doesn't allow us to determine anything about their individual areas. Statement (2) is insufficient, and the correct answer is (A).

4. For the triangle shown above, does $p = q = 60$?

   (1) $r = 180 - (p + r)$

   (2) $p = 60$

   ○ Statement (1) ALONE is sufficient, but statement (2) alone is not sufficient.
   ○ Statement (2) ALONE is sufficient, but statement (1) alone is not sufficient.
   ○ BOTH statements TOGETHER are sufficient, but NEITHER statement ALONE is sufficient.
   ○ EACH statement ALONE is sufficient.
   ○ Statements (1) and (2) TOGETHER are not sufficient.

4. **C** First, take a moment to rephrase the question. If $p = q = 60$, the triangle is equilateral. So, the question is equivalent to asking "Is the triangle equilateral?" Statement (1) is, by itself, insufficient to answer the question, although it does provide the very useful information that $r = q$. If you're comfortable working with triangles, you may have immediately read "180 minus the sum of p and r" as being equal to q. If not, you can prove this by doing some algebraic manipulation. Add $(p + r)$ to both sides to yield $r + p + r = 180$, but since 180 also equals $p + q + r$, you can combine the equations to get $r + p + r = p + q + r$. Subtract a p and a q from each side, and you're left with $r = q$. Nonetheless, this is still insufficient to answer the question. If r and q are both 60, the answer is "yes"; if they're both 45—remember, you can't trust the diagrams in Data Sufficiency—the answer is "no." We're down to BCE.

Statement (2), by itself, is also insufficient to answer the question; the only thing it tells us about q and r is their sum, which equals 120. Eliminate (B).

When we combine the statements, though, we can determine whether the triangle is equilateral. If r and q are equal and their sum is 120, then they, like p, equal 60. If all three angles equal 60, the triangle is equilateral, and the correct answer is (C).

MATH BIN 3

QUESTIONS

5. During a certain two-week period, a video rental store rented only comedies, dramas, and action movies. If 70 percent of the movies rented were comedies, and of the remaining movies rented, 5 times as many dramas as action movies were rented and A action movies were rented, then, in terms of A, how many of the movies rented were comedies?

- ○ $\dfrac{A}{14}$

- ○ $\dfrac{5A}{7}$

- ○ $\dfrac{7A}{5}$

- ○ $14A$

- ○ $35A$

6. x, y, and z are consecutive positive integers such that $x < y < z$. If the units digit of x^2 is 6 and the units digit of y^2 is 9, what is the units digit of z^2 ?

- ○ 0
- ○ 1
- ○ 2
- ○ 4
- ○ 5

EXPLANATIONS

5. **D** Since the problem never specifies how many videos were rented during the two-week period, this is a good opportunity to Plug In. Rather than plugging in a value for A and trying to determine the total number of videos rented—possible but problematic—let's Plug In an easy number, such as 100, for the total, and calculate the rest of the numbers from there.

If a total of 100 videos were rented in the two-week period, then 70 were comedies. Of the remaining 30, there were 5 times as many dramas as action movies, so that means 25 dramas and 5 action movies. We now know both the value for A, 5, and the target answer, 70. Only (D) yields 70 when 5 is plugged in for (A), so (D) is the correct answer.

6. **D** Because the units digit of x^2 is 6, the units digit of x must be either 4 or 6. Because x, y, and z are consecutive positive integers, the units digit of y is 5 if the units digit of x is 4. However, the units digit of y *can't* be 5 because the problem tells us that the units digit of y^2 is 9; if the units digit of y were 5, then the units digit of y^2 would also be 5. Therefore, the units digit of x is 6, the units digit of y is 7, and the units digit of z is 8. The units digit of z^2, then, is 4.

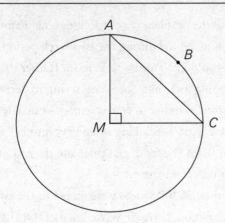

7. What is the area of the circle with center *M* shown above ?

(1) The length of *AC* is $8\sqrt{2}$.

(2) The length of arc *ABC* is 4π.

○ Statement (1) ALONE is sufficient, but statement (2) alone is not sufficient.
○ Statement (2) ALONE is sufficient, but statement (1) alone is not sufficient.
○ BOTH statements TOGETHER are sufficient, but NEITHER statement ALONE is sufficient.
○ EACH statement ALONE is sufficient.
○ Statements (1) and (2) TOGETHER are not sufficient.

7. **D** Statement (1) alone is sufficient to answer the question. Ordinarily, having one side of a right triangle isn't enough to solve for all three sides. However, since two of the sides of this triangle are also radii of the circle, this is no ordinary right triangle: It's an isosceles right triangle, also known as a 45-45-90 triangle. As such, knowing that the long side of the triangle is $8\sqrt{2}$ is enough to tell us that the short sides are both 8. Once we know the radius, we can solve for the area—64π, if you were wondering—and we're down to AD.

Statement (2) alone is also sufficient to answer the question. Arc *ABC*, since it's subtended (or "cut out") by a 90° angle, must represent $\frac{90}{360}$, or $\frac{1}{4}$, of the entire circumference. That gives us an entire circumference of 16π; from the circumference, we can find the radius, 8, and from there the area. The correct answer is (D).

MATH BIN 3

QUESTIONS

8. If 70 percent of the female and 90 percent of the male students in the senior class at a certain school are going on the senior trip and the senior class is 60 percent female, what percent of the senior class is going on the senior trip?

- ○ 82%
- ○ 80%
- ○ 78%
- ○ 76%
- ○ 72%

9. If P is a set of integers and 3 is in P, is every positive multiple of 3 in P ?

(1) For any integer in P, the sum of 3 and that integer is also in P.

(2) For any integer in P, that integer minus 3 is also in P.

- ○ Statement (1) ALONE is sufficient, but statement (2) alone is not sufficient.
- ○ Statement (2) ALONE is sufficient, but statement (1) alone is not sufficient.
- ○ BOTH statements TOGETHER are sufficient, but NEITHER statement ALONE is sufficient.
- ○ EACH statement ALONE is sufficient.
- ○ Statements (1) and (2) TOGETHER are not sufficient.

EXPLANATIONS

8. **C** This is a question about an unspecified amount, so it is a great opportunity to Plug In! Since the answers are percentages, let's Plug In 100 for the total number of seniors. That means we have 60 females, of whom 70%, or 42, are going on the senior trip; they'll be joined by 90% of the 40 males, which gives 36 males on the trip. That's a total of 42 + 36 = 78 students who are going on the trip. Seventy-eight out of our senior class of 100 is, of course, 78%, so the correct answer is (C).

9. **A** To find the answer to this yes-or-no question, Plug In for the two statements, starting with the one number that you know is in the set: 3. For Statement (1), if 3 is in the set, then 6 is in the set. If 6 is in the set, then 9 is also in the set. Using similar reasoning, it can be shown that every positive multiple of 3 is in the set. So, the answer to the question is "yes" and Statement (1) is sufficient. The possible answers are AD. For Statement (2), it can be shown that 3, 0, −3, −6 are in the set. But the positive multiples of 3 can be in the set, in which case the answer is to the question is "yes," or not in the set in which case the answer to the question is "no." So, Statement (2) is not sufficient. The answer is (A).

MATH BIN 3

QUESTIONS

10. A certain seafood restaurant gets a delivery of fresh seafood every day of the week. If the delivery company charges d dollars per delivery and c cents per delivered item and the restaurant has an average (arithmetic mean) of x items delivered per day, then which of the following is an expression for the total cost, in dollars, of one week's deliveries?

○ $\dfrac{7cdx}{100}$

○ $d + \dfrac{7cx}{100}$

○ $7d + \dfrac{xc}{100}$

○ $7d + \dfrac{7xc}{100}$

○ $7cdx$

EXPLANATIONS

10. **D** Since the answer choices contain variables, this is a good place to Plug In. Let's make $d = 10$, $c = 200$ (a particularly helpful number, because it allows us to work the problem in whole dollar amounts), and $x = 5$. If the restaurant has an average of 5 items per day delivered, then it had a total of 35 items delivered for the week. Multiplied by the 200 cents (or $2) charge per item, that's a total of $70 in per-item charges. When we add that amount to the $70 total for the per-delivery charges—7 deliveries at $10 per delivery—we get a total of $140 for the week. Our target answer, then, is 140; only (D) gives us 140 when we plug our values into our answer choices, and, therefore, (D) is the correct answer.

If you got (C), by the way, check your calculations for your target answer. You likely calculated the per-item charges as though x were the total, rather than the daily average, of the items delivered.

MATH BIN 3

QUESTIONS

11. Which of the following contains the interval two standard deviations from the mean of a set of data with an arithmetic mean of 46 and a standard deviation of 4 ?

- ◯ 38 to 46
- ◯ 38 to 54
- ◯ 42 to 50
- ◯ 44 to 48
- ◯ 46 to 50

EXPLANATIONS

11. **B**   Standard deviation is the measure of how greatly the individual elements in a data set vary from the arithmetic mean of the set. As a general rule, the more widely dispersed the data in a set, the greater the standard deviation.

For the GMAT, you mostly need to know that standard deviation is measured from the arithmetic mean of a data set. If a data set has an arithmetic mean of 10 and a standard deviation of 2, then 8 and 12 are the values that are exactly one standard deviation from the arithmetic mean of the set.

In this problem, the standard deviation is 4, and the question asks for an interval that covers two standard deviations from the arithmetic mean of 46. It's key here to remember that "two standard deviations" means two *in each direction*—that is, both above *and* below the mean. Thus, we need an interval that covers 2 × 4, or 8, from the mean in each direction: 46 − 8 = 38, so the bottom end of the interval is 38, and 46 + 8 = 54, so the top end of the interval is 54. The correct answer is (B).

If you chose (A), by the way, you accounted for only the two standard deviations below the mean. If you chose (E), you accounted only for the two standard deviations above the mean. And if you chose (C), you forgot to take two standard deviations in each direction.

MATH BIN 3

QUESTIONS

12. If a and b are positive integers, is a a multiple of b ?

(1) Every distinct prime factor of b is also a distinct prime factor of a.

(2) Every factor of b is also a factor of a.

○ Statement (1) ALONE is sufficient, but statement (2) alone is not sufficient.
○ Statement (2) ALONE is sufficient, but statement (1) alone is not sufficient.
○ BOTH statements TOGETHER are sufficient, but NEITHER statement ALONE is sufficient.
○ EACH statement ALONE is sufficient.
○ Statements (1) and (2) TOGETHER are not sufficient.

EXPLANATIONS

12. **B** To solve this yes-or-no problem, your best bet is to plug in values that meet the requirements given in the statements to determine whether Plugging In always yields the same answer to the question.

For Statement (1), for example, we could Plug In 4 for both a and b—that's one easy way to make sure that every prime factor of b is also a prime factor of a—and since every number is a multiple of itself, the answer to the question is "yes." However, if we leave $b = 4$ but make $a = 2$, we can still satisfy the requirement of Statement (1)—4 has only one prime factor, 2, which is also a prime factor of 2—but now our answer is "no." Since Statement (1) yields different answers, it's insufficient, and the possible answers are BCE.

Similar attempts in Statement (2), however, will always yield the answer "yes." We could, of course, again Plug In 4 for both variables, and we have our first "yes." If we leave $b = 4$, though, we can't make $a = 2$, since 4 isn't a factor of 2; a is a number such as 4 (which we've already used), 12, 16, or some other number that has 1, 2, and 4 as factors. Whichever one we pick, though, our answer is "yes"; Statement (2) is therefore sufficient, and the answer to the problem is (B).

MATH BIN 3

QUESTIONS

13. If Set X contains 10 consecutive integers and the sum of the 5 least members of the set is 265, then what is the sum of the 5 greatest members of the set?

   - ○ 290
   - ○ 285
   - ○ 280
   - ○ 275
   - ○ 270

14. If $a - b = c$, what is the value of b ?

   (1) $c + 6 = a$

   (2) $a = 6$

   - ○ Statement (1) ALONE is sufficient, but statement (2) alone is not sufficient.
   - ○ Statement (2) ALONE is sufficient, but statement (1) alone is not sufficient.
   - ○ BOTH statements TOGETHER are sufficient, but NEITHER statement ALONE is sufficient.
   - ○ EACH statement ALONE is sufficient.
   - ○ Statements (1) and (2) TOGETHER are not sufficient.

EXPLANATIONS

13. **A** We *could* solve this problem algebraically, although it's a bit of a chore. If we assign x to represent the smallest integer in the set, then $x + (x + 1) + (x + 2) + (x + 3) + (x + 4) = 265$, so $5x + 10 = 265$, $5x = 255$, and $x = 51$. The five least consecutive integers are thus 51 through 55; we can now add the five greatest consecutive integers, which are 56 through 60. The total is 290, and the correct answer is (A).

   A much simpler way to solve the problem, though, is to recognize that the difference between the sums of *any* two adjacent sets of five consecutive integers is the same; we can, therefore, find this difference using much smaller, easier-to-work-with numbers, and then add this difference to the total given in the problem. The sum of the integers from 1 to 5 is 15, and the sum of the integers from 6 to 10 is 40; our difference, thus, is 25, and 265 + 25 = 290.

14. **A** It can be a good idea to simplify before heading into the statements. If you have the equation $a - b = c$ and want b, then you could simply write it as $b = a - c$. Now, consider Statement (1) on its own. Statement (1) can be rewritten as $a - c = 6$. Since $a - c = b$ from the question stem, we know that $b = 6$. Statement (1) is sufficient, and we're down to AD. Statement (2) provides information about only one of the three variables in the original equation, so it cannot be sufficient on its own. The correct answer is (A).

$\{3, 5, 9, 13, y\}$

15. If the average (arithmetic mean) and the median of the set of numbers shown above are equal, then what is the value of y ?

 ○ 7
 ○ 8
 ○ 10
 ○ 15
 ○ 17

15. **D** This problem is a great opportunity to Plug In the Answers. Start with (C) and substitute 10 for y in the problem. The average of the numbers $\{3, 5, 9, 13, 10\}$ is 8, but the median of those numbers is 9. Eliminate (C). The value of y needs to be greater, so try (D), 15. The average of the numbers $\{3, 5, 9, 13, 15\}$ is 9, and the median of those numbers is also 9. We're done. The correct answer is (D).

16. For a certain foot race, how many different arrangements of medal winners are possible?

 (1) Medals will be given for 1st, 2nd, and 3rd place.

 (2) There are 10 runners in the race.

 ○ Statement (1) ALONE is sufficient, but statement (2) alone is not sufficient.
 ○ Statement (2) ALONE is sufficient, but statement (1) alone is not sufficient.
 ○ BOTH statements TOGETHER are sufficient, but NEITHER statement ALONE is sufficient.
 ○ EACH statement ALONE is sufficient.
 ○ Statements (1) and (2) TOGETHER are not sufficient.

16. **C** This is a permutation problem. Looking at Statement (1), it might seem enough to know that medals will be awarded for 1st, 2nd, and 3rd place. While some test takers might be quick to assume that there are $3 \times 2 \times 1$ possible arrangements of medal winners, until we know the number of runners, we don't know enough. The possible answers are BCE.

Statement (2) tells us the number of runners. Since we cannot use the information from Statement (1) while evaluating Statement (2), we now do not know how many medals are to be given. We're down to (C) or (E).

Putting the two statements together, we can now find out how many different arrangements of medal winners there are: $10 \times 9 \times 8 = 720$. The correct answer is (C).

MATH BIN 3

QUESTIONS	EXPLANATIONS

17. For the set of measurements 3, x_2, x_3, what is the value of x_3 ?

(1) The range of the set of measurements is 0.

(2) The standard deviation of the set of measurements is 0.

○ Statement (1) ALONE is sufficient, but statement (2) alone is not sufficient.
○ Statement (2) ALONE is sufficient, but statement (1) alone is not sufficient.
○ BOTH statements TOGETHER are sufficient, but NEITHER statement ALONE is sufficient.
○ EACH statement ALONE is sufficient.
○ Statements (1) and (2) TOGETHER are not sufficient.

17. **D** The range of any set of measurements is equal to the greatest item in the set minus the least. Statement (1) gives us a value for the range. If that value were anything other than 0, we would not be able to solve the problem based only on this statement. Because Statement (1) tells us that the range is 0, we actually know more than you might think about these three numbers. Because the problem tells us that the first measurement is 3, let's Plug In values for x_2 and x_3, just to see what happens. For example, if x_2 and x_3 both equal 5, the range does not equal 0. When you start Plugging In numbers, you realize that the only way for the range of these three numbers to be 0 is if each of the numbers is exactly the same. And because we know the first value is 3, that means both x_2 and x_3 equal 3 as well. The possible answers are AD.

Statement (2) tells us that all the measurements correspond exactly to the arithmetic mean— which tells us that all three measurements are equal to 3. The correct answer is (D).

18. An employer has 6 applicants for a programming position and 4 applicants for a manager position. If the employer must hire 3 programmers and 2 managers, what is the total number of ways the employer can make the selection?

○ 1,490
○ 132
○ 120
○ 60
○ 23

18. **C** In this combination problem, the employer's choice of a programmer can be written as

$$\frac{6 \times 5 \times 4}{3 \times 2 \times 1} \text{ or } 20$$

The employer's choice of a manager can be written as

$$\frac{4 \times 3}{2 \times 1} \text{ or } 6$$

To find the total number of ways she could make her selection, multiply the respective number of possibilities: $6 \times 20 = 120$. The correct answer is (C).

MATH BIN 3

QUESTIONS

19. On Monday, an animal shelter housed 55 cats and dogs, and by Friday exactly $\frac{1}{5}$ of the cats and $\frac{1}{4}$ of the dogs had been adopted. If no new cats or dogs were brought to the shelter during this period, what is the greatest possible number of pets that could have been adopted from the animal shelter between Monday and Friday?

- ◯ 11
- ◯ 12
- ◯ 13
- ◯ 14
- ◯ 20

EXPLANATIONS

19. **C** The question asks you for the greatest number of animals that could have been adopted from the shelter within the parameters of the problem. Because a greater proportion of dogs than cats was adopted, you should seek a scenario that maximizes the number of dogs adopted. You must also satisfy the other conditions of the problem, however; the number of cats, for example, must be a multiple of 5, because that is the only way that $\frac{1}{5}$ of the cats can be adopted. Because we want to maximize the number of dogs in the shelter, let's start by assuming the minimum possible number of cats, 5. This would leave 50 dogs in the shelter. This solution, unfortunately, is impossible; because 50 is not evenly divisible by 4, there cannot be 50 dogs in the shelter. Could there be 10 cats at the shelter? No, because this would leave 45 dogs, again making it impossible for exactly $\frac{1}{4}$ of the dogs to be adopted. 15 cats is the magic number, as it means there are 40 dogs. $\left(\frac{1}{5} \times 15\right) + \left(\frac{1}{4} \times 40\right) = 3 + 10 = 13$ animals. The correct answer is (C).

MATH BIN 3

QUESTIONS

20. If x is an integer, then which of the following statements about $x^2 - x - 1$ is true?

   - ◯ It is always odd.
   - ◯ It is always even.
   - ◯ It is always positive.
   - ◯ It is even when x is even and odd when x is odd.
   - ◯ It is even when x is odd and odd when x is even.

21. During a five-day period, Monday through Friday, the average (arithmetic mean) high temperature was 86 degrees Fahrenheit. What was the high temperature on Friday?

   (1) The average high temperature for Monday through Thursday was 87 degrees Fahrenheit.

   (2) The high temperature on Friday reduced the average high temperature for the five-day period by 1 degree Fahrenheit.

   - ◯ Statement (1) ALONE is sufficient, but statement (2) alone is not sufficient.
   - ◯ Statement (2) ALONE is sufficient, but statement (1) alone is not sufficient.
   - ◯ BOTH statements TOGETHER are sufficient, but NEITHER statement ALONE is sufficient.
   - ◯ EACH statement ALONE is sufficient.
   - ◯ Statements (1) and (2) TOGETHER are not sufficient.

EXPLANATIONS

20. **A** Because x is an integer, x must be either even or odd. If x is even, then $x^2 - x$ must also be even, and therefore $x^2 - x - 1$ is always odd. If x is odd, then $x^2 - x$ must be even, and again, $x^2 - x - 1$ is always odd.

You can also solve this problem by Plugging In. After Plugging In several values for x and calculating $x^2 - x - 1$, you will discover that the result is always odd. The correct answer is (A).

21. **D** The question stem tells us that the average high temperature for the five-day period was 86°; therefore, the sum of the high temperatures for those days was $5 \times 86 = 430°$. Statement (1) tells us that the average high temperature for the first four days was 87°; therefore, the sum of the high temperatures for those days was $4 \times 87 = 348°$. $430 - 348 = 82°$, the high temperature on Friday. Statement (1) is sufficient; the answer is AD. Statement (2) tells us that Friday's temperature reduced the average high for the five-day period by 1 degree. This means that the average high for the first four days was 87°; thus, Statement (2) is sufficient for the same reason that Statement (1) is sufficient. The correct answer is (D).

MATH BIN 3

QUESTIONS

22. What is the value of $x^2 - y^2$?

   (1) $x + y = 0$

   (2) $x - y = 2$

   ○ Statement (1) ALONE is sufficient, but statement (2) alone is not sufficient.
   ○ Statement (2) ALONE is sufficient, but statement (1) alone is not sufficient.
   ○ BOTH statements TOGETHER are sufficient, but NEITHER statement ALONE is sufficient.
   ○ EACH statement ALONE is sufficient.
   ○ Statements (1) and (2) TOGETHER are not sufficient.

23. If P is the perimeter of an equilateral triangle, which of the following represents the height of the triangle?

   ○ $\dfrac{P}{3}$

   ○ $\dfrac{P\sqrt{3}}{3}$

   ○ $\dfrac{P}{4}$

   ○ $\dfrac{P\sqrt{3}}{6}$

   ○ $\dfrac{P}{6}$

EXPLANATIONS

22. **A** Don't get caught making a careless assumption on this question. You may have immediately recognized that $x^2 - y^2$ factors to $(x + y)(x - y)$. Seeing that Statement (1) provides a value for $(x + y)$ and Statement (2) provides a value for $(x - y)$, you might have automatically assumed that the correct answer to this question is (C). Look more closely, however; Statement (1) tells you that $(x + y) = 0$. Zero times any number equals zero. Therefore, Statement (1) is sufficient to tell you that $(x + y)(x - y) = 0$. Statement (2), however, is not sufficient. Since Statement (2) says that $x - y = 2$, plug this number back into the factored expression from the question stem. Without the value for the other factor (or the values of x and y), Statement (2) cannot be used on its own to answer the question. The correct answer is (A).

23. **D** This is an excellent Plugging In problem. Plug In a value that is easily divisible by 3 for P; let's use 18. That would make the length of each side of the equilateral triangle 6.

Draw a height for the triangle. Note that the height of an equilateral triangle divides the triangle into two 30–60–90 triangles, each with a base of 3.

Now you can use the formula for the sides of a 30-60-90 triangle to determine that the height of the triangle is $3\sqrt{3}$ when $P = 18$. Finally, simply plug in 18 for P in every answer choice and eliminate those that do not yield a result of $3\sqrt{3}$. The correct answer is (D).

QUESTIONS

EXPLANATIONS

24. If 75 percent of all Americans own an automobile, 15 percent of all Americans own a bicycle, and 20 percent of all Americans own neither an automobile nor a bicycle, then what percent of Americans own *both* an automobile and a bicycle?

○ 0%
○ 1.33%
○ 3.75%
○ 5%
○ 10%

24. **E** This is a group formula problem. The group formula is Total = Group 1 + Group 2 – Both + Neither. Assume the total is 100. If there are 100 total Americans, then 75 own an automobile (which is Group 1), 15 own a bicycle (Group 2), and 20 own neither. So the equation now reads 100 = 75 + 15 – Both + 20. Solve for Both and discover that it equals 10. 10 is 10% of 100. The correct answer is (E).

25. Triangle *ABC* is an isosceles right triangle and triangle *DEF* is an equilateral triangle with height *EG*. What is the ratio of the area of *ABC* to the area of *DEF* ?

(1) The ratio of *BC* to *EG* is 1:1.

(2) The ratio of *AC* to *DF* is $\sqrt{3} : 2$.

○ Statement (1) ALONE is sufficient, but statement (2) alone is not sufficient.
○ Statement (2) ALONE is sufficient, but statement (1) alone is not sufficient.
○ BOTH statements TOGETHER are sufficient, but NEITHER statement ALONE is sufficient.
○ EACH statement ALONE is sufficient.
○ Statements (1) and (2) TOGETHER are not sufficient.

25. **D** The formula for the area of a triangle is $A = \dfrac{\text{base} \times \text{height}}{2}$. Therefore, if we know the ratio of the bases and the heights of these triangles, it would be safe to assume that we know enough to calculate the ratios of their areas. This makes (C) a very tempting answer, because Statement (1) provides the ratio of the heights of the two triangles and Statement (2) provides the ratio of the bases of the two triangles.

The reason that the answer to this question is (D) lies in the special nature of isosceles right triangles and equilateral triangles. Their sides are in a fixed proportion to one another, so when you have information about one side, you have information about all the sides and, consequently, the area of the triangles. For this reason, each statement is sufficient on its own.

To prove that to yourself, you can Plug In values for the sides of the triangles. For example, in Statement (1), the ratio of *BC* to *EG* is 1 to 1. So, let's say *BC* and *EG* are both one meter long. Since

QUESTIONS

EXPLANATIONS

ABC is isosceles, that means $AC = 1$, too, and the area of *ABC* is $\frac{1}{2}$. Since *DEF* is equilateral, that means *DG* and *GF* are each $\sqrt{3}$ and *DF* is $2\sqrt{3}$. Therefore, we can find the area of *DEF* ($\sqrt{3}$).

26. What is the value of integer x ?

    (1) $\sqrt[x]{64} = 4$

    (2) $x^2 = x + 6$

    ○ Statement (1) ALONE is sufficient, but statement (2) alone is not sufficient.
    ○ Statement (2) ALONE is sufficient, but statement (1) alone is not sufficient.
    ○ BOTH statements TOGETHER are sufficient, but NEITHER statement ALONE is sufficient.
    ○ EACH statement ALONE is sufficient.
    ○ Statements (1) and (2) TOGETHER are not sufficient.

26. **A** The only solution to the equation in Statement (1) is $x = 3$. That gets us down to AD.

    To determine whether Statement (2) is sufficient, subtract $2x + 8$ from both sides of the equation to get
    $$x^2 - x - 6 = 0$$
    This equation can be factored to
    $$(x - 3)(x + 2) = 0$$
    Thus, the equation has two solutions: x can equal 3 or –2. Statement (2) is not sufficient. The correct answer is (A).

MATH BIN 4

1. A rectangular garden with dimensions 20 feet by 30 feet is surrounded by a rectangular brick walkway of uniform width, as shown in the figure above. If the area of the walkway equals the area of the garden, what is the width of the walkway?

- ◯ 1 foot
- ◯ 3 feet
- ◯ 5 feet
- ◯ 8 feet
- ◯ 10 feet

1. **C**   To answer this question, first recognize that the area of the walkway can be calculated by subtracting the area of the smaller (white) rectangle from the larger rectangle in the figure. The difference between the areas of the two rectangles equals the area of the shaded region. This problem is ideal for Plugging In the Answers. Start with (C); if it is incorrect, you may be able to tell whether it is too large or too small, and you will be able to eliminate not only (C) but also two other answers.

If (C) is correct, then the walkway is 5 feet wide. With a walkway of that width, the dimensions of the large rectangle in the figure are 30 feet (the width of the garden—20 feet—plus 5 feet on each side to account for the width of the walkway) by 40 feet (the length of the garden—30 feet—plus 5 feet on each side to account for the width of the walkway). The area of the large rectangle, then, is 40 × 30 = 1,200 square feet, and the area of the shaded region is 1,200 − (20 × 30) = 1,200 − 600 = 600 square feet.

When the width of the walkway is 5 feet, the area of the walkway equals the area of the garden. That's the result we're looking for, so the correct answer is (C).

MATH BIN 4

QUESTIONS

2. If a fair two-sided coin is flipped 6 times, what is the probability that tails is the result at least twice but at most 5 times?

○ $\dfrac{5}{8}$

○ $\dfrac{3}{4}$

○ $\dfrac{7}{8}$

○ $\dfrac{57}{64}$

○ $\dfrac{15}{16}$

EXPLANATIONS

2. **C** As is often the case with difficult probability questions, the bottom part of the fraction—the total number of possibilities—is a permutation problem in itself. In this case, we need to figure out how many different outcomes we can get if we flip a coin 6 times. Since we have 6 events with 2 possible outcomes each, our total number of different outcomes is $2 \times 2 \times 2 \times 2 \times 2 \times 2$, or 2^6, or 64. Now we just need to figure out how many of those possibilities meet the requirement.

For this problem, however, since there are so many different ways to meet the requirement, we'll be better off figuring out how many outcomes *don't* meet our requirement; we can then subtract this number from the total of 64. There are only three ways to *not* meet the requirement of 2 to 5 tails on 6 flips—we could get 0, 1, or 6 tails—and these can be quickly and easily counted out. There is only one way to get 6 tails, and, likewise, there is only one way to get 0 tails, which is another way of saying 6 heads. That's two possibilities. And there are only six different ways to get tails once: The single tails can come up in the first spot, the second spot, and so on. That's 8 out of the total of 64 possible outcomes that don't meet our requirement, so 56 do. The probability, therefore, is $\dfrac{56}{64}$, which reduces to $\dfrac{7}{8}$. The correct answer is (C).

MATH BIN 4

QUESTIONS

3. The new recruits of a military organization who score in the bottom 16 percent on their physical conditioning tests are required to retest. If the scores are normally distributed and have an arithmetic mean of 72, what is the score at or below which the recruits are required to retest?

(1) There are 500 new recruits.

(2) 10 new recruits scored at least 82 on the physical conditioning test.

○ Statement (1) ALONE is sufficient, but statement (2) alone is not sufficient.
○ Statement (2) ALONE is sufficient, but statement (1) alone is not sufficient.
○ BOTH statements TOGETHER are sufficient, but NEITHER statement ALONE is sufficient.
○ EACH statement ALONE is sufficient.
○ Statements (1) and (2) TOGETHER are not sufficient.

EXPLANATIONS

3. **C** Statement (1) is not sufficient to answer the question by itself. It does let us determine *how many* recruits will have to retake the test, but we don't know anything about their scores. The possible answers are BCE. Statement (2) is also insufficient by itself—while those 10 recruits are certainly impressive, we don't know what part of the overall recruiting class they represent. We're down to (C) or (E).

When we combine the statements, though, we have enough information to answer the question. From Statements (1) and (2), it is possible to calculate that the 10 new recruits who scored at least 82 on the physical conditioning test make up the top 2% of the whole. Since the scores are normally distributed, the top 2% represents the third standard deviation above the mean. Because the top 2% represents the third standard deviation about the mean, there are two full standard deviations that occur before the top 2%. On a normally distributed curve, the first standard deviation is marked by 34% of the population, the second is marked by 14%, and the third is 2%. So, there are two full standard deviations in between the mean, 72, and the beginning of the third standard deviation (82). Because standard deviations in a normal curve are consistent values, each standard deviation begins 5 away from the last. So, the first standard deviation is represented by the values 72–77, the second is represented by 77–82, and the third is represented by 82–87. Now look at the question. The question is asking for the score that represents the bottom 16%, which is represented by the bottom two standard deviations. Since each standard deviation is worth 5, those who score at or below 67 represent the bottom 16%. The correct answer is (C).

MATH BIN 4

QUESTIONS

4. Each of the integers from 1 to 20 is written on a separate index card and placed in a box. If the cards are drawn from the box at random without replacement, how many cards must be drawn to ensure that the product of all the integers drawn is even?

    ○ 19
    ○ 12
    ○ 11
    ○ 10
    ○ 3

EXPLANATIONS

4. **C**   To determine how many cards must be drawn to ensure that the product is even, determine the worst-case scenario. Let's start by figuring out the maximum number of cards that can be drawn so that the product of the numbers on the cards is odd. The first card, obviously, is an odd-numbered card. If the second card is an odd-numbered card, then the product of the numbers on the cards is odd. If the third card is odd, then the product remains odd. As long as the numbers on the cards drawn are odd, the product of those numbers is odd. Thus, in the worst-case scenario, all ten odd numbered cards are drawn in succession. At this point, the eleventh card must be even, which would make the product of the 11 cards even. Therefore, 11 cards must be drawn to ensure an even product. The correct answer is (C).

MATH BIN 4

QUESTIONS

5. The average (arithmetic mean) of integers r, s, t, u, and v is 100. Are exactly two of the integers greater than 100 ?

(1) Three of the integers are less than 50.

(2) None of the integers is equal to 100.

○ Statement (1) ALONE is sufficient, but statement (2) alone is not sufficient.
○ Statement (2) ALONE is sufficient, but statement (1) alone is not sufficient.
○ BOTH statements TOGETHER are sufficient, but NEITHER statement ALONE is sufficient.
○ EACH statement ALONE is sufficient.
○ Statements (1) and (2) TOGETHER are not sufficient.

EXPLANATIONS

5. **E** This is a yes-or-no question. Statement (1) tells us that three of the five integers are less than 50. This information by itself does not ensure that the other two integers *are* greater than 100. Both remaining values *could* be greater than 100; the solution set {10, 20, 30, 140, 300}, for example, satisfies this condition. However, the set {1, 2, 3, 4, 490} *also* satisfies the conditions of the problem, and it contains only one value greater than 100. Statement (1) is insufficient on its own; the correct answer must be BCE. Statement (2) tells us only that none of the integers is equal to 100. By itself, this is clearly not sufficient to tell us that exactly two of the integers are greater than 100; eliminate (B). In fact, the statement provides no more useful information than that provided in Statement (1); both of the solutions provided above satisfy this statement as well. The correct answer is (E).

MATH BIN 4

QUESTIONS

6. Paul jogs along the same route every day at a constant rate for 80 minutes. What distance does he jog?

    (1) Yesterday, Paul began jogging at 5:00 P.M.

    (2) Yesterday, Paul had jogged 5 miles by 5:40 P.M. and 8 miles by 6:04 P.M.

    ⃝ Statement (1) ALONE is sufficient, but statement (2) alone is not sufficient.
    ⃝ Statement (2) ALONE is sufficient, but statement (1) alone is not sufficient.
    ⃝ BOTH statements TOGETHER are sufficient, but NEITHER statement ALONE is sufficient.
    ⃝ EACH statement ALONE is sufficient.
    ⃝ Statements (1) and (2) TOGETHER are not sufficient.

EXPLANATIONS

6. **B** Statement (1) clearly is not sufficient to answer the question because it tells us only Paul's starting time. The correct answer to this question must be BCE. Statement (2) tells us that Paul had jogged 5 miles by 5:40 P.M. and 8 miles by 6:04 P.M. You might be tempted to choose (C) at this point; after all, you now know when Paul began jogging and how far he had jogged at various intervals, so you could easily figure out how far he had run by 6:20 P.M., the end of the 80-minute period beginning at 5:00 P.M. Resist the temptation! Let's look more closely at Statement (2). It tells us that Paul covered 3 miles between 5:40 P.M. and 6:04 P.M. Thus, we know that Paul ran eight-minute miles during that 24-minute period. The question stem tells us that Paul jogs at a constant rate, and that he jogs for 80 minutes. Therefore, Statement (2), in combination with the question stem, provides all the information we need; Paul jogs eight-minute miles for 80 minutes, so the route along which he jogs is 10 miles long. The correct answer is (B).

QUESTIONS

7. The diagram above shows two wheels that drive a conveyor belt. The larger wheel has a diameter of 40 centimeters, and the smaller wheel has a diameter of 32 centimeters. If each wheel must rotate the exact same number of centimeters per minute, and the larger wheel makes r revolutions per minute, then, in terms of r, how many revolutions does the smaller wheel make per hour?

○ $\dfrac{1,280\pi}{3}$

○ $75r$

○ $48r$

○ $24r$

○ $\dfrac{64\pi}{3}$

EXPLANATIONS

7. **B**   Because the problem has variables in the answer choices, Plugging In is a great way to solve. Plug in an easy number, one that will make your calculations and answer checking simple. For the purposes of this explanation, let's set r equal to 2. With each rotation, each wheel rotates the length of its circumference. Thus, the wheel with diameter 40 centimeters rotates 40π centimeters with each rotation; the wheel with diameter 32 centimeters rotates 32π centimeters with each rotation. The larger wheel makes r revolutions per minute; because we've set r equal to 2, it makes 2 revolutions per minute and thus rotates 80π centimeters per minute. According to the problem, the smaller wheel must rotate the same distance. Therefore, the smaller wheel also rotates 80π centimeters per minute, meaning it rotates $60 \times 80\pi = 4,800\pi$ centimeters per hour. The smaller wheel covers 32π centimeters per rotation, so it must rotate $4,800\pi \div 32\pi = 150$ times per hour. Plug 2 in for r in each of the answer choices. The correct answer is (B), $75r$.

MATH BIN 4

QUESTIONS

8. An automobile dealership sells only sedans and coupes. It sells each in only two colors: red and blue. Last year, the dealership sold 9,000 vehicles, half of which were red. How many coupes did the dealership sell last year?

(1) The dealership sold three times as many blue coupes as red sedans last year.

(2) The dealership sold half as many blue sedans as blue coupes last year.

○ Statement (1) ALONE is sufficient, but statement (2) alone is not sufficient.
○ Statement (2) ALONE is sufficient, but statement (1) alone is not sufficient.
○ BOTH statements TOGETHER are sufficient, but NEITHER statement ALONE is sufficient.
○ EACH statement ALONE is sufficient.
○ Statements (1) and (2) TOGETHER are not sufficient.

EXPLANATIONS

8. **C** Create a table to solve this proportions question. It should look something like this:

	Red	Blue	TOTAL
Coupes			
Sedans			
TOTAL	4,500	4,500	9,000

The question stem tells us how many cars were sold last year. Because it tells us that half the cars sold were red, it also tells us the number of blue cars sold last year.

Statement (1) tells us: "The dealership sold three times as many blue coupes as red sedans last year." Enter this information into the table in algebraic terms:

	Red	Blue	TOTAL
Coupes		$3x$	
Sedans	x		
TOTAL	4,500	4,500	9,000

Because two unknowns—red coupes and blue sedans—remain, Statement (1) does not provide enough information to solve the problem. The correct answer is BCE.

Use the same procedure to test Statement (2): "The dealership sold half as many blue sedans as blue coupes last year":

	Red	Blue	TOTAL
Coupes		$2x$	
Sedans		x	
TOTAL	4,500	4,500	9,000

Again, two unknowns remain. *This* time, though, we have all the information we need to write a solvable equation. We know that $2x + x = 4,500$. Therefore x equals 1,500. We now know the following:

	Red	Blue	TOTAL
Coupes		3,000	
Sedans		1,500	
TOTAL	4,500	4,500	9,500

MATH BIN 4

QUESTIONS

EXPLANATIONS

Unfortunately, this still isn't enough information to answer the question. The answer is (C) or (E). Combine the information from the two statements. Statement (2) tells us that the dealership sold 3,000 blue coupes; combined with Statement (1), this tells us that the dealership sold 1,000 red sedans. We can now subtract 1,000 from 4,500 to determine that the dealership sold 3,500 red coupes. Therefore, it sold 6,500 coupes last year. The correct answer is (C).

9. At a college football game, $\frac{4}{5}$ of the seats in the lower deck of the stadium were sold. If $\frac{1}{4}$ of all the seats in the stadium are located in the lower deck, and if $\frac{2}{3}$ of all the seats in the stadium were sold, what fraction of the unsold seats in the stadium are in the lower deck?

○ $\frac{3}{20}$

○ $\frac{1}{6}$

○ $\frac{1}{5}$

○ $\frac{1}{3}$

○ $\frac{7}{15}$

9. **A** Solve this one using Plugging In. First, Plug In a number of seats for the entire stadium. Choose a number that divides easily by 3, 4, and 5. For the purposes of this explanation, let's say the stadium seats 60,000 people. The problem states that $\frac{2}{3}$ of all the seating in the stadium was sold, meaning that 40,000 of the 60,000 seats were sold. It also states that $\frac{1}{4}$ of the seating is located in the lower deck. Because $\frac{1}{4}$ of 60,000 is 15,000, that means the stadium has 15,000 seats in the lower deck. Of those 15,000 seats, according to the problem, $\frac{4}{5}$, or 12,000, were sold. The question asks what fraction of the unsold seats in the stadium were in the lower deck. Because 40,000 seats were sold in the entire stadium, a total of 20,000 were unsold; of the 20,000 unsold seats, $15,000 - 12,000 = 3,000$ were in the lower deck. The fraction $\frac{3,000}{20,000}$ reduces to $\frac{3}{20}$, so the correct answer is (A).

QUESTIONS

10. At Company *R*, the average (arithmetic mean) age of executive employees is 54 years old and the average age of non-executive employees is 34 years old. What is the average age of all the employees at Company *R* ?

   (1) There are 10 executive employees at Company *R*.

   (2) The number of non-executive employees at Company *R* is four times the number of executive employees at Company *R*.

   ○ Statement (1) ALONE is sufficient, but statement (2) alone is not sufficient.
   ○ Statement (2) ALONE is sufficient, but statement (1) alone is not sufficient.
   ○ BOTH statements TOGETHER are sufficient, but NEITHER statement ALONE is sufficient.
   ○ EACH statement ALONE is sufficient.
   ○ Statements (1) and (2) TOGETHER are not sufficient.

EXPLANATIONS

10. **B**   Statement (1) provides no information about the non-executive employees at Company *R*. It is not sufficient by itself, so we're down to BCE. Statement (2) provides a ratio of executive employees to non-executive employees at Company *R*. This information is sufficient on its own to determine the average age of all employees at Company *R*. Regardless of whether Company *R* has 2 executives and 8 non-executives or 200 executives and 800 non-executives, the resulting average for all employees is the same, because the proportional contribution of each group to the average remains fixed. The best way to prove this is simply to plug in some numbers and see for yourself. The average age of 1 executive and 4 non-executives is $\dfrac{54 + 4(34)}{5} = 38$. The average age of 30 executives and 120 non-executives is $\dfrac{30(54) + 120(34)}{150} = 38$. Thus, the correct answer is (B).

MATH BIN 4

QUESTIONS

11. If a, b, c, d, and x are all nonzero integers, is the product $ax \cdot (bx)^2 \cdot (cx)^3 \cdot (dx)^4$ negative?

(1) $a < c < x < 0$

(2) $b < d < x < 0$

- ○ Statement (1) ALONE is sufficient, but statement (2) alone is not sufficient.
- ○ Statement (2) ALONE is sufficient, but statement (1) alone is not sufficient.
- ○ BOTH statements TOGETHER are sufficient, but NEITHER statement ALONE is sufficient.
- ○ EACH statement ALONE is sufficient.
- ○ Statements (1) and (2) TOGETHER are not sufficient.

12. A four character password consists of one letter from the English alphabet and three different digits from 0 to 9. If the letter is the second or third character of the password, how many different passwords are possible?

- ○ 5,040
- ○ 18,720
- ○ 26,000
- ○ 37,440
- ○ 52,000

EXPLANATIONS

11. **A** Statment (1) tells us that a, c, and x are negative. Instinctively, we might conclude that this isn't enough information, because it tells us nothing about b or d. Look at the expression in the question stem again, though; b and d appear only in the expressions $(bx)^2$ and $(dx)^4$. Both of these expressions contain even exponents; we know, therefore, that these expressions are positive regardless of the values b and d represent, because nonzero integers raised to an even power are always positive. From Statement (1), we know that ax is positive (a negative times a negative equals a positive) and, similarly, that $(cx)^3$ is positive. Statement (1) is sufficient even though the answer to the question is "no." The possible answers are AD. Statement (2) provides no valuable information. The values of b and d do not matter, as they are only used in expressions that result in positive numbers. The values of a and c, however, do matter because they are raised to an odd exponent. Any number raised to an odd exponent retains the positive or negative nature of the original number. There is no way to ensure, then, that ax or cx, when raised to an odd exponent, is positive or negative. The correct answer is (A).

12. **D** According to the problem, an acceptable password consists of either *DLDD* or *DDLD*, where *D* represents a digit and *L* represents a letter of the alphabet. Remember also that the digits must be different. First, let's consider *DLDD*. The first character can be any of the ten digits, 0 through 9. The second character can be any of the 26 letters of the English alphabet. There are only 9 possible digits for the third character, because the third character cannot repeat the digit used for the first character. By the same reasoning, there are only 8 possible digits for the fourth character. Thus, there are $10 \times 26 \times 9 \times 8 = 18,720$ possible

MATH BIN 4

QUESTIONS

EXPLANATIONS

passwords that follow the *DLDD* pattern. Now consider *DDLD*. There are an equal number of possible passwords that follow this pattern. The first character can be any of 10 digits; the second character can be any of the 9 remaining digits; the third character can be any of the 26 letters of the alphabet; and the fourth character can be any of the remaining 8 digits.

$10 \times 9 \times 26 \times 8 = 18,720$. There are $18,720 + 18,720 = 37,440$ different passwords possible, and the correct answer is (D).

13. If *x* is a positive integer, is *x* divisible by 48 ?

(1) *x* is divisible by 8.

(2) *x* is divisible by 6.

○ Statement (1) ALONE is sufficient, but statement (2) alone is not sufficient.
○ Statement (2) ALONE is sufficient, but statement (1) alone is not sufficient.
○ BOTH statements TOGETHER are sufficient, but NEITHER statement ALONE is sufficient.
○ EACH statement ALONE is sufficient.
○ Statements (1) and (2) TOGETHER are not sufficient.

13. **E** This is a yes-or-no question. If we Plug In numbers for *x* in Statement (1), we can get both a "yes" answer (by Plugging In 48) and a "no" answer (by Plugging In 16), so the possible answers are BCE. The same is true with Statement (2). If *x* = 48, which is divisible by 6, the answer to the question is "yes." But, if *x* = 6, the answer to the question is "no." The possible answers are (C) or (E). Now, combine the statements. If *x* = 48, which is divisible by both 6 and 8, the answer to the question is "yes." However, if *x* = 24, which is also divisible by both 6 and 8, the answer to the question is "no." So, the statements are not sufficient when combined. Therefore, the correct answer is (E).

MATH BIN 4

QUESTIONS

$$\begin{array}{r} FGF \\ \times\ G \\ \hline HGG \end{array}$$

14. In the multiplication problem above, *F, G,* and *H* represent distinct odd digits. What is the value of the three-digit number *FGF* ?

- ○ 151
- ○ 161
- ○ 171
- ○ 313
- ○ 353

EXPLANATIONS

14. **A** At first it looks as though you'll have to substitute every odd digit for the three variables until you stumble onto the correct answer, but there's a trick to this problem that eliminates such guesswork. Look at the units column of the problem and you'll see that $F \times G$ yields a product with a units digit of *G*; therefore, it is quite possible that *F* is 1. Actually, you can go even further: *F must* equal 1, because *G* cannot equal 1 (otherwise, the product of this multiplication problem would be *FGF*, not *HGG*). Plus, if both *F* and *G* were odd digits greater than 1, the product of this multiplication problem would be a four-digit number. Because the product is the three-digit number *HGG*, *F* equals 1. You can now eliminate (D) and (E), and you also know that *G* must equal 5 or 7 (*G* cannot equal 6 because the problem says *G* must be an odd digit). When *G* equals 7, the product is a four-digit number; therefore, *G* is 5, and the correct answer is (A).

But you could have just plugged the answer choices into the problem, one at a time, to see which one works.

MATH BIN 4

QUESTIONS

15. A group of 20 friends formed an investment club, with each member contributing an equal amount to the general fund. The club then invested the entire fund, which amounted to d dollars, in Stock X. The value of the stock subsequently increased 40 percent, at which point the stock was sold and the proceeds divided evenly among the members. In terms of d, how much money did each member of the club receive from the sale? (Assume that transaction fees and other associated costs were negligible.)

- ○ $800d$
- ○ $\dfrac{7d}{5}$
- ○ $\dfrac{d}{20} + 40$
- ○ $\dfrac{d}{2}$
- ○ $\dfrac{7d}{100}$

EXPLANATIONS

15. **E** The variables in the answer choices should tell you that this is a great problem for Plugging In. Choose a value easily divisible by 20 (the number of friends in the group) and one for which percentages are easy to calculate (because the value of the stock increases by a percentage). Let's set d equal to 100. The general fund of $100, then, was invested in Stock X, which subsequently increased in value by 40 percent; thus, its value increased to $140. At this point, the club sold the stock and divvied up the proceeds. Each member received $140 ÷ 20 = $7 in the process. Therefore, when d equals 100, the correct answer choice yields a result of 7. Check each answer choice, Plugging In 100 for d. The correct answer is (E).

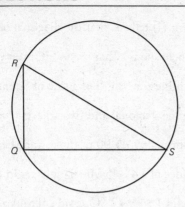

16. Triangle *QRS* is inscribed in a circle as shown above. Is *QRS* a right triangle?

(1) *RS* is a diameter of the circle.

(2) *QR* = 3 and *RS* = 5

⃝ Statement (1) ALONE is sufficient, but statement (2) alone is not sufficient.
⃝ Statement (2) ALONE is sufficient, but statement (1) alone is not sufficient.
⃝ BOTH statements TOGETHER are sufficient, but NEITHER statement ALONE is sufficient.
⃝ EACH statement ALONE is sufficient.
⃝ Statements (1) and (2) TOGETHER are not sufficient.

16. **A**   This problem requires you to clear two hurdles. First, you must remember a rule about inscribed angles in semicircles. Then, you must avoid succumbing to the power of suggestion. First, the rule about inscribed angles. Statement (1) tells us that *RS* is a diameter of the circle. That means we are dealing with two semicircles. The question stem tells us that triangle *QRS* is inscribed in a circle; thus, ∠*RQS* is inscribed. A triangle inscribed in a semicircle is always a right triangle. Therefore, ∠*RQS* measures 90°. Statement (1) is sufficient, and we're down to AD. Statement (2) can trick you if you don't forget all about Statement (1) first. It suggests that *QSR* is a right triangle, because the ratio of *QR* to *RS* recalls the familiar 3-4-5 triangle that satisfies the Pythagorean Theorem. However, Statement (2) does not preclude the possibility that *RS* is *not* a diameter and that therefore side *QS* does *not* measure 4. There is no way to determine whether *QRS* is a right triangle from Statement (2). The correct answer is (A).

MATH BIN 4

QUESTIONS

17. Square *G* has sides of length 4 inches. Is the area of Square *H* exactly one half the area of Square *G* ?

(1) The length of the diagonal of Square *H* equals the length of one side of Square *G*.

(2) The perimeter of Square *H* is twice the length of the diagonal of Square *G*.

○ Statement (1) ALONE is sufficient, but statement (2) alone is not sufficient.
○ Statement (2) ALONE is sufficient, but statement (1) alone is not sufficient.
○ BOTH statements TOGETHER are sufficient, but NEITHER statement ALONE is sufficient.
○ EACH statement ALONE is sufficient.
○ Statements (1) and (2) TOGETHER are not sufficient.

EXPLANATIONS

17. **D** Statement (1) tells us that the diagonal of Square *H* is 4 inches long. That is enough information to determine the length of a side of Square *H*, because the diagonal and two adjacent sides of a square form a 45-45-90 triangle, and the lengths of the sides of a 45-45-90 triangle are in the proportion $1 : 1 : \sqrt{2}$. One side of Square *H* has a length of $\dfrac{4}{\sqrt{2}} = \dfrac{4\sqrt{2}}{2} = 2\sqrt{2}$ inches. The area of Square *H* is 8 square inches, which is indeed half the area of Square *G*. We're down to AD. Statement (2) mentions the diagonal of Square *G*, which we know to be $4\sqrt{2}$ inches because the question stem tells us that the length of one side of Square *G* is 4 inches. Thus, the perimeter of Square *H* is $8\sqrt{2}$ inches, and the length of one side of Square *H* is $2\sqrt{2}$ inches. As in Statement (1), this information is sufficient to answer the question. The correct answer is (D).

MATH BIN 4

18. In a certain state, 70 percent of the counties received some rain on Monday, and 65 percent of the counties received some rain on Tuesday. No rain fell either day in 25 percent of the counties in the state. What percent of the counties received some rain on Monday and Tuesday?

- ○ 12.5%
- ○ 40%
- ○ 50%
- ○ 60%
- ○ 67.5%

18. **D** Use the group formula to solve this problem. The group formula is Total = Group 1 + Group 2 – Both + Neither. The problem specifies that the answer is the percent of counties that got rain on both days, so the answer depends on finding the "Both" category of the formula. Now, fill in the values for the formula. Plug In 100 for the total number of counties. Therefore, 70 counties received rain on Monday (which is Group 1), 65 counties received rain on Tuesday (Group 2), and 25 counties received no rain. Put these into the formula, so 100 = 70 + 65 – Both + 25. Solve the equation to find that Both = 60. 60 is 60% of 100, so the correct answer is (D).

19. *ABCD* is a rectangle with sides of length x centimeters and width y centimeters and a diagonal of length z centimeters. What is the perimeter, in centimeters, of *ABCD* ?

(1) $x - y = 7$

(2) $z = 13$

○ Statement (1) ALONE is sufficient, but statement (2) alone is not sufficient.
○ Statement (2) ALONE is sufficient, but statement (1) alone is not sufficient.
○ BOTH statements TOGETHER are sufficient, but NEITHER statement ALONE is sufficient.
○ EACH statement ALONE is sufficient.
○ Statements (1) and (2) TOGETHER are not sufficient.

19. **C** Statement (1) tells us that $x - y = 7$. An infinite number of combinations satisfy this equation, yielding an infinite number of perimeters for *ABCD*. Statement (1) is not sufficient, and we're down to BCE. Similarly, there are many different ways to draw a rectangle with diagonal 13. Not all of these rectangles have the same perimeter. Statement (2) is not sufficient by itself, and the correct answer is (C) or (E). At first glance, the two statements together don't appear to offer much more help. However, by applying a bit of algebraic trickery and the Pythagorean Theorem, we can wring more information from these two statements than is immediately apparent. Start by squaring Statement (1); this yields the equation $x^2 - 2xy + y^2 = 49$. The Pythagorean Theorem tells us that $x^2 + y^2 = z^2$, so we can use Statement (2) to substitute 13^2, or 169, for $x^2 + y^2$. This yields the equation $169 - 2xy = 49$, which can be simplified to $xy = 60$. There's just one more step. We know that $x^2 + y^2 = 169$, and we know that $xy = 60$. Thus, we know that $x^2 + 2xy + y^2 = 289$. The square root of $x^2 + 2xy + y^2$ is $(x + y)$, so we also know that $x + y = 17$ (it cannot equal -17 because x and y are centimeter lengths). This equation can be used in conjunction with Statement (1) to solve simultaneously for x and y, thus allowing you a way to calculate the perimeter of the rectangle. The correct answer is (C).

MATH BIN 4

QUESTIONS

20. Together, Andrea and Brian weigh p pounds and Brian weighs 10 pounds more than Andrea. If Andrea's dog, Cubby, weighs $\frac{p}{4}$ pounds more than Andrea then, in terms of p, what is Cubby's weight in pounds?

- ○ $\frac{p}{2} - 10$
- ○ $\frac{3p}{4} - 5$
- ○ $\frac{3p}{2} - 5$
- ○ $\frac{5p}{4} - 10$
- ○ $5p - 5$

EXPLANATIONS

20. **B** Variables in the answer choices mean it's time to Plug In. For the purposes of this problem, it's probably easiest to Plug In weights for Andrea and Brian, add them, and use the sum for the value of p. Remember to plug in values that conform to the rules of the problem; Brian must weigh exactly 10 pounds more than Andrea. Try to make p a value that is divisible by 4; that will make it easier to calculate Cubby's weight. Let's say Andrea weighs 45 pounds and Brian weighs 55 pounds. That makes p equal to 100, a nice, round number that is easily divisible by 4. Cubby weighs $\frac{p}{4}$ pounds more than Andrea, so he weighs 25 pounds more than Andrea, or 70 pounds. Plug 100 in for p in each of the answer choices and eliminate those that do not yield an answer of 70. The correct answer is (B).

MATH BIN 4

QUESTIONS

21. A first-grade teacher uses ten flash cards, numbered 1 through 10, to teach her students to order numbers correctly. She has students choose four flash cards at random and arrange the cards in ascending order. If she removes the cards numbered 2 and 4, how many different correctly ordered arrangements of the four selected cards are possible?

- ○ 70
- ○ 210
- ○ 336
- ○ 840
- ○ 1,680

EXPLANATIONS

21. **A** This question is easier than it first appears. At first glance, the restrictive rules—the cards must be arranged in order, some cards have been removed from the deck—seem to complicate the problem. In fact, they do not; because there is only one correct solution for each set of cards chosen, you need only figure out the number of possible combinations of the cards in order to determine the number of possible correct arrangements. The one-to-one correlation between combinations and correct solutions actually simplifies the problem. Because the teacher has removed two cards from the deck, only 8 cards remain. The values on the selected cards are immaterial and are presented merely as a distracter; the answer to this question is the same regardless of the values written on the two cards she removes. Make four spots for the cards chosen, then fill in the number of options for each spot: $8 \times 7 \times 6 \times 5$. Then, divide by the number of ways to arrange these four cards: $4 \times 3 \times 2 \times 1$. Reduce and solve to find 70. The correct answer is (A).

MATH BIN 4

QUESTIONS

22. If *A* and *B* are two-digit integers that share the same digits, except in reverse order, then what is the sum of *A* and *B* ?

(1) $A - B = 45$

(2) The difference between the two digits in each number is 5.

○ Statement (1) ALONE is sufficient, but statement (2) alone is not sufficient.
○ Statement (2) ALONE is sufficient, but statement (1) alone is not sufficient.
○ BOTH statements TOGETHER are sufficient, but NEITHER statement ALONE is sufficient.
○ EACH statement ALONE is sufficient.
○ Statements (1) and (2) TOGETHER are not sufficient.

23. A university awarded grants in the amount of either $7,000 or $10,000 to selected incoming freshmen. If the total amount of all such awards is $2,300,000, did the university award more $7,000 grants than $10,000 grants to its incoming freshmen?

(1) A total of 275 freshmen received grants in one of the two amounts.

(2) The amount of money awarded in $10,000 grants was $200,000 more than the amount of money awarded in $7,000 grants.

○ Statement (1) ALONE is sufficient, but statement (2) alone is not sufficient.
○ Statement (2) ALONE is sufficient, but statement (1) alone is not sufficient.
○ BOTH statements TOGETHER are sufficient, but NEITHER statement ALONE is sufficient.
○ EACH statement ALONE is sufficient.
○ Statements (1) and (2) TOGETHER are not sufficient.

EXPLANATIONS

22. E As you consider each statement, you might be tempted to think, "How many numbers can possibly satisfy all the constraints of the question stem *and* this statement?" Or, you may figure that both statements together, in addition to the information in the question stem, *must* be sufficient to answer the question. That, of course, is just what the test writers *expect* you to think. It turns out that several values satisfy each of the statements: 61 and 16; 72 and 27; 83 and 38; and 94 and 49 all satisfy Statements (1) and (2). Thus, neither statement is sufficient on its own, nor are they sufficient together. The correct answer is (E).

23. D This is a simultaneous equation problem dressed up as a word problem. The question stem tells us that two types of grants were awarded; it also provides the sum of the grants. Let's call the group of freshmen who received $7,000 grants *x* and the group of freshmen who received $10,000 grants *y*. The question stem tells us that $7,000x + 10,000y = 2,300,000$. That's one equation; to solve simultaneous equations, we need two equations. Statement (1) provides a second equation. That equation is $x + y = 275$. You can solve simultaneously—although, of course, you don't have to because this is Data Sufficiency, not Problem Solving—to determine that $x = 150$ and $y = 125$. Statement (1) is sufficient; the answer is (A) or (D). Statement (2) also provides a second equation. That equation is $10,000y = 7,000x + 200,000$. Again, you can solve to determine that $x = 150$ and $y = 125$. Choice (D) is the correct answer.

24. The figure shown above is a regular hexagon with center *H*. The shaded area is a parallelogram that shares three vertices with the hexagon and its fourth vertex is the center of the hexagon. If the length of one side of the hexagon is 8 centimeters, what is the area of the unshaded region?

   ○ $16\sqrt{3}$ cm³
   ○ 96 cm³
   ○ $64\sqrt{3}$ cm³
   ○ $96\sqrt{3}$ cm³
   ○ 256 cm³

24. **C** When a problem includes a regular hexagon, you know a lot more than you might think. That's because you can divide a regular hexagon into 6 congruent equilateral triangles, all meeting at the center of the hexagon. Furthermore, if you know the length of one side of an equilateral triangle, you can determine its area by dividing the equilateral triangle into two 30-60-90 triangles and applying the 30-60-90 ratios to determine the height of the equilateral triangle (the ratio of the sides of a 30-60-90 triangle is $1 : \sqrt{3} : 2$). The problem tells you that the length of one side of the hexagon is 8 centimeters. That means that the equilateral triangles that make up the hexagon have sides of 8 centimeters. Divide one into a 30-60-90 triangle and you'll get a triangle with sides $4 : 4\sqrt{3} : 8$; this tells you that the height of the equilateral triangle is $4\sqrt{3}$ and that its area is $\dfrac{8\left(4\sqrt{3}\right)}{2} = 16\sqrt{3}$ cm². The area of the unshaded region consists of four of the six equilateral triangles (the shaded region consists of the other two), so the area of the unshaded region is $4 \times 16\sqrt{3} = 64\sqrt{3}$ cm². The correct answer is (C).

MATH BIN 4

25. A fish tank contains a number of fish, including 5 Fantails. If two fish are selected from the tank at random, what is the probability that both will be Fantails?

   (1) The probability that the first fish chosen is a Fantail is $\frac{1}{2}$.

   (2) The probability that the second fish chosen is a Fantail is $\frac{4}{9}$.

   ○ Statement (1) ALONE is sufficient, but statement (2) alone is not sufficient.
   ○ Statement (2) ALONE is sufficient, but statement (1) alone is not sufficient.
   ○ BOTH statements TOGETHER are sufficient, but NEITHER statement ALONE is sufficient.
   ○ EACH statement ALONE is sufficient.
   ○ Statements (1) and (2) TOGETHER are not sufficient.

25. **D** To figure out this problem, you need to know the total number of fish. Looking at Statement (1) in combination with the question itself, you can see that if there are 5 Fantails, and the probability that the first selection is a Fantail is $\frac{1}{2}$; that means we actually know the total number of fish: $\frac{1}{2} = \frac{5}{x}$ or 10. You might think that the probability of the second fish being a Fantail is also $\frac{1}{2}$, but in fact that's not the case: There are only 9 fish left in total when the second selection is made, and there are only 4 possible Fantails from which to chose. So the probability of them both being chosen is $\frac{1}{2} \times \frac{4}{9}$, or $\frac{2}{9}$. We are down to AD.

Now, looking at Statement (2), if the probability that the second fish will be a Fantail is $\frac{4}{9}$, that means that the probability of the first fish being a Fantail is $\frac{5}{10}$, which means we can answer the question based on Statement (2) alone as well. The correct answer is (D).

VERBAL BIN 1

QUESTIONS

1. As its reputation for making acquisitions of important masterpieces has grown, the museum has increasingly turned down gifts of lesser-known paintings <u>they would in the past have accepted gratefully</u>.

  ○ they would in the past have accepted gratefully
  ○ they would have accepted gratefully in the past
  ○ it would in the past have accepted gratefully
  ○ it previously would have accepted gratefully in the past
  ○ that previously would have been accepted in the past

2. Over the past few decades, despite periodic attempts to reign in spending, currencies in South America <u>are devalued</u> by rampant inflation.

  ○ are devalued
  ○ are becoming more devalued
  ○ which have lost value
  ○ have become devalued
  ○ have since become devalued

3. A fashion designer's fall line for women utilizing new soft fabrics broke all sales records last year. To capitalize on her success, the designer plans to launch a line of clothing for men this year that makes use of the same new soft fabrics.

  The designer's plan assumes that

  ○ other designers are not planning to introduce new lines for men utilizing the same soft fabrics
  ○ men will be as interested in the new soft fabrics as women were the year before
  ○ the designer will have time to develop new lines for both men and women
  ○ the line for men will be considered innovative and daring because of its use of fabrics
  ○ women who bought the new line last year will continue to buy it this year

EXPLANATIONS

1. **C** The pronoun *they* in this stem sentence doesn't agree with the noun it refers to: the museum. In everyday speech, of course, we often say "they" when we are referring to a large institution—but on the GMAT, the test writers won't let us get away with such imprecision. Choices (A) and (B) can both be eliminated because they use the plural pronoun. Choices (D) and (E) both fix the problem in different ways, but both add a redundancy: There is no need to have "previously" and "in the past" in the same sentence. The correct answer is (C).

2. **D** This is a tense question. *Over the past few decades* implies a continued action over time—which needs the perfect tense. This eliminates choices (A) and (B). Choice (C) creates a sentence fragment. Choice (E) isn't bad, but the word *since* is a bit redundant because the sentence began with *over the past few decades*. The correct answer is (D).

3. **B** This is an analogy argument. The men's line is being introduced in the hope that men will like the new soft fabrics as much as women did the year before. The key word in the passage that might have alerted you to the analogy was the word *same*. The assumption on which this argument depends is that men and women will like the same new fabric. Choices (A), (C), (D), and (E) are all outside the scope of the argument. The correct answer is (B).

VERBAL BIN 1

4. The standard lamp is becoming outmoded, and <u>so too is the incandescent light bulb, it is Edison's miraculous invention to use</u> so much more energy than the new low-wattage halogen bulbs.

- ○ so too is the incandescent light bulb, it is Edison's miraculous invention to use
- ○ so too is the incandescent light bulb, Edison's miraculous invention that uses
- ○ so too the incandescent light bulb, Edison's miraculous invention using
- ○ also the incandescent light bulb, it is Edison's miraculous invention that uses
- ○ also the incandescent light bulb, which is Edison's miraculous invention to use

4. **B** This is basically an idiom question, but your checklist may first uncover a pronoun issue. The pronoun *it* clearly refers back to *light bulb*, but in this case the pronoun isn't actually necessary: *Edison's miraculous invention* refers directly back to *light bulb* without the need of a pronoun. This eliminates (A) and (D), both of which are actually run-on sentences. Next, you should turn your attention to the end of the underlined phrase. Do you have an invention *to use* energy ((A) and (E)), an invention *that uses* energy ((B) and (D)), or an invention *using* energy ((C))? If you said *that uses*, then you are doing just fine. Since we've already eliminated (D), the correct answer is (B).

5. Over the last 20 years, <u>the growth of information technology has been more rapid than any other business field</u>, but has recently begun to lag behind as newly emerging fields seem more enticing to new graduates.

- ○ the growth of information technology has been more rapid than any other business field
- ○ the growth of information technology has been more rapid than any other fields of business
- ○ information technology's growth has been more rapid than any other fields of business
- ○ the growing of information technology has been more rapid than that of any other business field
- ○ the growth of information technology has been more rapid than that of any other business field

5. **E** The clue that tells you this is a potential parallel construction problem is the word *than*. This sentence is supposed to compare the *growth* of information technology to the *growth* in other fields. However, as written, the sentence is comparing the *growth* of information technology directly to other fields. Once you spot this, you should immediately start looking for the replacement phrase, *that of*. Only two answer choices contain it, (D) and (E). However, (D) uses the awkward and unidiomatic phrase *the growing of information technology*. The correct answer is (E).

QUESTIONS

6. According to mutual fund sales experts, a successful year for a stock fund should result not only in increased investor dollars flowing into the fund, but also in increased investor dollars flowing into other mutual stock funds offered by the same company. However, while last year the Grafton Mutual Company's "Growth Stock Fund" beat average market returns by a factor of two and recorded substantial new investment, the other stock funds offered by Grafton did not report any increase whatsoever.

   Which of the following conclusions can properly be drawn from the statements above?

   ○ When one of the mutual funds offered by a company beats average market returns, the other mutual funds offered by that company will beat average market returns.
   ○ The mutual fund sales experts neglected to consider bond funds in formulating their theory.
   ○ The performance of the Grafton "Growth Stock Fund" was a result of a wave of mergers and acquisitions that year.
   ○ Investors currently dislike all stock mutual funds because of market volatility.
   ○ The success of one mutual fund is not the only factor affecting whether investors will invest in other mutual funds run by the same company.

7. With <u>less than thirty thousand dollars in advance ticket sales and fewer</u> acceptances by guest speakers than expected, the one-day symposium on art and religion was canceled for lack of interest.

   ○ less than thirty thousand dollars in advance ticket sales and fewer
   ○ fewer than thirty thousand dollars in advance ticket sales and less
   ○ fewer than thirty thousand dollars in advance ticket sales and fewer
   ○ lesser than thirty thousand dollars in advance ticket sales and fewer
   ○ less than thirty thousand dollars in advance ticket sales and as few

EXPLANATIONS

6. **E** This is a causal argument. According to experts, the high returns of one mutual fund *cause* investors to invest in other mutual funds run by the same company. However, in the case of the Grafton "family" of mutual funds, that was not the case. What conclusion can we draw from this? Keep (E), which asks us to consider that there might be alternate causes. Choices (A), (B), and (C) are outside the scope of the argument, while (D) is too extreme and illogical because the argument makes it clear that investors liked at least *one* stock mutual fund: Grafton's "Growth Stock Fund." The correct answer is (E).

7. **A** This question is about quantity words, as you probably suspected just from looking at the answer choices. When it comes to money, you use *fewer* if you are referring to the number of actual bills you have, but *less* if you are referring to the total amount and don't know the actual number of bills. This would get you down to (A) and (E). Acceptances, however, can be counted, so in the second half of the underlined portion of the underlined sentence, you would use *fewer*. If you were tempted by (E), you didn't notice that it created a new idiomatic error: Would you say as few *than* or as few *as*? That is, with (E) you would be

VERBAL BIN 1

QUESTIONS	EXPLANATIONS

saying "and as few acceptances by guest speakers than expected" when the idiom is "as few as" not "as few than." The correct answer is (A).

8. New technology now makes it feasible for computer call-in help desk services to route calls they receive to almost anywhere, theoretically allowing employees to work from home, without the need for a daily commute.

The adoption of this policy would be most likely to increase productivity if employees did not _____.

○ commute from a distance of fewer than 10 miles
○ commute by car as opposed to by rail
○ live in areas with dependable phone service
○ need to consult frequently with each other to solve callers' problems
○ have more than one telephone line

8. **D** The tricky part of this inference question is dealing with the "did not." Choice (A) is outside the scope of the argument because eliminating such a short commute would presumably not have much effect on productivity. Choice (B) is also outside the scope since the *method* of the commute employees would no longer have to make is probably irrelevant. If employees did not live in areas of dependable phone service, that would likely *decrease* productivity, so that eliminates (C). For similar reasons, eliminate (E); if employees did not have more than one phone line, it might decrease productivity since they would presumably get some personal calls at their place of residence. For (D), if employees needed to consult each other to answer callers' questions, they would be at a distinct disadvantage if they were all in separate locations. The correct answer is (D).

9. The port cities of England in the 19th century saw a renaissance of ship construction, with some innovative designs breaking new ground, stretching the limits of ship-building theory, and <u>received</u> acclaim from around the world.

○ received
○ it received
○ receiving
○ would receive
○ it had received

9. **C** This is a parallel construction question, in which the second half of the sentence contains a list of three actions, which all must be expressed in the same way. The three actions are *breaking, stretching,* and *received. Received* is underlined and does not match the other actions, so it must be changed to *receiving.* Eliminate (A), (B), (D), and (E), as they are not parallel to the other two verbs. The correct answer is (C).

QUESTIONS

10. According to a consumer research group survey, the majority of kitchen appliances purchased in the United States are purchased by men. This appears to belie the myth that women spend more time in the kitchen than men.

    The argument is flawed primarily because the author _____.

    ○ fails to differentiate between buying and using
    ○ does not provide information about the types of kitchen appliances surveyed
    ○ depends on the results of one survey
    ○ does not give exact statistics to back up his case
    ○ does not provide information on other appliances such as washers and dryers

11. <u>A contribution to a favorite charity being sent instead</u> of flowers when a colleague dies is becoming more the rule than the exception when it comes to funeral etiquette.

    ○ A contribution to a favorite charity being sent instead
    ○ A contribution being sent to a favorite charity as opposed
    ○ To send a contribution for a favorite charity instead
    ○ Sending a contribution to a favorite charity instead
    ○ Sending a contribution to a favorite charity as opposed

EXPLANATIONS

10. **A** The faulty assumption of this argument is that the buyers of the kitchen appliances are also the users of the kitchen appliances. We do not know that this is true. While more men may buy kitchen appliances, they are not necessarily the ones who use them. Choice (B) is wrong because knowing the individual types of kitchen appliances would not enhance the argument. Although (C) and (D) might seem tempting, the problem with this argument is not so much that the survey might not be representative, but rather that the author is using information about buying patterns to extrapolate how these appliances are later going to be used and by whom. Choice (E) is outside the scope of the argument. The correct answer is (A).

11. **D** The GMAT test writers have an aversion to the word *being*, which usually creates a passive voice. This eliminates (A) and (B). Generally, when a sentence begins with the infinitive verb form (*To send…*), you would need a parallel infinitive verb form in the second half of the sentence, which is not the case in (C) (which also uses the incorrect idiomatic expression *contribution for*). Choice (E) might seem tempting, except that the last two words—*as opposed*—don't go idiomatically with *of*. The correct answer is (D).

VERBAL BIN 1

Questions 12–15 are based on the following passage:

As a business model, the world of publishing has always been a somewhat sleepy enclave, but now all that seems poised to change. Several
Line companies have moved aggressively into a new
(5) business endeavor whose genesis comes from the question: Who owns the great works of literature?

Text-on-demand is not a completely new idea, of course. In the 1990s, the Gutenberg project sought volunteers to type literary classics that had
(10) expired copyrights into word processing files so that scholars would have searchable databases for their research. Most of the works of Shakespeare, Cervantes, Proust, and Molière were to be found free online by as early as 1995.

(15) However, now large-scale companies have moved into the market, with scanners and business plans, and are looking for bargain basement content. These companies are striking deals with libraries, and some publishers, to
(20) be able to provide their content, for a price, to individual buyers over the Internet.

At stake are the rights to an estimated store of 30 million books, most of which are now out of print. Many of these books are now also in the
(25) public domain, giving any company the right to sell them online. Still, a good portion of the books a general audience might actually want to buy is still under copyright. The urgent question: Who owns those copyrights? In the case of all too
(30) many books put out more than 20 years ago by now-defunct publishing companies, the answer is unclear—a situation the new text-on-demand companies are eager to exploit. An association of publishers has sued, claiming massive copyright
(35) infringement. The case is several years away from trial.

12. The primary purpose of the passage is to

○ present the results of a statistical analysis and propose further study
○ explain a recent development and explore its consequences
○ identify the reasons for a trend and recommend measures to address it
○ outline several theories about a phenomenon and advocate one of them
○ describe the potential consequences of implementing a new policy and argue in favor of that policy

12. **B** Process of Elimination is useful here. Does the author present a statistical analysis? No, so eliminate (A). While the author might be said to identify the reasons for a trend, does she recommend measures to address it? No, so eliminate (C). Does the author advocate anything whatsoever? No, so eliminate (D). Does the author argue in favor of any policy? No, so eliminate (E). The correct answer is (B).

QUESTIONS	EXPLANATIONS

13. It can be inferred from the passage that the works of Shakespeare, Cervantes, and Molière

○ are some of the most popular works of literature
○ are no longer copyrighted
○ are among the works for which the association of publishers is suing text-on-demand companies
○ do not currently exist as searchable databases
○ were owned by now-defunct publishing companies

13. B Look for information about the authors mentioned in the question: It's in the end of the second paragraph. Make sure to read the context and not just those lines. Based on the previous sentence, these books are examples of ones with expired copyrights that were typed and put online. This supports (B). Choices (A) and (E) might be true but cannot be inferred. Choice (C) is out of scope, as lawsuits apply to other works than the subject of this question. Choice (D) directly contradicts the passage. The correct answer is (B).

14. Which of the following is an example of a book that a text-on-demand company would not have to acquire the rights to?

○ A book still under copyright
○ A book more than 20 years old
○ A book in the public domain
○ A book a general audience might want to buy
○ A book not already owned by publishers the company has a deal with

14. C The passage states in the last paragraph that these companies want to exploit the unclear situation of who owns the copyrights to certain books. They would want to print something that is not under copyright, so it would be in the public domain, as the passage indicates in lines 25–26. For (B), the passage does not say that all books over 20 years old may be freely printed. The correct answer is (C).

QUESTIONS

15. It can be inferred from the passage that a common practice of text-on-demand companies is to

- ○ use scanners to find books they want to acquire
- ○ create business plans well before they have any actual business
- ○ buy content at premium prices
- ○ acquire the rights to books for as little as possible
- ○ attempt to supplant the role of traditional publishers

16. Exit polls, conducted by an independent organization among voters at five polling locations during a recent election, suggested that the incumbent mayor—a Democrat—was going to lose the election by a wide margin. But, in fact, by the time the final results were tabulated, the incumbent had won the election by a narrow margin.

Which of the following, if true, would explain the apparent contradiction in the results of the exit polls?

- ○ The people chosen at random to be polled by the independent organization happened to be Democrats.
- ○ The exit poll locations chosen by the independent organization were in predominantly Republican districts.
- ○ The exit polls were conducted during the afternoon, when most of the districts' younger voters, who did not support the incumbent mayor, were at work.
- ○ The incumbent mayor ran on a platform that promised to lower taxes if elected.
- ○ An earlier poll, conducted the week before the election, had predicted that the incumbent mayor would win.

EXPLANATIONS

15. D Use process of elimination. Choices (A) and (B) are recycled language—the passage mentions scanners and business plans but doesn't say that. Choice (C) is a reversal—the passage states that these companies are *looking for bargain basement content.* Choice (D) fits with this statement. Choice (E) is not supported because the passage doesn't explain what these practices have to do with *the role of traditional publishers.* The correct answer is (D).

16. B The key to this statistical argument is to understand that the sampling of the voters might not be representative of ALL the voters. Choice (A) says the voters chosen by the pollsters happened to be Democrats. But in that case, we would expect that the incumbent mayor, a Democrat, would have been predicted the winner of the election. Choice (C) says the exit poll was conducted at a time of day in which many people who disliked the mayor could not vote, implying that the actual election results for the incumbent would be worse, or at least no better. Choices (D) and (E) are outside the scope of the argument. Choice (B) gives a statistical reason for the skewed results: The exit polls were conducted in locations where the incumbent had little support—leaving open the possibility that his results would be stronger elsewhere. The correct answer is (B).

QUESTIONS

17. The spread of Avian flu from animals to humans has been well-documented, but less understood is the mechanism by which it is spread from one bird species to another. **In order to avoid a world-wide epidemic of Avian flu, scientists must make that study a first priority.** To solely tackle the human dimension of this possible pandemic is to miss half of the problem: its spread from one hemisphere to another.

    The bolded phrase plays which of the following roles in the argument above?

    ○ The bolded phrase states a premise of the argument.
    ○ The bolded phrase contradicts the author's main point.
    ○ The bolded phrase makes a statement that the author is about to contradict.
    ○ The bolded phrase states the author's conclusion.
    ○ The bolded phrase states an assumption the author is making.

18. Successful business leaders not only anticipate potential problems and have contingency plans <u>ready, instead proceeding as if they are likely to occur at any time</u>.

    ○ ready, instead proceeding as if they are likely to occur at any time
    ○ ready, but also proceed as if such problems are likely to occur at any time
    ○ ready, but also proceeding as if the occurrence of them is at any time likely
    ○ ready; they instead proceed as if their occurrence is likely at any time
    ○ ready; such problems are likely to occur at any time, is how they proceed

EXPLANATIONS

17. **D** Although there is no "therefore" or "hence" in front of it, the bolded phrase is the conclusion of the argument. The other phrases are premises of the argument. If you suspect a phrase may be the conclusion, it sometimes helps to imagine a "therefore" in front of it, to see if the sentence would make sense. If it does, chances are that's your conclusion. The correct answer is (D).

18. **B** The phrase *not only* must be followed by the phrase *but also* in order to complete the sentence properly. The answer must therefore be either (B) or (C). Choice (C) lacks parallel structure in the words *anticipate* and *proceeding*. Correctly formulated, this sentence should read *business leaders not only anticipate…but also proceed….* The correct answer is (B).

VERBAL BIN 1

QUESTIONS

19. An artist who sells her paintings for a fixed price decides that she must increase her income. Because she does not believe that customers will pay more for her paintings, she decides to cut costs by using cheaper paints and canvases. She expects that, by cutting costs, she will increase her profit margin per painting and thus increase her annual net income.

    Which of the following, if true, most weakens the argument above?

    ○ Other area artists charge more for their paintings than the artist charges for hers.
    ○ The artist has failed to consider other options, such as renting cheaper studio space.
    ○ The artist's plan will result in the production of inferior paintings which, in turn, will cause a reduction in sales.
    ○ If the economy were to enter a period of inflation, the artist's projected increase in income could be wiped out by increases in the price of art supplies.
    ○ The artist considered trying to complete paintings more quickly and thus increase production, but concluded that it would be impossible.

20. Although tapirs reared in captivity are generally docile and have even been kept as pets by South American villagers, <u>it is nonetheless a volatile creature</u> prone to unpredictable and dangerous temper tantrums.

    ○ it is nonetheless a volatile creature
    ○ it is nonetheless volatile creatures
    ○ being nonetheless volatile creatures
    ○ they are nonetheless a volatile creature
    ○ they are nonetheless volatile creatures

EXPLANATIONS

19. **C** To weaken an argument, look first at its conclusion. This argument concludes that the artist will *increase her profit margin...and thus increase her annual income* by using cheaper art supplies. Which answer choice undercuts this conclusion? Choice (C) does; if the artist's sales decrease, then her increased profit margin may not lead to an increase in annual income, because the decrease in sales may offset the increase in per-painting profit. The correct answer is (C).

20. **E** This is a pronoun agreement question. The subject of the sentence is *tapirs*; therefore, the pronoun that refers to the subject must be plural. The answer, therefore, must be (D) or (E). Choice (D) contains a new pronoun agreement error, because *they* is plural and *a volatile creature* is singular. Choice (C) has no pronoun at all. The correct answer is (E).

QUESTIONS

21. According to a recent report, the original tires supplied with the Impressivo, a new sedan-class automobile, wore much more quickly than tires conventionally wear. The report suggested two possible causes: (1) defects in the tires and (2) improper wheel alignment of the automobile.

Which of the following would best help the authors of the report determine which of the two causes identified was responsible for the extra wear?

○ A study in which the rate of tire wear in the Impressivo is compared to the rate of tire wear in all automobiles in the same class

○ A study in which a second set of tires, manufactured by a different company than the one that made the first set, is installed on all Impressivos and the rate of wear is measured

○ A study in which the level of satisfaction of workers in the Impressivo manufacturing plant is measured and compared to that of workers at other automobile manufacturing plants

○ A study that determines how often improper wheel alignment results in major problems for manufacturers of other automobiles in the Impressivo's class

○ A study that determines the degree to which faulty driving techniques employed by Impressivo drivers contributed to tire wear

EXPLANATIONS

21. **B** Because the report identifies two possible causes of the tire wear, the best answer must identify a study that focuses on one of these possible causes. Studies focusing on car models other than the Impressivo, (A) and (D), worker satisfaction, (C), or driver error, (E), are all irrelevant to this study. The study described in (B) removes one of the two possible causes. If the newly installed tires made by another manufacturer also turn out to wear abnormally, then the authors will have good reason to suspect that faulty alignment caused the initial problem. If the new tires wear normally, then they will know that the original tires were faulty. The correct answer is (B).

VERBAL BIN 1

QUESTIONS

Questions 22–25 are based on the following passage:

Founded at the dawn of the modern industrial era, the nearly forgotten Women's Trade Union League (WTUL) played an instrumental role
Line in advancing the cause of working women
(5) throughout the early part of the twentieth century. In the face of considerable adversity, the WTUL made a contribution far greater than did most historical footnotes.

The organization's successes did not come
(10) easily; conflict beset the WTUL in many forms. During those early days of American unions, organized labor was aggressively opposed by both industry and government. The WTUL, which represented a largely unskilled labor force, had
(15) little leverage against these powerful opponents. Also, because of the skill level of its workers as well as inherent societal gender bias, the WTUL had great difficulty finding allies among other unions. Even the large and powerful American
(20) Federation of Labor (AFL), which nominally took the WTUL under its wing, kept it at a distance. Because the AFL's power stemmed from its highly skilled labor force, the organization saw little economic benefit in working with the WTUL. The
(25) affiliation provided the AFL with political cover, allowing it to claim support for women workers; in return, the WTUL gained a potent but largely absent ally.

The WTUL also had to overcome internal
(30) discord. While the majority of the group's members were working women, a sizeable and powerful minority consisted of middle- and upper-class social reformers whose goals extended beyond labor reform. While workers argued that
(35) the WTUL should focus its efforts on collective bargaining and working conditions, the reformers looked beyond the workplace, seeking state and national legislation aimed at education reform and urban poverty relief as well as workplace issues.
(40) Despite these obstacles, the WTUL accomplished a great deal. The organization was instrumental in the passage of state laws mandating an eight-hour workday, a minimum wage for women, and a ban on child labor. It
(45) provided seed money to women who organized workers in specific plants and industries, and it also established strike funds and soup kitchens to support striking unionists. After the tragic Triangle Shirtwaist Company fire of 1911, the
(50) WTUL launched a four-year investigation whose conclusions formed the basis of much subsequent

EXPLANATIONS

workplace safety legislation. The organization also offered a political base for all reform-minded women, and thus helped develop the next
(55) generation of American leaders. Eleanor Roosevelt was one of many prominent figures to emerge from the WTUL.

The organization began a slow death in the late 1920s, when the Great Depression choked
(60) off its funding. The organization limped through the 1940s; the death knell eventually rang in 1950, at the onset of the McCarthy era. A turn-of-the-century labor organization dedicated to social reform, one that during its heyday was regarded by
(65) many as "radical," stood little chance of weathering that storm. This humble ending, however, does nothing to diminish the accomplishments of an organization that is yet to receive its historical due.

22. The primary purpose of this passage is to

○ describe the barriers confronting women in the contemporary workplace

○ compare and contrast the methods of two labor unions of the early industrial era

○ critique the methods employed by an important labor union

○ rebuke historians for failing to cover the women's labor movement adequately

○ call readers' attention to an overlooked contributor to American history

22. E Use Process of Elimination. Choice (A) is incorrect because the passage is focused on a historical group, not contemporary conditions. Choice (B) is incorrect because the passage is only about one union. Choice (C) is incorrect because the author doesn't critique the union's methods. Choice (D) is close but highlights why (E) is correct. The author notes that the WTUL is *nearly forgotten* but doesn't criticize historians for not drawing attention to it. The passage serves to remind readers of the WTUL. The correct answer is (E).

23. Which of the following best characterizes the American Federation of Labor's view of the Women's Trade Union League, as it is presented in the passage?

○ The WTUL was an important component of the AFL's multifront assault on industry and its treatment of workers.

○ Because of Eleanor Roosevelt's affiliation with the organization, the WTUL was a vehicle through which the AFL could gain access to the White House.

○ The WTUL was to be avoided because the radical element within it attracted unwanted government scrutiny.

○ The WTUL offered the AFL some political capital but little that would assist it in labor negotiations.

○ The WTUL was weakened by its hesitance in pursuing widespread social reform beyond the workplace.

23. D The passage states that the AFL was a *potent but largely absent ally*, and that the AFL *saw little economic benefit in working with the WTUL*, which served as *political cover* for the AFL. This does not support (A), (B), (C), or (E). The correct answer is (D).

24. Each of the following is cited in the passage as an accomplishment of the Women's Trade Union League EXCEPT

- ⭘ it organized a highly skilled workforce to increase its bargaining power
- ⭘ it contributed to the development of a group of leaders in America
- ⭘ it provided essential support to striking women
- ⭘ it helped fund start-up unions for women
- ⭘ it contributed to the passage of important social and labor reform legislation

24. **A** Search the passage for each answer choice. Choice (B) is in lines 54–55. Choice (C) is in lines 47–48. Choice (D) is in lines 45–46. Choice (E) is in lines 42–44. Choice (A) is not supported by the passage because in line 14 it states that the WTUL *represented a largely unskilled labor force.* The correct answer is (A).

25. The passage suggests which of the following about the "middle- and upper-class social reformers" mentioned in lines 32–33 ?

- ⭘ They did not understand, nor were they sympathetic to, the plight of poor women workers.
- ⭘ Their naive interest in Communism was ultimately detrimental to the Women's Trade Union League.
- ⭘ It was because of their social and political power that the Women's Trade Union League was able to form an alliance with the American Federation of Labor.
- ⭘ They represented only an insignificant fraction of the leadership of Women's Trade Union League.
- ⭘ They sought to advance a broad political agenda of societal improvement.

25. **E** The passage states that these women were a *powerful minority* within the WTUL and that they were *looking beyond the workplace* to influence legislation. Choices (A), (B), (C), and (D) are not supported by the text in this part of the passage, whereas (E) matches the meaning of the passage. The correct answer is (E).

VERBAL BIN 2

QUESTIONS

1. As its performance has risen on all the stock indexes, the bio-tech start-up has branched out into new markets to look for opportunities <u>they would previously have had to ignore</u>.

   ○ they would previously have had to ignore

   ○ they would have had to ignore previously

   ○ that previously they would have had to ignore

   ○ it previously would have had to ignore in past years

   ○ it would previously have had to ignore

2. Scientists wishing to understand the kinetic movements of ancient dinosaurs are today studying the movements of modern day birds, which many scientists believe are descended from dinosaurs. A flaw in this strategy is that birds, although once genetically linked to dinosaurs, have evolved so far that any comparison is effectively meaningless.

   Which of the following, if true, would most weaken the criticism made above of the scientists' strategy?

   ○ Birds and dinosaurs have a number of important features in common that exist in no other living species.

   ○ Birds are separated from dinosaurs by 65 million years of evolution.

   ○ Our theories of dinosaur movements have recently undergone a radical reappraisal.

   ○ The study of kinetic movement is a relatively new discipline.

   ○ Many bird experts do not study dinosaurs to draw inferences about birds.

EXPLANATIONS

1. **E** If you go through your mental checklist, you will probably spot the pronoun *they*. To whom does that pronoun refer? Even though there are a lot of plural nouns in the front half of the sentence, *they* must refer to the start-up company, which is singular. Never mind that many people in spoken English refer to a large company as *they*. On the GMAT, a singular noun needs a singular pronoun. That eliminates (A), (B), and (C). To choose between (D) and (E), look for a new error. That's what you'll find in (D), which uses both the words *previously* and *in the past*, creating a redundancy error. The correct answer is (E).

2. **A** In this passage, the author is questioning an analogical argument. To understand the kinetic movement of dinosaurs, says the argument, we should study the kinetic movement of birds, which are a lot like dinosaurs. The author is trying to weaken this analogy by saying that dinosaurs and birds are actually not very similar. Your job is to weaken the author's attempt to demonstrate that the argument is flawed. How do you do that? By showing that dinosaurs and birds *are* in fact alike. Choice (B), if anything, actually strengthens the author's criticism of the analogy. Choices (C) and (D) are outside the scope of the argument. Choice (E) seems to strengthen the author's criticism of the analogy. It is also out of scope since the fact that some bird experts don't study dinosaurs doesn't mean that dinosaur experts shouldn't study birds. Choice (A) shows how birds and dinosaurs are alike. The correct answer is (A).

VERBAL BIN 2

QUESTIONS

3. A factory in China has two options to improve efficiency: adding robotic assembly lines and subcontracting out certain small production goals that could be done more efficiently elsewhere. Adding robotic assembly lines will improve efficiency more than subcontracting some small production goals. Therefore, by adding robotic assembly lines, the factory will be doing the most that can be done to improve efficiency.

Which of the following is an assumption on which the argument depends?

○ Adding robotic assembly lines will be more expensive than subcontracting some small production goals.
○ The factory has a choice of robotic assembly lines, some of which might be better suited to this factory than others.
○ The factory may or may not decide to choose either alternative.
○ Efficiency cannot be improved more by using both methods together than by adding robotic assembly lines alone.
○ This particular factory is already the third most efficient factory in China.

4. <u>Just as the early NASA space explorers attempted on each flight to push the frontiers of our knowledge, so too</u> are the new private-consortium space explorers seeking to add to man's general understanding of the cosmos.

○ Just as the early NASA space explorers attempted on each flight to push the frontiers of our knowledge, so too
○ The early NASA space explorers attempted on each flight to push the frontiers of our knowledge, and in the same way
○ Like the case of the early NASA space explorers who attempted on each flight to push the frontiers of our knowledge, so too
○ As in the early NASA space explorers' attempts on each flight to push the frontiers of our knowledge, so too
○ Similar to the early NASA space explorers attempted on each flight to push the frontiers of our knowledge, so too

EXPLANATIONS

3. **D** As always, if you don't immediately grasp the reasoning behind an argument, scope is key to eliminating wrong answers. For example, the expense of implementing these goals, (A), was never mentioned and thus is outside the scope of the argument. The same goes for (B): Choosing between different types of robotic assembly lines is not part of this argument. As for (C), the argument does not depend on whether the two actions being considered are ever actually implemented—again it is outside the scope. And, come to think of it, so is (E), which tells us that the factory is already quite efficient; the argument is about making it *more* efficient. By using POE, you have your answer. However, here's the logic: The conclusion of the argument is that choosing *one* of these two methods will result in the factory becoming the most efficient that it can be. What the argument is ignoring is the possibility that the factory could be even more efficient if it implemented *both* changes. The correct answer is (D).

4. **A** The idiom *just as...so too* is correct as written. Each of the other choices uses variations on an unidiomatic expression instead. The correct answer is (A).

VERBAL BIN 2

QUESTIONS

5. A proposal for a new building fire safety code requires that fire-retardant insulation no longer be sprayed on steel girders in the factory, but be sprayed on once the girders have arrived at the building site. This will eliminate the dislodging of the insulation in transit and reduce fatalities in catastrophic fires by an estimated 20%.

Which of the following, if true, represents the strongest challenge to the new proposal?

○ The fire-retardant insulation will also be required to be one inch thicker than in the past.
○ Studies have shown that most dislodgement of insulation occurs after the girders arrive on site.
○ Catastrophic fires represent only 4% of the fires reported nationally.
○ The proposed safety code will add considerably to the cost of new construction.
○ In most of Europe, spraying fire-retardant insulation onto steel girders at the building site has been required for the past ten years.

6. An effort <u>to control the crippling effects of poverty in Brazil's interior cities, begun almost thirty years ago,</u> has been partially successful, despite the setback of a major drought and the interruption of aid during an extended economic crisis.

○ to control the crippling effects of poverty in Brazil's interior cities, begun almost thirty years ago,
○ begun almost thirty years ago for controlling the crippling effects of poverty in Brazil's interior cities,
○ begun for controlling the crippling effects of poverty in Brazil's interior cities almost thirty years ago,
○ at controlling the crippling effects of poverty in Brazil's interior cities begun almost thirty years ago,
○ that has begun almost thirty years ago to control the crippling effects of poverty in Brazil's interior cities,

EXPLANATIONS

5. **B** The words *strongest challenge* in the question mean that you are trying to weaken the argument. Choice (A), if anything, appears to support the argument rather than weaken it, so you can eliminate it. Choices (C) and (D) do seem negative toward the argument, but both are outside the scope, as is (E). For (B), if the insulation comes loose *after* the girders arrive on site, then making an effort to prevent its dislodgement in transit to the building site will not have any effect and will not necessarily reduce fatalities. The correct answer is (B).

6. **A** This is an idiom question. Do you attempt *to* do something, do you attempt *at* something, or do you attempt *for* something? Choice (E) uses the idiom correctly but creates a new tense error. The correct answer is (A).

QUESTIONS

7. A newly discovered disease is thought to be caused by a certain bacterium. However, recently released data note that the bacterium thrives in the presence of a certain virus, implying that it is actually the virus that causes the new disease.

   Which of the following pieces of evidence would most support the data's implication?

   ◯ In the absence of the virus, the disease has been observed to follow infection by the bacterium.
   ◯ The virus has been shown to aid the growth of bacteria, a process which often leads to the onset of the disease.
   ◯ The virus alone has been observed in many cases of the disease.
   ◯ In cases where the disease does not develop, infection by the bacterium is usually preceded by infection by the virus.
   ◯ Onset of the disease usually follows infection by both the virus and the bacterium.

8. The company was not even publicly traded until 1968, when the owner and founder sold it to David P. Markham, a private investor, who took the company public and established a long and generous policy of stock options for valued employees.

   ◯ who took the company public and established a long and generous policy of stock options for
   ◯ who, taking the company public, established a long and generous policy of stock options to
   ◯ who, when he took the company public, established a long and generous policy of stock options to
   ◯ who had taken the company public, establishing a long and generous policy of stock options as
   ◯ taking the company public and establishing a long and generous policy of stock options for

EXPLANATIONS

7. **C** The last line of this argument gives away its type: *...the virus that causes...* The cause of a certain disease was thought to be one thing, but now is believed to be something else. Recent evidence suggests that the cause is a virus (which also nourishes the bacterium once thought to be the cause of the disease). To support a causal argument, you take away possible alternate causes. Choice (C) does this by showing that while both virus and bacterium are often present at the same time, the virus has been found *without* the bacterium in many cases of the disease. Choice (A) directly contradicts this, suggesting that the bacterium is the sole cause. Choices (B) and (E) suggest that the virus plays a supporting role to the bacterium. Choice (D) is outside the scope of the argument. The correct answer is (C).

8. **A** The second half of this sentence contains a correctly constructed parallel list. The private investor *took* and *established*, both verbs in the simple past. In (B) and (D), the construction is less than parallel. In addition, several choices also use the unidiomatic *established...for* as opposed to *established... to*. In (E), the construction is parallel, but it now seems to modify *the owner and founder* rather than *Markham*. The correct answer is (A).

VERBAL BIN 2

QUESTIONS

9. Because of a quality control problem, a supplier of flu vaccines will not be able to ship any supplies of the vaccine for the upcoming flu season. This will create a shortage of flu vaccines and result in a loss of productivity as workers call in sick.

Which of the following, if true, most seriously weakens the argument above?

- ◯ The quality control problem of the supplier is not as severe as some experts had initially predicted.
- ◯ Other suppliers of flu vaccine have not been affected by the quality control problem.
- ◯ Last year there was also a shortage of flu vaccine available.
- ◯ The price of flu vaccines is expected to fall in the next ten years.
- ◯ The flu season is expected to last longer than usual this year.

EXPLANATIONS

9. **B** You might have been tempted by (A), which seems to weaken the argument by saying the quality control problem of the supplier is not as severe as experts had predicted. However, the initial predictions of experts are outside the scope of the argument, because they don't change the fact that this supplier will not be supplying any vaccines, regardless of how minor the problems might be. Similarly, what happened last year, (C), or what will happen in the next 10 years, (D), is also outside the scope of the argument; we want to know what will happen *this* year. Choice (E) seems to strengthen the argument since a longer flu season will presumably result in more people getting sick. For (B), if other suppliers have not been affected by quality control problems, then the overall shortage may be less severe. The correct answer is (B).

VERBAL BIN 2

QUESTIONS

10. Never before had the navy defeated <u>so many foes at once as it had in</u> the battle of Trafalgar in 1805.

○ so many foes at once as it had in
○ at once as many foes as
○ at once as many foes that there were in
○ as many foes at once as it did in
○ so many foes at once as that it defeated in

11. The changes that may be part of a general global warming trend include an increase in the frequency and severity of hurricanes, a gradual rise in sea level, <u>depleting the ozone layer, and raising the temperature of the earth</u>.

○ depleting the ozone layer, and raising the temperature of the earth
○ depleting the ozone layer, and a rise in the earth's temperature
○ a depletion of the ozone layer, and raising the earth's temperature
○ a depletion of the ozone layer, and a raise of the temperature of the earth
○ a depletion of the ozone layer, and a rise in the temperature of the earth

EXPLANATIONS

10. **D** This question is a swirling mixture of idiom and parallel comparison. The correct idiom in question: *as many…as*. When you say it out loud, does *so many…as* seem right? Of course, it's much easier to notice that it doesn't when the expression has already been pulled out of the problem for you. During the GMAT, you have to do your own pulling, but remember, you always have five sensational clues: the answer choices. Even if you initially have no idea what might or might not be wrong with this sentence, you can figure it out by scanning the answers; you'll see that you have a collection of *so many as*'s and *as many as*'s to choose from.

The other thing going on in this sentence, of course, is parallel comparison. Words such as *as* or *than* often mean a comparison is being made. The correct comparison would read: "Never before had a navy defeated as many foes at once as it *defeated*…," but as you know from reading our chapter on Sentence Correction, the test writers like to see if you know that you can replace the second verb with a replacement verb: *did*. The correct answer is (D).

11. **E** This sentence has what should be a parallel list of nouns, beginning with *an increase* and *a rise*, but then the last two items on the list are suddenly verb-like things: *depleting* and *raising*. Since it is the last two items that are underlined, these are the items that must change. Choices (A), (B), and (C) all have verb-like things in them. Choice (D), with two noun-like things, seems tempting at first, but do you say *a raise of the temperature*? Nope, it's unidiomatic. The correct answer is (E).

<u>Questions 12–16</u> are based on the following passage:

It has long been a tenet of business theory that the best decisions are made after careful review and consideration. Only after weighing all the options and studying projections, say most
(5) professors of business, can a practical decision be made.

Now, that model is being questioned by some business thinkers in the light of the theories of Malcolm Gladwell, who states that human beings
(10) often make better decisions in the blink of an eye.

It is, at first glance, a theory so counter-intuitive as to seem almost ludicrous. Behind any decision, Gladwell posits, there is a behind-the-scenes subconscious process in which the brain
(15) analyzes; ranks in order of importance; compares and contrasts vast amounts of information; and dismisses extraneous factors, seemingly almost instantaneously, often arriving at a conclusion in less than two seconds. Citing a multitude of
(20) studies and examples from life, Gladwell shows how that split-second decision is often better informed than a drawn-out examination.

Evanston and Cramer were the first to apply this theory to the business world. Evanston
(25) videotaped the job interviews of 400 applicants at different firms. He then played only 10 seconds of each videotape to independent human resources specialists. The specialists were able to pick out the applicants who were hired with an accuracy of
(30) over 90%.

Cramer took the experiment even further, using only five seconds of videotape, without sound. To his astonishment, the rate of accuracy with which the HR specialists were able to predict the
(35) successful applicants fell only to 82%.

Critics argue that these results illustrate a problem with stereotyping that impedes human resources specialists from hiring the best candidates even when they have the time to
(40) get below the surface: going for the candidate who "looks the part." Gladwell argues that, on the contrary, the human mind is able to make complicated decisions quickly and that intuition often trumps an extended decision-making
(45) process.

VERBAL BIN 2

QUESTIONS

12. The primary purpose of the passage is to

  ○ discuss reasons an accepted business theory is being reexamined
  ○ present evidence that resolves a contradiction in business theory
  ○ describe a tenet of business practices and how that tenet can be tested in today's economic environment
  ○ argue that a counter-intuitive new business idea is, in the final analysis, incorrect
  ○ present evidence that invalidates a new business model

13. According to the passage, all of the following are examples of the subconscious processes by which the brain makes a decision EXCEPT

  ○ analysis of information
  ○ ranking of information
  ○ comparison and contrast of information
  ○ rejecting information that is not pertinent
  ○ consulting a multitude of studies and examples

14. The author's attitude toward the long-held view that decisions should be made carefully over time expressed in lines 1–5 can best be described as

  ○ dismissive and scornful
  ○ respectful but questioning
  ○ admiring and deferential
  ○ uncertain but optimistic
  ○ condescending and impatient

EXPLANATIONS

12. **A** In this passage, the accepted practice of making thoughtful business decisions based on careful review is being questioned in light of a new theory. Both (D) and (E) imply that the author has rejected this new model. Choice (C) uses a catchy word from the passage (*tenet*) and fails to indicate that there is a new idea that goes against that tenet. Choice (B) implies that the contradiction between the theory of making decisions based on careful review and the theory of making split-second decisions has in fact been resolved. The correct answer is (A).

13. **E** Where do you find the key words *subconscious process*? In the third paragraph. Choices (A), (B), (C), and (D) are all paraphrases of examples of the processes cited in that paragraph. Only (E) is not. In fact, the multitude of studies and examples are cited in support of Gladwell's hypothesis. The correct answer is (E).

14. **B** Both (A) and (E) are too extreme to be the correct answer on the GMAT. But clearly, the new theory being described is an attempt to go beyond the conventional wisdom. The correct answer is (B).

QUESTIONS

15. The author most likely mentions the results of Cramer's extension of Evanston's experiment in order to

   ○ show that Cramer's hypothesis was correct, while Evanston's hypothesis turned out to be incorrect
   ○ show that Evanston's hypothesis was correct, while Cramer's hypothesis turned out to be incorrect
   ○ demonstrate that while both experiments were scientifically rigorous, neither ended up being scientifically valid
   ○ illustrate that the principle of subconscious decisions continues to work even when less information is available
   ○ demonstrate that Cramer's experiment was 8% more accurate than Evanston's, even though his subjects had less information to work with

16. It can be inferred that the critics referred to in line 36 believed the results of the two experiments had less to do with the innate decision-making of the subjects than with

   ○ the excellent decision-making of Evanston and Cramer
   ○ the expertise of Malcolm Gladwell, who originated the theory
   ○ not choosing candidates who "looked the part"
   ○ the use of videotape as a method of choosing candidates
   ○ their unconscious use of visual stereotypes in making their selections

EXPLANATIONS

15. **D** The information about Cramer's *extension* is in lines 31–35. Choices (A) and (B) are incorrect because the passage doesn't mention what the researchers' hypotheses were. Choice (C) is incorrect because the author doesn't say their work was invalid. Choice (D) in supported by the passage because Cramer found that with even less information the specialists were still highly successful at predicting. Choice (E) is incorrect; in Cramer's study the participants did somewhat worse with less information, not better. The correct answer is (D).

16. **E** The passage states that the critics believe that HR specialists prefer someone *who looks the part* and that is the reason successful candidates can be predicted from brief observations. This supports (E) because [looking] *the part* is the same as *visual stereotypes*. Watch out for trap answer (C), which is a reversal. The correct answer is (E).

17. The women's volleyball team at a local college finished fifth in its division, prompting the college to fire the team's general manager. The manager responded by suing the college, saying that the team's performance put it among the top teams in the country.

Which of the following statements, if true, would support the claim of the team's manager, and resolve the apparent contradiction?

○ The team won all of its "away" games during the season in question.
○ Attendance at the volleyball team's games was up 35% from the year before.
○ Of the starting team, three team members were unable to play for at least half the season because of injuries.
○ There are 80 teams in this particular volleyball team's division.
○ The team lost more games this year than it did the year before.

18. Country A recently broke off diplomatic relations with Country B when it was reported that Country B had been running a covert intelligence operation within the borders of Country A. While a spokesperson for Country B admitted the charge, the spokesperson said that it was common knowledge that all countries do this, and that Country A was no exception.

Which of the following inferences can be drawn from the argument above?

○ Country B should apologize and dismantle its intelligence operation in Country A.
○ The spokesperson for Country B claims that Country A engages in intelligence gathering too.
○ Because all countries engage in this practice, Country A's outrage was disingenuous.
○ Relations between Country A and Country B will be strained for some time.
○ Country B would be just as outraged if it was reported that Country A was running a covert intelligence operation with Country B's borders.

17. **D** The manager was apparently fired because of his team's end-of-season statistics. If this made you wonder if the statistics were actually representative, your thinking was right on the money. To support the manager's claim, we have to show that the team's fifth-place finish was actually better than it looked. Choices (A), (B), and (C), while generally positive about the team (and by extension, perhaps, its manager), are outside the scope of the argument. Choice (E) actually puts the team's performance in a more negative light. On the other hand, (D) puts the team's fifth-place finish in a very positive perspective: If the division was made up of 80 teams, finishing in fifth place is actually extremely good. The correct answer is (D).

18. **B** All of the answers to this inference question infer way too much to be the correct answer to a GMAT question—except for (B), which simply restates a sentence from the argument itself. Choice (A) says an apology is needed, which is way beyond the scope of this argument. Choice (C) goes further than the argument to make a value judgment. Choice (D) looks into the future, and (E) takes a "what if" position and builds on it. The correct answer is (B).

QUESTIONS

EXPLANATIONS

19. Because cellular telephones emit signals that can interfere with cockpit-to-control-tower transmissions, airplane passengers' use of these instruments <u>at all times that the airplane is in motion, even while on the ground, are</u> prohibited.

   ○ at all times that the airplane is in motion, even while on the ground, are

   ○ at all times during which the airplane, even while on the ground, is in motion, are

   ○ during airplane motion, even when it is on the ground, are

   ○ during times of the airplane being in motion, even on the ground, is

   ○ when the airplane is in motion, even while on the ground, is

19. **E** The subject of this sentence, *use*, is singular. Therefore, (A), (B), and (C) are incorrect; each states that *the passengers' use of these instruments… are prohibited*. Choice (D) is unidiomatic, and the phrase *even on the ground* is unnecessarily vague. Choice (E) is concise, clear, and employs the correct verb. The correct answer is (E).

20. In contrast to classical guitars, whose owners prefer the dulcet, rounded tones produced by nylon strings, <u>folk guitar owners prefer the bright and brassy sound</u> that only bronze or steel can create.

   ○ folk guitar owners prefer the bright and brassy sound

   ○ folk guitar owners prefer to get a sound that is bright and brassy

   ○ with a folk guitar, the owner gets the preferably bright and brassy sound

   ○ folk guitars produce a bright and brassy sound, which their owners prefer,

   ○ folk guitars produce a preferred bright and brassy sound for their owners

20. **D** Choices (A), (B), and (C) include a parallel comparison error; (A) and (B) compare *classical guitars* and *folk guitar owners*, while (C) compares a plural (*classical guitars*) and a singular (*a folk guitar*) noun. Choice (E) incorrectly suggests that the *bright and brassy* sound is universally preferred rather than preferred specifically by folk guitar owners. Furthermore, the placement of *for their owners* is unnecessarily confusing, as it separates two elements of the sentence that should be closely connected (*bright and brassy sound…that only bronze and steel can create*). Choice (D) corrects this error by setting the interceding phrase off with commas. The correct answer is (D).

Questions 21–22 are based on the following passage:

A system-wide county school anti-smoking education program was instituted last year. The program was clearly a success. Last year, the incidence of students smoking on school premises decreased by over 70 percent.

21. Which of the following assumptions underlies the argument in the passage?

○ Cigarettes are detrimental to one's health; once people understand this, they will quit smoking.

○ The doubling of the price of a pack of cigarettes last year was not the only cause of the students' altered smoking habits.

○ The teachers chosen to lead the anti-smoking education program were the most effective teachers in the school system.

○ The number of cigarettes smoked each day by those students who continued to smoke last year did not greatly increase.

○ School policy enforcers were less vigilant in seeking out smokers last year than they were in previous years.

21. **B** The argument presented is a causal argument. The significant underlying assumption of the argument, therefore, relates to the causal link between the anti-smoking education program and the reduction in smoking on school premises. The argument assumes that the program, and not some other set of circumstances, caused the reduction. It thus assumes that other possible causes—such as an increase in the price of cigarettes—were not substantial contributors to this result.

Process of Elimination is effective on this question, as it is on all Critical Reasoning questions. Because the argument hinges on one crucial piece of evidence—a decrease in the incidence of smoking on school premises—you can eliminate all answers that do not speak directly to that reduction. Thus, you can eliminate (A), (C), and (D). Choice (E), if true, would weaken the argument and therefore cannot be correct. The correct answer is (B).

VERBAL BIN 2

QUESTIONS	EXPLANATIONS

22. Which of the following, if true, would most seriously weaken the argument in the passage?

- ○ The author of this statement is a school system official hoping to generate good publicity for the anti-smoking program.
- ○ Most students who smoke stopped smoking on school premises last year continued to smoke when away from school.
- ○ Last year, another policy change made it much easier for students to leave and return to school grounds during the school day.
- ○ The school system spent more on anti-smoking education programs last year than it did in all previous years.
- ○ The amount of time students spent in anti-smoking education programs last year resulted in a reduction of in-class hours devoted to academic subjects.

22. C Once again, your focus should be on the evidence supporting the causal link between the anti-smoking education program and the reduction in smoking on school premises. What, other than the effectiveness of the program, would explain the reduced incidence of smoking on school premises? Choice (C) provides a possible alternate explanation: School policy made it easier for students to leave and return to campus. It is therefore possible, then, that the reduction in smoking on school premises was simply the result of students leaving school premises to smoke, then returning afterward.

Choice (B), while tempting, does not provide an alternate cause for the observed result. None of the other answers address the evidence supporting the conclusion of the passage; therefore, none of them truly weaken the argument. The correct answer is (C).

23. Mild exercise throughout pregnancy <u>may reduce the discomfort associated with pregnancy and result in</u> a speedier, easier birth, according to a recent study.

- ○ may reduce the discomfort associated with pregnancy and result in
- ○ may reduce the discomfort associated with pregnancy, with the result
- ○ may cause a reduction in the discomfort associated with pregnancy and as a result
- ○ might lead to a reduction in the discomfort associated with pregnancy and as a result
- ○ might reduce the discomfort associated with pregnancy and resulting in

23. A The sentence, as written, maintains correct parallel construction between *reduce the discomfort…* and *result in a speedier….* Each of the incorrect answers violates the rule of parallel construction. The correct answer is (A).

Questions 24–27 are based on the following passage:

What is it that keeps the developing world in an apparent state of perpetual poverty? Poor education, lack of basic medical care, and the
(Line) absence of democratic structures all certainly
(5) contribute to these nations' plight. However, according to Peruvian economist Hernando de Soto, the overriding cause is the overwhelming prevalence of black market activity, well outside the formal economy, in these countries. The losses
(10) incurred from this condition are twofold. First, they deny the government tax revenues which could be used to improve education, medical treatment, and government efficiency. More important, however, they deny earners the chance to accumulate assets
(15) recognized by law and thus prevent them from leveraging those assets to borrow. Reforming these nations' legal systems in order to confer ownership through titling, de Soto argues, would help the poor there access the assets their work
(20) should be generating. These assets could then be used to buy homes and construct businesses, thus building a more stable and prosperous economy. De Soto estimates the value of these assets, which he terms "dead capital," at nearly $10 trillion
(25) worldwide.

De Soto is not the first to locate the developing world's problems in the domain of property rights. Others have tried property rights reform and failed. According to de Soto, this is because
(30) his predecessors attempted to model their plans on existing, successful property rights systems. In other words, they tried to transplant American and British property law to an inhospitable host. De Soto argues that, within many of the extralegal
(35) markets of the developing world, mutually agreed upon rules for distributing assets and recognizing property rights already exist. Rather than force these markets to adjust to a new, foreign system of property titling, reformers should focus on
(40) codifying the existing systems wherever it is practical to do so. This would facilitate a quicker, more natural transition to an economy that builds wealth rather than squanders it.

QUESTIONS	EXPLANATIONS

24. The author's primary goal in the passage is to

- ◯ compare several failed attempts to address a problem
- ◯ respond to criticism of a new theory
- ◯ identify the problems inherent in a new economic theory
- ◯ describe a novel approach to an old problem
- ◯ compare different property rights systems in the industrial world

24. D Use POE. The author briefly mentions failed attempts, but it's not the main point of the passage, so (A) is incorrect. Choices (B) and (C) are incorrect because the author doesn't mention any criticisms or problems with the new theory. Choice (D) is supported by the passage because the author says that poverty is a *perpetual* problem and that de Soto's approach is different, or *novel*. Choice (E) is incorrect because while it is briefly mentioned, it's not the main point of the passage. The correct answer is (D).

25. According to the passage, de Soto believes that the quickest way to address poverty in the developing world is to

- ◯ increase funding for education
- ◯ build the infrastructure to support lending
- ◯ ensure medical care for all citizens
- ◯ aggressively root out corruption in government
- ◯ increase tax rates on all citizens in developing countries

25. B The passage states that de Soto feels it's a problem that the poor are prevented from borrowing (lines 15–16) and that by *reforming…legal systems…to confer ownership through titling* (16–20) the poverty would decrease. This supports (B). Some of the other answer choices are mentioned as problems in the developing world, but they aren't attributed to de Soto. The correct answer is (B).

26. The author's assertion that "reformers should focus on codifying the existing systems wherever it is practical to do so" (lines 39–41) suggests that

   ◯ in some instances, current systems are inadequate to meet the needs of a market economy
   ◯ these systems are already written down and need only be enacted as law
   ◯ where it is impractical to codify existing systems, countries should adopt American property law
   ◯ the existing systems are superior to those currently in use in modern industrialized countries
   ◯ improving education and medical care in these countries should take priority over reforming property laws

26. **A** The passage indicates that many of the black markets are already systems but aren't written into law. Choice (A) is supported by the quotation because it states *wherever possible*, so there may be some places that do not have sufficient systems to make into law. Choice (B) is a reversal—the passage states that the systems are not written. Choice (C) is incorrect because the author states that as a strategy *failed*. Eliminate (D) because the author makes no such comparison to those in industrialized countries. Choice (E) is the opposite of what is stated in the passage. The correct answer is (A).

27. The term "dead capital" (line 24) refers to

   ◯ loans that are never repaid
   ◯ failed investments in new businesses
   ◯ cities ruined by over-industrialization
   ◯ the proceeds of extralegal commerce
   ◯ property passed from generation to generation

27. **D** The passage refers *dead capital* back to these assets which ultimately are *the assets* [the poor's] *work should be generating*. The poor use black markets and thus do not receive the assets they would if their work were legal. This supports (D) because *extralegal* means outside of the law. The correct answer is (D).

VERBAL BIN 3

1. Unlike <u>Franklin D. Roosevelt's bootstrap program that helped</u> to restart economic growth in the 1930s through public works, Ronald Reagan proposed a program of trickle-down economics to restart the economy.

○ Franklin D. Roosevelt's bootstrap program that helped
○ Franklin D. Roosevelt and his bootstrap program which helped
○ Franklin D. Roosevelt, whose bootstrap program helped
○ the bootstrap program of Franklin D. Roosevelt that has helped
○ Franklin D. Roosevelt and his bootstrap program helping

1. **C** Part of what normally makes misplaced modifiers easy to spot is that the test writers generally ask you to fix the second phrase; this time, you have to fix the first phrase. The modifying phrase *Unlike FDR's bootstrap program* is supposed to modify the noun *Ronald Reagan*, which, of course, is not possible. You can't directly compare a program to a person. We could fix the second half of the sentence (*unlike FDR's program... Reagan's program...*), but since the second half of the sentence isn't underlined, we'll have to fix the first half. Choices (B) and (E) still directly compare FDR's program to Ronald Reagan. So does (D). Only (C) avoids the modifier error by directly comparing FDR to Reagan. The correct answer is (C).

2. In the 1970s, it became evident <u>that writing about someone else's research was much easier for social scientists who wanted to make a quick name for themselves</u> than it was to do their own research.

○ that writing about someone else's research was much easier for social scientists who wanted to make a quick name for themselves
○ that for social scientists who wanted to make a quick name for themselves, it was much easier to write about someone else's research
○ that for social scientists wanting to make a quick name for themselves, writing about someone else's research was much easier
○ for social scientists who wanted to make a quick name for themselves that writing about someone else's research was much easier
○ for social scientists who wanted to make a quick name for themselves, writing about someone else's research was much easier

2. **B** The problem in the stem sentence is that there are two actions that ought to be parallel but are not. *Writing* (about someone else's research) was easier than *to do* the research themselves. You could fix this two ways in the real world: *Writing* was easier than *doing*, or it was easier *to write* than *to do*. Each of the other answer choices mixes and matches these two ways incorrectly, except for (B). Putting the phrase *for social scientists* first, as (D) and (E) do, would not necessarily be wrong if the verbs were parallel. Choices (D) and (E) also do not have the idiom *evident that*. The correct answer is (B).

QUESTIONS

<u>Questions 3–4</u> are based on the following passage:

To improve the town's overcrowded school system, the town council has proposed an ambitious education plan to reduce classroom size and make capital improvements—a plan they intend to pay for with an increase in property taxes for homes valued over $500,000. Although the school system desperately needs improving, the town council's plan should be defeated because the majority of the people who would end up paying for the improvements receive no benefit from them.

3. Which of the following, if true, most strengthens the argument above?

- The town's school system is currently ranked among the worst in the state.
- Other towns nearby that have made similar capital improvements did not find that the improvements translated to a better quality of education.
- The town will need to spend additional money on an architect's plans for the capital improvements.
- An examination of the tax rolls shows that most homeowners in this category no longer have school-age children.
- Some homeowners will delay home improvement projects in order to keep the value of their homes below $500,000.

3. **D** The author is arguing to nix the plan to improve the schools. We want to strengthen his argument, but before we do, there is usually at least one answer choice that actually weakens the argument. It is helpful to get rid of these first, since they are usually easier to spot. In this case, (A) gives a compelling reason to *improve* the school system; eliminate it. Now, the reason the author gives for defeating the plan is that the people who pay for it will not benefit. To strengthen this argument, we need to show why this would be true. Choice (B) is against the school improvements, but for a different reason: in other towns, similar improvements didn't increase the quality of education. While important in the real world, this is slightly outside the scope of this argument. Choice (C) provides another possible negative of the plan, but again it doesn't show why the people who pay for it will not benefit. Choice (E) implies that taxpayers will delay their own capital improvements to avoid paying for the schools' capital improvements, but again this doesn't strengthen the author's particular argument— that the plan should be defeated because the people who must pay for it do not benefit. Choice (D) explains how this could be true: Most of the people slotted to pay for the school improvements don't even have school-age children. The correct answer is (D).

QUESTIONS

4. Which of the following, if true, provides the town council with the strongest counter to the objection that its plan is unfair?

- ○ Even with the proposed increase, property taxes in the town are well below the national average.
- ○ Paying for the school system improvements using existing town funds will result in shortfalls that will force the town into arrears.
- ○ The teachers in the town's school system receive some of the lowest salary packages in the immediate area, which is a major cause of attrition.
- ○ Smaller class sizes and capital improvements in a school system tend to increase property values in the surrounding community.
- ○ A feasibility study has shown that the cost of the improvements will likely be 20% higher than projected.

5. The rules of engagement under which a border patrol station can decide to use deadly force <u>includes responding to an invasionary incursion and the return of</u> hostile fire.

- ○ includes responding to an invasionary incursion and the return of
- ○ includes responding to an invasionary incursion and returning
- ○ include responding to an invasionary incursion and the return of
- ○ include a response to an invasionary incursion and the return of
- ○ include a response to an invasionary incursion and returning

EXPLANATIONS

4. **D** The author says the plan is unfair to the people who must pay for it. How do we counter that? By showing that they actually do receive a benefit. Before we weaken the author's argument, let's eliminate any answers that strengthen it. In this case, that means only (E). Now, (A) points out that property taxes would still be quite low even after the increase, but that doesn't mean the increase is fair. Choice (B) tells us why an alternate way to finance the improvements won't work, but it doesn't address the fairness of the way being discussed. Choice (C) tells us why the funds are urgently needed, but again doesn't show that the people who have to supply the funds actually would receive a benefit. Choice (D) finally gives us a reason the property tax increase might actually benefit those who pay for it: Good schools translates to higher property values. The correct answer is (D).

5. **D** As you know, GMAT test writers like to put as many words between the subject and the verb of a sentence as they can, in hopes that you will forget to check for agreement. The subject of this sentence was the plural *rules*. The verb was the singular *includes*. This eliminates (A) and (B). Choices (C) and (E) are not parallel because they mix verb-like forms with noun-like forms. The correct answer is (D).

VERBAL BIN 3

| QUESTIONS | EXPLANATIONS |

6. Although the word "phonetician" is popularly associated with Henry Higgins's task of improving the diction of Eliza Dolittle in *My Fair Lady*, in linguistics, <u>it is someone who studies</u> the formation of language.

  ○ it is someone who studies
  ○ it is a person studying
  ○ it refers to someone who studies
  ○ they are people who study
  ○ it is in reference to people who study

6. **C** The question here is: To what does the pronoun *it* refer? You might think it refers to *phonetician*, (in which case you might have thought the sentence was fine the way it was), but in fact it refers to *the word*. Choices (A), (B), and (D) could give the impression that *the word* is a person or persons. Choice (E) is awkward, and, like (D), needlessly uses the plural *people*. The correct answer is (C).

7. Experts studying patterns of shark attacks on humans have noted that attacks tend to diminish when the water temperature drops below 65 degrees Fahrenheit. Until recently, researchers believed this was because sharks prefer warmer water, and thus are present in fewer numbers in colder water. However, new research shows that sharks are present in equal numbers in cold and warm water.

Which of the following, if true, best explains the apparent paradox?

  ○ In general, humans prefer warm water.
  ○ Sharks' keen sense of smell is enhanced in cold water.
  ○ In the Pacific, shark attacks tend to occur more frequently in the daytime.
  ○ Of the more than 200 types of sharks present in the ocean, only three attack humans.
  ○ The average temperature of the earth's oceans is 55 degrees.

7. **A** We tend to try to explain shark attacks by thinking about the *shark's* behavior. But (A) points out that it takes two to tango. A shark attack requires one shark and one human to be attacked. One reason there might be fewer shark attacks on humans in cold water is that there are fewer humans swimming in cold water in the first place. If you were looking at (B) and saying, "Hmm, if a sharks' olfactory powers were enhanced by cold water, then presumably he'd be better at attacking," or if you were thinking that if his olfactory powers were enhanced he would know enough *not* to attack a human, then either way, you were having to think way too hard for this to be inside the scope. Choice (C) is outside the scope, too, since it is dealing with only one ocean and does not address temperature at all. Choice (D) provides extraneous information, and (E) does not help to explain the apparent paradox. The correct answer is (A).

8. As a result of surging economic indicators, most analysts upgraded the company's stock to a strong "buy," ignoring the advice of the head of a watchdog organization <u>who warned that the company's product would prove not only dangerous but</u> ineffective in the long run.

- ○ who warned that the company's product would prove not only dangerous but
- ○ warning that the company's product would prove not only dangerous and also
- ○ warning that the company's product would prove itself to be both dangerous and
- ○ who warned that the company's product would prove to be both dangerous and
- ○ who was warning that the company's product would prove not only dangerous but

8. **D** The sentence, as written, needs a *but also* to complement its *not only*. Choices (A) and (E) bite the dust. In (B), the same idiom comes into play, but this choice has bigger problems: Without the *who warned*, it is no longer clear who is doing the warning. Choice (C) can be eliminated for the same reason. The correct answer is (D).

QUESTIONS

9. MoviesNow! streaming service is projected to buy more licenses to stream more movies in the next 5 years than in any previous 5-year window. This is because MoviesNow!'s board of directors has encouraged the pursuit of subscribers who are parents of children under the age of 12 and the current selection of movies to stream in the MoviesNow! database is targeted at subscribers ages 18–35.

Which of the following, if true, would most strengthen the argument from MoviesNow!'s board of directors that they should pursue subscribers who are parents of children under the age of 12 ?

○ The board monitors the demographic targets of large advertising companies and chooses target audiences for their streaming service based off those trends.
○ A population study conducted by an independent research group has uncovered a large uptick in the number of parents who are raising children under the age of 12.
○ People aged 18–35 generally have less disposable income than other age demographics.
○ The licensing agreement MoviesNow! has with the largest movie production company is set to expire within the next 5 years.
○ The board of MoviesNow! is comprised of parents of children under the age of 12.

EXPLANATIONS

9. **B** This is a strengthen problem, as evidenced by the question asking which answer choice *would most strengthen the argument*. This argument uses a planning pattern, as evidenced by the presence of the plan of *MovieNow!'s board of directors*. The assumption of a planning reasoning pattern is that there are no problems with the plan. In this case, the assumption is that there are no problems with the plan to pursue *subscribers who are parents of children under the age of 12*. Because this is a strengthen question, the correct answer will provide information that makes the plan stronger, or removes a potential objection to the plan. Evaluate the answer choices individually. Choice (A) introduces *large advertising companies* and states that *the board monitors the demographic targets* of those companies to help *choose target audiences for their streaming service*. This choice is out of scope because it is not possible to know that the demographic targets of large advertising companies are the same demographics that the board of MoviesNow! is interested in pursuing. Eliminate (A). Choice (B) mentions a *population study conducted by an independent research group* that *uncovered a large uptick* in the demographic that the board of directors wants to pursue. If this information is true, then this is a good justification for the plan. Keep (B). Choice (C) mentions *people aged 18–35,* which is out of the scope of the question. Eliminate (C). Choice (D) mentions the *licensing agreement MoviesNow! has with the largest movie production company,* which is out of scope, so eliminate (D). Choice (E) could potentially weaken the argument, as if the board of directors is making choices based off their own demographic information and biases, then that is an alternate cause for the recommendation. Eliminate (E). The correct answer is (B).

QUESTIONS

10. A new influx of unprecedented private investment should create a bright new future for manned space exploration, <u>making the possibility of commercial space tourism much more viable than 10 years ago</u>.

   ○ making the possibility of commercial space tourism much more viable than 10 years ago

   ○ and make the possibility of commercial space tourism much more viable than 10 years ago

   ○ making the possibility of commercial space tourism much more viable than it was 10 years ago

   ○ and make the possibility of commercial space tourism much more viable than it was 10 years in the past

   ○ making the possibility of commercial space tourism much more viable than 10 years in the past

EXPLANATIONS

10. **C** The key word here is *than*—and if you spotted it, you knew to look for a parallel comparison problem. Two actions are being compared in this sentence, so we need the words "it was" after *than* to make that clear. If you spotted this error, you could eliminate (A), (B), and (E). Choice (D) might seem possible (and parallel in a different kind of way) until you get to the last words: *10 years in the past*. This is just not the same as *ago*. The correct answer is (C).

Questions 11–15 are based on the following passage:

As the American workforce gets grayer, age discrimination will likely become a more prominent issue in the courts. It is, of course, illegal to
Line discriminate against an employee because of his or
(5) her age, and yet it is not illegal to dismiss a worker because he has a high salary and expensive health care.

This apparent contradiction is at the heart of a raft of cases now making their way through the
(10) courts. The outcome of these cases will have broad implications for the workplace in the coming years. By 2020, the Bureau of Labor Statistics has projected that more than half of all workers will be over 40—many of whom, by dint of seniority and
(15) promotions, will be earning higher than median salaries, eligible for more stock options, and carrying higher health care costs as a result of a larger number of dependents and the increased cost of health care for older workers.
(20)   Is it any wonder that a bottom-line oriented business might want to shed these workers, whose productivity is likely to plummet in the next few years, even as they become more expensive employees?
(25)   Still, the legal challenges of implementing this policy are daunting. Businesses have the right to rate workers on their productivity and to rank them against their peers. But they are not allowed to prejudge individuals based on their sex, race, or
(30) age. Each worker must be treated on his or her own merits, rather than by how they fit into a larger profile of the group they belong to.

For companies looking to lay off these workers, the cost of making a mistake is high; while only
(35) one in three age discrimination suits are won by the plaintiff, the awards tend to be steep and the political fall-out harsh.

11. The primary purpose of the passage is to

   ○ advocate on behalf of the older American worker who could soon face dismissal
   ○ describe the origin of two theories of labor law and their effects on the workplace
   ○ present an overview of the legal ramifications of a practice some call discriminatory
   ○ describe the process by which America's workforce is getting older
   ○ describe the methods by which a company could reduce its bottom line

11. **C** Use POE. Choice (A) is incorrect because the passage describes a problem but doesn't *advocate*. Choice (B) is incorrect because the passage doesn't describe the origins of the ideas. Choice (C) is supported because the author maintains focus on the legal issues and states that some feel the practice is discriminatory. Choice (D) is incorrect because the passage isn't just about how people get older. Choice (E) is incorrect because it isn't the main focus of the passage. The correct answer is (C).

QUESTIONS

EXPLANATIONS

12. Which of the following best describes the organization of the second paragraph of the passage?

○ An assertion is made and then briefly contradicted.

○ A contradiction is stated and then quickly resolved.

○ A new theory is described and then qualified.

○ An apparent inconsistency is stated and its consequences outlined.

○ A conventional model is described and an alternative is introduced.

12. **D** The contradiction highlighted at the beginning of the second paragraph is not resolved or qualified; it is stated, and then its ramifications are outlined. The correct answer is (D).

13. Which of the following, if true, would most effectively weaken the author's assertion that a "bottom-line oriented business" might want to lay off older workers?

○ A new study shows that, on average, younger workers earn less and have lower associated medical costs than older workers.

○ Older workers have a higher rate of absenteeism than younger workers.

○ A new study shows that older workers are in fact more productive and have fewer medical expenses compared to younger workers.

○ A forecasted downturn in the economy will erode profits in may American businesses.

○ A new bill scheduled to become law will make it easier for employers to employ illegal aliens.

13. **C** To weaken the assertion that it might be in the interest of employers to lay off older people, it is necessary to show why employing older people would be good for companies. Choice (C) is the only answer that does so, suggesting that older employees are actually more productive and have fewer health care costs. The correct answer is (C).

VERBAL BIN 3

QUESTIONS

14. It can be inferred from the passage regarding the relationship between American companies and older Americans that

○ what is good for American companies is not necessarily good for older Americans

○ American companies are prohibited by law from practices that discriminate based on age

○ large monetary judgments from age discrimination suits might prove more expensive than paying older employees' salaries

○ by the year 2030, the percentage of older employees will be even higher than in the year 2020

○ some older employees may well be more productive than some younger employees

15. The author mentions all of the following as driving up the cost to employers for employing workers over the age of 40 EXCEPT

○ the cost of out-placement services
○ a larger number of dependents
○ increased cost of health care
○ higher median salaries
○ the cost of employee stock options

EXPLANATIONS

14. **B** Choice (A) is unsupported by the passage, so eliminate (A). Choice (B) is directly supported by the first paragraph of the passage, so keep (B). Choice (C) is a bit of an appeal to outside knowledge, and as true as it may be, it is not supported by the passage, so eliminate (C). Choices (D) and (E) are both out of the scope of the passage, so eliminate them both. The correct answer is (B).

15. **A** Use Process of Elimination. Choice (B) is mentioned in line 18. Choice (C) is in line 17. Choice (D) is in lines 15–16. Choice (E) is in line 16. The correct answer is (A).

QUESTIONS

16. A pharmaceutical company claims that its new drug promotes learning in children. To back up its claims, the company points to a study of 300 children who were given the drug, along with a control group of 300 children who were given a placebo. The 300 children who were given the drug reported that they were able to retain new information much more easily.

    Which of the following statements, if true, would most tend to weaken the claims of the pharmaceutical company?

    ○ The 300 children in the control group also reported that they were able to retain new information much more easily.
    ○ The drug has also been shown to prevent common skin rashes.
    ○ The drug has been proven to have severe side-effects.
    ○ The children in the study were not given any other medications during the study.
    ○ The children who were given the drug did better on cognitive measurement tests after the drug therapy than before.

EXPLANATIONS

16. **A** The drug company says its drug caused enhanced learning ability. To weaken this causal argument, look for an alternate cause. Choices (B), (D), and (E) appear to strengthen the argument, so we can eliminate them. Choice (C), while clearly a negative aspect of the drug, does not weaken the argument itself, which states simply that the drug enhances learning capability in children. Side effects are outside the scope of the argument. Choice (A) may not seem at first like an alternate cause, but if the control group (which did not receive the medicine) reported the exact same results as the children who did receive the drug, then clearly there is some other, as yet unnamed, alternate cause. The correct answer is (A).

17. In order to understand the dangers of the current real-estate bubble in Country *Y*, one has only to look to the real-estate bubble of the last decade in Country *Z*. In that country, incautious investors used the inflated value of their real estate as collateral in risky margin loans. When the real-estate market collapsed, many investors went bankrupt, creating a major recession. Country *Y* is in real danger of a similar recession if more-stringent laws restricting margin loans are not enacted promptly.

The answer to which of the following questions would be most useful in evaluating the significance of the author's claims?

○ Was the real estate in Country *Z* located principally in rural areas or was it located in more urban communities?

○ Could the bankruptcies in Country *Z* have been prevented by a private bailout plan by the nation's banks?

○ Does Country *Y* currently have any laws on its books regarding margin loans?

○ Are there business ties and connections between Country *Y* and Country *Z*?

○ Were there other factors in the case of Country *Y* that would make the comparison with Country *Z* less meaningful?

17. **E** To evaluate the significance of the author's claims, we need to recognize what kind of argument it is: an analogy. The author is saying that the situation in Country Y is analogous to that of Country Z. To weaken an analogy, you merely have to question whether the two situations were really analogous. Choices (A) and (B) are outside the scope of the argument. Choice (C) is incorrect because the author's argument stated that more-stringent laws were needed, making it irrelevant whether Country Y had any laws about this in the first place. Choice (D) goes off on an interesting tangent by asking if there were business ties between the two countries, but it does not weaken the argument's analogy. Only (E) questions whether the two situations are in fact analogous. The correct answer is (E).

18. Rules governing participation in a new extreme sports fantasy camp require <u>that applicants should be physically fit enough to endure the demanding</u> activities in which they will be engaging.

○ that applicants should be physically fit enough to endure the demanding

○ that applicants be physically fit enough to endure the demanding

○ applicants should have enough physical fitness to allow enduring the demands of

○ applicants are physically fit enough as to endure the demands of

○ physical fitness in applicants, enough for endurance of demanding

18. **B** This question tests two concepts. The first is idiomatic and concerns the word *require*. Because the word *require* indicates something that is compulsory (as opposed to optional), it cannot be followed by the word *should*; in other words, you can't require that something should happen, because then it's not really a requirement. This eliminates (A) and (C).

The second concept is a little more arcane. Requirements, like hypothetical situations posited in the future, take the subjunctive mood. In the subjunctive, the proper way to phrase the idea expressed in this sentence is *the rules require that applicants be physically fit*. The correct answer is (B).

QUESTIONS

19. During the summer of 2002, the Outer Banks <u>suffered a massive toad infestation, discouraging</u> many vacationers from visiting the area.

○ suffered a massive toad infestation, discouraging

○ suffered from a massive toad infestation and discouraged

○ suffered a massive infestation of toads, which discouraged

○ was suffering a massive infestation of toads and discouraging

○ had suffered from a massive toad infestation and this discouraged

20. A prolonged period of low mortgage rates resulted in a period of the most robust home sales ever. At the same time, the average sale price of resale homes actually dropped, when adjusted for inflation.

Which of the following, if true, would explain the apparent contradiction between the robust home sales and the drop in the average sale price of resale homes?

○ The inflation rate during this period exceeded the increase in the average salary, thus preventing many buyers from securing mortgages.

○ Resale homes represent the best value on the real estate market.

○ Without the adjustment for inflation, the price of resale homes actually increased by a very slight amount.

○ The decrease in mortgage rates was accompanied by a widening of the types of mortgages from which borrowers could choose.

○ The increase in home sales was due entirely to an increase in the sale of new homes.

EXPLANATIONS

19. **C** This question presents two ways to discuss the unfortunate toad incident on the Outer Banks. Was there a *massive toad infestation* or a *massive infestation of toads*? The second option is better, because the first leaves it unclear whether *massive* refers to the infestation or the toads themselves. Under the first option, it is theoretically possible that the Outer Banks was infested by a single 50-foot-tall toad. Thus, (A), (B), and (E) are all incorrect. Choice (D) incorrectly suggests that the Outer Banks, not the infestation of toads, discouraged vacationers. The correct answer is (C).

20. **E** During a period of robust home sales, one would expect the prices of all homes to increase; that would be the natural effect of the law of supply and demand. The question tells us, however, that the real price of resale homes during this period actually decreased. Thus, it is reasonable to assume that the demand for resale homes decreased. How can we resolve this apparent contradiction? If all the increased demand for homes was in the new home market, then it would be possible that the overall increase in home sales would not result in an increase in resale home prices and may, in fact, even accompany a drop in those prices. The correct answer is (E).

VERBAL BIN 3

21. Luis is taller than Rei. Kiko is taller than Marcus. Therefore, Kiko is taller than Rei.

    The conclusion drawn above is not supported by the argument; however, the addition of one additional piece of information would make the conclusion logically sound. All of the following could be that additional piece of information EXCEPT

    ○ Kiko is taller than Luis.
    ○ Luis is taller than Marcus.
    ○ Luis and Marcus are the same height.
    ○ Marcus and Rei are the same height.
    ○ Marcus is taller than Rei.

21. **B** This question is best solved by drawing a diagram to represent the information in the question stem.

We are looking for information that will allow us to draw the diagram

According to the question stem, four of the answer choices are sufficient to accomplish this. Your job is to find the one that is NOT sufficient.

Choice (A) is sufficient; if Kiko is taller than Luis and Luis is taller than Rei, Kiko must be taller than Rei.

Choice (B) is NOT sufficient; if Luis is taller than Marcus, then it is conceivable that Luis is taller than Kiko. Consequently, it is also possible that Rei, who is shorter than Luis, is also taller than Kiko; however, Rei may also be shorter. Use the diagrams we have already created to demonstrate, on your own, that (C), (D), and (E) are sufficient to make the conclusion logically sound. The correct answer is (B).

QUESTIONS

22. It has been estimated that <u>an increase in average regional temperature of even 0.5 degrees Fahrenheit could cost the southern United States more than $10 billion in lost agricultural income annually</u>.

- ⭘ an increase in average regional temperature of even 0.5 degrees Fahrenheit could cost the southern United States more than $10 billion in lost agricultural income annually
- ⭘ every year, $10 billion in agricultural income could be the cost to the southern United States as a result of an increase in the average temperature of the region of even 0.5 degrees Fahrenheit
- ⭘ the cost to the southern United States could be more than $10 billion in income from agriculture that results from a regional increase in average temperature of even 0.5 degrees Fahrenheit annually
- ⭘ annual income losses in agriculture of more than $10 billion could be the cost from increasing average temperatures in the southern United States of even 0.5 degrees Fahrenheit
- ⭘ annual income losses to the southern United States from the increase in average regional temperature of even 0.5 percent costing more than $10 billion in agricultural income each year

EXPLANATIONS

22. **A** Well, you've got five choices here and none is particularly good. Only four, however, contain grammatical errors, so the best way to proceed on a question like this one is to eliminate as many answer choices as you can, take your best guess from among the remaining answers, and move on. Choice (B) is an endless string of prepositions; furthermore, the placement of the phrase *of the region* between *increase in the average temperature* and *of even 0.5 degrees Fahrenheit* is needlessly confusing. Choice (C) incorrectly suggests that it is agriculture, and not lost income, that results from the temperature increase. In (D), *cost from* is unidiomatic; the correct phrasing is *cost of.* Choice (E) is redundant, as it refers to *annual losses* that occur *each year.* The correct answer is (A).

QUESTIONS

23. Within the Green Party, an internal debate is raging <u>among those who believe in compromising with mainstream politicians in order to achieve some goals with those who believe the party must not abandon any of its principles.</u>

   ○ among those who believe in compromising with mainstream politicians in order to achieve some goals with those who believe the party must not abandon any of its principles

   ○ among those who believe that achieving some goals requires compromise with mainstream politicians and those believing that none of the party's principles must be abandoned

   ○ between those believing in compromising with mainstream politicians in order to achieve some goals with those who believe the party must not abandon any of its principles

   ○ between those who believe in compromising with mainstream politicians in order to achieve some goals and those who believe the party must not abandon any of its principles

   ○ between those believing that achieving some goals means compromising with mainstream politicians and those who believe that the principles of the party must not be abandoned

EXPLANATIONS

23. **D** This is a tricky *between/among* question. The rule is that *between* is used to compare two items, *among* to compare three or more. Here we are talking about thousands of people, so you might think that *among* is the correct choice. However, because the sentence compares two groups of people, the correct answer is *between*. The argument is between the two groups, not among the thousands of people who make up those groups. Eliminate (A) and (B).

We can eliminate (C) because it is unidiomatic: It draws a comparison between one group *with* another when it should draw a comparison between one group *and* another. Choice (E) can be eliminated because it lacks parallel structure: It compares *those **believing** that achieving some goals…*and *those who **believe** that the principles of the party must not be abandoned*. The correct answer is (D).

24. In comparison to the drivers who live in Mountainview, a greater proportion of the drivers who live in Oak Valley exceed the speed limit regularly. This explains why there are more accidents each year in Oak Valley than in Mountainview.

All of the following statements, if true, weaken the conclusion drawn above EXCEPT:

○ Oak Valley has a greater proportion of blind intersections and sharp turns than has Mountainview.
○ There is a greater number of drivers in Oak Valley than in Mountainview.
○ Drivers in Mountainview must travel to Oak Valley to shop and work.
○ Per capita, there are fewer police officers monitoring traffic in Oak Valley than there are in Mountainview.
○ The roads are icier for a greater proportion of the year in Oak Valley than in Mountainview.

24. **D** Choice (D) may explain why people are more likely to exceed the speed limit in Oak Valley than in Mountainview, but it has no necessary correlation to the number of accidents in the two towns; therefore, it does nothing to weaken the conclusion that the greater proportion of speeders in Oak Valley results in a greater number of accidents there.

Choices (A) and (E) provide an alternate explanation: Driving conditions are poor, which certainly could contribute to accidents. Choice (B) indicates that there is much more traffic in Oak Valley, which could well explain why there are more traffic accidents there. Choice (C) states that many Mountainview residents travel to Oak Valley regularly; it is possible, then, that they, not the drivers who live in Oak Valley, cause the accidents. The correct answer is (D).

QUESTIONS

25. A study showed that only ten percent of American dog owners enroll their dogs in formal obedience training classes. More than 20 percent of these dog owners, the study also showed, participate in dog shows. Thus, it is obvious that people who train their dogs are more likely to participate in dog shows than are people who do not train their dogs.

The conclusion above is correct provided which of the following statements is also true?

○ It is impossible for a dog to compete in a dog show if the dog has not completed at least one formal obedience training class.
○ The proportion of dog owners who enroll their dogs in formal obedience training classes is representative of the proportion who train their dogs outside such classes.
○ Dog owners who participate in dog shows only train their dogs by enrolling them in formal obedience training lessons.
○ Participation in dog shows is a reliable indicator of how much attention a dog owner pays to his dog.
○ Only purebred dogs can participate in dog shows, so many owners who enroll their dogs in formal obedience training classes are excluded from this activity.

EXPLANATIONS

25. **B** The statement draws a conclusion about *people who train their dogs* based on statistics relating only to people who take their dogs to formal obedience training classes. In order for the statement to be correct, then, these statistics must be valid for all people who train their dogs, not only those who train them in formal classes. Choice (B) plugs this hole in the argument, thus making the conclusion necessarily true. The correct answer is (B).

QUESTIONS

26. A bullet train travels in excess of 150 miles per hour. Therefore, if a train travels slower than 150 miles per hour, it is not a bullet train.

   Which of the following most closely parallels the reasoning used in the argument above?

   ○ An orange ripens only on the vine. If it ripens on the vine, then it is not an orange.
   ○ Newspapers are often read by more than one person. Therefore, magazines are also likely to be read by more than one person.
   ○ An earthquake of 5.0 or above on the Richter scale causes massive damage. If there is not massive damage, then the earthquake did not attain a 5.0 or above.
   ○ A supersonic plane travels at speeds in excess of Mach 1. If it is not supersonic, then it will travel at speeds below Mach 1.
   ○ Fluoride generally prevents cavities. If there are no cavities, then there was no fluoride used.

EXPLANATIONS

26. **C** To answer this parallel-the-reasoning question, you have to break down the original argument, and then find an answer choice that mimics it exactly. In this case, the argument says a bullet train travels in excess of 150 miles per hour (if A, then B). Therefore, if a train travels less than 150 miles per hour, then it is not a bullet train (if not B, then not A). Now all you have to do is find an answer choice that mimics that reasoning exactly. Choice (A), broken down, reads, "if A, then B…so if B, then not A." This isn't it. Eliminate it. Choice (B) breaks down to "if A, then B… therefore C will also cause B." That's not it either. Choice (C) breaks down to "if A, then B…therefore if not B, then not A." Keep (C).
Choice (D) might seem tempting because it also has to do with a fast means of transportation, but what counts here is the reasoning: if A, then B…if not A, then not B. This is close, but no cigar. Choice (E) is also appealing; you may even think it mimics the argument exactly. But there's a trick. The first half of the sentence reads, "Fluoride generally prevents cavities" (if A, then B). Note that the B part is about the prevention—not the presence—of cavities. So the second half, "If there are no cavities, there was no fluoride," actually breaks down to "if B, then not A." The correct answer is (C).

NOTES

NOTES

NOTES

NOTES

BONUS MATERIALS

GMAT INSIDER

Admissions and Financial Aid Advice

While *Cracking the GMAT* will prepare you for your exam, GMAT Insider will help you navigate what comes next. The bonus materials included here contain invaluable information about what b-school is really like, wending your way through the financial aid and admissions processes, writing winning application essays, getting a job with an MBA, and more. Feel free to take advantage of this content, and we wish you the best of luck on your studies and preparation for business school.

Contents

Part 1

Is an MBA for You?

The MBA presents many opportunities but no guarantees. Whether you go to a first-tier full-time school across the country or to a less well-known, part-time school close to home, you'll acquire skills that could jumpstart a new career or take your existing career to levels that were previously unattainable. An MBA can be a ticket to power networks and recruiters, elite employers, and, of course, generous paychecks. It can transform you from low-level lackey to executive material in a mere 21 months, possibly fewer. But you could also end up with a mere piece of paper that doesn't help your career all that much, considering all your trouble—not to mention a very uncomfortable amount of debt.

The MBA is not remotely indispensable if you want to be a titan of industry, or even a vice titan. Don't let anyone tell you it is. Plenty of fabulously successful businesspeople who never bothered to get an MBA have done exceedingly well for themselves, including, just for example, Jeff Bezos, the founder of Amazon, and Steve Jobs, a co-founder of Apple. Mary Kay Ash, founder of Mary Kay Cosmetics; Bill Gates, co-founder of Microsoft; and Mark Zuckerberg, co-founder of Facebook, didn't even bother graduating from college, much less hitting b-school.

Of course, lots of really successful people in the business world do have MBAs. There's Phil Knight (Stanford, '62) who co-founded Nike. There's also George W. Bush (43rd president of the United States, Harvard, '75), Leonard A. Lauder (chairman emeritus of The Estée Lauder Companies Inc., Wharton '54), David Viniar (CFO and Executive Vice President of Goldman Sachs, Harvard '80), and banking bigwig Sallie Krawcheck (Columbia, '92). About a third of the CEOs at the biggest and best multinational firms have MBAs.

Most people who are thinking about getting an MBA aren't looking to start the most successful shoe company on the planet, or run for president, or preside over a large semiconductor chip-making company, though. Those accomplishments would be great, sure, but it would also be pretty swell just to become a fairly anonymous cog in upper management at an established company one day.

The first question you have to ask yourself if you are thinking of getting an MBA is big, basic, and blindingly obvious: Do you really want a career in business? If you are a writer or a scientist, an MBA isn't going to add much value unless, say, you want to write for the *Wall Street Journal* or you want to get into management at a big pharmaceutical conglomerate.

Provided that you can affirmatively answer that you want a business career, the next equally important question is: What exactly do you think an MBA is going to do for your career in business? In some niches of the business world (such as big consulting firms and big banks), virtually nobody is going to hire or seriously promote you unless you have this particular credential.

In other areas, though, such as trading, you can get by just fine with a bachelor's degree. So, what's an MBA going to do for you exactly? What barriers is it going to break down? Are you looking to gain credibility, accelerate your development, or move into a new job or industry? Are you simply looking to make more money? Are you looking for a promotion where you work now? How will an MBA help you reach those goals?

You Need a Plan

Don't go to business school unless you have a very firm idea about why you want to go to business school. Go to law school if you feel rudderless. (That's a joke, sort of.) We're not going to tell you that you can't go to b-school without some crazy 50-year life strategy and a laser-like industry focus, but it really will be better if you have some pretty concrete plans about your future as a businessperson, and some legitimate reasons for getting an MBA before you apply. It would be nice, for example, if you could declare that you are getting an MBA because you want to move from some technical area of expertise to, say, something finance-oriented, or even just that you want to move from a smaller firm to a larger one. Try to come up with something as defined and unambiguous as possible.

At the very least, you need to have a solid, coherent story that will impress an admissions staff. Knowing what you want doesn't just affect your decision to go, it also affects the quality of your application to various b-schools. Admissions committees favor applicants who have clear goals and objectives. They want a compelling story. Ideally, that story would even have the added benefit of being true because, obviously, you'll get more out of your education if you can find a school that offers the coursework and curriculum that fit your individual needs. Additionally, once you are actually enrolled, you'll be able to suck a lot more of the marrow out of your two years (or one year, or three, or whatever) if you have a clear objective in mind. If you're uncertain about your goals, you'll squander a lot of opportunities for career development, such as networking, mentoring, student clubs, and recruiter events.

WHY DO OTHER PEOPLE GO TO BUSINESS SCHOOL?

Networking. According to a survey by the Graduate Management Admission Council (the people who also bring you the GMAT), close to 50 percent of students enrolled in one- and two-year MBA programs say that networking opportunities most motivated them to pursue the degree. Business schools can provide an instant pedigree and amazing access. The cachet of an MBA opens doors to choice internships, blue-chip recruiters, and vast and loyal alumni networks. It's a veritable "in" for sectors such as private equity that tend to shut out the hoi polloi. There are also the professors on the faculty. They know people you want to know. The various business bigwigs who visit campus are good for even more contacts. And there are your classmates, who themselves have big ideas and vital connections.

To learn. Development of "the ability to control situations more effectively" is a very distant second in the Graduate Management Admission Council's survey of top reasons why people attend b-school. Graduate business schools teach the applied science of business. The best business schools combine the latest academic theories with pragmatic concepts and real-world solutions. They provide a very well-structured and fairly thorough grounding in operations, economics and accounting, finance, and marketing. B-schools also teach the analytical skills used to make complicated business decisions. You learn how to define the critical issues, apply analytical techniques, develop the criteria for decisions, and make decisions after evaluating their impact on other variables. Certainly, you'll get a slew of information from people who are vetted and qualified, and some of that information may even prove useful in your career. There is plenty of skills training as well. Business school stresses experiential learning. It's hands-on learning by doing, even if it's largely a sort of pseudo doing.

The prospect of interesting and exciting work. The prospect of finding better work to do motivates some b-school students. It's a remote third on the GMAC survey, just below the acquisition of management skills. Business school represents a nice, easy, fairly safe opportunity to reassess your career situation. One way or another, the job you have before you get an MBA will be among the principal factors influencing the job you get after you get your MBA. Nevertheless, the MBA route is a great way to catapult yourself into a different job or to move to a different industry altogether. An MBA is perhaps the only credential that allows you to make a lateral career move without reducing your income or your status. Many graduates use the degree to embark on entirely new career paths than those that brought them to the school; consultants become bankers, entrepreneurs become consultants, marketers become financiers, and so on. The MBA has been and will continue to be a terrific opportunity to reinvent yourself, and it's exceedingly common for people to make big professional changes once they get their degrees.

Part-time MBA and EMBA students are atypical. For part-time and executive MBA students, maintaining a marketable resume and learning how to manage more effectively are roughly tied for first place on the GMAC survey. Gaining confidence is a remote third among motivating factors for these students, and networking opportunities aren't nearly as coveted, for the obvious reasons that these students are already have positions in industry.

More money. Let's be honest here. Networking opportunities, management skills, and all the rest are great, but what a very high percentage of people ultimately want to do above all else with an MBA is make more money. There's definitely nothing wrong with that. We're talking about business, after all, not social work. And those three additional letters near your name can translate to a higher salary—sometimes a significantly higher salary—and all the trappings that come with it, particularly if you work or would like to work for a large, established company.

More prestige. Ideally, if you build a better mouse trap, the world will beat a path to your door. Actual, manifest accomplishment should be rewarded, right? Sadly, things don't always work that way. Status is a big deal and a fancy advanced degree confers status quickly and efficiently. Is that good and fitting? Maybe, maybe not, but the fact is that there's prestige attached to an MBA, particularly one from an exclusive, highly-ranked school. Your opinions are likely to carry more weight once you get the degree. Your resume might receive more attention. You might progress up the corporate ladder more quickly.

A NOTE FOR BUDDING ENTREPRENEURS

If you are a budding entrepreneur thinking about starting your own business, there are arguments both for and against getting an MBA.

The argument for b-school is that you'll be exposed to an array of different business issues and plenty of innovative management and leadership training. The greatest idea in the world is a loser if you don't know how to steer it to profitability. All of that instruction and coursework should equip you to turn your business idea into a cold, hard, cash-generating reality. Also, business school is all about networking and you are unlikely to find a better place to find capital and potential partners than an MBA program, especially if you are younger.

The argument against b-school for entrepreneurs is that the cost of getting an MBA is very high in one particularly critical aspect: time. If you go the traditional b-school route, you lose at least the better part of two precious years of working on and nurturing and growing your idea. Worse still, somebody else with pretty much the same idea might beat you to the market. The cost of getting an MBA is very high in the critical aspect of money too. You'll likely incur debt, which is a problem for any fledgling industrialist.

On top of all that, you'll probably learn to be more risk-averse—anathema to entrepreneurial gumption.

Getting a Job with an MBA

It's critically important to consider placement rates and the list of companies that typically recruit at the schools you consider. There is great variability in placement rates and starting salaries among schools. The industry you chose to work in strongly affects your job prospects, and several other factors also affect job placement and starting salary.

FACTORS THAT MATTER

Reputation. At the top programs, the lists of recruiters read like a "Who's Who" of American companies. The fancy-pants schools not only attract the greatest volume of recruiters, but they consistently get the attention of the companies where jobs tend to be most sought after. Traditionally heavy hirers such as investment banking and consulting companies continue to offer the highest starting salaries and signing bonuses, and recruiters from those firms gravitate to the name-brand schools. At the same time, there's something to be said for a homegrown MBA. Lesser-known, regional schools often have very strong relationships with local employers and industries. The business community in a given region often regards local b-schools (many of them state universities) very highly. Rutgers University in New Jersey, for instance, holds great sway at nearby, national employers such as Johnson & Johnson, providing graduates with a unique competitive advantage.

You. Your background and experiences also affect your success in securing a position. Important factors are academic standing, prior work experience, and the skills and knowledge you gained both during and before b-school. Intangibles matter too, such as your personal fit with the company. These days, prior experience is particularly important; it helps establish credibility and gives you an edge in competing for a position in a specific field. If your goal is to switch to a new industry, it's helpful if something on your resume ties your interest to the new profession. It's also smart to secure a summer job in the sector in which you want a career.

Student groups. On-campus clubs and organizations also play a big part in getting a job because they extend the recruiting efforts at many schools. Clubs host a variety of events that allow you to meet big kahunas, so that you can learn more about their industries and their specific companies. Clubs are also very effective at bringing in recruiters and other interested parties that do not recruit through traditional mainstream channels. For example, the high-tech, international, and entertainment student clubs provide career opportunities not available through the front door.

Alumni. The people who preceded you as graduates of an MBA program are also an important part of the b-school experience. While professors teach business theory and practice, alumni provide insight into the real business world. When you're ready to interview, alums can provide advice on how to get hired by the companies recruiting at your school. In some cases, they help you secure the interview and shepherd you through the hiring process. At the very least, alumni will help you get your foot in the door. A resume sent to an alum at a given company, instead of to "Sir or Madam" in the personnel department, has a much better chance of being noticed and acted on. Moreover, regional alumni clubs and alumni publications keep you plugged in after you graduate with class notes detailing who's doing what, where, and with whom. (It's that networking thing again.) Throughout your career, an active alumni relations department can give you continued support. Post-MBA executive education series, fund-raising events, and continued job placement efforts are all resources you can draw on for years to come.

Pluck. Finally, at the end of the day, getting a job once you have an MBA is pretty much the same as getting any other job. Persistence and initiative are always going to be helpful. Increasingly, even at the best schools, finding a job requires off-campus recruiting efforts and ferreting out the hidden jobs.

SOME BAD CAREER NEWS

There has been a pretty severe retrenchment of traditional MBA destinations (such as investment banks and consulting firms) in recent years. Do employers see the skill sets of today's MBAs bringing measurable value to their companies? In many cases, they don't. Companies big, small, and in-between just aren't hiring MBAs at anywhere near the level they did before the advent of the Great Recession. The business isn't there, so the revenue isn't there, so the jobs aren't available. According to a survey by the Graduate Management Admission Council, roughly 60 percent of traditional, full-time MBA students have offers by the spring of their second year. That's up nicely from the downright grim figure of 40 percent of a few years ago, but it's less than rosy.

Corporate recruitment strategy isn't what it used to be, either. Businesses are tightening their belts, fighting tooth and nail to stay competitive, and all manner of other bad clichés. Many companies in the consulting, finance, and consumer goods industries are opting to hire people with Bachelor's degrees instead of MBAs for management-track positions. Certainly, the salaries the companies must pay are lower. A typical hire out of college can expect to make a little more than $40,000 a year, while the average graduate of an MBA program can expect to make around $95,000. Younger applicants have fewer skills, but they are also less likely to have formed too many bad habits. Freshly-minted undergrads, with their minds full of mush, are more malleable. Companies get to start with a clean slate.

SOME GOOD CAREER NEWS

Check out The Princeton Review's latest rankings for "Best Career Prospects" in your Student Tools.

A recent Bloomberg *Businessweek* survey of 1,500 people who got their MBAs in 1992 found that salaries and bonuses are robust (at least for those people). A large number of the survey participants occupy executive positions in their respective companies. So that's some consolation.

It's also comforting to keep in mind the fact that hundreds of companies continue to visit and recruit from business school campuses. Job offers happen frequently and regularly. Recruiters exist in a symbiotic relationship with business schools. Employers maintain a strong presence on campus— even during an economic downturn—because doing so is in their best interests. When the good times eventually roll again, they'll want to have easy access to MBA programs. Consequently, MBA programs remain one of the most effective means to get yourself in front of recruiters and senior managers from the most desirable companies.

How many—and what kind—of offers will you receive? That's largely dependent on the appeal of your school to recruiters (which companies recruit on campus and how often they do so are statistics that will be readily available at any reputable school) and the particular industry you elect to pursue. For example, investment banks and consulting firms are always going to come to the schools for formal recruiting periods, whereas more off-the-beaten-path choices will require you to go off campus in search of opportunity.

At programs such as Chicago, Harvard, and Duke, six-figure salaries and sweet signing bonuses are still the norm for graduates. The majority of top grads receive a generous relocation package too. Indeed, if you were fortunate enough to have spent the summer between your first and second year at a consulting company, then you may also receive a "rebate" on your tuition. These companies often pick up your second-year tuition bill as well.

Types of Degree Programs

TWO-YEAR PROGRAMS

Traditional two-year MBA programs are ubiquitous, so they're the ones we've spent most of the time discussing here. They involve the same basic academic year, the same weekday classes, and the same long summer break that you've experienced since kindergarten.

ACCELERATED PROGRAMS

Accelerated MBA programs are faster versions of two-year programs. There's no summer vacation and holiday breaks are shorter. Course loads are higher; exams are frequent; and the whole experience is more rigorous and intensive. There's also no time for a summer job, which can be a big deal since many students hope summer jobs will lead to post-grad offers. Accelerated programs which typically last between 10 and 15 months are pretty standard in Europe, and they are becoming more common in the United States as well. Durations vary stateside. The accelerated program at Cornell University's Johnson School lasts a year (from May to May). Pepperdine's Graziadio School offers both 12-month and 15-month options. And finally, some full-time programs are basically accelerated programs. For example, it takes only 16 months to get an MBA at the Mays Business School at Texas A&M.

PART-TIME PROGRAMS

In conventional part-time MBA programs, you take classes on weekday nights and on the weekends. They last three years, sometimes longer. The process is essentially the same. You have access to the same professors, or at least a lot of them. It just takes longer and course loads are lighter. The obvious draw of part-time enrollment is that you get to keep your day job and the income it provides. The drawback is that networking and social opportunities are more limited. Also, part-time students aren't able to participate in on-campus recruiting events nearly as often as their full-time counterparts.

EXECUTIVE MBA PROGRAMS

EMBA programs are designed for managers and executives who already have fairly impressive full-time jobs and a higher level of professional experience. There are a few hundred EMBA programs to choose from around the world, and they tend to have a few essential features. Committing to a garden-variety EMBA program means spending every other Friday or so at school for, say, 20 months. That's important to consider because your boss will have to support your degree quest (or, at least, agree to your absence every other Friday). It's fair to say that EMBA programs have less rigorous admissions requirements as well. (Many don't even require a GMAT score.) Curricula are lighter and there are fewer course requirements. Also, EMBA programs vary a lot—and we mean a lot. Some schools are noted for finance, while others are all about entrepreneurship. At some schools, EMBA students rarely see rock-star professors; at other schools, those professors teach many classes. There's tremendous variance.

DUAL-DEGREE PROGRAMS

There's not much to say here since you probably have a solid understanding of what a dual degree entails. Dual MBA programs combine an MBA degree and another degree (typically a JD, or some additional master's degree). It's a way to cut costs and time, but the trade-off is that you'll be signing up for a ton of work. It's also worth noting that some business schools offer the opportunity to get a bachelor's degree in business as well as an MBA in five years (or perhaps four if you are ridiculously diligent). Obviously, dual-degree programs are cheaper and quicker than pursuing both degrees separately, but they still cost more in time and money than a single degree, so all the same caveats about deciding to attend apply. If you're considering a dual-degree program, make sure you know why you need both degrees to achieve your goals. While many graduates of these programs are very satisfied with their choices, anecdotally, we've also spoken with a number of grads who say that they really use only the MBA or their other degree, and that they would have been better off doing a single-degree track.

DISTANCE LEARNING PROGRAMS

The Internet is pretty awesome and many schools allow you to earn an MBA from the comfort of your own home (or wherever your computer is). It's an affordable alternative and it's nothing if not flexible. There are some drawbacks. You won't be able to take advantage of many networking opportunities from your living room, for example. On the job front, there's not going to be much at all in the way of recruitment. Also, taking classes on a campus retains a lot of snob appeal. Maybe that's sad and wrong, but it's reality. Finally, if you do decide on the distance learning route, be careful about the school you choose. Some of them are great. Others, not so much.

MBA Concentrations

Back in the day, it was enough just to earn your MBA and enter the working world a more knowledgeable and employable individual for it. Today, business represents an increasingly multifaceted and diverse world. It's much harder to be a jack of all trades. As a result, specialization is king across most MBA programs.

When you are looking at potential business schools, it's imperative to know whether they offer the concentration you're keen on. Here's an all-too-brief guide to some of the common ones.

Finance. The finance concentration is about money—how to manage it, make it, and make more of it. A specialization in finance will prepare you to make smart financial decisions for individuals, institutions, and companies.

Marketing. Marketing professionals anticipate consumer demands. They help to create products and services that consumers want, attract consumers to that product or service, and work to retain consumers over the long haul. They also have their hands in pricing and distribution, figuring out what stuff should cost and how to get it to customers.

Accounting. As an accounting specialist, you'll become an expert in the gathering and interpretation of financial data and the ways in which that data can affect a company.

Supply chain management. In a world of global suppliers and tight profit margins, effective supply chain management can mean the difference between profitability and bankruptcy. A specialization in supply chain management will prepare you to create and manage the entire selling process for any company with a good or service to vend.

International management. A concentration in international management will prepare you to succeed in today's global business environment. Many programs require students to spend a semester overseas, working at a company or studying at a partner university.

Entrepreneurship. A concentration in entrepreneurship offers you the chance to develop real business savvy, network with potential collaborators and investors, and try out new ideas with fewer risks than you'll encounter in the cold, unforgiving world outside the Ivory Tower.

Nonprofit management. Running a nonprofit requires the same skills you need to run any business: raising capital, managing an organization for maximum cost efficiency, and effectively delivering goods and services. It also requires some different skills, such as an understanding of nonprofit laws and policies, and an emphasis on fundraising, grant-writing, and campaigning, among other skills. Thus, the specialization.

Leadership. This concentration is designed to help you develop skills that are essential to success in any field: critical thinking, problem-solving, communicating, negotiating, and acting ethically in professional situations.

Healthcare administration. This specialization will teach you how the nation's very intricate and convoluted healthcare system works. It will also help you learn how to deal with the challenges facing healthcare organizations—from government agencies to hospitals to biotech, pharmaceutical, and medical technology companies.

Human resources management. In this concentration, you'll learn how to maximize human output in a business environment, from understanding individual behavior to designing effective management structures, training programs, and compensation schemes.

Part 2

Admissions

PREPARING TO BE A SUCCESSFUL APPLICANT

Get Good Grades

If you're still in school, concentrate on getting good grades. A high GPA says you've got not only brains but also discipline. It shows the admissions committee you have what you need to make it through the program. If you're applying directly from college or have limited job experience, your grades will matter even more. The admissions committee will have little else on which to evaluate you.

It's especially important that you do well in courses such as economics, statistics, and calculus. Success in these courses is more meaningful than success in classes like "Monday Night at the Movies" film appreciation. Of course, English is also important; b-schools want students who communicate well.

Strengthen Math Skills

Number-crunching is an inescapable part of b-school. If your work experience has failed to develop your quantitative skills, take an accounting or statistics course for credit at a local college or b-school. If you have a liberal arts background and did poorly in math, or got a low GMAT Quantitative score, this is especially important. Getting a decent grade will go a long way toward convincing the admissions committee you can manage the quantitative challenges of the program.

Work for a Few Years—But Not Too Many

Business schools have traditionally favored applicants who have worked full-time for several years. There are three primary reasons for this:

1. With experience comes maturity.

2. You're more likely to know what you want out of the program.

3. Your experience enables you to bring real-work perspectives to the classroom. Because business school is designed for you to learn from your classmates, each student's contribution is important.

Until recently, b-schools preferred to admit only those students with two to five years of work experience. The rationale was that at two years you have worked enough to be able to make a solid contribution, while beyond four or five, you might be too advanced in your career to appreciate the program fully. However, there is a new trend among top schools toward admitting "younger" applicants—that is, candidates with limited work experience as well as those straight from college.

Depending on the schools to which you're applying and the strength of your resume of accomplishments, you may not need full-time, professional work experience. Of course, there's a catch: The younger you are, the harder you'll have to work to supply supporting evidence for your case as a qualified applicant. Be prepared to convince admissions committees that you've already done some incredible things, especially if you're hailing straight from college.

If you've targeted top-flight schools such as Wharton, Columbia, or Stanford, applying fresh out of college is still a long shot. While your chances of gaining admission with little work experience have improved, your best shot is still to err on the conservative side and get a year or two of some professional experience under your belt.

If you're not interested in the big league or you plan on attending a local program, the number of years you should work before applying may vary. Research the admissions requirements at your target school. There's no doubt the MBA will jumpstart your career and have long-lasting effects on your business (and perhaps personal) outlook. If you're not ready to face the real world after college, plenty of solid b-schools will welcome you to another two years of academia.

There is one caveat to this advice, however. If your grades are weak, consider working at least three years before applying. The more professional success you have, the greater the likelihood that admissions committees will overlook your GPA.

Let Your Job Work for You

Many companies encourage employees to go to b-school. Some of these companies have close ties to a favored b-school and produce well-qualified applicants. If their employees are going to the kinds of schools you want to get into, these may be smart places to work.

Other companies, such as investment banks, feature training programs, at the end of which trainees go to b-school or leave the company. These programs hire undergraduates right out of school. They're known for producing solid, highly skilled applicants. Moreover, they're full of well-connected alumni who may write influential letters of recommendation.

Happily, the opposite tactic—working in an industry that generates few applicants—can be equally effective. Admissions officers look for students from underrepresented professions. Applicants from biotechnology, health care, not-for-profit, and even the Peace Corps are viewed favorably.

One way to set yourself apart is to have had two entirely different professional experiences before business school. For example, if you worked in finance, your next job might be in a different field, such as marketing. Supplementing quantitative work with qualitative experiences demonstrates versatility.

Finally, what you do in your job is important. Seek out opportunities to distinguish yourself. Even if your responsibilities are limited, exceed the expectations of the position. B-schools are looking for leaders.

March from the Military

A surprising number of b-school students hail from the military (although the armed forces probably had commanders in mind, not CEOs, when they designed their regimen). Military officers know how to be managers because they've held command positions. And they know how to lead a team under the most difficult of circumstances.

Because most have traveled all over the world, they also know how to work with people from different cultures. As a result, they're ideally suited to learn alongside students with diverse backgrounds and perspectives. B-schools with a global focus are particularly attracted to such experience.

The decision to enlist in the military is a very personal one. However, if you've thought of joining those few good men and women, this may be as effective a means of preparing for b-school as more traditional avenues.

HOW THE ADMISSIONS CRITERIA ARE WEIGHTED

Although admissions requirements vary among business schools, most rely on the following criteria: GMAT score, college GPA, work experience, your essays, letters of recommendation (academic and/or professional), an interview with an admissions representative, and your extracurriculars. The first four are generally the most heavily weighted. The more competitive the school, the less room there is for weakness in any area. Any component out of sync, such as a weak GMAT score, is potentially harmful.

Happily, the admissions process at business school is one where great emphasis is placed on getting to know you as a person. The essay component is the element that allows the schools to do just that. Your essays can refute weaknesses, fill in gaps, and in general, charmingly persuade an admissions board you've got the right stuff. They are the single most important criteria in business school admissions.

But as we've just said, they're not the only criteria. All pieces of your application must come together to form a cohesive whole. It is the entire application that determines whether you win admission.

Anticipate and Coordinate

The application process is very time consuming, so anticipating what you need to accomplish within the admissions time frame is critical. To make the best use of our advice, you should first contact each of the programs on your personal list of schools. Their standards and criteria for admission may vary, and you'll need to follow their specific guidelines. Please note that the less competitive a school is, the more easily you may be able to breeze through (or completely omit) the rigorous requirements we identify as crucial in the application process for the top programs.

In addition, business school applicants are often overwhelmed by how much they have to do to complete not only one, but several applications. Proper management of the process is essential, since there are so many factors to coordinate in each application.

You'll have to prep for the GMAT, then actually take the test, round up some writers for your recommendations, follow up with those chosen to write recommendations, make sure the recommendations are mailed in on time, have your college transcript sent, and finally, write the essays. Of course, some schools require an interview as well. What makes all of this particularly challenging is that many applicants have to do all of this while balancing the demands of a full-time job.

We know that it takes a supreme force of will to complete even one application. As grad school applications go, a top business school's is pretty daunting. So if you don't stay focused on the details and deadlines, you may drop the ball.

There are many common and incredibly embarrassing mistakes you can avoid with prudent early planning. These include allowing your recommenders to miss the deadline, submitting an application full of typos and grammatical errors, sending one school an essay intended for another, or forgetting to change the school name when using the same essay for several applications. Applicants who wind up cramming for the GMAT or squeezing their essay writing into several all-nighters end up seriously shortchanging themselves.

Apply Early

The best advice is to plan early and apply early. The former diminishes the likelihood of an accidental omission or a missed deadline. The latter increases your chances of acceptance.

The filing period ranges anywhere from six to eight months. The earlier you apply, the better your chances. There are a number of reasons for this:

First, there's plenty of space available early on. Many b-schools have rolling admissions, and as the application deadline nears, spaces fill up. The majority of applicants don't apply until the later months because of procrastination or unavoidable delays. As the deadline draws close, the greatest number of applicants competes for the fewest number of spaces.

Second, in the beginning, admissions officers have little clue about how selective they can be. They haven't reviewed enough applications to determine the competitiveness of the pool. An early application may be judged more on its own merit than on how it stacks up against others. This is in your favor if the pool turns out to be unusually competitive. Above all, admissions officers like to lock their classes in early; they can't be certain they'll get their normal supply of applicants. Admissions decisions may be more generous at this time.

Third, by getting your application in early you're showing a strong interest. The admissions committee is likely to view you as someone keen on going to their school.

To be sure, some admissions officers report that the first batch of applications tend to be from candidates with strong qualifications, confident of acceptance. In this case, you might not be the very first one on line; but being closer to the front is still better than getting lost in the heap of last-minute hopefuls.

Rounds vs. Rolling Admissions

Applications are processed in one of two ways: rounds or rolling admissions. Schools that use rounds divide the filing period into three or so timed cycles. Applications are batched into the round in which they are received and reviewed in competition with others in that round. A list of a b-school's round dates can be obtained by contacting its admissions office if it employs this method. Applications to schools with rolling admissions are reviewed on an ongoing basis as they are received.

GMAT and GPA

The GMAT and GPA are used in two ways. First, they're "success indicators" for the academic work you'll have to slog through if admitted—will you have the brainpower to succeed in the program? Second, they're used as benchmarks to compare each applicant to other applicants within the pool. At the more selective schools, you'll need a higher score and average to stay in the game.

Your college transcript is a major factor in the strength of your candidacy. Some schools focus more closely on the junior- and senior-year grades than the overall GPA, and most consider the reputation of your college and the difficulty of your course selections. A transcript loaded with offerings such as "Environmental Appreciation" and "The Child in You" won't be valued as highly as one packed with calculus and history classes.

The Essays

Admissions committees consider the essays the clincher, the swing vote on the admit/deny issue. Essays offer the most substantive information about who you really are. The GMAT and GPA reveal little about you, only that you won't crash and burn. Your work history provides a record of performance and justifies your stated desire to study business. But the essays tie all the pieces of the application together and create a summary of your experiences, skills, background, and beliefs.

The essays do more than give answers to questions. They create thumbnail psychological profiles. Depending on how you answer a question or what you present, you reveal yourself in any number of ways—creative, witty, open-minded, articulate, mature, to name a few. On the other hand, your essay can also reveal a negative side, such as arrogance, sloppiness, or an inability to think and write clearly.

For international students
If you are an international student, you may be required to submit a Test of English as a Foreign Language (TOEFL) score. For more information on the test and how The Princeton Review can help you prepare for it, visit **PrincetonReview.com/ k12/toefl-test-prep.** Or check out our test-prep book *Cracking the TOEFL IBT with CD.*

Visit your Student Tools for additional information on business school recommendations.

Letters of Recommendation

Letters of recommendation function as a reality check. Admissions committees expect them to support and reinforce what they're seeing in the rest of your application. When the information doesn't match up with the picture you've painted, it makes you look bad. Because you won't see the recommendation (it's sent in "blind"), you won't even know there's a problem. This can mean the end of your candidacy.

That's why you need to take extreme care in selecting your references.

Scan each application for guidelines on choosing your references—business schools typically request an academic and a professional reference. The academic reference should be someone who can evaluate your performance in an academic environment. It's better to ask an instructor, teacher's aide, or mentor who knew you well than a famous professor who barely knew your name.

The same holds true for your professional reference. Seek out individuals who can evaluate your performance on many levels. The reference will be far more credible. Finding the right person to write your professional reference, however, can be trickier. You may not wish to reveal to your boss early on that you plan on leaving, and if the dynamics of your relationship are not ideal (hey, it happens once in a while), he or she might not make an appropriate reference. If this is the case, seek out a boss at a former job or someone who was your supervisor at your current job but has since moved to another organization. Avoid friends, colleagues, and clients as references unless the school explicitly says it's okay.

Advise your writers on themes and qualities you highlighted in your application. Suggest that they include real-life examples of your performance to illustrate their points. In other words, script the recommendation as best you can. Your boss, even if he or she is your biggest fan, may not know what your recommendation should include.

A great recommendation is rarely enough to save a weak application from doom. But it might push a borderline case over to the "admit" pile. Mediocre recommendations can be damaging; an application that is strong in all other areas now has a weakness, an inconsistency.

A final warning on this topic: Procrastination is common here. Micromanage your references so that each recommendation arrives on time! If need be, provide packaging for an overnight letter, have your reference, seal it up, and then ship it out yourself.

The Interview

Not all business schools attach equal value to the interview. For some, it's an essential screening tool. For others, it's used to make a final decision on those caught somewhere between "admit" and "reject." Some schools may encourage, but not require, the interview. Others make it informative, with little connection to the admissions decision.

Like the letters of recommendation, an interview may serve as a reality check to reinforce the total picture. It may also be used to fill in the blanks, particularly in borderline cases.

If an interview is offered, take it. In person, you may be a more compelling candidate. You can use the interview to further address weaknesses or bring dull essays to life. Most importantly, you can display the kinds of qualities—enthusiasm, sense of humor, maturity—that can positively sway an admissions decision.

Act quickly to schedule your interview. Admissions departments often lack the time and staff to interview every candidate who walks through their doors. You don't want your application decision delayed by several months (and placed in a more competitive round or pool) because your interview was scheduled late in the filing period.

A great interview can tip the scale in the "admit" direction. How do you know if it was great? You were calm and focused. You expressed yourself and your ideas clearly. You developed a solid rapport with the interviewer.

A mediocre interview may not have much impact, unless your application is hanging on by a thread. In such a case, the person you're talking to (harsh as it may seem) is probably looking for a reason not to admit you, rather than a reason to let you in. If you feel your application may be in that hazy, marginal area, try to be extra-inspired in your interview.

Approach this meeting as you would a job interview. Remember, you're being sized up as a person in all of your dimensions. Here are a few tips to use during the interview.

- Dress and act the part of a professional but avoid being stiff or acting like a stuffed shirt.

- Limit your use of business jargon. Interviewers often hear a lot of the same generic answers. They are more interested in you being your witty, charming, natural self.

- Be personable and talk about your passions, such as hobbies or a recent trip you've taken. The idea is to get the interviewer thinking of you as someone who will contribute greatly to the quality of campus life.

Highlight your achievements and excellence, even in something like gourmet cooking, but avoid stunts, such as pulling out a platter of peppercorn pâté sautéed in anchovy sauce.

Part 3

Quotas, Recruitment, and Diversity

B-schools don't have to operate under quotas—governmental or otherwise. However, they probably try harder than most corporations to recruit diverse groups of people. Just as the modern business world has become global and multicultural, so too have b-schools. They must not only teach diversity in the classroom but also make it a reality in their campus population and, if possible, faculty.

Schools that have a diverse student body tend to be proud of it. They tout their success in profiles that demographically slice and dice the previous year's class by gender, race, and geographic and international residency. Prospective students can review this data and compare the diversity of the schools they've applied to.

However, such diversity doesn't come naturally from the demographics of the applicant pool. Admissions committees have to work hard at it. In some cases, enrollment is encouraged with generous financial aid packages and scholarships.

While they don't have quotas per se, they do target groups for admission, seeking a demographic balance in many areas. Have they admitted enough women, minorities, foreign students, marketing strategists, and liberal arts majors? Are different parts of the country represented?

As we've said before, the best b-schools tend to attract top talent, students, and recruiters to their campus. Women and minorities are the most sought-after groups targeted for admission. So it's no surprise that programs that report higher-than-average female and minority enrollments tend to be among the very best.

AN INITIATIVE FOR MINORITIES

Some schools report higher minority enrollments than others, so our advice is consistent: You need to thoroughly research the program you've set your sights on. Consider your goals. Do you simply want to attend the most prestigious program? How will social factors impact your goals and experiences on campus?

Most business schools aspire to diversify their programs. It's the number of minorities applying to business school that has remained consistently low. An initiative of the Graduate Management Admissions Council called The Diversity Pipeline Alliance (GMAC.com/Diversity) was formed to reverse this trend and increase the number of underrepresented minorities pursuing a business career. Much like the initiative for women, this organization plans a powerful marketing campaign with a pro-business career message for minority students from middle school to graduate school. It offers information on current opportunities for mentorships, internships, and financial assistance and provides an impressive roster of member organizations, services, and educational opportunities.

Minority enrollment at business schools is still quite low, so in all likelihood, you will not experience the dramatic upward shift in b-school demographics in the near future that initiatives such as the Diversity Pipeline Alliance hope to influence. However, by recognizing the disparity between the minority presence in the United States and minority involvement in business education and practice, we are working toward a solution.

As you make up your mind about where you want to go for b-school, know that the scenario is positive and that new infrastructures exist to support your business career.

FEMALE APPLICANTS AND STUDENTS

If you've toured the campus and classrooms of a business school, you may have noticed something: On average, roughly 70 percent of any given MBA program's students are male. It's not something business schools are happy with—far from it! In fact, it's something they are working to change as quickly as they can.

To check out which b-schools have the "Greatest Opportunity for Women," visit your Student Tools for the latest Business School Ranking lists.

Beyond showing significantly higher application volume, MBA programs of all types are seeing female applications increase. About 64 percent of full-time MBA programs have seen applications from women rise since 2006; the figure is 47 percent for part-time-programs and 50 percent for executive programs. While these numbers may not match the 50 percent male-to-female ratio of other graduate programs, closing the b-school gender gap is only a matter of time.

School Initiatives

How can we be sure that female enrollment will continue to increase? One reason is that getting women enthused about a career in business is a sky-high priority at business schools across the country these days. To wit, many business schools have launched their own women-only outreach and recruiting events. Columbia University hosts an annual "Women in Business" conference that brings together more than 700 alumnae, business leaders, students and prospective students to network and share ideas on achieving success in the marketplace. Linda Meehan, Assistant Dean for Admissions at Columbia Business School, knows that this outreach is working because "applicants walk away wowed by the extraordinary experience of being surrounded by so many intelligent, passionate and successful women." Events like these aim to dispel myths, discuss the perceived lack of role models, and help women make informed decisions.

Stanford's events, says Wendy Hansen, Associate Director of Admissions at the Stanford Business School, "focus on the educational experience, but also on the unique types of issues women have, such as: how does getting the MBA fit in with having a family or having a spouse? How do I make this experience fit in with my life?" Julia Min, Executive Director of Admissions at UC Berkeley's Haas School of Business, says attendees often find comfort in numbers. "Seeing such a large presence of women is empowering. They realize they're not in this alone, that there are other women around like them."

If all this sounds like good public relations, it is. Schools want to get the word out: MBAs offer women viable opportunities. But if the business schools are talking the talk, they're also walking the walk. There's nothing superficial about this campaign. Bit by bit, the MBA landscape for women is changing. Opportunities begin even before the first day of class. At Stanford, women admitted to the program are treated to one-on-one admit-lunches with female alumni. Once an admit gets to campus, she finds MBA life is chock-full of student-run women and management programs, support groups, retreats, executive conferences, mentoring programs, and other dedicated resources for women only.

For many years now, most business programs have had an on-campus Partners Club for spouses and significant others—a benefit to both female and male students. Newcomers to the business-school scene include groups like The Parents Club and Biz Kids where students can find family-oriented classmates and activities. Columbia University's Mother's Network is an initiative that provides a formal support network for new, current, and future b-school moms. Perhaps the most symbolic gesture of the increasing influence of women in business school is Stanford's provision of a private nursing room for MBA moms and their babies in its main classroom facility.

Our Advice

Look at the number of female MBA students attending your targeted school and evaluate whether you would feel comfortable there. Research the number and range of student organizations for women and speak with female MBAs about school life.

Part 4

Paying for Business School

HOW MUCH WILL IT COST?

To say that business school is an expensive endeavor is an understatement. In fact, to really gauge how expensive business school is, you need to look not only at your tuition costs and living expenses but also at the opportunity cost of foregoing a salary for the length of your program. Think about it: You'll have a net outflow of money.

But keep in mind that, unlike law school or medical school, business school is just a two-year program. Once those two years are over, you can expect to reap the rewards of your increased market value. Unfortunately, business school differs from law school and medical school in a much less desirable way as well—there are serious limitations on the amount of money available through scholarships and grants. Most business school students seeking financial aid will be limited to loans, and lots of them.

Try not to get too upset about borrowing the money for business school; think of it as an investment in yourself. But, like all investments, it should be carefully thought out. You need a law degree to practice law, and a medical degree to practice medicine, but a business degree is not required to work in business. That said, certain professional opportunities may be tougher to pursue without an MBA on your resume.

The Cost of B-School

So get out some paper, a pencil, and a calculator, and figure out how much it will cost you to attend school. What should you include? Your opportunity cost (lost income) and your cost of attending b-school (tuition and fees). One more thing: For a more accurate assessment of your investment, you should figure taxes into the equation by dividing tuition cost by 0.65 (this assumes taxes of about 35 percent). Why? Because in order to pay tuition of $35,000, you would have to make a pre-tax income of about $54,000. If you are lucky enough to have a source of aid that does not require repayment, such as a grant, scholarship, or wealthy benefactor, subtract that amount from the cost of attending b-school.

For example, if you currently make $60,000 and plan to attend a business school that costs $35,000 per year, your investment would be approximately $228,000.

$(60,000 \times 2) + [(35,000 \times 2)/0.65] = \$227,692.31$

Now say you receive an annual grant of $5,000. Your investment would now be approximately $212,300.

$(60,000 \times 2) + [(30,000 \times 2)/0.65] = \$212,307.69$

How Long Will it Take You to Recoup Your Investment?

To estimate this figure, you first need to estimate your expected salary increase post-MBA. Check out the average starting salaries for graduates of the programs you are looking at and adjust upward/downward based on the industry you plan to enter. Subtract your current salary from your expected salary and you'll get your expected salary increase.

Once you complete the step above, divide your investment (tuition and fees plus lost income) by your expected salary increase.

Going back to the example on the previous page, if your pre-MBA salary is $60,000 and you expect to make $80,000 when you graduate, your expected salary increase is $20,000 (a 33 percent increase). Let's assume you did not receive a grant and that your investment will be about $228,000.

228,000/20,000 = 11.4

It will take you approximately 11 years from the completion of the program to earn back your investment.

Keep in mind, these are approximations and don't take into account annual raises, inflation, and so on. But it is interesting, isn't it?

While business school is an expensive proposition, the financial rewards of having your MBA can be immensely lucrative as we discussed before. You won't be forced into bankruptcy if you finance it correctly. There are tried-and-true ways to reduce your initial costs, finance the costs on the horizon, and manage the debt you'll leave school with—all without selling your soul to the highest bidder.

Comparison Shopping

While cost shouldn't be the first thing on your mind when you are choosing a school, depending on your goals in getting an MBA, it might be fairly high on your list. Private schools aren't the only business schools. Many state schools have fantastic reputations. Regional schools may be more generous with financial aid. Tuition costs will vary widely between public and private schools, especially if you qualify as an in-state student. Keep in mind, however, that salary gains tend to be less dramatic at more regional schools.

HOW DO I FUND MY MBA?

The short answer: loans. Unless your company is underwriting your MBA, or you're able to pay your way in cash, you'll be financing your two years of business school through a portfolio of loans. Loans typically come in one of two forms: federal and private. Only a few of you will be lucky enough to qualify for, and get, grants and scholarships.

Anyone with reasonably good credit, regardless of financial need, can borrow money for business school. If you have financial need, you will probably be eligible for some type of financial aid if you meet the following basic qualifications:

- You are a United States citizen or a permanent U.S. resident.

- You are registered for Selective Service if you are a male, or you have documentation to prove that you are exempt.

- You are not in default on student loans already.

- You don't have a horrendous credit history.

International applicants to business school should take note: Most U.S. business schools will require all international students to pay in full or show proof that they will be able to pay the entire cost of the MBA prior to beginning the MBA program.

Federal Loans

The federal government funds federal loan programs. Federal loans are usually the "first resort" for borrowers because many are subsidized by the federal government and offer generous interest rates. Some do not begin charging you interest until after you complete your degree. Most federal loans are need-based, but some higher interest federal loans are available regardless of financial circumstances. Your business school's Financial Aid Office will determine what your need is, if any.

Private Loans

Private loans are funded by banks, foundations, corporations, and other associations. A number of private loans are targeted to aid particular segments of the population. You may have to do some investigating to identify private loans for which you might qualify. As always, contact your law school's Financial Aid Office to learn more.

Alternative Sources of Funding

We've already mentioned these in one form or other, but they are worthy of a bit more attention.

The first alternative is sponsorship by your employer or educational reimbursement. Not all companies treat this the same way, but if you are able to get your employer to kick in a portion of the cost, you are better off than before. But beware, this benefit also comes with strings attached. Most companies that pay for your MBA will require a commitment of several years upon graduation. If you renege, you could be liable for the full cost of your education. Others will require that you attend business school part-time, which you may or may not want to do. Often, part-time students are unable to participate in on-campus recruiting and networking efforts to the same extent as full-time students.

Educational reimbursement can come in another form as well. Some companies will provide sign-on bonuses to new MBAs that will cover the cost of a year's tuition. This is a fantastic development from the years of a robust economy, but it is by no means a guarantee during tougher times. Don't assume that you will have this option open to you just because it has been a common occurrence in past years.

The other "alternative" source of funding is a financial gift from family or another source. Either you have a resource that is willing and able to fund all or part of your MBA, or you don't. If you do, be thankful.

Applying for Financial Aid

In order to become eligible for financial aid of any kind, you will need to complete the Free Application for Federal Student Aid, also known as the FAFSA. You complete and submit this form after January 1 of the year in which you plan to enter business school. You should aim to complete and submit this form as soon as possible after the first of the year to avoid any potential delays. The FAFSA is available from a school's Financial Aid Office. You can also download the form directly from the website of the U.S. Department of Education at FAFSA.ed.gov. A third option is to use the FAFSA Express software (also downloadable from the website) and transmit the application electronically.

It is important to note that the form requires information from your federal income tax returns. Plan to file your taxes early that year.

In addition to the FAFSA form, most schools will have their own financial aid form that you will be required to complete and submit. These often have their own deadlines, so it is wise to keep careful track of all the forms you must complete and all their respective deadlines. Yes, it's a lot of paperwork, but get over it. You'll be much happier when the tuition bill arrives.

GUIDE TO FEDERAL LOANS

Stafford Loans

Stafford loans require you to complete the FAFSA form in order to qualify. These are very desirable loans because they offer low-interest rates capped at 5.31 percent (unsubsidized), with a loan fee of 1.066 percent, and are federally guaranteed. There is a limit to how much you can borrow in this program. Graduate and professional school students may borrow up to $20,500 per year from the unsubsidized Federal Stafford Loan. The cumulative loan limits are $138,500, including undergraduate debt (and no more than $65,500 in subsidized Federal Stafford loans). The aggregate amount includes any Stafford loans you may have from your undergraduate or other graduate studies.

Stafford loans come in two types: subsidized and unsubsidized. Subsidized loans are need-based as determined by your business school. They do not accrue interest while you are in school or in an authorized deferment period (such as the first six months after graduation). This cost is picked up by the government (hence the name "subsidized"). Repayment begins at that time. Unsubsidized loans are not need-based and do charge interest from the time of disbursement to the time of full repayment. You can pay the interest while you are in school or opt for capitalization, in which case the interest is added to the principal.

You will pay more in the long run if you choose capitalization. Interest payments may be tax deductible, so be sure to check. The standard repayment period for both is 10 years.

You will pay a small origination and guarantee fee for each loan, but this is not an out-of-pocket expense. It is simply deducted from the loan amount. Some schools will allow you to borrow the money under the Stafford program directly from them, while others will require you to borrow from a bank. For more information on federal loans, call the Federal Student Aid Information Center at 800-433-3243 or visit studentaid.ed.gov.

Perkins Loans

Perkins loans are available to graduate students who demonstrate exceptional financial need. The financial aid office will determine your eligibility for a Perkins Loan. If you qualify for a Perkins Loan as part of your financial aid package, take it. The loans are made by the schools and are repaid to the schools, although the federal government provides a large portion of the funds. You can borrow up to $8,000 for each year of graduate study up to a total of $60,000 (this includes any money borrowed under this program during undergraduate study). The interest rates on this loan are low, usually 5 percent. There are no fees attached. The grace period is nine months upon graduation.

Direct PLUS Loans

Direct PLUS loans are made available through schools, though the U.S. Department of Education is actually the lender. You may borrow up to the full cost of attendance as determined by your school, less any other financial aid received. Like other federal loans, Direct PLUS loans have a small origination fee and a fixed interest rate, which is currently 6.41 percent. These funds are paid directly to your school to cover tuition, fees, and room and board. Any remaining balance will be refunded to you to cover other expenses associated with your education—when a school determines the cost of attendance, books, travel, and other expenses are typically included.

PRIVATE/COMMERCIAL LOANS

This is expensive territory. Not only are interest rates high, but terms are also quite different from those found with federal loans. You may not be able to defer payment of interest or principal until after graduation. Origination and guarantee fees are also much higher since these loans are unsecured. After all, banks and other specialized lenders exist to loan money to folks like you, and unlike the federal government, want to make money doing it. If you go this route, shop around diligently. Think of it as good practice for your post-MBA executive career.

SCHOLARSHIPS AND GRANTS

The usual sources for this type of funding are alumni groups and civic organizations. This funding is limited, and actual awards tend to be small. Even if you benefited from generous scholarship funding as an undergraduate, it would be unwise to assume you'll have the same experience as a graduate student. But do investigate. You never know what's out there. Schools will frequently list any scholarships and grants that are available at the back of their financial aid catalog.

FOR MORE INFORMATION

Find out more about your financing options for business school education at PrincetonReview.com.

Part 5

What B-School Is Really Like

AN ACADEMIC PERSPECTIVE

The objective of all MBA programs is to prepare students for a professional career in business. One business school puts it this way:

Graduates should be all of the following:

- able to think and reason independently, creatively, and analytically

- skilled in the use of quantitative techniques

- literate in the use of software applications as management tools

- knowledgeable about the world's management issues and problems

- willing to work in and successfully cope with conditions of uncertainty, risk, and change

- astute decision makers

- ethically and socially responsible

- able to manage in an increasingly global environment

- proficient in utilizing technology as a mode of doing business

Sound like a tall order? Possibly. But this level of expectation is what business school is all about.

Nearly all MBA programs feature a core curriculum that focuses on the major disciplines of business: finance, management, accounting, marketing, manufacturing, decision sciences, economics, and organizational behavior. Unless your school allows you to place out of them, these courses are mandatory. Core courses provide broad functional knowledge in one discipline. To illustrate, a core marketing course covers pricing, segmentation, communications, product-line planning, and implementation. Electives provide a narrow focus that deepen the area of study. For example, a marketing elective might be entirely devoted to pricing.

Students sometimes question the need for such a comprehensive core program, but the functional areas of a real business are not parallel lines. All departments of a business affect each other every day. For example, an MBA in a manufacturing job might be asked by a financial controller why the company's product has become unprofitable to produce. Without an understanding of how product costs are accounted for, this MBA wouldn't know how to respond to a critical and legitimate request.

At most schools, the first term or year is devoted to a rigid core curriculum. Some schools allow first-years to take core courses side by side with electives. Still others have come up with an entirely new way of covering the basics, integrating the core courses into one cross-functional learning experience, which may also include sessions on topics such as globalization, ethics, and managing diversity. Half-year to year-long courses are team-taught by professors who will see you through all disciplines.

TEACHING METHODOLOGY

Business schools employ two basic teaching methods: case study and lecture. Usually, they employ some combination of the two. The most popular is the case study approach. Students are presented with either real or hypothetical business scenarios and are asked to analyze them. This method provides concrete situations (rather than abstractions) that require mastery of a wide range of skills. Students often find case studies exciting because they can engage in spirited discussions about possible solutions to given business problems and because they get an opportunity to apply newly acquired business knowledge.

On the other hand, lecturing is a teaching method in which—you guessed it—the professor speaks to the class and the class listens. The efficacy of the lecture method depends entirely on the professor. If the professor is compelling, you'll probably get a lot out of the class. If the professor is boring, you probably won't listen, which isn't necessarily a big deal since many professors make their class notes available online.

THE CLASSROOM EXPERIENCE

Professors teaching case methodology often begin class with a "cold call." A randomly selected student opens the class with an analysis of the case and makes recommendations for solutions. The cold call forces you to be prepared and to think on your feet.

No doubt, a cold call can be intimidating. But unlike law school, b-school professors don't use the Socratic Method to torture you, testing your thinking with a pounding cross-examination. They're training managers, not trial lawyers. At worst, particularly if you're unprepared, a professor will abruptly dismiss your contribution.

Alternatively, professors ask for a volunteer to open a case, particularly someone who has had real industry experience with the issues. After the opening, the discussion is broadened to include the whole class. Everyone tries to get in a good comment, particularly if class participation counts heavily toward the grade. "Chip shots"—unenlightened, just-say-anything-to-get-credit comments—are common. So are "air hogs," students who go on and on because they like nothing more than to hear themselves pontificate.

Depending on the school, class discussions can degenerate into wars of ego rather than ideas. But for the most part, debates are kept constructive and civilized. Students are competitive, but not offensively so, and learn to make their points succinctly and persuasively.

LIFE OUTSIDE OF CLASS

Business school is more than academics and a big-bucks job. A spirited community provides ample opportunity for social interaction, extracurricular activity, and career development.

Much of campus life revolves around student-run clubs. There are groups for just about every career interest and social need—from MBAs for a Greener America to the Small Business Club. There's even a group for significant others on most campuses. The clubs are a great way to meet classmates with similar interests and to get in on the social scene. They might have a reputation for throwing the best black-tie balls, pizza-and-keg events, and professional mixers. During orientation week, these clubs aggressively market themselves to first-years.

Various socially responsible projects are also popular on campus. An emphasis on volunteer work is part of the overall trend toward good citizenship. Perhaps to counter the greed of the 1980s, "giving back" is the b-school style of the moment. There is usually a wide range of options—from tutoring in an inner-city school to working in a soup kitchen to renovating public buildings.

Still another way to get involved is to work on a school committee. Here you might serve on a task force designed to improve student quality of life, or you might work in the admissions office and interview prospective students.

For those with more creative urges there are always the old standbys: extracurriculars such as the school paper, yearbook, or school play. At some schools, the latter is a dramatization of "b-school follies" and is a highlight of the year. Like the student clubs, these are a great way to get to know your fellow students.

Finally, you can play on intramural sports teams or attend the numerous informal get-togethers, dinner parties, and group trips. There are also plenty of regularly scheduled pub nights, just in case you thought your beer-guzzling days were over.

Most former MBA students say that going to b-school was the best decision they ever made. That's primarily because of non-academic experiences. Make the most of your classes, but take the time to get involved and enjoy yourself.

Part 6

The Importance of the Essay

An essay is a school's Rorschach test when considering your candidacy. Whether you're applying to business school, law school, or medical school, what you write says more about you than your GPA or test score.

Unlike the law or med school admissions processes, b-school admissions are unique in their request for many essays and their heavy weighting of those essays. Although grades and standardized tests are considered key benchmarks for admission, they function more as a threshold. Your stories are what close the deal one way or the other.

THE REAL YOU, REVEALED AND DISSECTED

In b-school admissions, the essays tie all the pieces of your application together. They weave a narrative of who you are and why you belong in a particular program. They provide a framework for your personal and professional activities, highlighting your choices and attitudes as well as your analytical and communication skills. They also reveal your character and integrity. That's because those onerous essay questions are designed to elicit thumbnail profiles of the real you, and together they are arguably the most heavily weighted criterion in the admissions process. For these reasons, the essays are invaluable screening tools.

At the top business schools, evaluating a candidate's character, genuine accomplishments, and potential has always been pivotal. That's because b-schools operate like micro-communities, and there is an expectation that you will work well and make connections within that community. Furthermore, the curriculum is designed so that you learn from your classmates. Therefore, each student's perspective, experience, and behavior is vital. B-school learning is also team-oriented, so a cooperative spirit (or lack thereof) says a lot about whether you're a strong fit for a particular program.

But perhaps most important, b-schools are a primary source of future business leaders. So attributes like honesty (yes, that includes what you put on your resume), leadership, and ethics matter. In the wake of Enron, WorldCom, Tyco, Lehman Brothers, and other corporate scandals, they matter more than ever. You can almost hear the collective b-school groan when the latest Wall Street violator turns out to be another MBA.

Figuring out whether you'll one day prove to be a source of pride or an embarrassment to your alma mater and the business community is the gray zone in admissions. So how does a b-school attempt to get at your true character and determine your potential as a business leader?

While it may be almost impossible to make such a prediction, the essays are good indicators of character strengths and flaws. So as you compose your stories, know that you're being looked at through many different lenses. B-schools are uniquely interested in characteristics beyond test scores. High on their list is emotional maturity, self-awareness, leadership ability, creativity, teamwork potential, and morality. Even the venerable Harvard Business School has a stated mission to do no less than "educate leaders who make a difference in the world." To screen for all these qualities, the schools rely on the essays. And herein lies the problem.

An Essay Can Be an Imperfect Screener

It may be difficult for an engineer who will one day launch an industry-transforming product to craft a compelling self-narrative. How many great business leaders might be disqualified from getting their MBA at a top school because their writing or storytelling skills are poor, or because at this young age they don't know how to show or articulate self-awareness in their essays?

In this way, the essays on b-school applications can be overreaching. But they're imperfect in other areas as well. When you consider the questions posed by the most selective programs, you realize that it's genuine frontline caretakers, like social and health care workers, who may best embody the value systems b-schools are looking for. It's by virtue of their chosen profession that caretakers demonstrate such value systems. For aspiring MBAs—also by virtue of their chosen profession—such redeeming qualities are often less evident.

Caught Between a Rock and a Hard Place

Ironically, success and financial reward are part of the b-school hype. Indeed, many schools are judged each year on their career placement statistics (translation: the number of grads who secure high-paying positions, and how quickly they do so), so they work hard to ensure that their statistics are competitive. But an applicant who articulates too much interest in the very pot of gold the MBA dangles may be penalized for lacking the softer skills b-schools desire these days.

The truth is that the negative aspect of the MBA stereotype might at times be true; many pre-MBAs are ambitiously preoccupied with success and financial reward. But why should that be considered unattractive? As you can see, these essay questions don't necessarily play to a would-be MBA's strengths. The essay writers of today need an advocate.

So how does one navigate between posturing as a sincere do-gooder and an ambitious future financial officer?

It's a difficult challenge. The majority of b-school applicants are deeper than their stereotypes would suggest. As we said before, they are reflective, accountable, and morally sound. Finessing all of those qualities in a series of short stories with strict word limits is no easy task.

How to Craft Your Essays

HIDDEN AGENDAS

Now that you know that the essays are used to check applicants for a range of qualities, it makes sense that each question on the application has a reason for being there. Even seemingly straightforward essay questions, such as those in the vein of, "Why do you want the MBA? Why do you want the degree at this juncture in your life? And why here?" have an agenda.

As essay questions go, these are fairly clear-cut. Although you'd probably rather do anything (including clean the bathroom) than sit down to suss out an honest and intelligible response, the task seems doable. So why do so many applicants fail to answer the question successfully? Because even a straightforward question needs to be thought through.

Here's the inside line: Schools consider this essay the ballast to your candidacy. They want to see well-crafted goals for your education and career outlined here. When I explain this to applicants, it surprises them. After all, they argue, b-school is a journey, and part of the journey is not knowing what lies ahead. Would-be MBAs treat this essay as an opportunity to share their excitement about the discovery. But if you're not sure where you're headed or why, it's nearly impossible to answer such questions convincingly.

It is critical that you present well-defined goals and expectations in your essays. At the best schools, admissions committees want you to lay down a compelling rationale for why you need the MBA and why their program specifically meets your needs. If you can't do that, then why should they award you one of their coveted spots? They want students who will value the resources at their program, not those in need of a two-year pit stop.

Half the battle in writing a winning essay is in knowing what the essay question is attempting to draw out, and we aim to offer some guidance in that respect. We don't want you to spend hours working on one question and completely miss the mark. Later on, we'll identify and translate commonly asked essay questions. But let there be no mistake about it, equally important to the content, or the "what" of the essay, is the "how."

THE "HOW" OF AN ESSAY IS IMPORTANT

Think of your essay-writing this way: All written communication lives or dies on the "how" in its message. The way you present yourself in your essays and frame your subject is crucial to the impression you create. Ever receive an apology letter that felt warm and real (as opposed to perfunctory)? Did it have a positive impact on how you felt about the person after you read it? If it did, you saw an example of a good use of "how."

Still not sure what the "how" is? It is

- the mood and tone in your writing

- your writing style and skill and the clarity of your thinking

- your ability to follow directions

- the judgment you use in selecting your subject matter

- the impact you leave on the reader

Tone and mood can communicate that you are candid, warm, friendly, and a true leader by example. It can also betray negativity, inappropriateness, or a lack of maturity.

There are many variables to the "how" of anyone's writing. There is no one formula we can hand off to you. What might work for one essay or one applicant won't necessarily work for another. The trick is to be self-aware.

WHAT YOUR ESSAYS SHOULD SAY ABOUT YOU

Applicants tend to place great emphasis on their accomplishments and strengths. But as we said before, there is more to writing an essay than this. You'll need to weave evidence of these favorable qualities into your essay so you can appear in the best possible light without boasting, lying, or being mushy or corny. In other words, the trick is to navigate between maintaining a modest position and showcasing your accomplishments.

As you compose your essays, remember to remain aware of what the details of your stories actually reveal about you.

Your essays should suggest that you are

- a leader
- humble
- mature
- goal-oriented
- creative
- dignified
- intelligent
- hard-working
- concerned for others
- team-oriented

- positive, with a can-do attitude
- introspective
- moral and ethical
- accountable
- able to learn from failure
- wise
- self-aware
- unique
- of sound mind and perspective

Your essays should avoid communicating that you are

- arrogant
- vain
- entitled
- egotistical
- competitive
- a perfectionist
- blindly ambitious
- angry or quick to blame
- immature

- overly bookish
- mediocre
- prejudiced regarding race and/or gender
- a poor or boring writer
- one who exercises poor judgment
- one who sets unrealistic goals

Take the favorable qualities from the first list that best describe you, and jot those down. It's time for you to find a vehicle through which to convey your finest features.

Consider what compelling stories you have to tell and sketch them out. Reflect on what each story says about you and what kind of picture each paints. Then when you sit down with your application, you'll start to draw connections between your stories and the questions that are asked of you.

Common Essay Questions (and What They're Really Asking)

CREATING PERFECTION TAKES TIME

> "Essays are the love letter of why a student wants to attend business school."
>
> —Julia Min, Director of MBA Admissions at Stern School of Business, New York University

No one ever said it was going to be easy. Depending on where you're applying and how prolific a writer you are, a b-school application will take anywhere from fifty to one hundred hours to complete. Sound excessive? Go ahead and try it. You'll probably scrap and rewrite an essay many times over. It takes time for thoughts to gestate. Indeed, it might feel like a fine wine ages faster than you write an essay.

You'll need to look at every essay question on each of your applications to determine how to optimally allocate your stories and anecdotes. One story might work well for either a leadership essay or an essay about failure. But you might have several good stories for leadership, and none for failure. Mapping out how you're going to allocate your anecdotes and stories is critical to your overall strategy.

Take a look at a recent year's essay questions from Harvard and Wharton below to get an idea of what you're up against. Keep in mind that not all schools will require you to write such exhaustive essays. The more selective a school is, the more rigid and demanding its standard for admission will be. That said, we're going to focus on the most brutal applications. They are the gold standard for essays, and their questions demand the greatest effort.

Harvard Business School

1. Discuss an experience that has had an impact on your development as a leader. (400-word limit)

2. What are your three most substantial accomplishments, and why do you view them as such? (600-word limit)

3. Recognizing that successful leaders are able to learn from failure, discuss a situation in which you failed and what you learned. (400-word limit)

4. Discuss an ethical dilemma that you experienced firsthand. How did you manage and resolve the situation? (400-word limit)

5. Provide a candid assessment of your strengths and weaknesses. (400-word limit)

6. What are your career aspirations, and how can Harvard Business School help you to reach them? (400-word limit)

7. (Optional) Is there any other information that you believe would be helpful to the Board in understanding you better and in considering your application? Please be concise.

The Wharton School, University of Pennsylvania

1. Describe how your experiences, both professional and personal, have led to your decision to pursue an MBA at the Wharton School this year. How does this decision relate to your career goals for the future? (1,000 words)

2. Describe a situation where leadership and teamwork were critical to the outcome of a project in which you were directly involved. What did you learn from the experience and how have you applied what you learned to other situations? (1,000 words)

3. Describe a personal achievement that has had a significant impact on your life. Give specific details. What did you learn from this experience? How did it help shape your understanding of yourself and the world around you? (500 words)

4. Please tell us something else about yourself that you feel will help the Admissions Committee know you better. (500 words)

READING BETWEEN THE LINES

Being a great storyteller and gifted writer can be a major advantage to the prospective b-school student. But be forewarned: A wonderful answer to a question not asked will not help you here. We can't stress enough that you must answer the question.

Each school has its own set of questions. Although posed differently, all search for the same insights. Here's a list of commonly asked questions and what's behind them.

Theme 1: Career Goals and the MBA

Describe your specific career aspirations. How will your goals be furthered by an MBA degree and by our MBA program in particular?

How do you feel the "X" school MBA degree can help you attain your specific career and personal goals for the five years after you graduate?

Discuss your career progression to date. What factors have influenced your decision to seek a general management education? Based on what you know about yourself at this time, how do you envision your career progressing after receiving the MBA degree? Please state your professional goals, and describe your plan to achieve them.

Translation: What do I want to be when I grow up, and how will the MBA get me there?

This may be the most important essay question. It lays out the reasons why you should be given one of the cherished spots in the program. Even if your post-MBA future is tough to envision, this question must be answered.

A good way to frame this essay is to discuss how the MBA makes sense in light of your background, skills, and achievements to date. Why do you need this degree? Why now? One common reason is being stymied in your work by a lack of skills that can be gained in their program. Or you may want to use the MBA as a bridge to the next step. For example, an actor who wants an MBA to prepare for a career in theater management. The more specific, the better.

It may be easier to provide specifics by breaking your plans into short-term and long-term objectives.

Don't be afraid to present modest goals. If you're in accounting and want to stay there, say so. Deepening your expertise and broadening your perspective are solid reasons for pursuing this degree. On the other hand, feel free to indicate that you'll use the MBA to change careers; 70 percent of all students at b-school are there to do just that.

If you aspire to lofty goals, like becoming a CEO or starting your own company, be especially careful that you detail a sensible, pragmatic plan. You need to show you're realistic. No one zooms to the top. Break your progress into steps.

Finally, this essay question asks how a particular program supports your goals. Admissions committees want to know why you've selected their school. That means you not only have to know, but also show, what's special about their program and how that relates specifically to your career aspirations. Hint: Many admissions officers say they can tell how much someone wants to go to their school by how well their essays are tailored to the offerings in their program.

Theme 2: Extracurriculars and Social Interaction—Our Nonwork Side

What do you do for fun?

What are your principal interests outside of your job or school?

What leisure and/or community activities do you particularly enjoy? Please describe their importance in your life.

Translation: Would we like to have you over for dinner? Do you know how to make friends? What are your special talents—the b-school Follies needs help. Are you well-balanced, or are you going to freak out when you get here?

B-school is not just about business, case studies, and careers. The best programs buzz with the energy of a student body that is talented and creative and that has personality. You won't be spending all your time in the library.

Are you interesting? Would you contribute to the school's vitality? Are you the kind of person other MBAs would be happy to meet? Describe activities you're involved in that might add something to the b-school community.

Are you sociable? B-school is a very social experience. Much of the work is done in groups. Weekends are full of social gatherings. Will you participate?

Initiate? Get along with others? Communicate that people, not just your job, are an important part of your life.

Can you perform at a high level without being a nerd?

B-school can be tough. It's important to know when to walk away and find some fun. Do you know how to play as hard as you work?

How well-rounded are you? Business leaders have wide-angle perspectives; they take in the whole picture. How deep or broad are your interests? A warning: Don't just list what you've done. Explain how what you've done has made you unique.

Theme 3: Whom You Most Admire

If you were able to choose one person from the business world, past or present, to be your personal professor throughout the MBA program, who would this person be and why?

Describe the characteristics of an exceptional manager, using an example of someone whom you have observed or with whom you have worked. Illustrate how his or her management style has influenced you.

Translation: What are your values? What character traits do you admire?

This is the curveball question. The committee isn't looking to evaluate your judgment in selecting some famous, powerful person in your firm or in the world. What they're really after, which you reveal in your selection of the person, are the qualities, attributes, and strengths you value in others, as well as in yourself. Some important qualities to address: drive, discipline, vision, ethics, and leadership. As always, provide specific examples. And avoid choosing anyone too obvious.

Since the person you select is not as important as what you say about him or her, your choices can be more humble. You might write about a current boss, business associate, or friend. Bad choices are your mother or father.

If you like, it's perfectly fine to go for a famous figure. Indeed, there may be about whose career and style you're passionate. Make sure your essay explains why you find this person so compelling.

Theme 4: Teamwork—How Do You Work with Others in a Group Setting?

At X School, a team, which consists of approximately five first-year students, is often assigned group projects and class presentations. Imagine that, one year from now, your team has a marketing class assignment due at 9:00 A.M. on Monday morning. It is now 10:00 P.M. on Sunday night—time is short, tension builds, and your team has reached an impasse. What role would you take in such a situation? How would you enable the team to meet your deadline? (Note: The specific nature of the assignment is not as important here as the team dynamic.) Feel free to draw on previous experiences, if applicable, in order to illustrate your approach.

Translation: We need cooperative, one-for-all-and-all-for-one students here. Are you cut out to be one, or are you a take-over type who has all the answers? Are you likely to help everyone get along and arrive at solutions? (We like those kinds of students.) Can you lead others to order and synergy? (We especially like leaders.) Or do you retreat or become a follower?

This, too, is a curveball question. But you can't afford to get it wrong. After the career goals question, it probably ranks as the most critical essay you write. Here the committee isn't looking to see how you save the team (so put yourself on ego alert as you sit down to write this one); they want to see how you can create an environment in which everyone contributes so that the sum is greater than its parts. Bottom line—the admissions committee is looking to see whether you have "emotional intelligence." Understand that schools today believe that emotional intelligence, the ability to navigate emotion-laden situations, is as important as strategic and analytical skills. This question is intended to illustrate this particular type of ability.

Expect to shift gears with this essay. Almost the entire application process thus far has asked you to showcase "me-me-me." Now the focus of your story needs to be on the "we" and how you made the "we" happen.

As you write your essay, consider that when you get to school, some team members will be from different countries where cultural attitudes play into team dynamics. Your sensitivity to these cultural differences, as well as to personality types, will go a long way toward demonstrating your emotional intelligence. For example, a team member hailing from a certain culture may withhold an opinion in an attempt to foster consensus. How can you help this person make a contribution? Likewise, consider differences among team members in terms of their academic and professional strengths. If the assignment is heavy on numbers, finance students may dominate teammates from softer sciences. How can you ensure that everyone feels valued? Teams are inspired to succeed when everyone is motivated and taking ownership within a context of respect.

Remember, the team in this particular essay is at an impasse, as most teams are at some point in time. Write about how you "unjammed" the jam. Ideas: A change of scene, food, twenty push-ups, a quick round-the-room confessional about why you came to b-school. Introducing some process is also useful; ground rules such as voting, speaking times, a division of labor, and a time line all create a method from the madness. Perhaps you encourage members to adopt roles—business or otherwise. Hint: The leader or CEO in this case might be your most soft-spoken team member. Whatever you do in this essay, be careful not to present yourself as the one who single-handedly gets the team dynamic going.

Theme 5: Diversity and What Makes You Unique

Our business school is a diverse environment. How will your experiences contribute to this?

During your years of study in the X program, you will be part of a diverse multicultural, multiethnic community within both the Business School and the larger university. What rewards and challenges do you anticipate in this environment, and how do you expect this experience to prepare you for a culturally diverse business world?

Translation: What about you is different in terms of your background, your experience, or your cultural or geographic heritage? Can we count on your unique voice and perspective in our wide-ranging classroom discussions? How will you support the diverse cultural climate we are fostering here?

This essay gets at two concerns for the admissions committee: How will you enrich the student body at this school? And what is your attitude toward others' diverse backgrounds? Today's business leaders must be able to make decisions in situations that cut across geographic and cultural boundaries. If your essay reveals that you have dinosaur-era, only-white-males-rule thinking, you're going to close the door on your candidacy.

So what if you are a white male? Or you have no immediate point of distinction? Maybe a grandparent or relative is an immigrant to this country and you can discuss the impact of his or her values on your life. Perhaps you are the first individual in your family to attend college or to attend graduate school. What does that mean to you? Perhaps you are involved in a meaningful or unusual extracurricular activity. How has this changed your perspective? Perhaps you did a business deal with a foreign country. What did you observe about that culture, and how did it affect your decisions?

Whatever you write about need not be dramatic—maybe you take art classes, coach a little league team, or race a motorcycle. Sound goofy? It's all in the framing. Racing a motorcycle might be about the physical and mental stamina, the ability to take risks, the commitment to learning something new.

This question can be relatively easy to answer if, of course, you have diversity or some unique element in your background. If you don't have something obvious, then you're going to have to dig a bit and find something you can amplify to suggest you bring a unique voice to the school.

Theme 6: Your Greatest Personal Achievement/Accomplishment

Describe a personal achievement that has had a significant impact on your life. In addition to recounting this achievement, please analyze how the event has changed your understanding of yourself, and how you perceive the world around you.

In reviewing the last five years, describe one or two accomplishments in which you demonstrated leadership.

Translation: Do you know what an achievement is? Have you done anything remarkable? What made it remarkable to you? Bonus points if you showed leadership or inspired others in some way.

This is one of those maddening essay questions because on the one hand, b-schools seek out applicants whose average age is twenty-seven (a relatively young age to have achieved much of anything). On the other hand, the schools want to know what miracles you've performed. Don't pull your hair out yet. There is a way out. Like all the others, this essay is just one more prove-to-us-you-have-some-character hoop you'll have to jump through. It's less about the achievement and more about who you are and how you see yourself.

Again, this question can be easy to answer if you have some clear accomplishment or event in your background. But if you're like the rest of us—you guessed it—you'll have to rely on framing.

Let's cover bad essay topics for achievements. Getting straight A's in college is not an achievement because everyone else at b-school has probably done the same. Surviving a divorce or breakup is a bad accomplishment topic. Personal stories are acceptable, but one taboo area is romance and marriage. If this is all you can come up with, you're going to look like you're as deep as a doughnut.

The accomplishment you choose might show some of the following qualities: character, sacrifice, humility, dedication, high personal stakes, perseverance over obstacles, insight, and learning. You need not have published a business article or won an award to answer this question. This essay is not about excellence of outcome, but what it took for you to reach some personal worthy objective. Maybe you didn't lead a sports team to a victory. The victory may be just that you made it onto the team.

Theme 7: Failure/What Mistakes Have You Made?

Discuss a non-academic personal failure. In what way were you disappointed in yourself? What did you learn from the experience?

Translation: Can you admit to a genuine failure? Do you have enough self-awareness to know what kind of failure is real? Can you learn from your mistakes? Do they lead to greater maturity and self-awareness? Do you take responsibility when the fault is yours?

Many applicants make the mistake of answering this question with a failure that is really a positive, such as "I'm a perfectionist and so therefore I was too demanding on a friend when she was in a crisis." Or they never really answer the question, fearful that any admission of failure will throw their whole candidacy into jeopardy. The truth is, if you don't answer this question with a genuine failure or mistake, one that the committee will recognize as authentic, you may have jinxed your application.

In this essay, you want to write about a failure that had some high stakes for you. Demonstrate what you learned from your mistake and how it helped you mature. What's the relevance to b-school here? Your ability to be honest, show accountability, and face your failures head-on reflects what kinds of decisions and judgments you will make as a business professional.

Can't think of a time you failed? Discuss the essay question with a friend or family member. An outsider's perspective may jog your memory. Remember, if your whole application has been about work, work, work, this is a great place to convince the committee you're a real person.

Theme 8: Ethics

Describe an ethical issue you have faced in your professional life and how you dealt with it. What was the outcome?

Translation: Do you even know what an ethical dilemma looks like? Are you tomorrow's corporate miscreant? What kinds of decisions and judgments might you make in your future practices as a business leader?

The last few years have brought attention to the ethical issues of the business world and the failure of corporate self-governance. In the aftermath of many high-profile scandals, b-schools don't want to turn out graduates who are fast into their suspenders, fast into a deal, and fast to swindle their clients and shareholders.

The above question tests your judgment, integrity, and perspective. It's most important to present a legitimate ethical dilemma here, one that has consequences. Applicants often write about the dilemma of not obeying a supervisor's orders because they wanted to do things their way, a known better way. But this is not an ethics problem (unless the order was improper or illegal); it's a management problem. Likewise, handing in a report to your boss that you know is full of errors is also not an ethical problem; it's a trivial, single-impact, easy-to-fix problem.

If you were thinking of telling a story like one of those mentioned above, it may be because you wanted to play it safe. This is one of those uncomfortable, hot-seat essays after all. But playing it safe here would only make you appear clueless or morally bereft.

This essay requires you to roll up your ethical shirtsleeves and get down in the dirt. True ethical issues are neither clean nor pretty. Don't shrink away from a discussion of failure here or present an overly optimistic, no-loose-ends solution.

It's key that you write about an ethical dilemma in which there was no easy course—one that entailed costs either way. For example, let's say you sold a product to a client and later discovered the product was faulty; your employer wanted you to keep mum. You'd built your sales relationships on trust and personal attention, so you wanted to be forthcoming. What did you do?

This essay must show that you can work through a complex ethical impasse, and it must highlight your sense of honor and conduct. This essay screams relevance. Make sure you shout back that you know right from wrong.

GMAT Insider comprises excerpts from the following titles:

Do I Need an MBA? Figuring Out if Business School Really Fits Your Future Needs, by Kal Chany and the Staff of The Princeton Review (Random House/Princeton Review Books)

The Best 296 Business Schools, 2015 Edition, by the Staff of The Princeton Review (Random House/Princeton Review Books)

Business School Essays That Made a Difference, 5th Edition, by Nedda Gilbert and the Staff of The Princeton Review (Random House/Princeton Review Books)

NOTES

NOTES